AF361948

Identification, Knowledge Engineering and Digital Modeling for Adaptive and Intelligent Control

Identification, Knowledge Engineering and Digital Modeling for Adaptive and Intelligent Control

Editors

Natalia Bakhtadze
Igor Yadykin
Andrei Torgashov
Nikolay Korgin

MDPI • Basel • Beijing • Wuhan • Barcelona • Belgrade • Manchester • Tokyo • Cluj • Tianjin

Editors

Natalia Bakhtadze
Russian Academy of Sciences
Russia

Igor Yadykin
V.A. Trapeznikov Institute of
Control Sciences
Russia

Andrei Torgashov
Institute of Automation and
Control Process FEB RAS
Russia

Nikolay Korgin
V.A. Trapeznikov Institute of
Control Sciences
Russia

Editorial Office
MDPI
St. Alban-Anlage 66
4052 Basel, Switzerland

This is a reprint of articles from the Special Issue published online in the open access journal *Mathematics* (ISSN 2227-7390) (available at: https://www.mdpi.com/journal/mathematics/special_issues/Identification_Knowledge_Engineering_Digital_Modeling_Adaptive_Intelligent_Control).

For citation purposes, cite each article independently as indicated on the article page online and as indicated below:

LastName, A.A.; LastName, B.B.; LastName, C.C. Article Title. *Journal Name* **Year**, *Volume Number*, Page Range.

ISBN 978-3-0365-8060-9 (Hbk)
ISBN 978-3-0365-8061-6 (PDF)

Contents

About the Editors

Natalia Bakhtadze

Professor, Dr. Natalia Bakhtadze, Head of the Identification Laboratory, Institute of Control Sciences of Russian Academy of Sciences, Moscow, Russia. Author of over 200 scientific publications. Areas of Interest: Identification of Control Systems; Estimation Theory; Adaptive Control; Model Predictive Control; Data Mining; Wavelet Analysis; Control of Technological Processes in Industry and Energy; Multi-Agent Systems. Member of the editorial board of several peer-reviewed journals ("Automation and Remote Control", "Advances in Systems Science and Applications" (Associate Editor-in-Chief), "Information Technology and Computing Systems" (Executive Editor), etc.). Vice-chair of IFAC TC 5.2. - Management and Control in Manufacturing and Logistics.

Igor Yadykin

Professor, Dr. Igor Yadykin, Institute of Control Sciences of Russian Academy of Sciences, Moscow, Russia. Author of over 250 scientific publications. Areas of Interest: power systems analysis; power systems simulation; adaptive and optimal control; mechanical engineering. Vice-chair of IFAC TC 6.3. Power and Energy Systems.

Andrei Torgashov

Dr. Sci. Andrei Torgashov, Principal Researcher, Institute of Automation and Control Processes FEB RAS, Vladivostok, Russia. Author of over 200 scientific publications. Areas of Interest: Process Control, System Identification, Process Modeling, Process Optimization, Model Predictive Control, Applied Statistics, PID Control, Stability Analysis, Control Systems Engineering, Statistical Data Analysis, Advanced Control Theory, Optimal Control, Modeling and Simulation, System Modeling, Advanced Control Systems APC.

Nikolay Korgin

Professor, Dr. Nikolay Korgin, Institute of Control Sciences of Russian Academy of Sciences, Moscow, Russia. Author of over 200 scientific publications. Areas of Interest: Mechanism Design; Game theory; Power Systems Analysis; Mechanical Engineering; Identification problems; Organizational Behavior; Mechanism Design; Organizational Theory; Organizational Management; Control Systems Engineering; Microeconomics; Strategic Management; Optimal Control; Strategic Planning; Leadership; Robustness; Human Resource Management; Organizational Development; Organizational Culture.

 *mathematics*

Editorial

Preface to the Special Issue on "Identification, Knowledge Engineering and Digital Modeling for Adaptive and Intelligent Control"—Special Issue Book

Natalia Bakhtadze

Institute for Control Sciences, Russian Academy of Sciences, 117806 Moscow, Russia; sung7@yandex.ru

Starting our work on this Special Issue, we assumed that the research results presented here would reflect the solutions to various problems related to production management; however, the set of identified problems showed that their solutions could be useful for a wider range of applications. Therefore, we have presented 14 articles covering various aspects of the new trends in adaptive and intelligent control and identification.

The results of research on the theories and methodologies of identification are presented. New methods for solving the problems of parametric and non-parametric identification are proposed, and the possibilities of using data mining and knowledge engineering methods for identifying control systems and building digital models of dynamic processes in real time are studied. Various aspects of constructing intelligent control systems with an identifier and reinforcement learning are discussed and the possibilities of intelligent model predictive control and its application to control objects of various natures, as well as stability problems, are investigated. Approaches to building models of strategic decision making under informational control are also proposed.

A general complex model is presented in [1] for collective dynamical strategic decision making with explicitly interconnected factors reflecting both the psychic (internal state) and behavioral (external action, result of activity) components of agents' activity under specified environmental and control factors. This model unifies and generalizes the approaches of game theory, social psychology, and the theory of multi-agent systems and control in organizational systems through a simultaneous consideration of both the internal and external parameters of the agents. Article [2] carries out a comparative analysis of the known methods for the synthesis of various control laws ensuring the invariance of the output (controlled) variable with respect to external disturbances, under various assumptions about their type and channels of acting on the control plant. Synthesis methods are presented by the example of a third-order nonlinear system with a single input and single output (SISO-system). For the systems where the matching conditions are not satisfied, the paper draws a conclusion on the expediency of introducing smooth and bounded nonlinear local feedbacks. In Ref. [3], the stability of bilinear systems is investigated using spectral techniques such as selective modal analysis. Predictive models of bilinear systems based on inductive knowledge extracted by big data mining techniques are applied with associative search of statistical patterns. In Ref. [4], the intelligent computational algorithms of evolutionary computing paradigms (ECPs) are presented, which effectively solve complex nonlinear optimization problems. The maximum-likelihood-based adaptive differential evolution algorithm (ADEA) is investigated for the identification of nonlinear Hammerstein output error (HOE) systems that are widely used for modeling various nonlinear processes in engineering and applied sciences. In Ref. [5], the stability of a bilinear system is investigated by the Gramian method. The paper shows that the state of a bilinear control system can be split uniquely into generalized modes corresponding to the eigenvalues of the dynamics matrix. The Gramians of the controllability and observability of a bilinear system can be divided into parts (sub-Gramians) that characterize the measure of these

Citation: Bakhtadze, N. Preface to the Special Issue on "Identification, Knowledge Engineering and Digital Modeling for Adaptive and Intelligent Control"—Special Issue Book. *Mathematics* **2023**, *11*, 1906. https://doi.org/10.3390/math11081906

Received: 3 April 2023
Accepted: 14 April 2023
Published: 18 April 2023

generalized modes and their interactions. In Ref. [6], the system identification properties of Dynamic Mode Decomposition (DMD) are studied. DMD is a popular data-driven framework for extracting linear dynamics from complex high-dimensional systems. In Ref. [7], a direct method for the synthesis of robust systems operating under parametric uncertainty in a control plant model is proposed. The developed robust control procedures are based on the assumption that the structural properties of the nominal system survive over the entire range of parameter changes. The authors in [8] show that for simulators providing vestibular stimulus, the automatic vestibular–ocular reflex (VOR) bodily function can objectively measure the accuracy of motion simulation. This requires a model of ocular response to enforced accelerations, which is offered in the paper. The model corresponds to a single-layer spiking differential neural network; its activation functions are based on the dynamic Izhikevich model of neuron dynamics.

The authors in [9] discuss the analysis and optimization of stochastic systems based on canonical wavelet expansions. A wavelet model for the calibration of essentially nonstationary stochastic processes and parameters is developed. In Ref. [10], a new algorithm is proposed for constructing an integral model of an input–output-type nonlinear dynamic system in the form of a quadratic segment of the Volterra integro-power series (polynomial). It examines the nonparametric identification of models using physically realizable piecewise linear test signals in the time domain.

In Ref. [11], a multi-output soft sensor for the industrial reactive distillation process of methyl tert-butyl ether (MTBE) is developed. Unlike the existing approaches, the paper offers soft sensors with filters to predict model errors, which are further considered as corrections in the final output forecasts. The authors in [12] consider the mathematical aspects of the problem of the optimal interception of a mobile search vehicle moving along random tacks on a given route and searching for a target, which travels parallel to this route. The interception problem was formulated as an optimal stochastic control problem, which was transformed to a deterministic optimization one.

The article [13] is aimed at numerical studies of inverse problems of experiment processing (identification of unknown parameters of mathematical models from experimental data) based on balanced identification technology. This technology uses the cross-validation root-mean-square error to select the values of the regularization parameters. The authors in [14] discuss the identification of plasma equilibrium reconstruction in D-shaped tokamaks on the basis of external magnetic plasma measurements. Such identification methods are aimed at increasing the speed of response when plasma discharges are relatively short, such as in the spherical Globus-M2 tokamak.

As Guest Editor of this Special Issue, I am grateful to the authors of these articles for their quality contributions, to the reviewers for their valuable comments, and to the administrative staff of MDPI for the support to complete this Special Issue. Special thanks to the Section Managing Editor Ms. Krystal Wang for her excellent collaboration and valuable assistance.

Funding: This research was funded by the Russian Science Foundation, grant number [19-19-00673-P].

Conflicts of Interest: The author declares no conflict of interest.

References

1. Novikov, D. Models of Strategic Decision-Making under Informational Control. *Mathematics* **2021**, *9*, 1889. [CrossRef]
2. Antipov, A.; Krasnova, S.; Utkin, V. Methods of Ensuring Invariance with Respect to External Disturbances: Overview and New Advances. *Mathematics* **2021**, *9*, 3140. [CrossRef]
3. Bakhtadze, N.; Yadikin, Y. Analysis and Prediction of Electric Power System's Stability Based on Virtual State Estimators. *Mathematics* **2021**, *9*, 3194. [CrossRef]
4. Hasnat, B.; Tariq, H.B.; Chaudhary, N.I.; Khan, Z.A.; Raja, M.A.Z.; Cheema, K.M.; Milyani, A.H. Maximum-Likelihood-Based Adaptive and Intelligent Computing for Nonlinear System Identification. *Mathematics* **2021**, *9*, 3199. [CrossRef]
5. Iskakov, A.; Yadykin, I. On Spectral Decomposition of States and Gramians of Bilinear Dynamical Systems. *Mathematics* **2021**, *9*, 3288. [CrossRef]

6. Heiland, J.; Unger, B. Identification of Linear Time-Invariant Systems with Dynamic Mode Decomposition. *Mathematics* **2022**, *10*, 418. [CrossRef]

7. Krasnova, S.; Kokunko, Y.; Utkin, A.; Utkin, V. Robust Stabilization via Super-Stable Systems Techniques. *Mathematics* **2022**, *10*, 98. [CrossRef]

8. Chairez, I.; Mukhamedov, A.; Prud, V.; Andrianova, O.; Chertopolokhov, V. Differential Neural Network-Based Nonparametric Identification of Eye Response to Enforced Head Motion. *Mathematics* **2022**, *10*, 855. [CrossRef]

9. Sinitsyn, I.; Sinitsyn, V.; Korepanov, E.; Konashenkova, T. Bayes Synthesis of Linear Nonstationary Stochastic Systems by Wavelet Canonical Expansions. *Mathematics* **2022**, *10*, 1517. [CrossRef]

10. Voscoboynikov, Y.; Solodusha, S.; Markova, E.; Antipina, E.; Boeva, V. Identification of Quadratic Volterra Polynomials in the "Input–Output" Models of Nonlinear Systems. *Mathematics* **2022**, *10*, 1836. [CrossRef]

11. Klimchenko, V.; Torgashov, A.; Shardt, Y.; Yang, F. Multi-Output Soft Sensor with a Multivariate Filter That Predicts Errors Applied to an Industrial Reactive Distillation Process. *Mathematics* **2021**, *9*, 1947. [CrossRef]

12. Galyaev, A.; Lysenko, P.; Rubinovich, E. Optimal Stochastic Control in the Interception Problem of a Randomly Tacking Vehicle. *Mathematics* **2021**, *9*, 2386. [CrossRef]

13. Sokolov, A.; Nikulina, I. Choice of Regularization Methods in Experiment Processing: Solving Inverse Problems of Thermal Conductivity. *Mathematics* **2022**, *10*, 4221. [CrossRef]

14. Mitrishkin, Y.; Korenev, P.; Konkov, A.; Kruzhkov, V.; Ovsiannikov, N. New Identification Approach and Methods for Plasma Equilibrium Reconstruction in D-Shaped Tokamaks. *Mathematics* **2022**, *10*, 40. [CrossRef]

 *mathematics*

Article

Models of Strategic Decision-Making under Informational Control

Dmitry Novikov

V.A. Trapeznikov Institute of Control Sciences, 117997 Moscow, Russia; novikov@ipu.ru; Tel.: +7-4953347569

Abstract: A general complex model is considered for collective dynamical strategic decision-making with explicitly interconnected factors reflecting both psychic (internal state) and behavioral (external-action, result of activity) components of agents' activity under the given environmental and control factors. This model unifies and generalizes approaches of game theory, social psychology, theories of multi-agent systems, and control in organizational systems by simultaneous consideration of both internal and external parameters of the agents. Two special models (of informational control and informational confrontation) contain formal results on controllability and properties of equilibriums. Interpretations of a general model are conformity (threshold behavior), consensus, cognitive dissonance, and other effects with applications to production systems, multi-agent systems, crowd behavior, online social networks, and voting in small and large groups.

Keywords: decision-making; psychic and behavioral components of activity; action; result of activity; equilibrium stability; consensus; threshold behavior; cognitive dissonance; conformity; informational control; informational confrontation

Citation: Novikov, D. Models of Strategic Decision-Making under Informational Control. *Mathematics* **2021**, *9*, 1889. https://doi.org/10.3390/math9161889

Academic Editor: Vassilis C. Gerogiannis

Received: 3 July 2021
Accepted: 7 August 2021
Published: 9 August 2021

Publisher's Note: MDPI stays neutral with regard to jurisdictional claims in published maps and institutional affiliations.

1. Introduction

What factors influence the decisions one makes? Each scientific domain gives its own answer, which is correct in the paradigm of its particular domain. For example, the *theory of individual decision-making* says that the main factor is the *utility* of the decision-maker. *Game theory* answers that it's a set of decisions made by others. *Psychology* says that it's a person's internal state (including their beliefs, attitudes, etc.). Table 1 contains factors of decision-making (columns), scientific domains (rows), and the author's subjective expert judgment on the degree (conventionally reflected by the number of plus signs in the corresponding cell) of taking into account the factors by the domains. Since all these domains are immense (but none of them explores a combination of more than two factors), references are given on several main books or representative survey papers.

In this paper, a model of strategic collective decision-making, which equally considers all of the factors listed in the columns of Table 1, is considered. The model includes explicit interconnected parameters, reflecting both psychic (state) and behavioral (action and activity result, see [1]) components of an *agent*'s activity. Following the methodology proposed in [2], we study the mutually influencing processes of the dynamics of the agent's internal states, actions, and activity results and the properties of the corresponding equilibria.

In decision-making, organizational systems control, and collective behavior, the traditional models of dynamics cover either *the behavioral components of activity* [1] (externally manifested, observable), the *actions* and (or) *activity results* of different agents [3], or *the psychic components of activity*, their *"internal states"* (opinions, beliefs, attitudes, etc.; see surveys in [4,5]), which are "internal" variables and are not always completely observable.

Table 1. Decision-making factors and related scientific domains.

Factor Scientific Domain	Utility	Action	Actionsof Others	Environment (and Results of Activity)	Internal State	History	Control
Individual decision-making [6,7]	+++	++		++	+	+	
Game theory [8], theory of collectivebehavior [9–11], behavioral economics [12]	++	+++	+++	+	+	+	+
Social psychology [13–16], Psychology of personality [17–19] Mathematical psychology [20–22]	+	++	+	++	+++	+	+
Multi-agent systems [23,24]		+++	+	++	++	+	+
Control theory (of social and organizational systems) [25,26]	++	++	++	+++	+	+	+++

In the general case, the strategic (goal-oriented) decisions of an agent can be affected by:

- his preferences as reflected by his objective or utility function;
- his actions and the results of activity carried out jointly with other agents;
- the state of an environment (the parameters that are not purposefully chosen by any of the agents);
- purposeful impacts (controls) from other agents.

The first three groups of sources of informational influence are "passive." The fourth source of influence—*control*—is active, and there may exist several agents affecting a given agent; see the model of informational confrontation in Section 6 below.

In the following paper, we introduce a general complex model of collective decision-making and control with explicit interconnected factors, reflecting both the psychic and behavioral components of activity. Some practical interpretations are conformity effects [10,11] as well as applications to production systems [25,27], multi-agent systems [23], crowd behavior [28], online social networks [29], and voting in small and large groups [9].

The main results are:

- The general model of decision-making, which embraces all the factors listed above, influencing the decisions made by a strategic agent (see Figure 1 and Equations (1)–(3));
- Particular cases of the general model, reflecting many effects well known in social psychology and organizational behavior: consensus, conformity, hindsight, cognitive dissonance, etc.;
- Two models (of informational control and informational confrontation) and formal results on controllability and the properties of equilibriums.

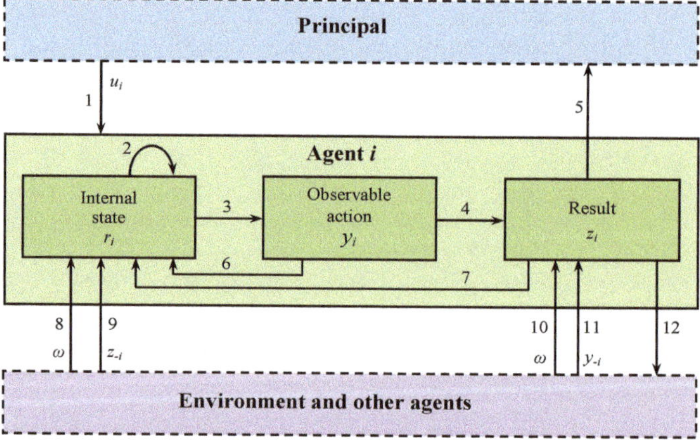

Figure 1. Structure of decision-making process [2].

This paper is organized as follows: in Section 2, the general structure of the decision-making process is considered. In Section 3, the well-known particular models of informational control, conformity behavior, etc., are discussed. In Section 4, the simple majority voting model is used as an example to present the original results on the mutually influencing processes of the dynamics of the agent's states and actions (the psychic and behavioral components of activity) and the properties of the corresponding equilibria. Section 5 is devoted to the model of informational confrontation between two agents, trying to control—influence on the third one—simultaneously in their own interests.

2. Decision-Making Model

Consider a set $N = \{1, 2, \ldots, n\}$ of interacting *agents*. Each agent is assigned a number (subscript). Discrete time instants (periods) are indicated by superscripts. Assume that there is a single control authority (*principal*) purposefully affecting the activity of different agents by *control* $\{u_i \in U_i\}$.

We introduce a parameter $r_i \in R_i$ (internal "*state*") of agent i, which reflects all his characteristics of interest, including his *personality structure* [1]. In applications, the agent's state can be interpreted as his *opinion*, *belief*, or *attitude* (e.g., his *assessment* of some object or agent), the effectiveness of his activity, the rate of his learning, the desired result of his activity, etc.

Let agent i choose *actions* from a set of admissible ones; A_i. His action is denoted by y_i ($y_i \in A_i$). The agent chooses their actions, and the *results* of their activity are realized accordingly, which is denoted by $z_i \in A_{zi}$, where A_{zi} is a set of admissible activity results of agent i. The agent's action and the result of his activity may mismatch due to *uncertainty factors*, including an *environment* with a state $\omega \in \Omega$ or the actions of other agents; see Figure 1.

The connection between the agent's action and the result of his activity may have a complex nature described by probability distributions, fuzzy functions, etc. [26]. For the sake of simplicity, assume that the activity result z_i of agent i is a given real-valued deterministic function $R_i(y_i, y_{-i}, \omega)$ that depends on his action, the vector $y_{-i} = (y_1, \ldots, y_{i-1}, y_{i+1}, \ldots, y_n)$ of actions of all other agents (the so-called *opponent's action profile* for agent i), and the environment's state ω. The function $R_i(\cdot)$ is called the *technological function* [27,30].

Suppose that each agent always knows his state, and his action is completely observable for him and all other agents.

Let agent i have *preferences* on a set A_{zi} of activity results. In other words, agent i has the ability to compare different results of his activity. The agent's preferences are described by his *utility function* (goal function, or payoff function) Φ_i: $A_{zi} \times R_i \to {}^{\circ 1}$: under a fixed state, of the two activity results, the agent prefers the one with the utility function of greater value. The agent's behavior is rational in the sense of maximizing his utility.

When choosing an action, the agent is guided by his preferences and how the chosen action affects the result of his activity. Given his state, the environment's state, and the actions of other agents, agent i chooses an action y_i^* maximizing his utility:

$$y_i^*(y_{-i}^*, r_i, \omega) \; = \; \arg\max_{y_i \in A_i} \Phi_i(R_i(y_i, y_{-i}^*, \omega), r_i), \; i \in N. \tag{1}$$

The expression (1) defines a *Nash equilibrium* of the agents' normal form game [8], in which they choose their actions once, simultaneously, and independently under *common knowledge* about the technological functions, utility functions, the states of different agents, and the environment's state [26].

The structure in Figure 1 is very general and covers, as particular cases, the following processes and phenomena:

- individual ($n = 1$) *decision-making* (arrow no. 3);
- *self-reflexion* (the arrow sequence 2–6, 7, 8–2);
- decision-making under *uncertainty* (the arrow sequence 8–3–4, 10);

- game-theoretic interaction of several agents and their *collective behavior* (the arrow sequence 4—11, 12);
- models of *complex activity* (the arrow sequence 1, 8–3–4, 10–5, 12);
- *control* of a single agent (the arrow sequence 1–3–4–5). Control consists of a purposeful impact on the set of admissible actions, the technological function, the utility function, the agent's state, or a combination of these parameters. Impact's purposefulness means that the agent chooses a required action, or a required result of his activity is realized. Depending on the subject of control, under fixed staff and structure of the system, there are institutional, motivational, and informational controls;
- control of several agents (the arrow sequence 1–3–4, 11–5);
- *social influence* [29] (the arrow sequence 1, 8, 9–2, 3); in particular, conformity effects [24];
- *learning during activity* [30] (the arrow sequence 2–3–4, 10–7);
- *learning* [30] (the arrow sequence 1, 2–3–4, 10–5, 7).

(Whenever several factors appear simultaneously in a process or phenomenon, the corresponding arrows in a sequence are conventionally separated by commas.)

Let us specify the decision-making model.

3. General Model

We introduce a series of assumptions. (Their practical interpretations are discussed below).

Assumption 1. $A_i = A_{zi} = R_i = U_i = [0, 1], i \in N.$

Assumption 2. $R_i(y_i, y_{-i}, \theta) = R(y_i, y_{-i}), i \in N.$

Assumption 3. *Under a fixed state r_i of agent i, his utility function Φ_i: $[0, 1]^2 \to \Re$ is single-peaked with the peak point $r_i, i \in N$ [26].*

Assumption 4. *The function $R(\cdot)$ is continuous, strictly monotonically increasing in all variables, and satisfies the unanimity condition:* $\forall a \in [0, \ 1] \ R(a, \dots, a) = a.$

Assumption 1 is purely "technical": as seen in the subsequent presentation, many results remain valid for a more general case of convex and compact admissible sets.

Assumption 2 is more significant, as it declares the following. First, the activity result (*collective decision*) $z = R(y_i, y_{-i})$ is the same for all agents. Second, there is no uncertainty about the environment's state. The agent's state determines his *preferences*——attitude towards the results of collective activity. The vector of individual results of the agents' activity depending, among other factors, on the actions of other agents can be considered by analogy. This line seems promising for future research. By Assumption 2, there is no uncertainty. Therefore, the dependence of the activity result (and the equilibrium actions of different agents) on the parameter ω is omitted.

According to Assumption 3, the agent's utility function, defined on the set of activity results, has a unique maximum achieved when the result coincides with the agent's state. In other words, the agent's state parameterizes his utility function, reflecting the goal of his activity. (Recall that a *goal* is a desired activity result [3].) Also, the agent's state can be interpreted as his *assessment*, *opinion*, or attitude [1] towards certain activity results; see the terminology of personality psychology in [1].

Assumption 4 is meaningfully transparent: if the goals of all agents coincide, then the corresponding result of their joint activity is achievable.

The expression (1) describes an agent's single decision (single choice of his action). To consider repetitive decision-making, we need to introduce additional assumptions. The decision-making dynamics studied below satisfy the following assumption.

Assumption 5. *The agent's action dynamics are described by the indicator behavior procedure [26]:*

$$y_i^t = \left(1 - \gamma_i^t\right) y_i^{t-1} + \gamma_i^t y_i^* \left(y_{-i}^{t-1}, r_i^t\right), \ t = 1, 2, \dots, \tag{2}$$

with given initial values (y_i^0, r_i^0), $i \in N$, *where* $\gamma_i^t \in (0,1]$ *are known constants. The action* $y_i^* \left(y_{-i}^{t-1}, r_i^t \right)$ *is called the local (current) position for the goal of agent i. In each period, the agent makes a "step" (proportional to* γ_i^t*) from his current state to his best response (1) to the action profile in the previous period.*

Assumption 6. *The agent's state dynamics are described by the procedure:*

$$r_i^t = \left[1 - b_i B_i \left(r_i^{t-1}, u_i^t \right) - c_i C_i \left(r_i^{t-1}, y_i^{t-1} \right) - d_i D_i \left(r_i^{t-1}, z^{t-1} \right) - e_i \right] r_i^{t-1} +$$

$$b_i B_i \left(r_i^{t-1}, u_i^t \right) u_i^t + c_i C_i \left(r_i^{t-1}, y_i^{t-1} \right) y_i^{t-1} + d_i D_i \left(r_i^{t-1}, z^{t-1} \right) z^{t-1} + e_i E_i \left(r_i^{t-1}, y_{-i}^{t-1} \right) \quad (3)$$

$$t = 1, 2, \ldots, i \in N.$$

Assumption 7. *The nonnegative constant degrees of trust* (b_i, c_i, d_i, e_i) *satisfy the constraints:*

$$b_i + c_i + d_i + e_i \leq 1, \ i \in N. \quad (4)$$

Assumption 8. *The trust functions* $B_i(\cdot)$, $C_i(\cdot)$, $D_i(\cdot)$, *and* $E_i(\cdot)$, $i \in N$, *have the domains* $[0, 1]$*; in addition,* $\forall a \in [0, 1]$ $E_i(a, \ldots, a) = a$, $i \in N$.

Assumption 9. *The nonnegative constant degrees of trust* (b_i, c_i, d_i, e_i) *and the trust functions* $B_i(\cdot)$, $C_i(\cdot)$, *and* $D_i(\cdot)$, $i \in N$, *satisfy the condition:*

$$\forall \, x_1, x_2, x_3, x_4 \in [0, 1] \ b_i B_i(x_1, x_2) + c_i C_i(x_1, x_3) + d_i D_i(x_1, x_4) + e_i, \ i \in N. \quad (5)$$

Assumptions 7–9 guarantee that the state of the dynamic system (2) and (3) stay within the admissible set.

The constant weights (b_i, c_i, d_i, e_i) possibly reflect the attitude (*trust*) of agent i to the corresponding *information source*, whereas the functions $B_i(\cdot)$, $C_i(\cdot)$, $D_i(\cdot)$, and $E_i(\cdot)$ reflect his trust in the information source. The factor $\left[1 - b_i B_i \left(r_i^{t-1}, u_i^t \right) - c_i C_i \left(r_i^{t-1}, y_i^{t-1} \right) - d_i D_i \left(r_i^{t-1}, z^{t-1} \right) - e_i \right]$ (see the first term on the right-hand side of the procedure (3)) conditionally reflects *the power of the agent's beliefs.*

Note that, for unitary values of the trust functions, the expression (3) also has a conditional probabilistic interpretation: with some probability, the agent does not change his state (opinion); with the probability b_i, the state becomes equal to the control and with the probability c_i, to his action, etc.

Let us present and discuss practical interpretations of the five terms on the right-hand side of the expression (3). According to (3), the state r_i^t of agent i in period t is a linear combination of the following parameters:

I. his state r_i^{t-1} in the previous period $(t - 1)$ (arrow no. 2 in Figure 1);

II. his action y_i^{t-1} in the previous period $(t - 1)$ (arrow no. 6 in Figure 1);

III. the actions y_{-i}^{t-1} and, generally, the activity results z_{-i}^{t-1} of other agents in the previous period $(t - 1)$ (arrows no. 11 and 9 in Figure 1, possibly indirect influence via the agent's activity result);

IV. the activity result z^{t-1} in the previous period $(t - 1)$ (arrow no. 7 in Figure 1);

V. the external impact (*control*) u_i^t applied to him in period t (arrow no. 1 in Figure 1).

Thus, the model (2)–(3) embraces both *external* (explicit) and *internal* (implicit) informational control of decision-making.

An example is the interaction of group members in an online social network. Based on their beliefs (states), they publicly express their opinions (assessments or actions) regarding some issue (phenomenon or process). In this case, the collective decision (opinion or assessment) may be, e.g., the average value of the expressed assessments (opinions). Some agents can apply informational control (without changing their states and actions); some honestly reveal their beliefs in assessments; some try to bring the collective assessment closer to their beliefs. The beliefs of some agents may "drift," depending on the current actions (both their own and other agents), control, and (or) collective assessment.

An equilibrium $y_i^*(a, \ldots, a) = r_i^* = a \in [0,1]$, $i \in N$, is called *unified*: the final decision and all states and actions of all agents are the same.

Under Assumptions 1–9, we have the following result:

Proposition 1 ([2]). *Let Assumptions 1–9 hold, and let all constant degrees of trust and trust functions be strictly positive. Without any control ($b_i = 0$, $i \in N$), a fixed point of the dynamic system (2) and (3) is the unified equilibrium.*

Really, substituting the unified equilibrium into the expressions (2) and (3), we obtain identities: the unified equilibrium satisfies (1) due to the properties of the utility function (see Assumption 3).

The unified equilibrium of the dynamic system (2) and (3) always exists, but its domain of attraction does not necessarily include all admissible initial states and actions. Moreover, it may be nonunique. Therefore, the properties of equilibria of the dynamic system (2) and (3) should be studied in detail, focusing on practically important particular cases.

4. Particular Cases

Several well-studied models represent particular cases of the dynamic model (2) and (3). Let us consider some of them; also, see the survey in [2].

4.1. Models of Informational Control

Models of informational control [29], in which the agent's opinions evolve under purposeful messages, e.g., from the *mass media*. In these models $c_i = d_i = e_i = 0$, $i \in N$:

$$r_i^t = \left(1 - b_i B_i\left(r_i^{t-1}, u_i^t\right)\right) r_i^{t-1} + b_i\, B_i\left(r_i^{t-1}, u_i^t\right) u_i^t,\ t = 1, 2, \ldots, i \in N.$$

The agent's state dynamics model (6) was adopted in the book [29] to pose and solve informational control problems.

The dynamics of opinions, beliefs, and attitudes of a personality can be described by analogy; see a survey of the corresponding models of personality psychology in [1,21].

4.2. Models of Consensus

Models of *consesus* (see [29] and surveys in [23,31]). In this class of models $b_i = c_i = d_i = 0$, and each agent averages their state with the states or actions of other agents:

$$E_i\left(r_i^{t-1}, y_{-i}^{t-1}\right) = e_i \sum_{j \in N \setminus \{i\}} e_{ij}\, \hat{E}_i\left(r_i^{t-1}, y_j^{t-1}\right) y_j^{t-1}.$$

In other words, the expression (3) takes the form:

$$r_i^t = (1 - e_i) r_i^{t-1} + e_i \sum_{j \in N \setminus \{i\}} e_{ij}\, \hat{E}_i\left(r_i^{t-1}, y_j^{t-1}\right) y_j^{t-1},\ t = 1, 2, \ldots, i \in N,$$

where the elements of the matrix $\|e_{ij}\|$ (the links between different agents) satisfy the condition $\sum_{j \in N \setminus \{i\}} e_{ij} = 1$, $i \in N$.

The existence conditions of equilibria can be found in [23,29].

4.3. Models of Conformity Behavior

Models of conformity behavior (see [9,11] and a survey in [28]). In this class of models, $b_i = c_i = d_i = 0$, $e_i = 1$ and each agent makes a binary choice between being active or passive ($A_i = \{0; 1\}$). Moreover, his action coincides with his state evolving as follows:

$$r_i^t = \begin{cases} 1, \ \sum\limits_{j \in N} e_{ij} y_j^{t-1} \geq \varsigma_i, \\ 0, \ \sum\limits_{j \in N} e_{ij} y_j^{t-1} < \varsigma_i, \end{cases} \ , \ t = 1, 2, \ldots, \ i \in N, \tag{6}$$

where $\varsigma_i \in [0,1]$ is the agent's *threshold*. The agent demonstrates *conformity behavior* [9,11]: he begins to act when the weighted share of active agents exceeds his threshold (the weights are the strengths of links between different agents). Otherwise, the agent remains passive. The dynamics of conformity behavior (6) were studied in the book [28].

In the models of informational control, consensus, and conformity behavior, the main emphasis is on the agent's states: his actions are not considered, or the action is assumed to coincide with the state.

4.4. Models of Social Influence

Models of social influence (see a meaningful description of social influence effects and numerous examples in [13,16]). On the one hand, the models of informational control, consensus, and conformity behavior can undoubtedly be attributed to the models of *social influence*. On the other hand, the general model (3) reflects other social influence effects known in *social psychology*, including the dependence of beliefs, relationships, and attitudes on the previous experience of the agent's activity [20–22].

Similar effects occur under *cognitive dissonance*: an agent changes his opinions or beliefs in dissonance with the performed behavior, e.g., with the action he chooses (see arrow no. 6 in Figure 1). In this case, an adequate model has the form:

$$r_i^t = \left(1 - c_i \, C_i\left(r_i^{t-1}, y_i^{t-1}\right)\right) r_i^{t-1} + c_i \, C_i\left(r_i^{t-1}, y_i^{t-1}\right) y_i^{t-1} \, , \ t = 1, 2, \ldots, \ i \in N,$$

($b_i = d_i = 0$, $e_{ij} = 0$). Within this model, the agent changes his state depending on the actions chosen.

Another example is *the hindsight effect* (explaining events by the retrospective view, "It figures"). This effect is the agent's inclination to perceive events that have already occurred or facts that have already been established, as obvious and predictable, despite insufficient initial information to predict them. In this case, an adequate model has the form:

$$r_i^t = \left(1 - d_i \, D_i\left(r_i^{t-1}, z^{t-1}\right)\right) r_i^{t-1} + d_i \, D_i\left(r_i^{t-1}, z^{t-1}\right) z^{t-1} \, , \ t = 1, 2, \ldots, \ i \in N,$$

($b_i = c_i = 0$, $e_{ij} = 0$). Within this model, the agent changes his state depending on the activity result (see arrow no. 7 in Figure 1).

The two models mentioned were considered in detail in [2].

5. Model of Voting

Consider a decision-making procedure by simple majority voting. Assume that the agents report their true opinions (actions) $y_i^t \in \{0; 1\}$: they either support a *decision* ($y_i^t = 1$) or not ($y_i^t = 0$). (Truth-telling means no strategic behavior.) The decision (the result of collective activity) is accepted ($z^t = 1$) if at least half of the agents voted for it; otherwise, the decision is rejected ($z^t = 0$): $z^t = I\left(\sum\limits_{j \in N} y_j^t \geq \frac{n}{2}\right)$, where $I(\cdot)$ denotes the indicator function. Examples are: election of some candidate or authority, support of resources or costs allocation variant, etc.

Agent i has a type (opinion or belief) $r_i^t \in [0,1]$ reflecting his inclination to support the decision. Assume that the agent chooses his action depending on his type: $y_i^t = I\left(r_i^{t-1} \geq \frac{1}{2}\right), i \in N$.

Let the dynamics of the agent's type be described by the procedure:

$$r_i^t = [1 - b_i - c_i - d_i] \, r_i^{t-1} + b_i \, u_i^t + c_i \, y_i^{t-1} + d_i \, z^{t-1}, \ t = 1, 2, \ldots, i \in N, \tag{7}$$

where $u_i^t \in [0, 1]$ is the *control* (i.e., informational influence via mass media, social media, or personal communication), and the nonnegative *constant degrees of trust* (b_i, c_i, d_i) satisfy the constraints:

$$b_i + c_i + d_i \leq 1, \ i \in N. \tag{8}$$

(Also, see the expression (3)).

Due to relations (8), the state of the dynamic system (7) stays within the admissible set $[0,1]^n$.

According to the expression (7), the type r_i^t of agent i in period t is a linear combination of the following parameters:

i. his type (opinion) r_i^{t-1} in the previous period $(t - 1)$ (the value $(1 - b_i - c_i - d_i)$ reflects *the strength of the agent's beliefs*);

ii. the external impact (*control*) u_i^t applied to him in period t;

iii. his action y_i^{t-1} in the previous period $(t - 1)$ (a change in the agent's type due to mismatch with the action chosen can be treated as *the cognitive dissonance effect*);

iv. the activity result z^{t-1} in the previous period $(t - 1)$ (a change in the agent's type due to mismatch with the collective decision can be treated as *conformity behavior*).

Within this model, an active system is controllable if the action of any agent can be changed to the opposite in finite time using admissible controls according to (7).

Let $\{r_i^0 \in [0, 1]\}$ be given initial types of all agents. Consider different modifications of the model (7), as described in Table 2.

Table 2. Modifications of model (7).

Modification	Control	Cognitive Dissonance	Conformity Behavior
1	−	−	−
2	+	−	−
3	−	+	−
4	−	−	+
5	+	+	−
6	+	−	+
7	−	+	+
8	+	+	+

Modification 1 corresponds to no influence on the types of any agents. In these conditions, the types are static: $r_i^t = r_i^0, t = 1, 2, \ldots, i \in N$.

Modification 2. Here the expression (7) takes the form $r_i^t = [1 - b_i] \, r_i^{t-1} + b_i \, u_i^t, t = 1, 2, \ldots, i \in N$.

Proposition 2. *In modification 2 with $b_i > 0, i \in N$, the system (7) is controllable. For $u_i^t \in \{0; 1\}$ and $b_i > max\left\{\frac{1/2 - r_i^0}{1 - r_i^0}; 1 - \frac{1}{2r_i^0}\right\}, i \in N$, the action of any agent can be changed to the opposite in one period.*

Lower bounds for constants $\{b_i\}$ in propositions 2, 4, 5, and 6 characterize minimal "strength" of informational control or minimal trust in the source of the control information to provide the system's controllability.

Modification 3. Here the expression (7) takes the form:

$$r_i^t = [1 - c_i]\, r_i^{t-1} + c_i\, y_i^{t-1}, \ t = 1,\, 2,\, \ldots,\, i \in N.$$

In this modification, the types of agents vary, but their actions and activity result are stationary: $y_i^t = y_i^0$, $z^t = z^0$, $t = 1, 2, \ldots, i \in N$. The agents become increasingly convinced of the correctness of their beliefs and initial action.

Modification 4. Here the expression (7) takes the form:

$$r_i^t = [1 - d_i]\, r_i^{t-1} + d_i\, z^{t-1}, \ t = 1,\, 2,\, \ldots,\, i \in N. \tag{9}$$

In this modification, the types and actions of agents vary, but the activity result is stationary: $z^t = z^0$, $t = 1, 2, \ldots, i \in N$. The prior majority of agents do not change their actions and, affecting those who prefer another alternative, gradually draw the latter to their side.

Proposition 3. *In modification 4 with $d_i > 0$, $i \in N$, for any initial conditions $\{r_i^0 \in [0,\, 1]\}$ the system (9) has the unique equilibrium z^0.*

Modification 5. Here the expression (7) takes the form:

$$r_i^t = [1 - b_i - c_i]\, r_i^{t-1} + b_i\, u_i^t + c_i\, y_i^{t-1}, \ t = 1,\, 2,\, \ldots,\, i \in N. \tag{10}$$

Writing the monotonicity condition for the agent's type depending on the control goal, we easily establish the following result.

Proposition 4. *In modification 5 with $b_i > c_i$, $i \in N$ the system (10) is controllable.*

Modification 6. Here the expression (7) takes the form:

$$r_i^t = [1 - b_i - d_i]\, r_i^{t-1} + b_i\, u_i^t + d_i\, z^{t-1}, \ t = 1,\, 2,\, \ldots,\, i \in N. \tag{11}$$

Writing the monotonicity condition for the agent's type depending on the control goal, we easily establish the following result:

Proposition 5. *In modification 6 with $b_i > d_i$, $i \in N$, the system (11) is controllable.*

Modification 7. Here there is no control, and the expression (7) takes the form:

$$r_i^t = [1 - c_i - d_i]\, r_i^{t-1} + c_i\, y_i^{t-1} + d_i\, z^{t-1}, \ t = 1,\, 2,\, \ldots,\, i \in N.$$

In this modification, the types of agents and, generally speaking, their actions vary, but the activity result is *stationary*: $z^t = z^0$, $t = 1, 2, \ldots, i \in N$. The prior majority of agents do not change their actions and, affecting those who prefer another alternative, possibly gradually draw the latter to their side (depending on the relation between the parameters c_i and d_i).

Modification 8. Here the type dynamics are described by the general expression (7). Writing the monotonicity condition for the agent's type depending on the control goal, we easily establish the following result:

Proposition 6. *In modification 8 with $b_i > 3\,(c_i + d_i)$, $i \in N$, the system (7) is controllable.*

Concluding this subsection, we also mention an interesting modification of the procedure (7): no control and *anti-conformists* (the agents choosing actions to obtain a result different from the majority's one):

$$r_i^t = [1 - c_i - d_i]\, r_i^{t-1} + c_i\, y_i^{t-1} + d_i \left(1 - z^{t-1}\right), \; t = 1, 2, \ldots, i \in N.$$

Example. Consider an illustrative example of three agents with the initial types $r_1^0 = 0.3$, $r_2^0 = 0.6$, and $r_3^0 = 0.4$ Assume that the cognitive dissonance effect is absent ($c_i = 0, i = \overline{1,3}$). The first agent does not change his type: $d_1 = 0$. The second and third agents are anti-conformists: $d_2 = 0.1$ and $d_3 = 0.1$. The dynamics of the agents' types (second and third agents) and activity result (unstable!) are shown in Figure 2.

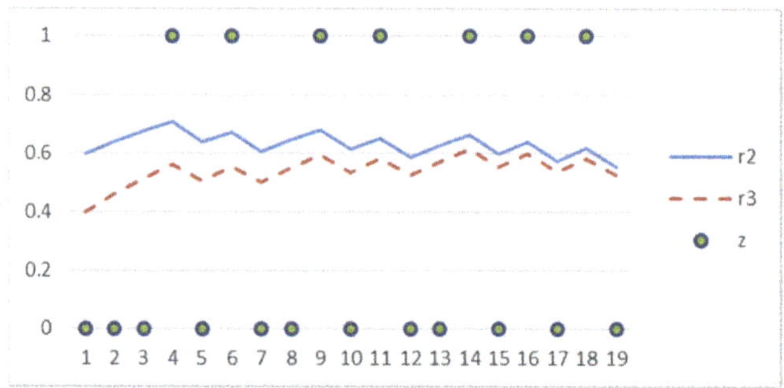

Figure 2. Dynamics of agents' types and activity result in the example.

6. Model of Informational Confrontation

Consider three agents: the first and second agents perform informational control (choose controls as their actions), affecting (due to the *informational influence*) the type (internal state—opinion or belief) of the third agent. The common activity result for all agents is the state of the third agent by a terminal period T.

Let the opinion r^t of the third agent in period t be a linear combination of his opinion and the opinions of the first and second agents in the previous period: $r^t = [1 - b_1 - b_2]\, r^{t-1} + b_1 r_1^{t-1} + b_2 r_2^{t-1}$. (All opinions have the range $[0, 1)$.)

Assume that the goals of the first and second agents are opposite (the first one is interested in turning r^t to state "0", while the second one—to state "1") and their states are invariable: $r_1^t \equiv 0, r_2^t \equiv 1$. Interpretations of agents states are the same as in Section 4 above.

If, in each period, the agents exchanged their opinions (true states), the opinion dynamics would be $r^t = [1 - b_1 - b_2]\, r^{t-1} + b_2$.

The controls of the first and second agents are to inform the third agent about their opinions in some periods. Therefore, we have:

$$r^t = \left[1 - b_1 I(y_1^t = 1) - b_2 I\left(y_2^t = 1\right)\right] r^{t-1} + b_1 I(y_1^t = 1)r_1^{t-1} + b_2 I(y_2^t = 1)r_2^{t-1}.$$

The sets of admissible actions have the form $y_i^t \in \{0; 1\}$, $i = \overline{1, 2}$, (such controls are called *binary*). Then $y_i^t = I(y_i^t = 1)$, $i = \overline{1, 2}$. Substituting $r_1^t \equiv 0, r_2^t \equiv 1$, we arrive at the following state dynamics of the third agent:

$$r^t = \left[1 - b_1 y_1^t - b_2 y_2^t\right] r^{t-1} + b_2 y_2^t, \; t = 1, 2, \ldots \tag{12}$$

where $b_1 + b_2 \leq 1$ and r^0 is a given initial state. (Also, see the expressions (3) and (7) above.) Let the first agent be interested in minimizing the terminal state r^T, whereas the second in maximizing it. Note that the consumption of resources and other costs are not included in the goal functions.

In a practical interpretation, the state of the third agent (his opinion, belief, or attitude towards some issue or phenomenon) is reduced by the first agent and increased by the second. There is an informational confrontation between the first and second agents, described by game theory. In the dynamic case considered below, we have a differential game; static models of informational confrontation and models of repeated games can be found in [28,29].

According to (12), the combinations, presented in Table 3, are possible in each period.

Table 3. The combinations of each period.

$y_1 = 0$	$y_2 = 0$	$\Delta r^t = 0$ (the state of the third agent is invariable)
$y_1 = 1$	$y_2 = 0$	$\Delta r^t = -b_1 \, r^{t-1} \leq 0$
$y_1 = 0$	$y_2 = 1$	$\Delta r^t = b_2(1 - r^{t-1}) \geq 0$
$y_1 = 1$	$y_2 = 1$	$\Delta r^t = b_2 - (b_1 + b_2) \, r^{t-1}$

In the latter case, the state of the third agent has a nonnegative increment if $b_2 \geq b_1 \frac{r^{t-1}}{1 - r^{t-1}}$. A differential counterpart of the difference Equation (12) has the form:

$$\dot{r}(t) = -[b_1 y_1(t) + b_2 y_2(t)] \, r(t) + b_2 y_2(t). \tag{13}$$

Assume that the actions of the first and second agents are subjected to the integral resource constraints (i.e., resources for customized publications in mass media or posts in social media, advertising costs, etc.)

$$\int_0^T y_i(t) \, dt \leq C_i, \ i = \overline{1,2}. \tag{14}$$

First, let us study several special cases.

Case 1 (control applied by the first agent only). Substituting $y_2^t \equiv 0$ or (and) $b_2 \equiv 0$ into (13), we obtain the differential equation $\dot{r}(t) = -b_1 \, y_1(t) \, r(t)$. Due to the constraint (14), the solution $r(t) = r^0 \exp\left\{-b_1 \int_0^t y_1(\tau) \, d\tau\right\}$ yields the estimate $r(T) = r^0 \exp\left\{-b_1 C_1\right\}$ of the terminal state, which is independent of the trajectory $y_1(t)$.

Case 2 (control applied by the second agent only). Substituting $y_1^t \equiv 0$ or (and) $b_1 \equiv 0$ into (13), we obtain the differential equation $\dot{r}(t) = b_2 \, y_2(t) \, (1 - r(t))$. Due to the constraint (14), the solution $r(t) = 1 - (1 - r^0) \exp\left\{-b_2 \int_0^t y_2(\tau) \, d\tau\right\}$ yields the estimate $r(T) = 1 - (1 - r^0) \exp\left\{-b_2 C_2\right\}$ of the terminal state, which is independent of the trajectory $y_2(t)$.

Case 3 (unlimited resources, both agents choose the actions $y_1^t \equiv 1, y_2^t \equiv 1$ in all periods). In this case, Equation (13) takes the form:

$$\dot{r}(t) = -[b_1 + b_2] \, r(t) + b_2. \tag{15}$$

The solution is given by:

$$r(t) = \frac{b_2}{b_1 + b_2} - \left(\frac{b_2}{b_1 + b_2} - r^0\right) e^{-(b_1 + b_2)t}. \tag{16}$$

The characteristic time is $\tau_0 \sim \frac{3}{b_1 + b_2}$, *and the asymptotic value is* $r^\infty = \frac{b_2}{b_1 + b_2}$.

Now, we return to the general case (13). Let $c_i(t) = \int_0^t y_i(\tau) d\tau \in [0; t]$, $c_i(T) \leq C_i$, $i = \overline{1,2}$, denote the resource consumption of agent i by a period t, representing a nondecreasing function of time. The choice of these functions by the first and second agents can be treated as their strategies.

The solution of Equation (13) is given by:

$$r(c_1(\cdot),\, c_2(\cdot), t) = \frac{r^0 + b_2 \int\limits_0^t y_2(\tau)\exp\{b_1 c_1(\tau) + b_2 c_2(\tau)\}d\tau}{\exp\{b_1 c_1(t) + b_2 c_2(t)\}}. \tag{17}$$

Consider the differential zero-sum two-person (antagonistic) game in normal form [32,33] of the first two agents. At the initial time instant of this game, the first and second agents choose their open-loop strategies $y_1(t)|_{t=0}^T$ and $y_2(t)|_{t=0}^T$, respectively, once, simultaneously, and independently of one another.

Further analysis will be restricted to the class of strategies with a single switch. In this class, at the initial time instant, the first and second agents simultaneously and independently choose some instants t_1 and t_2, respectively, when they start consuming their resource (apply controls) until complete exhaustion. Therefore, the open-loop strategies have the form:

$$y_i(t_i, C_i, t) = \begin{cases} 0,\, t < t_i; \\ 1,\, t \in [t_i, t_i + C_i]; \\ 0,\, t > t_i + C_i. \end{cases} \tag{18}$$

The functional (17) monotonically decreases in $c_1(\cdot)$ and increases in $c_2(\cdot)$. Hence, the first and second agents benefit from consuming the entire resource, and consequently, $t_1 \leq T - C_1$ and $t_2 \leq T - C_2$.

There are four possible relations among the parameters C_1, C_2, and T.

The first relation: $T \leq \min\{C_1;\, C_2\}$ (both agents have enough resources).

Here the Nash equilibrium strategies are: $\forall t \in [0, T]\ y_i^t \equiv 1,\, i = \overline{1,2}$, due to the monotonicity mentioned above.

The second and third relations: for some $i = \overline{1,2}$, $C_i \geq T_i$ and $C_{3-i} < T_i$.

Here, for agent i, the optimal strategy is: $\forall t \in [0,\, T]\ y_i^t \equiv 1$. For agent $(3 - i)$, the optimal switching instant t_{3-i} is the solution of a scalar optimization problem. The case $t_{3-i} = T - C_{3-i}$ is of practical interest. Note that the binary control is optimal under the constraints $y_i^t \in [0, 1],\, i = \overline{1,2}$, due to the linearity of (13) in the controls.

The fourth relation: $T > \max\{C_1;\, C_2\}$ (both agents lack resources).

Here the agents play a complete game. If $\tau_0 \ll \min\{C_1;\, C_2\}$, then the equilibrium of this game is $t_1^* = T - C_1,\, t_2^* = T - C_2$. Therefore, both agents start spending resources as late as possible, and the terminal value is $r(T) \approx r^\infty$. The same pair of strategies will be an equilibrium for $T \gg C_1 + C_2$ (when the quantities of resources are such that the controls are short-term on the scale of the period T). Practical interpretation is "save all reserves until the last decisive moment".

Hence, the results of this section give optimal strategies of the first two agents and characterize the equilibrium of their informational confrontation.

7. Conclusions

The main result is a general model (1)–(3) of joint dynamics of agents' actions and internal states, depending as on previous actions and states, as on the environment and the results of activity (see Figure 1). It allows combining methods and approaches of various decision-making paradigms, game theory, and social psychology to external and internal aspects of collective strategic decision-making.

Many known models and results of the above-mentioned scientific domains—reflecting the effects of consensus, threshold behavior, cognitive dissonance, informational influence, control, and confrontation—turn out to be the particular cases of the general model.

Three main directions seem prospective for future researches. First, the analysis of the general models in order to explore maximally general but analytical conditions for equilibrium existence, uniqueness, and its comparative statics. Second, generating new particular/applied models of collective activity and organizational behavior and management, taking into account not only "economical" rationality but psychological aspects as well. The third direction is the field of model identification and verification to put them closer to reality and practical applications.

Funding: This research received no external funding.

Data Availability Statement: Not applicable.

Conflicts of Interest: The author declares no conflict of interest.

References

1. Novikov, D. Control, activity, personality. *Adv. Syst. Sci. Appl.* **2020**, *20*, 113–135.
2. Novikov, D. Dynamics models of mental and behavioral components of activity in collective decision-making. *Large-Scale Syst. Control* **2020**, *85*, 206–237.
3. Belov, M.; Novikov, D. *Methodology of Complex Activity: Foundations of Understanding and Modelling*; Springer: Berlin/Heidelberg, Germany, 2020.
4. Banisch, S.; Olbrich, E. Opinion polarization by learning from social feedback. *J. Math. Sociol.* **2019**, *43*, 76–103. [CrossRef]
5. Flache, A.; MäS, M.; Feliciani, T.; Chattoe-Brown, E.; Deffuant, G.; Huet, S.; Lorenz, J. Models of social influence: Towards the next frontiers. *J. Artif. Soc. Soc. Simul.* **2017**, *20*, 31. [CrossRef]
6. Neumann, J.; Morgenstern, O. *Theory of Games and Economic Behavior*; Princeton University Press: Princeton, NJ, USA, 1944.
7. Fishburn, P. *Utility Theory for Decision Making*; R. E. Krieger Pub. Co: London, UK, 1979.
8. Myerson, R. *Game Theory: Analysis of Conflict*; Harvard University Press: London, UK, 1991.
9. Heckelman, J.; Miller, N. *Handbook of Social Choice and Voting*; Edward Elgar Publishing: London, UK.
10. Granovetter, M. Threshold models of collective behavior. *Am. J. Sociol.* **1978**, *83*, 1420–1443. [CrossRef]
11. Schelling, T. *Micromotives and Macrobehavior*; Norton & Co Ltd.: London, UK, 1978.
12. Dhami, S. *The Foundations of Behavioral Economic Analysis*; Oxford University Press: Oxford, UK, 2016.
13. Myers, D. *Social Psychology*, 12th ed.; McGraw-Hill: Columbus, OH, USA, 2012.
14. Perloff, R. *The Dynamics of Persuasion*, 6th ed.; Routledge: New York, NY, USA, 2017.
15. Zimbardo, P.; Leippe, M. *Psychology of Attitude Change and Social Influence*; McGraw-Hill: Columbus, OH, USA, 1991.
16. Cialdini, R. *Influence: Theory and Practice*, 5th ed.; Pearson: London, UK, 2008.
17. Sage. *The Sage Handbook of Personality Theory and Assessment. Vol. 1. Personality Theories and Models*; Sage Books: Los Angeles, CA, USA, 2008.
18. Schultz, D.; Schultz, S. *Theories of Personality*, 11th ed.; Cengage Learning: Boston, MA, USA, 2016.
19. Feist, J.; Feist, G. *Theories of Personality*, 9th ed.; McGraw-Hill Education: New York, NY, USA, 2017.
20. Allbaracin, D.; Shavitt, S. Attitudes and attitude change. *Annu. Rev. Psychol.* **2018**, *69*, 299–327. [CrossRef] [PubMed]
21. Hunter, J.; Danes, J.; Cohen, S. *Mathematical Models of Attitude Change*; Academic Press: Orlando, FL, USA, 1984.
22. Xia, H.; Wang, H.; Xuan, Z. Opinion dynamics: A multidisciplinary review and perspective on future research. *Int. J. Knowl. Syst. Sci.* **2011**, *2*, 72–91. [CrossRef]
23. Shoham, Y.; Leyton-Brown, K. *Multiagent Systems: Algorithmic, Game-Theoretical and Logical Foundations*; Cambridge University Press: Cambridge, UK, 2009.
24. Yakouda, M.; Abbel, W. Multi-Agent System: A Two-Level BDI Model Integrating Theory of Mind. *Int. J. Eng. Res. Technol.* **2020**, *9*, 208–216.
25. Burkov, V.; Goubko, M.; Kondrat'ev, V.; Korgin, N.; Novikov, D. *Mechanism Design and Management: Mathematical Methods for Smart Organizations*; Nova Science Publishers: New York, NY, USA, 2013.
26. Novikov, D. *Theory of Control in Organizations*; Nova Science Publishing: New York, NY, USA, 2013.
27. Belov, M.; Novikov, D. *Optimal Enterprise: Structures, Processes and Mathematics of Knowledge, Technology and Human Capital*; CRC Press: Boca Raton, FL, USA, 2021.
28. Breer, V.; Novikov, D.; Rogatkin, A. *Mob Control: Models of Threshold Collective Behavior*; Springer: Berlin/Heidelberg, Germany, 2017.
29. Chkhartishvili, A.; Gubanov, D.; Novikov, D. *Social Networks: Models of Information Influence, Control and Confrontation*; Springer: Berlin/Heidelberg, Germany, 2019.
30. Belov, M.; Novikov, D. *Models of Technologies*; Springer: Berlin/Heidelberg, Germany, 2020.
31. Minakowski, P.; Mucha, P.; Peszek, J. Density-induced consensus protocol. *Math. Models Methods Appl. Sci.* **2020**, *30*, 2389–2415. [CrossRef]
32. Gorelov, M.; Kononenko, A. Dynamic models of conflicts. III. Hierarchical games. *Autom. Remote Control.* **2015**, *76*, 264–277. [CrossRef]
33. Malsagov, M.; Ougolnitsky, G.; Usov, A. A differential Stackelberg game theoretic model of the promotion of innovations in universities. *Adv. Syst. Sci. Appl.* **2020**, *20*, 166–177.

mathematics

Article

Multi-Output Soft Sensor with a Multivariate Filter That Predicts Errors Applied to an Industrial Reactive Distillation Process

Vladimir Klimchenko [1], Andrei Torgashov [1,*], Yuri A. W. Shardt [2] and Fan Yang [3]

[1] Process Control Laboratory, Institute of Automation and Control Process FEB RAS, 5 Radio Str., Vladivostok 690041, Russia; volk@iacp.dvo.ru

[2] Department of Automation Engineering, Technical University of Ilmenau, 99084 Ilmenau, Germany; yuri.shardt@tu-ilmenau.de

[3] Beijing National Research Center for Information Science and Technology, Department of Automation, Tsinghua University, Beijing 100084, China; yangfan@tsinghua.edu.cn

* Correspondence: torgashov@iacp.dvo.ru; Tel.: +7-423-231-02-02

Abstract: The paper deals with the problem of developing a multi-output soft sensor for the industrial reactive distillation process of methyl tert-butyl ether production. Unlike the existing soft sensor approaches, this paper proposes using a soft sensor with filters to predict model errors, which are then taken into account as corrections in the final predictions of outputs. The decomposition of the problem of optimal estimation of time delays is proposed for each input of the soft sensor. Using the proposed approach to predict the concentrations of methyl sec-butyl ether, methanol, and the sum of dimers and trimers of isobutylene in the output product in a reactive distillation column was shown to improve the results by 32%, 67%, and 9.5%, respectively.

Keywords: soft sensing; multivariate filter; reactive distillation

Citation: Klimchenko, V.; Torgashov, A.; Shardt, Y.A.W.; Yang, F. Multi-Output Soft Sensor with a Multivariate Filter That Predicts Errors Applied to an Industrial Reactive Distillation Process. *Mathematics* **2021**, *9*, 1947. https://doi.org/10.3390/math9161947

Academic Editor: Michal Fečkan

Received: 20 June 2021
Accepted: 13 August 2021
Published: 15 August 2021

Publisher's Note: MDPI stays neutral with regard to jurisdictional claims in published maps and institutional affiliations.

1. Introduction

As the size and complexity of industrial systems increases, there is a need to accurately measure most process variables. Unfortunately, not all variables can be accurately measured using online hard sensors. For certain variables, such as concentration or density, the only accurate measurements can be obtained by manually taking samples and analyzing them in a laboratory. One solution to this problem is the development of soft sensors, which take the easy-to-measure variables and create models to predict the hard-to-measure variables [1].

All soft sensor systems consist of a process model that takes the easy-to-measure variables and provides an estimate of the hard-to-measure variables. These models can be constructed using methods ranging from linear regression to principal component analysis and support vector machines. Although the main focus has been on the development of the soft sensor models [2–5], advanced soft sensor systems have also a bias update term that can take any slowly sampled information to update the soft sensor prediction [1]. This bias update term is normally designed as some function of the difference between the predicted and measured values [6]. Of note, it should be mentioned that the measured values are often sampled very slowly and with considerable time delay. This means that during the points at which there are no updates, the previously available bias value is used. When such a system is properly designed, it can provide good tracking of the process, i.e., the predicted and measured values are close to each other.

Recently, it has been suggested that instead of only using the available slowly sampled data for updating the bias term, it should be possible to also model the historical errors and use them to predict the future errors [7]. It has been shown that such an approach can improve the overall performance of the soft sensor system. However, there still remain issues with how best to model and implement this predictive bias update term.

Furthermore, there are issues with incorporating time delays into this approach since they will greatly increase the size of the required search space.

Therefore, this paper will examine the development of a predictive bias update term for a nonlinear system using dimension reduction. The proposed approach will be tested using data from an industrial reactive distillation column that produces methyl tert-butyl ether (MTBE).

2. Background

Consider the soft sensor system shown in Figure 1, where u_t is the input, y_t is the measured (true) output, $\hat{y}_{m,t}$ the predicted soft sensor value, $\hat{y}_{\alpha,t}$ and $\hat{y}_{\beta,t}$ are intermediate soft sensor values, G_p is the true process, $\hat{G}_p$ is the soft sensor process model, and G_B is the bias update term. It can be noted that purpose of the bias update term is to take the information from the measured values and correct the output of the soft sensor system. This comes primarily from the unknown disturbances and the inherent plant-model mismatch.

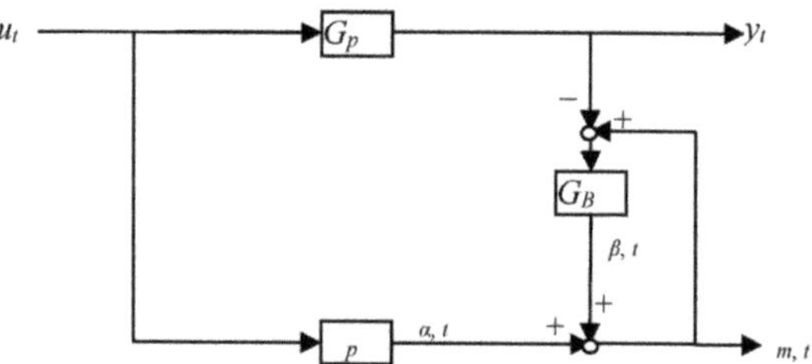

Figure 1. Soft sensor system of interest [1].

Another approach to this problem is to re-arrange the bias update term so that it contains a predictive model that can predict the errors between the measured and predicted values. This re-arrangement is shown in Figure 2, where the predicted value from the soft sensor is corrected based on the modeled errors of the system. The question becomes how to design this model so that the best predictions can be obtained.

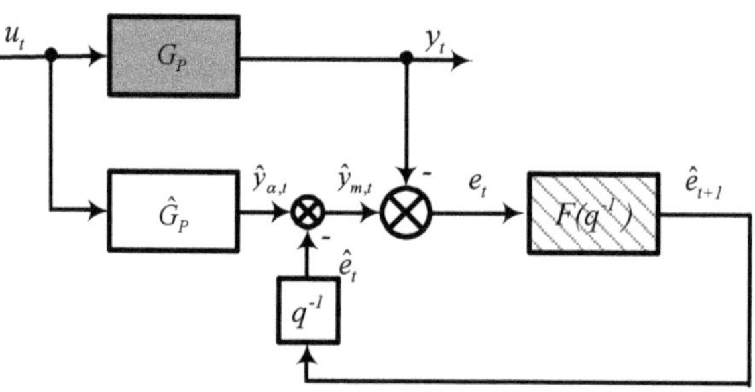

Figure 2. Bias update term as a predictive model with feedback: ▆—plant, ▨—predictive model.

For prediction of time series, the Box-Jenkins methodology is traditionally used, according to which the time series model is found in the class of autoregressive-moving average (ARMA) models, i.e., is considered a rational algebraic function of the backward shift operator. The flexibility of the ARMA class makes it possible to find parsimonious models, i.e., the adequacy of the evaluated model is achieved with a small number of estimated parameters. Since this property is especially important for empirical models, the Box-Jenkins methodology is widely used to solve various practical problems. This approach is adopted in this paper.

In industrial processes, where it is desired to implement the model on programmable logic control (PLC) units, the complexity of the model $\hat{G}_p$ can be an issue. Therefore, this paper will consider a simple model for $\hat{G}_p$ of the form

$$y_t = b_0 + bx_t + e_t \tag{1}$$

where b are the parameters to be estimated and x_t is the input(s). Model (1) can be improved by taking into account possible delays of the output variables relative to inputs. Consider the following model for a multi-output soft sensor

$$y_{t,m} = b_m\, u_m\,(t,\,\tau_m) + e_{t,m} \tag{2}$$

where $t = 1, 2, \ldots, n$; $m = 1, 2, 3$ (the number of outputs m is given by the industrial production team and reflecting the key quality indices of MTBE product). Vector $b_m = (b_{m,\,1}, b_{m,\,2}, \ldots, b_{m,\,10})$ is a row vector of unknown coefficients; $\tau_m = (\tau_{m,\,1}, \tau_{m,\,2}, \ldots, \tau_{m,\,10})$ is a row vector of unknown time delays; $u_m\,(t,\,\tau_m) = (u_{t,\,m,\,1}, u_{t,\,m,\,2}, \ldots, u_{t,\,m,\,10})^{\mathrm{T}}$; $u_{t,\,m,\,k}$ is the measurement of the x_k value at time $t - \tau_{m,\,k}$ with $k = 1, 2, \ldots, 10$. Please note that it has been assumed here that the maximal time delay is 10 samples and justified from the industrial process dynamics point of view. However, it can easily be extended to arbitrary values.

Solving model (2) by minimizing the mean squared error (MSE) gives an estimate for the unknown parameters $\hat{b}_m$ and $\hat{\tau}_m$. The MSE depends not only on the coefficients b_m, but also on the delays τ_m, i.e.,

$$D_{em}(b_m\,\tau_m) = \frac{1}{n}\sum_{t=1}^{n}\{y_{tm} - b_m u_m(t,\,\tau_m)\}^2,\ m = 1, 2, 3 \tag{3}$$

Thus,

$$\left(\hat{b}_m,\,\hat{\tau}_m\right) = \underset{b_m,\,\tau_m}{\arg\min}\, D_{em}(b_m,\,\tau_m). \tag{4}$$

Please note that if $D_{em}(b_m^*,\,\tau_m^*) = \underset{b_m,\,\tau_m}{\min}\, D_{em}(b_m,\,\tau_m)$, than $D_{em}(b_m^*,\,\tau_m^*) = \underset{b_m}{\min} D_{em}(b_m,\,\tau_m^*)$.

Consequently,

$$\underset{b_m,\,\tau_m}{\min}\, D_{em}(b_m,\,\tau_m) = \underset{\tau_m}{\min}\left\{\underset{b_m}{\min} D_{em}(b_m,\,\tau_m)\right\} = \underset{\tau_m}{\min} D_{em}(\hat{b}_m,\,\tau_m) \tag{5}$$

Furthermore, the estimates $\hat{b}_m$ are found using standard regression analysis which gives

$$\hat{b}_m = \left\{\left(\mathbf{U}_m^{\mathrm{T}}\mathbf{U}_m\right)^{-1}\mathbf{U}_m^{\mathrm{T}}\mathbf{Y}_m\right\}^{\mathrm{T}},\ m = 1, 2, 3 \tag{6}$$

where $\mathbf{Y}_m$ is the m-th column of the matrix $\mathbf{Y}$; $\mathbf{U}_m$ is a matrix with dimension $n \times 10$, whose t-th row is the row $u_m\,(t,\,\tau_m)^{\mathrm{T}}$.

Since all variables are measured at discrete moments in time, the gradient descent methods cannot be directly applied to minimize the objective function $D_{em}(\hat{b}_m,\,\tau_m)$ for the argument τ_m. However, this difficulty can be avoided by calculating D_{em} for any values of the elements of the vector τ_m by interpolating between the nearby nodes of the discrete grid. Interpolation with a large search space dimension is a difficult problem. Among the various characteristics of the algorithms used, such properties as visibility and relative simplicity come to the fore. Therefore, in this situation, the most preferable is the polynomial interpolation.

2.1. Error Modeling

If the $e_{t,\,m}$ error were known at time $t-1$, then using Equation (2), it would be possible to predict the $y_{t,\,m}$ variable with absolute accuracy. Unfortunately, the $e_{t,\,m}$ error is not known in advance, but it can be predicted using any statistical patterns found in the sequence $e_{1,\,m}, e_{2,\,m}, \ldots$. This error prediction can be used as a correction to model (2) as shown in Figure 2, therefore improving the prediction accuracy of the $y_{t,m}$ output variable. To evaluate a predictive model for the sequence $e_{1,\,m}, e_{2,\,m} \ldots$, let us consider the class of ARMA models. Let us introduce the predicted process as the output of an invertible linear filter, called a shaping filter, driven by white noise, i.e., a process with a constant spectral density. In this case, the transfer function of the shaping filter is considered a rational algebraic function of the backward shift operator, i.e.,

$$
e_t = \frac{\prod\limits_{l=1}^{N_n}\left(1 - H_l q^{-1}\right)}{\prod\limits_{k=1}^{N_d}\left(1 - G_k q^{-1}\right)} \varepsilon_t \tag{7}
$$

where ε_t and e_t are values of the input and output processes of the shaping filter at time t; N_n is the order of the moving average; N_d is the order of the autoregressive component; H_l, G_k are constants (generally speaking, complex-valued); and q^{-1} is the backshift operator. The stationarity and invertibility conditions, which are necessary to predict the e_t process, are [8]

$$
|G_k| < 1,\ k = 1, \ldots, N_d;\ |H_l| < 1,\ l = 1, \ldots, N_n \tag{8}
$$

The flexibility of the ARMA class provides the possibility of finding parsimonious models, i.e., the adequacy of the constructed model is achieved with a relatively small number of estimated parameters. Since this property is especially important for empirical models, the models with the structure given in Equation (7) and their variants are widely used for solving practical problems.

The filter for predicting the e_t process can be found using the prediction error method (PEM) [9]. Expanding the brackets in Equation (7) gives

$$
e_t = \frac{\left(1 - \theta_1 q^{-1} - \ldots - \theta_{N_n} q^{-N_n}\right)}{\left(1 - \eta_1 q^{-1} - \ldots - \eta_{N_d} q^{-N_d}\right)} \varepsilon_t \tag{9}
$$

where θ_l and η_k are the model parameters. It is assumed that the polynomials in the numerator and denominator have no common roots, since otherwise it would be possible to reduce the common multipliers in the numerator and denominator of Equation (7).

The PEM function finds the parameter values that minimize the predictive MSE of the e_t process for given polynomial orders (N_n, N_d) and the initial estimates of the parameters θ_l and η_k. It is possible to choose suitable orders of the polynomials based on sample estimations of the spectral density of the considered process. Recall that the frequency response of the shaping filter is the value of Equation (7) on a circle of unit radius centered on the origin and the spectral density $S(\omega)$ of the output process e_t is equal to the product of the variance of the input process and the square of the frequency response modulus, i.e., [10]

$$
S(\omega) = \sigma_\varepsilon^2 \frac{\prod\limits_{l=1}^{N_n}\left(1 - H_l e^{-j\omega}\right) \prod\limits_{l=1}^{N_n}\left(1 - \overline{H}_l e^{j\omega}\right)}{\prod\limits_{k=1}^{N_d}\left(1 - G_k e^{-j\omega}\right) \prod\limits_{k=1}^{N_d}\left(1 - \overline{G}_k e^{j\omega}\right)}, \tag{10}
$$

where σ_ε^2 is the variance of random process ε_t and $\overline{H_l}$ and $\overline{G_k}$ are the complex conjugates of the constants H_l and G_k. Furthermore, since we desire that our filter be invertible, it follows that for the model

$$\varepsilon_t = \frac{\prod_{k=1}^{N_d}(1 - G_k q^{-1})}{\prod_{l=1}^{N_n}(1 - H_l q^{-1})} e_t \tag{11}$$

the e_t process is invertible if the absolute values of all the H_l constants are less than one. Similarly, if the absolute values of all the G_k constants is less than one, then the e_t process is stationary [8]. Thus, although multiple processes can have the same spectral density, there is only one that is both stationary and invertible.

Once the general model has been obtained, we can rewrite it as an infinite impulse response model, i.e.,

$$e_t = \varepsilon_t + \sum_{k=1}^{\infty} \psi_k \varepsilon_{t-k} \tag{12}$$

where ψ is an impulse response coefficient. Since we know that the general model converges [8], it follows that we only need a finite number of terms in Equation (12). Furthermore, we note that

$$e_{t-i} = \varepsilon_{t-i} + \sum_{k=1}^{\infty} \psi_k \varepsilon_{t-i-k} \tag{13}$$

which implies that for any positive i the random variables ε_t and e_{t-i} are uncorrelated (since the process ε_t is white noise). Therefore, successively multiplying both sides of Equation (12) by the values of the corresponding process at delays i and taking expectations, we obtain equations for finding the initial estimates of the parameters that involve the covariances of the errors for different lags [10]. Obviously, since the true covariances are not known, they will need to be replaced by the sample estimates. This method of estimating the coefficients does not lead to too large error as long as the absolute values of the parameters of model (7) are not too close to the boundary of unit circle centered on the origin. Thus, it is possible to design the required filter.

2.2. Filter Design

Let $e_t = (e_{t,1}, e_{t,2}, \ldots, e_{t,N})^{\mathrm{T}}$ be an N-dimensional stationary process of the soft sensor's errors whose shaping filter transfer matrix is $F_0(q^{-1})$, i.e.,

$$e_t = F_0(q^{-1})\varepsilon_t \tag{14}$$

where q^{-1} is the backshift operator; $\varepsilon_t = (\varepsilon_{t,1}, \varepsilon_{t,2}, \ldots, \varepsilon_{t,N})^{\mathrm{T}}$ is an N-dimensional vector of white noise; and $F_0(q^{-1}) = [f_{km}(q^{-1})]$ is an $N \times N$ matrix function, whose entries denoted as $f_{km}(q^{-1})$ are the rational transfer function from $\varepsilon_{t,m}$ to $e_{t,k}$. Thus, it is desired to construct the filter that will predict e_{t+1} given the past values.

Let $P(q^{-1})$ be the desired one-step ahead predictor transfer matrix, $\hat{e}_{t+1} = P(q^{-1})e_t$ the prediction of the vector e_{t+1} at time t, and $\tilde{e}_{t+1} = e_{t+1} - \hat{e}_{t+1}$ the error of the prediction obtained with the aid of the filter $P(q^{-1})$. Then

$$\tilde{\varepsilon}_t = e_t - \hat{e}_t = e_t - q^{-1}\hat{e}_{t+1} = e_t - q^{-1}P\left(q^{-1}\right)e_t = \left[I_N - q^{-1}P\left(q^{-1}\right)\right]e_t \tag{15}$$

where I_N is identity matrix of order N. Consequently, the filter in the square brackets transforms the initial series into the prediction error series. If the random vector $\tilde{\varepsilon}_t$ includes components correlated with those of the vector $\tilde{\varepsilon}_{t-j}$ at some $j > 0$, we can predict the errors $\tilde{\varepsilon}_t$ using the known previous errors. Using those predictions as corrections to the $\tilde{e}_t$ that were obtained, we could improve the accuracy of the predictions. Hence, in order to maximize the predictor accuracy, we must find a $P(q^{-1})$ such that the errors $\tilde{\varepsilon}_t$ are uncorrelated with the errors $\tilde{\varepsilon}_{t-j}$ at any $j > 0$ with some nonzero correlation between the components of $\widetilde{\varepsilon}_t$ (i.e., at $j = 0$) being admissible. In other words, the time series $\widetilde{\varepsilon}_t$ must be N-dimensional white noise. Consequently, $I_N - q^{-1}P(q^{-1}) = F_0^{-1}(q^{-1})$, from which it follows that $P(q^{-1}) = q[I_N - F_0^{-1}(q^{-1})]$.

Thus, the predictor transfer matrix $P(q^{-1})$ can be expressed through the transfer matrix of the shaping filter $F_0(q^{-1})$. The matrix $F_0(q^{-1})$ can be found from

$$G(q^{-1}) = F_0(q^{-1})F_0^{\mathrm{T}}(q), \tag{16}$$

where $G(q^{-1}) = [g_{km}(q^{-1})]$, $g_{km}(q^{-1})$ is the q-transform of the statistical estimate of the cross-covariance function of the time series $e_{t,k}$ and $e_{t,m}$ (in particular, when $m = k$, g_{mm} is a q-transform of the sample covariance function, i.e., the autocovariance generating function (AGF) of the time series e_{tm}).

The algorithm for finding $F_0(q^{-1})$ is simplified by decomposing it into N stages. At the kth stage, a shaping filter $F_k(q^{-1})$ of the k-dimensional process $(e_{t,\,1}, e_{t,\,2}, \ldots, e_{t,\,k})^{\mathrm{T}}$ is found. At this stage, the filter $F_{k-1}(q^{-1})$, found at the $(k-1)$th stage, is used in order to transform the matrix $G_k(q^{-1}) = F_k(q^{-1})F_k^{\mathrm{T}}(q)$ so that its transform contains nonzero elements in only one line, one column, and on the main diagonal. This technique substantially simplifies the procedure of spectral factorization (finding the matrix function $F_k(q^{-1})$) [11].

The proposed approach allows us to identify the vector time series transfer matrix without resorting to a complicated phase state representation. This advantage is used to obtain an adequate model with relatively few estimated parameters for the initial time series shaping filter $F_0(q^{-1})$. Simultaneously, the model for the transfer matrix of the inverse filter $F_0^{-1}(q^{-1})$, which transforms the initial time series into the white noise, is also found.

The algorithm for constructing both the shaping filter $F_0(q^{-1})$ and its inverse $F_0^{-1}(q^{-1})$ is described in [11]. Based on this algorithm, the sequence of prediction errors $\widetilde{\varepsilon}_t$ should be N-dimensional white noise. However, since in practice, the true characteristics of the original process are not known, but only their estimates, containing inevitable statistical errors, in reality, the properties of the sequence $\widetilde{\varepsilon}_t$ can be significantly different from the properties of white noise. Thus, to verify the optimality of the resulting model $P(q^{-1})$ of the predictive filter, a criterion is needed to test the hypothesis that the process $\widetilde{\varepsilon}_t$ is N-dimensional white noise. To construct such a criterion, we can transform the process $\widetilde{\varepsilon}_t$ in such a way that its spectral density matrix is diagonal. Such a transformation is achieved by means of a rotation of axes in the N-dimensional variable space $\widetilde{\varepsilon}_1, \widetilde{\varepsilon}_2, \cdots, \widetilde{\varepsilon}_N$ [12]. Since the variances of these variables can be made equal to each other by normalization, without loss of generality, we suppose that spectral density matrix of the noise $\widetilde{\varepsilon}_t$ is an $N \times N$ identity matrix I_N.

Consider a univariate sequence $\zeta_k = \widetilde{\varepsilon}_{t-j,m}$, where $k = jN + m$. Please note that each pair couple (j, m) determines one k and each k determines one pair couple (j, m). Consequently, $\widetilde{\varepsilon}_t$ is multivariate white noise if and only if ζ_k is univariate white noise. It is known that the spectral density of univariate white noise is constant [8,13]. Thus, testing the hypothesis that $\widetilde{\varepsilon}_t$ is multivariate white noise is reduced to testing the hypothesis on the constancy of the spectral density of a univariate sequence. This hypothesis can be tested using Kolmogorov's criterion [14].

Please note that only a time series containing prediction errors is used as the initial information for constructing a predictor with the proposed approach. Information about the model with which the predictions were obtained is not used. Therefore, this approach is applicable to any predictive model that involves errors, regardless of the specific properties of the model used.

2.3. Summary of the Proposed Approach

Thus, the proposed procedure for developing the model can be summarized as follows:

Step 1: Create an initial sample $u_t, y_t, t = 1, 2, \ldots, K$. If the plant is already functioning then the initial sample consists of the historical values of u_t, y_t. Otherwise, the initial sample is forming during the trial period of the plant. The initial sample is divided into training and testing datasets.

Step 2: Based on the data included in the training sample, the coefficients and delays of the model given by Equation (2) are estimated via solving optimization problem (4).

Step 3: Based on the data included in the training sample, the errors for the model and the corresponding sample spectrum of errors are calculated.

Step 4: Based on the sample spectrum, the order of the ARMA model is selected in order to predict the unknown future error given the known current and past errors.

Step 5: The least squares method is used to find the values of the ARMA model parameters.

Step 6: The ARMA model obtained is used as the predictive filter $F(q^{-1})$ in the feedback loop of the compensator (bias update term) as shown in Figure 2.

Step 7: If the resulting soft sensor improves the accuracy of the prediction for the test sample then it can be recommended for practical use.

Please note that the obtained predictive filter model can be recommended for further use for the same plant on the data of which it was built. As for the approach, it will certainly be successful if the sequence of errors of the plant is a stationary (or close to it) process. In addition, the class of successful applicability of this approach can be extended to those plants, for whose errors it is possible to find an invertible transformation that brings the sequence of errors to a stationary process. The quality of the developed model should be checked on a test sample that was not used at the stage of the model training.

3. Industrial Application of the Proposed Method

Industrial methyl tert-butyl ether (MTBE) production occurs in a reactive distillation unit, as shown in Figure 3. The feed containing isobutylene and methanol (MeOH) enters the column. The distillate (D) is a lean butane-butylene fraction with a certain amount of MeOH. The raffinate is the heavy product MTBE that is withdrawn from the bottom part of the column. Table 1 shows the main process variables for the industrial unit. The goal is to develop a soft sensor for the prediction of the concentrations of methyl sec-butyl ether (MSBE), MeOH, and the sum of dimers and trimers of isobutylene (DIME) in the bottom product MTBE.

The measured values of output y_m and input x_k variables at the time moment t are denoted as $y_{tm}, x_{tk}; m = 1, 2, 3; k = 1, 2, \ldots, 10;$ and $t = 1, 2, \ldots, n$. The existing measurements may be used for development of a predictive model of the form

$$y_t = b_0 + bx_t + e_t, \quad t = 1, 2, \ldots, n \tag{17}$$

where $y_t = (y_{t,1}, y_{t,2}, y_{t,3})^{\mathrm{T}}; x_t = (x_{t,1}, x_{t,2}, \ldots, x_{t,10})^{\mathrm{T}}; b$ is a matrix of the model parameters $[b_{mk}]$ of dimension $3 \times 10; b_0 = (b_1, b_2, b_3)^{\mathrm{T}}$ is a vector of the constant biases; $e_t = (e_{t,1}, e_{t,2}, e_{t,3})^{\mathrm{T}}$ is a vector of the residuals, and the superscript T denotes the transpose. Since Equation (17) can be rewritten as

$$(y_t - \bar{y}) = b(x_t - \bar{x}) + e_t \tag{18}$$

where $\bar{y} = \frac{1}{n} \sum_{t=1}^{n} y_t, \bar{x} = \frac{1}{n} \sum_{t=1}^{n} x_t$, then expectations of all the elements of vectors y_t, x_t, and e_t, as well as biases vector b_0, may be considered to be equal to zero without loss of generality.

Although the elements of matrix b are unknown, they are easily estimated using the ordinary least squares (OLS) method, which gives [10]

$$\hat{b} = \left\{ \left(\mathbf{X}^{\mathrm{T}}\mathbf{X} \right)^{-1} \mathbf{X}^{\mathrm{T}}\mathbf{Y} \right\}^{\mathrm{T}} \tag{19}$$

where $\mathbf{X} = [x_{tk}]; \mathbf{Y} = [y_{tm}]; m = 1, 2, 3; k = 1, 2, \ldots, 10;$ and $t = 1, 2, \ldots, n$.

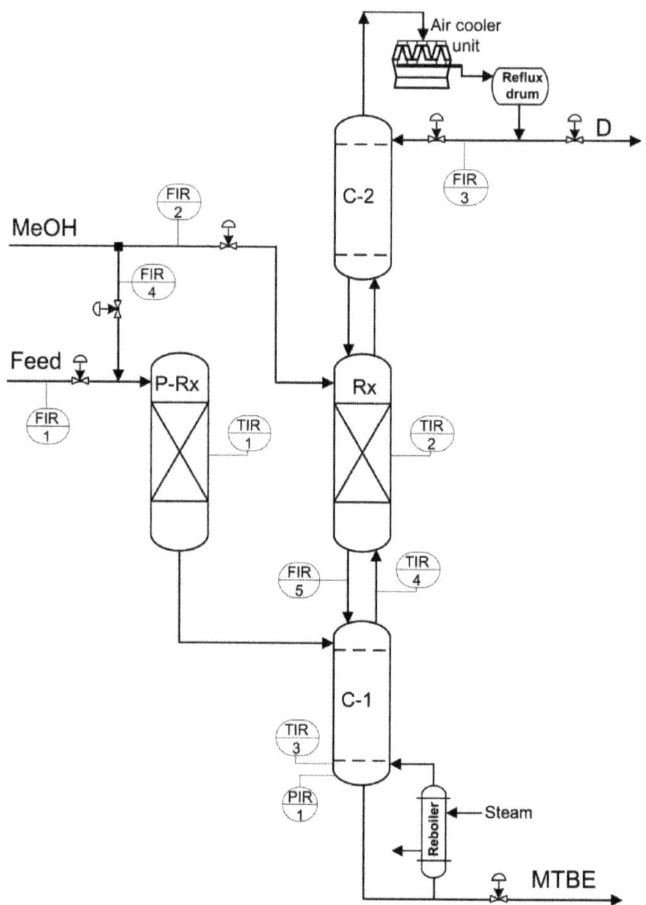

Figure 3. Reactive distillation unit of MTBE production.

Table 1. Soft sensor input and output variables.

Description of Process Variable	Notation	SS Variable
Feed flowrate, m^3/s	FIR-1	x_1
MeOH flowrate to Rx, m^3/s	FIR-2	x_2
Reflux flowrate, m^3/s	FIR-3	x_3
MeOH flowrate to P-Rx, m^3/s	FIR-4	x_4
Bottoms flowrate from Rx, m^3/s	FIR-5	x_5
Bottom pressure, MPa	PIR-1	x_6
Temperature in P-Rx, K	TIR-1	x_7
Temperature in Rx, K	TIR-2	x_8
Bottom temperature, K	TIR-3	x_9
Vapor flow temp. from $C-1$, K	TIR-4	x_{10}
Concentration of MSBE in MTBE, wt.%	-	y_1
Concentration of MeOH in MTBE, wt.%	-	y_2
Concentration of DIME in MTBE, wt.%	-	y_3

For the training sample containing $n = 400$ measurements, the following estimates were obtained:

$$\bar{x} = (51.8154\ 1.8747\ 52.1154\ 3.0859\ 51.9866\ 0.7580\ 60.7100$$
$$66.4516\ 136.3077\ 64.5725)^{\mathrm{T}}$$

$$\bar{y} = (0.5440\ 0.1461\ 0.0595\ )^{\mathrm{T}}$$

$$\hat{b} = \begin{pmatrix} -0.0151 & 0.2383 & -0.0342 & 0.1401 & 0.0476... \\ -0.0173 & 0.0794 & 0.0281 & 0.1191 & -0.0171... \\ -0.0080 & 0.1118 & -0.0061 & 0.0537 & 0.0134\ \ldots \\ -1.7361 & 0.0430 & -0.0012 & -0.1019 & 0.0388 \\ 2.9800 & -0.0093 & -0.0072 & -0.1333 & 0.0353 \\ 0.3490 & 0.0215 & -0.0011 & -0.0467 & 0.0098 \end{pmatrix}.$$

The estimated MSE vector for the model (17) is $(0.0094\ 0.0095\ 0.0021)^{\mathrm{T}}$, while the vector of sample estimates of variances of the output variables is $(0.0321\ 0.0184\ 0.0047)^{\mathrm{T}}$.

Let R^2_m be a sample estimate of the coefficient of determination, i.e., the estimate of a fraction of variance of the dependent variable y_m explained by model (18), i.e.,

$$R^2_m = 1 - \frac{D_{e,m}}{D_m} \tag{20}$$

where D_m is a sample estimate of the variance of the output variable y_m, $D_{e,m}$ is the mean squared value of the $e_{t,m}$ errors, and $m = 1, 2, 3$. This gives $R^2_1 = 0.7061$, $R^2_2 = 0.4822$, and $R^2_3 = 0.5467$.

Assuming a sampling time of one hour, the estimates of the delay vector $\hat{\tau}_1$ for predicting the output variable y_1 is

$$\hat{\tau}_1 = (4.83\ 0\ 2.00\ 5.00\ 1.83\ 0\ 2.00\ 0.83\ 1.00\ 2.00)$$

and the estimate of the coefficient vector is equal to

$$\hat{b}_1 = (0.0002\ 0.1341 - 0.0360\ 0.0064\ 0.0451 - 2.3289\ 0.0519 - 0.0029 - 0.0819\ 0.0442)$$

with $D_{e,1}(\hat{b}_1, \hat{\tau}_1) = 0.0091$.

Similarly, for variables y_2 and y_3, we obtain

$$\hat{\tau}_2 = (0.33\ 0.33\ 1.67\ 4.50\ 0.50\ 0.67\ 0.33\ 0.50\ 0.50\ 1.67)$$

$$\hat{b}_2 = (-0.0263\ 0.1481\ 0.0315\ 0.1947 - 0.0168\ 3.4223 - 0.0064 - 0.0092 - 0.1513\ 0.0385);\ D_2\left(\hat{b}_2, \hat{\tau}_2\right) = 0.0088$$

$$\hat{\tau}_3 = (4.17\ 0\ 0.83\ 4.33\ 0.83\ 0.50\ 2.00\ 0.67\ 0.83\ 1.00)$$

$$\hat{b}_3 = (-0.0021\ 0.0811 - 0.0070 - 0.0016\ 0.0130\ 0.3795\ 0.0259 - 0.0015 - 0.0455\ 0.0098);\ D_3\left(\hat{b}_3, \hat{\tau}_3\right) = 0.0020$$

The sample estimate of the coefficient of determination to predict the output variable y_m denoted by R^2_{Lm} is $R^2_{L1} = 0.7160$; $R^2_{L2} = 0.5200$; $R^2_{L3} = 0.5726$.

The effect of delay accounting was evaluated on a test sample containing 167 measurements. As a result, the MSE of the predictions of output variables y_1, y_2 and y_3 decreased by 23%, 10%, and 3%, respectively.

Now, let us consider modeling the error term. From the spectral density of the errors for $e_{t,1}$ and $e_{t,3}$ shown in Figures 4 and 5, it can be seen that the maximum within the interval $[0, 0.5]$ Hz indicates the presence in the denominator of the spectral density function $S(\omega)$ a factor $(1 - Ge^{-j\omega})$ with a complex-valued constant G. Since the sampling time is equal to 12 h, the frequency unit $1/(12\ \mathrm{h})$ is used instead of Hz. However, for the practical application of the filter given by Equation (9), it is necessary that all the coefficients be real [8]. Therefore, the denominator of density $S(\omega)$ must contain a factor

$(1 - \overline{G}e^{-j\omega})$ along with a factor $(1 - Ge^{-j\omega})$. If the frequency response models for $e_{t,1}$ and $e_{t,3}$ processes are limited to these two factors (assuming the numerator is equal to one), then the corresponding spectral density of the second-order autoregressive process approximates well the sample estimates of the spectrum of $e_{t,1}$ and $e_{t,3}$ processes at different values of G. However, the insufficiently rapid decrease of the spectral density in the high-frequency region justifies the inclusion in the denominator of the model another multiplier with a real value of the constant G.

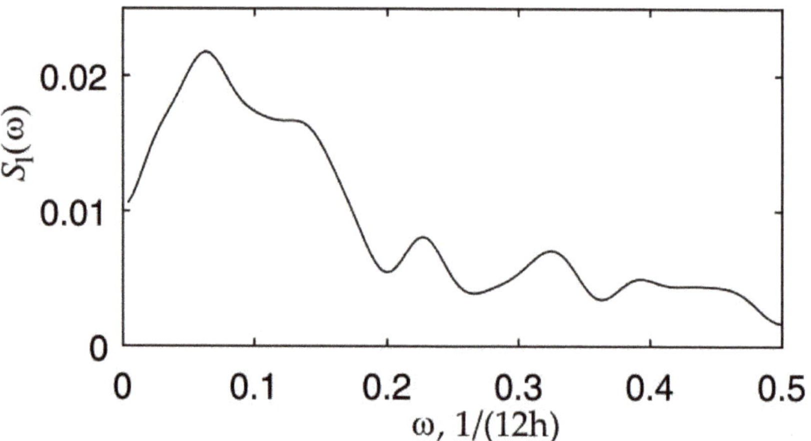

Figure 4. Sample spectrum of the process $e_{t,1}$.

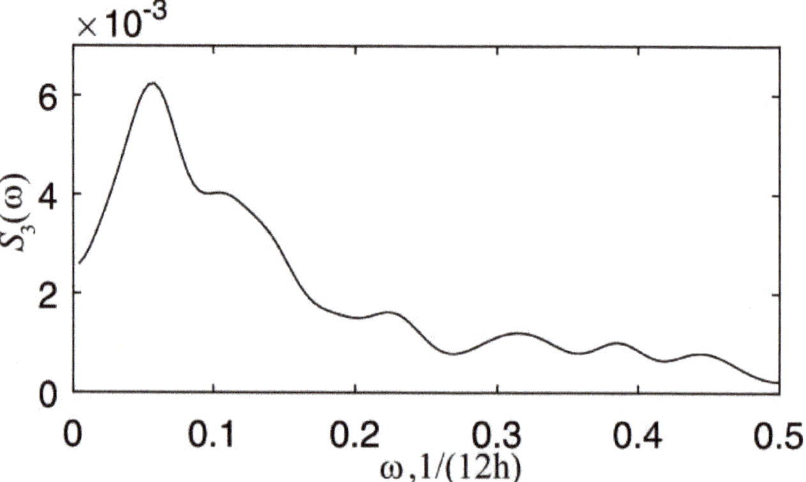

Figure 5. Sample spectrum of the process $e_{t,3}$.

In Figure 6, which shows the spectral density for the $e_{t,2}$ errors, the sample spectrum of this time series resembles the spectrum of a first-order autoregressive process [15–17]. However, we note that the stochastic process is not uniquely determined by its spectral density [8]. Therefore, as previously mentioned, we need to include two additional constraints that the resulting model be invertible and realizable. This will ensure that we have a unique model.

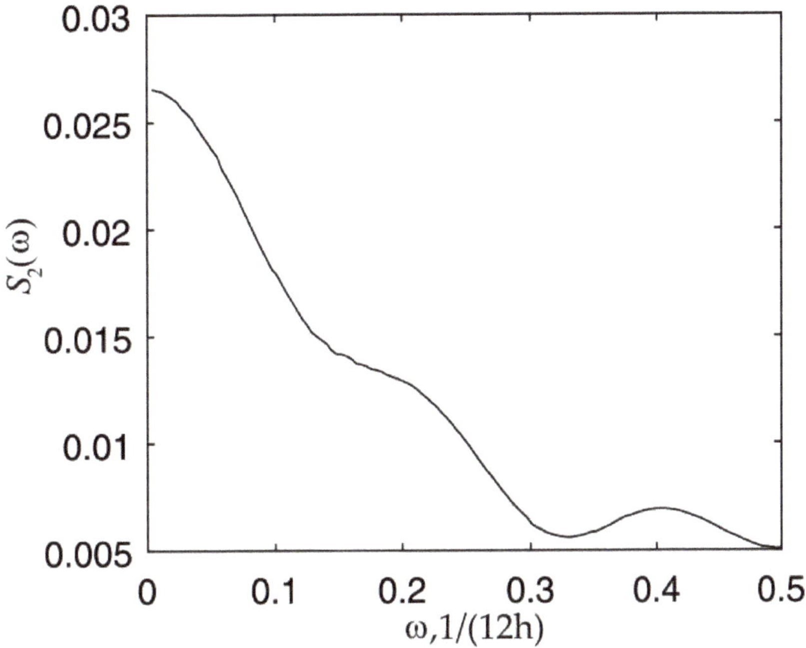

Figure 6. Sample spectrum of the process $e_{t,\,2}$.

Based on the theoretical properties of the process, the error models are

$$e_{t,\,1} - \eta_{11}e_{(t-1),\,1} - \eta_{21}e_{(t-2),\,1} - \eta_{31}e_{(t-3),\,1} = \varepsilon_{t,\,1} \tag{21}$$
$$e_{t,\,2} - \eta_{12}e_{(t-1),\,2} = \varepsilon_{t,\,2}$$

$$e_{t,\,3} - \eta_{13}e_{(t-1),\,3} - \eta_{23}e_{(t-2),\,3} - \eta_{33}e_{(t-3),\,3} = \varepsilon_{t,\,3}$$

where η are the parameters to be determined. These parameters can be found using the approach presented in Section 2.2 by multiplying the finite impulse response model by the delayed errors and taking the expectations. For example, for e_1, this gives

$$\gamma_i = \eta_{11}\gamma_{i-1} + \eta_{21}\gamma_{i-2} + \eta_{31}\gamma_{i-3},\, i = 1, 2, 3 \tag{22}$$

where $\gamma_i = \mathrm{cov}(e_{t1}, e_{(t-i)1}) = \gamma_{-i}$.

For the process $e_{t,\,1}$, the estimates of the coefficients η_{11}, η_{21} and η_{31} are, respectively, equal to 0.4131, -0.0093, and -0.0528. These values were used as the initial guesses passed to the PEM function. As a result of calculations, the model parameters were found to be: $\eta_{11} = 0.4175$, $\eta_{21} = 0.03234$, $\eta_{31} = -0.07026$. The initial value of coefficient η_{12} is 0.3748 and its final value is $\eta_{12} = 0.3758$.

Similarly, using Equation (22), the initial guesses were $\eta_{13} = 0.5142$, $\eta_{23} = -0.0507$, and $\eta_{33} = -0.0207$ to give final values of $\eta_{13} = 0.5151$, $\eta_{23} = -0.02676$, and $\eta_{33} = -0.03246$.

The performance of predictive filter models obtained from the analysis of the training dataset is validated using the testing sample. Figures 7–9 compare the predictions against the true values, where the solid line shows the true $e_{t,\,m}$ errors and the dashed line their predicted values for $m = 1, 2,$ and 3. At the time point t on the x-axis, the corresponding error $e_{t,\,m}$ and the predicted error $\hat{e}_{t,m}$ computed at $t - 1$.

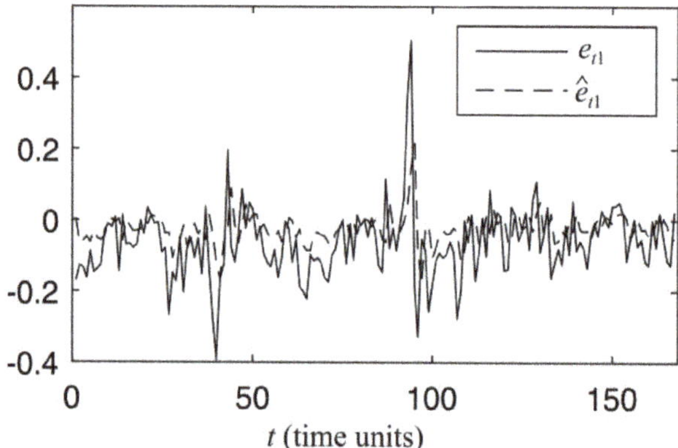

Figure 7. Prediction of the process $e_{t,1}$.

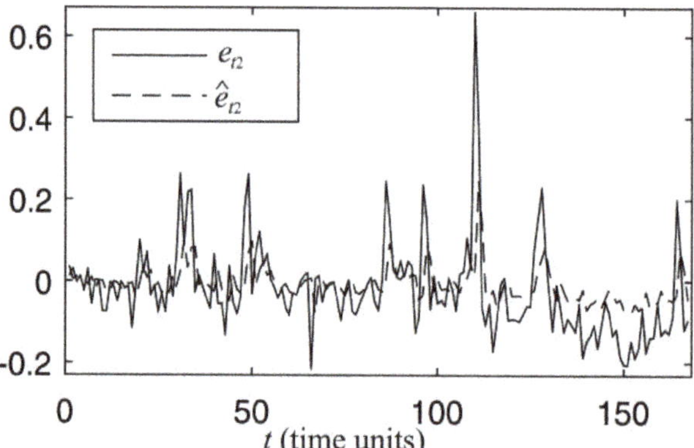

Figure 8. Prediction of the process $e_{t,2}$.

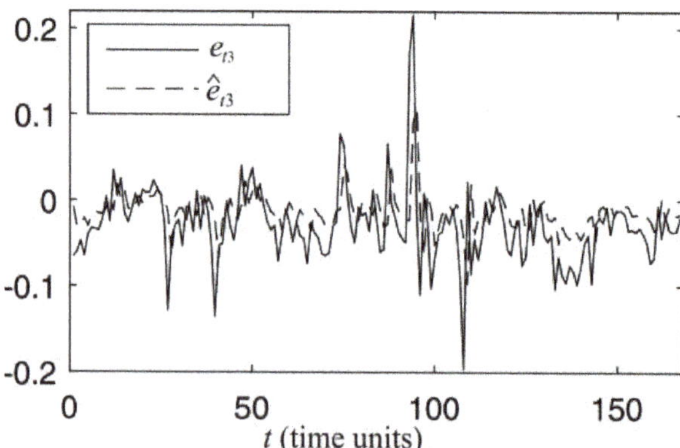

Figure 9. Prediction of the process $e_{t,3}$.

Figures 10–12 compare the performance of the soft sensors with the proposed filter for error prediction and a traditional method, in which adaptive bias term is calculated based on the moving window (MW) approach [18]. It can be seen that the filter provides better tracking of the process values, therefore improving the accuracy of the overall soft sensor system reducing the MSE of the output variables y_1, y_2, and y_3 by 32%, 67%, and 9.5%, respectively.

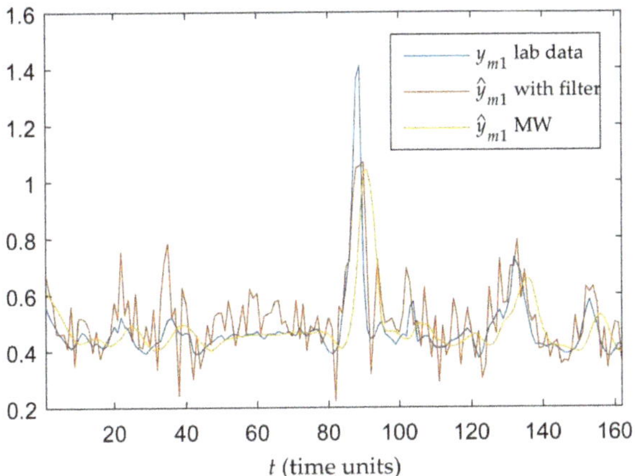

Figure 10. Estimation of y_{m1}.

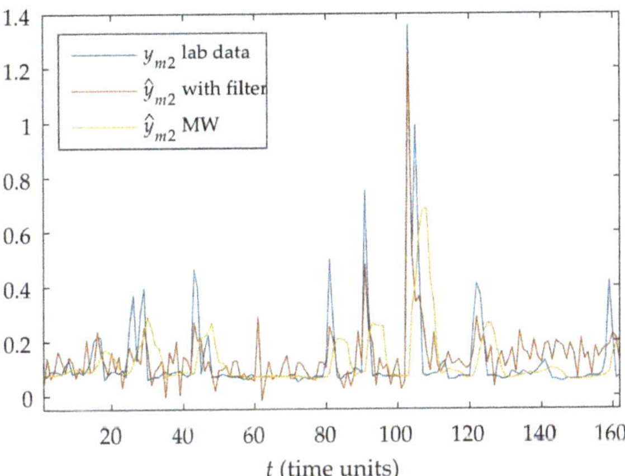

Figure 11. Estimation of y_{m2}.

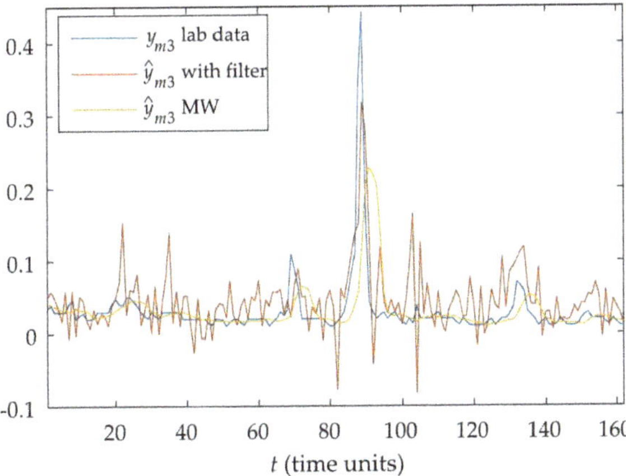

Figure 12. Estimation of y_{m3}.

4. Conclusions

This paper proposed a new approach to handling the bias update term in a soft sensor system. Rather than purely using available samples, the new bias update term seeks to predict what the errors will be in the future. Tests of this approach on a reactive distillation column show that the approach can handle the errors well. However, the predictive filters used only work for areas without serious disturbances or outliers.

Therefore, it makes sense to consider more complex models for the predictive filters including models with an additional component in the form of some flow, for example, Poissonian flow, of events (outliers). If the flow of outliers is added to the process model then the intensity of this flow needs to be estimated. In this case, the number of outliers in the training dataset should be sufficient to estimate the intensity of the flow of outliers with acceptable accuracy.

Author Contributions: Conceptualization, all; methodology, Y.A.W.S., A.T., V.K.; software, A.T.; validation, A.T., Y.A.W.S.; formal analysis, all; resources, F.Y., V.K.; writing—original draft preparation, Y.A.W.S., A.T.; writing—review and editing, all; funding acquisition, F.Y., V.K., Y.A.W.S. All authors have read and agreed to the published version of the manuscript.

Funding: This research was funded by RFBR and NSFC (grant numbers 21-57-53005 and 62111530057) and National Science and Technology Innovation 2030 Major Project (grant No.2018AAA0101604) of the Ministry of Science and Technology of China.

Data Availability Statement: Data can be obtained by contacting the authors.

Conflicts of Interest: The authors declare no conflict of interest.

References

1. Shardt, Y.A.W. *Data Quality Assessment for Closed-Loop System Identification and Forecasting with Application to Soft Sensors*; University of Alberta Press: Ed-monton, AB, Canada, 2012; Available online: https://era.library.ualberta.ca/items/8382f12a-8960-4508-9ede-0679e021394b (accessed on 2 January 2021).
2. Bakirov, R.; Babrys, B.; Fay, D. Multiple adaptive mechanisms for data-driven soft sensors. *Comput. Chem. Eng.* **2017**, *96*, 42–54. [CrossRef]
3. Funatsu, K. Process control and soft sensors. In *T. Engel, & J. Gasteiger, Applied Chemoinformatics: Achievements and Future Opportunities*; Wiley-VCH: Weinheim, Germany, 2018; pp. 571–584.
4. Kim, S.; Kano, M.; Hasebe, S.; Takimi, A.; Seki, T. Long-term industrial applications of inferential control based on just-in-time soft-sensors: Economical impact and challenges. *Ind. Eng. Chem. Res.* **2013**, *52*, 12346–12356. [CrossRef]
5. Torgashov, A.; Skogestad, S. The use of first principles model for evaluation of adaptive soft sensor for multicomponent distillation unit. *Chem. Eng. Res. Des.* **2019**, *151*, 70–78. [CrossRef]
6. Griesing-Scheiwe, F.; Shardt, Y.A.; Pérez-Zuñiga, G.; Yang, X. Soft Sensor Design for Restricted Variable Sampling Time. *J. Process. Control.* **2020**, *92*, 310–318. [CrossRef]
7. Klimchenko, V.V.; Samotylova, S.A.; Torgashov, A.Y. Feedback in a predictive model of a reactive distillation process. *J. Comput. Syst. Sci. Int.* **2019**, *58*, 637–647. [CrossRef]
8. Box, G.E.; Jenkins, G.M.; Reinsel, G.C.; Ljung, G.M. *Time Series Analysis: Forecasting and Control*; Wiley: Hoboken, NJ, USA, 2016.
9. Ljung, L. *System Identification*; Prentice Hall: Englewood Cliffs, NJ, USA, 1987.
10. Shardt, Y.A.W. *Statistics for Chemical and Process Engineers*; Springer: Berlin/Heidelberg, Germany, 2015.
11. Klimchenko, V.V. Decomposition of the multi-dimensional time series identification problem. *Autom. Remote. Control.* **2008**, *69*, 845–857. [CrossRef]
12. Anderson, T.W. *An Introduction to Multivariate Statistical Analysis*, 3rd ed.; John Wiley: New York, NY, USA, 2003.
13. Brillinger, D.R. *Time Series: Data Analysis and Theory*; SIAM: Philadelphia, PA, USA, 2001.
14. Marsaglia, G.; Tsang, W.W.; Wang, J. Evaluating Kolmogorov's Distribution. *Stat. Softw.* **2003**, *8*, 1–4. [CrossRef]
15. Hoff, J.C. *A Practical Guide to Box-Jenkins Forecasting*; Lifetime Learning Publications: Belmont, CA, USA, 1983.
16. Hannan, E.J.; Deistler, M. *Statistical Theory of Linear Systems*; John Wiley and Sons: New York, NY, USA, 1988.
17. Marple, S.L. *Digital Spectral Analysis*, 2nd ed.; Courier Dover Publications: Chicago, IL, USA, 2019.
18. Kadlec, P.; Grbic, R.; Gabrys, B. Review of adaptation mechanisms for data-driven soft sensors. *Comput. Chem. Eng.* **2011**, *35*, 1–24. [CrossRef]

Article

Optimal Stochastic Control in the Interception Problem of a Randomly Tacking Vehicle

Andrey A. Galyaev *, Pavel V. Lysenko and Evgeny Y. Rubinovich

Institute of Control Sciences of RAS, 117997 Moscow, Russia; pashlys@yandex.ru (P.V.L.);
rubinvch@ipu.ru (E.Y.R.)
* Correspondence: galaev@ipu.ru

Abstract: This article considers the mathematical aspects of the problem of the optimal interception of a mobile search vehicle moving along random tacks on a given route and searching for a target, which travels parallel to this route. Interception begins when the probability of the target being detected by the search vehicle exceeds a certain threshold value. Interception was carried out by a controlled vehicle (defender) protecting the target. An analytical estimation of this detection probability is proposed. The interception problem was formulated as an optimal stochastic control problem, which was transformed to a deterministic optimization problem. As a result, the optimal control law of the defender was found, and the optimal interception time was estimated. The deterministic problem is a simplified version of the problem whose optimal solution provides a suboptimal solution to the stochastic problem. The obtained control law was compared with classic guidance methods. All the results were obtained analytically and validated with a computer simulation.

Keywords: optimal stochastic control; path planning; 2D random search; interception

Citation: Galyaev, A.A.; Lysenko, P.V.; Rubinovich, E.Y. Optimal Stochastic Control in the Interception Problem of a Randomly Tacking Vehicle. *Mathematics* **2021**, *9*, 2386. https://doi.org/10.3390/math9192386

Academic Editors: Natalia Bakhtadze, Igor Yadykin, Andrei Torgashov and Nikolay Korgin

Received: 30 August 2021
Accepted: 22 September 2021
Published: 25 September 2021

Publisher's Note: MDPI stays neutral with regard to jurisdictional claims in published maps and institutional affiliations.

1. Introduction

Search problems have become increasingly popular recently and have attracted a significant number of researchers [1–5]. The search process is considered to be that of exploring a certain area of a physical space in order to detect a searched object (SO) in this area with the search vehicle (SV) using various types of physical sensors. The basis for solving these problems is a symbiosis of models and methods from multiple branches of science, which allows establishing causal relationships among the search conditions, the physical characteristics of the SOs, and the search results.

Mathematical formulations of search problems can include various criteria [6,7] with the goal of the minimization or maximization of these criteria. All search problems can be divided into two groups according to the SO's type: it can be stationary or mobile. The problems of the first type (Chapter 2 of [1]) are easier to solve than the problems of mobile SOs (Chapter 3 of [1,5]), since the parameters of their movement may be unknown to the SV. The problems of the second type have become popular in recent years due to the development of unmanned vehicles such as unmanned aerial vehicles (UAVs) or unmanned underwater vehicles (UUVs), operating in a largely unpredictable and uncertain marine environment [1,8].

The practical applications of such autonomous vehicles and search problems can vary from environmental monitoring and geological exploration to combat and reconnaissance tasks. Therefore, the parameters of the mathematical models can vary greatly depending on the different characteristics of real-world objects and their operating conditions. The problem considered in this article can be applied to objects in the marine environment such as UUVs or autonomous surface vehicles (ASVs), which can serve as both the SO and SV in the model under discussion.

The search can be performed by one [3,5] or several SVs [9,10]. If the SV and SO are on conflicting sides and the search itself is undesirable for the SO [11,12], then we can talk about the so-called threat environment [13,14]. Several SVs can be connected in a network structure and form a dynamically changing threat map [10,15]. The task of the SO (UUV or UAV) in this case is to avoid these threats while moving. The trajectory planning problem can be formulated for the SO when the threat mapping is known. If the dynamics of the SO is also known, then these problems are classical problems of deterministic optimal control.

If the SV presents a danger to the SO, the problem of interception can be considered. There is a vast class of such problems with various formulations and models of the moving vehicles. These models may include restrictions on the maneuverability of the vehicles [16–18]. Moreover, the problem can be considered optimal if any criterion, as for example, the intercept time, must be minimized [19–21]. In most problems studied in the literature, the intercepted vehicle moves along a given programmed trajectory [22]. Meanwhile, real vehicles as a rule move in a stochastic way, and this case is considered in the presented article.

The article relates to various branches of mathematics, such as stochastic control, guidance, information processing and search, and optimization, and is devoted to the problem of the optimal interception of an SV that moves randomly on tacks along a given course and searches for a target SO. The interception is carried out by a controlled mobile vehicle protecting the target SO. The presence of an arbitrarily maneuvering search vehicle requires an adequate mathematical formalization in the form of a stochastic control problem. The maneuvering process can be conveniently formalized using a jump-like Markov process with a given state vector and a given matrix of the transition intensities between these states. Such a model allows us to describe the trajectory of the SV in the form of a linear stochastic differential equation, which makes it possible to obtain the equations of the evolution of the mathematical expectation and variance. These equations allow us to formulate the problem of SV interception by the controlled vehicle with the criterion of a predicted miss or with a given mathematical expectation of a miss at the final position of the SV [16–21]. The purpose of the article is to find an interception trajectory of the controlled defender vehicle as a result of solving the optimal stochastic control problem and comparing this trajectory with classical guidance algorithms such as the pursuit guidance method and the method of proportional navigation guidance [23–25].

The considered problem belongs to the "attacker–target–defender" type [26–28], the essence of which is a counteraction to the SV (attacker) from the SO (target), which can be a certain strategically important mobile vehicle, by using an autonomous attacking robotic complex (defender), for example an UAV or UUV.

In this article, by SV, we mean a vehicle moving programmatically or randomly on a plane equipped with a circular detection zone of a fixed radius. The goal of the SV is to detect the SO, i.e., to cover the point of the plane depicting the SO with its detection zone and maximize some functional that characterizes the reliability of detecting the SO in this zone. The reliability of the detection (probability of correct classification) of the SV may depend on various physical factors, in particular on the time spent by the SO in the detection zone, its current distance from the SV, the direction of the velocity vector of the SO, etc. [29].

We considered the SO to be able to observe the real trajectory of the SV and evaluate the characteristics of its movement, i.e., current coordinates and components of the velocity vector. At some point in time, the SO releases a mobile defender, which moves autonomously and stealthily and does not have a communication channel with the SO. It was also assumed that the defender can evaluate the current motion characteristics of the SV using its passive onboard sensors. The stealthiness of the defender is provided, in particular, with its low velocity.

The proposed work has the following structure. In Section 2, the model of the SV with a given detection zone is considered. Section 3 contains a statistic description of the detection probability of the SO moving along a straight-line trajectory. In Section 4, the interception problem is formulated as an optimal stochastic control problem. This problem is analytically solved in Section 5, and the obtained results are discussed and illustrated with simulation examples in Section 6. Section 7 concludes the article and suggests the direction for future work.

2. Model of the SV's Movement on Tacks

The search system consists of one SV, which has a circle detection zone of radius R. The SV moves piecewise-rectilinearly on a plane, tacking randomly around the line of the general course. The origin O of the stationary Cartesian coordinate system XOY is situated in the initial position of the SV, as shown in Figure 1. This coordinate system is oriented in such a way that its OX axis coincides with the line of the general course of the SV.

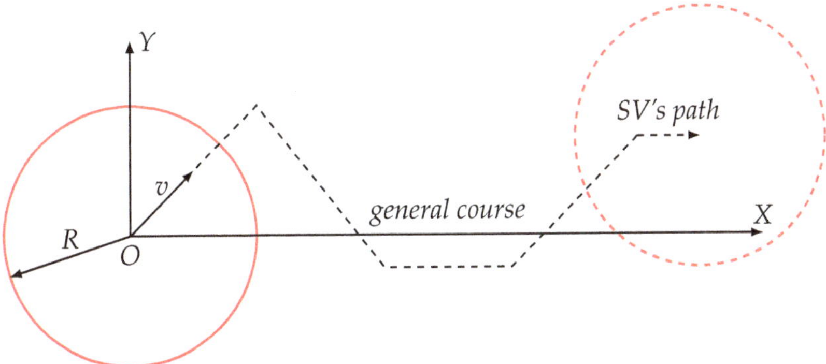

Figure 1. The SV's trajectory.

The SV moves on tacks in accordance with the following law:

$$\begin{cases} \dot{x}_{SV} = v_x = v \cos \alpha, \\ \dot{y}_{SV} = v_y = \theta_t v \sin \alpha, \end{cases} \tag{1}$$

where α is the specified tacking angle, v is the SV's search speed, and θ_t is a random jump-like Markov process. The component of the SV's velocity vector $\vec{v}$ along the line of the general course is constant:

$$v_x = \text{const.}$$

Figure 2 shows a velocity diagram of the SV. As follows from (1), tacking was performed by periodically changing the velocity component v_y according to a random Markov process θ_t with a finite vector of states $J = (j_1, j_2, \ldots, j_n)$ and a given matrix of the transition intensities between these states Λ. This article discusses the case of processes with three states $J = (-1, 0, 1)$. This means that the SV's velocity vector can coincide with the general course line ($\theta_t = 0$) or deviate from it by a constant angle equal to $\pm\alpha$ (when $\theta_t = \pm 1$), as shown in Figure 2.

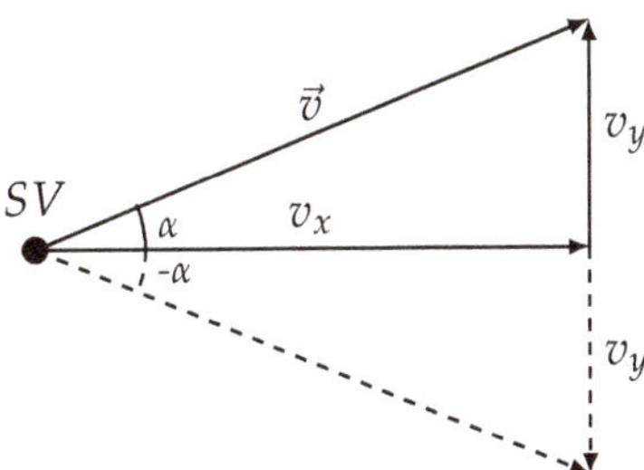

Figure 2. Velocity diagram of the SV.

We considered transitions between process states equally possible with transition intensity matrix:

$$\Lambda = \lambda \begin{pmatrix} -2 & 1 & 1 \\ 1 & -2 & 1 \\ 1 & 1 & -2 \end{pmatrix}, \tag{2}$$

corresponding to the state vector J. The variable λ here is $\lambda = 1/\tau_0$, where τ_0 is the average time of the SV being on one tack. This model generates random trajectories that have the approximate shape shown in Figure 1.

For the mathematical formulation of the stochastic optimization problem, it is convenient to study the Gaussian Markov analog instead of the jump-like process θ_t. This diffusion process Θ_t has the same mathematical expectation and correlation function as the process θ_t. It follows from the theory of jump-like Markov processes that Θ_t allows the stochastic Ito differential [30]:

$$d\Theta_t = -D\Theta_t dt + \sigma dw_t, \tag{3}$$

where w_t is a standard Wiener process and D, σ are constants related to the original Markov process θ_t: $D \triangleq 3\lambda$ and $\sigma \triangleq 2\tan\alpha\sqrt{\lambda}$.

3. Detection Probability of the SO Moving at a Constant Velocity

Firstly, let us consider the task of detecting a target SO (target) with the SV, whose dynamics is described in Section 2. The following model was investigated. The target moves at a constant speed parallel to the general course line of the SV at a distance l from it.

The initial distance between the vehicles along the general course is L, so the initial Cartesian distance is $\sqrt{L^2 + l^2}$. The SV is moving according to (1), where θ_t is a random Markov process with the state vector J and the transition matrix Λ from (2). The target moves according to the law:

$$\begin{cases} \dot{x} = -u, \\ \dot{y} = 0, \end{cases} \tag{4}$$

where u is its constant velocity.

The target will be detected if the distance between it and the SV becomes less than R. To simplify the model, let us assume that the detection is successful when the target's and SV's x-coordinates become equal at some point in time: $x_{SV}(\vartheta) = x(\vartheta)$, and the inequality $|y_{SV}(\vartheta) - y(\vartheta)| \leq R$ is satisfied for the y coordinates.

The rendezvous instant ϑ is defined as:

$$\vartheta = \frac{L}{v\cos\alpha + u}. \tag{5}$$

The probability of detection will be determined by including the y_{SV} coordinate in the interval $[l - R, l + R]$, namely:

$$\mathbf{P}_{\text{det}} = \mathbf{P}\{l - R \leq y_{SV}(\vartheta) \leq l + R\} = \mathbf{P}\left\{ \frac{l-R}{v\sin\alpha} \leq \int_0^\vartheta \theta_s\, ds \leq \frac{l+R}{v\sin\alpha} \right\}. \tag{6}$$

As mentioned in (3), the random jump-like Markov process θ_t can be replaced with its Gaussian Markov analog Θ_t, which has the same mathematical expectation and correlation function as the process θ_t.

Further, instead of calculating the random integral (6), we estimated the target detection probability by the SV through the analytical approximation of probability histograms, obtained in the numerical simulation. We assumed that at the instant $t_0 = 0$, the target is situated in the position $E^0 = (L, l)$ and $L \gg 1$ (as shown in Figure 3) and the velocity of the target $u < 1$.

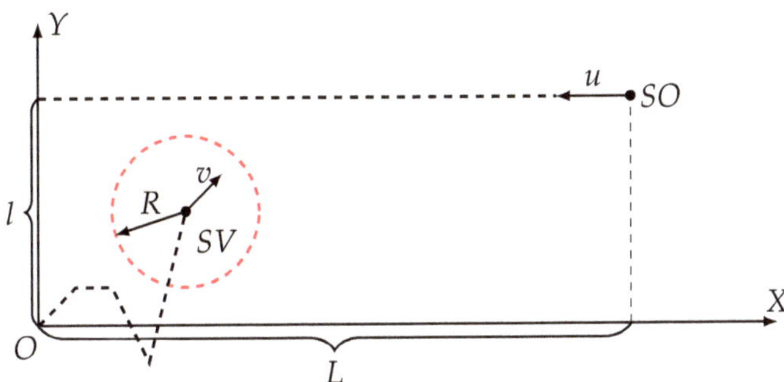

Figure 3. Relative positions of the SV and SO.

Due to the latter assumption, the SV's detection zone can be considered as a flat-line segment with the length of the diameter instead of the circle. Thus, the detection probability can be estimated as the probability of meeting the target with this segment.

The histograms of the distribution density of the y_{SV} coordinate obtained in the interval $[l - \Delta l, l + \Delta l]$ for some small Δl are well approximated by the symmetric density of the Gaussian distribution. Figure 4 depicts the histogram of the probability of meeting between the target and SV and the corresponding density of the Gaussian distributions: $\mathcal{N}(0, \sigma_1^2)$ for $\sigma_1 = 0.705$ for the case $L = L_1 = 5$ (Figure 4a) and $\mathcal{N}(0, \sigma_2^2)$ for $\sigma_2 = 0.993$ for the case $L = L_2 = 10$ (Figure 4b). The histograms were constructed as a result of computer simulation of the movement of the target and SV for 10,000 implementations of the SV trajectory corresponding to $\lambda = 5/3$.

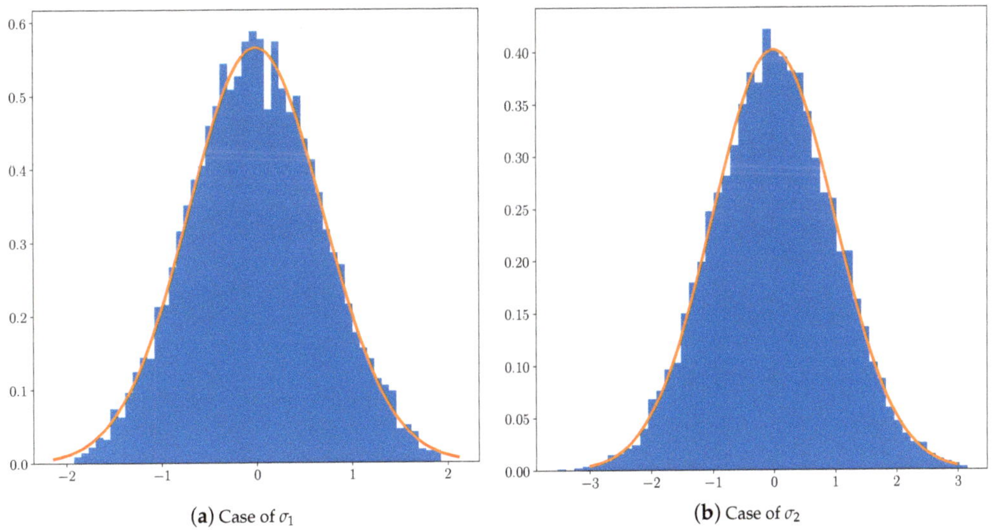

(a) Case of σ_1 (b) Case of σ_2

Figure 4. Histograms of the probability detection distribution density of the target moving at a constant velocity.

These graphs allowed us to estimate the SV's detection probability $\mathbf{P}_{\text{det}}$ at its various initial positions. Now, Equation (6) may be approximated as:

$$\mathbf{P}_{\text{det}} = \mathbf{P}\{l - R \leq y_{SV}(\vartheta) \leq l + R\} = \frac{1}{\sqrt{2\pi}\sigma_i} \int_{l-R}^{l+R} \exp\left(-y^2/(2\sigma_i^2)\right) dy, \tag{7}$$

where σ_i corresponds to various parameters (L_i, l_i, u_i). In particular, when $l = l_1 = 1.5$ and $l = l_2 = 2.5$ for L_1 and L_2, respectively, these probabilities are presented in Table 1. In all cases, the velocity of the target is $u = 0.3$. All values are given in a normalized scale.

Table 1. The detection probability of the target $\mathbf{P}_{\text{det}}$ at its various initial positions $E^0 = (L, l)$.

L	l	$\mathbf{P}_{\text{det}}$
5	1.5	0.238
5	2.5	0.017
10	1.5	0.304
10	2.5	0.065

Next, we introduced a certain threshold value (security threshold) $h < 1$ of the permissible detection probability of $\mathbf{P}_{\text{det}}$, for example $h = 0.07$. The situation with $\mathbf{P}_{\text{det}} \leq h$ is considered *safe*. In this case, the target continues to move in a straight line without changing its course and speed. If $\mathbf{P}_{\text{det}} > h$, then the situation is considered *dangerous*. It was assumed that in the case of a dangerous situation, the target (to prevent the negative consequences of possible detection) uses the mobile defender mentioned in the Introduction, whose task is to intercept the SV with a minimum standard error at a given point in the plane relative to the SV.

The minimization of this miss is associated with the solution of the following optimal stochastic control problem.

4. Optimal Stochastic Control Problem

The problem was considered in a moving Cartesian coordinate system $X_t O_t Y_t$, where the origin O_t is associated with the current position P^t of the SV and the axis $O_t X_t$ is directed parallel to the SV's general course. The current position of the defender E_2^t is given by a two-dimensional vector Z_2^t directed from $O_t \triangleq P^t$ to E_2^t.

Terminal position E_2^θ of the defender is defined by a given two-dimensional vector d, as shown in Figure 5. An auxiliary vector $\eta_t \triangleq Z_2^t - d$ was introduced for a more convenient formulation of the defender's optimal control problem.

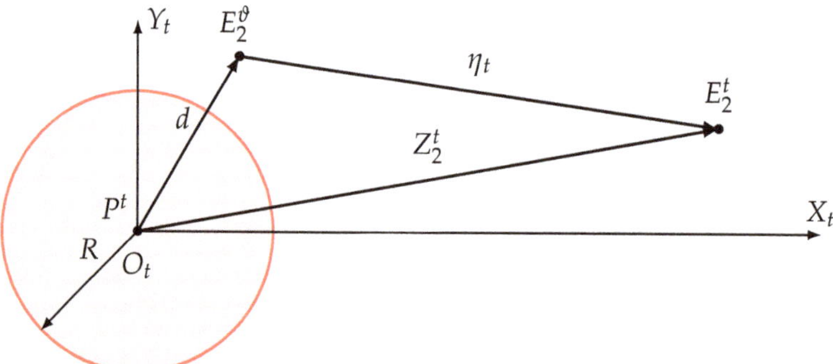

Figure 5. Geometry of the problem.

In the selected coordinate system, the equations of the relative motion of the defender–SV system have the form:

$$\dot{Z}_2^t = u_t - \begin{pmatrix} 1 \\ \Theta_t \end{pmatrix}, \qquad u_t = \begin{pmatrix} u_x^t \\ u_y^t \end{pmatrix}, \tag{8}$$

where Θ_t is from (3) and the initial position of Z_2^0 were set. The two-dimensional velocity vector u_t of the defender plays the role of the control and is subject to the restrictions:

$$|u_t| \leq \beta < 1 \tag{9}$$

with the specified constant β.

In terms of the auxiliary vector η_t introduced above, the equations of motion (8) take the compact form:

$$\dot{\eta}_t = u_t + A + B\Theta_t, \quad \eta_0 \triangleq Z_2^0, \tag{10}$$

where:

$$A = \begin{pmatrix} -1 \\ 0 \end{pmatrix}, \quad B = \begin{pmatrix} 0 \\ -1 \end{pmatrix}. \tag{11}$$

At the terminal moment ϑ, the following condition must be met:

$$\mathbf{E}\eta_\vartheta = 0, \tag{12}$$

where $\mathbf{E}$ is the sign of the mathematical expectation. As a criterion, we took the terminal functional:

$$\mathbf{E}G(\eta_\vartheta, \Theta_\vartheta) \to \min_{u_t}, \tag{13}$$

where:

$$G(\eta_\vartheta, \Theta_\vartheta) = \eta_\vartheta^2 + \gamma\Theta_\vartheta. \tag{14}$$

In (13) and (14), the summand η_ϑ^2 characterizes the standard deviation of the defender from the end of the vector d at the terminal moment ϑ. The term $\gamma\mathbf{E}\Theta_\vartheta$, where γ is a given constant, plays the role of an additional terminal penalty for the "convenient" or "inconvenient" tack of the SV at the time of ϑ. Here, the words "convenient" or "inconvenient" are used in the following sense. The tack of the SV at the time of ϑ is considered "convenient" if $\Theta_\vartheta < 0$, i.e., the component of the velocity of the SV along the OY axis is negative (the SV is moving away from the line of the movement of the target E_1). Otherwise, we considered the tack of the SV "inconvenient".

5. Optimal Stochastic Control

5.1. Reduction of the Optimal Stochastic Control Problem to the Deterministic One

It is known that solving stochastic optimization problems in real time is associated with certain difficulties [30]. For this reason, instead of the original stochastic problem (3), (9)–(14), we solved its deterministic analog. To construct this analog, we need the following auxiliary results.

The solution of Equation (3) has the form:

$$\Theta_t = e^{-Dt}\Theta_0 + \sigma \int_0^t e^{-D(t-s)} dw_s. \tag{15}$$

Integration (15) leads to the equation:

$$\int_0^t \Theta_s ds = \frac{\Theta_0}{D}\left(1 - e^{-Dt}\right) + \frac{\sigma}{D}\int_0^t \left(1 - e^{-D(t-s)}\right) dw_s. \tag{16}$$

Now, let us calculate the value of the criterion (13) with an arbitrary permissible program control u_t and the parameter ϑ fixed at the moment $t_0 = 0$. To this end, we integrated the equations of motion (10) taking into account (16). We have:

$$\eta_\vartheta = \eta_0 + A\vartheta + B\frac{\theta_0}{D}\left(1 - e^{-D\vartheta}\right) + B\frac{\sigma}{D}\int_0^\vartheta \left(1 - e^{-D(\vartheta-s)}\right) dw_s + \int_0^\vartheta u_s ds. \tag{17}$$

From (12) and (17) follows:

$$\mathbf{E}\eta_\vartheta = \eta_0 + A\vartheta + B\frac{\Theta_0}{D}\left(1 - e^{-D\vartheta}\right) + \int_0^\vartheta u_s ds = 0. \tag{18}$$

Finally, from (17) and (18), we obtain:

$$\mathbf{E}\,\eta_\vartheta^2 = \frac{\sigma^2}{D^2}\left[\vartheta - \frac{2}{D}\left(1 - e^{-D\vartheta}\right) + \frac{1}{2D}\left(1 - e^{-2D\vartheta}\right)\right]. \tag{19}$$

Thus, the (13) criterion takes the form:

$$\mathbf{EG} = \frac{\sigma^2}{D^2}\left[\vartheta - \frac{2}{D}\left(1 - e^{-D\vartheta}\right) + \frac{1}{2D}\left(1 - e^{-2D\vartheta}\right)\right] + \gamma e^{-D\vartheta}\Theta_0 \to \min_{u_t}. \tag{20}$$

Now, we transformed (18) by introducing a two-dimensional vector ξ_t subordinate to the equation:

$$\dot{\xi}_t = A + B\Theta_0 e^{-Dt} + u_t \tag{21}$$

with boundary conditions:

$$\xi_0 = \eta_0, \qquad \xi_\vartheta = 0. \tag{22}$$

In terms of the vector ξ_t, the desired deterministic analog is the following auxiliary problem of optimal (deterministic) control, which includes the equations of motion (21), boundary conditions (22), control constraints (9), and terminal criterion $F(\vartheta) \to \min\limits_{u_t}$, where $F(\vartheta)$ denotes the right-hand side of (20) with the excluded additive constants $-2\sigma^2/D^3$ and $\sigma^2/(2D^3)$:

$$F(\vartheta) \triangleq \frac{\sigma^2}{D^2}\left[\vartheta + \frac{2}{D}e^{-D\vartheta} - \frac{1}{2D}e^{-2D\vartheta}\right] + \gamma e^{-D\vartheta}\Theta_0 \to \min_{u_t}. \tag{23}$$

5.2. Pontryagin's Maximum Principle in the Auxiliary Optimal Problem (23)

To solve the auxiliary problem, we used Pontryagin maximum principle (PMP) [31]. According to the procedure of PMP, firstly, we constructed the Hamiltonian:

$$H = \lambda_\xi \cdot \left(A + B\theta_0 e^{-Dt}\right) + \lambda_\xi \cdot u_t \to \max_{u_t}. \tag{24}$$

Here, the dot between the two-dimensional vectors means a scalar product, and $\lambda_\xi = \lambda_\xi(t)$ is a conjugate variable corresponding to the phase variable ξ_t. From (24), we found the explicit form of the optimal control (here and further, the * symbol indicates the optimal controls):

$$u_t^* = \beta\frac{\lambda_\xi(t)}{|\lambda_\xi(t)|}. \tag{25}$$

The conjugate variable satisfies [31]:

$$\dot{\lambda}_\xi(t) = -\frac{\partial H}{\partial \xi}(t) = 0; \tag{26}$$

hence $\lambda_\xi(t) = \lambda_\xi = \text{const}$, which leads to $u_t^* = u^* = \text{const}$ with $|u^*| = \beta$. In other words, the program motion of the controlled object is implemented in a straight line with the maximum possible speed. The transversality conditions at instant ϑ are given by:

$$\delta F(\vartheta) + \lambda_\xi \cdot \delta\xi - H\delta\vartheta = 0, \tag{27}$$

where according to (23):

$$\delta F(\vartheta) = \frac{\partial F(\vartheta)}{\partial\vartheta}\delta\vartheta = \frac{\sigma^2}{D^2}\left[1 - 2e^{-D\vartheta} + e^{-2D\vartheta}\right]\delta\vartheta - \gamma De^{-D\vartheta}\theta_0\,\delta\vartheta. \tag{28}$$

Following (27), (28):

$$H(\vartheta) = \frac{\sigma^2}{D^2}\left[1 - 2e^{-D\vartheta} + e^{-2D\vartheta}\right] - \gamma D e^{-D\vartheta}\theta_0. \tag{29}$$

Integrating (21), taking into account (22), gives:

$$\eta_0 + A\vartheta + B\frac{\theta_0}{D}\left(1 - e^{-D\vartheta}\right) + u^*\vartheta = 0 \tag{30}$$

that naturally coincides with (18) under $u_t = u^*$.

Next, we put

$$\begin{cases} u^* \triangleq \beta(\cos\varphi, \sin\varphi), & \text{with} \quad \varphi = \text{const}, \\ \eta_0 \triangleq (x_0, y_0). \end{cases} \tag{31}$$

Then, from (30) and (31), we have in a componentwise form of the system of two equations with respect to φ and ϑ:

$$\begin{cases} x_0 - \vartheta + \beta\vartheta\cos\varphi = 0, \\ y_0 + \beta\vartheta\sin\varphi - \dfrac{\theta_0}{D}\left(1 - e^{-D\vartheta}\right) = 0. \end{cases} \tag{32}$$

From (32) follows:

$$\begin{cases} \cos\varphi = (\vartheta - x_0)(\beta\vartheta)^{-1}, \\ \sin\varphi = \left[\dfrac{\Theta_0}{D}\left(1 - e^{-D\vartheta}\right) - y_0\right](\beta\vartheta)^{-1}, \end{cases} \tag{33}$$

where ϑ can be found as the least-positive root of the equation, following from the identical equality $\cos^2\varphi + \sin^2\varphi = 1$ with respect to the right parts of (33), namely:

$$(\vartheta - x_0)^2 + \left[\frac{\Theta_0}{D}\left(1 - e^{-D\vartheta}\right) - y_0\right]^2 = \beta^2\vartheta^2. \tag{34}$$

Formulas (33) and (34) allow us to find the velocity components of the controlled object and the time interval $[0, \vartheta]$ of its motion from the initial position to the end of the vector d.

If $D\vartheta$ in (34) is sufficiently large, then the term $e^{-D\vartheta}$ is close to zero and can be omitted. In this case, (34) takes the form:

$$(\vartheta - x_0)^2 + \left(\frac{\Theta_0}{D} - y_0\right)^2 = \beta^2\vartheta^2. \tag{35}$$

Then, the instant ϑ can be found as the least root of the square Equation (35):

$$\vartheta = \frac{x_0 - \sqrt{x_0^2 - (1 - \beta^2)\left(x_0^2 + \left(\dfrac{\Theta_0}{D} - y_0\right)^2\right)}}{1 - \beta^2}. \tag{36}$$

To construct a positional optimal control (feedback control) of the defender, the current moment t was taken as the initial t_0, the current position (x_t, y_t) was taken as the initial (x_0, y_0), and the current value of Θ_t—for the initial Θ_0; after that, the instantaneous direction of the vector u_t^* of the defender's velocity was calculated using the formulas (31) taking into account (33) and (36). Next, u_t^* was recalculated at the rate of updating the current information. Note that at a high rate of updating this information, it may be quite justified to use the piecewise program control of the defender, in which its control is recalculated only at certain moments called correction moments with intervals between them Δt_u. During these intervals, the defender moves programmatically according to control u_t^*, calculated in the previous step.

6. Examples

To demonstrate the effectiveness of the obtained optimal control, a numerical simulation was performed for two approaches for studying the interaction between the defender and SV. These approaches differ in the mathematical description of the evolution of the y-component of the SV's velocity. In the first (discrete) approach, this component is piecewise constant and its evolution is described as a jump-like Markov process θ_t with three states $(1, 0, -1)$ and the transition intensity matrix Λ from (2). The description of this process is given in the beginning of Section 2. In the second (continuous) approach, an evolution of the y-component of the SV's velocity vector is set by Gaussian process Θ_t, i.e., continuous diffusion process (3).

In both approaches, the control of the defender was obtained through Equations (31), (33), and (36). In other words, the control of the defender is always calculated according to the continuous diffusive model (3) of the evolution of the y-component of the SV's velocity vector. Strictly speaking, as this control law is the result of the solution of the continuous problem, it should not always successfully solve the discrete problem, simulated in the first approach. The idea of these experiments is to apply the solution of the continuous problem, which can be solved analytically, to the similar discrete practical model, which cannot be studied in the same convenient way. In all experiments, vector d was considered to be null, i.e., the defender has to intercept the SV.

Both approaches to the simulation are shown in further examples, which were devoted to two different applications of the studied interception problem.

The realization of diffusive process Θ_t was acquired in Maple with the package for stochastic equations. An approximate formula for ϑ (36) was used for the stochastic differential Equation (15). Thus, Maple allows integrating this equation numerically and obtaining the optimal trajectory of the defender, as well as the random trajectory of the SV corresponding to the process with the appropriate mathematical expectation and dispersion.

A more practical discrete jump-like process θ_t was simulated in Python script. The movement of the SV and defender was computed with a very small discretization step Δt, which is the quality of the simulation. At each step, the SV, according to the model from Section 3, can change the direction of its v_y velocity component with probability $2\lambda\Delta t$ or not change it with probability $(1 - 2\lambda\Delta t)$. However, in practice, this model is not very useful. This process is identical to a Gaussian process: the time of another SV tack is sampled exponentially with mathematical expectation $1/\lambda$, and the direction of the vertical velocity for this tack is chosen from two directions, different from the current one with probability $1/2$. The defender, on the other hand, has its own parameter Δt_u and corrects its control law according to (36) every interval Δt_u, considering the current positions to be initial.

6.1. Intrusion in the Detection Zone

The first application is the intrusion of the SV's detection zone by the defender to distract the SV from the target. In normalized scale, these parameters are:

$$R = 1, \quad v_x = 1, \quad \tau_0 = 0.6.$$

Let $\tan \alpha = 0.5$. Then, the parameters for Gauss process Θ_t are:

$$\lambda = \frac{1}{\tau_0} \approx 1.67, \quad D = 3\lambda \approx 5, \quad \sigma = 2 \tan \alpha \sqrt{\lambda} = 1.29.$$

In the coordinate system associated with the initial position of the SV, the initial coordinates of the defender's position are $(10, 1)$ in the normalized scale. The velocity of the defender was chosen as $\beta = 0.5$. The probability of the detection of the target following a parallel course from this coordinates equals $\mathbf{P}_{\text{det}} = 0.5$, which is higher than the accepted security threshold $h = 0.07$. Thus, according to the above-described security concept, the target must use a mobile defender.

The results of this experiment are shown in Figure 6. The red line depicts the trajectory of the defender, whereas the blue one, that of the SV. Figure 6a shows the evolution of the y-component of the SV's velocity according to Markov jump-like process θ_t. Figure 6b shows the trajectories of the vehicles for the diffusion approximation Θ_t of the process θ_t. In Figure 6a, the black ellipse depicts the circular detection zone of radius R, which looks ellipsoidal due to the different scale of the OX and OY axes. In the case of the discrete model, the parameter Δt_u is equal to τ_0. In the case of the continuous model, the calculation of the defender's optimal control is performed in time with the SV's information updating, i.e., almost continuously (Δt_u equals the simulation discretization step).

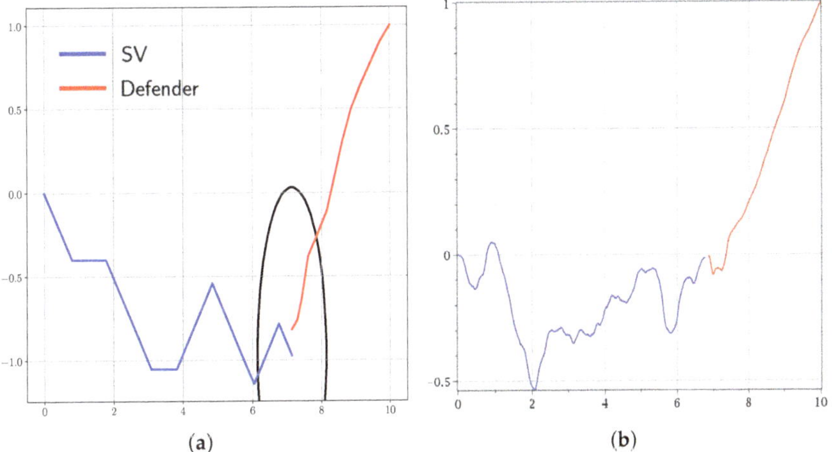

Figure 6. Intrusion of the SV's detection zone. (**a**) SV and defender trajectories corresponding to the path of θ_t; (**b**) SV and defender trajectories corresponding to the path of Θ_t.

For the estimation of time ϑ, Equation (36) was used. According to (36), interception time $\vartheta = 7$, which means $e^{-D\vartheta} \approx 0$, i.e., $1 - e^{-D\vartheta} \approx 1$, so u_t can be found from Equations (31), (33), and (36). One can see in Figure 6 that the trajectories of the defender for the discrete and continuous models of the SV's movement were quite close. The difference of the trajectories in the final sections was due to the significant duration of the interval Δt_u between the updates of the information about the SV and, thereby, the corrections of the defender's program control in the discrete approach.

As one can see, the problem of interception was solved successfully, as the defender moving from the initial position with the found u control finally occurred in the close vicinity of the SV.

6.2. Destruction of the SV

The second application is the task of the destruction of the SV using the defender. To complete this task, the defender must come close enough to the SV. In the normalized scale:

$$R = 1, \quad v_x = 1, \quad \tau_0 \approx 60.$$

Let $\tan \alpha = 0.5$. Therefore:

$$\lambda = 0.017, \quad D = 0.05, \quad \sigma = 0.13.$$

In the coordinate system associated with the initial position of the SV, the initial coordinates of the defender are $(300, 20)$ in the normalized scale. The velocity of the defender was chosen as $\beta = 0.5$. As the target moves parallel to the general course of the SV, then the detection probability $\mathbf{P}_{\text{det}}$ equals $\mathbf{P}_{\text{det}} = 0.37 > h = 0.07$; thus, using the defender is justified.

The results of the modeling are presented in Figure 7. As in the first example, Figure 7a corresponds to the discrete approach to the simulation and the process θ_t, and Figure 7b relates to the continuous approach and the process Θ_t.

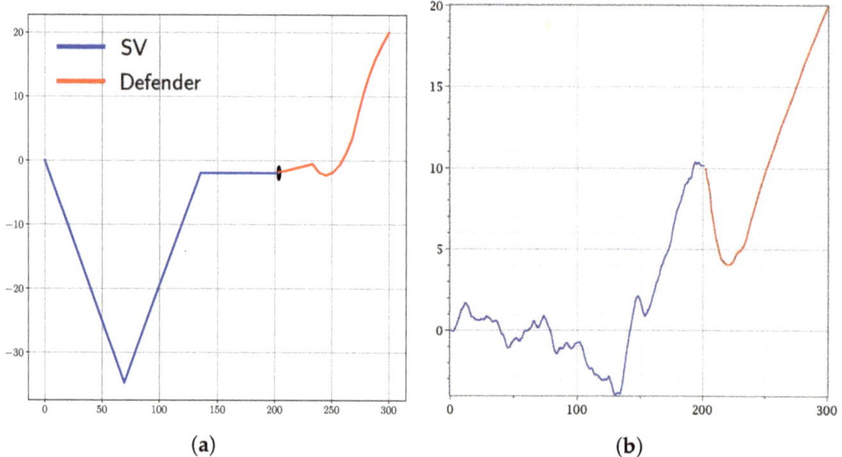

(a)

(b)

Figure 7. Destruction of the SV. (**a**) SV and defender trajectories corresponding to the path of θ_t; (**b**) SV and defender trajectories corresponding to the path of Θ_t.

The accuracy of the interception of the SV by the defender or the so-called terminal miss obviously depends on the parameter Δt_u—the time interval between corrections of the defender's control. Figure 8 presents the results of different simulations of the interception of the SV by the defender for the discrete approach. Figure 8a corresponds to the case of $\Delta t_u = \tau_0$. A sufficient miss of the defender can be explained by the relatively significant duration Δt_u of its movement without control correction and the "inconvenient" realization of the tack, which combined with the velocity advantage ($\beta < 1$) allowed the SV to avoid interception by the defender. However, decreasing the parameter Δt_u helped achieve more satisfactory results, as shown in Figure 8b. For two similar realizations of process θ_t (blue lines), the trajectories of the controlled defender (red lines) were clearly very different with dependence on the parameter Δt_u (τ_0 and $\tau_0/10$, respectively).

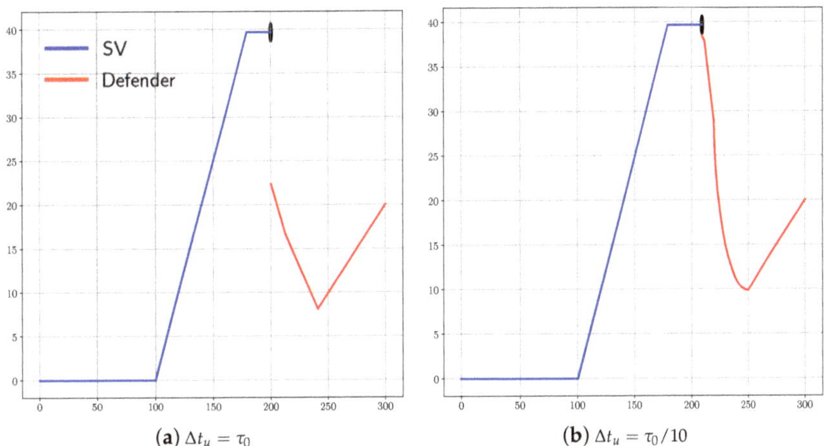

(**a**) $\Delta t_u = \tau_0$ (**b**) $\Delta t_u = \tau_0/10$

Figure 8. Interception trajectories with different values of Δt_u.

6.3. Comparison with Classic Guidance Methods

The optimal control law of the defender obtained here was compared with classic guidance methods, mentioned in the Introduction, such as the pursuit guidance method and parallel guidance, which is a specific case of the proportional navigation guidance method. On average, our method gave better results than the others. In Figure 9, a typical realization of different simulated guidance methods is presented. The orange line designates the trajectory of the defender, acting according to the pursuit guidance method; the red line denotes the trajectory generated by the parallel guidance algorithm; the blue graph shows the SV's movement. The defender, controlled according to Equations (31), (33) and (36), has a green trajectory. Dashed lines illustrate the distances on the Y axis between the SV and defender at instant ϑ when their X-coordinates coincide.

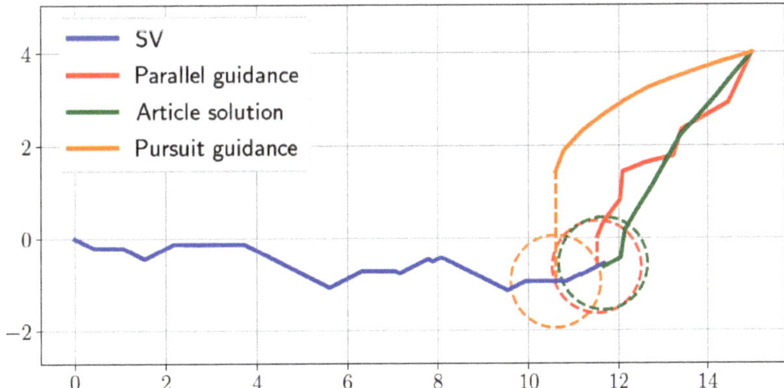

Figure 9. Comparison of different guidance methods.

As one can see, the green defender was closer to the SV than the others. Classic guidance methods are effective when the pursuer velocity is higher than the one of the evader. That is not the case in the current study, because the defender's velocity β was less than the velocity of the SV. Moreover, the classic guidance methods are not intended to be use for intercepting stochastic targets, unlike the control law obtained in this article as a solution of the stochastic optimal control problem.

7. Conclusions

The article considered one "attacker–target–defender"-type problem of the interaction on a plane between the search system, consisting of one search vehicle with the circle detection zone, and the mobile searched object. The search vehicle tacked randomly along a given general course towards the searched object, and its movement was described using a Markov jump-like process. The searched object had a mobile defender onboard, which can be used for the distraction and destruction of the search vehicle, if it presents a danger to the searched object in the sense of its detection. The feature of this problem is that the defender has lower dynamic capabilities in comparison to the searching vehicle being intercepted.

It was shown that, being stochastic in nature, the optimal control problem of the interception of a search vehicle can be transformed into the classic deterministic problem of optimal control in the class of piecewise-programmatic controls. The optimal time of interception was estimated, and an optimal control law was found. The examples of the numerical simulations for both the discrete and continuous (stochastic and deterministic) problems were presented to reveal the efficiency of the designed results. Furthermore, a comparison with the interception solutions, based on classic guidance laws, was presented.

In the future, it is planned to consider a similar problem statement with a group of search vehicles instead of one.

Author Contributions: Conceptualization, A.A.G. and E.Y.R.; methodology, A.A.G. and E.Y.R.; software, P.V.L.; validation, A.A.G., P.V.L. and E.Y.R.; formal analysis, A.A.G., P.V.L. and E.Y.R.; investigation, A.A.G. and E.Y.R.; writing—original draft preparation, A.A.G., P.V.L. and E.Y.R.; writing—review and editing, A.A.G., P.V.L. and E.Y.R.; visualization, P.V.L.; supervision, A.A.G. and E.Y.R.; project administration, A.A.G.; funding acquisition, A.A.G. All authors have read and agreed to the published version of the manuscript.

Funding: This paper was partially supported by the Program of Basic Research of RAS.

Institutional Review Board Statement: Not applicable.

Informed Consent Statement: Not applicable.

Data Availability Statement: Data sharing not applicable.

Conflicts of Interest: The authors declare no conflict of interest.

Abbreviations

The following abbreviations are used in this manuscript:

SO	Searched object
SV	Search vehicle
UAV	Unmanned aerial vehicle
UUV	Unmanned underwater vehicle
ASV	Autonomous surface vehicle

References

1. Stone, L.D.; Royset, J.O.; Washburn, A.R. *Optimal Search for Moving Targets*; Springer International Publishing: Cham, Switzerland, 2016.
2. Meghjani, M.; Manjanna, S.; Dudek, G. Multi-target search strategies. In Proceedings of the 2016 IEEE International Symposium on Safety, Security, and Rescue Robotics (SSRR), Lausanne, Switzerland, 23–27 October 2016; pp. 328–333.
3. Youngchul, B. Target searching method in the chaotic mobile robot. In Proceedings of the 23rd Digital Avionics Systems Conference, Salt Lake City, UT, USA, 24–28 October 2004; Volume 12, pp. 7–12.
4. Austin, D.J.; Jensfelt, P. Using multiple Gaussian hypotheses to represent probability distributions for mobile robot localization. In Proceedings of the 2000 ICRA, Millennium Conference, IEEE International Conference on Robotics and Automation, San Francisco, CA, USA, 24–28 April 2000; pp. 1036–1041.
5. Galyaev, A.A.; Lysenko P.V.; Yakhno V.P. Optimal Path Planning for an Object in a Random Search Region. *Autom. Remote Control* **2018**, *79*, 2080–2089. [CrossRef]

6. Shaikin, M.E. On statistical risk funstional in a control problem for an object moving in a conflict environment. *J. Comput. Syst. Sci. Int.* **2011**, *1*, 22–31.

7. Sysoev, L.P. Criterion of detection probability on trajectory in the problem of object motion control in threat environment. *Control Probl.* **2010**, *6*, 65–72.

8. Andreev, K.V.; Rubinovich, E.Y. Moving observer trajectory control by angular measurements in tracking problem. *Autom. Remote Control* **2016**, *77*, 106–129. [CrossRef]

9. Wettergren, T.A.; Baylog, J.G. Collaborative search planning for multiple vehicles in nonhomogeneous environments. In Proceedings of the OCEANS 2009, Biloxi, MS, USA, 26–29 October 2009; pp. 1–7.

10. Wang, Y.; Hussein, I.I. *Search and Classification Using Multiple Autonomous Vehicles*; Springer: London, UK, 2012.

11. Galyaev, A.A.; Maslov, E.P. Optimization of a mobile object evasion laws from detection. *J. Comput. Syst. Sci. Int.* **2010**, *49*, 560–569. [CrossRef]

12. Galyaev, A.A.; Maslov, E.P. Optimization of the Law of Moving Object Evasion from Detection under Constraints. *Autom. Remote Control* **2012**, *73*, 992–1004. [CrossRef]

13. Zabarankin, M.; Uryasev, S.; Pardalos, P. *Optimal Risk Path Algorithms Cooperative Control and Optimization*; Murphey, P., Ed.; Kluwer Acad: Dordrecht, The Netherlands, 2002; Volume 66, pp. 271–303.

14. Sidhu, H.; Mercer, G.; Sexton, M. Optimal trajectories in a threat environment. *J. Battlef. Technol.* **2006**, *9*, 33–39.

15. Dogan, A.; Zengin, U. Unmanned Aerial Vehicle Dynamic-Target Pursuit by Using Probabilistic Threat Exposure Map. *J. Guid. Control Dyn.* **2006**, *29*, 723–732. [CrossRef]

16. Meyer, Y.; Isaiah, P.; Shima, T. On dubins paths to intercept a moving target. *Automatica* **2015**, *53*, 256–263. [CrossRef]

17. Zheng, Y.; Chen, Z.; Shao, X.; Zhao, W. Time-optimal guidance for intercepting moving targets by dubins vehicles. *Automatica* **2021**, *128*, 109557. [CrossRef]

18. Buzikov, M.E.; Galyaev, A.A. Time-minimal interception of a moving target by dubins car. *Autom. Remote Control* **2021**, *82*, 745–758. [CrossRef]

19. Guelman, M.; Shinar, J. Optimal guidance law in the plane. *J. Guid. Control Dyn.* **1984**, *7*, 471–476. [CrossRef]

20. Glizer, V.Y. Optimal planar interception with fixed end conditions: Closed-form solution. *J. Optim. Theory Appl.* **1996**, *88*, 503–539. [CrossRef]

21. Gopalan, A.; Ratnoo, A.; Ghose, D. Time-optimal guidance for lateral interception of moving targets. *J. Guid. Control Dyn.* **2016**, *39*, 510–525. [CrossRef]

22. Manyam, S.G.; Casbeer, D.W. Intercepting a target moving on a racetrack path. In Proceedings of the 2020 International Conference on Unmanned Aircraft Systems (ICUAS), Athens, Greece, 1–4 September 2020; pp. 799–806.

23. Siouris, G.M. *Missile Guidance and Control Systems*; Springer: New York, NY, USA, 2004.

24. Lin, C.F. *Modern Navigation, Guidance, and Control Processing*; Prentice Hall: Hoboken, NJ, USA, 1991.

25. Palumbo, N.F.; Blauwkamp, R.; Lloyd, J. Basic Principles of Homing Guidance. *Johns Hopkins APL Tech. Digest.* **2010** , *29*, 25–41.

26. Pachter, M.; Garcia, E.; Casbeer, D.W. Active target defense differential game. In Proceedings of the 52nd Annual Allerton Conference on Communication, Control, and Computing, Montlcello, IL, USA, 30 September–3 October 2014; pp. 46–53.

27. Pachter, M.; Garcia, E.; Casbeer, D.W. Active Target defense differential game with a fast Defender. In Proceedings of the American Control Conference (ACC), Chicago, IL, USA, 1–3 July 2015; pp. 3752–3757.

28. Zhang, J.; Zhuang, J. Modeling a Multi-target Attacker-defender Game with Multiple Attack Types. *Reliab. Eng. Syst. Saf.* **2019**, *185*, 465–475. [CrossRef]

29. Galyaev, A.A.; Dobrovidov, A.V.; Lysenko, P.V.; Shaikin, M.E.; Yakhno, V.P. Path Planning in Threat Environment for UUV with Non-Uniform Radiation Pattern. *Sensors* **2020**, *20*, 2076. [CrossRef] [PubMed]

30. Krichagina, N.V.; Liptser, R.S.; Rubinovich, E.Y. Kalman filter for Markov processes. In *Statistics and Control of Stochastic Processes*; Publ. Div.: New York, NY, USA, 1985; pp. 197–213.

31. Ross, I.M. *A Primer on Pontryagin's Principle in Optimal Control*; Collegiate Publishers: San Francisco, CA, USA, 2009.

 *mathematics*

Article

Methods of Ensuring Invariance with Respect to External Disturbances: Overview and New Advances

Aleksey Antipov [1,*], Svetlana Krasnova [1] and Victor Utkin [2]

[1] Laboratory of Systems with Discontinuous Control, V.A. Trapeznikov Institute of Control Sciences of Russian Academy of Science, 117997 Moscow, Russia; skrasnova@list.ru

[2] E.S. Pyatnitskiy Laboratory of Dynamics of Nonlinear Control Processes, V.A. Trapeznikov Institute of Control Sciences of Russian Academy of Science, 117997 Moscow, Russia; viktorutkin013@gmail.com

* Correspondence: scholess18@mail.ru; Tel.: +7-(495)-198-1720 (ext. 1577)

Abstract: In this paper, we carry out a demonstration and comparative analysis of known methods of the synthesis of various control laws ensuring the invariance of the output (controlled) variable with respect to external disturbances under various assumptions about their type and channels of acting on the control plant. Methods of the synthesis are presented on the example of a third-order nonlinear system with single input and single output (SISO-systems), dynamic feedback synthesis is presented at a descriptive level and the focus is on procedures of static feedback synthesis. For the systems in which the matching conditions are not satisfied, it is concluded that it is expedient to introduce smooth and bounded nonlinear local feedbacks. Within the framework of the block control principle, we developed an iterative procedure of synthesis of S-shaped sigmoid feedbacks for such systems. Nonlinear local feedbacks ensure stabilization of the output variable with the given accuracy and settling time as in a system with traditionally used linear local feedbacks with high gains. However, in contrast to it, sigmoid functions do not lead to a large overshoot of state variables and control actions.

Keywords: external disturbances; invariance; block control principle; decomposition; high-gain factors; sliding mode control; sigmoid function

Citation: Antipov, A.; Krasnova, S.; Utkin, V. Methods of Ensuring Invariance with Respect to External Disturbances: Overview and New Advances. *Mathematics* **2021**, *9*, 3140. https://doi.org/10.3390/math9233140

Academic Editors: Natalia Bakhtadze, Igor Yadykin, Andrei Torgashov and Nikolay Korgin

Received: 10 November 2021
Accepted: 3 December 2021
Published: 6 December 2021

Publisher's Note: MDPI stays neutral with regard to jurisdictional claims in published maps and institutional affiliations.

1. Introduction

The basic issue of automatic control theory is the tracking problem, which consists in a convergence of the output variables to the reference admissible signals with the given performance of the transient and steady-state processes. The main efforts of researchers are aimed at solving this problem for the control plants, operating under the action of external uncontrolled disturbances. The methods of the synthesis of invariant systems used at the present stage are quite diverse. However, their effectiveness and applicability depend on many factors. Firstly, our goal is to systematize the existing methods of disturbance suppressing and compensating, to formalize the requirements on the degree of certainty of the control plant, at which it is advisable to use one or another approach. We also present the methods of synthesizing the corresponding control laws. The results of the survey are presented in Sections 2 and 3. Secondly, in Section 4 we propose a new, more universal approach to the synthesis of invariant systems with nonlinear feedback, in which the advantages of classical methods are concentrated. Moreover, this approach gives an effective result in cases where classical methods are not applicable.

To strengthen the methodological component of the presented material, we will consider all the stated approaches specifically on the example of a single-channel nonlinear minimum-phase system of the third order operating under the action of external uncontrolled disturbances. The given synthesis procedures for a third-order system fully describe all the features of the presented methods. Therefore, the algorithms can be easily extended to similar systems of a higher order. In this sense, without loss of generality, the considered control plant model can be interpreted as one of the subsystems of external dynamics equations of a multichannel system [1]

For the sake of presentation simplicity, let us suppose that the mathematical model of control plant has a relative degree of three and is representable in the following canonical input-output form:

$$\begin{aligned}
\dot{x}_1 &= x_2 + \eta_1(t), \\
\dot{x}_2 &= x_3 + \eta_2(t), \\
\dot{x}_3 &= f(x) + b(x)u + \eta_3(t),
\end{aligned} \tag{1}$$

where $x = (x_1, x_2, x_3)^{\mathrm{T}} \in X \subset R^3$ is measured state vector, X is open bounded region; $x_1 \in R$ is controlled variable (output), $u \in R$ is control action (input); $b(x) \neq 0$, $x \in X$ is the structural requirement, needed for system controllability. In the system (1) $\eta_i(t)$ are unknown functions of time that depend on external deterministic disturbances and other uncertainties in the description of the control plant model, which are bounded in modulus by known constants:

$$\left|\eta_i(t)\right| \leq H_i = \mathrm{const} > 0,\ t \geq 0,\ i = \overline{1,3}. \tag{2}$$

The assumptions about the smoothness/non-smoothness of these functions, as well as the requirements of definiteness of $f(x)$, $b(x)$ will be refined further.

Note that the output variable $x_1(t)$ can represent a tracking error which is the residual between the controlled variable and the given signal. We can assume that the analytical form of the given signal is not known, there are only its measured current values. Then its derivative is assumed to be an unknown bounded function that is additively included in $\eta_1(t)$.

It should be understood that in the presence of persistent disturbances $\eta_{1,2}(t)$, stabilization of all state variables of the system (1) is not possible for any control law. In a closed system, the variables $x_2(t)$ and $x_3(t)$ will have to describe the external actions $\eta_1(t)$ and $\eta_2(t)$ correspondingly. Therefore, for the system (1), the problem of feedback synthesis, ensured stabilization of only the output variable $x_1(t)$, is posed, which in the general case can be achieved with some accuracy,

$$|x_1(t)| \leq \Delta_1,\ t \geq t_1. \tag{3}$$

Further, it is assumed that the value $\Delta_1 > 0$ is given. The settling time $t_1 > 0$ depends on the initial conditions. In addition, the requirement on the given settling time often leads to cumbersome constructions and conservative estimates on the regulator parameters selection. Therefore, in the review section, we consider sufficient conditions for solving the posed problem (3) without the given settling time. A complete solution of the problem (3) will be given in the presentation of the author's method.

Then, for the system (1) the known and new methods of solving the posed problem are considered under various assumptions. The article is structured as follows. In Section 2, we consider a particular case of system (1), when an external disturbance acts on the same channel as the control (matched disturbance). The methods of synthesis and the results of a comparative analysis of the following approaches of solving the problem (3) are presented:

- Dynamic feedback and disturbance compensation by using its estimate in combined control;
- Static feedback and complete suppression of disturbance using discontinuous controls and organizing a sliding mode;
- Static feedback and suppression of disturbance with a given accuracy using linear control with high-gain factors;
- Static feedback and suppression of disturbance with a given accuracy using piecewise linear continuous control.

In Section 3, we deal with the system (1) with unmatched disturbances. The main attention is paid to the case when external disturbances are not smooth. For the solution of the posed problem (3), a standard procedure of block synthesis of linear local feedbacks with high-gain factors is presented. The advantages and disadvantages of this method are described, and a conclusion about the advisability of introducing smooth and bounded nonlinear feedbacks in practical applications is made.

In Section 4 a new approach developed by the authors and implemented in practical applications is presented. Sufficient conditions of the posed problem (3) solution for the given settling time are formalized, and a constructive procedure of block synthesis of nonlinear sigmoid local feedbacks is developed. In the conclusion, the prospect for the further development of the results presented in Section 4 is indicated.

2. Feedback Synthesis Methods in a System with a Matched Disturbance

The most developed case in the automatic control theory means that functions with parametric uncertainties and external disturbances are affine and act in the control space. In this case, the disturbances are said to be matched with the control and the matching conditions are satisfied. For example, for a linear system

$$\dot{x} = Ax + Bu + Q\eta(t)$$

matching conditions have a form [1,2]

$$\mathrm{Im}Q \subset \mathrm{Im}B \Leftrightarrow \mathrm{rank}B = \mathrm{rank}(B \ Q).$$

This means that the columns of the matrix Q are a linear combination of the columns of the matrix B, therefore, the original system can be represented as

$$\dot{x} = Ax + B(u + \Lambda\eta), Q = B\Lambda.$$

For the system (1), the matching conditions take a form

$$\eta_i(t) \equiv 0, \ t \geq 0, \ i = 1, \ 2 \tag{4}$$

Thus, in this section, we consider a special case of the system (1) and (4)

$$\begin{aligned}
\dot{x}_1 &= x_2, \\
\dot{x}_2 &= x_3, \\
\dot{x}_3 &= f(x) + b(x)u + \eta_3(t),
\end{aligned}$$

where the requirements on the smoothness of the functions $f(x)$, $\eta_3(t)$ are generally not imposed.

Note that if $x_1(t)$ is a tracking error, then $x_2(t)$ and $x_3(t)$ are the first and second derivatives of the tracking error, which depend on the first and second derivatives of a given signal and are supposed to be known functions of time. Uncertainty is allowed only for the third derivative of the given signal, which is bounded and additively included in $\eta_3(t)$.

In contrast to the general case, in Systems (1) and (4) with matched disturbance it is possible to ensure the stabilization of all state variables using:

(i) Dynamic feedback and disturbance compensation;
(ii) Static feedback and disturbance suppression.

According to the first approach, firstly, the complete definiteness of the factor $b(x)$ before control is required. Secondly, we need to estimate the unknown disturbance $\eta_3(t)$ using any method to ensure asymptotically decreasing of the estimation error $\Delta\eta(t) = \eta_3(t) - \hat{\eta}_3(t)$ or its convergence to some small vicinity of zero rather quickly,

$$\lim_{t \to +\infty} \Delta\eta(t) = 0 \text{ or } |\Delta\eta(t)| \leq \delta, \ t \geq t_0, \ 0 < t_0 < t_1.$$

The obtained estimate $\hat{\eta}_3(t)$ is used for the synthesis of combined control

$$u = -(\phi(x) + \hat{\eta}_3(t))/b(x),$$

where $\phi(x)$ is a stabilizing component. If the function $f(x)$ is complete defined, then we can linearize the closed system by feedback

$$u = -\frac{1}{b(x)}\left(f(x) + \hat{\eta}_3(t) + \sum_{i=1}^{3} c_i x_i\right), \tag{5}$$

where $c_i > 0$ are the coefficients of stable polynomial $\lambda^3 + c_3\lambda^2 + c_2\lambda + c_1$.

The closed system (1), (4) and (5) has a form

$$\begin{aligned}
\dot{x}_1 &= x_2, \\
\dot{x}_2 &= x_3, \\
\dot{x}_3 &= -c_1 x_1 - c_2 x_2 - c_3 x_3 + \Delta\eta(t),
\end{aligned}$$

where, in the general case, the given control accuracy (3) is ensured. Particularly, when estimate error decreases, an asymptotic stabilization of all state vector and, hence, the output variable

$$\lim_{t \to +\infty} x_1(t) = 0, \tag{6}$$

is occurred. In both cases by the selection of $c_i > 0$ we can ensure the required characteristics of the transient process of the output variable.

The standard approach of obtaining an estimate of an external disturbance $\hat{\eta}_3(t)$ is to expand the state space using a dynamic model, simulating the action of external disturbance, and construction of extended observer [3–5]. In the case of parametric uncertainty of the control plant model, the identification and adaptation algorithms are additionally used to estimate the unknown parameters [6–8].

However, the implementation of these approaches will lead to large estimation errors if the parameters and disturbances vary significantly during the operation of the control plant, and the used model does not describe these changes adequately. On the other side, taking into account all possible variations of external disturbances will lead to an unacceptable expansion of the dynamic model, a significant complication of the controller, and an increase in computing time of the control signal. An alternative to introducing a model of external influences is the construction of an observer based on the model of the control plant, which allows to obtain the estimates of unknown inputs without their dynamical model under certain conditions [9–12].

The second approach of invariance ensuring does not require the external disturbance estimation and consists in it suppressing by discontinuous controls with the organization of sliding modes or continuous feedbacks with high-gain factors. As a rule, these are linear controls.

To organize the sliding mode in the system (1) and (4), it is necessary to specify the switching surface (plane)

$$s = c_1 x_1 + c_2 x_2 + x_3,$$

where $c_{1,2} > 0$ are the coefficients of the stable polynomial $\lambda^2 + c_2\lambda + c_1$, and introduce the discontinuous control law

$$u = -M\mathrm{sign}(b(x))\mathrm{sign}(s), \quad \mathrm{sign}(b(x)) = \mathrm{const},$$

where $M = \mathrm{const} > 0$ is the amplitude of discontinuous control, $\mathrm{sign}(s)$ is the sign function

$$\mathrm{sign}(s) = \left[\begin{array}{l} -1, \ s < 0, \\ +1, \ s > 0, \end{array}\right.$$

which value is undefined when $s = 0$, but it bounded on interval $[-1; 1]$.

Within the framework of this method, complete certainty of $f(x)$, $b(x)$ is not required, but the boundaries of their varying are assumed to be known

$$|f(x(t))| \leq F,$$
$$0 < b_{min} \leq |b(x)| \leq b_{max}, \ x \in X, t \geq 0 \tag{7}$$

A sufficient condition of sliding mode occurrence on the plane $s = 0$ has the form of inequality $s\dot{s} < 0$ [12–14], where

$$\dot{s} = c_2 s - c_2 c_1 x_1 + (c_1 - c_2^2)x_2 + f(x) - M|b(x)|\text{sign}(s) + \eta_3(t),$$
$$|c_2 s(t) - c_2 c_1 x_1(t) + (c_1 - c_2^2)x_2(t)| \leq C, \ t \geq 0.$$

They are satisfied when we select amplitude from the inequality

$$M > (C + F + H_3)/b_{min}. \tag{8}$$

When determining the upper estimate C of the admissible region of initial conditions $|x(0)| \leq X_0$, it is necessary to estimate the region of variation of closed system variables

$$\dot{x}_1 = x_2,$$
$$\dot{x}_2 = -c_1 x_1 - c_2 x_2 + s$$

with respect $|s(t)| \leq |s(0)|$, $t \geq 0$.

When (8) is valid, the requirement $s\dot{s} \leq |s|(C + F + H_3 - Mb_{min}) < 0$ is satisfied, and the sliding mode arises on the plane $s = 0$ in a finite time $t > t_0, 0 < t_0 < t_1$. In the sliding mode, the dynamic order of the closed system decreases

$$\dot{x}_1 = x_2,$$
$$\dot{x}_2 = -c_1 x_1 - c_2 x_2, \ s(t) = 0, \ t \geq t_0,$$

and the stability of the accepted polynomial implies asymptotic stabilization of the output variable (6).

Thus, according to this method, the synthesis problem is divided into two successively solved subproblems of lower dimension:

(i) The selection of switching plane parameters $c_{1,2} > 0$ at which the reduced second-order system is stable;

(ii) Selection of the amplitude of discontinuous control (8), at which stabilization of the virtual elementary system of the first order is ensured. This decomposition simplifies the synthesis of a controller for the multidimensional system with vector control. The main advantage of the method is that motion in the sliding mode does not depend on the operator of the control plan, external matched disturbances and is determined by the selection of the switching surface. The disadvantages include the need to calculate the upper estimate C in systems with a constant amplitude of discontinuous control, if the factor $b(x)$ before control contains undefined parameters. Such estimates are always conservative and lead to excessive consumption of control resources in a sliding mode.

$$\dot{s} = c_2 s - c_2 c_1 x_1 + (c_1 - c_2^2)x_2 + f(x) - M|b(x)|\text{sign}(s) + \eta_3(t)$$

Note that the use of discontinuous controls is natural in the presence of electrical inertia-less actuators that function exclusively in the key mode. In this case, the implementation of constant amplitude is a standard technical solution. Now let us consider systems in which there are no electrical actuators and only continuous control is permissible. Another method, based on disturbance suppression, is to use linear controls with high-gain factors [14–16]. For system (1) and (4) we introduce linear feedback instead of discontinuous control

$$u = -k\mathrm{sign}(b(x))s, \ \mathrm{sign}(b(x)) = \mathrm{const},$$

where $k = \mathrm{onst} > 0$ is a high-gain factor inversely proportional to the desired accuracy of suppression of matched disturbances and uncertainties: $|s(t)| \leq \Delta, \ t \geq t_0, 0 < t_0 < t_1$. With respect,

$$\dot{s} = c_2 s - c_2 c_1 x_1 + (c_1 - c_2^2)x_2 + f(x) - k|b(x)|s + \eta_3(t),$$
$$\left|(c_1 - c_2^2)x_2(t) - c_2 c_1 x_1(t)\right| \leq C_1, \ t \geq 0$$

the selection of the high-gain factor from inequality

$$k > \frac{C_1 + F + H_3}{\Delta b_{\min}} + \frac{c_2}{b_{\min}} \tag{9}$$

will ensure that sufficient condition $s\dot{s} \leq |s|(C_1 + F + H_3 - (kb_{\min} - c_2)|s|) < 0$ is satisfied outer the region $|s(t)| \leq \Delta$, in which the variable $s(t)$ converges in a finite time. When $t \geq t_0$, the closed system can be represented in the form

$$\dot{x}_1 = x_2,$$
$$\dot{x}_2 = -c_1 x_1 - c_2 x_2 + s, \ |s(t)| \leq \Delta, \tag{10}$$

which ensures the control goal (3), where Δ_1 depend on Δ and accepted $c_{1,2}$.

Note, if we exactly know $f(x), \ b(x)$, the combined control laws can be formed, which resources will be used only on the suppression of external disturbances. Selected based on the virtual system $\dot{s} = c_1 x_2 + c_2 x_3 + f(x) + b(x)u + \eta_3(t)$ combine control law

$$u = -(c_1 x_2 + c_2 x_3 + f(x) + M\mathrm{sign}(s) \, [\text{or } ks])/b(x)$$

leads to the closed system

$$\dot{x}_1 = x_2,$$
$$\dot{x}_2 = -c_1 x_1 - c_2 x_2 + s,$$
$$\dot{s} = -M\mathrm{sign}(s) \, [\text{or } -ks] + \eta_3(t)$$

and when $M > H_3$ [or $k > H_3/\Delta$] ensure the fulfillment (6) [or (3)].

The main restriction of the synthesis method of systems with high-gain factors is that it is unrealizable in practical applications. To satisfy the constraints on control actions, the continuous piecewise linear controls in the form of saturation functions are used [17,18], which are the hybrid of linear and discontinuous controls. These functions are bounded, and they tend to a sign function with the increasing of high-gain factors. Consequently, in the closed system saturation functions ensure similar properties as in the systems, operating in sliding mode, and with some accuracy.

For system (1) and (4) let us consider feedback in the form of saturation function

$$u = -M\mathrm{sign}(b(x))\mathrm{sat}(\bar{k}s), \ \mathrm{sign}(b(x)) = \mathrm{const},$$

where $M = \mathrm{const} > 0$ is the amplitude, $\bar{k} = \mathrm{const} > 0$ is the high-gain factor

$$M\mathrm{sat}(\bar{k}s) = \left[\begin{array}{l} M\mathrm{sign}(\bar{k}s), \ |s| > 1/\bar{k}, \\ M\bar{k}s, \ |s| \leq 1/\bar{k}. \end{array} \right.$$

Amplitude is selected so as in a system with discontinuous control (8), that ensures $|s(t)| \leq 1/\bar{k} \leq \Delta, \ t > t_0$, when $|s(0)| > 1/\bar{k}$. Selection of $\bar{k} \geq 1/\Delta$ ensures the desired stabilization accuracy, and as a result, the fulfillment of (10) and (3).

Significantly, that in contrast to a discontinuous control law with constant amplitude, which value does not vary in modulus during all control process, the values of saturation control automatically decrease in modulus in the steady-state mode (this fact is also valid for linear continues control). It occurs due to the stabilization of state variables, and when $t > t_1$, the control signal describes only external disturbance $\eta_3(t)$ with small not-decreasing components.

Thus, the combined control makes it possible to compensate for external matched disturbances, but for this, it is necessary to obtain their estimates and identify the unknown parameters of the system. In the case when the combined control cannot be realized, it remains to use the control aimed at suppressing external disturbances and model uncertainties. The selection of the type of control depends on the properties of the system and the existing design requirements on the smoothness and boundness.

3. Block Synthesis of Linear Local Feedbacks in System with Unmatched Disturbances

The most difficult are the control plants with unmatched disturbances (when conditions (4) are not satisfied), which cannot be compensated or suppressed by true control. In the tracking problem, these disturbances also include the derivatives of the reference signals. In addition, the problem of ensuring invariance with respect to disturbances is posed only for controlled outputs (tracking errors), since the remaining variables have to describe the corresponding external influences. According to the classical approach of the synthesis of a tracking system under the assumption of the smoothness of external influences, the state space is expanded due to the generators of reference and external influences, as well as the corresponding dynamic observers and identifiers of parameters [1]. In this case, the dynamic order of the closed system can increase by a factor of five or more times (in comparison with the dimension of the control plant model) if the external disturbances (and the corresponding autonomous models) vary significantly during the control process. If it is possible to formulate a model that accurately describes the dynamics of external disturbances, then asymptotic stabilization of tracking errors is theoretically achieved by expanding the state space.

Another approach is to represent the model of the control plant in the canonical or block input-output form, with the differentiation of external signals. In the process of obtaining this form, mixed variables are generated, which are the functions of state variables with additive external influences and their derivatives [19,20]. For system (1) under the assumption of differentiability of external disturbances $\eta_{1,2}(t)$, the canonical system in mixed variables has the form

$$
\begin{aligned}
\dot{\bar{x}}_1 &= \dot{\bar{x}}_2, \\
\dot{\bar{x}}_2 &= \bar{x}_3, \\
\dot{\bar{x}}_3 &= f(x) + b(x)u + \bar{\bar{\eta}}_3(t),
\end{aligned}
\tag{11}
$$

where

$$
\bar{x}_1 = x_1,\ \bar{x}_2 = x_2 + \eta_1(t),\ \bar{x}_3 = x_3 + \eta_2(t) + \dot{\eta}_1(t),\ \bar{\bar{\eta}}_3(t) = \eta_3(t) + \dot{\eta}_2(t) + \ddot{\eta}_1(t).
$$

In the last equation of the system (11), the initial variables x are left in the arguments of the functions $f(x)$, $b(x)$ for the convenience of synthesis. Structurally, system (11) repeats system (1), (4) with matched disturbances, since all uncertainties are concentrated in the control space and are subject to compensation or suppression using the control laws presented in Section 2.

The feature of this approach of ensuring invariance is that the problem of evaluating external influences separately is not considered, the autonomous models that generate them are not introduced into the constructions. Assuming that the output variable $\bar{x}_1 = x_1$, is measured, an observer is constructed based on the transformed system (11) with an indefinite input. Due to the suppression function of corrective action of the observer, it gives an estimate of mixed variables and uncertainties to form feedback and leads to an increase in the dynamic order of closed system by no more than twice. As a rule, in this case, ε-invariance of the output variable with respect to external unmatched disturbances is achieved.

However, the mentioned approaches are not applicable in the case when external unmatched disturbances and other model uncertainties are not smooth enough and cannot be differentiated. An example is shock loads and dry friction forces when controlling mechanical objects, taking into account the dynamics of actuators [21–25]. In the particular case, when a non-smooth disturbance is separated from the true control by one integrator, it can be suppressed using "vortex" control with continuous and discontinuous components. The result is achieved due to the organization of an oscillatory transient process in the system, in which part of the state variables automatically compensates for the influence of unknown terms [26].

In the general case, when external unmatched disturbances act on the control plant, the estimation, and compensation or suppression of which are not possible by true control, it remains to use the possibilities of disturbance suppression using local feedbacks. The methodological basis for the implementation of this approach is the decomposition methods and the block control principle [16,27]. According to this approach, using a non-degenerate change of variables, the equations of external dynamics are reduced to a block input-output form with an affine occurrence of fictitious and true controls. It consists of elementary blocks, in each of which the dimension of the controlled variables is equal to the rank of the matrix before the fictitious controls, which are the variables of the next block. For the general case of a controllable minimum-phase nonlinear system of the n-th order with affine external influences η, the block form is the following [20]:

$$\dot{x}_1 = f_1(x_1) + B_1(x_1)x_2 + Q_1(x_1)\eta;$$
$$\dot{x}_i = f_i(x_1, \ldots, x_i) + B_i(x_1, \ldots, x_i)x_{i+1} + Q_i(x_1, \ldots, x_i)\eta, \; i = \overline{2, r-1};$$
$$\dot{x}_r = f_r(x_1, \ldots, x_r) + B_r(x_1, \ldots, x_r)u + Q_r(x_1, \ldots, x_r)\eta,$$

where $B_i \in R^{p_i \times p_{i+1}}, i = \overline{1, r-1}, B_r \in R^{p_r \times p_r}, Q_i \in R^{p_i \times 1}, \dim x_i = \mathrm{rank} B_i = p_i, i = \overline{1, r}$, $p_1 + p_2 + \ldots + p_r = n$.

Sequentially (from top to bottom) formed stabilizing local feedbacks in each block are provided by the selection of true control. When a block form is obtained, external influences are not differentiated and do not participate in transformations, but with a block organization, they become matched with fictitious controls. Then, with an appropriate selection of fictitious controls, it is possible to stabilize the output variables with some accuracy.

Let us explain the essence of the block control principle using the example of system (1), which, as we see, is a special case of the block form and consists of three elementary blocks of the first order. In the first and second equations, the variables x_2 and x_3, respectively, are treated as fictitious controls, with which the bounded disturbances η_1 and η_2 are matched, respectively. The smoothness requirement is not imposed on external disturbances. The question arises about the selection of the form of stabilizing functions in fictitious and true controls, that would ensure the invariance of the output variable with respect to external disturbances by suppressing them.

As shown above, the classical methods of suppressing external and parametric bounded disturbances acting in the control space are: (1) continuous linear feedbacks with high-gain factors; (2) discontinuous controls bounded in modulus with the organizations of sliding modes. In addition, only controls of the first type (due to their smoothness) can be used to form local feedbacks. We emphasize once again that with the help of linear local feedbacks in a system with unmatched disturbances, it is possible to ensure stabilization of the controlled variable only with certain accuracy (3).

For system (1), let us consider the standard step-by-step procedure of block synthesis of linear local feedbacks with high-gain factors under the action of unmatched bounded disturbances [16]. It consists of the following stages: (1) introduction of local feedbacks (stabilizing fictitious controls) by non-degenerate change of variables of the original system (1) to residuals between real and adopted fictitious controls; (2) the selection of the control law; (3) setting the parameters of the feedback that meets the control goal. We represent the first stage in the form of the following procedure, which for system (1) consists of three steps and is similarly extended to systems of any order presented in the block form of controllability.

Procedure 1 : Non-degenerate transformation with the introduction of linear local feedbacks.

Step 1. In the first equation of system (1), we introduce linear local feedback $x_2^* = -k_1 x_1$, $k_1 = \text{const} > 0$ and the residual between the actual and the selected fictitious control

$$e_2 = x_2 - x_2^* = x_2 + k_1 x_1. \tag{12}$$

Taking into account the notation $e_1 = x_1$ and (12), the first equation of System (1) takes the form

$$\dot{e}_1 = -k_1 e_1 + e_2 + \eta_1. \tag{13}$$

Step 2. Let us write the differential equation for the residual (12) by (1) and (13)

$$\dot{e}_2 = x_3 + \eta_2 + k_1 \dot{e}_1 = -k_1^2 e_1 + k_1 e_2 + x_3 + \eta_2 + k_1 \eta_1,$$

where we form a combined fictitious control with a linear stabilizing component $x_3^* = k_1^2 e_1 - k_2 e_2$, $k_2 = \text{const}$, $k_2 > k_1$ and a residual between the actual and the selected fictitious control

$$e_3 = x_3 - x_3^* = x_3 - k_1^2 e_1 + k_2 e_2. \tag{14}$$

With respect (14), the second equation of the system (1) takes the form

$$\dot{e}_2 = -(k_2 - k_1)e_2 + e_3 + \eta_2 + k_1 \eta_1. \tag{15}$$

Step 3. Let us write the differential equation for the residual (14) by (1) and (15)

$$\dot{e}_3 = f(x) + b(x)u + \eta_3(t) - k_1^2 \dot{e}_1 + k_2 \dot{e}_2 = k_1^3 e_1 - (k_1^2 + k_2^2 - k_2 k_1)e_2 + k_2 e_3 + \\ + f(x) + b(x)u + \eta_3 + k_2 \eta_2 + (k_2 k_1 - k_1^2)\eta_1. \tag{16}$$

The procedure is over.

Thus, we have obtained system (13), (15) and (16) using a nondegenerate linear transformation of the system (1). The final transformation matrix is obtained as a result of the product of the transformation matrices performed at the first (12) and second (14) steps of the procedure (in the indicated order)

$$P = \begin{pmatrix} 1 & 0 & 0 \\ 0 & 1 & 0 \\ -k_1^2 & k_2 & 1 \end{pmatrix} \begin{pmatrix} 1 & 0 & 0 \\ k_1 & 1 & 0 \\ 0 & 0 & 1 \end{pmatrix} = \begin{pmatrix} 1 & 0 & 0 \\ k_1 & 1 & 0 \\ k_1 k_2 - k_1^2 & k_2 & 1 \end{pmatrix}, \ \det P \neq 0$$

For simplicity of presentation, we will consider the case of complete definiteness of functions $f(x)$, $b(x)$, which allows us to accept a combined true control in the form

$$u = -(k_1^3 e_1 - (k_1^2 + k_2^2 - k_2 k_1)e_2 + k_2 e_3 + f(x) + \varphi(e_3))/b(x). \tag{17}$$

The closed system (13) and (15)–(17) takes the form

$$\begin{aligned} \dot{e}_1 &= -k_1 e_1 + e_2 + \eta_1, \\ \dot{e}_2 &= -(k_2 - k_1)e_2 + e_3 + \eta_2 + k_1 \eta_1, \\ \dot{e}_3 &= -\phi(e_3) + \eta_3 + k_2 \eta_2 + (k_2 k_1 - k_1^2)\eta_1. \end{aligned} \tag{18}$$

The stabilizing component $\phi(e_3)$ of the control law (17) must ensure the suppression of the linear combination of disturbances $\eta_3 + k_2 \eta_2 + (k_2 k_1 - k_1^2)\eta_1$ and the stabilization of the variable e_3. For this, either discontinuous control or linear with high-gain factors or their piecewise-linear continuous hybrid in the form of a saturation function is applied, namely:

$$\begin{aligned} &(1)\ \phi(e_3) = M\mathrm{sign}(e_3);\\ &(2)\ \phi(e_3) = k_3 e_3;\\ &(3)\ \phi(e_3) = M\mathrm{sat}(\bar{k}_3 e_3), \end{aligned} \tag{19}$$

where $M, k_3, \bar{k}_3 = \mathrm{const} > 0$. Note that the control laws (19) are formed by the variable e_3 (14), which is a linear combination of the measured state variables of the original system (1).

As shown above, in the first case (19) when the amplitude is selected based on the inequality

$$M > H_3 + k_2 H_2 + (k_2 k_1 - k_1^2) H_1 \tag{20}$$

the sufficient condition $e_3 \dot{e}_3 < 0$ is satisfied. The sliding mode arises on the plane $e_3 = 0$ in a finite time $t > t_0 > 0$, and the dynamical order of the system is reduced. In the second case (19), a high-gain factor is selected taking into account the specified stabilization accuracy similarly to (9), namely:

$$k_3 > \frac{H_3 + k_2 H_2 + (k_2 k_1 - k_1^2) H_1}{\Delta_3}. \tag{21}$$

In the third case (19), the lower bounds of the parameter's selection of the piecewise linear control have the form (20) and $\bar{k}_3 > 1/\Delta_3$, $\Delta_3 > 0$. In both the second and third cases, the convergence of the variable to some neighborhood of zero is ensured

$$|e_3(t)| \leq \Delta_3,\ t > t_0. \tag{22}$$

Using (22), let us consider the procedure of selection the high-gain factors $k_1 > 0$, $k_2 > 0$ based on the second Lyapunov method. We introduce a candidate on the Lyapunov function as the sum of two terms $V = V_1 + V_2$, $V_i = \frac{1}{2}e_i^2$, $i = 1, 2$, and estimate their derivatives by (2), (13) and (15):

$$\begin{aligned} e_1 \dot{e}_1 &\leq |e_1|(|e_2| + H_1 - k_1|e_1|),\\ e_2 \dot{e}_2 &\leq |e_2|(|e_3| + H_2 + k_1 H_1 - (k_2 - k_1)|e_2|). \end{aligned} \tag{23}$$

It follows from inequalities (23) that sufficient stability conditions $\dot{V} < 0$ are met if the high-gain factors satisfy the inequalities

$$\begin{aligned} k_1 &> \tfrac{H_1 + \Delta_2}{\Delta_1},\ |e_3| \leq \Delta_3,\ |e_2| \leq \Delta_2,\ |e_1| > \Delta_1,\\ k_2 &> \tfrac{H_2 + k_1 H_1 + \Delta_3}{\Delta_2} + k_1,\ |e_3| \leq \Delta_3,\ |e_2| > \Delta_2. \end{aligned} \tag{24}$$

Thus, first, we set the desired accuracy of the stabilization Δ_i, $i = \overline{1, 3}$ of the virtual variables $e = (e_1, e_2, e_3)^{\mathrm{T}}$. Then, with a sequential (from top to bottom) selection of high-gain factors based on inequalities (24) and (21), the variables of the closed system (18) and (19) sequentially (from bottom to top) converge into the given neighborhoods of zero

$$|e_3(t)| \leq \Delta_3 \Rightarrow |e_2(t)| \leq \Delta_2 \Rightarrow |e_1(t)| \leq \Delta_1, \tag{25}$$

and the control goal (3) is achieved. When selecting the high-gain factors, one should take into account that as the k_1 increases, the accuracy improves (3) (in the limited case $\Delta_1 \to 0$ when $k_1 \to +\infty$) and the settling time decreases. However, due to the unboundedness of linear controls, this leads to the well-known problem of large overshoot [28]. On the other hand, in practical applications control resources are always bounded, so there is an upper bound of the selection of $k_1 \leq k_{1\max}$ and the corresponding minimum achievable tracking error $\Delta_{1,\min} \leq \Delta_1$.

The bounded control in the form of a saturation function is not smooth. On the one hand, it is not an obstacle when these functions are used in corrective actions of observers of the state of systems with disturbances [20,29]. However, on the other hand, it narrows the possibilities of its application as fictitious controls in practical problems.

Summing up, we can conclude that for the universal formation of invariant local feedbacks and the practical realizability of control Algorithms, it is advisable to use smooth analogs of the saturation function. These include transcendental S-shaped functions: arctangent, hyperbolic tangent, logistic function, etc. The odd hyperbolic tangent $\text{th}(x) = 1 - 2/(\exp(2x) + 1)$ appears to be a constructive tool for the analysis and synthesis of nonlinear control. This bounded function depends on the exponent, its derivatives are also bounded everywhere and are recursively expressed through the antiderivative.

In this paper, a modification of the hyperbolic tangent, which is more convenient for constructions, is used in the form of a sigmoid function $\sigma(x) = -\text{th}(-x/2)$. Its properties and the corresponding synthesis procedure developed by the authors are presented in the next section and constitute the main result of this work.

4. Block Synthesis of Nonlinear Local Feedbacks in Systems with Unmatched Disturbances

Let us consider a smooth and bounded sigmoid function

$$\sigma(kx) = \frac{2}{1 + \exp(-kx)} - 1, \ k = \text{const} > 0,$$

which is defined on the whole number axis and has the following properties: $\sigma(-kx) = -\sigma(kx)$, $\sigma(kx) \underset{x \to 0}{\sim} kx/2$, $\sigma(kx) \underset{k \to +\infty}{\sim} \text{sign}(x)$. In its argument, a factor k is specially introduced, which plays a role of a high-gain factor in a small neighborhood of zero in further constructions. The derivative of the sigmoid function has a recursive form:

$$\sigma'(kx) = k(1 - \sigma^2(kx))/2 > 0, \ x \in R, \sigma'(-kx) = \sigma'(kx).$$

To simplify the analysis of a nonlinear sigmoid function, let us establish its analogy with a piecewise linear saturation function. Consider some neighborhood of zero with radius $\Delta > 0$. The following estimates

$$\begin{aligned}
\sigma(k\Delta) &< |\sigma(kx)| < 1, \ 0 < \sigma'(kx) < \sigma'(k\Delta), \ |x| > \Delta; \\
\tfrac{\sigma(k\Delta)|x|}{\Delta} &\leq |\sigma(kx)| \leq \sigma(k\Delta), \ \sigma'(k\Delta) \leq \sigma'(kx) \leq \sigma'(0) = \tfrac{k}{2}, \ |x| \leq \Delta
\end{aligned} \tag{26}$$

are valid for the sigmoid function and its derivative in the indicated intervals. Inequalities (26) demonstrate that when $|x| > \Delta$ the sigmoid function is close to a constant, and when $|x| \leq \Delta$ it is close to a linear function. To formalize the abscissa of the specified division, we introduce the parameter $c = \text{const} > 0$: $|x| = \Delta = c/k$, which is advisable to select from the interval

$$k\Delta = c \in [1.3; 3], \tag{27}$$

where ± 1.3 are the abscissas of the inflection points of the first derivative $\sigma'''(\pm 1.3) = 0$, and $\sigma(\pm 1.3) \approx \pm 0.57$, $\sigma'(\pm 1.3) \approx 0.34k$; ± 3 are the abscissas of the vertices of the sigmoid function, in which its curvature reaches its maximum, while $\sigma(\pm 3) \approx \pm 0.9$, $\sigma'(\pm 0.9) \approx 0.095k$ [19].

For the convenience of calculations, we take

$$c = 2.2; \ \sigma(c) \approx 0.8; \ \frac{1}{\sigma(c)} \approx 1.25; \ \sigma'(c) \approx 0.18k. \tag{28}$$

Using (28), estimates (26) take the following form:

$$\begin{aligned}
0.8 &< |\sigma(kx)| < 1, \ 0 < \sigma'(kx) < 0.18k, \ |x| > c/k, \ c = 2.2; \\
\tfrac{0.8k|x|}{c} &= 0.36k|x| \leq |\sigma(kx)| \leq 0.8, \ 0.18k \leq \sigma'(kx) \leq \sigma'(0) = \tfrac{k}{2}, \ |x| \leq c/k.
\end{aligned} \tag{29}$$

Let us explain the idea of using sigmoid feedback and the selection of its parameters in the problem of ensuring invariance using the example of an elementary system with external disturbance

$$\dot{x} = \eta(t) + u, \tag{30}$$

where $x \in R$ is the state variable, $\eta(t)$ is the external disturbance, which is described by a deterministic, unknown, but bounded function of a time. The requirement of smoothness is not imposed on it, it is sufficient that it be piecewise continuous. The problem of stabilizing system (30) with a given accuracy using the sigmoid control

$$u = -m\sigma(kx) \tag{31}$$

with a constant amplitude $m = \text{onst} > 0$ and high-gain factor $k = \text{const} > 0$ is posed.

Lemma 1. *If in system (30), (31) the external disturbance is bounded by a known constant $|\eta(t)| \leq H = \text{const} > 0$, $t \geq 0$, then for any arbitrary small $\Delta > 0$, $T > 0$ and any initial values $x(0)$ from some bounded domain $X_0 \geq |x(0)|$ there are positive real numbers $\bar{k}$ u $\bar{m}$, such that for any $k \geq \bar{k}$, $m \geq \bar{m}$, the following inequality is valid*

$$|x(t)| \leq \Delta, \ t \geq T. \tag{32}$$

Proof. Let us introduce the parametric dependence (27), then, with respect to (28) and (29), the following lower estimates are valid for control (31) on the indicated intervals. To analyze the stability of closed system (30) and (31), we use the second Lyapunov method. Let us introduce a candidate on the Lyapunov function $V = x^2/2$ and estimate its derivative on the indicated intervals taking into account (33).

$$|u(x)| = |m\sigma(kx)| \geq \left[\begin{array}{l} 0.8m, \ |x| > \Delta, \\ 0.8mk|x|/2.2, \ |x| \leq \Delta \end{array} \right. \tag{33}$$

$$\dot{V} = x(\eta(t) - m\sigma(kx)) \leq \left[\begin{array}{l} |x|(H - 0.8m), \ |x| > \Delta, \\ |x|(H - 0.8mk|x|/2.2), \ |x| \leq \Delta. \end{array} \right. \tag{34}$$

It follows from (34) that the derivative of the Lyapunov function is negative if the feedback parameters satisfy the following conditions:

$$\begin{aligned} 0.8m > H &\Leftrightarrow m > 1.25H, \\ k > \frac{H}{0.8m} \cdot \frac{2.2}{\Delta}. \end{aligned} \tag{35}$$

The fulfillment of the first inequality (35) means that the state variable will converge into the region $|x| \leq \Delta$ or will not leave it if it was there initially. In addition, the fulfillment of the second inequality guarantees stabilization with a given accuracy (32), namely:

$$|x| \leq \frac{H}{0.8m}\Delta < \Delta.$$

Using $0 < H/(0.8m) < 1$, it is possible to simplify the lower bound for selection a high-gain factor in comparison with the second inequality (35) and take

$$k \geq \bar{k} = 2.2/\Delta. \tag{36}$$

In the general case $|x(0)| > \Delta$ to guarantee the achievement of the state variable of a given region in a given time $T > 0$, let us increase the lower bound of selection of amplitude. With respect to the estimate of the solution of system (30) and (31) on the interval $t \in [0; T]$

$$|x(t)| \leq |x(0)| + (H - 0.8m)T \leq \Delta. \tag{37}$$

we obtain

$$m \geq \bar{m} = 1.25\left(\frac{X_0 - \Delta}{T} + H\right), \ X_0 > \Delta. \tag{38}$$

Thus, we defined such $\bar{k}$ (36) and $\bar{m}$ (38) that for any $k \geq \bar{k}$, $m \geq \bar{m}$, the stabilization of the state variable with the given accuracy and for the given time (32) is ensured in the closed system (30) and (31). Lemma 1 is proved. □

As you can see, the sigmoid control, as well as the piecewise-linear saturation function, is bounded everywhere and contains two adjustable parameters. The selection of the amplitude provides the given time of convergence of the controlled variable to a certain neighborhood of zero, and the selection of a high-gain factor provides the radius of this area, i.e., the given stabilization accuracy. In a first-order system, the transient process is monotonic.

We use the results obtained in Lemma 1 to stabilize the output variable of system (1) taking into account (2) and (7) under the following assumptions: the requirements of smoothness of external disturbances are not imposed, the functions $f(x)$, $b(x)$ are not required to be completely defined, the sign of $b(x)$ is constant and known. In further constructions, we will take into account the given settling time (3), which is guaranteed for all initial values of the variables from the bounded admissible region

$$|x_1(0)| \leq X_1, \ |x_2(0)| \leq X_2, \ |x_3(0)| \leq X_3. \tag{39}$$

As a methodological basis of the synthesis procedure, we use the block control principle, demonstrated in Section 3 for the synthesis of linear feedbacks. Let us emphasize that the idea of the approach proposed below is similar to the backstepping [30]. The main differences of our approach are that it does not require smoothness of functions $f(x)$, $b(x)$, and $\eta_i(t)$, $i = \overline{1,3}$; we use static feedback, do not expand the state space, and do not aim to obtain estimates of the existing uncertainties. To avoid large overshoot, which is typical for linear feedbacks with high-gain factors, we will select stabilizing fictitious controls in the form of smooth and bounded sigmoid functions

$$x_i^* = -m_{i-1}\sigma(k_{i-1}e_{i-1}), \ k_{i-1} = \text{const} > 0, \ m_{i-1} = \text{const} > 0, \ i = 2, \ 3,$$

where e_2 and e_3 are the residuals between the variables x_2 and x_3, respectively, and the selected fictitious controls

$$e_i = x_i - x_i^* = x_i + m_{i-1}\sigma(k_{i-1}e_{i-1}), \ i = 2, \ 3, e_1 = x_1. \tag{40}$$

For uniformity, true control is also accepted as a sigmoid function

$$u = -\text{sign}(b)m_3\sigma(k_3e_3), \ k_3 = \text{const} > 0, \ m_3 = \text{const} > 0 \tag{41}$$

Note that to simplify the computational implementation, instead of (41), one can also use a continuous, bounded, but non-smooth saturation function or discontinuous control in systems with electric actuators as a true control.

Also note that, unlike Procedure 1 with linear transformations in changes of variables (40) and control law (41), we did not compensate the nonlinear components that do not depend on external disturbances in order not to complicate the control function.

Let us rewrite closed system (1), (41) with respect to residuals (40)

$$\begin{aligned}
\dot{e}_1 &= -m_1\sigma(k_1e_1) + e_2 + \eta_1, \\
\dot{e}_2 &= -m_2\sigma(k_2e_2) + e_3 + \eta_2 + \Lambda_1, \\
\dot{e}_3 &= -|b(x)|m_3\sigma(k_3e_3) + f(x) + \eta_3 + \Lambda_2,
\end{aligned} \tag{42}$$

where terms

$$\Lambda_i = m_i\frac{k_i(1 - \sigma^2(k_ie_i))}{2}\dot{e}_i, \ i = 1, \ 2, \tag{43}$$

are the derivatives of the corresponding fictitious controls, which arise in the transition to the new coordinate basis (40).

There is no need to change the arguments of functions $b(x)$ and $f(x)$ in the last equation of transformed system (42) since constraints (7) are specified in terms of the variables of the original system (1), and the specific of these functions do not matter for the formation of control law (41).

We will perform feedback synthesis according to the block approach in terms of virtual system (42). The idea is that sigmoid fictitious and true controls introduced into each subsystem using non-degenerate change of variables (40) and feedback (41) serve to suppress external uncontrolled disturbances. This will ensure the stabilization of the residuals e_i, $i = \overline{1,3}$ with any given accuracy. By virtue of the inverse change of variables (40), namely, this means that in the closed system (1) with nonlinear control (41), which is realized in the form

$$u = -\mathrm{sign}(b)m_3\sigma(k_3(x_3 + m_2\sigma(k_2(x_2 + m_1\sigma(k_1x_1))))), \tag{44}$$

in the steady-state, the variables $x_2(t)$ and $x_3(t)$ describe external disturbances $\eta_1(t)$ and $\eta_2(t)$, accordingly. In addition, the stabilization accuracy of the output variables of both systems will be the same. Thus, the fulfillment of the objective condition in closed system (42) and (41)

$$|e_1(t)| \leq \Delta_1, \, t \geq t_1, \tag{45}$$

is equivalent to solving the problem (3).

As shown in Section 3, the block approach in multidimensional systems consists in sequentially solving elementary synthesis problems in subsystems (blocks) similar to (30). However, only the last subsystem is directly regulated by the true control, and in the rest, the variables of the next block act as fictitious controls. As a consequence, in the general case of nonzero initial conditions only in the last block, a monotonic transient process is guaranteed.

Sufficient conditions of the existence of feedback parameters m_i, k_i, $i = 1, 2, 3$ that ensure the fulfillment of objective condition (45) in the system (42) are formulated in Lemma 2. In the process of constructive proof, a step-by-step procedure of adjusting the amplitudes of sigmoid controls was formalized, in which the decomposition principle is implemented [31,32].

Lemma 2. *Let us consider closed system (1), (44), presented in the form (42) using non-degenerate changes of variables. If conditions (2) and (7) are satisfied for this system, then for any initial values of variables from the bounded domain (39) and for any, arbitrarily small $\Delta_1 > 0$, $t_1 > 0$, there are real numbers $\overline{k}_i > 0$, $i = \overline{1,3}$, $0 < \overline{m}_i < \overline{\overline{m}}_i$, $i = 1, 2$, $\overline{m}_3 > 0$, such that for any $k_i \geq \overline{k}_i$, $m_i : \overline{m}_i < m_i \leq \overline{\overline{m}}_i$, inequality (45) is satisfied.*

Constructive Proof. According to the ideology of the block approach, in the closed system (42) it is necessary to provide the following sequence of convergence of residuals:

$$|e_3| \leq \Delta_3 \, (t \geq t_3 > 0) \Rightarrow |e_2| \leq \Delta_2 \, (t \geq t_2 > t_3) \Rightarrow |e_1| \leq \Delta_1 \, (t \geq t_1 > t_2), \tag{46}$$

where $\Delta_1 > 0$, $t_1 > 0$ are the given (45), $\Delta_{2,3} > 0$ are assigned arbitrarily. The dependences $t_{2,3}$ on the initial conditions and accepted $\Delta_{2,3} > 0$ are established in the course of the proof.

Lemma 1 demonstrates the existence of $\overline{k}_i > 0$, $i = \overline{1,3}$ such as for any $k_i \geq \overline{k}_i$, $i = \overline{1,3}$ the desired radii $\Delta_{1,2,3} > 0$ (46) of neighborhoods of zero are guaranteed, at which the residuals converge in the indicated times (46). With respect (28) and similarly to (36), we fix the values of high-gain factors based on the inequalities

$$k_i^* \geq \overline{k}_i = 2.2/\Delta_i, \, i = \overline{1,3}. \tag{47}$$

In (47) and below, using the symbol $*$ in the superscript, we will denote specific accepted numerical values of the parameters.

Increasing the accepted values k_i^* leads to a decrease in the stabilization errors of residuals. The convergence of the residuals into the established areas in the specified time (46) is ensured by selection m_i, $i = \overline{1,3}$.

The stabilization of system (42) is carried out "from the bottom up" (46). Sufficient conditions of the selection of amplitudes, similar to the first inequality in (35), are valid when the indicated conditions are met:

$$
\begin{aligned}
&0.8m_1 > H_1 + \Delta_2, \ |e_2| \le \Delta_2 \\
&0.8m_2 > H_2 + |\Lambda_1| + \Delta_3, \ |e_3| \le \Delta_3, \\
&0.8b_{\min}m_3 > F + H_3 + |\Lambda_2|.
\end{aligned}
\tag{48}
$$

The fulfillment of (47) and (48) ensures the sequential stabilization of the residuals with a given accuracy without taking into account the convergence time, which depends on the initial conditions. In a particular case, the fulfillment of (47) and (48) will ensure $|e_i(t)| \le \Delta_i$, $i = \overline{1,3}$ at $t \ge 0$, i.e., the goal of control (45) is achieved.

In the tracking system, the following variants of the initial conditions are also subject of interest: if $|e_3(0)| \le \Delta_3, |e_2(0)| > \Delta_2$, then the transient process of $e_2(t)$ will be monotonical; if $|e_i(0)| \le \Delta_i$, $i = 2, 3$, $|e_1(0)| > \Delta_1$, then the transient process of $e_1(t)$ will be without overshoot.

In the rest of the particulars, as well as in the general case $|e_i(t)| > \Delta_i$, $i = \overline{1,3}$, within the framework of these constructions, a monotonic transient process is guaranteed only for the variable $e_3(t)$.

Until the variables of the lower blocks of system (42) reach the specified neighborhoods (46), the variables of the upper blocks grow in absolute value and reach their maximum value no later than at the following times:

$$
|e_3(t)| \le |e_3(0)| = e_{3,\max}, |e_2(t)| \le |e_2(t_3)| = e_{2,\max}, |e_1(t)| \le |e_1(t_2)| = e_{1,\max}, \ t \ge 0 \tag{49}
$$

By (39) and (40), we estimate the ranges of initial values of the variables of system (42)

$$
|e_1(0)| \le X_1, \ |e_i(0)| \le X_i + m_{i-1}, \ i = 2, 3 \tag{50}
$$

Using (42), (48) and (50) and taking into account that the proper motions in closed system (42) are stable, we estimate the maximum values (49)

$$
\begin{aligned}
&e_{1,\max} \le X_1 + (e_{2,\max} - \Delta_2)t_2, \\
&e_{2,\max} \le X_2 + m_1 + (e_{3,\max} - \Delta_3)t_3, \\
&e_{3,\max} \le X_3 + m_2.
\end{aligned}
\tag{51}
$$

To ensure the given convergence time, it is necessary to increase the lower bounds of the selection of amplitudes (48). First, we give estimates of the derivatives of fictitious controls (43). They differ at different intervals and depend on the corresponding estimates of the derivatives of the sigmoid functions and the derivatives of the corresponding residuals (42). Using (48), for the derivatives of the residuals, the following estimates are valid:

$$
\begin{aligned}
&t \in [0; t_2) : |\dot{e}_1(t)| \le \underbrace{H_1 + \Delta_2}_{<0.8m_1} + e_{2,\max} - \Delta_2 + m_1 < 2m_1 + e_{2,\max} - \Delta_2, \\
&t \ge t_2 : |\dot{e}_1(t)| \le H_1 + \Delta_2 + m_1 < 2m_1; \\
&t \in [0; t_3) : |\dot{e}_2(t)| = \underbrace{H_2 + |\Lambda_1| + \Delta_3}_{<0.8m_i} + e_{3,\max} - \Delta_3 + m_2 < 2m_2 + e_{3,\max} - \Delta_3, \\
&t \ge t_3 : |\dot{e}_2(t)| = H_2 + |\Lambda_1| + \Delta_3 + m_2 < 2m_2.
\end{aligned}
\tag{52}
$$

For the derivative of the sigmoid function, by (29) on the indicated intervals, we have

$$
\begin{aligned}
&|e_i(t)| > c/k_i, \ t \in [0; t_i) : \ 0 < 0.5k_i(1 - \sigma^2(k_i e_i)) < 0.18k_i, \\
&|e_i(t)| \le c/k_i, \ t \ge t_i \ 0.18k_i \le 0.5k_i(1 - \sigma^2(k_i e_i)) \le 0.5k_i, \ i = 1, 2
\end{aligned}
\tag{53}
$$

Combining (52) and (53), we obtain estimates of the derivatives of fictitious controls (43) on the indicated intervals

$$|\Lambda_i| = m_i \frac{k_i(1 - \sigma^2(k_i e_i))}{2}|\dot{e}_i| \leq \left[\begin{array}{l} 0.36k_i m_i^2 + 0.18k_i m_i(e_{i+1,\max} - \Delta_{i+1}), \ t \in [0; \ t_{i+1}); \\ 0.36k_i m_i^2, \ t \in [\,t_{i+1}; \ t_i); \\ k_i m_i^2, \ t \geq t_i; \ i = 1, 2 \end{array} \right.$$

To uniformly accept as an estimate

$$|\Lambda_i| \leq k_i m_i^2, \ t \geq 0; \ i = 1, 2, \tag{54}$$

we need to provide $0.18k_i m_i(e_{i+1,\max} - \Delta_{i+1}) \leq 0.64k_i m_i^2 \Rightarrow e_{i+1,\max} - \Delta_{i+1} \leq 3.5m_i$, $i = 1, 2$. For this we introduce constraints on the peak values of the residuals, slightly lowering the limiting estimates for the convenience of calculations:

$$e_{i,\max} \leq 3m_{i-1} + \Delta_i, \ i = 1, 2 \tag{55}$$

For consistency, limitation on the overshoot of the output variable also can be introduced:

$$|e_1(0)| \leq X_1 < e_{1,\max} \leq E_1. \tag{56}$$

In a particular case $|e_1(0)| < \Delta_1$, the implementation of $e_{1,\max} \leq E_1 = \Delta_1$ provides $|e_1(t)| \leq \Delta_1, \ t \geq 0$.

With respect (55) and (56), inequalities (51) take the form

$$\begin{aligned} e_{1,\max} &\leq X_1 + 3m_1 t_2 \leq E_1, \\ e_{2,\max} &\leq X_2 + m_1 + 3m_2 t_3 \leq 3m_1 + \Delta_2, \\ e_{3,\max} &\leq X_3 + m_2 \leq 3m_2 + \Delta_3, \end{aligned} \tag{57}$$

whence additional conditions follow, which must be taken into account when selecting $t_{2,3}$ ($0 < t_3 < t_2 < t_1$) and amplitudes of fictitious controls:

$$0 < m_1 \leq \frac{E_1 - X_1}{3t_2}, \ 0 < m_2 \leq \frac{2m_1 + \Delta_2 - X_2}{3t_3}; \tag{58}$$

$$m_1 > \frac{X_2 - \Delta_2}{2}, \ m_2 > \frac{X_3 - \Delta_3}{2}. \tag{59}$$

Note that, according to constructions (48) $m_{i-1} > \Delta_i, \ i = 2,3$, while $\Delta_i > 0, \ i = 2,3$ can be accepted less or more than values X_i. The requirement of smallness is not imposed on them. To simplify the calculations, one can initially fix $\Delta_i = X_i, \ i = 2, 3$, which removes the need to check the fulfillment of conditions (59).

In the general case $\Delta_i < X_i, i = 2, 3$, the inequalities of the lower bound of the selection of amplitudes m_i will contain two basic components. Due to the first component m_{i1}, as well as m_3, similarly to (38), the convergence of residuals $e_1(t)$, $e_2(t)$, $e_3(t)$ on intervals $[t_2; t_1]$, $[t_3; t_2]$, $[0; t_3]$, respectively, from the peak values (51), (57) into the given areas in a given time (46) is ensured. The second component m_{i2} provides the implementation of constraints (59). In addition, in contrast to the amplitude of the true control m_3, which is selected only based on the lower estimate, there are upper constraints on the selection of the amplitudes of the fictitious controls (58).

Let us formalize a step-by-step procedure of sequential, "top-down" selection of the amplitudes of sigmoid controls and admissible times $t_{2,3}$ for the given Δ_1, t_1, assigned E_1 (56), $\Delta_{2,3} > 0$, and adopted on their basis $k_i^*, i = \overline{1,3}$ (47). During the procedure, variation of free parameters is allowed.

Procedure 2. Selection of sigmoid feedback amplitudes

Step 1. Using (57), the first inequality (48) takes the form

$$0.8m_1 \geq \frac{X_1 + 3m_1 t_2 - \Delta_1}{t_1 - t_2} + H_1 + \Delta_2 \Rightarrow m_{11} \geq \frac{X_1 - \Delta_1 + (H_1 + \Delta_2)(t_1 - t_2)}{0.8t_1 - 3.8t_2},$$

whence the constraint on the selection $0 < t_2 < t_1$ follows:

$$0.8t_1 - 3.8t_2 > 0 \Rightarrow t_2 < 0.2t_1. \tag{60}$$

Based on (60), we select $t_2^* > 0$ and substitute it into the double inequality

$$\max\{m_{11}; m_{12}\} < \overline{m}_1 < \overline{\overline{m}}_1, \tag{61}$$

$$m_{11} = \frac{X_1 - \Delta_1 + (H_1 + \Delta_2)(t_1 - t_2^*)}{0.8t_1 - 3.8t_2^*}, \quad m_{12} = \frac{X_2 - \Delta_2}{2}, \quad \overline{\overline{m}}_1 = \frac{E_1 - X_1}{3t_2^*}. \tag{62}$$

If inequality (61) is satisfied, then we fix t_2^*, $m_1^* \in (\overline{m}_1; \overline{\overline{m}}_1]$ and go to the second step. If (61) is not satisfied, arbitrary parameters should be varied. This can be performed in two ways.

First way. If it is required to ensure accepted E_1 (56), then we vary Δ_2 and/or t_2. If with the initially accepted $0 < t_2^* < 0.2t_1$ inequality $m_{12} > m_{11}$ (62) is valid, then by increasing Δ_2 (up to $\Delta_2 = X_2$) it is necessary to ensure $m_{11} > m_{12}$. If with the new Δ_2^* the inequality (61) is not valid and initially $m_{11} > m_{12}$, then we decrease t_2^*. The critical value $\bar{t}_2 > 0 : m_{11}(\bar{t}_2) = \overline{\overline{m}}_1(\bar{t}_2)$ exists and equals

$$\bar{t}_2 = \frac{\sqrt{p_2^2 - 4p_1 p_3} - p_2}{2p_1},$$

$$p_1 = -3(H_1 + \Delta_2),$$
$$p_2 = 0.8(E_1 - X_1) + 3(E_1 - \Delta_1 + (H_1 + \Delta_2)t_1),$$
$$p_3 = -0.8(E_1 - X_1)t_1.$$

From the limit relation

$$\lim_{t_2 \to +0} m_{11}(t_2) = \frac{X_1 - \Delta_1 + (H_1 + \Delta_2)t_1}{0.8t_1} = \text{const} < \lim_{t_2 \to +0} \frac{E_1 - X_1}{3t_2} = +\infty, \tag{63}$$

it follows that $\overline{\overline{m}}_1$ can be made arbitrarily large and for any $t_2^* > 0 : 0 < t_2^* < \bar{t}_2$ inequality (61) will be satisfied.

Thus, by reducing t_2, it is possible to provide any sufficiently small overshoot in the output variable (56). However, this can lead to a significant increase in the lower bounds of the selection of amplitudes in the following blocks.

Second way. If we abandon the accepted E_1 (56) and increase its value

$$E_1 > \overline{E} = X_1 + 3m_1^* t_2^*, \tag{64}$$

where $\overline{E}$ is the minimum possible overshoot of the output variable with the initial accepted value $0 < t_2^* < 0.2t_1$, then one can arbitrarily increase the upper bound $\overline{\overline{m}}_1$ of the selection of the amplitude (61).

Step 2. The second inequality (46) is ensured by selection m_2. With respect (54), (57), the second inequality (48) takes the form

$$0.8m_2 \geq \frac{X_2 + m_1^* + 3m_2 t_3 - \Delta_2^*}{t_2^* - t_3} + H_2 + k_1^*(m_1^*)^2 + \Delta_3 \Rightarrow$$
$$m_{21} \geq \frac{X_2 + m_1^* - \Delta_2^* + (H_2 + k_1^*(m_1^*)^2 + \Delta_3)(t_2^* - t_3)}{0.8t_2^* - 3.8t_3}, \tag{65}$$

whence follows a constraint on the selection $0 < t_3 < t_2^*$, similar to (60)

$$0.8t_2^* - 3.8t_3 > 0 \Rightarrow t_3 < 0.2t_2^*. \tag{66}$$

Based on (66), we select $t_3^* > 0$ and substitute it into the double inequality

$$\max\{m_{21}; m_{22}\} < \overline{m}_2 < \overline{\overline{m}}_2, \tag{67}$$

where $m_{21}(t_3^*)$ (65),

$$m_{22} = \frac{X_3 - \Delta_3}{2}, \quad \overline{\overline{m}}_2 = \frac{2m_1^* + \Delta_2^* - X_2}{3t_3^*}. \tag{68}$$

If (67) is satisfied, then we fix t_3^*, $m_2^* \in (\overline{m}_2; \overline{\overline{m}}_2]$ and go to the third step. If (67) is not fulfilled, arbitrary parameters Δ_3 and/or t_3 should be varied. If initially $m_{22} > m_{21}$, then by increasing Δ_3 (up to $\Delta_3 = X_3$) we need to ensure $m_{21} > m_{22}$. If with new Δ_3^* the inequality (67) is not satisfied or initially $m_{21} > m_{22}$, then we decrease t_3^*. The critical value $\bar{t}_3 > 0 : m_{21}(\bar{t}_3) = \overline{\overline{m}}_2(\bar{t}_3)$ exists and equals

$$\bar{t}_3 = \frac{\sqrt{q_2^2 - 4q_1q_3} - q_2}{2q_1},$$

$$\begin{aligned}
q_1 &= -3(H_2 + k_1^*(m_1^*)^2 + \Delta_3), \\
q_2 &= 3(3m_1^* + (H_2 + k_1^*(m_1^*)^2 + \Delta_3)t_2^*) + 0.8(2m_1^* + \Delta_2 - X_2), \\
q_3 &= -0.8(2m_1^* + \Delta_2 - X_2)t_2^*.
\end{aligned} \tag{69}$$

From a limit relation similar to (63), namely

$$\lim_{t_3 \to +0} m_{21}(t_3) = \frac{X_2 + m_1^* - \Delta_2^* + (H_2 + k_1^*(m_1^*)^2 + \Delta_3)t_2^*}{0.8t_2^*} = \text{const} < \lim_{t_3 \to +0} \frac{2m_1^* + \Delta_2^* - X_2}{3t_3} = +\infty$$

it follows that for any $t_3^* > 0 : 0 < t_3^* < \bar{t}_3$ inequality (48) is valid.

Note that at the second step (as opposed to the first), the fulfillment of (67) can be ensured only in the indicated way. Increasing the upper limit $\overline{\overline{m}}_2$ by increasing m_1^* will also lead to an increase in the lower limit $\overline{m}_2(m_{21})$, and at a faster rate.

Allowable values t_3^*, m_2^*, Δ_3^* and $k_3^*(\Delta_3^*)$ are fixed, and then we go to the third step.

Step 3. Using (54), (57), the third inequality (48) takes a form similar to (38)

$$m_3 \geq \overline{m}_3 = \frac{1.25}{b_{\min}}\left(\frac{X_3 + m_2^* - \Delta_3^*}{t_3^*} + F + H_3 + k_3^*(m_2^*)^2\right). \tag{70}$$

Based on (70), let us fix m_3^*. The amplitude adjustment procedure is complete.

Thus, there are exist such $\bar{k}_i > 0$, $i = \overline{1, 3}$(47), $0 < \overline{m}_i < \overline{\overline{m}}_i$, $i = 1, 2$(61), (62) and (67) and $\overline{m}_3 > 0$ (70), that for all $k_i \geq \bar{k}_i$, $m_i : \overline{m}_i < m_i \leq \overline{\overline{m}}_i$, $\forall m_3 \geq \overline{m}_3$ the variables in closed system (42) sequentially converge into the indicated regions within the specified time (46), which ensures the fulfillment of the target condition. Lemma 2 is proved. $\square$

The theoretical significance of the obtained results is as follows. It is shown that it is fundamentally possible to ensure any arbitrary small stabilization error of the output variable with any sufficiently small overshoot (56) in any arbitrary small time for any admissible initial conditions (39). However, it must be understood that a decrease in target characteristics (45) will lead to an increase in the parameters of the controller and the values of fictitious and true controls in the transient process, which is undesirable in real automatic control systems.

We can easily extend the procedure presented in the proof of Lemma 2 to n-dimensional canonical systems with one input. Accordingly, without restrictions, this approach is applicable to MIMO systems with m outputs, in which: (i) the number of inputs is not less than outputs; (ii) the system is representable in the form of m input-output subsystems with one input, in which the matrix before the controls has full rank; (iii) there is no internal dynamics subsystem or its solutions are bounded (i.e., the system is a minimum phase). The more general case of MIMO systems requires additional research.

5. Discussion

The main result of this work is the use of S-shaped smooth sigmoid functions in the feedback loop as fictitious and true controls when unmatched non-smooth disturbances act on the system. The parameters of the nonlinear stabilizing controller are iteratively selected at the stage of synthesis based on inequalities obtained from the worst possible values of the parameters of the control plant and the boundaries of changes in external influences. This approach does not require reconfiguring the controller when internal and external factors change within acceptable limits. Thus, it simplifies the structure of the controller and decreases the formation time of the control signal, since additional identification of unknown parameters, a compilation of models, and the use of an external disturbance observer are not required. In the process of regulation, the sigmoid fictitious and true controls converge to the unknown bounded external signals matched with them in a finite time and repeat their shape with a predetermined accuracy. Thus, a mechanism of suppressing disturbances, including those that are not into the space of true control, is automatically implemented, which ensures the invariance of the output (controlled) variable.

The boundness of sigmoid feedbacks is their undoubted advantage over the traditionally used linear feedbacks with high-gain factors, leading to a large overshoot. In the paper [33], the results of comparative analysis and modeling of systems with linear and nonlinear local feedbacks operating under uncertainty conditions are shown. In [34,35], the results of modeling closed systems with sigmoid local feedbacks as applied to various electromechanical control plants are presented. The disadvantages of the method include a more complex computational implementation compared to a linear control. However, given the constantly increasing power of modern control microprocessors, this is not a serious obstacle to the use of nonlinear functions in automatic control systems of modern and promising technical objects.

Due to the organization of local feedbacks, the state variables of the closed initial system will "track" bounded sigmoid signals, while the maximum deviations of fictitious controls from "reference influences" are bounded (51). This fact is a prerequisite for the creation of analytical methods of the synthesis of invariant systems, taking into account design constraints on the state and control variables. The solution of this problem is the subject of future research by the authors.

Author Contributions: Conceptualization, methodology, S.K. and V.U.; validation, investigation, formal analysis, A.A. and S.K.; writing—original draft preparation, S.K.; writing—review and editing, A.A. and V.U. All authors have read and agreed to the published version of the manuscript.

Funding: This research received no external funding.

Conflicts of Interest: The authors declare no conflict of interest.

References

1. Wonham, W.M. *Linear Multivariable Control: A Geometric Approach*; Springer: Berlin/Heidelberg, Germany, 1979.
2. Drazenovic, B. The Invariance Conditions in Variable Structure Systems. *Autom. Remote Control* **1969**, *5*, 287–295.
3. Nikiforov, V.O. Adaptive nonlinear tracking with complete compensation of unknown disturbances. *Eur. J. Control* **1998**, *4*, 132–139. [CrossRef]
4. Bobtsov, A.A. Output control algorithm with the compensation of biased harmonic disturbances. *Autom. Remote Control* **2008**, *69*, 1289–1296. [CrossRef]
5. Andrievsky, B.; Furtat, I. Disturbance Observers: Methods and Applications. I. Methods. *Autom. Remote Control* **2020**, *81*, 1563–1610. [CrossRef]
6. Alexandrov, A.G.; Chestnov, V.N.; Alexandrov, V.A. Identification Based Control for Wind Turbine. *IFAC-PapersOnLine* **2017**, *50*, 2272–2277. [CrossRef]
7. Krstic, M.; Kanellakopoulos, I.; Kokotovic, P. *Nonlinear and Adaptive Control Design*; Wiley: Hoboken, NJ, USA, 1995.
8. Yin, L.; Deng, W.; Yang, X.; Yao, J. Finite-Time Output Feedback Control for Electro-Hydraulic Servo Systems with Parameter Adaptation. *Machines* **2021**, *9*, 214. [CrossRef]

9. Xie, Y.; Zhang, X.; Jiang, L.; Meng, J.; Li, G.; Wang, S. Sliding-mode Disturbance Observer-based Control for Fractional-Order System with Unknown Disturbances. *Unmanned Syst.* **2020**, *8*, 193–202. [CrossRef]

10. Levant, A. Higher-order sliding modes, differentiation and output-feedback control. *Int. J. Control* **2003**, *76*, 924–941. [CrossRef]

11. Hall, C.; Shtessel, Y. Sliding Mode Disturbance Observer-Based Control for a Reusable Launch Vehicle. *J. Guid. Control Dyn.* **2006**, *29*, 1315–1328. [CrossRef]

12. Edwards, C.; Spurgeon, S. *Sliding Mode Control: Theory and Applications*; Taylor & Francis Ltd.: Oxfordshire, UK, 1998; p. 237.

13. Utkin, V.I.; Guldner, J.; Shi, J. *Sliding Mode Control in Electromechanical Systems*; CRC Press: New York, NY, USA, 2009.

14. Khalil, H. *Nonlinear Systems*; Prentice Hall: Upper Saddle River, NY, USA, 2002; p. 750.

15. Tsypkin, Y.; Polyak, B. High-Gain Robust Control. *Eur. J. Control* **1999**, *5*, 3–9. [CrossRef]

16. Utkin, V.A. Invariance and Independence in Systems with Separable Motion. *Autom. Remote Control* **2001**, *62*, 1825–1843. [CrossRef]

17. Slotine, J.E. Sliding controller design for non-linear systems. *Int. J. Control* **1984**, *40*, 421–434. [CrossRef]

18. Campos, E.; Monroy, J.; Abundis, H.; Chemori, A.; Creuze, V.; Torres, J. A nonlinear controller based on saturation functions with variable parameters to stabilize an AUV. *Int. J. Nav* **2019**, *11*, 211–224. [CrossRef]

19. Krasnova, S.A.; Mysik, N.S. Cascade synthesis of a state observer with nonlinear correcting influences. *Autom. Remote Control* **2014**, *75*, 263–280. [CrossRef]

20. Krasnova, S.A.; Utkin, V.A.; Utkin, A.V. Block approach to analysis and design of the invariant nonlinear tracking systems. *Autom. Remote Control* **2017**, *78*, 2120–2140. [CrossRef]

21. Hinrichsen, F.; Larnder, C. Combined viscous and dry friction damping of oscillatory motion. *Am. J. Phys.* **2018**, *86*, 577. [CrossRef]

22. Feng, H.; Qiao, W.; Yin, C.; Yu, H.; Cao, D. Identification and compensation of non-linear friction for a electro-hydraulic system. *Mech. Mach. Theory* **2019**, *141*, 1–13. [CrossRef]

23. Hidalgo, M.; Garcia, C. Friction compensation in control valves: Nonlinear control and usual approaches. *Control Eng. Pract.* **2018**, *58*, 42–53. [CrossRef]

24. Huang, S.; Liang, W.; Tan, K.K. Intelligent Friction Compensation: A Review. *IEEE/ASME Trans. Mechatron.* **2019**, *24*, 1763–1774. [CrossRef]

25. Delibas, B.; Koc, B. A method to realize low velocity movability and eliminate friction induced noise in piezoelectric ultrasonic motors. *IEEE/ASME Trans. Mechatron.* **2020**, *25*, 2677–2687. [CrossRef]

26. Kochetkov, S.A.; Utkin, V.A. Providing the Invariance Property on the Basis on Oscillation Modes. *Dokl. Math.* **2013**, *88*, 618–623. [CrossRef]

27. Loukianov, A.G. Nonlinear block control with sliding mode. *Autom. Remote Control* **1998**, *7*, 916–933.

28. Polyak, B.T.; Tremba, A.A.; Khlebnikov, M.V.; Shcherbakov, P.S.; Smirnov, G.V. Large deviations in linear control systems with nonzero initial conditions. *Autom. Remote Control* **2015**, *76*, 957–976. [CrossRef]

29. Kokunko, Y.G.; Krasnova, S.A.; Utkin, V.A. Cascade Synthesis of Differentiators with Piecewise Linear Correction Signals. *Autom. Remote Control* **2021**, *82*, 1144–1168. [CrossRef]

30. Li, Y. Command Filter Adaptive Asymptotic Tracking of Uncertain Nonlinear Systems with Time-Varying Parameters and Disturbances. *IEEE Trans. Automat. Contr.* **2021**, 1. [CrossRef]

31. Danik, Y.E.; Dmitriev, M.G.; Makarov, D.A. Stabilizing Regulators for Nonlinear Continuous Systems of Large Dimension Using the Asymptotics of the Matrix Algebraic Riccati Equations Solutions. In Proceedings of the Eleventh International Conference "Management of Large-Scale System Development", Moscow, Russia, 1–3 October 2018; pp. 1–4.

32. Yurkevich, V.D. Tracking Control of PWM Non-affine Nonlinear Systems via Singular Perturbation Approach. *IFAC-PapersOnLine* **2015**, *48*, 854–859. [CrossRef]

33. Kochetkov, S.A.; Krasnova, S.A.; Antipov, A.S. Cascade Synthesis of Electromechanical Tracking Systems with Respect to Restrictions on State Variables. *IFAC PapersOnLine* **2017**, *50*, 1042–1047.

34. Krasnova, S.A.; Antipov, A.S. Hierarchical Design of Sigmoidal Generalized Moments of Manipulator under Uncertainty. *Autom. Remote Control* **2018**, *79*, 554–570. [CrossRef]

35. Antipov, A.S.; Krasnova, S.A. Block-Based Synthesis of a Tracking System for a Twin-Rotor Electromechanical System with Constraints on State Variables. *Mech. Solids* **2021**, *56*, 43–56.

Article

Analysis and Prediction of Electric Power System's Stability Based on Virtual State Estimators

Natalia Bakhtadze * and Igor Yadikin

V.A. Trapeznikov Institute of Control Sciences, 65 Profsoyuznaya, 117997 Moscow, Russia; jadikin1@mail.ru
* Correspondence: sung7@yandex.ru; Tel.: +7-916-544-2259

Abstract: The stability of bilinear systems is investigated using spectral techniques such as selective modal analysis. Predictive models of bilinear systems based on inductive knowledge extracted by big data mining techniques are applied with associative search of statistical patterns. A method and an algorithm for the elementwise solution of the generalized matrix Lyapunov equation are developed for discrete bilinear systems. The method is based on calculating the sequence of values of a fixed element of the solution matrix, which depends on the product of the eigenvalues of the dynamics matrix of the linear part and the elements of the nonlinearity matrixes. A sufficient condition for the convergence of all sequences is obtained, which is also a BIBO (bounded input bounded output) systems stability condition for the bilinear system.

Keywords: Gramian method; bilinear system process identification; generalized Lyapunov equation; knowledgebase; associative search models; wavelet analysis

1. Introduction

Stability estimators (soft sensors) are increasingly used in mode planning and supervisory control in present day electric power systems (EPS) [1–19]. Due to the growing popularity of distributed generation and renewable energy sources (RES) in EPS, its operation modes may approach the stability limits. It is, therefore, necessary to improve both predictive modeling techniques and the methods of analysis and preventive control not only for small deviation modes, but also for essentially nonlinear ones [14,20–23]. Bilinear systems are the closest ones to the essentially nonlinear class among all nonlinear systems. Therefore, research methods for bilinear systems have been actively developed over recent decades [2–5,20,21,24–28]. Spectral methods of stability analysis, in particular, selective modal analysis, are widely used in the design and operation of EPS [16,18,22,23].

This article presents the results of the development of these methods and their extension over the class of bilinear EPS models. This will expand their application area [7,8,19,21,28]. To create bilinear models of discrete stationary dynamical systems, digital identification methods and associative search algorithms are used, based on the intelligent analysis of big data obtained from system operation monitoring.

The work [13] develops the Poincaré normal form method for analyzing the stability of energy systems based on continuous dynamical systems with smooth nonlinearities. This approach can be considered to be an alternative to stability estimator development. The article [21] uses a virtual model of energy system's inertia to control the frequency in a system with a high level of microgrid penetration that shows the possibility of using stability estimators not only for stability monitoring tasks, but also for controlling the frequency of low-frequency oscillations.

In [26], Volterra equations are proposed for analyzing the stability of power systems with renewable energy sources. As against [26], Volterra equations are used by the authors for developing digital twins of bilinear models for EPS. The work [27] shows an effective method of Lyapunov stability indices for studying small-signal stability of EPS, which can be used to solve problems discussed in our article.

Citation: Bakhtadze, N.; Yadikin, I. Analysis and Prediction of Electric Power System's Stability Based on Virtual State Estimators. *Mathematics* **2021**, *9*, 3194. https://doi.org/10.3390/math9243194

Academic Editor: Ioannis Dassios

Received: 5 October 2021
Accepted: 7 December 2021
Published: 10 December 2021

Publisher's Note: MDPI stays neutral with regard to jurisdictional claims in published maps and institutional affiliations.

Separable spectral expansions of discrete Lyapunov equations are obtained for MISO LTI (multiple input single output linear time invariant) discrete dynamical systems governed by state equations in controllability and observability forms. A method and an algorithm for the element-wise solution of the generalized matrix Lyapunov equation are developed for discrete bilinear systems. The method is based on calculating the sequence of values of a fixed element of the solution matrix, which depends on the product of the eigenvalues of the dynamics matrix of the linear part and the elements of the nonlinearity matrixes. The new method is a spectral version of the iterative method used for solving this equation.

The new method changes the very computing paradigm: sequences of elements are now calculated instead of decision matrixes. In addition to this paradigm change, the method changes the approach to studying the stability of the initial nonlinear model of the power system. The convergence of all sequences of elements means BIBO stability of the original system in a wider area than the area of "small-signal stability of power systems", as well as identify new indicators of stability in this area.

For developing bilinear models of discrete stationary dynamical systems of this class, the authors propose digital identification methods and associative search algorithms, based on the intelligent analysis of big data collected during system operation.

Computing speed is the key advantage of such identification techniques against the known methods of bilinear model development. The off-line training of the identification system is carried out in advance; further, in the course of real-time operation, the current values of model parameters are obtained using the knowledge accumulated at the training phase [29]. This is done by choosing analogs from the appropriate cluster [18]. It should be noted that the associative search method creates a new linear model at each time step. Section 2 shows how such a model can be further used for digital bilinear model development. In Section 6, an example of obtaining the values of the parameters of linear associative models is cited. In future studies, it is planned to develop a version of this method for the non-stationary case.

2. Knowledge-Based Bilinear Models of Discrete Stationary Dynamic Systems

The essence of the machine learning procedure is as follows [9]. For the current time instant k, a set of impacts u_k ($u_k \in \mathbb{R}^m$) on the stationary system during the time interval $T = \{k - T, k - T + 1, \ldots, k\}$, is divided into clusters (together with the corresponding values of the outputs y_{k-i}, $i = 0, \ldots, T$). The clustering procedure is carried out with reference to the distance between the vectors. For the current vector u_k, a set of vectors u_{k-i} and the corresponding outputs y_{k-i} are collected within the corresponding cluster. Next, a system of linear equations is formed for the unknown coefficients and the output y_k. Unlike traditional regression models, this model does not contain all the prehistory, but rather especially selected vectors (the closest to the current input vector subject to a certain criterion) named "associations".

The least squares method provides a solution to this system of equations, which is optimal if the conditions of the Gauss-Markov theorem are met [30]. Statistical independence of the model variables is a condition of this theorem, which is not met for closed-loop systems. The transition to a system of simultaneous linear equations can be done in particular per the Moore-Penrose procedure [31,32]. As a result, a pseudo-solution of the original system of equations can be obtained such that the resulting linear model will have accuracy admissible for a wide range of applications.

It should be noted that the described identification algorithm generates point models, the best ones for the nonlinear system under investigation at a time instant. Therefore, unlike traditional identification algorithms, we do not improve a single model ad infinitum, rather we deal with a sequence of digital ad hoc models; each one is the best fit at the specific time instant subject to the chosen criterion.

Another feature of the models obtained by machine learning is the fact that if the corresponding model accuracy requirements are met, then the solution does not need to be found every time, it can be rather "found" in the cluster, which contains the current vector u_k. This can be the "nearest neighbor", or a vector selected in some other way, in particular, the cluster's centroid.

If it is nevertheless necessary to solve a system of linear equations, it will be possible in the near future using quantum algorithms.

Machine learning procedures are carried out off-line, at the training stage. Therefore, this identification algorithm demonstrates high speed.

There is a class of essentially nonlinear systems, for which the accuracy of point linear models may be insufficient. This class can include nonlinear systems described by the following equations:

$$\dot{x}(t) = f(x, u, t) = f(x, t) + b(x)u(t), \ x(0) = 0$$
$$y(k) = Cx(k), \tag{1}$$

where $x(t)$ is the state vector of the system, $x(t) \in \mathbb{R}^n$, f and b are nonlinear functions. Models of such systems in the form of:

$$\dot{x}(t) = ax(t) + Nx(t)u(t) + bu(t) \tag{2}$$

where $ax(t) + bu(t)$ is the system's linear part, are called *bilinear models*.

If the matrix $B \in \mathbb{R}^{n \times m}$, the system can be represented as

$$\dot{x}(t) = Ax + \sum_{\gamma=1}^{m} N_\gamma x u_\gamma + Bu,$$
$$y = Cx, \tag{3}$$

or, in the discrete case:

$$x(k+1) = Ax(k) + \sum_{\gamma=1}^{m} N_\gamma x(k)u_\gamma(k) + Bu(k), \ x(0) = 0,$$
$$y(k) = Cx(k), \tag{4}$$

where $x \subset \mathbb{R}^n$, $y \in \mathbb{R}^1$, $u \in \mathbb{R}^m$, A, B, C, N_γ are matrices of appropriate dimensions.

Equation (4) can be rewritten as:

$$x(k+1) = [A \vdots N_1 \vdots \cdots \vdots N_m]\tilde{x}(k) + Bu(k), \tag{5}$$

where

$$\tilde{x}(k) = \begin{bmatrix} x(k) \\ x(k) \cdot u_1(k) \\ \cdots \\ x(k) \cdot u_m(k) \end{bmatrix} \in \mathbb{R}^{1 \times (n \times (m+1))}. \tag{6}$$

Thus, we get the representation:

$$x(k+1) = \tilde{A}\tilde{x}(k) + Bu(k),$$
$$\tilde{A} = [A \vdots N_1 \vdots \cdots \vdots N_m], \tag{7}$$

where:

$$\tilde{x}(k) = D^n \cdot x(k),$$

$$D^n = \begin{bmatrix} D^{0n} \\ \cdots \\ D^{nn} \end{bmatrix}, \ D^{0n} = \begin{bmatrix} 1 & \cdots & 0 \\ \vdots & 1 & \vdots \\ 0 & \cdots & 1 \end{bmatrix}, \ D^{in} = \begin{bmatrix} u_i(k) & \cdots & 0 \\ \vdots & u_i(k) & \vdots \\ 0 & \cdots & u_i(k) \end{bmatrix}, \ i = 1, \ldots, n.$$

For simplicity, we assume that $m = n$. Otherwise, the matrices N_i are padded with zero rows so that the number of rows is equal to n.

Then Equation (4) can be represented as

$$x(k+1) = \tilde{A}D^n x(k) + Bu(k). \tag{8}$$

Furthermore, to identify the parameters of the system, we will carry out the transition from a state-space model to a linear input-output model. This transition is a standard procedure described, e.g., in [33]. The identification is carried out using the associative search algorithm together with the Moore-Penrose procedure [31,32], which delivers a solution to a system of linear equations with the statistical dependence of the components of the vector $\tilde{x}$.

Returning to the canonical form of the model results in an estimate of all parameters, i.e., the updated bilinear model. The ability to determine the system's state and output for various control impacts enables the usage of identification models for predicting the approach to stability boundaries in advance.

3. Controllability and Observability Gramians of Discrete Stationary Bilinear Systems

Let the model (4) of a discrete stationary dynamical system be obtained as a result of identification using the algorithms described in Section 2. We will assume that it belongs to the class of MISO LTI systems.

Consider a MISO LTI discrete stationary dynamical system in the form:

$$\begin{aligned} x(k+1) &= Ax(k) + Bu(k), \ x(0) = 0, \\ y(k) &= Cx(k), \end{aligned} \tag{9}$$

where $x \in \mathbb{R}^n, y \in \mathbb{R}^1, u \in \mathbb{R}^m$

We will consider real matrices of the corresponding sizes A, B, C. Let us assume that the system (9) is stable, fully controllable and fully observable, all eigenvalues of matrix A are different. Consider discrete algebraic Lyapunov equations associated with Equation (9) in the form:

$$\begin{aligned} AP^c A^* + BB^* &= P^c, \\ A^* P^o A + C^* C &= P^o. \end{aligned}$$

Consider a bilinear discrete stationary dynamical system in the form:

$$\begin{aligned} x(k+1) &= Ax(k) + \sum_{\gamma=1}^{m} N_\gamma x(k)u_\gamma(k) + Bu(k), \ x(0) = 0, \\ y(k) &= Cx(k), \end{aligned} \tag{10}$$

where $x \in \mathbb{R}^n, y \in \mathbb{R}^1, u \in \mathbb{R}^m$, A, B, C, N_γ are matrices of appropriate dimensions. One of the most important properties of control systems is the controllability. In [4,5], controllability and observability Gramians of discrete bilinear dynamical systems were introduced and iterative algorithms for their computation were proposed. Let us denote:

$$\begin{aligned} P_1(k_1) &= A^{k_1} B, \\ P_i(k_1, \ldots, k_i) &= A^{k_i}[N_1 P_{i-1} N_2 P_{i-1} \ldots N_m P_{i-1}], \ i \geq 2, \end{aligned}$$

The controllability Gramian of a bilinear system is defined as follows:

$$P = \sum_{i=1}^{\infty} \sum_{k_i=0}^{\infty} \cdots \cdots \sum_{k_i=0}^{\infty} P_i P_i^T. \tag{11}$$

It was shown in [5] that if the spectrum of A belongs to the interior of the unit circle, then, under certain additional conditions, the solutions to the following two Lyapunov generalized matrix equations:

$$APA^* + BB^* + \sum_{j=1}^{m} N_j P N_j^* = P, \tag{12}$$

$$A^*QA + C^*C + \sum_{j=1}^{m} N_j Q N_j^* = Q, \tag{13}$$

are the Gramians of controllability and observability. The Gramian of controllability of a bilinear system is the limiting solution

$$P = \lim_{i \to \infty} P_i \tag{14}$$

obtained as a result of the implementation of the following iterative procedure

$$AP_1 A^* - P_1 = -BB^*,$$

$$AP_i A^* - P_i + \sum_{j=1}^{m} N_j P_{i-1} N_j^* = 0, \ i = 2, \dots \infty. \tag{15}$$

Similarly, the observability Gramian of a bilinear system is the limiting solution obtained by implementing a similar iterative procedure. The disadvantage of such procedures is that the resulting limiting solution is not always the corresponding Gramian of the bilinear system.

Our goal is to create improved iterative algorithms for calculating the Gramians of bilinear systems and to develop a method and algorithms for calculating the stability indices of bilinear systems based on them. To achieve this goal, it is proposed to change the computation paradigm by transferring computations from the matrixes to their elements in the course of iterations.

The very idea of the element-wise computation of Gramians is not new: for example, the method for vectorizing the solution of generalized matrix Lyapunov equations is based on it [3,5]. However, the calculation of sequences of numeric elements of Gramian matrixes will reveal new patterns of sequences behavior, for example, the formation of geometric progressions of elements. This will allow investigating the behavior of sequences for small, medium and large matrixes and develop new approaches to approximate calculations. Another argument in favor of the element-wise approach is that this approach to calculating the spectral decompositions of Gramians of linear continuous systems was previously proposed in [7] and has shown its effectiveness.

4. Iterative Methods for Calculating the Solutions of the Generalized Lyapunov Equations for Canonical State form Equations

Consider further the spectral methods of Gramians calculating for discrete linear systems. These methods were studied in early works [1–3,7,11] Consider a MIMO LTI discrete system reduced using a non-degenerate coordinate transformation to the diagonal form of the dynamics matrix

$$x = T x_d \ x_d(k+1) = \Lambda x_d(k) + B_d u(k), \ y_d(k) = C_d x_d(k),$$
$$\Lambda = T^{-1}AT, \ B_d = T^{-1}B, \ C_d = CT, \tag{16}$$

or

$$A = \begin{bmatrix} u_1 & u_2 \cdots & u_n \end{bmatrix} \begin{bmatrix} z_1 & 0 & 0 & 0 \\ 0 & z_2 & & 0 \\ 0 & & \ddots & \\ 0 & 0 & & z_n \end{bmatrix} \begin{bmatrix} v_1^* \\ v_2^* \\ \vdots \\ v_n^* \end{bmatrix} = T\Lambda T^{-1}, \; TV = VT = I, \quad (17)$$

where the matrix T consists of the right eigenvectors u_i, and matrix T^{-1} consists of the left eigenvectors v_i^* corresponding to the eigenvalues z_i. The last equality is a condition for eigenvectors normalization.

In particular, in [8], the spectral decompositions of Gramian controllability and observability matrixes for LTI MIMO discrete stable systems with a simple spectrum are as follows:

$$P^c = \sum_{k=1}^{n} \sum_{\rho=1}^{n} P_{k,\rho}^c, \; P_{k,\rho}^c = \sum_{\eta=0}^{n-1} \sum_{j=0}^{n-1} \frac{z_k^j z_\rho^\eta}{N(z_k) N(z_\rho)} \cdot \frac{1}{1 - z_\rho z_k} A_j B B^T A_\eta^T, \quad (18)$$

$$P^o = \sum_{k=1}^{n} \sum_{\rho=1}^{n} P_{k,\rho}^o, \; P_{k,\rho}^o = \sum_{\eta=0}^{n-1} \sum_{j=0}^{n-1} \frac{z_k^j z_\rho^\eta}{N(z_k) N(z_\rho)} \cdot \frac{1}{1 - z_\rho z_k} A_\eta^T C^T C A_j, \quad (19)$$

where z_k, z_ρ are the roots of the characteristic equation, A_j, A_η^T are the Faddeev matrices. For the Lyapunov equations of the same diagonalized systems of the form:

$$\Lambda P_d^c \Lambda^* + B_d B_d^* = P_d^c, V_d = B_d B_d^*,$$
$$\Lambda^* P_d^o \Lambda + C_d^* C_d = P_d^o, W_d = C_d^* C_d,$$

we have the following formulas for spectral decomposition:

$$P_{d,\rho k}^c = \frac{1}{1 - z_\rho z_k} R_k B_d B_d^* R_\rho^*, \; \forall z : |z| < 1, \quad (20)$$

$$P_{d,\rho k}^o = \frac{1}{1 - z_\rho z_k} R_k^* C_d^* C_d R_\rho, \; \forall z : |z| < 1, \quad (21)$$

where R_k are the residues of the resolvent of the matrix Λ in the eigenvalues of the matrix z_k. The elements "ρk" of the sub-Gramian matrixes (20)–(21) satisfy the formulas:

$$p_{d\rho k}^c = \frac{1}{1 - z_\rho z_k} v_{d\rho k}, \; p_{d\rho k}^o = \frac{1}{1 - z_\rho z_k} w_{d\rho k}. \quad (22)$$

When transforming Equation (4) by decomposing the matrix A in its eigenvalues (16)–(17), we obtain the equations

$$x_d(k+1) = \Lambda x_d(k) + \sum_{\gamma=1}^{m} N_{d\gamma} x_d(k) u_\gamma(k) + B_d u(k), \; x_d(0) = 0,$$
$$y(k) = C_d x(k). k = 0, 1, 2 \ldots \quad (23)$$

$$N_{d\gamma} = T N_\gamma.$$

Definition 1. *Consider the following matrix and vector identities:*

$$A \equiv \sum_{i,j} a_{ij} 1_{ij}, \; \{a\} \equiv \sum_{i} a_i 1_i, \; 1_{ij} = e_i e_j^T, \; 1_i = e_i,$$

where the unit vector is as follows:

$$e_i = \begin{bmatrix} 0 \ldots & 0 & 1 & 0 & \ldots 0 \end{bmatrix}^T.$$

We call the above decompositions of matrixes and vectors *separable decompositions*. The separability property means the change in the very paradigm of solution computing: the transition from the matrix-vector consideration to the element-wise one.

Let us derive a formula for spectral decomposition of Gramian for the dynamics matrix of the system, transformed into the canonical controllability form using a linear nondegenerate transformation of coordinates with the following matrix:

$$R_c^F, \quad x = R_c^F x_c.$$

We assume full-controllability and full-observability conditions are fulfilled. Furthermore, we consider the channel "γ" MISO LTI of the linear system in the canonical controllability form:

$$x_c(k+1) = A_c^F x_c(k) + b_\gamma^F u(k), \ x_c(0) = 0,$$
$$y(k) = c_\gamma^F x(k), k = 0,1,2\ldots \tag{24}$$

$$A_c^F = \begin{bmatrix} 0 & 1 & 0 & & 0 \\ 0 & 0 & 1 & & 0 \\ 0 & 0 & & 1 & 0 \\ 0 & 0 & 0 & 0 & 1 \\ -a_0 & -a_1 & -a_2 & \ldots & -a_{n-1} \end{bmatrix}, \ b_\gamma^F = \begin{bmatrix} 0 & 0 & \ldots & 0 & 1 \end{bmatrix}^T, N_{c\gamma}^F = \left(R_c^F\right)^{-1} N_\gamma.$$

$$c_\gamma^F = \begin{bmatrix} \xi_0 & \xi_1 & \cdots & \xi_{n-2} & \xi_{n-1} \end{bmatrix}.$$

The following relations are valid:

$$R_c^F = \begin{bmatrix} B & AB & \ldots & \ldots & A^{n-1}B \end{bmatrix} \begin{bmatrix} a_1 & a_2 & & a_{n-1} & 1 \\ a_2 & a_3 & a_{n-1} & 1 & \\ & a_{n-1} & & & 0 \\ a_{n-1} & 1 & & 0 & 0 \\ 1 & 0 & 0 & 0 & 0 \end{bmatrix},$$

$$\left(R_c^F\right)^{-1} A R_c^F = A^F, \left(R_c^F\right)^{-1} B = B^F, C R_c^F = C^F.$$

Lemma 1. *Consider a linear discrete MISO system in the form (2) represented by equations in the canonical form of controllability of the form (24). Let us further consider the decomposition of the dynamics matrix A^F resolvent into a segment of the Faddeev series of the form*

$$\left(Iz - A^F\right)^{-1} = \sum_{j=0}^{n-1} \frac{A_j^F z^j}{N(z)},$$

where: $N(z)$ is a characteristic polynomial, A_j^F is Faddeev matrix, $j = 1,2,\ldots n$.

The elements of the last column of the matrix A_j^F satisfy the statements:

$$\left\{a_{n-k,n}^F\right\}^T = e_{n-k}^T, \ k = 0,1,2\ldots,n-1. \tag{25}$$

Comment. *Note, first that the decomposition of the resolvent in the Faddeev series form does not require calculating the eigenvalues of the dynamics matrix A^F. Second, the transfer function of the "γ" channel of the linear part is determined by the formula:*

$$V_\gamma^{Fln} = \begin{bmatrix} \xi_0 & \xi_1 & \cdots & \xi_{n-2} & \xi_{n-1} \end{bmatrix} \left(Iz - A^F\right)^{-1} b_\gamma^F, \ b_\gamma^F = \begin{bmatrix} 0 & \cdots & 0 & 1 \end{bmatrix}^T,$$

hence it follows that it is determined only by the elements of the last column of the matrix A^F.

Proof. Consider the expansion of the resolvent of the matrix A^F in the form of a segment of the Faddeev series

$$\left(Iz - A^F \right)^{-1} = \frac{\sum_{j=0}^{n-1} A_j^F z^j}{N(z)}.$$

We will accept

$$N(z) = z^n + a_{n-1} z^{n-1} + \cdots a_1 z + a_0, \; R_j = A_{j-1}^F, \; j = 1, 2, \ldots n.$$

We apply the method of mathematical induction. An iterative algorithm for calculating the Faddeev matrixes and the coefficients of the characteristic equation has the form at the first step [17]:

$$a_n = 1, \; R_n = A_{cn-1}^F = I,$$

at the step "k":

$$a_{n-k} = -\frac{1}{k} tr \left(A^F R_{n-k+1} \right), \; R_{n-k} = a_{n-k} I + A^F R_{n-k+1}, \; k = 1, 2, \ldots n.$$

Consider the formation of the last column of matrixes A_{n-k}^F.
The first step:

$$A_{cn-1}^F = I.\left\{ a_{n-1,n}^F \right\} = \begin{bmatrix} 0 & 0 & \cdots & 0 & 1 \end{bmatrix}^T.$$

The second step:

$$A_{cn-2}^F = \begin{bmatrix} 0 & 1 & 0 & & 0 \\ 0 & 0 & 1 & & 0 \\ 0 & 0 & & 1 & 0 \\ 0 & 0 & 0 & 0 & 1 \\ -a_1 & -a_2 & \cdots & -a_{n-2} & 0 \end{bmatrix}, \; \left\{ a_{cn-2,n}^F \right\} = \begin{bmatrix} 0 & \cdots & 0 & 1 & 0 \end{bmatrix}^T.$$

Suppose that for step "$k-1$", the last column of the matrix $A_{cn-(k-1)}^F$ has the form:

$$\left\{ a_{cn-(k-1),n}^F \right\} = \begin{bmatrix} \underbrace{0}_{1} & \cdots & \underbrace{0}_{n-(k-2)} & \underbrace{1\ldots}_{n-(k-1)} & \underbrace{0}_{n} \end{bmatrix}^T.$$

We introduce the notation:

$$A_c^F A_{cn-(k-1)}^F = S, \; S = \begin{bmatrix} \{s_1\} & \{s_2\} & \cdots & \{s_n\} \end{bmatrix}.$$

The last column of the matrix is:

$$\{s_n\} = \begin{bmatrix} \underbrace{0}_{1} & \cdots & \underbrace{1}_{n-k} & \underbrace{0.}_{n-(k-1)} & \underbrace{-a_{cn-(k-1),n}^F}_{n} \end{bmatrix}^T.$$

In accordance with the Faddeev—Le Verrier algorithm, we have:

$$\left\{ a_{cn-k,n}^F \right\} = \begin{bmatrix} \underbrace{0}_{1} & \cdots & \underbrace{1}_{n-k} & \underbrace{0}_{n-(k-1)} & \underbrace{0}_{n} \end{bmatrix}^T.$$

$\square$

Corollary 1. *Without loss of generality, we assume m = 1. The general formulas (9) of spectral decompositions for the controllability Gramians of the linear system transformed in the canonical controllability form, taking into account the Lemma 1, acquire a simpler form:*

$$P^{cF} = \sum_{k=1}^{n} \sum_{\rho=1}^{n} P_{k,\rho}^{cF}, \quad P_{k,\rho}^{cF} = \sum_{\eta=0}^{n-1} \sum_{j=0}^{n-1} \frac{z_k^j z_\rho^\eta}{\dot{N}(z_k) \dot{N}(z_\rho)} \frac{1}{1 - z_\rho z_k} e_{j+1} e_{\eta+1}^T. \tag{26}$$

A similar approach can be used to derive a formula for spectral decompositions for observability Gramians of the MISO system transformed in the canonical form of observability. In this case, the following formulas are valid [18]:

$$x = R_0^F x_o,$$

$$R_0^F = \left\{ \begin{bmatrix} a_1 & a_2 & & a_{n-1} & 1 \\ a_2 & a_3 & a_{n-1} & 1 & \\ & a_{n-1} & & & 0 \\ a_{n-1} & 1 & & 0 & 0 \\ 1 & 0 & 0 & 0 & 0 \end{bmatrix} \begin{bmatrix} c \\ cA \\ \vdots \\ cA^{n-1} \end{bmatrix} \right\}^{-1}.$$

Let us use (16) and consider the formation of the expression $A_{oj}^{FT} c^{FT} c^F A_{oj}^F$. In accordance with duality principle, due to the complete controllability and observability, the following formula is valid:

$$c^F A_{oj}^F = \left(A_{cj}^F \right)^T b^F. \tag{27}$$

Substituting (27) into (19), we obtain the expression:

$$P^{oF} = \sum_{k=1}^{n} \sum_{\rho=1}^{n} P_{k,\rho}^{oF} = \sum_{\eta=0}^{n-1} \sum_{j=0}^{n-1} \frac{z_k^j z_\rho^\eta}{\dot{N}(z_k) \dot{N}(z_\rho)} \frac{1}{1 - z_\rho z_k} e_{j+1} e_{\eta+1}^T, \quad P^{oF} = P^{cF}. \tag{28}$$

The Gramians of the original system are related to the Gramians of the systems transformed into canonical forms as follows

$$R_c^F P^{cF} R_c^{FT} = P^c, \quad \left(R_o^{FT} \right)^{-1} P^{oF} \left(R_o^F \right)^{-1} = P^o.$$

Please note that in this case the expressions of the Gramians and sub-Gramians of controllability and observability depend only on the eigenvalues of the dynamics matrix. In addition, the proposed approach using canonical forms made it possible to simplify the general formulas significantly.

5. Separable Spectral Method and Algorithm for Solving the Generalized Lyapunov Equation

Theorem 1. *Consider a MISO (multiple input single output) discrete bilinear stationary system in the form (4) [3–5,24].*

(1)　Let the matrix A be a Hurwitz one with the simple spectrum,
(2)　Let the vector $u(k)$ be bounded:

$$\|u(k)\| = \sqrt[2]{\sum_{i=1}^{m} |u_i(k)|^2} < M.$$

(3) There exist real numbers α, ρ such that the following inequalities hold:

$$\|A\| \le \alpha\rho^i, \; i = 0,1,2,\ldots,$$
$$\rho < i, \alpha > 0,$$
$$M < \sqrt{1 - \rho^2\alpha^{-1}}.$$

(4) Suppose, in addition, the following conditions are satisfied:

$$\left| \frac{p_{ij}^{C\,bln(k+1)}}{p_{ij}^{C\,bln(k)}} \right| \le \overline{N}L < 1, \; \forall k, \nu, \mu, j, \eta, \gamma, \tag{29}$$

where

$$\overline{N} = \sup n^2 \underbrace{|n_{d\nu i}^{\gamma}||n_{d\nu j}^{\gamma}|}_{\nu,\mu,j,\eta,\gamma}, \; L = \left| (1 - z_{\nu max}z_{\nu max}{}^{*})^{-1} \right|. \tag{30}$$

In (30), $z_{\nu max}$ denotes the maximum eigenvalue of the dynamics matrix of the linear part of the system.

Then, there also exists a uniquely following separable iterative spectral solution to the generalized Lyapunov equation (12) for the diagonalized system (16):

$$p_d^{(k)ij} = \left(\sum_{\nu,\mu} p_{d\nu\mu}^{(k-1)ij} \right) \left[(1 - z_\nu z_\mu)^{-1} n_{d\nu i}^{\gamma} n_{d\mu j}^{\gamma} \right], \; k = 2,3,\ldots\infty. \tag{31}$$

$$\forall \nu, \mu, i, j = 1,2,\ldots n; \gamma = 1,2,\ldots m.$$

Sequences of partial sums (31) converge uniformly and absolutely to the corresponding elements of the solution matrix of the generalized Lyapunov equation (12) if the conditions of the theorem are satisfied. The controllability Gramian of the original bilinear system P^{cbln} is related to the controllability Gramian of the diagonalized bilinear system P_d^{cbln} as follows

$$T P_d^{cbln} T^T = P^{cbln}. \tag{32}$$

Proof. Consider an iterative process, which develops the solution of (31).

Step 1. Let us consider the forming of the right-hand side of the generalized Lyapunov equation for the case $m = 1$. We do not need the matrix of the Lyapunov equation solution of the linear part; rather we need a separable spectral decomposition of this solution in the pair spectrum of the matrix [18]:

$$P_d^{bln(1)} = \sum_{\gamma=1}^{m} \sum_{\nu=1}^{n} \sum_{\mu=1}^{n} \frac{v_{d,\gamma\nu\mu}}{1 - z_\nu z_\mu} 1_{\nu\mu}. \tag{33}$$

Step 2. Consider the formation of the right-hand side of the generalized Lyapunov equation with the example of the matrix $N_d^{\gamma} 1_{ij} (N_d^{\gamma})^T$:

$$N_d^{\gamma} 1_{ij} (N_d^{\gamma})^T = \sum_{\nu=1}^{n} \sum_{\mu=1}^{n} n_{d,\nu i}^{\gamma} n_{\mu j}^{\gamma} 1_{\nu\mu}, \tag{34}$$

The solution of the Lyapunov equation takes at Step 2 the form:

$$P_d^{bln(2)} = \sum_{\gamma=1}^{m} \sum_{\nu=1}^{n} \sum_{\mu=1}^{n} \frac{1}{1 - z_\nu z_\mu} \left(n_{d,\nu i}^{\gamma} n_{d\mu j}^{\gamma} \right) p_{\nu\mu}^{bln(1)ij\gamma} 1_{\nu\mu}.$$

Proceeding in a similar way and taking into account the summation of sub-Gramians over the index "γ", we obtain a formula for calculating the matrix of the Gramian kernel of the order "k" at step "k".

$$p_d^{bln(k)ij\gamma} = \sum_{\nu,\mu} r^{(k)ij\gamma} p_{\nu\mu}^{(k-1)ij\gamma} 1_{\nu\mu}, \quad r^{(k)ij\gamma} = \left[(1 - z_\nu z_\mu)^{-1} n_{d\nu i}^\gamma n_{d\mu j}^\gamma\right], \tag{35}$$

$$p_{d\nu\mu}^{(k)ij\gamma} = \left(\sum_{\nu,\mu} p_{d\nu\mu}^{(k-1)ij\gamma}\right)\left[(1 - z_\nu z_\mu)^{-1} n_{d\nu i}^\gamma n_{d\mu j}^\gamma\right], \ k = 2,3,\dots\infty,$$

$$\forall \nu,\mu,i,j = 1,2,\dots n; \gamma = 1,2,\dots m. \tag{36}$$

$\square$

This proves the theorem's statement about the iterative spectral decomposition of the solution in the case of solution convergence. Let us show that under the conditions of Theorem 2, the convergence of the sequences is absolute and uniform. To this end, we construct a majorizing sequence for the elements of the sub-Gramian matrixes. Suppose that conditions (29)–(30) are satisfied. For all converging sequences' elements "ij", the following conditions must be satisfied:

$$\left|p_d^{(k)ij\gamma}\right| \leq \left|p_d^{(k-1)ij\gamma}\right| \dots \leq \left|p_d^{bln(1)ij\gamma}\right| \leq \underset{ij}{max}\left|p_d^{bln(1)ij\gamma}\right| = M_{max}^{ij\gamma}.$$

Let us introduce the notation $M_{max} = \underset{ij\gamma}{max} M_{max}^{ij\gamma}$. For the matrix N_d^γ, the exact upper bound of the products exists:

$$n^2\left|n_{d\nu j}^\gamma\right|\left|n_{d\mu\eta}^\gamma\right| \leq \overline{N}, \ \overline{N} > 0, \ \forall \gamma,\nu,i,\mu,j: \ \gamma,\nu,i,\mu,j = 1,2,\dots n.$$

In addition, in addition, due to the stability of the linear part, the exact upper bound exists for the functions:

$$L = \underset{\nu\mu}{max}\left|(1 - z_{\nu max} z_{\nu max}{}^*)^{-1}\right|, \ L > 0, \ \forall \nu,\mu,: \ \nu,\mu = 1,2,\dots n,$$

where $z_{\nu max}$ is the maximum eigenvalue of the dynamics matrix of the system's linear part. Therefore, the following inequality holds:

$$\left|\frac{p_{dij}^{cbln(k+1)}}{p_{dij}^{cbln(k)}}\right| \leq \overline{N}L \ \forall \gamma,\nu,i,\mu,j: \ \gamma,\nu,i,\mu,j = 1,2,\dots n.$$

We choose a single majorant for all numerical sequences in the form:

$$S_0, S_1,\dots S_k.$$

$$S_k = M_{max}^{ij\gamma} n^2 \left[\underset{\nu\mu}{max}\left|(1 - z_{\nu max} z_{\nu max}{}^*)^{-1}\right| \underset{\nu\mu ij\gamma}{max}\left|n_{d\nu i}^\gamma n_{d\mu j}^\gamma\right|\right]^{k-1}.$$

$$k = 2,3,\dots\infty.$$

Obviously, with such a choice, according to (36), the following inequality holds:

$$\left|p_{d\nu\mu}^{(k)ij\gamma}\right| < S_k, \ \forall k,i,j,\nu,\mu,\gamma. \tag{37}$$

It follows thereof that under conditions (29)–(30), the inequality

$$\left| \frac{p_{dij}^{bln(k+1)}}{p_{dij}^{bln(k)}} \right| \leq \frac{S_{k+1}}{S_k} < 1, \tag{38}$$

is valid.

The majorizing sequence for all sub-Gramians of the bilinear system forms a geometric progression with positive terms. In accordance with the convergence criterion for geometric progressions, it converges if the following condition is satisfied:

$$\overline{N}L < 1.$$

In accordance with the Weerstrass test (37)–(38), the sequences of partial sums $p_{dij}^{cbln(k)}$ converge uniformly and absolutely. The uniqueness of the iterative solution under conditions (1)–(3) was proved in [5].

The Gramians method can be used simultaneously for state monitoring and control of large-scale power systems, in particular, for static stability analysis, for developing stability estimators, detecting dangerous free and forced oscillations, and assessing the resonant interaction of dangerous oscillations [1,7–10].

Algorithm of the spectral iterative solution of the generalized Lyapunov equation of the form (12) is as follows:

Step 1. Calculate the spectrum of the dynamics matrix of the linear part, check the stability of the linear part, the absence of multiple roots of the characteristic equation. Find a non-degenerate coordinate transformation that transforms the dynamics matrix of the linear part into a diagonal matrix. Let us transform the equations of the bilinear system (9) to the diagonal form.

Step 2. Check the fulfillment of conditions (1)–(4) of Theorem 1.

Step 3. By analyzing conditions (4), we identify the numerical sequences of elements of the matrixes of the kernels of the spectral expansion of the matrixes of the solution of the generalized Lyapunov equation, which are critical from the point of view of convergence.

Step 4. Using algorithm (34), we compute the sequences of elements "ij" of the matrixes of the kernels of the Gramian expansion of the bilinear system at each step. We aggregate the elements of the sequences into the matrixes of the kernels of the decomposition of the bilinear system Gramian. We estimate the accuracy of the solution.

Step 5. Using Formula (32), we calculate the Gramian matrix of the original bilinear system.

Comment. In [3,5,20,24], various versions of the generalized Lyapunov equation solutions are proposed using conditions (1)–(3) given in Theorem 1., but the similarity transformation of the dynamics matrix of the linear part to the diagonal form is not used, and the separable spectral decomposition is not used solutions of the Lyapunov equation of the linear part and the generalized Lyapunov equation for a bilinear system. Such a technique allows one to switch from calculating decision matrixes at separate iterations to calculating sequences of their elements.

As is known [2], the necessary and sufficient condition for energy stability of the system in terms of the square of the H_2 norm of the linear system transfer function $G(z)$ has the form:

$$\|G(z)\|_2^2 = \mathrm{tr} C P^c C^{\mathrm{T}} = \mathrm{tr} B^{\mathrm{T}} P^o B < +\infty.$$

Therefore, we define the stability loss risk functional of a bilinear system as:

$$J(z_1, z_2, \ldots, z_n) = \mathrm{tr} C P^{cbln} C^{\mathrm{T}} = \mathrm{tr} B^{\mathrm{T}} P^{obln} B. \tag{39}$$

As the system approaches the stability threshold caused by the approaching of the characteristic equation roots to the imaginary axis, the risk functional approaches the infinity. Let us define the acceptable risk of stability loss of the bilinear system as:

$$J^{(\gamma)}(z_1, z_2, \ldots, z_n, \gamma) = M_{\gamma perm}, \ \gamma = 1, 2, \ldots m.$$

We will consider any system as conditionally *unstable* if all its roots lie in a unit circle, but the functional of the stability loss risk (39) exceeds the established acceptable risk value. Accordingly, we will consider the system conditionally stable if:

$$J^{(\gamma)}(z_1, z_2, \ldots, z_n, \gamma) < M_{\gamma perm}. \ \gamma = 1, 2, \ldots m. \tag{40}$$

The inequalities (40) define a set of energy functionals, the boundedness whereof guarantees the BIBO stability of the bilinear system. Conditions (1)–(4) of the theorem are sufficient conditions for the BIBO stability of the bilinear system and, at the same time, sufficient conditions for the boundedness of the energy functionals $J^{(\gamma)}$.

It is easy to see that inequalities (40) determine the stability conditions for a bilinear energy system in a wider range as against the traditional selective modal analysis. The analysis of expressions (37), (38) shows that the elements of the numerical sequences for the Gramian of the bilinear system converge at different rates, the guaranteed estimate whereof is specified by expressions (29)–(30).

This estimate depends on the choice of the "γ" channel, on the values of the elements of the nonlinearity matrixes for a specific channel, and on the proximity of the product of two eigenvalues of the linear part to unity. Sufficient conditions for BIBO stability of a bilinear system were obtained earlier in [3,5,24]. Theorem 1 establishes additional sufficient conditions (29)–(30) that guarantee the existence of not only a matrix for the solution of the generalized Lyapunov equation, but also of complete controllability and observability properties for the bilinear system.

6. Case Studies

The increased requirements for speed, accuracy and control capabilities under conditions of uncertainty in the presence of various kinds of disturbances in the control systems of production processes in industry and the electric power industry have demonstrated the inadequacy of the capabilities of traditional approaches to the synthesis of automatic control systems. Methods of identification synthesis, in which models are developed on the basis of data mining and machine learning, are gaining more and more popularity [18].

The authors have developed an intelligent system designed to dynamically assess the state of facilities in the power system [34]. The system is underpinned by intelligent algorithms of grid dynamics identification with automatic on-line self-tuning based on the data from monitoring systems.

State estimation models for power facilities with on-line model tuning are based on data monitoring and application of a predictive method for state estimation—the associative search method.

The acquisition, storage, processing, displaying, analysis and documenting of the information are executed in real time based on the data from automated power generation, distribution and consumption systems and supervisory control, monitoring and accounting. Figure 1 demonstrates power dynamic estimation for a certain facility in the power system.

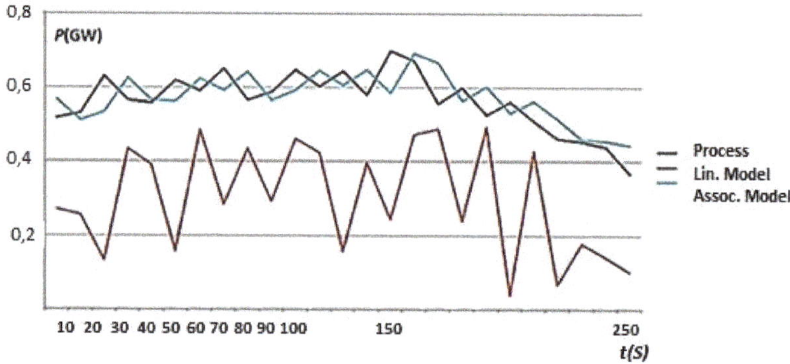

Figure 1. Power dynamic estimation.

In Figure 1, we have:

- the black line represents the dynamics of the real process;
- the red line shows the result in a linear model;
- and the blue line shows the result obtained by associative search model.

Figure 1 shows how a more accurate estimate of a real process dynamics can be obtained using the associative search model, compared with the classical linear models.

7. Conclusions

Predictive bilinear models of discrete dynamical systems are obtained using the associative search algorithm. The method is based on the use of machine learning procedures and inductive knowledge (associative patterns) extraction from historical data. The method features high algorithmic speed, since the main computational load falls on the training stage.

According to the proposed scheme, we, at first, obtain a bilinear model of a nonlinear dynamic object, and then analyze the stability. The advantages of the scheme are the accuracy and speed of the identification algorithm. Section 6 demonstrates the operation of the associative search algorithm. It shows that for nonlinear systems the models obtained through this algorithm are more accurate as against the ones obtained using traditional linear techniques.

Furthermore, according to our scheme, separable spectral expansions of discrete Lyapunov equations are obtained for MISO LTI discrete dynamical systems governed by state equations in controllability and observability forms. A method and an algorithm for the element-wise solution of the generalized matrix Lyapunov equation are developed for discrete bilinear systems. The new method is a spectral version of the well-known iterative method used for solving this equation.

A sequence of values is calculated for a fixed element of the solution matrix. The element depends on the eigenvalues product of the dynamics matrix of the linear part and the elements of the nonlinearity matrixes. A sufficient condition for the convergence of all sequences is obtained, which is also a BIBO stability condition for a bilinear system.

The article discusses MIMO, MISO, and SISO classes of bilinear systems of the form (10) but does not consider bilinear systems with distributed parameters. In the future, the authors intend to extend the new method over this class of systems. Time-variant systems will be also investigated.

Author Contributions: Conceptualization, N.B. and I.Y.; methodology, N.B. and I.Y.; formal analysis, N.B. and I.Y.; investigation, N.B. and I.Y.; writing—original draft preparation, N.B. and I.Y.; writing—review and editing, N.B. and I.Y.; visualization N.B. and I.Y.; supervision, N.B. and I.Y.; project administration, N.B. and I.Y.; funding acquisition, N.B. and I.Y. All authors have read and agreed to the published version of the manuscript.

Funding: The APC was funded by the Russian Science Foundation. This work was supported by the Russian Science Foundation project no. 19-19-00673 and by the Russian Foundation for Basic Re-search (RFBR), project number 21-57-53005.

Institutional Review Board Statement: Not applicable.

Informed Consent Statement: Not applicable.

Data Availability Statement: Not applicable.

Conflicts of Interest: The authors declare no conflict of interest.

References

1. Yadykin, I.; Bakhtadze, N.; Lototsky, V.; Maximov, E.; Sakrutina, E. Stability Analysis Methods of Discrete Power Supply Systems in Industry. *IFAC PaperOnLine* **2016**, *49*, 355–359. [CrossRef]
2. Antoulas, A.C. *Approximation of Large-Scale Dynamical Systems*; SIAM Press: Philadephia, PA, USA, 2005.
3. Benner, P.; Damm, T. Lyapunov equations, Energy Functionals and Model Order Reduction of Bilinear and Stochastic Systems. *SIAM J. Control Optim.* **2011**, *49*, 686–711. [CrossRef]
4. Alessandro, P.D.; Isidori, A.; Ruberti, A. Realization and structure theory of bilinear dynamic systems. *SIAM J. Control* **1974**, *12*, 517–535. [CrossRef]
5. Zhang, L.; Lam, J.; Huang, B.; Yang, G.H. On Gramians and balanced truncation of discrete—time bilinear systems. *Int. J. Control* **2003**, *76*, 414–427. [CrossRef]
6. Polyak, B.T.; Khlebnikov, M.V.; Rapoport, L.B. *Mathematical Theory of Automatic Control*; LENAND: Moscow, Russia, 2019. (In Russian)
7. Yadykin, I.; Galyaev, A. On the Methods for Calculation of Gramians and Their Use in Analysis of Linear Dynamic Systems. *Autom. Remote Control.* **2013**, *74*, 207–224. [CrossRef]
8. Yadykin, I.B.; Iskakov, A.B. Spectral Decompositions for the Solutions of Sylvester, Lyapunov, and Krein Equations. *Doklady Math.* **2017**, *95*, 103–107. [CrossRef]
9. Bakhtadze, N.; Kulba, V.; Lototsky, V.; Maximov, E. Identification Methods Based on Associative Search Procedure. *Control Cybernetics* **2011**, *2*, 6–18.
10. Yadykin, I.; Lototsky, V.; Bakhtadze, N.; Maximov, E.; Nikulina, I. Soft Sensors of Power Systems Stability Based on Predictive Models of Dynamic Discrete Bilinear Systems. *IFAC PapersOnLine* **2018**, *51*, 897–902. [CrossRef]
11. Hauksdóttir, S.; Sigurðsson, S.P. The continuous closed form controllability Gramian and its inverse. In Proceedings of the 2009 American Control Conference Hyatt Regency Riverfront, St. Louis, MO, USA, 10–12 June 2009; pp. 5345–5351.
12. Sauer, P.W.; Pai, M.A. *Power System Dynamics and Stability*; Printice Hall: New Jersey, NJ, USA, 1998.
13. Ugwuanyi, N.S.; Kestelyn, X.; Marinescu, B.; Thomas, O. Power System Nonlinear Modal Analysis Using Computationally Reduced Normal Form Method 4. *Energies* **2020**, *13*, 1249. [CrossRef]
14. Gibbard, M.J.; Pourbeick, P.; Vowless, D.J. *Small Signal Stability, Control and Dynamic Performance of Power Systems*; University Adelaide Press: Adelaide, Australia, 2015.
15. Voropai, N.I.; Tomin, N.V.; Sidorov, D.N.; Kurbatsky, V.G.; Panasetsky, D.A.; Zhukov, A.V.; Efimov, D.N.; Osak, A.B. A suite of intelligent tools for early detection and prevention of blackouts in power interconnections. *Autom. Remote Control.* **2018**, *79*, 1741–1755. [CrossRef]
16. Garofalo, F.; Iannelli, L.; Vasca, F. Participation Factors and their Connections to Residues and Relative Gain Array. *IFAC Proc. Vol.* **2002**, *35*, 125–130. [CrossRef]
17. Faddeev, D.K.; Faddeeva, V.N. *Computational Methods of Linear Algebra*; Freeman: San-Francisco, CA, USA, 2016.
18. Bahtadze, N.; Yadykin, I. Discrete Predictive Models for Stability Analysis of Power Supply Systems. *Mathematics* **2020**, *8*, 1943. [CrossRef]
19. Mellodge, P. *A Practical Approach to Dynamical Systems for Engineers*; Elsevier: Oxford, UK, 2016.
20. Benner, P.; Breiten, T. Krylov-Subspace Based Model Reduction of Nonlinear Circuit Models Using Bilinear and Quadratic-Linear Approximations. In *Progress in Industrial Mathematics at ECMI 2010. Mathematics in Industry*; Günther, M., Bartel, A., Brunk, M., Schöps, S., Striebel, M., Eds.; Springer: Berlin/Heidelberg, Germany, 2012.
21. Golpîra, H.; Messina, A.R.; Bevrani, H. Emulation of Virtual Inertia to Accommodate Higher Penetration Levels of Distributed Generation in Power Grids. *IEEE Trans. Power Syst.* **2019**, *34*, 3384–3394. [CrossRef]
22. Hamzi, B.; Abed, E.H. Local modal participation analysis of nonlinear systems using Poincare linearization. *Nonlinear Dyn.* **2020**, *99*, 803–811. [CrossRef]
23. Häger, U.; Rehtanz, C.; Voropai, N. (Eds.) *Monitoring, Control and Protection of Interconnected Power Systems*; Springer: Berlin/Heidelberg, Germany, 2014.
24. Siu, T.; Schetzen, M. Convergence of Volterra series representation and BIBO stability of bilinear systems. *Int. J. Syst. Sci.* **1991**, *22*, 2679–2684. [CrossRef]

25. Shaker, H.R.; Takavori, M. Generalized Hankel Interaction Index Array for Control Structure Selection for Discrete-Time MIMO Bilinear Processes and Plants. In Proceedings of the 2014 IEEE 53rd Annual Conference on Decision and Control (CDC), Los Angeles, CA, USA, 15–17 December 2014; pp. 3149–3154.
26. Sidorov, D.; Muftahov, I.; Tomin, N.; Karamov, D.; Panasetsky, D.; Dreglea, A.; Liu, F.; Foley, A. Dynamic Analysis of Energy Storage With Renewable and Diesel Generation Using Volterra Equations. *IEEE Trans. Ind. Inform.* **2020**, *16*, 3451–3459. [CrossRef]
27. Iskakov, A.B.; Yadykin, I.B. Lyapunov modal analysis and participation factors applied to small-signal stability of power systems. *Automatica* **2021**, *132*, 109814. [CrossRef]
28. Lubbok, J.; Bansal, V. Multidimensional Laplace transforms for solution of nonlinear equation. *Proc. IEEE* **1969**, *116*, 2075–2082. [CrossRef]
29. Vapnik, V.N. *The Nature of Statistical Learning Theory*; Springer: Berlin, Germany, 1995.
30. Shaffer, J.P. The Gauss-Markov Theorem and random regressors. *Am. Stat.* **1991**, *45*, 269–273. [CrossRef]
31. Moore, E. On the reciprocal of the general algebraic matrix. *Bull. Am. Math. Soc.* **1920**, *26*, 394–395.
32. Penrose, R. A generalized inverse for matrices. *Proc. Camb. Philos. Soc.* **1955**, *51*, 406–413. [CrossRef]
33. Polyak, B.; Shcherbakov, P. *Robust Stability and Control*; Nauka: Moscow, Russia, 2002. (In Russian)
34. Bakhtadze, N.; Maximov, E.; Maximova, N. Digital Identification Algorithms for Primary Frequency Control in Unified Power System. *Mathematics* **2021**, *9*, 2875. [CrossRef]

 *mathematics*

Article

Maximum-Likelihood-Based Adaptive and Intelligent Computing for Nonlinear System Identification

Hasnat Bin Tariq [1], Naveed Ishtiaq Chaudhary [1], Zeshan Aslam Khan [1], Muhammad Asif Zahoor Raja [2,*], Khalid Mehmood Cheema [3] and Ahmad H. Milyani [4]

[1] Department of Electrical Engineering, International Islamic University, Islamabad 44000, Pakistan; hasnat.msee143@iiu.edu.pk (H.B.T.); naveed.ishtiaq@iiu.edu.pk (N.I.C.); zeshan.aslam@iiu.edu.pk (Z.A.K.)
[2] Future Technology Research Center, National Yunlin University of Science and Technology, 123 University Road, Section 3, Douliou, Yunlin 64002, Taiwan
[3] School of Electrical Engineering, Southeast University, Nanjing 210096, China; kmcheema@seu.edu.cn
[4] Department of Electrical and Computer Engineering, King Abdulaziz University, Jeddah 21589, Saudi Arabia; ahmilyani@kau.edu.sa
* Correspondence: rajamaz@yuntech.edu.tw

Citation: Tariq, H.B.; Chaudhary, N.I.; Khan, Z.A.; Raja, M.A.Z.; Cheema, K.M.; Milyani, A.H. Maximum-Likelihood-Based Adaptive and Intelligent Computing for Nonlinear System Identification. *Mathematics* **2021**, *9*, 3199. https://doi.org/10.3390/math9243199

Academic Editors: Natalia Bakhtadze, Igor Yadykin, Andrei Torgashov and Nikolay Korgin

Received: 11 November 2021
Accepted: 9 December 2021
Published: 11 December 2021

Abstract: Most real-time systems are nonlinear in nature, and their optimization is very difficult due to inherit stiffness and complex system representation. The computational intelligent algorithms of evolutionary computing paradigm (ECP) effectively solve various complex, nonlinear optimization problems. The differential evolution algorithm (DEA) is one of the most important approaches in ECP, which outperforms other standard approaches in terms of accuracy and convergence performance. In this study, a novel application of a recently proposed variant of DEA, the so-called, maximum-likelihood-based, adaptive, differential evolution algorithm (ADEA), is investigated for the identification of nonlinear Hammerstein output error (HOE) systems that are widely used to model different nonlinear processes of engineering and applied sciences. The performance of the ADEA is evaluated by taking polynomial- and sigmoidal-type nonlinearities in two case studies of HOE systems. Moreover, the robustness of the proposed scheme is examined for different noise levels. Reliability and consistent accuracy are assessed through multiple independent trials of the scheme. The convergence, accuracy, robustness and reliability of the ADEA are carefully examined for HOE identification in comparison with the standard counterpart of the DEA. The ADEA achieves the fitness values of 1.43×10^{-8} and 3.46×10^{-9} for a population size of 80 and 100, respectively, in the HOE system identification problem of case study 1 for a 0.01 nose level, while the respective fitness values in the case of DEA are 1.43×10^{-6} and 3.46×10^{-7}. The ADEA is more statistically consistent but less complex when compared to the DEA due to the extra operations involved in introducing the adaptiveness during the mutation and crossover. The current study may consider the approach of effective nonlinear system identification as a step further in developing ECP-based computational intelligence.

Keywords: adaptive differential evolution; evolutionary computing; Hammerstein; nonlinear system identification

1. Introduction

1.1. Background and Motivation

System identification or parameter estimation involves the approximation of unknown variables of the system, and this concept provides the foundation for solving different engineering, science and technology problems [1]. Most real-time systems are nonlinear and complex in nature. There are many applications for nonlinear systems in science and engineering, such as the inverted pendulum system [2], motion control of a motor driven robot [3], average dwell-time switching [4], tail-control missile system [5], and weather station systems [6].

Nonlinear systems can be described through different nonlinear models, including the Volterra series [7], Wiener series [8], NARMAX model [9], Wiener model [10–12] and Hammerstein model [13], etc. Researchers revealed the strong relations between different nonlinear models and the Volterra series [14]. Sidorov et al. contributed significantly in the theory and applications of Volterra equations by proposing different methods [15–17] and exploring the applications in power system operations and energy storage systems [18]. The Volterra series can also represent the Hammerstein model, and Kibangou et al. [19] described Hammerstein model through Volterra series representation and identified the coefficients of the Hammerstein model using the Volterra series. The Hammerstein model has a simpler structure with easier identification than the Volterra series [20]. Therefore, the Hammerstein model is often used to represent a wide class of nonlinear systems [21–24].

The Hammerstein structure, presented in Figure 1, belongs to a class of input nonlinear systems (INL) where a nonlinear block is cascaded with a linear block. Different local and global search algorithms were proposed for the identification of INL models. Local search algorithms are easy to implement but prone to become stuck in local minima. Local search algorithms include the key term separation technique for the parameter estimation of the Hammerstein-controlled autoregressive system [25]; impulse response, constrained, least-square support vector machine modeling for multiple-input and multiple-output Hammerstein system identification [26]; fractional calculus-based adaptive techniques [27,28]; and the parameter estimation problems of input-nonlinear-output error autoregressive systems, based on the key variable separation technique and the auxiliary model-based identification [29], whereas global search techniques effectively handle the local minima issues. The global search methods based on evolutionary and swarm optimization heuristics are effectively applied for the parameter estimation of different-input nonlinear systems, such as genetic algorithms, which are used for the parameter estimation of nonlinear, Hammerstein-controlled autoregressive systems [30]. Meta-heuristic computing techniques are used for the parameter estimation of Hammerstein-controlled auto-regressive, moving-average systems using differential evolution, genetic algorithms, pattern searches and simulated annealing algorithms [31]. Evolutionary computational heuristics are presented for the parameter estimation problem of nonlinear Hammerstein-controlled, auto-regressive systems through a global search competency of the backtracking search algorithm, differential evolution, and genetic algorithms [32]. The neural networks and fuzzy-logic-based, computational, intelligent approaches are also used to solve complex system identification problems [33–37].

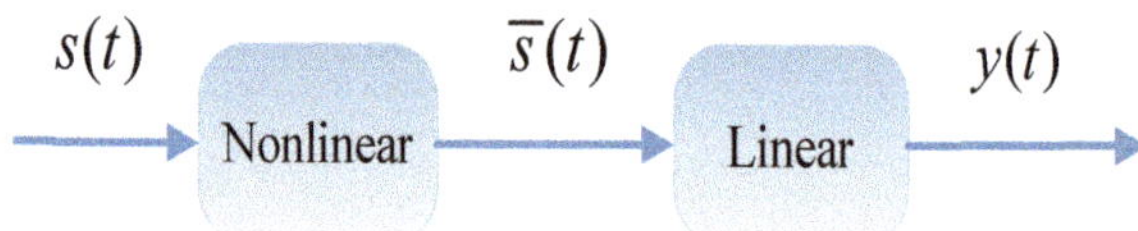

Figure 1. Block Diagram of INL systems.

The DEA was also effectively applied to INL systems, and it showed better results than its standard counterparts [38]. Recently, a new variant of the DEA called the maximum-likelihood-based adaptive DEA (ADEA) was proposed [39] for linear systems. The ADEA showed an improved performance compared to the standard DAE in terms of convergence speed and accuracy. The increasing complexity of nonlinear systems requires a continuous search for more accurate and reliable computing algorithms. Thus, the enhanced performance of the DEA and ADEA inspired authors to investigate the behavior of these algorithms for effective INL system identification.

1.2. Objectives and Contribution

In this study, the performance of the DEA and ADEA in terms of correctness, robustness, and convergence, is examined for different nonlinearities, as well as noise levels, in INL systems. The most important contributions of this study are as follows:

- A novel application of the evolutionary computing paradigm through maximum-likelihood-based adaptive, differential, evolution algorithm, ADEA, is explored for efficient optimization in nonlinear system identification.
- The ADEA is developed by introducing the concept of adaptiveness in the mutation and crossover operators of the standard DEA approach.
- The convergence, accuracy and robustness analyses of the ADEA are conducted for different types of nonlinearities and noise levels considered in two case studies of nonlinear systems.
- The reliability of the ADEA is tested in comparison with the standard counterpart of the DEA through executing multiple independent executions of both schemes.
- The ADEA is statistically more consistent than the DEA but less complex due to the extra operations involved in introducing the adaptiveness during the mutation and crossover.

1.3. Paper Outline

The rest of the paper is presented as follows: the INL-based system model of the Hammerstein output error (HOE) structure is given in Section 2. The differential evolution based proposed schemes are presented in Section 3. The simulation results for two case studies of HOE systems are provided in Section 4. The main conclusions and some future research directions are listed in Section 5.

2. Mathematical Model of HOE Systems

Figure 2 shows the block diagram of the HOE model [40].

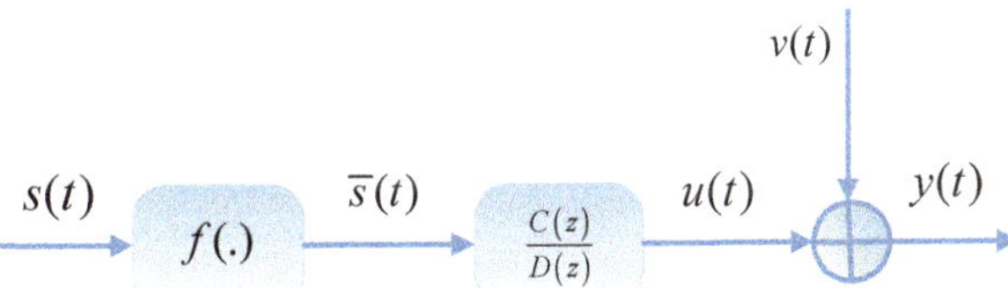

Figure 2. Mathematical structure of HOE system.

The input–output relation of HOE system in Figure 2 is represented as:

$$y(t) = u(t) + v(t) \tag{1}$$

where $y(t)$ represents the systems' output, $v(t)$ denotes the additive noise, and $u(t)$ denotes noise-free output, defined as:

$$u(t) = \frac{C(z)}{D(z)}\,\overline{s}(t) \tag{2}$$

$\overline{s}(t)$ shows the nonlinear block's output and is defined as a nonlinear function of the system input $s(t)$ with a known basis: $\gamma_1,\ \gamma_2, \ldots,\ \gamma_m$,

$$\overline{s}(t) = f(s(t)) = e_1\gamma_1(s(t)) + e_2\gamma_2(s(t)) + \ldots + e_m\gamma_m(s(t)) \tag{3}$$

or:

$$\overline{s}(t) = \sum_{j=1}^{m} e_j\gamma_j(s(t)) \tag{4}$$

Substituting (3) in (2) yields:

$$u(t) = \frac{C(z)}{D(z)}e_1\gamma_1(s(t)) + e_2\gamma_2(s(t)) + \cdots + e_m\gamma_m(s(t)) \tag{5}$$

where $D(z)$ and $C(z)$ represents the polynomials with shifting operator as: $z^{-1}[z^{-1}\,y(t) = y(t-1)]$

$$D(z) = 1 + d_1 z^{-1} + d_2 z^{-2} + \ldots + d_n z^{-n}$$
$$C(z) = c_1 z^{-1} + c_2 z^{-2} + \cdots + c_n z^{-n} \tag{6}$$

The output of the HOE can be expressed in terms of information and parameter vectors, where the information vector containing the input and output delay terms is denoted by $w(t)$ and the corresponding parameter vector of the HOE is defined as [40]:

$$\theta = [d, c, e]^{\mathrm{T}} \epsilon \mathcal{R}^{n_0}$$

where $n_0 = 2n + m$ and the variables in the parameter vector are:

$$d = [d_1, d_2, \ldots\ldots\ldots\ldots d_n]^{\mathrm{T}} \epsilon \mathcal{R}^n$$

$$c = [c_1, c_2, \ldots\ldots\ldots\ldots c_n]^{\mathrm{T}} \epsilon \mathcal{R}^n$$

$$e = [e_1, e_2, \ldots\ldots\ldots\ldots e_m]^{\mathrm{T}} \epsilon \mathcal{R}^m$$

The block diagram of the identification of the nonlinear system modelled through the block-oriented HOE structure shown in Figure 2, by using the proposed evolutionary algorithms, is shown in Figure 3. The objective is to minimize the error $z(t)$ between the desired response and the estimated response by exploiting the proposed evolutionary computing approach, such that $y(t)$ approaches $\hat{y}(t)$.

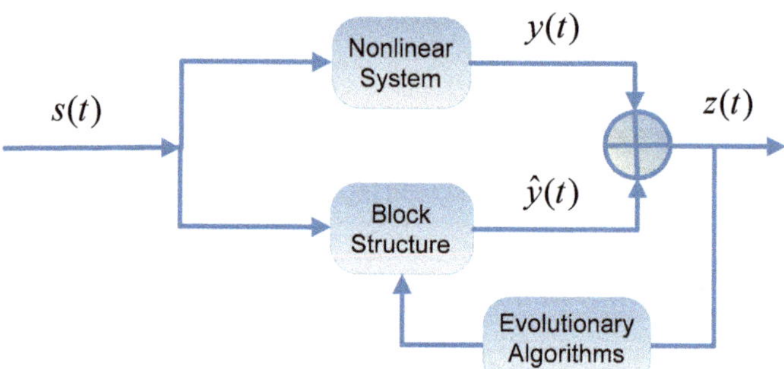

Figure 3. Identification model of nonlinear systems.

3. Proposed Methodology

In this section, the proposed methodology based on the DEA and ADEA with maximum-likelihood criteria are presented for the identification of the HOE system given in Section 2.

3.1. Differential Evolution Algorithm (DEA)

The DEA is one of the most broadly exploited algorithms in ECP, developed by Rainer Stron and Kenneth Price in 1995 [41]. This is a population-based algorithm which has the ability to solve global optimum problems. Due to its usefulness and efficiency, this algorithm is applied to various problems, such as the parameter estimation of Hammerstein control autoregressive systems [38], deep belief network [42], effective long short-term memory for electricity price prediction [43], parameter estimation of solar cells [44], effective electricity energy consumption forecasting using an echo state network [45]. In this study, a recently introduced maximum-likelihood-based adaptive DEA is exploited for HOE identification and the maximum-likelihood-based DEA is used for the purpose of comparison [39]. The flowchart describing the main steps of the DEA is presented in Figure 4.

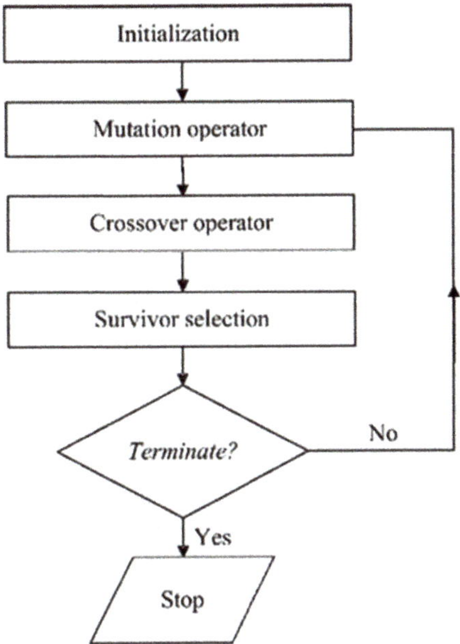

Figure 4. Flowchart of the DEA.

3.2. Adaptive Differential Evolution Algorithm (ADEA)

Different variants of the DEA are proposed through introducing the adaptivity in the process of mutation and crossover. These adaptive DEA variants are effectively exploited to solve many nonlinear problems, such as those involving photovoltaic models and other optimization problems [46–54]. The main steps of the adaptive DEA are similar to the simple DEA that starts from population initialization, mutation, crossover, selection and then termination. The only aspect which differs is the adaptiveness factor of both the mutation and crossover processes. Recently, a maximum-likelihood-criterion-based adaptive DEA, i.e., ADEA, was proposed, where the fitness value is calculated by the maximum-likelihood-criterion function [39]. In ADEA, the values of mutation and crossover process change automatically according to the generation (T). The pseudocode of the ADEA is presented in Algorithm 1, whereas the stepwise mechanism involved in the learning of the ADEA is as follows:

Step 1. Initialization:

Set the generation t = 1 and set the initial population $P_{i,0}$.

Given the population size Np, the mutation Factor F and the maximum generation T.

Step 2. Data Collection:

Collect the calculated data $\{w_i\,(1),\, w_i\,(2),\, \ldots,\, w_i\,(N)\}$ and $\{y_i\,(1),\, y_i\,(2),\, \ldots,\, y_i\,(N)\}$.

Step 3. Adaptive Mutation Operation:

Calculate the mutation vector $V_{i.a,t}$ using $L = \exp(1 - \frac{T}{T+1-t})$; AMF $= F \cdot 2^L$;

$V_{i.a,t} = p_{i.X1,t-1} + \text{AMF} \cdot (p_{i.X2,t-1} - p_{i.X3,t-1})$;

Step 4. Adaptive Crossover Operation:

Read $V_{i.a,j,t}$ from mutation vector $V_{i.a,t} = [V_{i.a,1,t},\, V_{i.a,2,t},\, \ldots,\, V_{i.a,D,t}]^{T}$; and read $p_{i.a,j,t-1}$ from target vector $p_{i.a,t-1} = [p_{i.a,1,t-1},\, p_{i.a,2,t-1},\, \ldots,\, p_{i.a,D,t-1}]^{T}$; to create the crossover vector $U_{i.a,t}$.

For t = 1, the adaptive crossover probability Pc will be Pc $= \frac{1+\cos(t)}{2}$; and for t = 2l the adaptive crossover probability Pc will be Pc $= \frac{1+\cos(t-1)}{2}$;

Step 5. Selection Procedure:

Compute the maximum-likelihood criterion function of $\boldsymbol{U}_{i.a,t}$ and $\boldsymbol{p}_{i.a,t-1}$ using the equations:

$$J(\boldsymbol{U}_{i.a,t}) = \tfrac{1}{N} \sum_{t=1}^{N} \left[\boldsymbol{y}_i(t) - \boldsymbol{w}_i^T(t)\boldsymbol{U}_{i.a,t}\right]^2; \; J(\boldsymbol{p}_{i.a,t-1}) = \tfrac{1}{N} \sum_{t=1}^{N} \left[\boldsymbol{y}_i(t) - \boldsymbol{w}_i^T(t)\boldsymbol{p}_{i.a,t-1}\right]^2;$$

- Develop the target vector $\boldsymbol{p}_{i.a,t}$.

Step 6. Optimal Target Vector:

- Compute the optimal target vector $\boldsymbol{p}_{i.best,t}$.
- Using equations $J(\boldsymbol{p}_{i.a,t}) = \tfrac{1}{N} \sum_{t=1}^{N} \left[\boldsymbol{y}_i(t) - \boldsymbol{w}_i^T(t)\boldsymbol{p}_{i.a,t}\right]^2; \; \boldsymbol{p}_{i.best,t} = \arg\min_{\boldsymbol{p}_{i.a,t}} J(\boldsymbol{p}_{i.a,t});$

Step 7. Iteration:

- If $t > T$, then let $t := t + 1$ and go back to Step 2; otherwise, obtain the optimal target vector $\boldsymbol{p}_{i.best,t}$.

Algorithm 1 Pseudo-code of the ADEA

Input: Collect data $\{\boldsymbol{w}_i(1), \boldsymbol{w}_i(2), \dots, \boldsymbol{w}_i(N)\}$ and $\{\boldsymbol{y}_i(1), \boldsymbol{y}_i(2), \dots, \boldsymbol{y}_i(N)\}$. Given the population size Np, the mutation factor F and maximum generation T. Let the generation $t = 1$.
Output: $\boldsymbol{p}_{i,best,t}$

(1) **for** $a = 1 : Np$ **do**
(2)   **for** $j = 1 : D$ **do**
(3) $p_{i.a,j,0} = \text{rand}(0, 1)$
(4)   **end**
(5) $p_{i.a,0} = \left[p_{i.a,1,0}, \; p_{i.a,2,0}, \dots, \; p_{i.a,D,0}\right]^T$
(6) **end**

(7) $P_{i,0} = \left[p_{i.1,0}, \; p_{i.2,0}, \dots, \; p_{i.Np,0}\right]^T$
(8) **for** $t = 1 : T$ **do**
(9)   **for** $i = 1 : Np$ **do**
(10) $X1 = \text{randperm}(Np, 1)$
(11)   **while** $X1 = p$ **do**
(12) $X1 = \text{randperm}(Np, 1)$
(13)   **end**
(14)   **X2 = randperm(Np, 1)**
(15)   **while** $X2 = p$ or $X2 = X1$ **do**
(16) $X2 = \text{randperm}(Np, 1)$
(17)   **end**
(18) $X3 = \text{randperm}(Np, 1)$; **while** $X3 = p$ or $X3 = X1$ or $X3 = X2$ **do**
(19) $X3 = \text{randperm}(Np, 1)$
(20)   **end**
(21) $L = \exp\left(1 - \frac{T}{T+1-t}\right)$; $AMF = F \cdot 2^L$; $V_{i.a,t} = p_{i.X1,t-1} + AMF \cdot (p_{i.X2,t-1} - p_{i.X3,t-1})$
(22) **if** $t = 1$ or $t = 2l$ **then**
(23) $Pc = \frac{1+\cos(t)}{2}$
(24) **else**
(25) $Pc = \frac{1+\cos(t-1)}{2}$
(26) **end**
(27) $V_{i.a,t} = \left[V_{i.a,1,t}, \; V_{i.a,2,t}, \dots, \; V_{i.a,D,t}\right]^T$; $p_{i.a,t-1} = \left[p_{i.a,1,t-1}, \; p_{i.a,2,t-1}, \dots, \; p_{i.a,D,t-1}\right]^T$
(28) **for** $j = 1 : D$ **do**
(29)   **if** $\text{rand}(0, 1) \leqslant Pc$ or $j = \text{randperm}(D, 1)$ **then**
(30) $U_{i.a,j,t} = V_{i.a,j,t}$
(31)   **else**
(32) $U_{i.a,j,t} = p_{i.a,j,t-1}$
(33)   **end**
(34) **end**

Algorithm 1 Pseudo-code of the ADEA

(35) $U_{i.a,t} = \left[U_{i.a,1,t}, U_{i.a,2,t}, \ldots, U_{i.a,D,t} \right]^T$

(36) $J(U_{i.a,t}) = \frac{1}{N} \sum_{t=1}^{N} \left[y_i(t) - w_i^T(t) U_{i.a,t} \right]^2$

(37) $J(p_{i.a,t-1}) = \frac{1}{N} \sum_{t=1}^{N} \left[y_i(t) - w_i^T(t) p_{i.a,t-1} \right]^2$

(38) **if** $J(U_{i.a,t}) > J(p_{i.a,t-1})$ **then**

(39) $\qquad p_{i.a,t} = U_{i.a,t}$

(40) **else**

(41) $\qquad p_{i.a,t} = p_{i.a,t-1}$

(42) **end**

(43) $J(p_{i.a,t}) = \frac{1}{N} \sum_{t=1}^{N} \left[y_i(t) - w_i^T(t) p_{i.a,t} \right]^2$

(44) $p_{i.best,t} = arg\ min_{p_{i.a,t}}\ J(p_{i.a,t})$

(45) **End**

---

4. Simulation and Performance Analyses

This section includes the simulation results of two case studies for HOE system identification using DEA and ADEA. The simulations for both algorithms are performed in MATLAB. The identification of HOE systems is performed by considering different noise levels, as well as various sets of generation size and diverse population size, while the results are presented in a variety of convergence graphs and multiple statistical analyses. The input $s(t)$ for this system is taken as a zero mean and unit variance, while noise $v(t)$ is an additive noise. The performance of algorithms in terms of convergence speed, accuracy, robustness and reliability is evaluated through fitness function formulation. The equation for the fitness function is given below:

$$\text{Fitness} = \text{mean}(\mathbf{y} - \hat{\mathbf{y}})^2$$

where $\mathbf{y}$ represents the desired response and $\hat{\mathbf{y}}$ is the estimated response through proposed evolutionary algorithms. The optimal parameter settings for DAE and ADAE technique are presented in Table 1.

Table 1. Parameter settings of DEA and ADEA.

Sr. No.	Type of Parameter	DEA	ADEA
1	Number of variables	8	8
2	Mutation factor	0.25	Adaptive
3	Crossover probability	0.8	Adaptive
4	Lower bound	−2	−2
5	Upper bound	2	2

4.1. Case Study 1

The desired response for case study 1 of the HOE system is obtained through a set of parameters taken in [40]. The performance of the ADEA is assessed by considering two type of nonlinearities and different noise levels in the HOE system. The performances of DEA and ADEA in terms of fitness are initially investigated for the variable size of generations (400, 600, 800) and populations (50, 100, 150). The detailed results with polynomial-type nonlinearity are presented in Table 2. It is observed from the fitness values in Table 2 that, for the given generations size (400, 600, 800), the fitness of both algorithms decreases with the increase in population size. Furthermore, both methods achieved minimum fitness values for largest generation sizes. It is observed that the ADEA showed an improved performance compared to the DEA for almost all generations and population sizes. The best fitness achieved by ADEA for 800 generations with 150 population size is 7.08×10^{-15}.

Table 2. Comparison of DEA and ADEA with respect to generations and population size for polynomial-type nonlinearity in case study 1.

Generations (T)	Population Size (Np)	DEA Fitness	ADEA Fitness
	50	1.32×10^{-4}	2.33×10^{-6}
400	100	2.89×10^{-6}	7.86×10^{-9}
	150	3.41×10^{-10}	6.63×10^{-9}
	50	1.09×10^{-4}	3.44×10^{-7}
600	100	2.44×10^{-7}	4.21×10^{-11}
	150	4.53×10^{-9}	3.33×10^{-12}
	50	5.16×10^{-5}	6.54×10^{-9}
800	100	1.01×10^{-6}	3.24×10^{-14}
	150	2.26×10^{-9}	7.08×10^{-15}

The fitness-based learning curves for different generations and population sizes with polynomial-type nonlinearity are shown in Figure 5. Figure 5a–c represent the learning curves for DEA with different generations and population size, whereas Figure 5d–f denote learning curves for ADEA with variations in generations and population size. Figure 5a–c show that the DEA aachieved a fast and accurate convergence for a large number of generations and population sizes, but a slight difference in convergence is observed for DEA until 100 generations with different populations are reached. Likewise, Figure 5d–f show that the ADEA also accomplished minimum fitness values for more generations and populations.

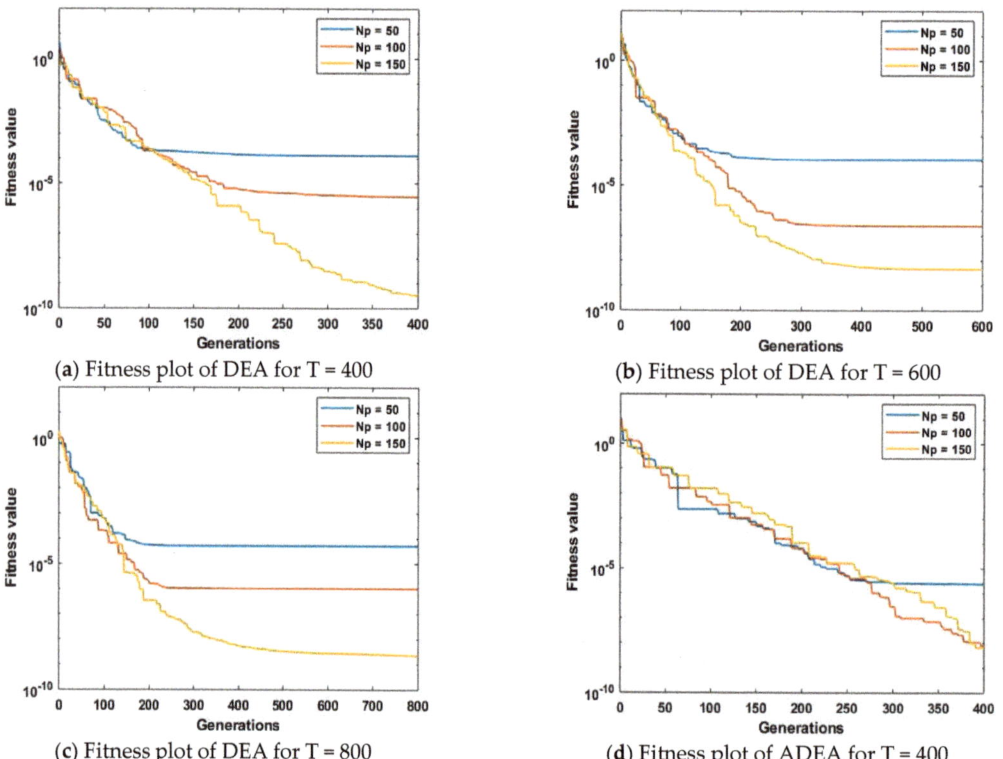

(a) Fitness plot of DEA for T = 400

(b) Fitness plot of DEA for T = 600

(c) Fitness plot of DEA for T = 800

(d) Fitness plot of ADEA for T = 400

Figure 5. *Cont.*

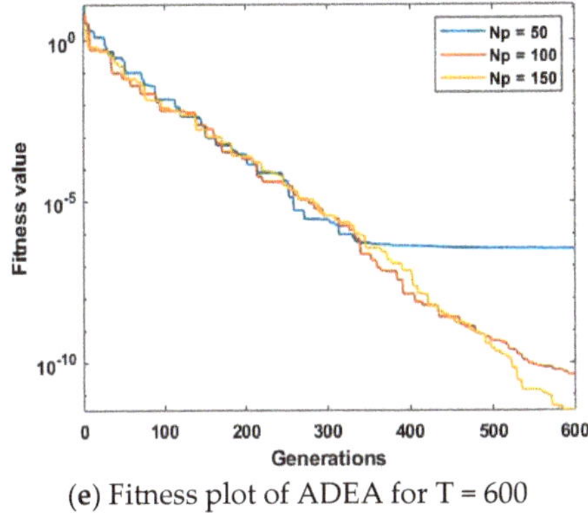

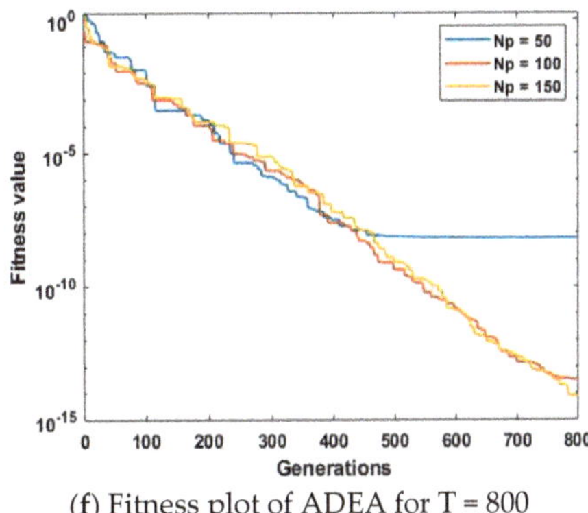

(**e**) Fitness plot of ADEA for T = 600   (**f**) Fitness plot of ADEA for T = 800

Figure 5. Fitness plots of DEA vs. ADEA, with respect to generations and population size for polynomial-type nonlinearities in case study 1.

The performance of DAE and ADAE is further examined for three noise variances (0.09, 0.05, 0.01) with fixed population sizes, (50, 80, 100) and a changing size of generations. To analyze the methods in terms of optimal fitness, the results with polynomial-type nonlinearity are provided in Table 3 for three noise levels, as well as three different populations. It is witnessed from the fitness values in Table 3 that both the DEA and ADEA accomplished a significant performance in terms of fitness for small values of noise variances along with a different number of populations. However, both methods did not perform significantly for higher noise variances with different population sizes. The optimal fitness achieved by both DEA and ADEA with a noise variance of 0.01 and population size of 100 is 2.12×10^{-6} and 8.69×10^{-10}, respectively.

Table 3. Comparison of DEA and ADEA with respect to noise variance and fixed population size for polynomial-type nonlinearity in case study 1.

Noise Variance	Population Size (Np)	DEA Fitness	ADEA Fitness
	50	2.84×10^{-3}	5.02×10^{-3}
0.09	80	4.94×10^{-3}	3.73×10^{-3}
	100	3.71×10^{-3}	4.21×10^{-3}
	50	2.01×10^{-4}	1.13×10^{-5}
0.05	80	1.30×10^{-5}	9.05×10^{-6}
	100	1.44×10^{-5}	8.68×10^{-6}
	50	1.11×10^{-4}	3.03×10^{-8}
0.01	80	8.22×10^{-6}	9.18×10^{-10}
	100	2.12×10^{-6}	8.69×10^{-10}

The learning curves for the fitness achieved with polynomial-type nonlinearity, three noise variances and three population variations are presented in Figure 6. Learning curves for DEA and ADEA are shown in Figures 6a–c and 6d–f, respectively. Figure 6a–c show that the convergence and steady-state performance of the DEA increases with the reducing population size, noise variance and generations and vice versa. Similar behavior was shown by the ADEA for lower noise levels and smaller population sizes. Moreover, ADEA accomplishes optimal fitness for generations, twice that of the DEA.

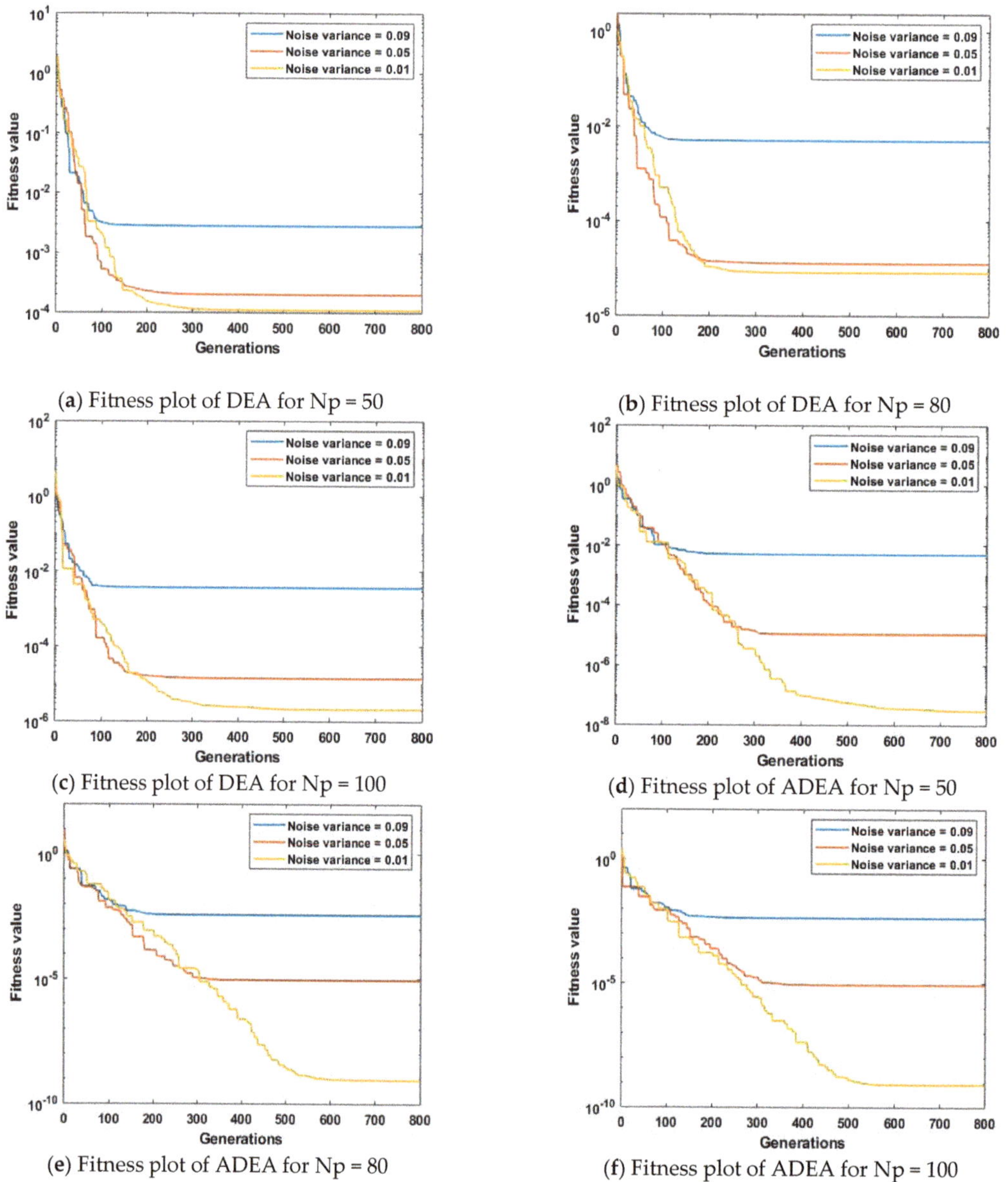

(a) Fitness plot of DEA for Np = 50

(b) Fitness plot of DEA for Np = 80

(c) Fitness plot of DEA for Np = 100

(d) Fitness plot of ADEA for Np = 50

(e) Fitness plot of ADEA for Np = 80

(f) Fitness plot of ADEA for Np = 100

Figure 6. Fitness plots of DEA vs. ADEA with respect to noise variance and population size for polynomial-type nonlinearities in case study 1.

The fitness with regard to MSE for both DEA and ADEA is also evaluated by introducing sigmoidal-type nonlinearity to the HOE system. The investigations are made for different populations (50, 100, 150) and generations (400, 600, 800). The comparison of fitness results between DEA and ADEA for the HOE system under consideration with sigmoidal-type nonlinearity are shown in Table 4. It is seen from the MSE results shown in Table 4 that the performances of DEA and ADEA increase with the increase in population size for various generations (400, 600, 800). The optimal fitness of both algorithms is accomplished for the largest values of generations and populations. The relative performance, in terms of minimum value of fitness achieved by both methods with respect to particular generations and populations, is not consistent. The minimum fitness attained by DEA and ADEA with a maximum number of generations and populations is 6.26×10^{-11} and 3.24×10^{-9}, respectively.

Table 4. Performance comparison of DEA and ADEA with regard to generations and population size for sigmoidal-type nonlinearity in case study 1.

Generations (T)	Population Size (Np)	DEA Fitness	ADEA Fitness
	50	7.14×10^{-5}	1.77×10^{-4}
400	100	9.44×10^{-6}	1.37×10^{-5}
	150	8.89×10^{-7}	1.41×10^{-4}
	50	2.08×10^{-5}	1.18×10^{-4}
600	100	3.82×10^{-7}	3.40×10^{-8}
	150	8.54×10^{-8}	8.18×10^{-9}
	50	1.10×10^{-5}	1.21×10^{-7}
800	100	5.17×10^{-7}	4.63×10^{-8}
	150	6.26×10^{-11}	3.24×10^{-9}

The learning plots representing fitness for sigmoidal-type nonlinearity with variations of generation and population are shown in Figure 7. The fitness curves for DEA are shown in Figure 7a–c and the learning curves for ADEA are given in Figure 7d–f. A similar trend in performance of DEA and ADEA is noticed from Figure 7a–f regarding convergence speed and final estimated accuracy. Both methods exhibit fast convergence for smaller population and generation size. However, they have achieved optimal fitness for bigger values of population and generation.

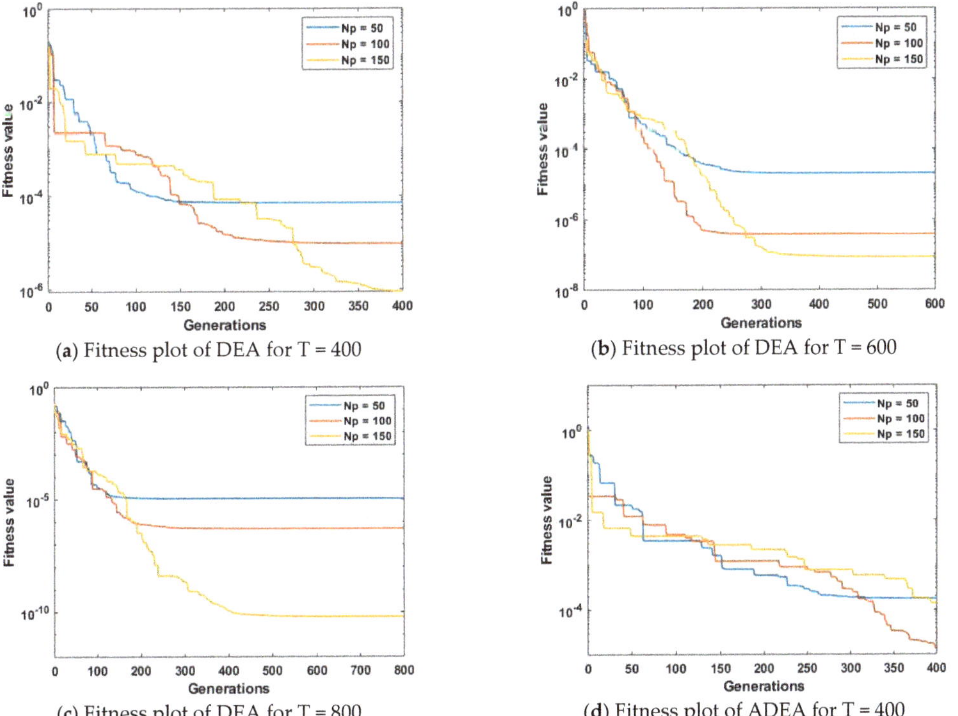

(a) Fitness plot of DEA for T = 400

(b) Fitness plot of DEA for T = 600

(c) Fitness plot of DEA for T = 800

(d) Fitness plot of ADEA for T = 400

Figure 7. *Cont.*

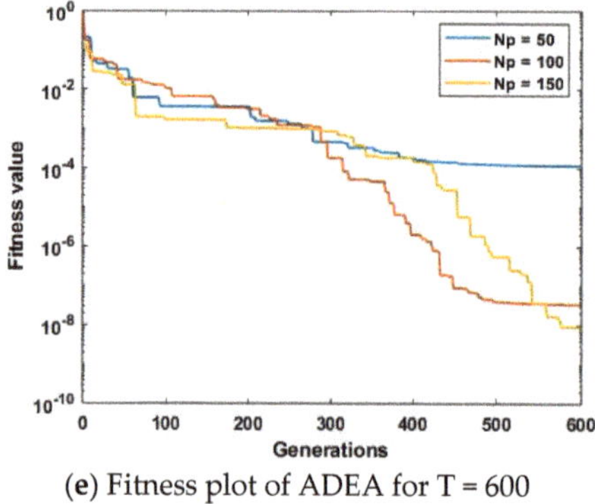

(**e**) Fitness plot of ADEA for T = 600

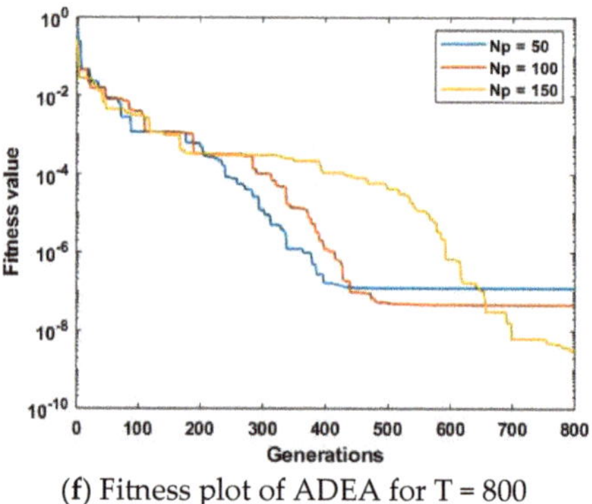

(**f**) Fitness plot of ADEA for T = 800

Figure 7. Fitness curves of DEA vs. ADEA with regard to generations and population size for sigmoidal-type nonlinearities in case study 1.

The behavior of DEA and ADEA methods in terms of minimal fitness achieved with sigmoidal-type nonlinearity for the HOE system is also assessed by fixing the three population sizes, i.e., [50, 80, 100] against three noise variances [0.09, 0.05, 0.01] and different generations set. The optimal fitness attained for different noise levels and population sizes are presented in Table 5. It is observed that both DEA and ADEA performed well for smallest value of noise by obtaining optimal fitness of 1.67×10^{-7} and 3.46×10^{-9}, respectively.

Table 5. Performance comparison of DEA and ADEA with regard to noise variance and population size for sigmoidal-type nonlinearity in case study 1.

Noise Variance	Population Size (Np)	DEA Fitness	ADEA Fitness
	50	5.60×10^{-3}	6.79×10^{-3}
0.09	80	3.60×10^{-3}	5.37×10^{-3}
	100	3.70×10^{-3}	3.82×10^{-3}
	50	5.50×10^{-5}	1.91×10^{-5}
0.05	80	8.68×10^{-6}	1.29×10^{-5}
	100	9.04×10^{-6}	8.27×10^{-5}
	50	1.67×10^{-7}	6.63×10^{-7}
0.01	80	8.74×10^{-6}	1.43×10^{-8}
	100	5.49×10^{-7}	3.46×10^{-9}

Figure 8 shows the fitness-based learning curves with sigmoidal-type nonlinearity for various noise levels, population sizes, and different generations. The learning curves for DEA, shown in Figure 8a–c, demonstrate that DEA performs effectively in terms of convergence rate for low noise variances with the maximum number of populations. DEA achieves a fast convergence by increasing the generation size up to 200, whereas the graphs in Figure 8d–f show a fast convergence rate for ADEA up to 600 generations with low noise levels, e.g., 0.01, and a small population size, e.g., 50.

4.2. Case Study 2

The desired response for case study 2 of the HOE system is obtained through a set of parameters taken in [55]. The performance of the ADEA is assessed by considering two type of nonlinearities and different noise levels in the HOE system.

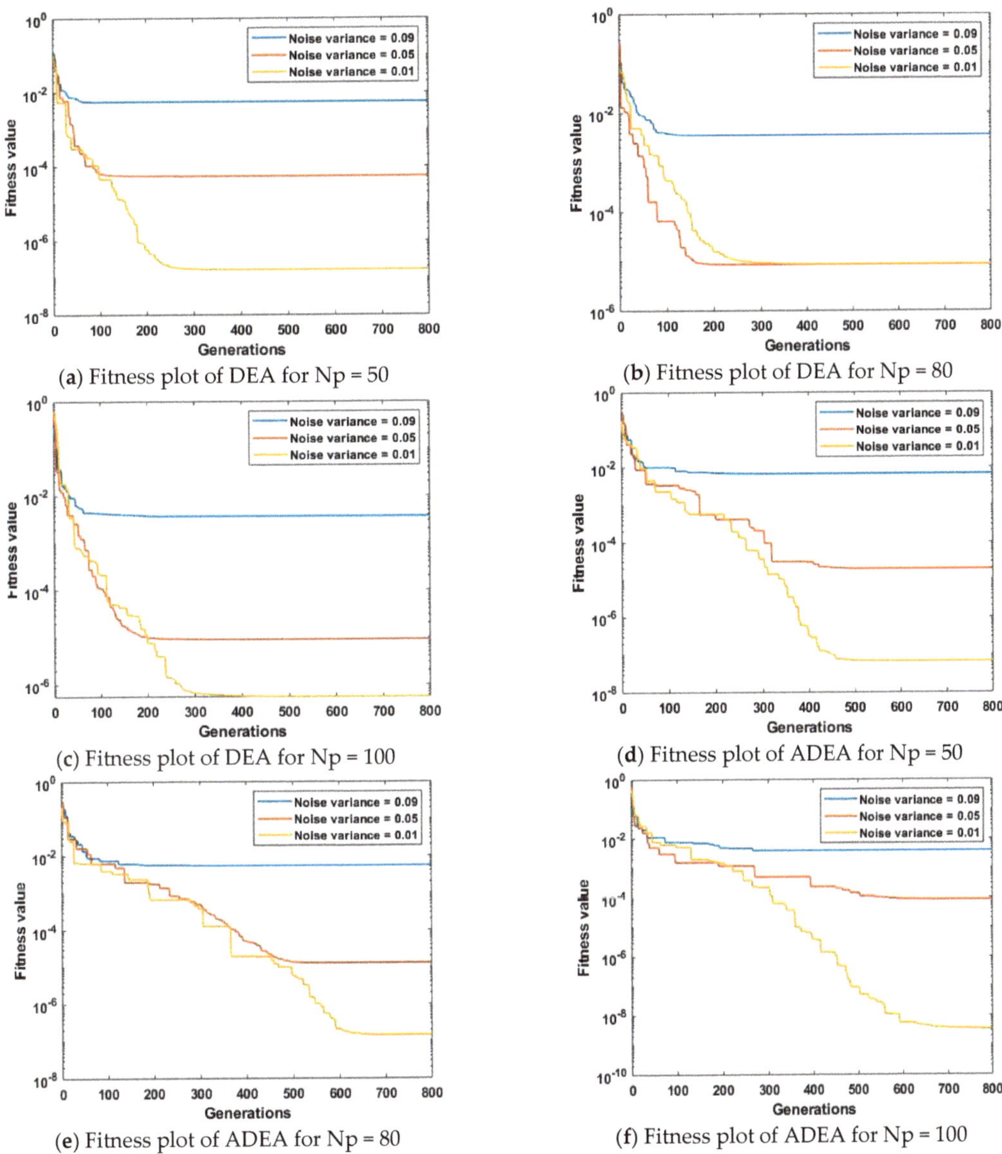

Figure 8. Fitness curves of DEA vs. ADEA with regard to noise variance and population size for sigmoidal-type nonlinearities in case study 1.

In case study 2, the methods DEA and ADEA are assessed for various populations, (50, 100, 150) and generations (400, 600, 800) using two types of nonlinearities: polynomial and sigmoidal. The performance outcomes of DEA and ADEA for polynomial- and sigmoidal-type nonlinearities are shown in Tables 6 and 7 respectively. Tables 6 and 7 show that the performance of both DEA and ADEA for different numbers of generations increases for both types of nonlinearities with an increase in the population size. Moreover, the best performance of both methods is achieved for a larger generation size. For polynomial-type nonlinearity, the minimum fitness values achieved by DEA and ADEA are 6.32×10^{-19}

and 6.84×10^{-12}, respectively, whereas the minimum fitness values accomplished by DEA and ADEA for sigmoidal-type nonlinearity are 7.68×10^{-12} and 3.78×10^{-12}, respectively.

Table 6. Comparison of DEA and ADEA with respect to generations and population size for polynomial-type nonlinearity.

Generations (T)	Population Size (Np)	DEA Fitness	ADEA Fitness
	50	6.60×10^{-5}	5.04×10^{-4}
400	100	3.39×10^{-5}	2.06×10^{-6}
	150	$2.12 \times 10^{-1}1$	9.71×10^{-7}
	50	8.87×10^{-4}	1.54×10^{-3}
600	100	7.26×10^{-7}	9.41×10^{-9}
	150	7.01×10^{-16}	1.69×10^{-9}
	50	1.65×10^{-4}	4.00×10^{-4}
800	100	9.14×10^{-8}	9.87×10^{-12}
	150	6.32×10^{-19}	6.84×10^{-12}

Table 7. Comparison of DEA and ADEA with respect to generations and population size for sigmoidal-type nonlinearity in case study 2.

Generations (T)	Population Size (Np)	DEA Fitness	ADEA Fitness
	50	1.46×10^{-3}	2.51×10^{-5}
400	100	3.18×10^{-5}	4.79×10^{-7}
	150	1.04×10^{-5}	1.90×10^{-7}
	50	2.34×10^{-4}	3.30×10^{-5}
600	100	3.88×10^{-6}	3.67×10^{-7}
	150	4.66×10^{-10}	4.37×10^{-9}
	50	5.55×10^{-4}	5.84×10^{-10}
800	100	2.31×10^{-7}	5.03×10^{-10}
	150	7.68×10^{-12}	3.78×10^{-12}

Figures 9 and 10 show fitness-based learning curves with different populations and generations for polynomial-type and sigmoidal-type nonlinearities, respectively. Figure 9 shows that both DEA and ADEA show fast convergence for a smaller population and generation size, but both methods obtained better steady-state performance for larger population and generation sizes. A similar performance trend was shown by DEA and ADEA in Figure 10 for sigmoidal-type nonlinearity.

To prove the robustness of DEA and ADEA, the performance of both techniques was evaluated for different noise variances (0.09, 0.05, 0.01), variable generation sizes and three population sizes (50, 80, 100). The optimal results achieved by DEA and ADEA with polynomial- and sigmoidal-type nonlinearities for three noise variances and populations are presented in Tables 8 and 9, respectively. It is seen from the fitness values shown in Tables 8 and 9 that both DEA and ADEA obtained optimal fitness values for the smallest value of noise level. Furthermore, the performance of both methods in terms of fitness is increased by increasing the population size for different noise levels. The optimum fitness values achieved by DEA and ADEA with polynomial-type nonlinearity and smallest value of noise (0.01) are 1.03×10^{-6} and 5.02×10^{-10}, respectively. However, the minimum fitness values accomplished by DEA and ADEA with a sigmoidal-type nonlinearity are 1.09×10^{-9} and 1.39×10^{-7}, respectively.

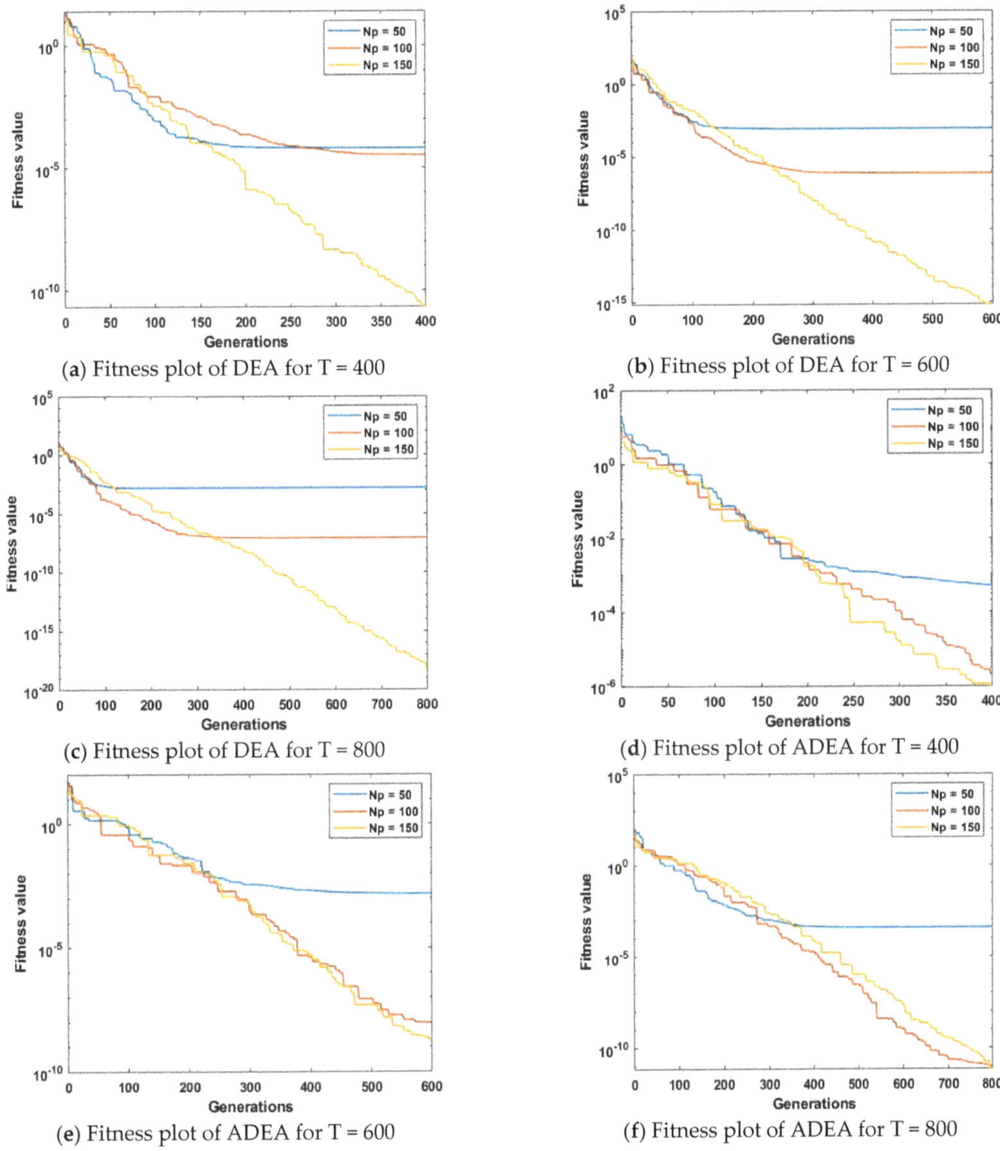

(**a**) Fitness plot of DEA for T = 400

(**b**) Fitness plot of DEA for T = 600

(**c**) Fitness plot of DEA for T = 800

(**d**) Fitness plot of ADEA for T = 400

(**e**) Fitness plot of ADEA for T = 600

(**f**) Fitness plot of ADEA for T = 800

Figure 9. Fitness plots of DEA vs. ADEA with respect to generations and population size for polynomial-type nonlinearities in case study 2.

The fitness-based learning curves for polynomial- and sigmoidal-type nonlinearities with three noise variances, three populations and varying generation sizes are shown in Figures 10 and 11, respectively. Figures 10a–c and 11a–c represent the performance-based learning curves of DEA; Figures 10d–f and 11d–f denote the plots for ADEA with different settings. Figure 9 shows that the convergence rate of both DEA and ADEA with polynomial-type nonlinearity increases by increasing the population size and decreasing the noise level, as well as generation size, while both methods accomplished an optimum steady-state performance for the smallest value of noise, a larger population, and larger generation size. A similar performance was demonstrated by both methods for sigmoidal-type nonlinearity, as shown in Figure 12.

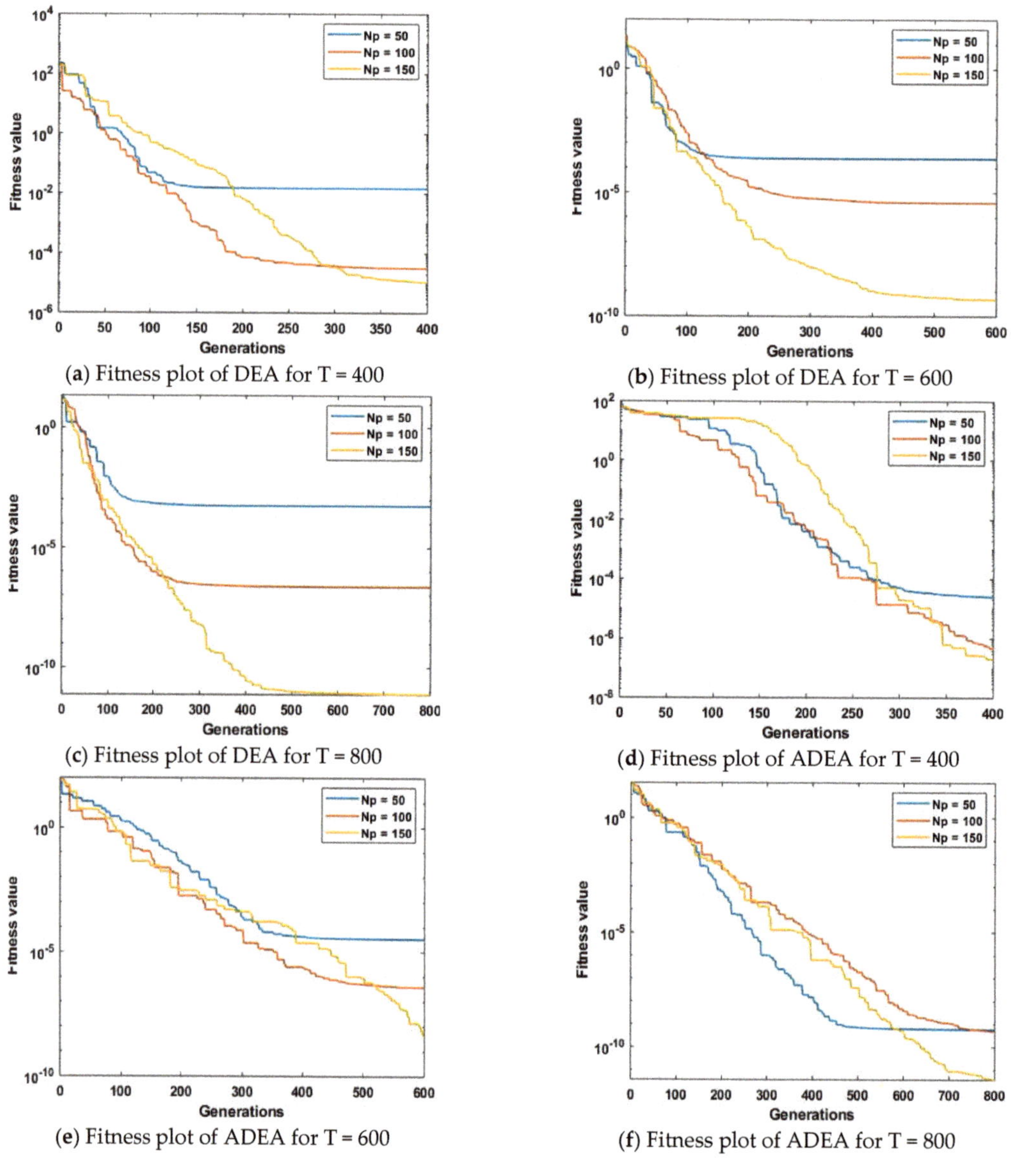

Figure 10. Fitness plots of DEA vs. ADEA with respect to generations and population size for sigmoidal-type nonlinearity in case study 2.

Table 8. Comparison of DEA and ADEA with respect to noise variance and fixed population size for polynomial-type nonlinearity.

Noise Level	Population Size (Np)	DEA Fitness	ADEA Fitness
	50	0.013	4.23×10^{-3}
0.09	80	0.008	2.91×10^{-3}
	100	0.001	1.98×10^{-3}
	50	4.89×10^{-5}	1.05×10^{-5}
0.05	80	8.97×10^{-4}	7.46×10^{-6}
	100	3.57×10^{-5}	5.01×10^{-6}
	50	1.54×10^{-6}	8.66×10^{-8}
0.01	80	1.03×10^{-6}	8.66×10^{-10}
	100	3.40×10^{-6}	5.02×10^{-10}

Table 9. Comparison of DEA and ADEA with respect to noise variance and fixed population size for sigmoidal-type nonlinearities in case study 2.

Noise Variance	Population Size (Np)	DEA Fitness	ADEA Fitness
	50	1.36×10^{-3}	4.60×10^{-3}
0.09	80	3.90×10^{-3}	3.29×10^{-3}
	100	2.70×10^{-3}	1.59×10^{-3}
	50	5.28×10^{-5}	1.14×10^{-5}
0.05	80	8.80×10^{-6}	2.63×10^{-5}
	100	4.61×10^{-6}	3.97×10^{-6}
	50	2.58×10^{-5}	1.54×10^{-7}
0.01	80	1.09×10^{-9}	4.39×10^{-6}
	100	4.20×10^{-7}	1.39×10^{-7}

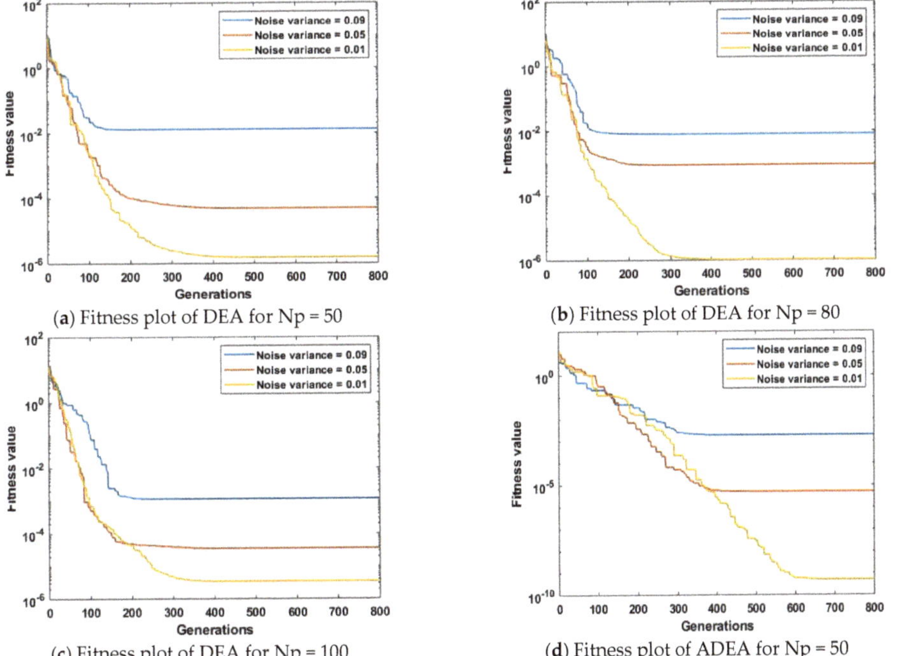

(**a**) Fitness plot of DEA for Np = 50

(**b**) Fitness plot of DEA for Np = 80

(**c**) Fitness plot of DEA for Np = 100

(**d**) Fitness plot of ADEA for Np = 50

Figure 11. *Cont.*

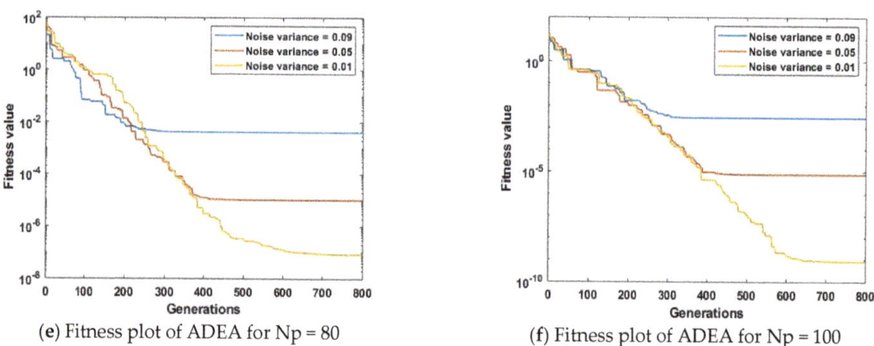

(**e**) Fitness plot of ADEA for Np = 80   (**f**) Fitness plot of ADEA for Np = 100

Figure 11. Fitness plots of DEA vs. ADEA with respect to noise variance and population size for polynomial-type nonlinearities in case study 2.

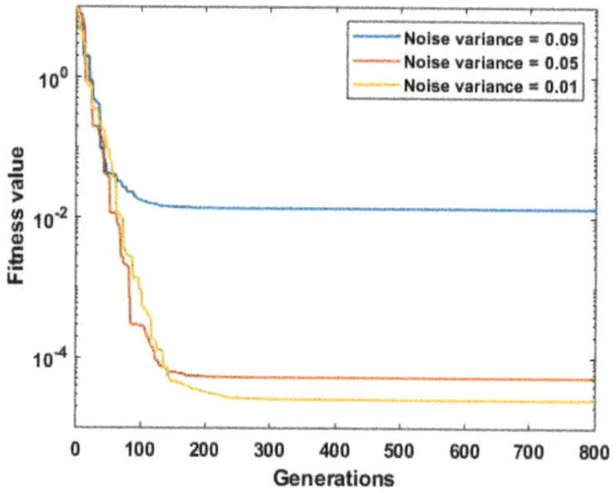

(**a**) Fitness plot of DEA for Np = 50 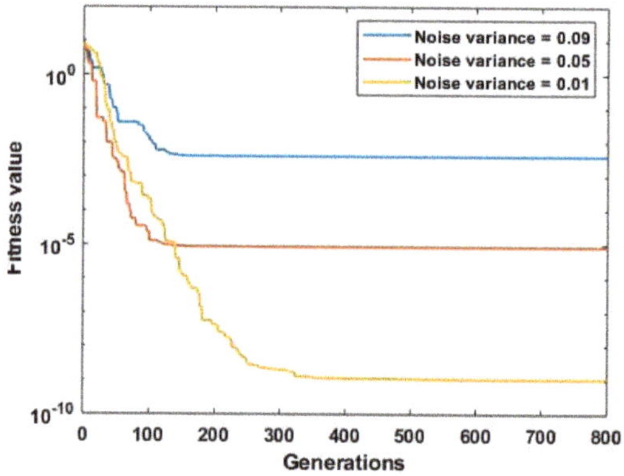   (**b**) Fitness plot of DEA for Np = 80

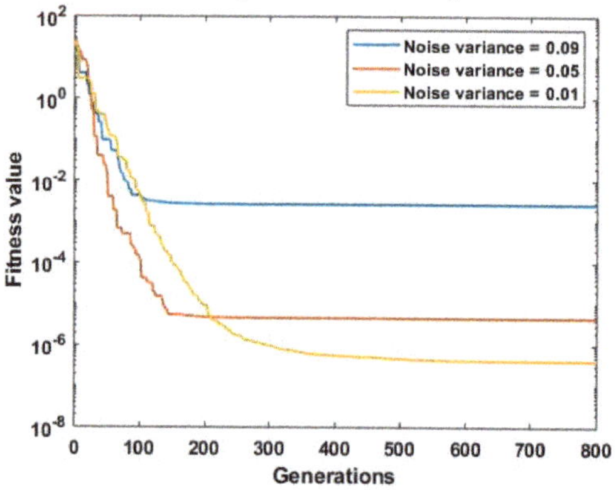

(**c**) Fitness plot of DEA for Np = 100 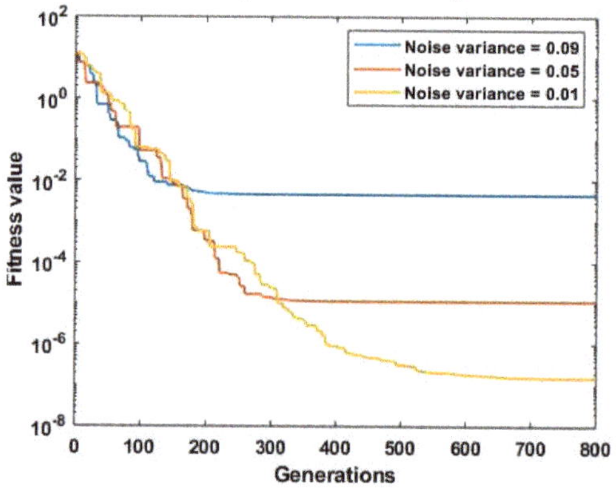   (**d**) Fitness plot of ADEA for Np = 50

Figure 12. *Cont.*

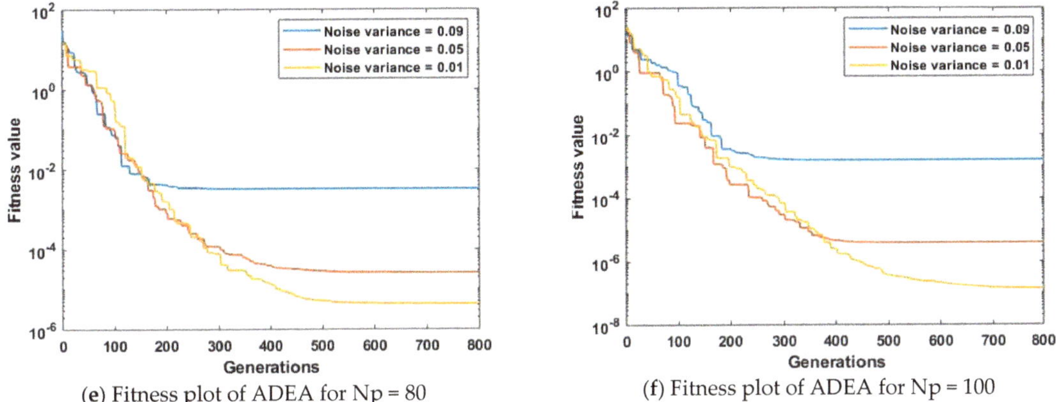

(**e**) Fitness plot of ADEA for Np = 80   (**f**) Fitness plot of ADEA for Np = 100

Figure 12. Fitness plots of DEA vs. ADEA with respect to noise variance and population size for sigmoidal-type nonlinearities in case study 2.

4.3. Statistical Study of DEA and ADEA

The statistical investigations of DEA and ADEA for various numbers of runs, with different noise variances, fixed population sizes, and constant generation sizes are shown in Figure 13. It is witnessed from Figure 13a–c that, for all values of noise variances, ADEA is more convergent than DEA, and the optimal fitness achieved by ADEA is much better than that of DEA for all noise variances. It is also noticed that the performance of both DEA and ADEA only slightly degrades by increasing the noise level.

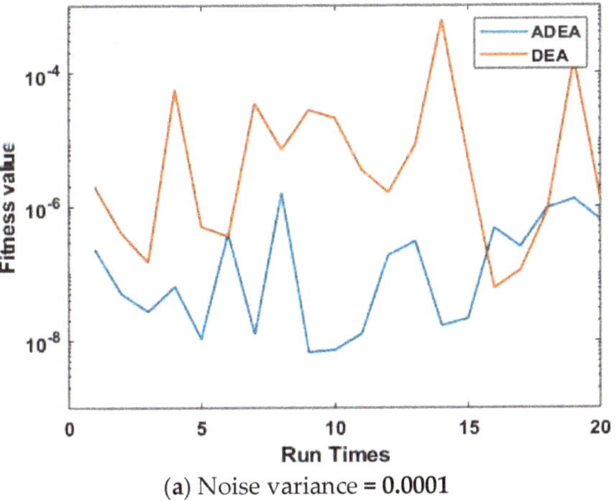

(**a**) Noise variance = 0.0001

Figure 13. *Cont.*

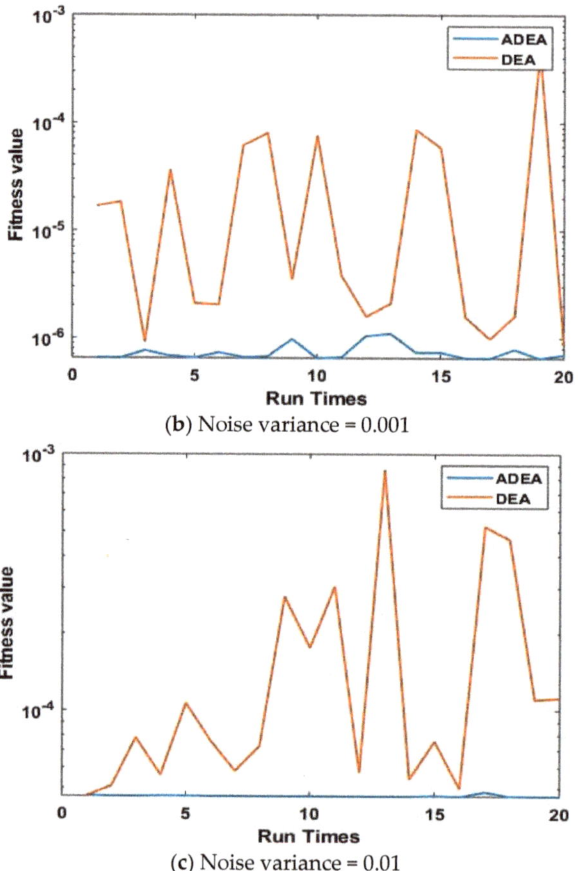

(b) Noise variance = 0.001

(c) Noise variance = 0.01

Figure 13. Statistical analyses plots of DEA and ADEA for Np = 100, T = 500 and multiple noise variances.

It is observed from the detail results presented for the two case studies that the proposed evolutionary algorithms can be effectively utilized for nonlinear systems identification with polynomial- and sigmoidal-type nonlinearities. The proposed evolutionary algorithms identify the unknown HOE system through optimizing the fitness function that makes the difference between the desired and the estimated response approach to zero. However, the optimal fitness value is not required to correspond to the same set of parameters taken to generate the desired response since, in practical applications, only the desired response is available, rather than the set of parameters.

5. Conclusions

The following are the conclusions drawn from the extensive simulation results presented in the last section:

The evolutionary, computing, paradigm-based DEA and ADEA are effectively used for the nonlinear system identification of Hammerstein output error structures. The DEA and ADEA are accurate and convergent for different nonlinearities, based on polynomial- and sigmoidal-type nonlinearities. The robustness of the DEA and ADEA is established for different levels of external disturbances. However, the accuracy of both algorithms decreases by increasing the noise level. The performance of both DEA and ADEA improves by increasing the population size and generation count, but at the cost of a higher computational budget. The reliable inferences regarding the performance of the DEA and ADEA are drawn through statistical analyses based on 20 independent executions of the algorithms. The convergence speed of the ADEA is slightly slower than the DEA due to the crossover and mutation adaptiveness factor. In comparison, the ADEA is more accurate and statistically consistent compared to the DEA, but at the cost of a little more complexity due to the extra operations involved in introducing the adaptiveness during the mutation and crossover steps. The presented study is a step further in the domain of nonlinear system identification through the use of intelligent computing based on evolutionary algorithms.

In future, the application of the proposed methodology can be investigated for solving nonlinear supply energy systems [56], industrial reactive distillation processes [57], power supply systems [58] and delivery systems [59]. Moreover, the other recently introduced evolutionary algorithms [60] and fuzzy predictive control [61–64] can be used for efficient nonlinear system identification.

Author Contributions: Conceptualization, N.I.C. and Z.A.K.; methodology, H.B.T., N.I.C. and M.A.Z.R.; software, H.B.T.; validation, M.A.Z.R. and Z.A.K.; resources, H.B.T., K.M.C. and A.H.M.; writing—original draft preparation, H.B.T.; writing—review and editing, N.I.C., Z.A.K. and M.A.Z.R.; supervision, N.I.C. and Z.A.K.; project administration, K.M.C. and A.H.M.; funding acquisition, K.M.C. and A.H.M. All authors have read and agreed to the published version of the manuscript.

Funding: This research received no external funding.

Institutional Review Board Statement: Not applicable.

Informed Consent Statement: Not applicable.

Data Availability Statement: Not applicable.

Acknowledgments: Not applicable.

Conflicts of Interest: The authors declare no conflict of interest.

References

1. Beck, J.V.; Arnold, K.J. *Parameter Estimation in Engineering and Science*; John Wiley & Sons: Hoboken, NJ, USA, 1977.
2. Su, X.; Xia, F.; Liu, J.; Wu, L. Event-triggered fuzzy control of nonlinear systems with its application to inverted pendulum systems. *Automatica* **2018**, *94*, 236–248. [CrossRef]
3. Yao, J.; Deng, W. Active disturbance rejection adaptive control of uncertain nonlinear systems: Theory and application. *Nonlinear Dyn.* **2017**, *89*, 1611–1624. [CrossRef]
4. Niu, B.; Ahn, C.K.; Li, H.; Liu, M. Adaptive control for stochastic switched nonlower triangular nonlinear systems and its application to a one-link manipulator. *IEEE Trans. Syst. Man Cybern. Syst.* **2017**, *48*, 1701–1714. [CrossRef]
5. Sun, R.; Na, J.; Zhu, B. Robust approximation-free prescribed performance control for nonlinear systems and its application. *Int. J. Syst. Sci.* **2018**, *49*, 511–522. [CrossRef]
6. Chakour, C.; Benyounes, A.; Boudiaf, M. Diagnosis of uncertain nonlinear systems using interval kernel principal components analysis: Application to a weather station. *ISA Trans.* **2018**, *83*, 126–141. [CrossRef]
7. Benamor, A.; Messaoud, H. A new adaptive sliding mode control of nonlinear systems using Volterra series: Application to hydraulic system. *Int. J. Model. Identif. Control* **2018**, *29*, 44–52. [CrossRef]
8. Da Silva, S.; Cogan, S.; Foltête, E. Nonlinear identification in structural dynamics based on Wiener series and Kautz filters. *Mech. Syst. Signal Process.* **2010**, *24*, 52–58. [CrossRef]
9. Billings, S.A. *Nonlinear System Identification: NARMAX Methods in the Time, Frequency, and Spatio-Temporal Domains*; Wiley: West Sussex, UK, 2013.
10. Ławryńczuk, M.; Tatjewski, P. Offset-free state-space nonlinear predictive control for Wiener systems. *Inf. Sci.* **2020**, *511*, 127–151. [CrossRef]
11. Ławryńczuk, M. MPC Algorithms Using Input-Output Wiener Models. In *Nonlinear Predictive Control Using Wiener Models*; Springer: Cham, Switzerland, 2022; pp. 71–141.
12. Ławryńczuk, M. MPC of State-Space Benchmark Wiener Processes. In *Nonlinear Predictive Control Using Wiener Models*; Springer: Cham, Switzerland, 2022; pp. 309–336.
13. Boubaker, S. Identification of nonlinear Hammerstein system using mixed integer-real coded particle swarm optimization: Application to the electric daily peak-load forecasting. *Nonlinear Dyn.* **2017**, *90*, 797–814. [CrossRef]
14. Cheng, C.M.; Peng, Z.K.; Zhang, W.M.; Meng, G. Volterra-series-based nonlinear system modeling and its engineering applications: A state-of-the-art review. *Mech. Syst. Signal Process.* **2017**, *87*, 340–364. [CrossRef]

15. Sidorov, D.N.; Sidorov, N.A. Convex majorants method in the theory of nonlinear Volterra equations. *Banach J. Math. Anal.* **2012**, *6*, 1–10. [CrossRef]
16. Noeiaghdam, S.; Sidorov, D.; Wazwaz, A.M.; Sidorov, N.; Sizikov, V. The Numerical Validation of the Adomian Decomposition Method for Solving Volterra Integral Equation with Discontinuous Kernels Using the CESTAC Method. *Mathematics* **2021**, *9*, 260. [CrossRef]
17. Sidorov, D.; Muftahov, I.; Tynda, A. Numerical solution of fractional Volterra integral equation with piecewise continuous kernel. In *Journal of Physics: Conference Series*; IOP Publishing: Bristol, UK, 2021; Volume 1847, p. 012011.
18. Sidorov, D.; Muftahov, I.; Tomin, N.; Karamov, D.; Panasetsky, D.; Dreglea, A.; Liu, F.; Foley, A. A dynamic analysis of energy storage with renewable and diesel generation using Volterra equations. *IEEE Trans. Ind. Inform.* **2019**, *16*, 3451–3459. [CrossRef]
19. Kibangou, A.Y.; Favier, G. Tensor analysis-based model structure determination and parameter estimation for block-oriented nonlinear systems. *IEEE J. Sel. Top. Signal Process.* **2010**, *4*, 514–525. [CrossRef]
20. Cheng, C.M.; Dong, X.J.; Peng, Z.K.; Zhang, W.M.; Meng, G. Kautz basis expansion-based Hammerstein system identification through separable least squares method. *Mech. Syst. Signal Process.* **2019**, *121*, 929–941. [CrossRef]
21. Holcomb, C.M.; de Callafon, R.A.; Bitmead, R.R. Closed-Loop Identification of Hammerstein Systems with Application to Gas Turbines. *IFAC Proc. Vol.* **2014**, *47*, 493–498. [CrossRef]
22. AitMaatallah, O.; Achuthan, A.; Janoyan, K.; Marzocca, P. Recursive wind speed forecasting based on Hammerstein Auto-Regressive model. *Appl. Energy* **2015**, *145*, 191–197. [CrossRef]
23. Liang, T.; Dinavahi, V. Real-Time System-on-Chip Emulation of Electro-Thermal Models for Power Electronic Devices Via Hammerstein Configuration. *IEEE J. Emerg. Sel. Top. Power Electron.* **2017**, *6*, 203–218. [CrossRef]
24. Le, F.; Markovsky, I.; Freeman, C.T.; Rogers, E. Recursive identification of Hammerstein systems with application to electrically stimulated muscle. *Control. Eng. Pract.* **2012**, *20*, 86–396. [CrossRef]
25. Ding, F.; Chen, H.; Xu, L.; Hayat, T. A hierarchical least squares identification algorithm for Hammerstein nonlinear systems using the key term separation. *J. Frankl. Inst.* **2018**, *355*, 3737–3752. [CrossRef]
26. Castro-Garcia, R.; Agudelo, O.M.; Suykens, J.A. Impulse response constrained LS-SVM modelling for MIMO Hammerstein system identification. *Int. J. Control.* **2018**, *92*, 908–925. [CrossRef]
27. Chaudhary, N.I.; Zubair, S.; Aslam, M.S.; Raja, M.A.Z.; Machado, J.T. Design of momentum fractional LMS for Hammerstein nonlinear system identification with application to electrically stimulated muscle model. *Eur. Phys. J. Plus* **2019**, *134*, 407. [CrossRef]
28. Chaudhary, N.I.; Raja, M.A.Z.; He, Y.; Khan, Z.A.; Machado, J.T. Design of multi innovation fractional LMS algorithm for parameter estimation of input nonlinear control autoregressive systems. *Appl. Math. Model.* **2021**, *93*, 412–425. [CrossRef]
29. Xiong, W.; Ding, F. Iterative identification algorithms for input nonlinear output error autoregressive systems. *Int. J. Control. Autom. Syst.* **2016**, *14*, 140–147.
30. Raja, M.A.Z.; Shah, A.A.; Mehmood, A.; Chaudhary, N.I.; Aslam, M.S. Bio-inspired computational heuristics for parameter estimation of nonlinear Hammerstein controlled autoregressive system. *Neural Comput. Appl.* **2018**, *29*, 1455–1474. [CrossRef]
31. Mehmood, A.; Chaudhary, N.I.; Zameer, A.; Raja, M.A.Z. Novel computing paradigms for parameter estimation in Hammerstein controlled auto regressive auto regressive moving average systems. *Appl. Soft Comput.* **2019**, *80*, 263–284. [CrossRef]
32. Mehmood, A.; Chaudhary, N.I.; Zameer, A.; Raja, M.A.Z. Backtracking search optimization heuristics for nonlinear Hammerstein controlled auto regressive auto regressive systems. *ISA Trans.* **2019**, *91*, 99–113. [CrossRef]
33. Mohammadi Moghadam, H.; Mohammadzadeh, A.; Hadjiaghaie Vafaie, R.; Tavoosi, J.; Khooban, M.H. A type-2 fuzzy control for active/reactive power control and energy storage management. *Trans. Inst. Meas. Control.* **2021**, 01423312211048038. [CrossRef]
34. Tavoosi, J.; Mohammadzadeh, A.; Jermsittiparsert, K. A review on type-2 fuzzy neural networks for system identification. *Soft Comput.* **2021**, *25*, 7197–7212. [CrossRef]
35. Tavoosi, J.; Suratgar, A.A.; Menhaj, M.B.; Mosavi, A.; Mohammadzadeh, A.; Ranjbar, E. Modeling Renewable Energy Systems by a Self-Evolving Nonlinear Consequent Part Recurrent Type-2 Fuzzy System for Power Prediction. *Sustainability* **2021**, *13*, 3301. [CrossRef]
36. Tavoosi, J.; Shirkhani, M.; Abdali, A.; Mohammadzadeh, A.; Nazari, M.; Mobayen, S.; Bartoszewicz, A. A New General Type-2 Fuzzy Predictive Scheme for PID Tuning. *Appl. Sci.* **2021**, *11*, 10392. [CrossRef]
37. Tavoosi, J.; Zhang, C.; Mohammadzadeh, A.; Mobayen, S.; Mosavi, A.H. Medical Image Interpolation Using Recurrent Type-2 Fuzzy Neural Network. *Front. Neuroinformatics* **2021**, *15*, 667375. [CrossRef]
38. Mehmood, A.; Aslam, M.S.; Chaudhary, N.I.; Zameer, A.; Raja, M.A.Z. Parameter estimation for Hammerstein control autoregressive systems using differential evolution. *Signal Image Video Process.* **2018**, *12*, 1603–1610. [CrossRef]
39. Cui, T.; Xu, L.; Ding, F.; Alsaedi, A.; Hayat, T. Maximum likelihood-based adaptive differential evolution identification algorithm for multivariable systems in the state-space form. *Int. J. Adapt. Control. Signal Process.* **2020**, *34*, 1658–1676. [CrossRef]
40. Pouliquen, M.; Pigeon, E.; Gehan, O. Identification scheme for Hammerstein output error models with bounded noise. *IEEE Trans. Autom. Control.* **2015**, *61*, 550–555. [CrossRef]
41. Stron, R.; Price, K. Differential evolution—A simple and efficient adaptive scheme for global optimization over continuous space. *J. Glob. Optim.* **1997**, *11*, 341–359. [CrossRef]
42. Deng, W.; Liu, H.; Xu, J.; Zhao, H.; Song, Y. An improved quantum-inspired differential evolution algorithm for deep belief network. *IEEE Trans. Instrum. Meas.* **2020**, *69*, 7319–7327. [CrossRef]

43. Peng, L.; Liu, S.; Liu, R.; Wang, L. Effective long short-term memory with differential evolution algorithm for electricity price prediction Energy 2018, 162, 1301–1314. *Energy* **2017**, *162*, 1301–1314. [CrossRef]
44. Biswas, P.P.; Suganthan, P.N.; Wu, G.; Amaratunga, G.A.J. Parameter estimation of solar cells using datasheet information with the application of an adaptive differential evolution algorithm. *Renew. Energy* **2019**, *132*, 425–438. [CrossRef]
45. Wang, L.; Hu, H.; Ai, X.-Y.; Liu, H. Effective electricity energy consumption forecasting using echo state network improved by differential evolution algorithm. *Energy* **2018**, *153*, 801–815. [CrossRef]
46. Li, S.; Gu, Q.; Gong, W.; Ning, B. An enhanced adaptive differential evolution algorithm for parameter extraction of photovoltaic models. *Energy Convers. Manag.* **2020**, *205*, 112443. [CrossRef]
47. Peng, Y.; He, S.; Sun, K. Parameter identification for discrete memristive chaotic map using adaptive differential evolution algorithm. *Nonlinear Dyn.* **2021**, 1–13. [CrossRef]
48. Ramli, M.A.M.; Bouchekara, H.R.E.H.; Alghamdi, A.S. Optimal sizing of PV/wind/diesel hybrid microgrid system using multi-objective self-adaptive differential evolution algorithm. *Renew. Energy* **2018**, *121*, 400–411. [CrossRef]
49. Mohamed, A.W.; Suganthan, P.N. Real-parameter unconstrained optimization based on enhanced fitness-adaptive differential evolution algorithm with novel mutation. *Soft Comput.* **2018**, *22*, 3215–3235. [CrossRef]
50. Sakr, W.S.; L-Sehiemy, R.A.E.; Azmy, A.M. Adaptive differential evolution algorithm for efficient reactive power management. *Appl. Soft Comput.* **2017**, *53*, 336–351. [CrossRef]
51. Wang, S.; Li, Y.; Yang, H.; Liu, H. Self-adaptive differential evolution algorithm with improved mutation strategy. *Soft Comput.* **2018**, *22*, 3433–3447. [CrossRef]
52. Wang, S.; Li, Y.; Yang, H. Self-adaptive differential evolution algorithm with improved mutation mode. *Appl. Intell.* **2017**, *47*, 644–658. [CrossRef]
53. Fu, C.M.; Jiang, C.; Chen, G.S.; Liu, Q.M. An adaptive differential evolution algorithm with an aging leader and challengers mechanism. *Appl. Soft Comput.* **2017**, *57*, 60–73. [CrossRef]
54. Mohamed, A.W. Solving large-scale global optimization problems using enhanced adaptive differential evolution algorithm. *Complex Intell. Syst.* **2017**, *3*, 205–231. [CrossRef]
55. Ding, F.; Shi, Y.; Chen, T. Auxiliary model-based least-squares identification methods for Hammerstein output-error systems. *Syst. Control. Lett.* **2007**, *56*, 373–380. [CrossRef]
56. Bakhtadze, N.; Yadykin, I.; Maximov, E.; Maximova, N.; Chereshko, A.; Vershinin, Y. Forecasting the Risks of Stability Loss for Nonlinear Supply Energy Systems. *IFAC-Pap.* **2021**, *54*, 478–483. [CrossRef]
57. Klimchenko, V.; Torgashov, A.; Shardt, Y.A.; Yang, F. Multi-Output Soft Sensor with a Multivariate Filter That Predicts Errors Applied to an Industrial Reactive Distillation Process. *Mathematics* **2021**, *9*, 1947. [CrossRef]
58. Bakhtadze, N.; Yadikin, I. Discrete Predictive Models for Stability Analysis of Power Supply Systems. *Mathematics* **2020**, *8*, 1943. [CrossRef]
59. Bakhtadze, N.; Karsaev, O.; Sabitov, R.; Smirnova, G.; Eponeshnikov, A.; Sabitov, S. Identification models in flexible delivery systems for groupage cargoes. *Procedia Comput. Sci.* **2020**, *176*, 225–232. [CrossRef]
60. Ramos-Pérez, J.M.; Miranda, G.; Segredo, E.; León, C.; Rodríguez-León, C. Application of Multi-Objective Evolutionary Algorithms for Planning Healthy and Balanced School Lunches. *Mathematics* **2021**, *9*, 80. [CrossRef]
61. Mohammadzadeh, A.; Kumbasar, T. A new fractional-order general type-2 fuzzy predictive control system and its application for glucose level regulation. *Appl. Soft Comput.* **2020**, *91*, 106241. [CrossRef]
62. Mosavi, A.; Qasem, S.N.; Shokri, M.; Band, S.S.; Mohammadzadeh, A. Fractional-order fuzzy control approach for photovoltaic/battery systems under unknown dynamics, variable irradiation and temperature. *Electronics* **2020**, *9*, 1455. [CrossRef]
63. Vafaie, R.H.; Mohammadzadeh, A.; Piran, M. A new type-3 fuzzy predictive controller for MEMS gyroscopes. *Nonlinear Dyn.* **2021**, *106*, 381–403. [CrossRef]
64. Qasem, S.N.; Ahmadian, A.; Mohammadzadeh, A.; Rathinasamy, S.; Pahlevanzadeh, B. A type-3 logic fuzzy system: Optimized by a correntropy based Kalman filter with adaptive fuzzy kernel size. *Inf. Sci.* **2021**, *572*, 424–443. [CrossRef]

mathematics

MDPI

Article

On Spectral Decomposition of States and Gramians of Bilinear Dynamical Systems

Alexey Iskakov * and Igor Yadykin

V.A. Trapeznikov Institute of Control Sciences of RAS, 117997 Moscow, Russia; jad@ipu.ru
* Correspondence: isk_alex@mail.ru or iskalexey@gmail.com

Abstract: The article proves that the state of a bilinear control system can be split uniquely into generalized modes corresponding to the eigenvalues of the dynamics matrix. It is also shown that the Gramians of controllability and observability of a bilinear system can be divided into parts (sub-Gramians) that characterize the measure of these generalized modes and their interactions. Furthermore, the properties of sub-Gramians were investigated in relation to modal controllability and observability. We also propose an algorithm for computing the Gramians and sub-Gramians based on the element-wise computation of the solution matrix. Based on the proposed algorithm, a novel criterion for the existence of solutions to the generalized Lyapunov equation is proposed, which allows, in some cases, to expand the domain of guaranteed existence of a solution of bilinear equations. Examples are provided that illustrate the application and practical use of the considered spectral decompositions.

Keywords: bilinear systems; eigenmode decomposition; spectral expansions; generalized Lyapunov equation; Gramians; observability; controllability; small-signal analysis; numerical algorithm

Citation: Iskakov, A.; Yadykin, I. On Spectral Decomposition of States and Gramians of Bilinear Dynamical Systems. *Mathematics* **2021**, *9*, 3288. https://doi.org/10.3390/math9243288

Academic Editor: Jaume Giné

Received: 4 November 2021
Accepted: 10 December 2021
Published: 17 December 2021

Publisher's Note: MDPI stays neutral with regard to jurisdictional claims in published maps and institutional affiliations.

1. Introduction

Monitoring the state of various technical, social, and biological systems using non-linear mathematical models and modern information technology is a widely relied upon trend in the development of modern civilization. An example is the state estimation and control in modern electric power systems. Renewable energy sources and distributed generation, electric vehicles and charging networks, and the increased use of power electronics pose new challenges for the monitoring and controling of complex oscillations in energy systems [1]. New problems require the development of new methods for the analysis of non-linear dynamic systems, including computational methods for their solutions.

Bilinear control systems represent an important class of non-linear systems, which are linear in inputs and states, but they are not linear in both. Research in the field of non-linear and "weakly non-linear" control systems described by the Volterra series dates back more than half a century. In [2], a theory of realization was developed, and structural decompositions of the Gramians of bilinear systems were investigated; furthermore, explicit representations of the Gramian of a bilinear system were obtained in the form of a Volterra series, and the conditions for its convergence were investigated. In [3,4], the multivariate Laplace transform was used to construct a solution for systems with smooth non-linearities. In [5], an iterative solution of the generalized Lyapunov equation was obtained, which was first used to analyze the state of an electric power system. It was shown that a solution to this equation exists if the linear part of the bilinear system is stable, and the input signal and non-linearity matrices are bounded in the norm. In [6], these results were generalized for multiple-input and multiple-output (MIMO) dynamical systems.

Research in the field of bilinear control systems is closely related to the problem of model order reduction (MOR) by constructing an approximating model of a lower dimension. Among the methods for solving this problem, we note balanced truncation, singular decomposition, the Krylov subspace method, optimal methods for the H_2-norm of

Gramians, and hybrid methods. For most of the methods, iterative algorithms for their implementation have been developed, and conditions for the existence and uniqueness of the solution of the corresponding generalized Lyapunov equations have been established [6–9]. In these studies, the squared H_2-norm of Gramians of the bilinear system was used, and its spectral expansions using singular values were obtained. To estimate the error between the full and reduced models, energy functionals were introduced, and the corresponding H_2-norm optimal algorithms for the interpolation of bilinear systems were proposed.

Modal analysis and selective modal analysis are among the main methods for analyzing the stability of electric power systems with small deviations from the steady state. These methods involve identifying dominant weakly stable modes of the power system and are widely used in combination with other linear and non-linear analysis methods [1,10]. To assess bilinear effects in power systems analysis, the technique of normal forms [11], modal series methods [12], and bilinear approximation [13] are used. These methods consider the higher-order terms of the Taylor expansion in the system approximation and use normal Poincaré forms. In [14], a method was proposed for the fast computation of normal forms, considering the interaction of dominant modes. Ref. [15] proposes a hybrid method combining selective modal analysis and Koopman mode decomposition.

In contrast to these methods, in this study, we consider the spectral decomposition, not for the instantaneous dynamics of state variables, but for the Lyapunov functions, which characterize the L_2-norms of variables or signals in the time domain. This approach allows us to consider the non-linear effects associated with the accumulation of influence over time. For linear dynamic systems, Lyapunov functions are usually associated with the controllability and observability Gramians, which characterize the integrated energy of the input and output signals. The concept of Gramians was further generalized and interpreted for deterministic bilinear systems using energy functionals [16]. For linear systems, ref. [7] obtained singular expansions for infinite Gramians of controllability and observability based on the diagonalization of the dynamics matrix. A more general form of the spectral decomposition of Gramians into components (sub-Gramians) corresponding to the individual eigenvalues of the system or their pairwise combinations was proposed in [17,18]. In [19], the spectral expansions for the Gramians of controllability and observability were generalized to the case of bilinear continuous systems.

The purpose of this study is to develop and provide a rationale for the application of the spectral expansions of the Gramians proposed in [19] for the analysis and monitoring of bilinear systems. As the state of a bilinear system is not the sum of eigenmodes as in the linear case, a number of important theoretical questions arise. How should eigenmodes be viewed and interpreted in a bilinear system? What interpretation can be given to the spectral expansions of the Gramians in [19]? What is their connection with the expansion of the Gramians in linear systems?

Main Contribution

As spectral expansions of states of bilinear systems are closely related to the corresponding expansions of states of linear systems, in Section 2, we first consider the concepts of modal controllability and observability for a linear dynamical system. The following new results were obtained: Criteria for modal controllability and observability are proposed (Propositions 3 and 5), and a relation is established between the eigenmodes of the linear system and sub-Gramians of controllability and observability (Propositions 7 and 9).

The main theoretical results are presented in Section 3. We show that the solution of a bilinear system under any control can be split uniquely into generalized modes corresponding to the eigenvalues of the dynamics matrix (Proposition 11). The definitions of sub-Gramians are proposed in a new form, and their relationship with the definitions in [19] are clarified (Property 4). The conditions for the existence of sub-Gramians (Property 1) and their consistency with the concept of sub-Gramians in linear theory (Property 3) are established.

In [19], expressions for sub-Gramians were proposed in the form of solutions to the modal Lyapunov equations. In this study, the same quantities are derived as the sums of squared convolution kernels arising in the Volterra series expansion of the state of the bilinear system. Moreover, it is proved (in Property 4) that if these quantities exist, then for a stable matrix of dynamics, they coincide with the definition in [19]. Although the new definition of sub-Gramians essentially coincides with the definition in [19], it allows us to establish a relation between sub-Gramians and the corresponding generalized modes of a bilinear system, namely, to prove that sub-Gramians characterize some measure of the corresponding generalized eigenmodes and their pairwise scalar products (Proposition 5) under the condition that controls are small enough. From a theoretical point of view, this result provides a conceptual justification for the concept of sub-Gramians for bilinear systems. From the point of view of applications, it allows one to make energy-based estimates of individual generalized modes and their pairwise interactions in the system. Such estimates, in turn, can become the basis for stability analysis and optimal control in bilinear dynamical systems.

Section 4 proposes an iterative algorithm for computing the Gramians and sub-Gramians based on the element-wise computation of the solution matrix on an eigenvector basis. This algorithm is similar to the algorithms in [20]. However, based on the proposed algorithm, a novel criterion for the existence of solutions to the generalized Lyapunov equation is formulated (Theorem 4), which, in some cases, allows the expansion of the domain of guaranteed existence of a solution of bilinear equations. At the end of Section 4, some examples that illustrate the application and practical use of the considered spectral decompositions are presented.

2. Spectral Expansions of Gramians of Linear Systems

2.1. Eigenmode Decompositions of the Dynamics of a Linear System

In this section, we consider the eigen-decomposition of the dynamics of a linear stationary system, which will be required for further presentation. Consider a linear dynamical system of the form

$$\begin{cases} \dot{x} = A\,x + B\,u \\ \quad\; y = C\,x \end{cases},\tag{1}$$

where $x \in \mathbb{R}^n$ is the state vector, and $y \in \mathbb{R}^l$, $u \in \mathbb{R}^m$ are the output signal and control, respectively. A, B, C are real matrices. Suppose that the dynamics matrix A has a simple spectrum $\sigma(A) = \{\lambda_1, \lambda_2, \ldots, \lambda_n\}$.

Proposition 1. *A matrix A with a simple spectrum can be represented as*

$$A = \lambda_1\,R_1 + \lambda_2\,R_2 + \cdots + \lambda_n\,R_n,\tag{2}$$

where R_i are the matrices of residues in the decomposition of the resolvent of matrix A:

$$(Is - A)^{-1} = \frac{R_1}{s - \lambda_1} + \frac{R_2}{s - \lambda_2} + \cdots + \frac{R_n}{s - \lambda_n}.\tag{3}$$

Proof. When all eigenvalues are distinct, the residue matrices of the resolvent of matrix A can be calculated using the normalized right and left eigenvectors as $R_i = u_i v_i^T$ (see [21]). Then, representation (2) directly follows from the eigen decomposition of matrix A. $\square$

From the representation of the residue matrices through the eigenvectors and the orthogonality of the eigenvectors, it follows that the residue matrices R_i satisfy the following the orthogonality property:

$$R_i\,R_j = R_i\,\delta_{ij},\tag{4}$$

where δ_{ij} is the Kronecker delta. Thus, representation (2) of matrix A is *separable* in the sense that all terms in it are orthogonal to each other in accordance with (4). If the matrices R_i of residues are known, then using (2)–(4), one can easily find all the powers of the matrix A

$$A^k = \sum_i \lambda_i^k R_i, \quad k = 0, \pm 1, \pm 2, \ldots, \tag{5}$$

and the summation index here and in the following are assumed to be from one to n. Substituting (5) into the Taylor expansion of the matrix exponent of A, we obtain

$$e^{At} = \sum_i R_i e^{\lambda_i t}. \tag{6}$$

Proposition 2 (Eigenmode decomposition). *Solution, control, and output signal of linear system (1) are separable with respect to the eigenmodes, i.e., there is a representation*

$$x(t) = \sum_i x_i(t), \quad u(t) = \sum_i u_i(t), \quad y(t) = \sum_i y_i(t), \quad \text{where}$$

$$x_i(t) = R_i x(t) = R_i e^{\lambda_i t} x_0 + B e^{\lambda_i t} \int_{t_0}^{t} e^{-\lambda_i \tau} u_i(\tau) d\tau, \tag{7}$$

$$u_i(t) = B^{\#} R_i B u(t), \quad y_i(t) = C x_i(t) = C R_i x(t),$$

$x_0 = x(t_0)$ *is the initial position of the system, and* $B^{\#}$ *denotes the Moore–Penrose inverse. The system (1) splits into separate subsystems*

$$\begin{cases} \dot{x}_i(t) = \lambda_i \, x_i(t) + B \, u_i(t) \\ \quad y_i(t) = C \, x_i(t) \end{cases}, \quad i = 1, \cdots, n. \tag{8}$$

Recall that the Moore–Penrose inverse matrix $B^{\#}$ exists and is unique for any complex or real matrix B and it is defined by four conditions: (i) $BB^{\#}B = B$, (ii) $B^{\#}BB^{\#} = B^{\#}$, (iii) $BB^{\#}$ is Hermitian, and (iv) $B^{\#}B$ is Hermitian.

Proof. The expression (7) for $x_i(t) = R_i x(t)$ is obtained by multiplying the solution to (1):

$$x(t) = e^{At} x_0 + e^{At} \int_{t_0}^{t} e^{-A\tau} B \, u(\tau) \, d\tau$$

on the left by R_i, taking into account property (4) and also that $R_i e^{At} = R_i e^{\lambda_i t}$, $e^{-A\tau} = \sum_j R_j e^{-\lambda_j \tau}$, $B u_i(\tau) = R_i B u(\tau)$. If we differentiate (7), we obtain (8). $\square$

The expression (7) for $x_i(t) = R_i x(t)$ determines the dynamics of the *eigenmode* corresponding to the eigenvalue λ_i in system (1). The corresponding mode in the output signal is determined by the expression $y_i(t) = C x_i(t)$.

2.2. Modal Observability and Controllability of a Linear System

In this section, by analogy with the classical definitions of an observable and controllable linear system, we introduce the corresponding concepts for individual eigenmodes. We also establish simple criteria for modal controllability and observability for a linear stationary system (1).

Definition 1. *The mode corresponding to the eigenvalue* λ_i *is* **observable** *in the linear system (1) at the moment* t_0, *when* $y_i(t, t_0, x_0, u = 0) \equiv 0$ *at* $t \geq t_0$ *if, and only if,* $x_i(t_0) = 0$.

According to (7), the observability of a mode in a stationary system (1) is entirely determined by the matrices R_i and C. Therefore, we can also discuss the *modal observability of a pair* $\{C, R_i\}$. For stationary systems, modal observability can be verified using the following simple criterion.

Proposition 3. *The mode corresponding to* λ_i *in the linear system (1) is observable. if, and only if,* $C R_i \neq 0$.

Proof. If the stationary pair $\{C, R_i\}$ is modally observable, then $CR_i x_0 \neq 0$ holds for any $R_i x_0 \neq 0$, that is, for some $x_0 \neq 0$, $CR_i x_0 \neq 0$ is fulfilled, and therefore $CR_i \neq 0$. If $CR_i \neq 0$, then there is some $x_0 \neq 0$ such that $CR_i x_0 \neq 0$. Let us now choose an arbitrary $R_i \tilde{x}_0 \neq 0$. It is easy to show that the vectors $R_i x_0$ and $R_i \tilde{x}_0$ are both eigenvectors of matrix A corresponding to the eigenvalue λ_i. Because, by assumption, the spectrum of $\sigma(A)$ is simple, these vectors are proportional, that is, $R_i \tilde{x}_0 = \alpha R_i x_0$, $\alpha \in \mathbb{C}$. Therefore, $CR_i \tilde{x}_0 = \alpha CR_i x_0 \neq 0$, that is, the pair $\{C, R_i\}$ is modally observable. $\square$

One can check the observability of the system by checking the observability of its individual modes.

Proposition 4. *The stationary system* (1) *is observable (identifiable) if, and only if, each mode is observable (identifiable).*

Proof. It follows from the definitions and equivalence of the following statements

$$\forall i: \quad y_i(t, t_0, x_0, u = 0) \equiv 0 \text{ at } t \geq t_0 \ <=> \ y(t, t_0, x_0, u = 0) \equiv 0 \text{ at } t \geq t_0 \, ;$$

$$\forall i: \ x_i(t_0) = 0 \ <=> \ x(t_0) = 0. \quad \square$$

However, individual modes can be observable when the dynamical system (1) as a whole is unobservable.

Similarly, one can consider the concept of modal controllability and obtain a criterion for modal controllability.

Definition 2. *The mode corresponding to the eigenvalue λ_i in the linear system* (1) *is **controllable**, if for each event $(t_0, x_0 = x_i(t_0))$, there is a control $u(t)$, which brings the system to the zero state in a finite time.*

For stationary systems, modal controllability can be verified using the following simple criterion.

Proposition 5. *The mode corresponding to λ_i in the linear system* (1) *is controllable if, and only if, $R_i B \neq 0$.*

Proof. If $R_i B = 0$, then it follows from (7) that mode $x_i(t)$ is not controllable. If $R_i B \neq 0$, then $u(t)$ can always be chosen, such that

$$\int_{t_0}^{t_0 + T} e^{-\lambda_j \tau} u(\tau) d\tau = \begin{cases} u_i^0, & j = i \\ 0, & j \neq i \end{cases}, \quad R_i x_0 = -R_i B u_i^0, \quad j = 1, \ldots, n$$

Then, in a finite time T, the control $u(t)$ brings the system from state $x_i(t_0) = R_i x_0$ to the zero state, i.e., the eigen-mode corresponding to λ_i is controllable. $\square$

According to Proposition 5, the controllability of a mode in a stationary system is entirely determined by the matrices R_i and B. Thus, we can discuss *the modal controllability of the stationary pair $\{R_i, B\}$*. The controllability of the system can be verified by checking the controllability of its individual modes.

Proposition 6. *A stationary linear system* (1) *is controllable if, and only if, each mode is controllable.*

Proof. If the system (1) is controllable, then each of its modes, by definition, is also controllable. Consider a system in which each mode can be controlled. Let at the moment t_0, it is in the state $x_0 \neq 0$. Let us choose modal control in the form

$$u(t) = \sum_i u_i(t), \quad u_i(t) = \begin{cases} u_i^0 f_i(t), & t \in [t_0, t_0 + T] \\ 0, & t \notin [t_0, t_0 + T] \end{cases}, \tag{9}$$

where the set of scalar functions $f_1, f_2, \cdots, f_n$ satisfies the condition

$$\forall i, k = 1, \cdots, n \; : \; \int_{t_0}^{t_0+T} e^{-\lambda_k t} f_i(t)dt = \delta_{ik} = \begin{cases} 0, & i \neq k \\ 1, & i = k \end{cases}. \tag{10}$$

As functions f_i, for example, one can always choose piecewise constant functions on n sections of the interval $t \in [t_0, t_0 + T]$. Substituting the control $u(t)$ from (9) and (10) into the solution to (1),

$$x(t) = e^{At} x_0 + e^{At} \int_{t_0}^{t} e^{-A\tau} Bu(\tau)d\tau \,,$$

we obtain

$$x(t) = \sum_i x_i(t) = \sum_i (R_i x_0 + R_i B u_i^0) e^{-\lambda_i t}, \quad t \geq t_0 + T. \tag{11}$$

Because all eigenvalues λ_i are simple, the vectors $R_i x_0$ and $R_i B u_i^0$ coincide up to a scalar factor with the corresponding right eigenvector of the system. In addition, according to Proposition 5, $R_i B \neq 0$ for all i. Therefore, it is always possible to choose vectors u_i^0, such that $x(t) \equiv 0, t \geq t_0 + T$ in (11). Thus, system (1) is controllable. $\square$

The choice of the control $u(t)$ in the form (9–10) also proves the following property:

Corollary 1. *If an individual mode of system (1) is controllable, then there is a control $u_i(t)$ that allows one to change this eigenmode arbitrarily on any finite interval without changing other eigenmodes of the solution.*

Note that individual modes can be controllable even when the dynamical system as a whole is uncontrollable.

2.3. Spectral Decompositions of Gramians of a Linear System

In this section, we recall the basic facts about the observability and controllability Gramians of the linear system (1) and their spectral expansions, and also offer a meaningful interpretation of the corresponding spectral components in these expansions.

The Gramians of controllability and observability of a stable linear system (1) are, respectively, the quantities

$$P_C = \int_0^\infty e^{At} BB^T e^{A^T t} dt, \quad P_O = \int_0^\infty e^{A^T t} C^T C e^{At} dt, \tag{12}$$

which are also solutions of the corresponding Lyapunov equations

$$A P_C + P_C A^T = -BB^T, \quad A^T P_O + P_O A = -C^T C. \tag{13}$$

If $x_0 = x(0)$ is the initial state of system (1), then the integral energy of the output signal at zero control is determined by the observability Gramian

$$\int_0^\infty y^T(t) y(t) dt = x_0^T P_O x_0. \tag{14}$$

If the state x_0 is reachable, then the minimum energy for bringing the system from the zero state to x_0 and the corresponding optimal control $\hat{u}(t)$ are determined by the inverse matrix of the controllability Gramian

$$\inf_{x(-\infty)=0} \int_{-\infty}^{0} \hat{u}^T(t)\hat{u}(t)dt = x_0^T P_C^\# x_0, \quad \hat{u}(t) = B^T e^{-A^T t} P_C^\# x_0, \quad -\infty < t < 0, \tag{15}$$

where $P_C^{\#}$ is the Moore–Penrose inverse.

In [17], the spectral decompositions of Gramians (12) were proposed. In [18], they were generalized to a more general class of solutions of the matrix Krein equations. The eigenterms of the expansions are represented using the residues of the resolvent of the matrix A. Let us formulate this result for Equation (13) in the following form:

Theorem 1 ([18]). *If $\lambda_i^* + \lambda_j \neq 0$ for all $\lambda_i, \lambda_j \in \sigma(A)$, Then, for any matrices B and C, there is a unique solution of the Lyapunov Equation (13), and it is presented in the form*

$$P = \sum_{i=1}^{n} \tilde{P}_i = \sum_{i,j=1}^{n} P_{ij}, \quad \tilde{P}_i = \sum_{j=1}^{n} P_{ij}, \tag{16}$$

where the spectral components for the controllability and observability Gramians, respectively, are given by

$$\tilde{P}_i^C = -\left\{ R_i B B^T (\lambda_i I + A^*)^{-1} \right\}_{Herm}, \quad P_{ij}^C = \left\{ \frac{-1}{\lambda_i + \lambda_j^*} R_i B B^T R_j^* \right\}_{Herm}, \tag{17}$$

$$\tilde{P}_i^O = -\left\{ R_i^* C^T C (\lambda_i^* I + A)^{-1} \right\}_{Herm}, \quad P_{ij}^O = \left\{ \frac{-1}{\lambda_i^* + \lambda_j} R_i^* C^T C R_j \right\}_{Herm}, \tag{18}$$

where $\{\cdot\}_{Herm}$ denotes the Hermitian part of the matrix, and R_i and R_j are the matrix residues (3) that correspond to the eigenvalues λ_i and λ_j.

The eigenterms $\tilde{P}_i$ and P_{ij} in expressions (16) are called in [17] *the sub-Gramians and pairwise sub-Gramians*, respectively. They characterize the contribution of the corresponding eigenmodes or their pairs to the energy variation of the system, determined by the corresponding Gramian over an infinite time interval. The following statement holds:

Proposition 7 (Interpretation of observability sub-Gramians). *For system (1) with zero control, the value $x_0^T \tilde{P}_i^O x_0$ is the cross-correlation between the output signal $y(t)$ and its i-th modal component at a lag of zero. The value $x_0^T P_{ij}^O x_0$ is the cross-correlation between the i-th and j-th modal components of the output signal at a lag of zero.*

Proof. Considering that $y(t) = Ce^{At} x_0$ and $y_i(t) = CR_i e^{\lambda_i t} x_0$, we obtain

$$\frac{1}{2} \int_0^\infty (y_i^* y + y^* y_i) dt = \frac{1}{2} x_0^T \int_0^\infty (e^{\lambda_i^* t} R_i^* C^T Ce^{At} + e^{A^T t} C^T C R_i e^{\lambda_i t}) dt\, x_0 = x_0^T \tilde{P}_i^O x_0$$

Similarly, we directly verify that $\frac{1}{2} \int_0^\infty (y_i^* y_j + y_j^* y_i) dt = x_0^T P_{ij}^O x_0$. $\square$

Similar to the Lyapunov Equation (13) hold for Gramians, the corresponding *modal Lyapunov equations* hold for sub-Gramians.

Proposition 8. *Under the conditions of Theorem 1, the observability sub-Gramians $\tilde{P}_i^O$ and P_{ij}^O in expansions (16) and (18) satisfy the following modal Lyapunov equations:*

$$A^T \tilde{P}_i^O + \tilde{P}_i^O A = -\frac{1}{2}\left(R_i^* C^T C + C^T C R_i \right), \tag{19}$$

$$A^T P_{ij}^O + P_{ij}^O A = -\frac{1}{2}\left(R_i^* C^T C R_j + R_j^* C^T C R_i \right). \tag{20}$$

Proof. This is verified by the direct substitution of (18) into (19) and (20). $\square$

Similar statements are proved for controllability sub-Gramians.

Proposition 9 (Interpretation of controllability sub-Gramians). *For system* (1) *and reachable state* x_0, *consider problem* (15) *of finding the required control* $\hat{u}(t)$ *with the minimum energy. Then, the value* $x_0^T (P_C^\#)^T \tilde{P}_i^C P_C^\# x_0$ *is the cross-correlation between the optimal control* $\hat{u}(t)$ *and its i-th modal component at a lag of zero. The value* $x_0^T (P_C^\#)^T P_{ij}^C P_C^\# x_0$ *is the cross-correlation between the the i-th and j-th modal components of the optimal control at a lag of zero.*

Proposition 10. *Under the conditions of Theorem 1, the controllability sub-Gramians* $\tilde{P}_i^C$ *and* P_{ij}^C *in* (16) *and* (17) *satisfy the following modal Lyapunov equations:*

$$A\tilde{P}_i^C + \tilde{P}_i^C A^T = -\frac{1}{2}\left(R_i BB^T + BB^T R_i^*\right),$$

$$AP_{ij}^C + P_{ij}^C A^T = -\frac{1}{2}\left(R_i BB^T R_j^* + R_j BB^T R_i^*\right).$$

3. Spectral Decompositions of Gramians of a Bilinear Control System

In this section, we extend the results obtained for linear systems to the case of bilinear control systems. In particular, we introduce the concept of *a generalized eigenmode* and prove that the state of the bilinear system can be uniquely split into generalized modes corresponding to the eigenvalues of the dynamics matrix. Further, we recall some known facts about the controllability and observability Gramians of bilinear systems and propose their *spectral decomposition* into parts (sub-Gramians) corresponding to the spectrum of the dynamics matrix. We prove that individual sub-Gramians characterize some measure of the corresponding generalized eigenmodes or their pairwise scalar products.

3.1. Partitioning the Solution into Generalized Modes of the Matrix A

Consider a bilinear control system of the form [5,6]

$$\dot{x}(t) = Ax(t) + \sum_{j=1}^m N_j x(t)u_j(t) + Bu(t), \quad y(t) = Cx(t), \tag{21}$$

where $x(t) \in \mathbb{R}^n$, $u(t) \in \mathbb{R}^m$, $y(t) \in \mathbb{R}^l$ are the state, input, and output vectors, respectively, and $A, N_1, \cdots, N_m, B$, and C are the real matrices. Assume that the initial state is $x(0) = 0$, and the system input satisfies $u(t) = 0$, $t < 0$. Then, the solution of (21) can be considered as a solution to the following recursive system of linear equations:

$$\dot{x}^{(1)}(t) = Ax^{(1)}(t) + Bu(t),$$

$$\dot{x}^{(k)}(t) = Ax^{(k)}(t) + \sum_{j=1}^m N_j x^{(k-1)}(t)u_j(t) + Bu(t), \quad k = 2,3,\cdots \tag{22}$$

Solving the systems (22) sequentially, we obtain

$$x^{(1)}(t) = \int_0^\infty e^{A\tau_1} Bu(t-\tau_1)d\tau_1,$$

$$x^{(2)}(t) = x^{(1)}(t) + \sum_{j_2=1}^m \int_0^\infty \int_0^\infty e^{A\tau_2}.N_{j_2}e^{A\tau_1} Bu(t-\tau_2-\tau_1)u_{j_2}(t-\tau_2)d\tau_1 d\tau_2, \quad \cdots,$$

$$x^{(k)}(t) = x^{(k-1)}(t) + \sum_{j_2,\cdots,j_k=1}^m \int_0^\infty \cdots \int_0^\infty e^{A\tau_k} N_{j_k} \cdots e^{A\tau_2}.N_{j_2}e^{A\tau_1} Bu(t-\tau_1-\cdots-\tau_k)$$

$$u_{j_2}(t-\tau_2\cdots-\tau_k)\cdots u_{j_k}(t-\tau_k)\,d\tau_1 d\tau_2 \cdots d\tau_k, \quad k = 3,\cdots \tag{23}$$

It was proved in [22] that if the sequence $x^{(k)}(t)$ in (23) converges (that is, the corresponding *Volterra series* of corrections converges), then it converges to the solution of (21), that is,

$$x(t) = \lim_{k\to\infty} x^{(k)}(t). \tag{24}$$

It was proved in [23] that this sequence always converges if matrix A is stable, input control is bounded, and all the matrices N_j are sufficiently bounded in norm. In what follows, we assume that the corresponding Volterra series converges, and the limit (24) exists.

From (23), it follows that the solution to the bilinear system (21) is constructed as the sum of (i) the solution of its linear part $x^{(1)}(t)$, (ii) the bilinear correction $x^{(2)}(t) - x^{(1)}(t)$ generated by the linear part, (iii) the bilinear correction $x^{(3)}(t) - x^{(2)}(t)$ generated by the first correction, etc. Moreover, all non-linear corrections of the form $x^{(k)}(t) - x^{(k-1)}(t)$, $k = 2, 3, \cdots$ are integral transformations of the linear part $x^{(1)}(t)$ of order k with respect to control, that is,

$$x(t) = x^{(1)}(t) + \sum_{k=1}^{\infty} F^k x^{(1)}(t), \quad \text{where}$$

$$Fx(t) = \sum_{j=1}^{m} \int_0^{\infty} e^{A\tau} N_j\, x(t-\tau)\, u_j(t-\tau)\, d\tau. \tag{25}$$

Moreover, according to our assumption, the integral operator F in (25) is a contraction.

The solution $x^{(1)}(t)$ of the linear part of the system (21) can be divided into eigenmodes of the matrix A, in accordance with the definitions (7) in Section 2.1.

$$x^{(1)}(t) = \sum_i x_i^{(1)}(t), \quad \text{where}$$

$$x_i^{(1)}(t) = R_i\, x^{(1)}(t) = \int_0^{\infty} e^{\lambda_i \tau} R_i\, B\, u(t-\tau)\, d\tau, \tag{26}$$

where R_i is the residue matrix in (3) corresponding to λ_i.

Definition 3. *The **generalized mode** of the bilinear system (21) corresponding to the eigenvalue λ_i of the matrix A is the sum of the mode $x_i^{(1)}(t)$ of the linear part of the system and non-linear corrections generated by this mode, obtained in the course of solving the recursive system (22), i.e.,*

$$x_i(t) = x_i^{(1)}(t) + \sum_{k=1}^{\infty} F^k x_i^{(1)}(t), \tag{27}$$

where the integral operator F is defined in (25) and is assumed to be a contraction, and $x_i^{(1)}$ is defined in (26).

The significance of Definition 3 is justified by the following statement.

Proposition 11. *Let the initial state of the bilinear system (21) $x(0) = 0$, which satisfies $u(t) = 0$, $t < 0$, and the Volterra series in (23) converges. Then, the solution of (21) is uniquely split into generalized modes (27), corresponding to the eigenvalues of matrix A.*

$$x(t) = \sum_i x_i(t). \tag{28}$$

Proof. By constructing the sequence in (23),

$$x^{(k)}(t) = x^{(1)}(t) + \sum_{j=1}^{k-1} F^j x^{(1)}(t)$$

According to Proposition 2, the solution of the linear part $x^{(1)}(t)$ is uniquely decomposed into eigenmodes

$$x^{(1)}(t) = \sum_{i=1}^{n} x_i^{(1)}(t)$$

Since the integral operator F is linear, we obtain

$$x^{(k)}(t) = \sum_{i=1}^{n} x_i^{(1)}(t) + \sum_{j=1}^{k-1} F^j\left(\sum_{i=1}^{n} x_i^{(1)}(t)\right) = \sum_{i=1}^{n}\left(x_i^{(1)}(t) + \sum_{j=1}^{k-1} F^j x_i^{(1)}(t)\right) = \sum_{i=1}^{n} x_i^{(k)}(t)$$

If Volterra series $\sum_k(x^{(k)}(t) - x^{(k-1)}(t))$ in (23) converges, then according to [22], the sequence $\{x^{(k)}(t)\}$ converges to the solution of (21). Due to the convergence of the sequence $\{x^{(k)}(t)\}$, the sequences $\{x_i^{(k)}(t)\}$ for each i also converge to $x_i(t)$ in (27), since they are obtained by multiplying $\{x^{(k)}(t)\}$ by constant matrices R_i. Therefore, taking the limit $k \to \infty$ in the previous equation, we obtain the assertion of the proposition. $\square$

3.2. Spectral Decompositions of Gramians

The concept of controllability and observability Gramians for a bilinear system was studied in [2]. The controllability Gramian of system (21) is defined as

$$P_C = \sum_{k=1}^{\infty} P^{(k)} = \sum_{k=1}^{\infty} \int_0^{\infty} \cdots \int_0^{\infty} G_k BB^T G_k^T d\tau_1 \cdots d\tau_k, \quad \text{where}$$

$$G_1 = e^{A\tau_1}, G_k(\tau_1 \cdots \tau_k) = e^{A\tau_k}[N_1 G_{k-1}, \cdots, N_m G_{k-1}], \quad k = 2, 3, \cdots \tag{29}$$

It characterizes the *input-to-state energy* of the system [16]. Additionally, the following statements hold:

Theorem 2 ([6]). *The controllability (observability) Gramian exists if (i) A is stable, such that* $||e^{At}|| \le \beta e^{-\alpha t}, t \ge 0, \alpha, \beta > 0.$ *(ii)* $||\sum_{\gamma=1}^{m} N_\gamma N_\gamma^T|| < 2\alpha/\beta^2.$

Theorem 3. *If matrix A is stable and the controllability Gramian exists, then (i) system (1) is controllable if, and only if, $P_C > 0$ [2], and (ii) the Gramian P_C satisfies the generalized Lyapunov equation [5]*

$$AP_C + P_C A^T + \sum_{\gamma=1}^{m} N_\gamma P_C N_\gamma^T = -BB^T. \tag{30}$$

A study in [6] (in Proposition 1) also showed that if the matrix A is stable, then the terms of the series $P^{(k)}$ in (29) can be found as successive solutions of the following recursive system of linear Lyapunov equations:

$$AP^{(1)} + P^{(1)} A^T + BB^T = 0,$$

$$AP^{(k)} + P^{(k)} A^T + \sum_{\gamma=1}^{m} N_\gamma P^{(k)} N_\gamma^T = 0, \quad k = 2, 3, \cdots \tag{31}$$

The following useful addition can be made to this statement.

Proposition 12. *The controllability Gramian (29) of the bilinear system (21) is the sum of the controllability Gramian $P^{(1)}$ of the linear part and the integrals of the Gram matrices formed by convolution kernels that arise when calculating the non-linear corrections $x^{(k)}(t) - x^{(k-1)}(t)$, $k = 2, 3, \cdots$ in the recursive solution to system (22).*

Proof. According to (31), $P^{(1)}$ in (29) is the controllability Gramian of the linear part of the system (21), and the other terms $P^{(k)}$ are calculated in (29) as integrals of the Gram matrices:

$$P^{(k)} = \int_0^{\infty} \cdots \int_0^{\infty} G_k BB^T G_k^T dt_1 \cdots dt_k,$$

and it can be verified that these Gram matrices

$$G_k BB^T G_k^T = \sum_{j_k=1}^{m} e^{A\tau_k} N_{j_k} G_{k-1} BB^T G_{k-1}^T N_{j_k}^T e^{A^T \tau_k} = \cdots =$$

$$\sum_{j_2,\cdots,j_k=1}^{m} e^{A\tau_k} N_{j_k} \cdots e^{A\tau_2} N_{j_2} e^{A\tau_1} BB^T e^{A^T \tau_1} N_{j_2}^T e^{A^T \tau_2} \cdots N_{j_k}^T e^{A^T \tau_k}$$

are formed by convolution kernels, arising when calculating the corrections $x^{(k)}(t) - x^{(k-1)}(t)$, $k = 2, 3, \cdots$ in (23). $\square$

Definition 4. *Controllability sub-Gramians and pairwise sub-Gramians of the bilinear system* (21) *are, respectively, the matrices*

$$\tilde{P}_i^C = \sum_{k=1}^{\infty} \tilde{P}_i^{(k)} = \frac{1}{2} \sum_{k=1}^{\infty} \int_0^{\infty} \cdots \int_0^{\infty} G_k (R_i BB^T + BB^T R_i^*) G_k^T d\tau_1 \cdots d\tau_k , \tag{32}$$

$$P_{ij}^C = \sum_{k=1}^{\infty} P_{ij}^{(k)} = \frac{1}{2} \sum_{k=1}^{\infty} \int_0^{\infty} \cdots \int_0^{\infty} G_k (R_i BB^T R_j^* + R_j BB^T R_i^*) G_k^T d\tau_1 \cdots d\tau_k , \tag{33}$$

where R_i and R_j are the residue matrices in (3) *corresponding to the eigenvalues λ_i and λ_j of matrix A, and the matrices G_k are defined in* (29).

We now establish some basic properties of sub-Gramians (32) and (33) in Definition 4.

Property 1. *Under the conditions of Theorem 2, sub-Gramians* (32) *and* (33) *exist.*

Proof. Under the conditions of Theorem 2, the series in (32) and (33) are formed using the same contracting operator F as a series (29) in the definition of Gramian. Therefore, sub-Gramians exist. $\square$

Suppose, further, that the matrix A is stable and controllability sub-Gramians (32) and (33) exist. Then the following properties are satisfied.

Property 2. *The sum over all sub-Gramians is Gramian* (29)

$$P_C = \sum_{i=1}^{n} \tilde{P}_i^C = \sum_{i,j=1}^{n} P_{ij}^C , \quad \tilde{P}_i^C = \sum_{j=1}^{n} P_{ij}^C . \tag{34}$$

Proof. This is verified by the direct summation of expressions (32) and (33) considering the uniform convergence of the series and integrals and the property of residue matrices $\sum_i R_i = I$. $\square$

Property 3 (Consistency with linear theory)**.** *The sub-Gramians $\tilde{P}_i^{(1)}$ and $P_{ij}^{(1)}$ in* (32) *and* (33) *are the controllability sub-Gramians of the linear part of system* (21) *in accordance with the definitions* (17) *of Section* 2.3.

Property 4. *Controllability sub-Gramians of the bilinear system in* (32) *and* (33) *satisfy the corresponding generalized modal Lyapunov equations*

$$A\tilde{P}_i^C + \tilde{P}_i^C A^T + \sum_{\gamma=1}^{m} N_\gamma \tilde{P}_i^C N_\gamma^T = -\frac{1}{2} \left(R_i BB^T + BB^T R_i^* \right) , \tag{35}$$

$$AP_{ij}^C + P_{ij}^C A^T + \sum_{\gamma=1}^{m} N_\gamma P_{ij}^C N_\gamma^T = -\frac{1}{2} \left(R_i BB^T R_j^* + R_j BB^T R_i^* \right) . \tag{36}$$

Proof. We can directly verify that when A is stable, the terms $\tilde{P}_i^{(k)}$ in (32) can be obtained from the following Lyapunov equations:

$$A\tilde{P}_i^{(1)} + \tilde{P}_i^{(1)} A^T + \frac{1}{2}\left(R_i BB^T + BB^T R_i^*\right) = 0,$$

$$A\tilde{P}_i^{(k)} + \tilde{P}_i^{(k)} A^T + \sum_{\gamma=1}^{m} N_\gamma \tilde{P}_i^{(k-1)} N_\gamma^T = 0, \quad k = 2, 3, \cdots$$

We sum the first K equations. Because we assumed that sub-Gramians exist, that is, the series in (32) and (33) converge, then, the series $\sum_{k=1}^{K} \tilde{P}_i^{(k)}$ converges uniformly as $K \to \infty$. Taking the limit $K \to \infty$, we obtain (35). Similarly, we obtain (36). $\square$

Corollary 2. *If Equation (30) has a unique solution and the sub-Gramians $\tilde{P}_i^C$ and P_{ij}^C exist, then they are defined as unique solutions to (35) and (36).*

Proof. According to Property 4, sub-Gramians must satisfy (35) and (36). If (30) has a unique solution, then the operator on the left-hand side of (30) is non-singular. Therefore the sub-Gramians $\tilde{P}_i^C$ and P_{ij}^C are defined uniquely by (35) and (36) for any matrix on the right-hand side. $\square$

Choose the input control satisfying the conditions $u(t) = 0, t < 0$ and $\int_0^\infty |u(t)|^2 dt = M^2 < 1$. Consider the set of vector functions

$$\Omega_u = \left\{ f(t) : f(t) = \sum_{k=0}^{\infty} F^k f^{(1)}(t), \ f^{(1)}(t) = \int_0^\infty G_1(\tau) B_f u(t-\tau) d\tau \right\},$$

where operator F is defined in (25), $G_1(\tau) = e^{A\tau}$ as in (29), and B_f is a matrix of appropriate dimensions. Then for any $x, y \in \Omega_u$ we define the scalar product as

$$(x,y)_\Omega = \sum_{k=1}^{\infty} M^{2k} \cdot \text{Trace}\left(\int_0^\infty \cdots \int_0^\infty G_k B_x B_y^* G_k^T \, d\tau_1 \cdots d\tau_k \right), \tag{37}$$

where G_k are defined as in (29). This definition satisfies the axioms of linearity, commutativity and positive definiteness. Then, the following analog of Proposition 7 holds for the sub-Gramians of the bilinear system.

Property 5. *Suppose that in the bilinear system (21), the initial state is $x(0) = 0$, and the control satisfies the condition $u(t) = 0, t < 0$. Then, for a sufficiently small control $\int_0^\infty |u(t)|^2 dt = M^2 < 1$, the trace of controllability sub-Gramian $\tilde{P}_i^C$ estimates from above the value of the dot product (37) of a solution vector $x(t)$ with generalized mode $x_i(t)$ in (28), and the trace of pairwise sub-Gramian P_{ij}^C estimates from above the value of the dot product of a generalized mode $x_i(t)$ with generalized mode $x_j(t)$*

$$|(x, x_j)_\Omega| \leq |\text{Trace } \tilde{P}_i^C|,$$

$$|(x_i, x_j)_\Omega| \leq |\text{Trace } P_{ij}^C|. \tag{38}$$

The *observability Gramian* and *observability sub-Gramian* of system (21) are defined in a similar manner. Properties similar to Properties 1–5 are satisfied for them. *Gramian of observability* is defined as

$$P_O = \sum_{k=1}^{\infty} P^{(k)} = \sum_{k=1}^{\infty} \int_0^\infty \cdots \int_0^\infty Q_k^T C^T C Q_k d\tau_1 \cdots d\tau_k, \quad \text{where}$$

$$Q_1 = e^{A\tau_1}, \ Q_k(\tau_1 \cdots \tau_k) = \left[N_1^T Q_{k-1}^T, \cdots, N_m^T Q_{k-1}^T \right]^T e^{A\tau_k}, \quad k = 2, 3, \cdots \tag{39}$$

Definition 5. *Observability sub-Gramians and pairwise sub-Gramians* of the bilinear system (21) are, respectively, the matrices

$$\tilde{P}_i^O = \sum_{k=1}^{\infty} \tilde{P}_i^{(k)} = \frac{1}{2} \sum_{k=1}^{\infty} \int_0^{\infty} \cdots \int_0^{\infty} Q_k^T (R_i^* C^T C + C^T C R_i) Q_k \, d\tau_1 \cdots d\tau_k, \tag{40}$$

$$P_{ij}^O = \sum_{k=1}^{\infty} P_{ij}^{(k)} = \frac{1}{2} \sum_{k=1}^{\infty} \int_0^{\infty} \cdots \int_0^{\infty} Q_k^T (R_i^* C^T C R_j + R_j^* C^T C R_i) Q_k \, d\tau_1 \cdots d\tau_k. \tag{41}$$

The observability sub-Gramians satisfy the following *modal Lyapunov equations*:

$$A^T \tilde{P}_i^O + \tilde{P}_i^O A + \sum_{\gamma=1}^{m} N_\gamma^T \tilde{P}_i^O N_\gamma = -\frac{1}{2}\left(R_i^* C^T C + C^T C R_i\right),$$

$$A^T P_{ij}^O + P_{ij}^O A + \sum_{\gamma=1}^{m} N_\gamma^T P_{ij}^O N_\gamma = -\frac{1}{2}\left(R_i^* C^T C R_j + R_j^* C^T C R_i\right).$$

4. Iterative Algorithms for Computing Gramians and Sub-Gramians

In this section, we propose iterative algorithms for computing the Gramians and sub-Gramians for bilinear control systems based on the element-wise computation of the solution matrix on an eigenvector basis. Similar formulas for linear systems were proposed in [24]. Based on the proposed iterative procedure, we introduce a new criterion for the existence of solutions to generalized Lyapunov equations, which in some cases allows us to expand the region of guaranteed existence of solutions in comparison with the estimate of Theorem 2. The proposed criterion, however, uses more detailed information on the coefficients of matrices $N\gamma$ and eigenvalues of matrix A.

4.1. Algorithm for the Element-Wise Computation of Gramian in the Eigenvector Basis

Assume that the matrix A in (21) has a simple spectrum $\sigma(A) = \{\lambda_1, \lambda_2, \cdots, \lambda_n\}$ and the following eigenvalue decomposition

$$A = U\Lambda V, \quad UV = VU = I, \tag{42}$$

where $\Lambda = diag\{\lambda_1, \lambda_2, \cdots, \lambda_n\}$. The columns of matrix U are composed of the normalized right eigenvectors of matrix A, and the rows of matrix V are the normalized left eigenvectors. Then, the Lyapunov Equation (30) in the eigenbasis takes the form

$$\Lambda \tilde{P}_C + \tilde{P}_C \Lambda^* + \sum_{\gamma=1}^{m} \tilde{N}_\gamma \tilde{P}_C \tilde{N}_\gamma^T = -\tilde{Q}, \tag{43}$$

where $\tilde{P}_C = V P_C V^*$, $\tilde{Q} = V B B^T V^*$, $\tilde{N}_\gamma = V N_\gamma U$, and $(\cdot)^*$ denotes the Hermitian conjugation. The iterative procedure (31) for solving Equation (43) in the eigenbasis of matrix A takes the form

$$\Lambda \tilde{P}^{(1)} + \tilde{P}^{(1)} \Lambda^* = -\tilde{Q},$$

$$\Lambda \tilde{P}^{(k)} + \tilde{P}^{(k)} \Lambda^* = -\sum_{\gamma=1}^{m} \tilde{N}_\gamma \tilde{P}^{(k)} \tilde{N}_\gamma^*, \quad k = 2, 3, \cdots, \tag{44}$$

$$\tilde{P}_C = \sum_{k=1}^{\infty} \tilde{P}^{(k)}, \quad P_C = U \tilde{P}_C U^*,$$

where $\tilde{P}^{(k)} = V P^{(k)} V^*$. Let $(v_i^\gamma)^T = e_i^T \tilde{N}_\gamma$ be the i-th raw matrix $\tilde{N}_\gamma$, where e_i is the i-th column of the unit matrix. Then, (44) can be written in terms of the matrix components as

$$\left(\tilde{P}^{(1)}\right)_{ij} = \frac{-1}{\lambda_i + \lambda_j^*}\left(\tilde{Q}\right)_{ij},$$

$$\forall k > 1: \quad \left(\tilde{P}^{(k)}\right)_{ij} = -\sum_{\gamma=1}^{m} \frac{-v_i^{\gamma}\,\tilde{P}^{(k-1)}\left(v_j^{\gamma}\right)^{T}}{\lambda_i + \lambda_j^*}, \quad P_C = U\left(\sum_{k=1}^{\infty} \tilde{P}^{(k)}\right)U^*, \tag{45}$$

4.2. Novel Criterion for the Existence of Gramians

The iterative procedure (45) assumes an appropriate *criterion for the existence of Gramian* P_C, which is based on the convergence of its elements in an iterative process.

Theorem 4. *The controllability Gramian P_C in (29) exists if (i) the matrix A is stable, and (ii) the inequality holds*

$$\sqrt{\sum_{i,j} q_{ij}^2} < 1, \quad q_{ij} = \sum_{\gamma=1}^{m} \frac{|v_i^{\gamma}| \cdot |v_j^{\gamma}|}{|\lambda_i + \lambda_j^*|}, \quad i,j = 1, \cdots, n, \tag{46}$$

where the vectors $v_i^{\gamma} = U^* N_{\gamma}^T V^* e_i$, the matrices V, U are defined in (42), and λ_i, λ_j are the eigenvalues of the matrix A. Under the above conditions, the Gramian P_C can be obtained using an iterative algorithm (45).

Proof. For the proof, we use the Frobenius norm $||\cdot||_F$. From expressions (45), it follows that

$$\left| v_i^{\gamma}\,\tilde{P}^{(k-1)}\left(v_j^{\gamma}\right)^{T} \right| \le |v_i^{\gamma}| \cdot |v_j^{\gamma}| \cdot ||\tilde{P}^{(k-1)}||_F,$$

$$\left|\left(\tilde{P}^{(k)}\right)_{ij}\right| \le q_{ij}||\tilde{P}^{(k-1)}||_F, \quad ||\tilde{P}^{(k)}||_F \le \sqrt{\sum_{i,j} q_{ij}^2} \cdot ||\tilde{P}^{(k-1)}||_F$$

Thus, under (46), the series $\sum_{k=1}^{\infty} \tilde{P}^{(k)}$ in (44) is bounded from above by a converging geometric progression, and therefore converges. Adding the K equations in (44) and taking the limit $K \to \infty$, we obtain a solution to the generalized Lyapunov equation in the eigenvector basis (43). If the series $\sum_{k=1}^{\infty} \tilde{P}^{(k)}$ converges in the iterative procedure (44) on an eigenbasis, then the corresponding series $\sum_{k=1}^{\infty} P^{(k)}$ converges in procedure (31). According to [6] (Proposition 1), if the matrix A is stable, then the terms of the series defining the Gramian P_C in (29) are calculated using terms $P^{(k)}$ obtained in the iterative procedure (31), that is, $P_C = \sum_{k=1}^{\infty} P^{(k)}$. Hence, the Gramian P_C exists. $\square$

The conditions for the existence of a solution in the Lyapunov Equation (30), established in Theorem 2 [6], are based on the characteristics of the matrices as a whole, whereas Theorem 4 uses the convergence criterion, which is based on more detailed information about the coefficients of the matrices N_{γ} and the eigenvalues of the matrix A. Therefore, we can expect that the criterion of Theorem 4 will allow, in general, to expand the domain of guaranteed existence of a solution in comparison with the criterion of Theorem 2. Let us compare them using an illustrative example.

Example 1. *Consider the following generalized Lyapunov equation with parameter ϵ:*

$$\begin{pmatrix} -1 & 0 \\ 0 & -2 \end{pmatrix} \cdot P + P \cdot \begin{pmatrix} -1 & 0 \\ 0 & -2 \end{pmatrix} + \epsilon^2 \begin{pmatrix} 1 & 1 \\ 0 & 1 \end{pmatrix} \cdot P \cdot \begin{pmatrix} 1 & 0 \\ 1 & 1 \end{pmatrix} = \begin{pmatrix} -3 & -3 \\ -3 & -3 \end{pmatrix} \tag{47}$$

In the notation of Theorem 2, we have

$$\alpha = \beta = 1, \quad NN^T = \epsilon^2 \begin{pmatrix} 2 & 1 \\ 1 & 1 \end{pmatrix}, \quad (NN^T)^2 = \epsilon^4 \begin{pmatrix} 5 & 3 \\ 3 & 2 \end{pmatrix},$$

$$||NN^T||_F = \sqrt{trace((NN^T)^2)} = \epsilon^2 \sqrt{7}.$$

The condition for the existence of a solution to Equation (47) *established by Theorem 2 takes the form*

$$||NN^T|| < 2\alpha/\beta^2, \quad \epsilon^2 < 2/\sqrt{7} \approx 0.756.$$

In the notation of Theorem 4, we have

$$\lambda_1 = -1, \ \lambda_2 = -2, \ |v_1| = \sqrt{2}, \ |v_2| = 1, \ (q)_{ij} = \epsilon^2 \begin{pmatrix} 1 & \sqrt{2}/3 \\ \sqrt{2}/3 & 1/4 \end{pmatrix}.$$

The condition for the existence of a solution to Equation (47) *established by Theorem 4 takes the form*

$$\sqrt{\sum_{i,j} q_{ij}^2} = \epsilon^2 \sqrt{217/144} < 1, \quad \epsilon^2 < 12/\sqrt{217} \approx 0.815.$$

In this example, the criterion of Theorem 4 allows us to expand the domain of guaranteed existence of solutions (47) *in comparison with the criterion of Theorem 2. However, the application of this criterion requires more detailed information about the system.*

We calculate the solution to Equation (47) using the iterative algorithm (45) for $\epsilon = 0.5$. In this case, we obtain

$$\tilde{P}^{(1)} = \begin{pmatrix} 1.5 & 1 \\ 1 & 0.75 \end{pmatrix}, \quad \tilde{P}^{(2)} = \begin{pmatrix} 0.5312 & 0.1458 \\ 0.1458 & 0.04687 \end{pmatrix},$$

$$\tilde{P}^{(3)} = \begin{pmatrix} 0.1089 & 0.01614 \\ 0.01614 & 0.002930 \end{pmatrix}, \quad \tilde{P}^{(4)} = \begin{pmatrix} 0.01599 & 0.001589 \\ 0.001589 & 0.0001831 \end{pmatrix},$$

$$\tilde{P} \approx \sum_{k=1}^{4} \tilde{P}^{(k)} = \begin{pmatrix} 2.15609 & 1.1635 \\ 1.1635 & 0.79998 \end{pmatrix}. \tag{48}$$

The criterion of Theorem 2 guarantees convergence with the common ratio of geometric progression $q = \epsilon^2 \sqrt{7}/2 \approx 0.3307$, and the relative accuracy of the solution (48) after four iterations is not worse than $q^4/(1-q) \approx 0.0179$, that is, 1.79%.

The criterion of Theorem 4 guarantees convergence with the common ratio of geometric progression $q = \epsilon^2 \sqrt{217/144} \approx 0.3069$ and the relative accuracy of solution (48) after four iterations is not worse than $q^4/(1-q) \approx 0.0128$, that is, 1.28%.

In this case, the exact solution to (47) and the actual error after four iterations are as follows:

$$P = \begin{pmatrix} 832/385 & 64/55 \\ 64/55 & 4/5 \end{pmatrix}, \ P - \tilde{P} = \begin{pmatrix} -0.0049 & -0.00014 \\ -0.00014 & 0.00002 \end{pmatrix}, \ ||P - \tilde{P}||_F = 0.0049$$

that is, for $||P||_F = 2.83$, the relative accuracy of the solution (48) is 0.17%.

4.3. Iterative Algorithm for Computing Sub-Gramians

Modal Lyapunov Equations (35) and (36) for the controllability sub-Gramians differ from Equation (30) for the Gramian P_C only on the right-hand side. Therefore, to apply the iterative procedure (45) to compute the sub-Gramians $\tilde{P}_i^C$ and P_{ij}^C, the matrix $\tilde{Q} = VBB^T V^*$ in the first Equation (45) must be replaced with matrices

$$\tilde{Q}_i = \frac{1}{2}V(R_iBB^T + BB^T R_i^*)V^* \quad \text{and} \quad Q_{ij} = \frac{1}{2}V(R_iBB^T R_j^* + R_jBB^T R_i^*)V^*,$$

respectively. The elements of these matrices in the eigenvector basis are calculated as

$$(\tilde{Q}_i)_{pr} = \frac{1}{2}(\delta_{ip} + \delta_{ir})(\tilde{Q})_{pr} \quad \text{and,} \quad (\tilde{Q}_{ij})_{pr} = \frac{1}{2}(\delta_{ip}\delta_{jr} + \delta_{jp}\delta_{ir})(\tilde{Q})_{pr},$$

where δ_{ls} is the Kronecker delta. Substituting these expressions into the iterative procedure (45) instead of $(\tilde{Q})_{pr}$, we obtain the following iterative procedure for *computation of sub-Gramians $\tilde{P}_i^C$ in* (35)

$$\left(\tilde{P}_i^{(1)}\right)_{pr} = -\frac{1}{2} \cdot \frac{1}{\lambda_p + \lambda_r^*}(\delta_{ip} + \delta_{ir})(\tilde{Q})_{pr},$$

$$\forall k > 1: \quad \left(\tilde{P}_i^{(k)}\right)_{pr} = \sum_{\gamma=1}^{m} \frac{-v_p^\gamma \tilde{P}_i^{(k-1)}\left(v_r^\gamma\right)^T}{\lambda_p + \lambda_r^*}, \tag{49}$$

$$\tilde{P}_i^C = U\left(\sum_{k=1}^{\infty} \tilde{P}_i^{(k)}\right)U^*,$$

and an iterative procedure for *computation of pairwise sub-Gramians P_{ij}^C in* (36)

$$\left(\tilde{P}_{ij}^{(1)}\right)_{pr} = -\frac{1}{2} \cdot \frac{1}{\lambda_p + \lambda_r^*}(\delta_{ip}\delta_{jr} + \delta_{jp}\delta_{ir})(\tilde{Q})_{pr},$$

$$\forall k > 1: \quad \left(\tilde{P}_{ij}^{(k)}\right)_{pr} = \sum_{\gamma=1}^{m} \frac{-v_p^\gamma \tilde{P}_{ij}^{(k-1)}\left(v_r^\gamma\right)^T}{\lambda_p + \lambda_r^*}, \tag{50}$$

$$P_{ij}^C = U\left(\sum_{k=1}^{\infty} \tilde{P}_i^{(k)}\right)U^*.$$

Sufficient conditions for the applicability of iterative procedures (49) and (50) are the same as those for the iterative procedure (44) established in Theorem 2 or in Theorem 4.

Example 2. *To illustrate the definition of sub-Gramians and algorithms for their computation, we calculate the controllability sub-Gramians for Equation (47) with $\epsilon = 1/2$. As was established in Example 1, the Gramian P exists, and according to Property 1, all sub-Gramians also exist. According to Property 2, the Gramian is split into sub-Gramians in the form*

$$P = P_1 + P_2 = \begin{pmatrix} 144/77 & 6/11 \\ 6/11 & 0 \end{pmatrix} + \begin{pmatrix} 112/385 & 34/55 \\ 34/55 & 4/5 \end{pmatrix} = \begin{pmatrix} 832/385 & 64/55 \\ 64/55 & 4/5 \end{pmatrix}$$

$$P = P_{11} + P_{12} + P_{21} + P_{22} = \begin{pmatrix} 12/7 & 0 \\ 0 & 0 \end{pmatrix} +$$

$$\begin{pmatrix} 12/77 & 6/11 \\ 6/11 & 0 \end{pmatrix} + \begin{pmatrix} 12/77 & 6/11 \\ 6/11 & 0 \end{pmatrix} + \begin{pmatrix} 52/385 & 4/55 \\ 4/55 & 4/5 \end{pmatrix}.$$

Moreover, the sub-Gramians themselves, according to Property 4, can be calculated from the corresponding modal Lyapunov Equations (35) and (36), respectively.

Example 3. *For completeness, we present an example of using sub-Gramians to analyze a bilinear model of an electric power system from [20]. As a test bilinear model, the 17th-order model from [5] was used for two interconnected power systems, each area having one steam and one hydro unit. In a test experiment, the contribution of generalized eigenmodes (28) and their pair interactions to the small-signal perturbation energy of the system was estimated based on the coefficient α, which characterized the magnitude of all bilinear terms. To illustrate the process of selecting eigenmodes that are sensitive to bilinear effects, as well as the selection of areas of linear and bilinear behavior of* *the system, consider Figure 1. One can see the Frobenius norm of sub-Gramians $\tilde{P}_i$ for generalized eigenmodes as a function of the weighting coefficient α. The behavior of the spectral components indicates the range of applicability of the linear model in general and reveals particular eigenmodes that are sensitive to bilinear effects. The arrowhead in Figure 1 indicates the threshold between the linear and bilinear behavior of the system at $\alpha \approx 4.17$. This threshold can be defined from the condition that the difference between the norms of "linear" and full sub-Gramians corresponding to some eigenmode reaches a certain percentage. In this case, we can see in Figure 1 that the most sensitive to bilinear effects are the S15 and S14 modes. At $\alpha \approx 4.17$ the norm of their sub-Gramians has increased by 17% and 15%, respectively. The modes S1 and S4/S5 are also sensitive to bilinear effects. The norms of their sub-Gramians have increased by 6.6% and 4.6%, respectively. Other modes are less sensitive, and can be considered in the linear approximation, as long as the norms of their sub-Gramians remain less than the chosen threshold value. The threshold, after which the non-linear behavior of the eigenmode must be considered, can be determined individually for each mode. This information can be used for small-signal or transient stability analyses. A detailed description of the model, test experiment, and its results can be found in [5,20].*

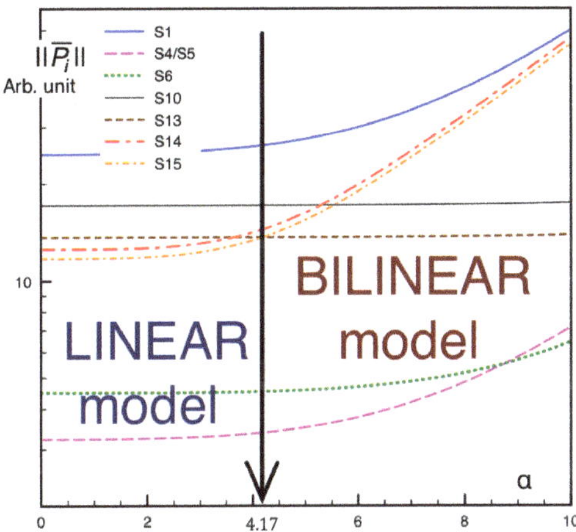

Figure 1. The Frobenius norm of sub-Gramians $\tilde{P}_i$ for generalized eigenmodes as a function of the weighting coefficient α in the test experiment in [20].

5. Discussion

In this study, we show that (i) the solution of a bilinear system can be split uniquely into generalized modes corresponding to the eigenvalues of the dynamics matrix, and (ii) the controllability and observability Gramians can be split into "sub-Gramians" that characterize the magnitude of these generalized modes and their pairwise interactions. This characterization, however, was proven only for small enough input control. A similar condition arises when establishing the relationship between the Gramians and the energy of states in the system in [16] and, apparently, it is typical for bilinear systems.

In contrast to the spectral expansions of the instantaneous dynamics of a bilinear system in [11–13], the spectral expansions of the L_2-norms of states and signals considered in this paper can be useful for analyzing the non-linear effects associated with the accumulation of the influence of disturbances over time. Therefore, the practical significance of the obtained results is that they allow the characterization of the contribution of generalized modes or their pairwise combinations to the asymptotic dynamics of the integrated perturbation energy in bilinear systems. In particular, the norm of the obtained sub-Gramians increases when the frequencies of the corresponding oscillating modes approximate each other. Thus, the proposed decompositions may provide a new fundamental approach for quantifying resonant modal interactions in bilinear systems.

When the bilinear effects decrease, the proposed expansions allow a smooth transition to the linear case (see Property 3). This property can be useful in determining the range of applicability of a linear model and identifying generalized eigenmodes that are sensitive to bilinear effects and require "non-linear refinement" of their dynamics. It can be expected that in some large systems, there will be only a few such modes. Therefore, a non-linear examination of their dynamics will not take much time when real-time state estimation is required. The first test experiment with a bilinear model of an electric power system in [20] showed that the proposed spectral decompositions allow one to determine the range of applicability of linear model in general and to reveal particular generalized eigenmodes that sensitive to bilinear effects.

Although this study focuses on continuous bilinear systems, the results obtained can be extended to different classes of systems. First, they can be extended to discrete dynamical systems. In the linear case, this was partially performed in [18]. Meanwhile, the generalized Lyapunov equations that we consider for deterministic bilinear systems can be naturally associated with stochastic linear control systems (see [8]). Therefore, the results of spectral decomposition of Gramians can immediately be carried over to this class of systems. In this case, the results must be interpreted in terms of probabilities. Finally, the equations considered in this study can describe a special class of linear parameter-varying systems that can be reformulated as bilinear dynamical systems [9]. In this case, the interpretation of the spectral decompositions must include the effect of parameter variation.

It should be noted that the main object of research in this study is matrix Lyapunov equations, that is, matrix equations. An alternative approach is to apply the apparatus of linear matrix inequalities and semi-definite programming [25]. Therefore, another possible area of research is the combination of these approaches. In terms of applications, the authors plan to apply the developed methods to study the stability of electric power systems using linear and non-linear graph models. Another emerging area is the analysis of the stability of neural networks, including the use of Lyapunov functions [26,27]. The dissipativity principle in the synchronization of neural networks is very similar to the synchronization of generators in power systems. Therefore, the application of the developed methods to the problem of synchronization of neural networks is another possible direction for future research.

Author Contributions: A.I. and I.Y. contributed equally on the development of the theory and their respective analysis. All authors have read and agreed to the published version of the manuscript.

Funding: This research was funded by the Russian Science Foundation, grant number 19-19-00673.

Institutional Review Board Statement: Not applicable.

Informed Consent Statement: Not applicable.

Data Availability Statement: Not applicable.

References

1. Häger, U.; Rehtanz, C.; Voropai, N.I. *Monitoring, Control and Protection of Interconnected Power Systems*; Springer: New York, NY, USA, 2014; 391p.
2. D'Alessandro, P.; Isidori, A.; Ruberti, A. Realization and structure theory of bilinear dynamic systems. *SIAM J. Control.* **1974**, *12*, 517–535. [CrossRef]
3. Pupkov, K.A.; Kapalin, V.I.; Yushchenko, A.S. *Functional Series in the Theory of Nonlinear Systems*; Nauka: Moscow, Russia, 1976; 448p. (In Russian)
4. Flagg, G.M.; Gugercin, S. Multipoint Volterra Series Interpolation and H2 Optimal Model Reduction of Bilinear Systems. *SIAM J. Matrix Anal. Appl.* **2015**, *36*, 549–579. [CrossRef]
5. Al-Baiyat, S.; Farag, A.S.; Bettayeb, M. Transient approximation of a bilinear two-area interconnected power system. *Electr. Power Syst. Res.* **1993**, *26*, 11–19. [CrossRef]
6. Zhang, L.; Lam, J. On the H_2 model reduction of bilinear systems. *Automatica* **2002**, *38*, 205–216. [CrossRef]
7. Antoulas, A.C. *Approximation of Large-Scale Dynamical Systems: Advances in Design and Control*; SIAM: Philadephia, PA, USA, 2005; 479p.

8. Benner, P.; Breiten, T. Interpolation-based H2-model reduction of bilinear control systems. *SIAM J. Matrix Anal. Appl.* **2012**, *33*, 859–881. [CrossRef]

9. Benner, P.; Cao, X.; Schilders, W. A bilinear H2 model order reduction approach to bilinear parameter-varying systems. *Adv. Comput. Math.* **2019**, *45*, 2241–2271. [CrossRef]

10. Gibbard, M.J.; Pourbeik, P.; Vowles, D.J. *Small-Signal Stability, Control and Dynamic Performance of Power Systems*; University of Adelaide Press: Adelaide, Australia, 2015.

11. Jang, G.; Vittal, V.; Kliemann, W. Effect of nonlinear modal interaction on control performance: Use of normal forms technique in control design, Part 1: General theory and procedure. *IEEE Trans. Power Syst.* **1998**, *13*, 401–407. [CrossRef]

12. Pariz, N.; Shanechi, H.M.; Vaahedi, E. Explaining and validating stressed power systems behavior using modal series. *IEEE Trans. Power Syst.* **2003**, *18*, 778–785. [CrossRef]

13. Arroyo, J.; Betancourt, R.; Messina, A.R.; Barocio, E.D. Development of bilinear power system representations for small-signal stability analysis. *Electr. Power Syst. Res.* **2007**, *77*, 1239–1248. [CrossRef]

14. Ugwuanyi, N.S.; Kestelyn, X.; Thomas, O.; Marinescu, B.; Messina, A.R. New Fast Track to Nonlinear Modal Analysis of Power System Using Normal Form. *IEEE Trans. Power Syst.* **2020**, *35*, 3247–3257. [CrossRef]

15. Hamzi, B.; Abed, E.H. Local modal participation analysis of nonlinear systems using Poincaré linearization. *Nonlinear Dyn.* **2020**, *99*, 803–811. [CrossRef]

16. Benner, P.; Damm, T. Lyapunov equations, energy functionals, and model order reduction of bilinear and stochastic systems. *SIAM J. Control. Optim.* **2011**, *49*, 686–711. [CrossRef]

17. Yadykin, I.B.; Iskakov, A.B.; Akhmetzyanov, A.V. Stability analysis of large-scale dynamical systems by sub-Gramian approach. *Int. J. Robust. Nonlin. Control* **2014**, *24*, 1361–1379. [CrossRef]

18. Yadykin, I.B.; Iskakov, A.B. Spectral Decompositions for the Solutions of Sylvester, Lyapunov, and Krein Equations. *Dokl. Math.* **2017**, *95*, 103–107. [CrossRef]

19. Yadykin, I.B.; Iskakov, A.B. Spectral decompositions for the solutions of Lyapunov equations for bilinear dynamical systems. *Dokl. Math.* **2019**, *100*, 501–504. [CrossRef]

20. Iskakov, A.B.; Yadykin, I.B. Analysis of a bilinear model of an electric power system using spectral decompositions of Lyapunov functions. *IFAC-PapersOnLine* **2020**, *53*, 13514–13519. [CrossRef]

21. Garofalo, F.; Iannelli, L.; Vasca, F. Participation Factors and their Connections to Residues and Relative Gain Array. *IFAC Proc. Vol.* **2002**, *35*, 125–130. [CrossRef]

22. Bruni, C.; Dipillo, G.; Koch, G. On the mathematical models of bilinear systems. *Ric. Di Autom.* **1971**, *2*, 11–26.

23. Siu, T.; Schetzen, M. Convergence of Volterra series representation and BIBO stability of bilinear systems. *Int. J. Syst. Sci.* **1991**, *22*, 2679–2684. [CrossRef]

24. Yadykin, I.; Galyaev, A. On the methods for calculation of Gramians and their use in analysis of linear dynamic systems. *Autom. Remote Control* **2013**, *74*, 207–224. [CrossRef]

25. Khlebnikov, M.V. Quadratic Stabilization of Bilinear Control Systems. *Autom. Remote Control* **2016**, *77*, 980–991. [CrossRef]

26. Vadivel, R.; Hammachukiattikul, P.; Gunasekaran, N.; Saravanakumar, R.; Dutta, H. Strict dissipativity synchronization for delayed static neural networks: An event-triggered scheme. *Chaos Solitons Fractals* **2021**, *150*, 111212. [CrossRef]

27. Gunasekaran, N.; Thoiyab, N.M.; Zhu, Q.; Cao, J.; Muruganantham, P. New Global Asymptotic Robust Stability of Dynamical Delayed Neural Networks via Intervalized Interconnection Matrices. *IEEE Trans. Cybern.* **2021**. [CrossRef] [PubMed]

mathematics

Article

New Identification Approach and Methods for Plasma Equilibrium Reconstruction in D-Shaped Tokamaks

Yuri V. Mitrishkin [1,2,*,†], Pavel S. Korenev [2,†], Artem E. Konkov [2,†], Valerii I. Kruzhkov [1,2,†] and Nicolai E. Ovsiannikov [1,2,†]

1. Faculty of Physics, Lomonosov Moscow State University, Moscow 119991, Russia; kruzhkov.vi14@physics.msu.ru (V.I.K.); ovsjannikov.ne15@physics.msu.ru (N.E.O.)
2. V.A. Trapeznikov Institute of Control Sciences of Russian Academy of Sciences, Moscow 117997, Russia; korenev.pavel@physics.msu.ru (P.S.K.); konkov@physics.msu.ru (A.E.K.)
* Correspondence: mitrishkin.yv19@physics.msu.ru
† These authors contributed equally to this work.

Abstract: The paper deals with the identification of plasma equilibrium reconstruction in D-shaped tokamaks on the base of plasma external magnetic measurements. The methods of such identification are directed to increase their speed of response when plasma discharges are relatively short, like in the spherical Globus-M2 tokamak (Ioffe Inst., St. Petersburg, Russia). The new approach is first to apply to the plasma discharges data the off-line equilibrium reconstruction algorithm based on the Picard iterations, and obtain the gaps between the plasma boundary and the first wall, and the second is to apply new identification methods to the gap values, producing plasma shape models operating in real time. The inputs for on-line robust identification algorithms are the measurements of magnetic fluxes on magnetic loops, plasma current, and currents in the poloidal field coils measured by the Rogowski loops. The novel on-line high-performance identification algorithms are designed on the base of (i) full-order observer synthesized by linear matrix inequality (LMI) methodology, (ii) static matrix obtained by the least square technique, and (iii) deep neural network. The robust observer is constructed on the base of the LPV plant models which have the novelty that the state vector contains the gaps which are estimated by the observer, using input and output signals. The results of the simulation of the identification systems on the base of experimental data of the Globus-M2 tokamak are presented.

Keywords: tokamak; plasma equilibrium reconstruction; linear plasma models; identification; state observer; LMI; least square technique; deep neural network

Citation: Mitrishkin, Y.V.; Korenev, P.S.; Konkov, A.E.; Kruzhkov, V.I.; Ovsiannikov, N.E. New Identification Approach and Methods for Plasma Equilibrium Reconstruction in D-Shaped Tokamaks. *Mathematics* **2022**, *10*, 40. https://doi.org/10.3390/math10010040

Academic Editors: Igor Yadykin, Andrei Torgashov, Nikolay Korgin and Natalia Bakhtadze

Received: 21 November 2021
Accepted: 19 December 2021
Published: 23 December 2021

Publisher's Note: MDPI stays neutral with regard to jurisdictional claims in published maps and institutional affiliations.

1. Introduction

Tokamaks [1], toroidal vessels with magnetic coils (Figure 1), originated at the I.V. Kurchatov Institute of Atomic Energy in the USSR and spread around the world to solve the problem of controlled thermonuclear fusion: obtaining energy from the fusion of the light elements nuclei. The most promising devices for solving this problem are vertically elongated tokamaks with increased gas-kinetic pressure (D-shaped tokamaks) (Figure 1). Plasma (the fourth state of matter) vertically elongated by an external magnetic field is unstable in the vertical direction, and it is necessary to use automatic feedback control systems to keep it near the first tokamak wall.

In our studies, we developed, modeled, and applied control systems of plasma position, current and shape for various tokamaks: ITER (International Thermonuclear Experimental Reactor, Cadarache, France) [2,3], T-15MD (tokamak created at NRC "Kurchatov Institute", Moscow, Russia, planned to be launched in the near future) [4–6], Tuman-3 (toroidal installation with adiabatic compression) [3,4], Globus-M2 (spherical tokamak) [4,7,8] (operating at Ioffe Physics and Technology Institute of RAS, St. Petersburg, Russia), T-11M (operating circular tokamak) [9], and IGNITOR (JSC "SSC RF TRINITI", Troitsk, Russia) [10].

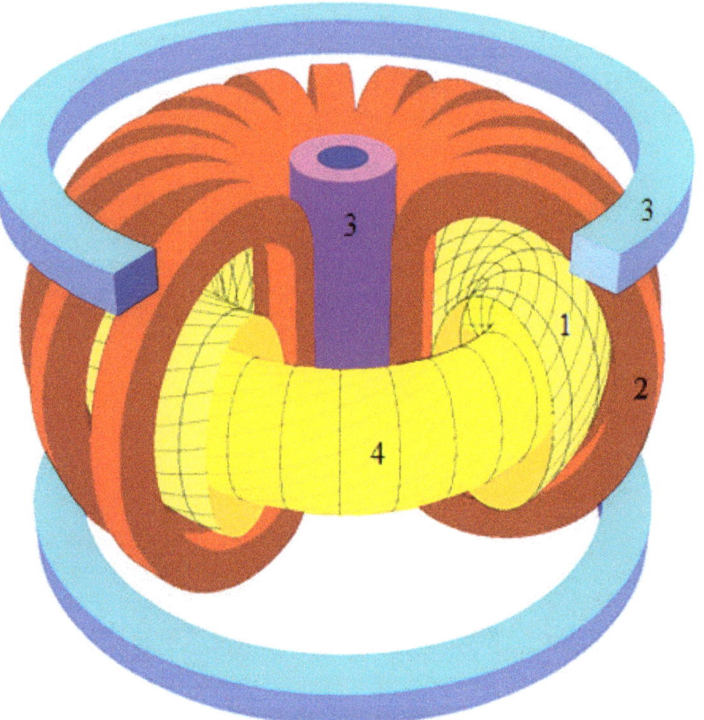

Figure 1. Vertically elongated tokamak without iron core: 1 is the VV; 2 is the toroidal field coil; 3 are the poloidal field inner and outer coils; 4 are plasma and helical magnetic lines (©ITER Project Center (Russia): https://www.iterrf.ru/index.php/istoriya-sozdaniya-proekta, accessed on 21 December 2021).

Since optical reconstruction codes such as OFIT [11] are not available in many tokamaks, the plasma boundary in D-shaped tokamaks usually is not measured directly but rather reconstructed from the external measurements. There are a number of codes which are able to solve that problem, off-line and on-line [12]. The most popular of them are EFIT (equilibrium fitting) [13], which uses the Picard iterations [14] and which is applied on-line on a set of tokamaks, such as DIII-D, NSTX (U.S.), EAST (China), KSTAR (S. Korea) and RTLIUQE [15] used on TCV (Switzerland). These codes were adopted for ITER.

In this work, the new plasma equilibrium reconstruction algorithms are to be inserted into the plasma position, current, and shape feedback control system of the Globus-M2 tokamak. In Figure 2, one can see the digital model of that system [16] where the plasma equilibrium reconstructed algorithm is to be identified by the new methods proposed in the paper.

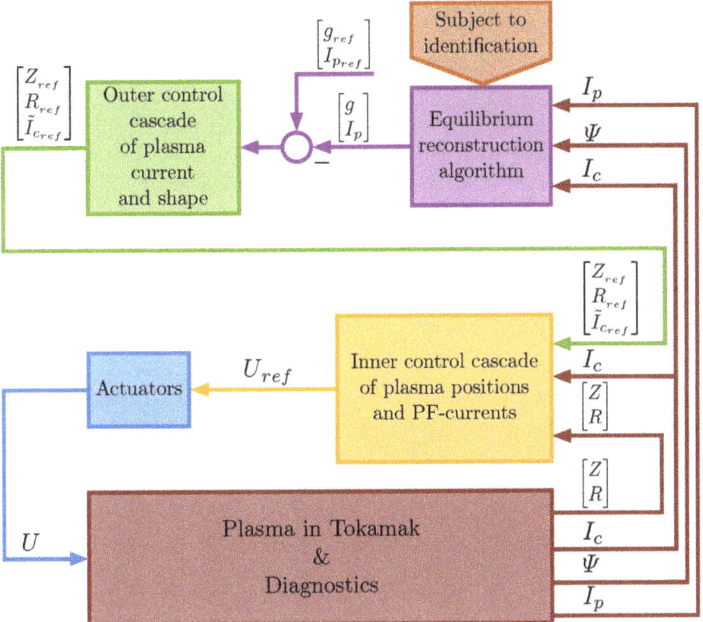

Figure 2. Structure scheme of the plasma position, current and shape control system of Globus-M2 tokamak.

2. Reconstructing Plasma Equilibria from External Magnetic Measurements

A tokamak is an axially symmetrical device, so the tokamak plasma equilibrium is described in the poloidal plane (r, z), typically in terms of the poloidal magnetic flux distribution $\Psi(r, z)$, which is defined as the flux of the magnetic field vector $\vec{B}$ through a surface S bounded by the line $(r = const, z = const)$:

$$\Psi(r, z) = \frac{1}{2\pi} \iint_S \vec{B} d\vec{S}. \tag{1}$$

The magnetic field lines, along which plasma particles move, lie on the flux surfaces $\Psi(r, z) = const$; therefore, the boundary of the magnetically confined plasma can be found as the largest closed flux surface.

The toroidal current density J_φ in the tokamak is connected with the poloidal flux through the linear second-order partial differential equation [1]:

$$-\mu_0^{-1} \left(\frac{\partial}{\partial r} \frac{1}{r} \frac{\partial}{\partial r} + \frac{1}{r} \frac{\partial^2}{\partial z^2} \right) \Psi = J_\varphi. \tag{2}$$

The boundary conditions for the equation are obtained from the definition and the physical meaning of the poloidal flux:

$$\Psi|_{r=0} = 0, \ \Psi|_{r=\infty} = 0. \tag{3}$$

When the right-hand side of the Equation (2) is known, it can be solved with the standard numerical methods, for example, using the corresponding Green's function G [17]:

$$\Psi(r,z) = \iint J_\varphi(r',z')G(r,z,r',z')dr'dz',$$

$$G(r,z,r',z') = \frac{\mu_0}{\pi}\sqrt{\frac{rr'}{k^2}}\left(\left(1-\frac{k^2}{2}\right)K(k^2) - E(k^2)\right),$$

where K and E are the elliptic integrals of the first and the second kind respectively, and

$$k^2 = \frac{4rr'}{(r+r')^2 + (z-z')^2}.$$

In practice, the plasma current distribution and the induced currents in the conductive Vacuum Vessel (VV) of the tokamak are often not available for real-time reconstruction and must be identified together with the poloidal flux distribution from the external magnetic measurements, which include coil currents $I_1,\ldots,I_{N_c}$, total plasma current I_p measured by Rogowski coils and poloidal flux values Ψ at finite number of points $\{(r_1,z_1),\ldots,(r_{N_l},z_{N_l})\}$ by magnetic loops outside the plasma.

Hence, the plasma equilibrium reconstruction problem is to find plasma area S_p, plasma current distribution J_p and induced current density J_v such that:

$$\chi^2 = \left(I_p - \int J_p dS\right)^2/\sigma_p^2 + \sum_{j=1}^{N_l}(\Psi_j - \Psi(r_j,z_j))^2/\sigma_j^2 \xrightarrow[J_p,J_v]{} min, \tag{4}$$

where σ_p and σ_j are uncertainties of the plasma current and poloidal flux at j^{th} magnetic loop, $\Psi(r,z)$ is the solution of the Equation (2) with boundary conditions (3) and the right-hand side:

$$J_\varphi(r,z) = \begin{cases} J_p, & (r,z) \in S_p, \\ I_k N_k/S_k, & (r,z) \in S_k, \quad k=1,\ldots,N_c, \\ J_v & (r,z) \in S_v, \end{cases}$$

S_k and S_v are the area occupied by the kth coil and the VV, respectively, N_k is the number of turns of the kth coil.

Optionally, coil current measurements may also be considered uncertain and accounted in the functional (4) by terms $\left(I_k - I_k^{measured}\right)^2/\sigma_{I_k}^2, k=1,\ldots,N_c$. The functional may also include other measurements that can be expressed in terms of the currents and the magnetic flux. Finally, as the plasma equilibrium reconstruction problem is ill-posed in the sense of Hadamard, the functional may include a regularization term.

To find the plasma shape in the Globus-M2 tokamak (Figure 3), the flux-current distribution identification (FCDI) code was used [14]. The FCDI code applies the following expression for the plasma toroidal current density, obtained from the plasma force balance equations [1,14]:

$$J_p = rp'(\Psi) + \frac{1}{\mu_0 r}F(\Psi)F'(\Psi).$$

where p is plasma pressure and F is poloidal current defined analogous to poloidal flux (1):

$$F = \frac{\mu_0}{2\pi}\iint_S \vec{J}d\vec{S}.$$

The Picard iteration method is used to find the poloidal flux distribution. Since F and p depend only on poloidal flux, on each iteration, the FCDI code approximates the plasma current density by polynomials of the poloidal flux from the previous iteration:

$$p'(\Psi) = \sum_{k=0}^{N_p} c_k^{(p)} \Psi^k,$$

$$F(\Psi)F'(\Psi) = \sum_{k=0}^{N_F} c_k^{(F)} \Psi^k.$$

Similarly, the VV currents are approximated as a linear combination of some basis functions, for example, orthogonal VV current modes [18]:

$$J_v = \sum_{k=0}^{N_v} c_k^{(v)} J_k.$$

The coefficients of the J_p polynomials and the J_v basis function regression are found then by minimizing the error functional (4) which can be written in the matrix form:

$$\chi^2 = \|Ac - b\|^2.$$

Here, c is the $N \times 1$ column-vector of the coefficients $c^{(p)}, c^{(F)}, c^{(v)}$, $N = N_p + N_F + N_v$, A is the $M \times N$ matrix, where M is the number of magnetic measurements used, and b is the $N \times 1$ column-vector. To regularize the problem, the SVD truncation method is used to minimize the quadratic functional [19]. After the coefficients are determined, the corresponding poloidal flux distribution is calculated, which is used for the polynomials construction on the next iteration. The iterations are continued until the error χ^2 is sufficiently small or the maximal number of iterations is reached.

Figure 3. Globus-M2 tokamak (©Ioffe Physics and Technology Institute of RAS, St. Petersburg, Russia).

3. Experimental Data

The FCDI code was applied to 50 discharges of the Globus-M2 tokamak. For each discharge, there are magnetic measurements available $y^{(1)}, y^{(2)}, \ldots, y^{(50)}$, which include currents in the 8 control coils (Horizontal Field Coil, Vertical Field Coil, Central Solenoid, Poloidal Field Coil 1, upper and lower sections of the Poloidal Field Coil 2, Poloidal Field Coil 3 and Correcting Coil) (Figure 4), poloidal magnetic flux from 21 loops, vertical dipole magnetic flux (difference between magnetic flux above and below plasma), horizontal dipole magnetic flux (difference between magnetic flux on the left and on the right of the plasma), and quadrupole magnetic flux (expressed as $\psi(L_1) - \psi(L_2) + \psi(L_3) - \psi(L_4)$, with location of loops L_1–L_4 shown in Figure 4) so that $y^{(i)} \in \mathbb{R}^{33 \times s_i}$, $i \in [1; 50]$, where each $s_i = T_i / \tau$, T_i is the duration of the discharge, τ is the discretization step. Here, the discretization step is the time step between the reconstructed off-line equilibria. It is constrained only by the discretization time of the experimental measurements.

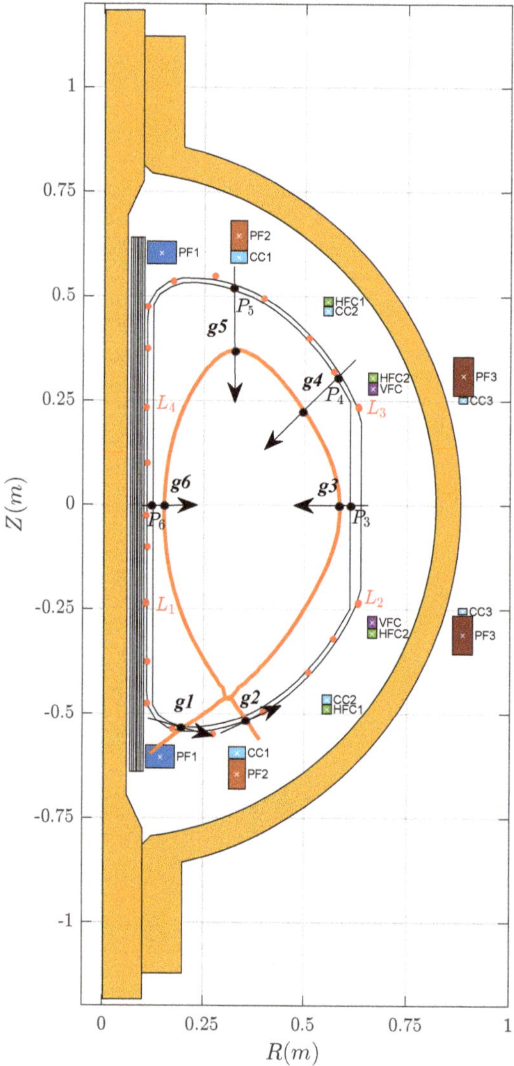

Figure 4. Poloidal system of the Globus-M2 tokamak and plasma boundary with strike points *g1*, *g2* and gaps *g3*–*g6*.

From these data, the FCDI code obtains plasma current distribution and plasma boundary coordinates for the divertor phases of the discharges. The calculated plasma shapes are represented by the positions of 2 strike points (g_1, g_2) on the VV and values of 4 gaps $(g_3\text{–}g_6)$ between plasma and VV (Figure 4) $g^{(1)}, g^{(2)}, \ldots, g^{(50)}$; $g^{(i)} \in \mathbb{R}^{6 \times s_i}$. The strike points are points of intersection of the poloidal flux isoline, which bounds the plasma and the VV. Their coordinates g_1 and g_2 are calculated as the distance from point P_6 in Figure 4 along the VV. The gap g_3 is calculated as the distance between point P_3 on the VV outer wall and the plasma boundary on the horizontal line, g_4 is the distance between P_4 and the plasma boundary on the 45° line, g_5 is the distance between P_5 and the plasma boundary along the vertical line, and g_6 is the distance between point P_6 on the VV inner wall and the plasma along the horizontal line. The $g_1\text{–}g_6$ values describe plasma shape in the LSND (lower single null divertor) configuration, typical for the Globus-M2 tokamak. Other configurations may require different sets of descriptors, but the identification methods described below are applicable all the same.

4. Plasma Model

The plasma dynamics is described by Faraday's law equations:

$$\frac{d}{dt}\Phi(J_p, I) + RI = U, \tag{5}$$

and force balance equation

$$\vec{F}(J_p, I) = 0. \tag{6}$$

The measured fluxes and the plasma shape are determined by currents in the tokamak:

$$\begin{aligned} \Psi &= \Psi(J_p, I), \\ g &= g(J_p, I). \end{aligned} \tag{7}$$

Here, $I = [I_c^\mathrm{T}, I_v^\mathrm{T}, I_p]^\mathrm{T}$, Φ, R, and U are respectively the column-vector of currents, column-vector of magnetic flux, diagonal matrix of electrical resistance and column-vector of the voltage applied to the control coils, VV, and plasma $\vec{F}$ is the force acting on the plasma, g is the column vector of strike points positions on the VV and the gaps between the plasma and VV, Ψ is the column vector of the fluxes measured by the tokamak diagnostics. The plasma mass is neglected.

The magnetic flux vector can be expressed as $\Phi(J_p, I) = M(J_p)I$, where M is the inductance matrix. The dependence of the inductance matrix M, force $\vec{F}$ and plasma shape g on plasma current distribution J_p is nonlinear but for the small deviations from the reconstructed equilibrium, the linearized model is sufficient. Assuming that plasma can rigidly move in vertical and radial directions, the linearized Equations (5)–(7) take form:

$$M\frac{dI}{dt} + \frac{\partial \Phi}{\partial \vec{r}_p}\frac{d\vec{r}_p}{dt} + R\delta I = \delta U,$$

$$\frac{\partial \vec{F}}{\partial I}\delta I + \frac{\partial \vec{F}}{\partial \vec{r}_p}\delta \vec{r}_p = 0,$$

$$\delta \Psi = \frac{\partial \Psi}{\partial I}\delta I + \frac{\partial \Psi}{\partial \vec{r}_p}\delta \vec{r}_p,$$

$$\delta g = \frac{\partial g}{\partial I}\delta I + \frac{\partial g}{\partial \vec{r}_p}\delta \vec{r}_p,$$

where $\vec{r}_p$ is the radius-vector $\vec{r}_p = [r_p, z_p]^\mathrm{T}$ of plasma center of mass, δ denotes deviation from the scenario value.

Introducing state vector $x = \delta I = [\delta I_c^{\mathrm{T}}, \delta I_v^{\mathrm{T}}, \delta I_p]^{\mathrm{T}}$, input vector $u = \delta U$ and output vector of plasma and coil currents, gaps, and fluxes deviations $y = [\delta I_p, \delta I_c^{\mathrm{T}}, \delta \Psi^{\mathrm{T}}, \delta g^{\mathrm{T}}]^{\mathrm{T}}$, the LPV (linear parameter varying) model takes the standard state-space form:

$$\begin{cases} \dot{x}(t) = A_m(J_p, t)x(t) + B_m(J_p, t)u(t), \\ y(t) = C_m(J_p, t)x(t). \end{cases} \tag{8}$$

The reconstructed plasma current distributions J_p are used to calculate series of linear models $\{A, B, C\}_{nm}$ describing plasma dynamics in each considered discharge. Here, index n denotes time moment t_n for which the model is obtained

$$A_{nm} = A_m(J_p, t_n), B_{nm} = B_m(J_p, t_n), C_{nm} = C_m(J_p, t_n), n = 1, \ldots, N_m,$$

where $t_1, \ldots, t_{N_m}$ correspond to the time points of the divertor phase of the mth tokamak discharge with the time step of 1 ms and index m denotes the serial number of discharge. This represents the LPV model (8) as an array of LTI (linear time invariant) models. During modeling each discharge, a linear interpolation is performed between time points from t_1 to t_{N_m}.

The models have 24 states, 8 inputs, and 39 outputs. Each obtained model has a single real positive pole.

Although the models include expressions for the gaps as the outputs, the gaps are not directly measured on the tokamak, so it may be convenient to apply state-space coordinate transformation, replacing any 6 currents with gaps in the state vector and removing gaps from the outputs. Furthermore, use the ZOH (zero-order hold) for discretization with sample time $T_s = 0.1$ ms such that

$$t(T_s k) \le t \le t(T_s k + T_s), k \in \mathbb{Z},$$

$$A_{nm}^d = \exp(A_{nm} T_s), B_{nm}^d = A_{nm}^{-1}(A_{nm}^d - I)B_{nm}, C_{nm}^d = C_{nm}.$$

The final array of discrete-time models in the state-space form is obtained

$$\begin{cases} x(T_s k + T_s) = A_{nm}^d x(T_s k) + B_{nm}^d u(T_s k), \\ y(T_s k) = C_{nm}^d x(T_s k). \end{cases} \tag{9}$$

The models have 8 inputs $u = \delta U$, 24 states $x = [\delta g^{\mathrm{T}}, \delta \hat{I}^{\mathrm{T}}]^{\mathrm{T}}$ consisting of 6 gaps and truncated to 18 elements current vector $\hat{I}$, 33 outputs $y = [\delta I_p, \delta I_c^{\mathrm{T}}, \delta \Psi^{\mathrm{T}}]^{\mathrm{T}}$ directly corresponding to the values measured by the diagnostics at Globus-M2 tokamak: plasma current, 8 currents in control coils, poloidal magnetic flux from 21 loops, quadrupole magnetic flux, and vertical and horizontal dipole magnetic flux. The inclusion of the gaps in the state vector is convenient for some applications, one of which is described in the next section.

5. Plasma Shape Identification by Robust Observer Synthesized by LMI

The idea of gap estimation with a robust discrete state observer is as follows. Using the FCDI code, a series of LPV models for a series of plasma discharges is computed. The gaps are included in the state vector of all linear models, and the output vector includes the signals measured by the magnetic diagnostics system of the tokamak. Then, using the LMI method, a unified state observer is synthesized, which provides minimal error between states and state estimates for a series of LPV models.

The synthesized observer can be used in a real experiment, with experimental signals connected to its input as shown in Figure 5.

The unified observer for an array of linear models of the plant ensures the minimum error between the state vectors and state estimation and consequently between the gaps values and gaps estimation over the entire discharge duration. This further guarantees the robust behavior of the synthesized plasma shape control system.

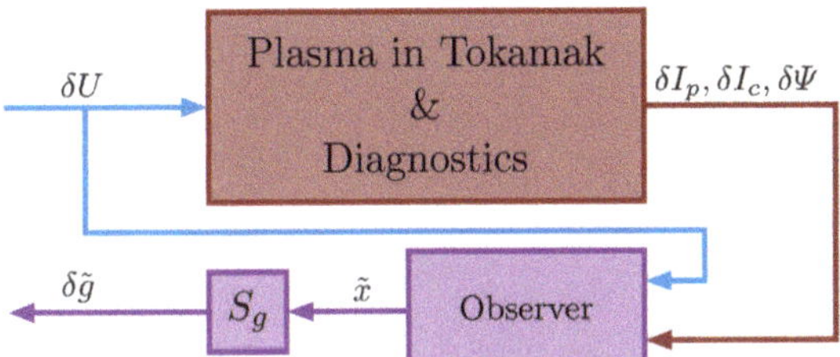

Figure 5. Robust observer synthesized via LMIs for use in a real experiment. The red vector signal includes experimental signals obtained by the magnetic diagnostic system. The blue vector signal includes voltages on the poloidal coils. The yellow signal contains states estimation, which includes gaps estimation.

The state equation of the full-order discrete-time observer [20] is given as follows

$$\tilde{x}(T_s k + T_s) = A^d \tilde{x}(T_s k) + B^d u(T_s k) + L\left(y(T_s k) - C^d \tilde{x}(T_s k)\right),$$

where $\tilde{x}$ is the state estimation vector of discrete-time state-space plant model $\{A^d, B^d, C^d\}$, T_s is the sample time and L is the matrix of the observer.

Then it is necessary to perform the transition to the error equation of the observer

$$e(T_s k + T_s) = \left(A^d - LC^d\right) e(T_s k),$$

where $e = x - \tilde{x}$ is the error between the states and state estimations.

The matrix inequalities systems for the observer synthesis are obtained using the generalized Lyapunov theorem [21]

$$\begin{cases} X \succ 0, \\ R(X, V) = L_{\mathbb{D}} \otimes X + M_{\mathbb{D}} \otimes \left(X(A^d - LC^d)\right) + M_{\mathbb{D}}^{\mathsf{T}} \otimes \left(X(A^d - LC^d)\right)^{\mathsf{T}} \prec 0, \end{cases}$$

where the symbol "$\otimes$" denotes the Kronecker product.

The poles of the observer are placed in the $\mathbb{D}$-region formed by the disk with the characteristic function

$$F_{\mathbb{D}}(s) = L_{\mathbb{D}} + sM_{\mathbb{D}} + \bar{s}M_{\mathbb{D}}^{\mathsf{T}} < 0,$$

where

$$L_{\mathbb{D}} = \begin{bmatrix} -0.5 & 0 \\ 0 & -0.5 \end{bmatrix}, \quad M_{\mathbb{D}} = \begin{bmatrix} 0 & 1 \\ 0 & 0 \end{bmatrix}. \tag{10}$$

The choice of this $\mathbb{D}$-region is due to the need, on the one hand, to provide shorter transition times in the observer compared to the plant model, and on the other hand, the $\mathbb{D}$-region should not be too small; otherwise, it would be impossible to find a solution of the LMI system for the array of plant models.

The synthesizable observer should qualitatively estimate the states for each LTI model from (9), which is obtained from the LPV model (8) for the mth plasma discharge. In addition, the same observer should qualitatively estimate the states for several LPV models corresponding to several discharges. In this approach, the robust performance of the synthesized observer is achieved.

The LMI system for obtaining the observer matrix for the array of models in state-space (9) with the replacement of $V = XL$ is as follows

$$
\begin{cases}
X \succ 0, \\
R_1(X,V) = L_\mathbb{D} \otimes X + M_\mathbb{D} \otimes \left(XA_{11}\right) + M_\mathbb{D}^\mathsf{T} \otimes \left(XA_{11}\right)^\mathsf{T} \\
\qquad\qquad - M_\mathbb{D} \otimes \left(VC_{11}\right) - M_\mathbb{D}^\mathsf{T} \otimes \left(VC_{11}\right)^\mathsf{T} \prec 0, \\
\qquad\qquad \vdots \\
R_r(X,V) = L_\mathbb{D} \otimes X + M_\mathbb{D} \otimes \left(XA_{nm}\right) + M_\mathbb{D}^\mathsf{T} \otimes \left(XA_{nm}\right)^\mathsf{T} \\
\qquad\qquad - M_\mathbb{D} \otimes \left(VC_{nm}\right) - M_\mathbb{D}^\mathsf{T} \otimes \left(VC_{nm}\right)^\mathsf{T} \prec 0,
\end{cases}
\tag{11}
$$

where $n = 1,\ldots,N_m$, $m = 1,\ldots,M$ and $r = 1,\ldots,N_m M$.

The LMI system (11) includes $N_m M + 1$ LMIs, and it must be solved with respect to the two unknown matrices, X and V. The matrix of the observer is defined as

$$
L = X^{-1}V.
$$

Finally, the gap estimation vector $\delta\tilde{g}$ is obtained as follows

$$
\delta\tilde{g} = S_g\tilde{x},
$$

where S_g (Figure 5) is the gaps estimation selection matrix from the state vector estimation

$$
S_g = \begin{bmatrix} I_6 & 0_{6,18} \end{bmatrix},
$$

where I_6 is the identity matrix and $0_{6,18}$ is the zeros matrix of the appropriate size.

The comparison of the gaps variations δg derived by LPV model obtained from the FCDI code and the gaps variations estimation $\delta\tilde{g}$ obtained by the robust observer synthesized via LMIs for plasma discharge #37263 is shown in Figure 6.

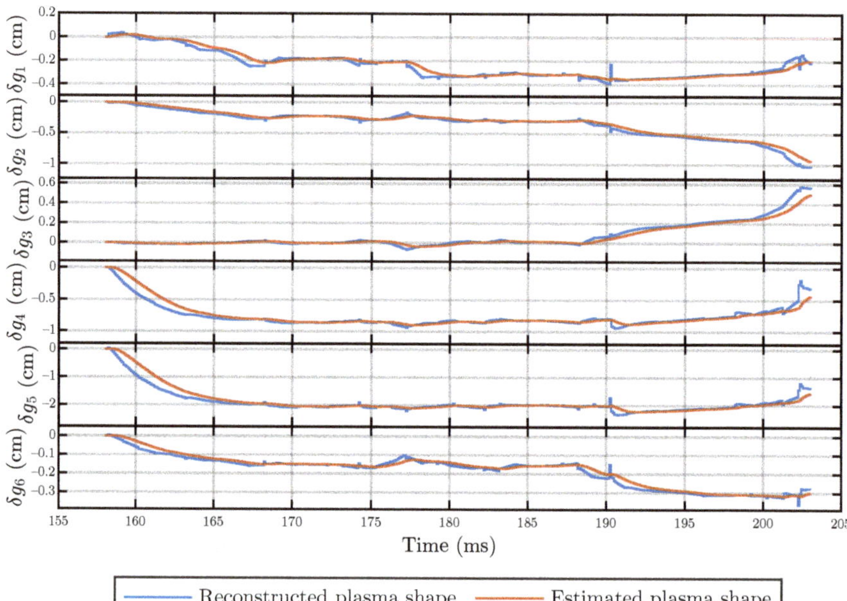

Figure 6. Comparison of gaps variations δg derived by LPV model obtained from the FCDI code (blue line) and estimation of gap variations $\delta\tilde{g}$ obtained from robust observer synthesized by LMIs (red line). Globus-M2 discharge #37263.

6. Static Matrix Plasma Shape Identification

The idea of the static matrix plasma shape estimation is that at any time moment $j \in [1; s_i]$ of any discharge $i \in [1; 50]$, the plasma shape estimation $\hat{g}_j^{(i)} \in \mathbb{R}^6$ may be obtained by multiplication of the measurable signals at this time moment $y_j^{(i)} \in \mathbb{R}^{33}$ and matrix $K \in \mathbb{R}^{6 \times 33}$ summing the base gap values $\tilde{g} \in \mathbb{R}^6$. As this takes place, the matrix K and vector $\tilde{g}$ are constant for all plasma discharges:

$$\hat{g}_j^{(i)} = Ky_j^{(i)} + \tilde{g}, \quad K = const, \quad \tilde{g} = const, \quad \hat{g}_j^{(i)} \in \mathbb{R}^6, \tag{12}$$

The matrix K and vector $\tilde{g}$ are obtained by the minimization of the summed squared differences between the estimated and the reconstructed values of all 6 gaps in all 50 discharges at all time moments:

$$E(K, \tilde{g}) = \sum_{i=1}^{50} \sum_{k=1}^{6} \sum_{j=1}^{s_i} (\hat{g}_{jk}^{(i)} - g_{jk}^{(i)})^2 = \sum_{i=1}^{50} \sum_{k=1}^{6} \sum_{j=1}^{s_i} (Ky_j^{(i)} + \tilde{g} - g_{jk}^{(i)})^2 \xrightarrow[K,\tilde{g}]{} min, \tag{13}$$

where $\hat{g}^{(i)} = [\hat{g}_1^{(i)}, \hat{g}_2^{(i)}, \dots, \hat{g}_{s_i}^{(i)}] \in \mathbb{R}^{6 \times s_i}$ is the matrix estimation of ith discharge gaps, $g^{(i)} = [g_1^{(i)}, g_2^{(i)}, \dots, g_{s_i}^{(i)}] \in \mathbb{R}^{6 \times s_i}$ is the matrix of the reconstructed values of ith discharge gaps. If $y^{(i)} = [y_1^{(i)}, y_2^{(i)}, \dots, y_{s_i}^{(i)}] \in \mathbb{R}^{6 \times s_i}$ is the matrix of measurable signals of the ith discharge so $r^{(i)}(\tilde{g}) = [\tilde{g}, \tilde{g}, \dots, \tilde{g}] \in \mathbb{R}^{6 \times s_i}$ is the matrix with the same columns $\tilde{g}$. Equation (12) can be rewritten in the matrix form,

$$\hat{g}^{(i)} = Ky^{(i)} + r^{(i)}(\tilde{g}), \quad \hat{g}^{(i)} \in \mathbb{R}^{6 \times s_i}. \tag{14}$$

Equation (13) can be rewritten in matrix form as follows:

$$E(K, \tilde{g}) = \sum_{i=1}^{50} \|\hat{g}^{(i)} - g_k^{(i)}\|^2 \xrightarrow[K,\tilde{g}]{} min. \tag{15}$$

Let $Y = [y^{(1)}, y^{(2)}, \dots, y^{(50)}]$; $Y \in \mathbb{R}^{33 \times S}$, where $S = \sum_{i=1}^{50} s_i$, $G = [g^{(1)}, g^{(2)}, \dots, g^{(50)}]$; $G \in \mathbb{R}^{6 \times S}$ and $\hat{G} = [\hat{g}^{(1)}, \hat{g}^{(2)}, \dots, \hat{g}^{(50)}]$; $\hat{G} \in \mathbb{R}^{6 \times S}$. Matrix Y contains all measurements, matrix G is all reconstructed gaps. Since $\hat{G} = [\hat{g}^{(1)}, \hat{g}^{(2)}, \dots, \hat{g}^{(50)}] = [Ky^{(1)} + r, Ky^{(2)} + r, \dots, Ky^{(50)} + r]$, problems (14) and (15) are equivalent to

$$\begin{aligned} \hat{G}(K, \hat{g}) &= KY + R(\tilde{g}), \quad \hat{G} \in \mathbb{R}^{6 \times S} \\ E(K, \tilde{g}) &= \|\hat{G}_k(\hat{g}) - G_k\|^2 \xrightarrow[K,\tilde{g}]{} min \end{aligned} \Rightarrow \begin{aligned} K(\tilde{g}) &= (G - R(\tilde{g}))Y^+ \\ Y^+ &= (Y^T Y)^{-1} Y^T \end{aligned} \tag{16}$$

where $R(\tilde{g}) = [\tilde{g}, \tilde{g}, \dots, \tilde{g}] \in \mathbb{R}^{6 \times S}$ is the matrix with the corresponding columns $\tilde{g}$. If $\tilde{g}$ is known, then the problem is the overdetermined system of linear equations and can be solved by the generalized inverse matrix: $K(\tilde{g}) = (G - R(\tilde{g}))Y^+$. Then $\hat{G}(\tilde{g}) = K(\tilde{g})Y + R(\tilde{g})$. Problem (16) is equivalent to:

$$E(\tilde{g}) = \|\hat{G}_k(\tilde{g}) - G_k\|^2 \xrightarrow[\tilde{g}]{} min. \tag{17}$$

This problem can be solved by the iterative gradient method:

$$\tilde{g}' = \tilde{g} - \gamma \nabla E(\tilde{g}). \tag{18}$$

This is done to obtain matrix K and the base gap values using the data of 50 discharges of the Globus-M2 tokamak. The calculated base gap values are

$$\tilde{g}_1 = 0.5235\,\text{m},\ \tilde{g}_2 = 0.6264\,\text{m},\ \tilde{g}_3 = 0.0217\,\text{m},$$
$$\tilde{g}_4 = 0.1058\,\text{m},\ \tilde{g}_5 = 0.1590\,\text{m},\ \tilde{g}_6 = 0.0278\,\text{m}.$$
(19)

The obtained matrix K and base gap values are tested on the discharge #37712 that was not used for identification (Figure 7). The mean squad error (MSE) of all gaps estimation at all moments of time is $1.5 \times 10^{-5}\,\text{m}^2$.

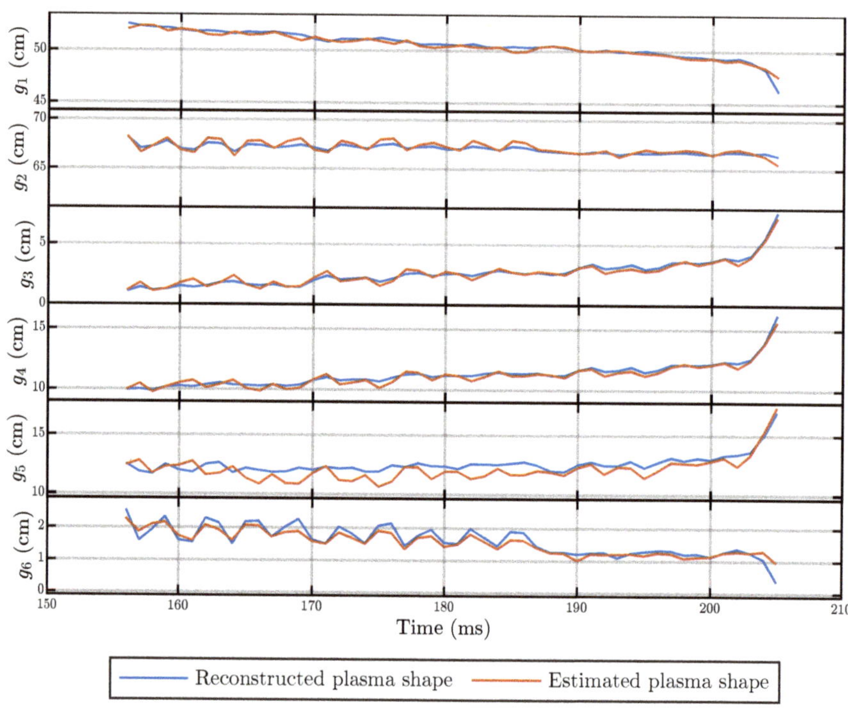

Figure 7. Estimation of the gap values in the discharge #37712 of the Globus-M2 spherical tokamak.

7. Neural Network for Plasma Shape Identification

In this section, the identification system based on an artificial neural network is proposed. It is assumed that the input and the output data can be linked using some unknown function f. Neural networks are well known for their ability to approximate unknown functions [22]. Attempts to apply them to plasma research in tokamaks began as early as the 1990s. Several major results have been achieved, including the tasks of plasma equilibrium reconstruction [23–26]. However, the vast majority of studies use feed-forward neural networks with multiple hidden layers to approximate the unknown mapping function, which have not shown good results in this problem in the area of generalization to various unknown discharges. To improve this ability, this paper proposes an approach using an encoder–decoder network structure [27].

Neural networks are based on the concept of artificial neurons. The first concept was proposed by Rosenblat [28], called perceptron. It receives inputs $(X_1, X_2, .., X_n)$ and sums it with weights $(W_1, W_2, .., W_n)$. Then the special function, named the transfer function, is applied to this sum product. The result of the transfer function is the output of the neuron. The most simple neural network, called multilayer perceptron, consists of three layers of neurons: the first one gets the input data, the second one is hidden and processes this data, and the third one is an output layer (Figure 8).

To approximate an unknown function f, a neural network needs to be trained on some given data. The better approximation is achieved by adjusting weights of network's neurons to minimize the value of the loss function, which is computed between the network output and groundtruth values.

In this work, the input and output data are represented as time sequences. Each point in time corresponds to a vector of features, so the data can be described by the matrix with dimensions of time intervals and parameters. The dimensionality in time is equal to 4110, i.e., there are 4110 data vectors at each time point of discharge. The time step is 6.38×10^{-5} s, so the entire signal is 0.262154 s. The variation in the absolute values of the various parameters, particularly the coil currents, is quite large, so the normalized values are used. They are obtained by subtracting the average value over the entire time sequence from each value of a particular parameter, and then dividing the result by the standard deviation.

However, the time dimension length is not fixed, as the plasma shape parameters are only determined during the divertor phase, when the strike points and corresponding values g_1 and g_2 exist. The start time and duration of this phase are not known from the available for the real-time reconstruction diagnostic (currents and magnetic fluxes) and require further determination.

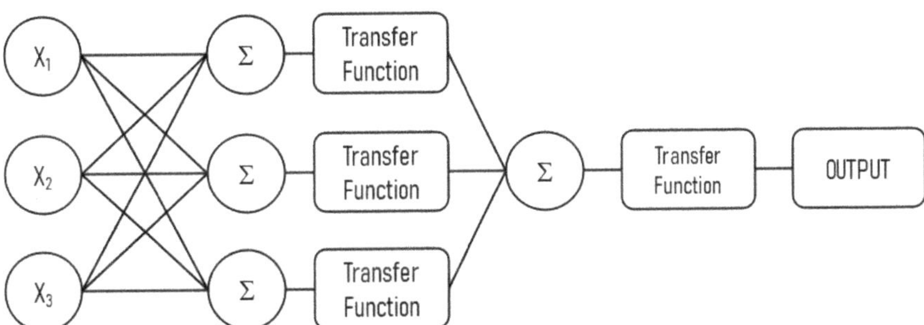

Figure 8. Multilayer perceptron.

In general, the plasma shape identification problem is dynamic, i.e., the gap values at some point in time during the divertor phase depend not only on the values of magnetic fluxes and coil currents at the same point in time, but also on the values at previous time steps. Therefore, to determine the required parameters, it is advisable to use recurrent-based neural networks. However, it is not practical to use the entire input signal in such a network for several reasons. First, the longer the sequence of the data fed to the recurrent network input, the longer the training and prediction processes, which are important factors in real-time identification. Second, the coordinate values are only significantly affected by data over a relatively small time range. Based on this, the task can be divided into two subtasks. The first one is to determine whether a given moment in time is a divertor phase. The second one is calculation of the required parameters during the already known divertor phase. The first subtask can be solved using a simple feed forward network without the use of recurrence blocks because it is a classification problem, not a regression problem, unlike the second one. In addition, the first subtask is only necessary to limit the length of the input signal to the recurrent network and achieve a simultaneous increase in system speed and improved positioning accuracy.

The values of magnetic fluxes through the loops and coil currents are fed into the network separately. Each input is processed by a densely connected layer, whose outputs are then concatenated. The merged result is fed into two densely connected layers with a dropout between them. This solution is designed to combat overtraining, which has a significant impact in this task because the signals provided for training have a similar structure. The output of the network is the probability that the current time moment belongs to the divertor phase (Figure 9).

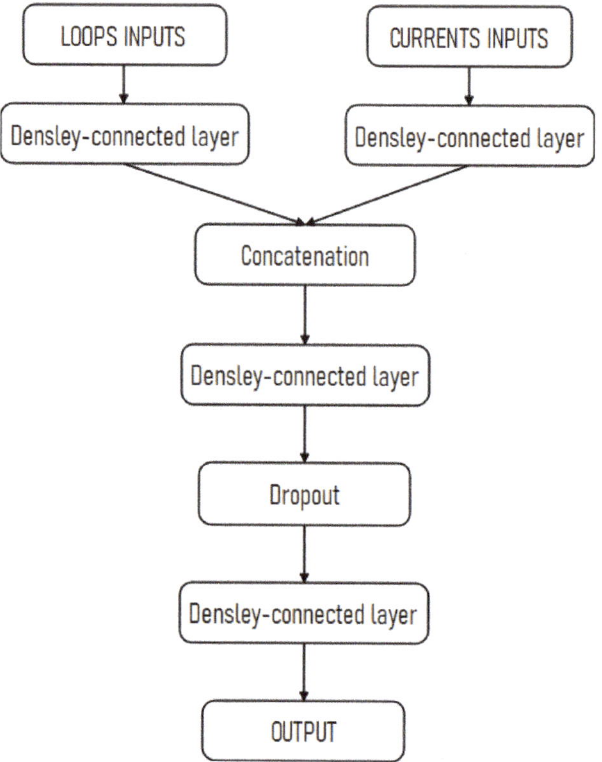

Figure 9. FNN model.

After this, the binary crossentropy is used as the loss function to measure the difference between the network output and training data

$$BCS(\Theta, y) = -y \log(x) + (1 - y) \log(1 - x),$$

where Θ is the neural network parameters, x is the network's output value, and y is a label.

The sigmoid function is taken as a transfer function of the output neuron and RelU for the neural network hidden layer ones

$$\mathrm{sigm}(S) = \frac{1}{1 + e^{-S}}.$$

The Adam [29] optimization algorithm with learning rate $\alpha = 0.0001$ is used to minimize the loss function. Learning takes place on 50 discharges and the remaining one is left for tests. To measure how often output values match with groundtruth values, the binary accuracy function is utilized. The obtained accuracy of the identification of the divertor phase for all time points equals 0.986 (Figure 10).

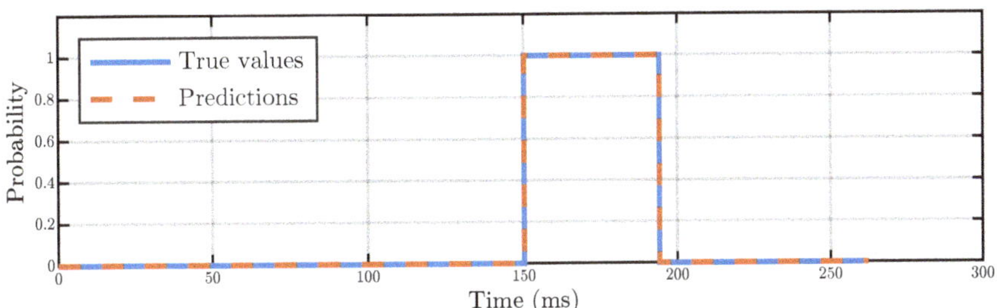

Figure 10. Divertor phase of the test discharge #37270.

The second subtask is to determine the required gap values during the divertor phase. As mentioned above, the recurrent neural network based on an encoder–decoder architecture [27] can combat this problem. This type of networks allows to capture temporal dependencies both in input and output data and build mapping between them. The first major block-encoder-created state describing input signal and the second block decoder is responsible for mapping the data into an output sequence. Both the encoder and decoder consist of GRU cells [30].

Figure 11 shows the encoder–decoder network schematic diagram. The network input is divided into two parts: encoder input and decoder input. An input signal is a sequence of vectors with the values of magnetic fluxes and currents, and it is applied to the encoder input. The decoder input can vary. Therefore, it is best to set the decoder input to 0, which will make it work with the dependencies passed to it by the encoder.

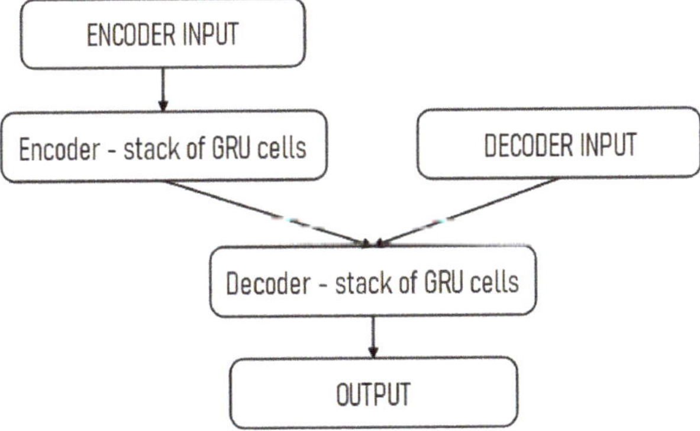

Figure 11. Encoder–decoder model.

The MSE as loss function and linear function as transfer function for the output neuron have the best performance for this regression problem.

$$MSE(\tilde{g}, g) = \frac{1}{N} \sum_{i=1}^{N} (\tilde{g}_i - g_i)^2, \qquad (20)$$

where $\tilde{g}_i$ are the network's estimation of gaps and coordinates, g_i are the groundtruth values, and N is the number of values.

This network is also trained on 50 signals and tested on the remaining one. Figure 12 shows the results for the required plasma parameters during the divertor phase of the discharge #37270.

The deviation is calculated for all values of each gap using the MSE. The results obtained have the order of 10^{-5}.

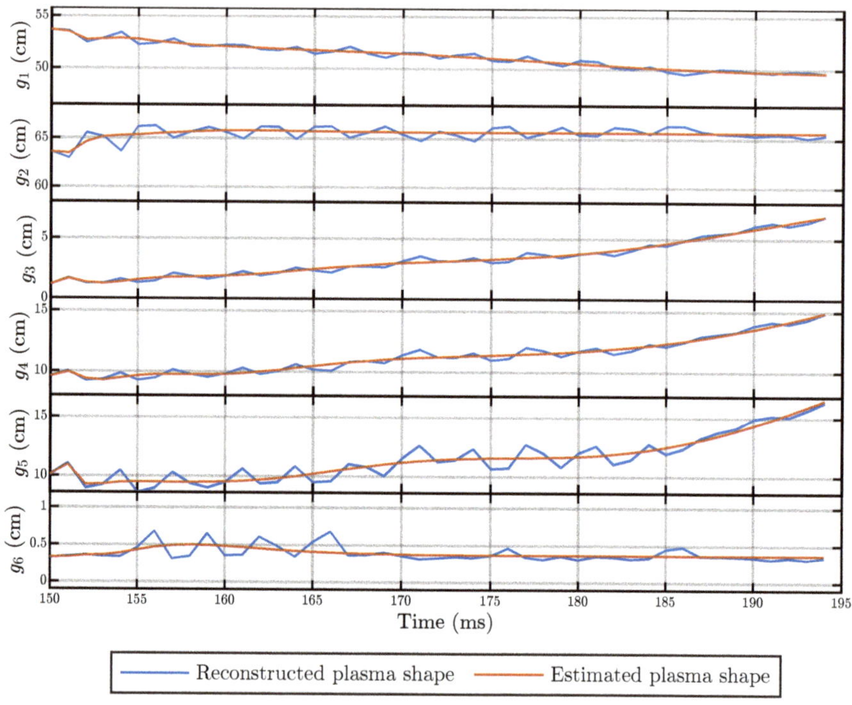

Figure 12. Neural network estimation of the gap values. Discharge #37270 of the Globus-M2 spherical tokamak.

8. Real Time Simulation of Identification Systems

To develop and realize plasma control systems for tokamaks, it is effective to apply so-called digital twins with real and digital control systems (Figure 13). This idea is used intensively in the industry because it gives a lot of advantages for the design, modeling, and application of control systems in real time. The digital twin is the interface between the digital and real world because it can have the ability to link physical and virtual worlds in real time, which provides more a realistic and holistic measurement of unforeseeable and unpredictable scenarios [31].

All signals from the magnetic diagnostics system of the tokamak are analog, which are then digitized by passing through an analog–digital converter (ADC). We can simulate the signal digitization process on our real-time test bed (Figures 14 and 15).

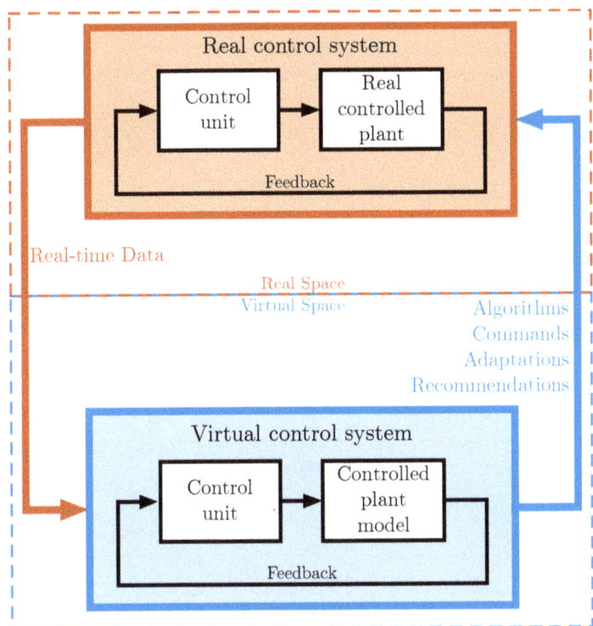

Figure 13. Digital twin containing a real dynamical plant with real feedback controller and virtual dynamical plant with a real feedback controller closed by the feedback of information flows: real-time data and algorithms, commands, adaptations, and recommendations.

Figure 14. Real-time test bed for plasma control in tokamaks. The test bed consists of two Speedgoat performance real-time target machines that are connected in feedback: one computer plays the role of the controlled plant model and the other one is the MIMO controller (https://www.ipu.ru/press-center/62866, accessed on 21 December 2021).

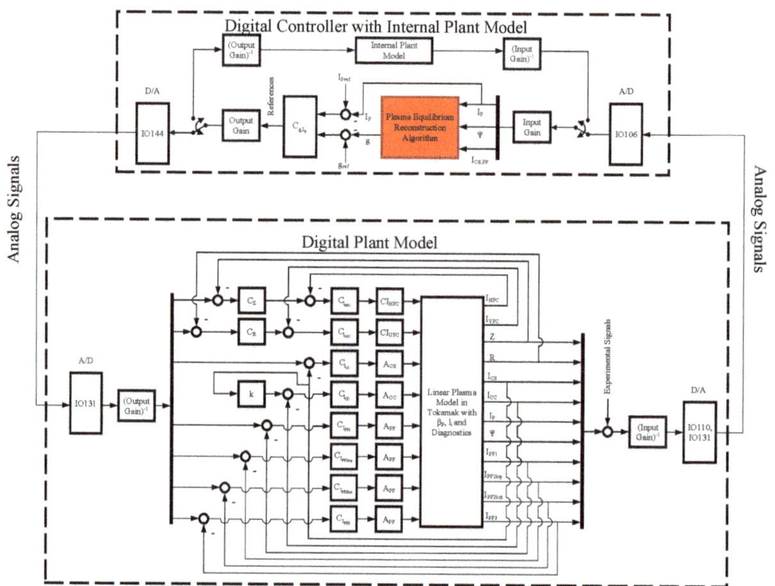

Figure 15. Scheme of digital twin of Globus-M2. The block with plasma equilibrium reconstruction algorithm is marked by red color.

In Figure 13, one can see the digital twin containing the real dynamical plant with the real feedback controller in the real space and the virtual dynamical plant with the real feedback controller in the virtual space. Between these spaces, there is a feedback of information flows that offers the opportunity to use the results obtained on the digital feedback system for the real control system, and vice versa. The data flows between an existing physical object and a digital object are fully integrated in both directions, which one might refer to as a digital twin [32]. The digital twin in the paper consists of the spherical Globus-M2 tokamak with a plasma feedback control system and a test bed with a digital controlled plant model and a feedback controller. The test bed was created by Lomonosov Moscow State University, Trapeznikov Institute of Control Sciences (Moscow), and Ioffe Institute (St. Petersburg). A photo of the test bed for Globus-M2 that is operating in real time is given in Figure 14. In Figure 15, one can see the test bed scheme in detail consisting of the digital plant model and the digital controller with an internal plant model for controller tuning. The digital plant model contains the plasma model in the tokamak and a set of feedback loops for plasma horizontal and vertical position control, for currents control in the poloidal field coils. The digital controller contains plasma equilibrium reconstruction algorithm as well as plasma current and shape controller.

This connection of the two real-time target machines is real and reliable. The real-time test bed is away from sources of powerful electromagnetic radiation, and all of its components have high-quality protection by means of shielding and grounding.

The two identification algorithms described in this paper are applied on the real-time testbed. Figure 16 shows the real-time running of a robust observer synthesized via LMIs. Figure 17 shows the real-time running of the identification algorithm with the static matrix. Real-time simulations are performed with a sample time of 0.1 ms.

These signals demonstrate the workability of two new approaches to reconstruct plasma equilibrium in real time on the test bed. That means important value of these signals in Figures 16 and 17.

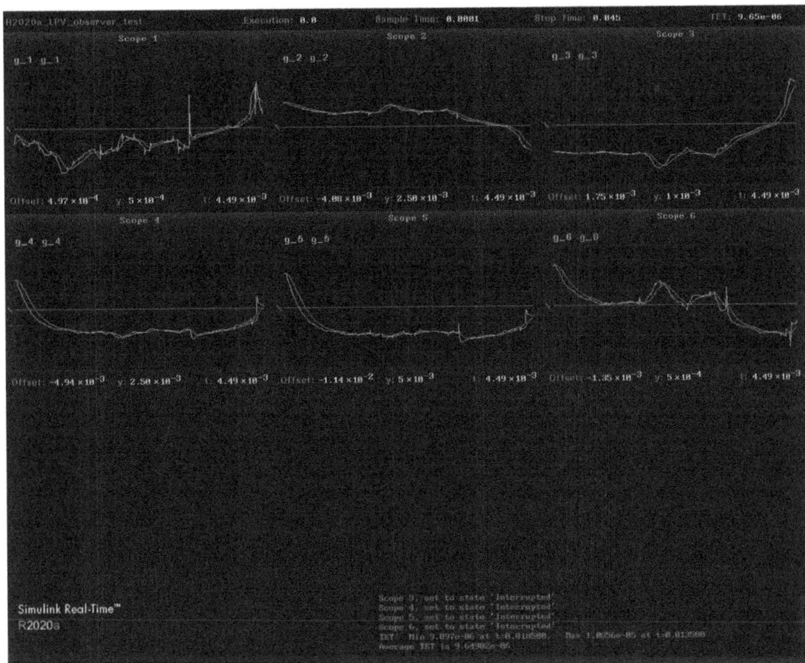

Figure 16. Real-time simulation of gaps variations δg derived by LPV model obtained from the FCDI code (blue line) and estimation of gap variations $\delta \tilde{g}$ obtained from robust observer synthesized by LMIs (red line). Discharge #37263.

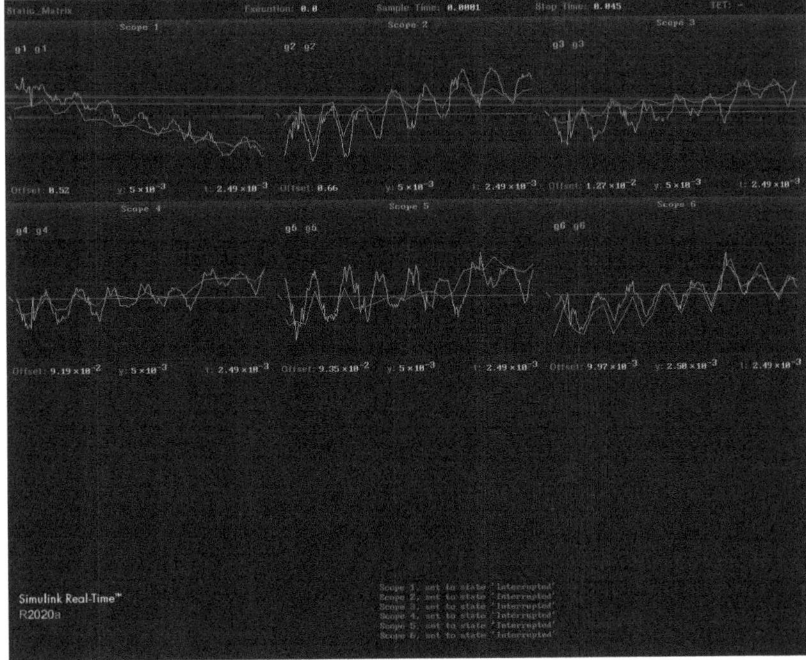

Figure 17. Real-time simulation of gaps g derived by LTI model obtained from the FCDI code (blue line) and estimation of gaps $\tilde{g}$ obtained from static matrix (red line). Discharge #37263.

9. Comparison of Identification Algorithms

Table 1 shows the comparison results of the different gap identification algorithms. For each gap g and an estimate of this gap $\tilde{g}$, the value of the MSE (20) is calculated. For each algorithm, the value of the TET (task execution time) in the real-time simulation is given.

Table 1. Comparison of identification results.

	$MSE(\tilde{g}, g) \cdot 10^{-6}$ m^2						
Algorithms	g_1	g_2	g_3	g_4	g_5	g_6	**TET, μs**
Robust Observer	0.06	0.16	0.08	0.43	1.92	0.02	9.7
Static Matrix	9.61	11.44	5.51	6.98	50.66	3.04	6.3
Neural Network	6.48	30.18	4.54	7.64	37.18	0.76	60

The FCDI code has an execution time of approximately 25 ms, which is too slow for real-time applications at Globus-M2 tokamak. To apply a plasma shape identification algorithm in real time, the algorithm must have an execution time of less than 1 ms, preferably less than 0.1 ms. All algorithms in Table 1 satisfy that criteria.

The MSE of the robust observer is 100 times smaller than other algorithms. This advantage is due to the fact that the observer is the dynamic model in the state-space form with 24 states. It contains 24 integrators with the help of which the error between the states of the plant model and the estimates of the states at the observer's output is fast minimized. The time it takes to minimize the error is determined by the location of the observer's poles. The observer's poles are defined by the $\mathbb{D}$-region (10).

The disadvantages of using the observer include the fact that it requires the use of scenario values of currents and fluxes, i.e., values relative to which the deviations from gaps are calculated. Other algorithms use the full values of experimental signals as inputs. The synthesis of the observer is possible only in the presence of linear models of the plasma in the tokamak as (9). Linear plant models can be derived only for deviations of currents and fluxes from the scenario values.

The fastest of these estimation algorithms of the gaps between the plasma boundary and the first wall is the static matrix algorithm with a TET of 6.3 μs because it is the simplest and requires only matrix-vector multiplication. The neural network algorithm is attractive because it can be adapted to a large number of discharges during experiments.

10. Discussion

In this work, the authors developed the original direction of plasma equilibrium reconstruction in D-shaped tokamaks using the magnetic measurements outside the hot plasma [33]. The basic criteria of this development are speed of response and accuracy. In practice, there is a set of such approaches, mentioned in the Introduction, which are used on working D-shaped tokamaks all over the world. Some of them use Picard iterations or current filaments methods. However, they rely only on the measurements outside plasma and most do not use the information from the database of the previous plasma discharges. If one uses this information, it may be possible to increase the speed of plasma equilibrium reconstruction. Moreover, when the history information of the plasma discharges is used, one can apply various reconstruction approaches from very simple ones, such as approximation with static matrices, to complex ones, such as artificial neural networks, which can be adjusted by and learn from dynamic processes. It gives a chance to improve not only the process of plasma identification on-line, but to understand the patterns of plasma processes from the experiment. These patterns cannot be deduced from the theory of high-temperature plasma physics because the plasma in a magnetic field is an extremely complicated object. These patterns represent the relationships between the gaps, which are the outputs of the plasma equilibrium reconstruction algorithm applied off-line to a set of plasma discharges and the inputs of this algorithm. The input signals are the measured fluxes on the magnetic loops, the currents in the CS/PF coils, and the plasma current. Then, one can use these patterns to apply any plasma reconstruction algorithms with the highest speed of response, e.g., state observers, static matrices, neural networks, and others. This activity is similar to machine learning techniques, where the search process is automated on big data [34]. In future, we can use these patterns for effective plasma control systems design with the fast plasma equilibrium reconstruction algorithms in the feedback with the usage of our new testbed for the installation of plasma control systems in real time on operating tokamaks [16].

11. Conclusions

The development of the fusion problem is moving forward but not very quickly because the plasma in tokamaks is an extremely complicated plant. In spite of that, the technologies in this field have had great progress and new technologies are appearing. One of these directions is plasma diagnostics to which our research belongs. The algorithms of plasma equilibrium reconstruction, such as ones using static matrix, state observer, and artificial neural network, can be included into the feedback of plasma shape control. The first real-time test of these algorithms is done on the digital model of the plasma shape control system (Figures 2 and 15). After that, the control system can be used in a real experiment on the Globus-M2 tokamak by means of a controller based on the third machine of the digital complex shown in Figures 14 and 15. The third machine will be connected to the tokamak as the control unit of the real control system, like in Figure 13. The real control system will interact with the virtual control system shown in Figures 14 and 15, realizing the concept of the digital twin shown in Figure 13. This approach is in line with the digital twins which are applied in Industry 4.0 [35].

In any case, there is a critical point in this new identification approach. The point is that this approach greatly increases the response rate of plasma equilibrium reconstruction, but the estimation accuracy may not be as high as, for example, in the filaments (current rings) approach. So, the designer of the magnetic plasma control system should choose what is more adequate for the specific control problem since the plasma equilibrium reconstruction algorithm is included in the feedback (Figure 15).

12. Patents

The authors received the patent of the RF on the approach of modeling plasma magnetic control systems with the plasma equilibrium reconstruction algorithm in feedback #2702137 with the priority from 28 April 2017 [36]. The next application for the RF patent was submitted for the structure and approach of the digital testbed under the number 2021128495.

Author Contributions: Conceptualization, Y.V.M.; methodology, Y.V.M. and P.S.K.; software, P.S.K., A.E.K., V.I.K. and N.E.O.; validation, P.S.K., A.E.K., V.I.K. and N.E.O.; formal analysis, P.S.K., A.E.K., V.I.K. and N.E.O.; investigation, P.S.K., A.E.K., V.I.K. and N.E.O.; resources, P.S.K., A.E.K., V.I.K. and N.E.O.; data curation, P.S.K., A.E.K., V.I.K. and N.E.O.; writing—original draft preparation, Y.V.M., P.S.K., A.E.K., V.I.K. and N.E.O.; writing—review and editing, Y.V.M. and P.S.K.; visualization, Y.V.M., P.S.K., A.E.K., V.I.K. and N.E.O.; supervision, Y.V.M.; project administration, Y.V.M.; funding acquisition, Y.V.M. All authors have read and agreed to the published version of the manuscript.

Funding: This research was funded by the Russian Science Foundation (RSF) under grant number 21-79-20180.

Institutional Review Board Statement: Not applicable.

Informed Consent Statement: Not applicable.

Data Availability Statement: Restrictions apply to the availability of these data. Data was obtained from Ioffe Physics and Technology Institute of RAS (St. Petersburg, Russia) and are available from: https://globus.rinno.ru (accessed on 21 December 2021) with the permission of Ioffe Physics and Technology Institute of RAS.

Acknowledgments: The authors are grateful to their colleagues from Ioffe Institute in St. Petersburg (Russia) for their help in supporting us with the experimental data of plasma behavior in the tokamak Globus-M/M2 in line with the grant of Russian Science Foundation #21-79-20180.

Conflicts of Interest: The authors declare no conflict of interest. The funders had no role in the design of the study; in the collection, analyses, or interpretation of data; in the writing of the manuscript, or in the decision to publish the results.

Abbreviations

The following abbreviations are used in this manuscript:

PF	Poloidal Field
VV	Vacuum Vessel
ITER	International Thermonuclear Experimental Reactor
EFIT	Equilibrium Fitting
FCDI	Flux-Current Distribution Identification
SVD	Singular Value Decomposition
LMI	Linear Matrix Inequality
LTI	Linear Time-Invariant
LPV	Linear Parameter-Varying
TET	Task Execution Time
MSE	Mean Square Error

References

1. Wesson, J. *Tokamaks*, 3rd ed.; Clarendon Press: Oxford, UK, 2004.
2. Mitrishkin, Y.V.; Korostelev, A.Y.; Dokuka, V.N.; Khayrutdinov, R.R. Synthesis and simulation of a two-level magnetic control system for tokamak-reactor plasma. *Plasma Phys. Rep.* **2011**, *37*, 279–320. [CrossRef]
3. Mitrishkin, Y. *Upravleniye Plazmoi v Eksperimentalnikh Termoyadernikh Ustanovkakh: Adptivniye Avtokolebatelniye i Robustniye Sistemi Upravleniya [Plasma Control in Experimental Thermonuclear Installations: Adaptive Auto-Oscillation and Robust Control Systems]*; KRASAND: Moscow, Russia, 2016. (In Russian)
4. Mitrishkin, Y.; Kartsev, N.; Kuznetsov, E.; Korostelev, A. *Metodi i Sistemi Magnitnogo Upravleniya Plazmoi v Tokamakakh [Methods and Systems of Plasma Magnetic Control in Tokamaks]*; KRASAND: Moscow, Russia, 2020. (In Russian)
5. Mitrishkin, Y.V.; Kartsev, N.M.; Zenkov, S.M. Stabilization of unstable vertical position of plasma in T-15 tokamak. I. *Autom. Remote Control* **2014**, *75*, 281–293. [CrossRef]
6. Mitrishkin, Y.V.; Kartsev, N.M.; Zenkov, S.M. Stabilization of unstable vertical position of plasma in T-15 tokamak. II. *Autom. Remote Control* **2014**, *75*, 1565–1576. [CrossRef]
7. Mitrishkin, Y.V.; Prokhorov, A.A.; Korenev, P.S.; Patrov, M.I. Plasma magnetic time-varying nonlinear robust control system for the Globus-M/M2 tokamak. *Control Eng. Pract.* **2020**, *100*, 104446. [CrossRef]
8. Mitrishkin, Y.; Prokhorov, A.; Korenev, P.; Patrov, M. Hierarchical robust switching control method with the Improved Moving Filaments equilibrium reconstruction code in the feedback for tokamak plasma shape. *Fusion Eng. Des.* **2019**, *138*, 138–150. [CrossRef]
9. Kuznetsov, E.A.; Mitrishkin, Y.V.; Kartsev, N.M. Current inverter as self-oscillating actuator in applications for plasma position control systems in the Globus-M/M2 and T-11M tokamaks. *Fusion Eng. Des.* **2019**, *143*, 247–258. [CrossRef]
10. Mitrishkin, Y.; Korenev, P.; Konkov, A.; Kartsev, N.; Smirnov, I. New horizontal and vertical field coils with optimised location for robust decentralized plasma position control in the IGNITOR tokamak. *Fusion Eng. Des.* **2021**, accepted.
11. Hommen, G.; de Baar, M.; Nuij, P.; McArdle, G.; Akers, R.; Steinbuch, M. Optical boundary reconstruction of tokamak plasmas for feedback control of plasma position and shape. *Rev. Sci. Instrum.* **2010**, *81*, 113504. [CrossRef]
12. Beghi, A.; Cenedese, A. Advances in real-time plasma boundary reconstruction: From gaps to snakes. *IEEE Control Syst. Mag.* **2005**, *25*, 44–64. [CrossRef]
13. Lao, L.L.; St. John, H.; Stambaugh, R.D.; Kellman, A.G.; Pfeiffer, W. Reconstruction of current profile parameters and plasma shapes in tokamaks. *Nucl. Fusion* **1985**, *25*, 1611–1622. [CrossRef]
14. Korenev, P.; Mitrishkin, Y.; Patrov, M. Rekonstrukciya ravnovesnogo raspredeleniya parametrov plazmy tokamaka po vneshnim magnitnym izmereniyam i postroenie lineinykh plazmennykh modelei [Reconstruction of equilibrium distribution of tokamak plasma parameters by external magnetic measurements and construction of linear plasma models]. *Mechatronics Autom. Control* **2016**, *17*, 254–265. (In Russian)
15. Coda, S.; Ahn, J.; Albanese, R.; Alberti, S.; Alessi, E.; Allan, S.; Anand, H.; Anastassiou, G.; Andrèbe, Y.; Angioni, C.; et al. Overview of the TCV tokamak program: Scientific progress and facility upgrades. *Nucl. Fusion* **2017**, *57*, 102011. [CrossRef]
16. Mitrishkin, Y.V. Plasma magnetic control systems in D-shaped tokamaks and imitation digital computer platform in real time for controlling plasma current and shape. *Adv. Syst. Sci. Appl.* **2021**, *21*, 1–14.

17. Ariola, M.; Pironti, A. *Magnetic Control of Tokamak Plasmas*, 2nd ed.; Springer: Berlin, Germany, 2016.
18. Lazarus, E.; Lister, J.; Neilson, G. Control of the vertical instability in tokamaks. *Nucl. Fusion* **1990**, *30*, 111–141. [CrossRef]
19. Forsythe G.; Malcolm M.; Moler, C. *Computer Methods for Mathematical Computations*; Prentice Hall: Englewood Cliffs, NJ, USA, 1977.
20. Duan, G.R.; Yu, H.H. *LMIs in Control Systems*; CRC Press: Boca Raton, FL, USA, 2013.
21. Chilali, M.; Gahinet, P.; Apkarian, P. Robust pole placement in LMI regions. *IEEE Trans. Autom. Control* **1999**, *44*, 2257–2270. [CrossRef]
22. Cybenko, G. Approximation by superpositions of a sigmoidal function. *Math. Control Signals Syst.* **1992**, *5*, 455. [CrossRef]
23. Lister, J.B.; Schnurrenberger, H. Fast non-linear extraction of plasma equilibrium parameters using a neural network mapping. *Nucl. Fusion* **1991**, *31*, 1291. [CrossRef]
24. Coccorese, E.; Morabito, C.; Martone, R. Identification of noncircular plasma equilibria using a neural network approach. *Nucl. Fusion* **1994**, *34*, 1349. [CrossRef]
25. Windsor, C.G.; Todd, T.N.; Trotman, D.L.; Smith, M.E.U. Real-time electronic neural networks for iter-like multiparameter equilibrium reconstruction and control in compass-d. *Fusion Technol.* **1997**, *32*, 416–430. [CrossRef]
26. Zhu, Z.J.; Guo, Y.; Yang, F.; Xiao, B.J.; Li, J.G. Estimation of plasma equilibrium parameters via a neural network approach. *Chin. Phys. B* **2019**, *28*, 125204. [CrossRef]
27. Sutskever, I.; Vinyals, O.; Le, Q.V. Sequence to sequence learning with neural networks. In *Advances in Neural Information Processing Systems*; MIT Press: Cambridge, MA, USA, 2014; pp. 3104–3112.
28. Rosenblatt, F. The perceptron: A probabilistic model for information storage and organization in the brain. *Psychol. Rev.* **1958**, *65*, 386. [CrossRef]
29. Kingma, D.P.; Ba, J. Adam: A method for stochastic optimization. *arXiv* **2014**, arXiv:1412.6980.
30. Chung, J.; Gulcehre, C.; Cho, K.; Bengio, Y. Empirical evaluation of gated recurrent neural networks on sequence modeling. *arXiv* **2014**, arXiv:1412.3555.
31. Singh, M.; Fuenmayor, E.; Hinchy, E.P.; Qiao, Y.; Murray, N.; Devine, D. Digital Twin: Origin to future. *Appl. Syst. Innov.* **2021**, *4*, 36. [CrossRef]
32. Kritzinger, W.; Karner, M.; Traar, G.; Henjes, J.; Sihn, W. Digital Twin in manufacturing: A categorical literature review and classification. *IFAC-PapersOnLine* **2018**, *51*, 1016–1022. [CrossRef]
33. Mitrishkin, Y.; Kartsev, N.; Prokhorov, A.; Pavlova, E.; Korenev, P.; Konkov, A.; Kruzhkov, V.; Ivanova, S. Tokamak plasma models development for plasma magnetic control systems design by first principle equations and identification approach. *Procedia Comput. Sci.* **2021**, *186*, 466–474. [CrossRef]
34. Shalev-Shwartz, S.; Ben-David, S. *Understanding Machine Learning: From Theory to Algorithms*; Cambridge University Press: New York, NY, USA, 2013. [CrossRef]
35. Parrott, A.; Warshaw, L. *Industry 4.0 and the Digital Twin: Manufacturing Meets Its Match*; Deloitte University Press: New York, NY, USA, 2017.
36. Mitrishkin, Y.; Prohorov, A.; Korenev, P.; Patrov, M. Sposob Formirovfniya Modeli Magnitnogo Upravleniya Formoy i Tokom Plasmi s Obratnoy Svyazyu v Tokamake. [Method of Formation of the Model of Magnetic Control of Plasma Shape and Current with Feedback in a Tokamak]. Patent for Invention of the Russian Federation No. 2702137, 28 April 2017. (In Russian)

 *mathematics*

Article

Robust Stabilization via Super-Stable Systems Techniques

Svetlana A. Krasnova, Yulia G. Kokunko, Victor A. Utkin and Anton V. Utkin *

V.A. Trapeznikov Institute of Control Sciences of RAS, 117997 Moscow, Russia; skrasnova@list.ru (S.A.K.); juliakokunko@gmail.com (Y.G.K.); viktorutkin013@gmail.com (V.A.U.)
* Correspondence: utkin-av@rambler.ru; Tel.: +7-(495)-198-17-20 (ext. 1577)

Abstract: In this paper, we propose a direct method for the synthesis of robust systems operating under parametric uncertainty of the control plant model. The developed robust control procedures are based on the assumption that the structural properties of the nominal system are conserved over the entire range of parameter changes. The invariant-to-parametric-uncertainties transformation of the initial model to a regular form makes it possible to use the concept of super-stable systems for the synthesis of a stabilizing feedback. It is essential that the synthesis of super-stable systems is carried out not on the basis of assigning eigenvalues to the matrix of the close-loop system, but in terms of its elements. The proposed approach is applicable to a wide class of linear systems with parametric uncertainties and provides a given degree of stability.

Keywords: parametric uncertainty; robust control; super-stability; regular form; decomposition

1. Introduction

Citation: Krasnova, S.A.; Kokunko, Y.G.; Utkin, V.A.; Utkin, A.V. Robust Stabilization via Super-Stable Systems Techniques. *Mathematics* **2022**, *10*, 98. https://doi.org/10.3390/math10010098

Academic Editors: Natalia Bakhtadze, Igor Yadykin, Andrei Torgashov and Nikolay Korgin

Received: 18 November 2021
Accepted: 22 December 2021
Published: 28 December 2021

Publisher's Note: MDPI stays neutral with regard to jurisdictional claims in published maps and institutional affiliations.

The problem of stabilizing the state variables of dynamic automatic control plants is a fundamental problem, the formulation and solution of which served as the basis for the formation and development of control theory. Classical methods of control theory, in particular modal control, are based on the assumption of an accurate description of the mathematical model of the control process and the environment of its operation. In reality, there is often parametric uncertainty in the mathematical model of control plants, in particular due to the discarding of residual terms of higher order in the linearized models. This leads to the need to consider a parametrically indeterminate model when synthesizing feedback and to set the robust control problem. Many researchers are currently paying increased attention to control problems in conditions of parametric uncertainty. The direct way to solve the stabilization problem is to obtain estimates of unknown parameters of the control plant model, either directly using the parametric identification theory [1,2], or indirectly, based on the adaptation theory [3,4]. After obtaining estimates of unknown parameters, it becomes possible to use well-developed modal control methods. Another trend in solving the problem of stabilization of parametrically uncertain systems refers to the currently actively developing theory of robust control, in which we can roughly define two main fields: problems of analysis and problems of synthesis. Classical methods for analyzing open-loop systems include results on interval stability of polynomials [5,6], robust frequency methods [7], the D-partition technique [8], H_∞ optimization methods [9], and others. Direct and very effective methods of robust control include the use of sliding-mode technique [10] and deep feedback [11]. Note that both methods provide the independence of motions in the sliding mode (slow motions) only from the matching uncertainties. It should be noted that usually on the problem statement step of these approaches, no assumptions are made about the structural properties of the controllability of the system. These methods of robust theory allow us to establish only the fact of system stability and do not give a direct answer to the question of the nature of convergence, which reduces their practical value.

This paper considers a different approach to robust stabilization, where a guaranteed stability margin for linear stationary systems with interval parameter uncertainty is achieved using linear state feedback. The methodological basis of the developed approach is the synthesis of super-stable closed systems [12], and decomposition is based on the transformation of the control plant model to a regular form [13]. It is essential that in these approaches, the results are expressed in terms of matrix elements rather than their eigenvalues. Possibilities for extending this approach are available by using the block approach [14–16].

The paper has the following structure. Section 2 considers parametrically certain linear stationary systems. As a methodological basis for further discussion, the procedure of modal synthesis based on transformation to a regular form is presented. For the particular case of a regular form, which consists of two elementary subsystems, we formalize a procedure for the synthesis of a stabilizing feedback that ensures super-stability of the closed-loop system in the new coordinate basis and a guaranteed stability margin in the initial system. Section 3 considers a significant practical class of linear stationary systems, in which, for all values of uncertain parameters from intervals with known bounds, the structural controllability properties defined by the nominal system are conserved. For a class of systems with a controllability indicator equal to two, we formalize rank requirements for the structure of indeterminate matrices, in case of which the indeterminate system is reduced to a regular form regardless of the unknown parameters. Sufficient conditions for the feasibility of robust control are formalized. The procedure for synthesizing a stabilizing feedback is also formalized. In this case, the super-stability of the system is ensured in the coordinate basis of a regular form, and for the original system, a given stability margin is provided in all intervals of uncertain parameters. Section 4 contains numerical examples to illustrate the developed theoretical results.

2. Parametrically Certain Systems

2.1. The Elementary Control Problem

A mathematical model of a linear stationary control plant is considered

$$\dot{x} = Ax + Bu, \tag{1}$$

where $x \in R^n$ is measurable state vector, $u = \mathrm{col}(u_1, \ldots, u_m) \in R^m$ is control vector; $A \in R^{n \times n}$, $B \in R^{n \times m}$ are constant known matrices, and pair (A, B) is controllable.

For system (1), there is a problem of stabilization by means of a linear static feedback

$$u = Fx, \tag{2}$$

resulting in a closed-loop system

$$\dot{x} = (A + BF)x = A_0 x. \tag{3}$$

Typical for a linear system is the modal control problem, in which the choice of the feedback matrix $F \in R^{m \times n}$ must assign a given spectrum σ_d to the closed-loop matrix

$$\sigma_\mathrm{d} = \sigma(A_0) = \left\{ \lambda_i \in C : \det(\lambda_i I_n - A_0) = 0, i = \overline{1, n} \right\}, \ \mathrm{Re}\lambda_i(A_0) < 0, i = \overline{1, n}, \tag{4}$$

which ensures asymptotic convergence of the state vector to the zero equilibrium position

$$\lim_{t \to +\infty} x(t) = \vec{0}.$$

In Formula (4) and below, I is unit matrix of a given dimension.

In general, the following problems arise when solving the modal control problem:

(1) by assigning only eigenvalues in a closed system (3), it is not always possible to achieve the desired transients of the state variables;

(2)   in multidimensional systems with vector control, there are certain computational difficulties in synthesis, called the "curse of dimensionality";

(3)   full parametric certainty of the matrices A and B is required.

The first two problems can be solved in some special cases of system (1). These include elementary systems with full-rank control.

Definition 1. *System (1) is called elementary if the number of controls in it is not less than the dimensionality of the state vector and the control matrix has a full rank:*

$$\dim u = m \geq n = \dim x, \ \mathrm{rank} B_{n \times m} = n.$$

The synthesis problem in the elementary system is also called elementary, because the feedback matrix is directly found from the matrix equation $A + BF = A_0$, such as

$$m > n : F = B^{+}(A_0 - A); \ m = n : \ F = B^{-1}(A_0 - A), \tag{5}$$

where in the first expression B^{+}—pseudo-inverse matrix B, $BB^{+}B = B$. In the elementary system, the matrix B rows are linearly independent, hence $B_{n \times m} B^{+}_{m \times n} = I_n$ and $B^{+} = B^T(BB^T)^{-1}$ [17].

Thus, in the elementary system, at first, the synthesis problem (5) is solved in terms of matrix elements rather than their eigenvalues. Second, one can easily provide the desired transients in all state variables by choosing a reference matrix of simple structure, in a Jordanian form or diagonal form. In the latter case, the transient process of each state variable will be monotonous with a given rate of convergence to zero, which is determined by the values of the diagonal elements of the reference matrix.

The advantages of systems with full control are obvious, but in practice, usually the control problem is not elementary. In the next subsection, the procedure of nonsingular linear transformations is given, which allows extracting an elementary subsystem with full control from the initial system of general form.

2.2. Synthesis of Modal Control Based on a Regular Form

We will consider the general case of system (1), where the number of controls is less than the dimension of the state vector and $0 < \mathrm{rank} B_{n \times m} = m_0 \leq m < n$, i.e., out of n matrix rows B only m_0 are basic. For such a system, there is an equivalent representation in a new coordinate basis, which is called a regular form (RF) with respect to the control [13,18]. In this form, the elementary subsystem with full control is singled out. The point of the corresponding linear nonsingular transformation is grouping of basis rows and zeroing linearly dependent rows of the matrix B.

Definition 2. *A regular form with respect to the control vector is an equivalent representation of system (1),* $\mathrm{rank} B_{n \times m} = m_0 \leq m < n$ *in the form of two subsystems*

$$\begin{aligned} \dot{x}_1 &= A_{11}x_1 + A_{12}x_2, \\ \dot{x}_2 &= A_{21}x_1 + A_{22}x_2 + B_2 u, \end{aligned} \tag{6}$$

which are obtained as a result of nonsingular variable change

$$Tx = \overline{x} = \begin{pmatrix} x_1 \\ x_2 \end{pmatrix}, \ \det T_{(n \times n)} \neq 0, x_1 \in R^{n-m_0}, \mathrm{rank} B = \mathrm{rank} B_2 = \dim x_2 = m_0$$

and similarity transformation

$$TAT^{-1} = \overline{A} = \begin{pmatrix} A_{11(n-m_0) \times (n-m_0)} & A_{12(n-m_0) \times m_0} \\ A_{21(m_0 \times (n-m_0))} & A_{22(m_0 \times m_0)} \end{pmatrix}, TB = \overline{B} = \begin{pmatrix} O_{(n-m_0) \times m} \\ B_{2(m_0 \times m)} \end{pmatrix}.$$

Here and further in the text, O is the zero matrix of the corresponding dimension.

The second subsystem of system (6) contains full-rank control, which is a condition for the solution of the elementary control problem in this subsystem; similar to (5), pair (A_{22}, B_2) is obviously controllable. In the first subsystem of system (6), which in the general case is not elementary, the vector x_2 is considered virtual control action. If system (1) pair (A, B) is controllable, then due to invariance of the controllability property to nonsingular linear transformations, this means that in the first subsystem of (6) the pair (A_{11}, A_{12}) is also controllable.

Note that there can be several sets of basis rows in matrix B, so in general there are several equivalent realizations of the regular form (6) for a particular system. They differ by the values of the matrix elements $\overline{A}$ and B_2, but all have the same structure, in that the first subsystem has no control, and the second has a dynamic order m_0 and is elementary.

Based on the regular form, the problem of synthesis of modal control is decomposed into two successively solvable subproblems of lesser dimensions than the original system. In the first subsystem $n - m_0$ with virtual control x_2, the problem of assigning a part of a given spectrum (4) is solved. The derived linear local feedback is introduced by a nonsingular linear transformation, and the assignment of the second part of the spectrum is provided by a real linear control u, meaning the elementary synthesis problem of dimension m_0 is solved. As a result, a linear control law for the variables of the transformed system will be obtained. Using the resulting transformation matrix, it should be presented with respect to the state variables of the initial system in the form (2). According to the property of invariance of the roots of the characteristic equation to nondegenerate linear transformations, the characteristic polynomials (and hence the spectrum) of matrices of closed-loop initial and transformed systems will be equal to each other. Let us present these transformations in the form of a step-by-step description.

Procedure 1. Synthesis of modal control based on transition to a regular form.

1. Nonsingular transformation of system (1) to the regular form (6).

    1.a. Grouping basis rows of the matrix B and forming matrix $B_{2(m_0 \times m)}$.
    If necessary, rearrange the matrix B rows in a way that m_0 of its last rows are linearly independent, and perform an appropriate variable change, in which the transformation matrix is a permutation matrix $T_{p(n \times n)}$, $\det T_p \neq 0$:

$$T_p B = \widetilde{B} = \begin{pmatrix} \widetilde{B}_1 \\ B_2 \end{pmatrix}, T_p x = \widetilde{x} = \begin{pmatrix} \widetilde{x}_1 \\ x_2 \end{pmatrix}, \widetilde{x}_1 \in R^{n-m_0}, T_p A T_p^{-1} = \widetilde{A} = \begin{pmatrix} \widetilde{A}_{11} & \widetilde{A}_{12} \\ \widetilde{A}_{21} & \widetilde{A}_{22} \end{pmatrix}, \tag{7}$$

$$\mathrm{rank} B = \mathrm{rank} B_2 = \dim x_2 = m_0.$$

System (1) will be represented in the following equivalent form:

$$\dot{\widetilde{x}}_1 = \widetilde{A}_{11} \widetilde{x}_1 + \widetilde{A}_{12} x_2 + \widetilde{B}_1 u, \quad \dot{x}_2 = \widetilde{A}_{21} \widetilde{x}_1 + \widetilde{A}_{22} x_2 + B_2 u. \tag{8}$$

If no permutations are required, then $T_p = I$, and to obtain the system (8), the appropriate notation is introduced.

1.b. Zeroing out the linearly dependent rows of a matrix B.
If in system (8) $\widetilde{B}_{1(n-m_0) \times m} \neq O$, then the matrix $\widetilde{B}_1$, which consists of linearly dependent rows of a matrix B_2, needs to be reset to zero. It is required that as a result of partial change of the variables,

$$x_1 = \widetilde{x}_1 - B_2^* x_2, \ x_1 \in R^{n-m_0}. \tag{9}$$

In the new subsystem relative to x_1 control was absent, as follows

$$\dot{x}_1 = \dot{\widetilde{x}}_1 - B_2^* \dot{x}_2 = (\widetilde{A}_{11} - B_2^* \widetilde{A}_{21}) \widetilde{x}_1 + (\widetilde{A}_{12} - B_2^* \widetilde{A}_{22}) x_2 + (\widetilde{B}_1 - B_2^* B_2) u \Rightarrow \widetilde{B}_1 - B_2^* B_2 = O.$$

From the resulting matrix equation, we have

$$m_0 < m : B_2^* = \widetilde{B}_1 B_{2(m \times m_0)}^+, \ B_2^+ = B_2^T (B_2 B_2^T)^{-1}; \ m_0 = m : B_2^* = \widetilde{B}_1 B_{2(m \times m)}^{-1}. \tag{10}$$

The corresponding transformation of partial variable change (9) has the form

$$T_a \widetilde{B} = T_a \begin{pmatrix} \widetilde{B}_1 \\ B_2 \end{pmatrix} = \overline{B} = \begin{pmatrix} O \\ B_2 \end{pmatrix}, \det T_{a(n \times n)} \neq 0, \ T_a \widetilde{x} = T_a \begin{pmatrix} \widetilde{x}_1 \\ x_2 \end{pmatrix} = \overline{x} = \begin{pmatrix} x_1 \\ x_0 \end{pmatrix}, T_a \widetilde{A} T_a^{-1} = \overline{A}$$

$$, \ T_a = \begin{pmatrix} I_{n-m_0} & -B^*_{2(n-m_0) \times m_0} \\ O_{m_0 \times (n-m_0)} & I_{m_0} \end{pmatrix}, T_a^{-1} = \begin{pmatrix} I_{n-m_0} & B^*_{2(n-m_0) \times m_0} \\ O_{m_0 \times (n-m_0)} & I_{m_0} \end{pmatrix} \tag{11}$$

and leads system (8) to the regular form (6). If in system (8) $\widetilde{B}_{1(n-m_0) \times m} = O$, it corresponds exactly to the regular form (6) and $T_a = I$.

The sequence of the above transformations of system (1) to the regular form (6) is

$$Tx = T_a(T_p x) = \overline{x}, \ T = T_a T_p, \tag{12}$$

where some cases may be $T_p = I$ and/or $T_a = I$. Clearly, the equality $T_p = T_a = I$ occurs in mathematical models that are initially of the regular form (6), and this situation is typical of many practical applications.

Procedure 2. Decomposition synthesis of modal control based on RF.

2.a. Synthesis of fictitious control in the first RF subsystem.

We have to choose $n - m_0$ values from a given spectrum σ_d (4) so as not to disconnect complex-conjugate pairs, if any. If an odd $n - m_0$ and/or m_0 is required to break the complex-conjugate pair, then the decomposition will have to be dropped, and a different synthesis method should be used. Otherwise, this method will produce a complex feedback matrix (2), which is not acceptable in practical applications.

If the above choice is possible, in the first subsystem of system (6) we form a linear virtual control $x_2 = F_1 x_1$ and obtain the local feedback matrix

$$F_{1(m_0 \times (n-m_0))} : A_1 = A_{11} + A_{12} F_1, \sigma(A_1) \subset \sigma_d. \tag{13}$$

Due to the controllability of the pair (A_{11}, A_{12}), this problem has a solution. In the particular case $\operatorname{rank} A_{12} = \dim x_1 = n - m_0 \leq m_0$, when also the first subsystem is elementary, then similarly to (5) we can assign in it both a given spectrum and a given matrix of own movements. In the general case, problem (13) is not elementary, but the dimensions of the desired matrix are smaller than when solving problem (3) in the original system (1), (2), where $\dim F = m \times n$.

Remark 1. *In many applications, the transition to the RF simplifies the synthesis procedure sufficiently, and it is possible to simply represent the initial system in the form of two subsystems. In general case for large-dimensional systems, one can continue the mentioned transformations and in the first subsystem of (6) allocate in a similar way an elementary subsystem with respect to virtual control x_2, etc. As a result, the first subsystem of system (6) will be represented as associated elementary subsystems (blocks) with full-rank virtual controls, which are the variables of the following block. The form in this case is called the block form of controllability, on the basis of which the synthesis problem is divided into consecutive elementary control problems* [14].

In order to implement the local relation of variables that has been formed, we need to introduce a mismatch between the real control and the selected virtual control by means of partial variable change

$$x_2 = F_1 x_1, \ e_1 := x_1, \ e_2 = x_2 - F_1 x_1, \ e_2 \in R^{m_0} \tag{14}$$

and the corresponding linear transformation

$$T_e \overline{x} = \begin{pmatrix} x_1 \\ x_2 \end{pmatrix} = e = \begin{pmatrix} e_1 \\ e_2 \end{pmatrix}, \ T_e = \begin{pmatrix} I_{(n-m)} & O_{(n-m_0) \times m_0} \\ -F_{1(m_0 \times (n-m_0))} & I_{m_0} \end{pmatrix}, T_e^{-1} = \begin{pmatrix} I_{(n-m_0)} & O_{(n-m_0) \times m_0} \\ F_{1(m_0 \times (n-m_0))} & I_{m_0} \end{pmatrix},$$

$$\det T_{e(n \times n)} \neq 0, T_e \overline{A} T_e^{-1} = A_e = \begin{pmatrix} A_1 & A_{12} \\ C_{21} & C_{22} \end{pmatrix}, T_e \overline{B} = T_e \begin{pmatrix} O \\ B_2 \end{pmatrix} = \begin{pmatrix} O \\ B_2 \end{pmatrix}. \tag{15}$$

As a result, RF with local relation closed-loop will be obtained:

$$\dot{e}_1 = A_1 e_1 + A_{12} e_2,$$
$$\dot{e}_2 = C_{21} e_1 + C_{22} e_2 + B_2 u. \tag{16}$$

2.b. Synthesis of real control by variables of transformed systems.

Next, the local feedback generated in the first subsystem of (16) must be provided by the real control. For the second elementary subsystem of (16) we have to compose a reference matrix $A_{2(m_0 \times m_0)}$ with m_0 with eigenvalues from the rest of the given spectrum $\sigma(A_1) \cup \sigma(A_2) = \sigma_d$, and form a feedback on the variables of the transformed system:

$$m_0 < m: \ u = B_2^+(-C_{21}e_1 - C_{22}e_2 + A_2 e_2) = Ke;$$
$$m_0 = m: \ u = B_2^{-1}(-C_{21}e_1 - C_{22}e_2 + A_2 e_2) = Ke. \tag{17}$$

System (16), with closed-loop by control (17), will take the form

$$\dot{e}_1 = A_1 e_1 + A_{12} e_2, \ \dot{e}_2 = A_2 e_2. \tag{18}$$

Its matrix has an upper triangular block structure

$$\begin{pmatrix} A_1 & A_{12} \\ O & A_2 \end{pmatrix}$$

and is stable according to (4), and its eigenvalues meet the characteristic equation $\det(\lambda I - A_1)\det(\lambda I - A_2) = 0$.

2.c. A modal control law based on the state of the initial system.

Finally, based on (17), it is necessary to form a feedback on the variables of the original systems (1) and (2), since it is these variables that are measured. By substitutions of variables (7), (11), and (15), the resulting transformation matrix and the resulting modal control law (2) are as follows:

$$T_e T_a T_p x = e, \ u = Ke = Fx, F_{m \times n} = K T_e T_a T_p, \tag{19}$$

which provides (3), (4), and a solution to the stabilization problem.

Modal control synthesis is complete.

As stated in subsection 2.a, full parametric certainty of the matrices A and B is required to implement modal control, which limits its applicability in practical applications, as models of real-world control plants often depend on unknown parameters.

In such cases, the requirements of the closed-loop system are relaxed, and the stability margin, which is one of the key quality indicators of the transition process, is considered as the target condition. The problem is to synthesize a linear feedback (2), which provides in the closed-loop system (3) a stability margin not less than a given $\eta_d > 0$:

$$\min\{-\mathrm{Re}\lambda_i(A + BF)\}_{i=\overline{1,n}} = \eta \geq \eta_d. \tag{20}$$

As a methodological basis for problem (20), we will use the concept of super-stability of the system, which is defined in terms of matrix elements using inequalities rather than characteristic Equation (4), which is a precondition for using this concept in solving robust control problems in systems with uncertain parameters.

Definition 3 ([12]). *Matrix $A = (a_{ij}) \in R^{n \times n}$ and, consequently, the system $\dot{x} = Ax$ are called super-stable if A is a negative-diagonal-dominated matrix, i.e., all the elements of its main diagonal are negative numbers $a_{ii} < 0$, $i = \overline{1, n}$, which are greater in absolute value than the sum of the modules of the non-diagonal elements in the row:*

$$\min\left\{ -a_{ii} - \sum_{j=1, j \neq i}^{n} |a_{ij}| \right\}_{i=\overline{1,n}} = v > 0, \tag{21}$$

where v has the meaning of a margin of super-stability.

The statements in Lemma 1 below are rather obvious. However, we will present a rigorous proof of them, because they are important for further discussion.

Lemma 1. *Any super-stable matrix $A = (a_{ij}) \in R^{n \times n}$, (21) is Hurwicz, and its stability margin $\min\{-\mathrm{Re}\lambda_i(A)\}_{i=\overline{1,n}} = \eta > 0$ is as much as the margin of her super-stability (21), i.e.,*

$$\eta \geq v. \tag{22}$$

Proof 1. According to Gershgorin's theorem [17], each of the eigenvalues λ of matrix A is always located in one of the circles of the complex plane $|a_{ii} - \lambda| \leq \sum_{j=1, j \neq i}^{n} |a_{ij}|, i = \overline{1, n}$ centered at a_{ii} and with a radius of $\sum_{j=1, j \neq i}^{n} |a_{ij}|$. Each eigenvalue λ of matrix A corresponds to the eigenvector h: $\sum_{j=1}^{n} a_{ij}h = \lambda h, i = \overline{1, n}$. Let $|h_k| = \max_i |h_i| > 0$; then,

$$|a_{kk} - \lambda||h_k| = \left| \sum_{i, j \neq k}^{n} a_{kj}h_i \right| \leq |h_k| \sum_{j \neq k}^{n} |a_{kj}| \text{ and } |a_{kk} - \lambda| \leq \sum_{j \neq k}^{n} |a_{kj}|.$$

It follows that if the matrix A is super-stable and $-a_{kk} > \sum_{j \neq k}^{n} |a_{kj}|$, then each of its eigenvalues lies in the left half-plane of the complex plane, i.e., matrix A is Hurwitz and its stability margin is defined as $\eta = -\mathrm{Re}\lambda_0 = \min\{-\mathrm{Re}\lambda_i(A)\} > 0$.

Let λ_0 be a real simple eigenvalue of the matrix A, to which corresponds the eigenvector $\overline{h}_0 = (h_1, \ldots, h_n)^T$, $\lambda_0 \overline{h}_0 = A\overline{h}_0$, and for the k-th ($k = 1, 2, \ldots, n$) element we have: $\lambda_0 h_k = \sum_{j=1}^{n} a_{kj}h_j$. Let h_k be an element with a maximum module $\overline{h}_0$: $|h_k| = \max\{|h_i|\}_{i=\overline{1,n}}$.

Then, a fair estimate is $|\lambda_0||h_k| \geq |a_{kk}||h_k| - \sum_{j=1, j \neq k}^{n} |a_{kj}||h_j| \geq |h_k|(|a_{kk}| - \sum_{j=1, j \neq k}^{n} |a_{kj}|) = |h_k|v$, whence it follows $\eta = |\lambda_0| \geq v$, inequality (20) is satisfied. The case of $\mathrm{Re}\lambda_0$ corresponds to a pair of complex-conjugate eigenvalues, and the estimate becomes $|\mathrm{Re}\lambda_0||h_k| \geq |a_{kk}||h_k| - \sum_{j=1, j \neq k}^{n} |a_{kj}||h_j| \geq |h_k|v$ inequality (26) is satisfied.

In the case of an multiple-eigenvalue λ_0, similar estimates hold for all linearly independent eigenvectors corresponding to a given eigenvalue. Lemma 1 is proved. $\square$

In a controllable linear system with certain parameters, it is always possible to achieve stability with state feedback, but super-stability is rarely achieved due to a lack of control actions. In this sense, the only obvious exceptions are elementary systems.

As it is shown in subsection 2.a, it is possible to provide any reference matrix A_0, including a super-stable one, in a closed-loop system using feedback (2) and (5), if the parameters of the elementary system are known. Let us note that a diagonal matrix with negative elements $A_0 = \mathrm{diag}\{a_i\}, a_i < 0, i = \overline{1, n}$ is a special case of a super-stable matrix, where $\min\{|a_i|\} = \min\{-\lambda_i(A_0)\} = \eta = v$.

Let us distinguish a class of nonelementary linear systems, for the stabilization of which with a given stability margin (20) we can interconnectively apply the concept of super-stability and decomposition synthesis based on the transition to the RF. This class includes a particular case of controllable systems (1), in which RF (6) will consist of two elementary subsystems. The possibility of such a representation is contained in the rank structure of the controllability matrix.

If system (1), where $0 < \mathrm{rank} B_{n \times m} = m_0 \leq m < n$, is controllable, its controllability matrix is of full rank:

$$\mathrm{rank}(B \ \ AB \ \ A^2 B \ \ \ldots \ \ A^{n-m_0} B)_{n \times m(n-m_0+1)} = n. \tag{23}$$

The rank structure of the controllability matrix (23) is characterized by a controllability index and a controllability indicator [19]. If the rank of the controllability matrix (23) is increased according to the following scheme:

$$\begin{aligned}
\mathrm{rank} B &= m_0 \neq 0, \ \mathrm{rank}(B \ \ AB) = m_0 + m_1, \ m_0 \geq m_1 \neq 0, \\
\mathrm{rank}(B \ \ AB \ \ A^2 B) &= m_0 + m_1 + m_2, \ m_1 \geq m_2 \neq 0, \ldots, \\
\mathrm{rank}(B \ \ AB \ \ \ldots \ \ A^r B) &= m_0 + m_1 + \ldots + m_r, \ m_{r-1} \geq m_r \neq 0, \\
\mathrm{rank}(B \ \ AB \ \ \ldots \ \ A^r B \ \ A^{r+1} B) &= m_0 + m_1 + \ldots + m_r + 0 \Rightarrow \\
\Rightarrow \mathrm{rank}(B \ \ AB \ \ \ldots \ \ A^{r+1} B \ \ A^{r+2} B) &= m_0 + m_1 + \ldots + m_r + 0 + 0,
\end{aligned} \tag{24}$$

then pair $(A, \ B)$ corresponds to a specific set of natural numbers $m_0, \ldots, m_r$:

$$\mathrm{rank}(B \ \ AB \ \ \ldots \ \ A^r B) = m_0 + m_1 + \ldots + m_r = n, \ m_0 \geq m_1 \geq \ldots \geq m_r, \ r \leq n - m_0, \tag{25}$$

which are called the indexes of controllability of the pair $(A, \ B)$. $m_i \in N$, $i = \overline{0, r}$ is the number of linearly independent matrix columns $A^i B$, which form the basis of the controllability matrix, compiled according to the specified scheme; $r + 1$ is controllability indicator of pair $(A, \ B)$, the number of its controllability indices. $\square$

Lemma 2. *If the controllability matrix of a linear controlled system (1) has a controllability indicator equal to two,*

$$\mathrm{rank} B_{(n \times m)} = m_0 \neq 0, \ \mathrm{rank}(B \ \ AB)_{n \times 2m} = m_0 + m_1 = n, \ m_0 \geq (n - m_0), \tag{26}$$

then, using the nondegenerate replacement of variables (12), system (1) will be represented in RF (6), in which not only the second, but also the first subsystem will be elementary with respect to the virtual control,

$$\mathrm{rank} A_{12(n-m_0) \times m_0} = n - m_0. \tag{27}$$

Proof 2. Let us rearrange the blocks of the controllability matrix (26) without performing a rearrangement inside the blocks $W_{(n \times 2m)} = (A B \ B)$. For convenience, we denote $AB = P$. Let us multiply this matrix from the left by the transition matrix to RF (12). According to (7) and (12), the matrix obtained as a result of multiplication can be represented in the following form:

$$TW = T_a T_p (P \ B) = T_a \begin{pmatrix} \widetilde{P}_1 & \widetilde{B}_1 \\ \widetilde{P}_2 & \widetilde{B}_2 \end{pmatrix} = \begin{pmatrix} P_{1(n-m_0) \times m} & O \\ P_2 & B_{2(m_0 \times m)} \end{pmatrix} = \overline{W},$$

where $P_1 = \widetilde{P}_1 - \widetilde{B}_1 B_2^+ \widetilde{P}_2$. By design, $\mathrm{rank} W_{(n \times 2m)} = n$, and $\mathrm{rank} B = \mathrm{rank} B_{2(m_0 \times m)} = m_0$. When multiplied by the nonsingular matrix $\det T_{(n \times n)} \neq 0$, the rank does not change and $\mathrm{rank} \overline{W}_{(n \times 2m)} = n$, which is why matrix P_1 is of full rank:

$$\mathrm{rank} P_{1(n-m_0) \times m} = n - m_0. \tag{28}$$

Considering that the matrices $W_{n \times 2m}$ and $\overline{W}_{n \times 2m} = TW$ are of full rank and consist of linearly independent rows, there are pseudo-inverse matrices for them, and

$$W_{2m \times n}^+ : \ WW^+ = I_n, \ \overline{W}^+ = (TW)^+ = \begin{pmatrix} P_{1(m \times (n-m_0))}^+ & O \\ \times & B_{2(m \times m_0)}^+ \end{pmatrix}. \tag{29}$$

In Formula (29) and further in the text, the symbol $\times$ denotes matrices, the type of which does not affect the structural properties.

Taking (27) into account, the similarity transformation of the matrix A to RF $TAT^{-1} = \overline{A}$ can be represented as

$$TAT^{-1} = T\,AWW^{+}\,T^{-1} = T\,AW(TW)^{+} = (TAW)\overline{W}^{+},$$

where $TAW = TA(AB\ B) = T(A^2B\ AB)$, $AB = P$. Then,

$$TAT^{-1} = (T(A^2B\ AB))\overline{W}^{+} = \begin{pmatrix} \times & P_1 \\ \times & \times \end{pmatrix}\begin{pmatrix} P_1^{+} & O \\ \times & B_2^{+} \end{pmatrix} = \begin{pmatrix} \times & P_1 B_2^{+} \\ \times & \times \end{pmatrix} = \begin{pmatrix} A_{11} & A_{12(n-m_0)\times m_0} \\ A_{21} & A_{22} \end{pmatrix},$$

where $A_{12(n-m_0)\times m_0} = (P_1 B_2^{+})_{(n-m_0)\times m_0}$ due to (28), (29), and $\operatorname{rank}(P_1 B_2^{+})_{(n-m_0)\times m_0} = n - m_0$, so equality (27) is satisfied. Lemma 2 is proved. $\square$

Let us extend (without proof) the results of Lemma 2 to controlled systems of general form (25).

A consequence of Lemma 2 is as follows. If condition (25) is satisfied in system (1), then it can be represented in the block form of controllability, which consists of $r + 1$ elementary blocks of dimension $m_0, m_1, \ldots m_r$ by a linear nonsingular transformation $Tx = (x_1, \ldots, x_{r+1})$, $\det T \neq 0$, $x_1 \in R^{m_r}$, $x_2 \in R^{m_{r-1}}$, $\ldots$, $x_{r+1} \in R^{m_0}$. Matrix T can be found by transforming the matrix W to the bottom-triangular block form with matrices of full rank on the main diagonal:

$$TW = T(A^rB \ldots AB\ B) = \overline{W} = \begin{pmatrix} P_r & \ldots & O & O & O \\ \ldots & \ldots & \ldots & \ldots & \ldots \\ & & \ldots & P_2 & O & O \\ & & & \ldots & P_1 & O \\ & & & \ldots & & P_0 \end{pmatrix}, \tag{30}$$

where $\operatorname{rank}P_{0(m_0\times m)} = m_0$, $\operatorname{rank}P_{i(m_i\times m_{i-1})} = m_i$, $i = \overline{1, r}$.

Just as in the procedure of converting to the RF (6), the essence of the transformations is that successively in each block B, AB, $\ldots$, $A^{r-1}B$, one needs to group m_i basis rows of matrix P_i by transpositions (similar to (7)) and zero out the top linearly dependent lines (similar to (11)). In this case, the leftmost block A^rB can be discarded, since its elements do not participate in the formation of the matrix T.

For the selected class of systems (1), (26), it is possible to provide a guaranteed stability margin (24) by providing super-stability of the closed system (18) in a new coordinate basis, where the reference matrices A_1, A_2 can be assigned arbitrarily. Selecting these matrices diagonally

$$A_1 = \operatorname{diag}\left\{a_i^1\right\}_{i=\overline{1, n-m_0}}, \quad A_2 = \operatorname{diag}\left\{a_i^2\right\}_{i=\overline{1, m_0}}, \tag{31}$$

on the one hand, excludes the presence of complex-conjugate eigenvalues in the matrix of the closed system, but, on the other hand, simplifies the computational aspect of the synthesis. Then, for any parameters satisfying the non-strict inequalities

$$\nu \geq \eta_{\mathrm{d}}, \quad a_i^1 \leq -\left(\nu + \sum_{j=1}^{m_0}\left|a_{ij}^{12}\right|\right), \quad A_{12} = (a_{ij}^{12}), \quad i = \overline{1, n-m_0}; \quad a_i^2 \leq -\nu > 0, \quad i = \overline{1, m_0}, \tag{32}$$

the closed-loop system (18) will be super-stable with a margin of super-stability $\nu \geq \eta_{\mathrm{d}}$.

As it was noted, the property of super-stability is formulated in terms of matrix elements (21) rather than their eigenvalues, so it is not invariant to linear transformations, and the initial closed system (1), (19), (31), (32) in general case will not be super-stable. However, because of (22), it guarantees stabilization with a stability margin at least equal to the one given in (20).

In the next section, we consider the possibility of synthesis of robust control of parametrically uncertain systems in the context of the proposed approach.

3. Parametrically Uncertain Systems

3.1. Elementary Control Problem

This section considers the problem of stabilization of linear stationary systems operating under interval parameter uncertainty

$$\dot{x} = (A + \hat{A})x + (B + \hat{B})u, \, x \in R^n, \, u \in R^m, \, m < n, \tag{33}$$

where matrices elements $A = (a_{ij})$, $i, j = \overline{1, n}$, $B = (b_{ij})$, $i = \overline{1, n}$, $j = \overline{1, m}$, which define the nominal system (1), are known, and pair (A, B) is controllable. Elements of matrices $\hat{A} = (\hat{a}_{ij})$ and $\hat{B} = (\hat{b}_{ij})$ are constant but unknown; their values belong to closed intervals with known boundaries:

$$a_{ij\min} \leq \hat{a}_{ij} \leq a_{ij\max}, \, i, j = \overline{1, n}; b_{ij\min} \leq \hat{b}_{ij} \leq b_{ij\max}, \, i = \overline{1, n}, \, j = \overline{1, m}.$$

In the following, to simplify the explanation, we will assume that the values of the uncertain elements are in intervals symmetric with respect to zero

$$a_{ij} - \widehat{a}_{ij} \leq a_{ij} + \hat{a}_{ij} \leq a_{ij} + \widehat{a}_{ij}, \, i, j = \overline{1, n}; b_{ij} - \widehat{b}_{ij} \leq b_{ij} + \hat{b}_{ij} \leq b_{ij} + \widehat{b}_{ij}, \, i = \overline{1, n}, \, j = \overline{1, m}. \tag{34}$$

Then, the values of the matrix elements of the system (33) will be in closed intervals with known bounds, symmetrical for the corresponding nominal values

$$a_{ij} - \widehat{a}_{ij} \leq a_{ij} + \hat{a}_{ij} \leq a_{ij} + \widehat{a}_{ij}, \, i, j = \overline{1, n}; b_{ij} - \widehat{b}_{ij} \leq b_{ij} + \hat{b}_{ij} \leq b_{ij} + \widehat{b}_{ij}, \, i = \overline{1, n}, \, j = \overline{1, m}.$$

It is supposed that pair $((A + \hat{A}), (B + \hat{B}))$ is controllable in all acceptable intervals of parameter uncertainty, and moreover, the rank structures of the controllability matrices of the nominal system (1) and the parametrically perturbed system (33) are the same. This requirement is due to practical considerations. The uncertain system model (33) describes the functioning of a real control plant, and, for example, the failure to meet the condition $\operatorname{rank} B = \operatorname{rank}(B + \hat{B})$ indicates a "faulty" actuator or damaged communication with the control plant.

In a general case, the solution of the modal control problem with the assignment of a given spectrum (4) in the system (33) is not possible. We set the problem of synthesis of linear feedback (2), providing stabilization of the system (33) at all acceptable values of uncertain parameters (34) with stability margin not less than the given one $\eta_d > 0$, i.e., providing in a closed-loop system

$$\min\{-\operatorname{Re}\lambda_i[(A + \hat{A}) + (B + \hat{B})F]\}_{i=\overline{1,n}} = \eta \geq \eta_d. \tag{35}$$

We first investigate the possibility of solving the problem (35) for parametrically uncertain elementary systems of two types. The first type of the considered elementary systems are the systems with known control matrix

$$\dot{x} = (A + \hat{A})x + Bu, \, \dim u = m \geq n = \dim x = \operatorname{rank} B, \tag{36}$$

which are obviously controllable. No additional requirements are imposed on them. Variable states with uncertain coefficients cannot be compensated for by feedback, so the control law can be formed in two ways:

$$u = Fx = B^+(K - A)x \text{ or } u = Fx = B^+Kx, \, K = \operatorname{diag}(k_i)_{i=\overline{1,n}}. \tag{37}$$

In (37) and below we consider the general case of a rectangular matrix B. In a special case $m = n$, instead of B^+, matrix B^{-1} should be used. The corresponding closed-loop systems have the following form:

$$\dot{x} = (K + \hat{A})x \text{ or } \dot{x} = (K + A + \hat{A})x. \tag{38}$$

Obviously, the choice of matrix elements K can provide super-stability of systems (38) with any stability margin $\nu > 0$. To achieve the control goal (35), let us assume $\nu \geq \eta_{\mathrm{d}}$. Then, for any k_i, satisfying the inequalities

$$k_i \leq -(\eta + \sum_{j=1}^{n} \widehat{a}_{ij}) \text{ or } k_i \leq -(\eta + a_{ii} + \widehat{a}_{ij} + \sum_{j=1, j \neq i}^{n} (|a_{ij}| + \widehat{a}_{ij})), \, i = \overline{1, n}, \qquad (39)$$

matrices of systems (38) will be super-stable (21), which due to (22) and $\nu \geq \eta_{\mathrm{d}}$ solves the problem (35).

In practical applications, in order to save control resources, the first method of feedback generation is recommended (37), and the calculated values of the super-stability margin and k_i take on the basis of equalities $\nu = \eta_{\mathrm{d}}$ and (39).

Consider the general case of parametrically uncertain elementary systems

$$\dot{x} = (A + \hat{A})x + (B + \hat{B})u, \, \dim u = m \geq n = \dim x = \mathrm{rank} B, \qquad (40)$$

where the elements of the undefined matrices satisfy (34), but additional constraints must be imposed on the matrix $\hat{B}$ so that the system remains controllable.

Remark 2. *In a first-order system $\dot{x} = (a + \hat{a})x + (b + \hat{b})u$, the condition $b \neq 0$ is added to a basic requirement $b + \hat{b} \neq 0$. From a theoretical point of view, the situation is acceptable when $\mathrm{sign}(b) \neq \mathrm{sign}(b + \hat{b})$, and the problem (35) has a solution. However, in models of real control plants the parameters have a certain physical meaning, so the following conditions are proposed:*

$$b \neq 0, b + \hat{b} \neq 0 \text{ and } \mathrm{sign}(b) = \mathrm{sign}(b + \hat{b}) \Rightarrow |b| > \widehat{b} \Leftrightarrow 1 > \widehat{b}/|b|. \qquad (41)$$

The conditions (41) are characteristic of adequate models of parametrically uncertain control plants, in which the uncertainty intervals have "reasonable" bounds with respect to the nominal system parameters.

Then, the control law

$$u - k\mathrm{sign}(b + \hat{b})x \qquad (42)$$

will result in a closed-loop system $\dot{x} = (a + \hat{a} + k|b + \hat{b}|)x$, and the choice of gain based on inequality $k \leq -(\eta_{\mathrm{d}} + a + \widehat{a})/(|b| - \widehat{b})$ provides a given margin of safety.

The condition under which the multidimensional system (40) is not only controllable, but also preserves the structural property of the nominal system, namely, it remains elementary, appears as

$$\mathrm{rank} B = \mathrm{rank}(B + \hat{B}) = n. \qquad (43)$$

When making any of the requirements for uncertain matrices in (43) and below, it is assumed by default that these requirements are met for all values of uncertain elements from the allowable ranges (34).

However, as will be shown below, in the used approach the fulfillment of (43) is necessary but not sufficient to solve the problem (35).

Due to the parametric uncertainty of the control matrix in system (40), even state variables with certain coefficients cannot be compensated for by feedback, so we form a one-parameter control law in the form

$$u = Fx = kB^{+}Sx, \, k = \mathrm{const}, \, S = \mathrm{diag}\{\mathrm{sign}(1 + l_{ii})\}_{i=\overline{1,n}}, \, L_{(n \times n)} = \hat{B}B^{+} = (l_{ij}) . \qquad (44)$$

From the form of the matrix of the closed-loop system (40), (44),

$$\dot{x} = [A + \hat{A} + k(I_n + L)S]x , \qquad (45)$$

the choice of matrix S is clear. It contains the signs of the diagonal elements of the matrix $I + L$. The conditions for these signs to be constant for all acceptable values of the matrix $\hat{B}$ uncertain parameters are formulated in Lemma 3.

Lemma 3. *If in system (45), the matrix $I_n + L$ has a predominant diagonal*

$$\min\{|1 + l_{ii}| - \sum_{j=1, j \neq i}^{n} |l_{ij}|\}_{i=\overline{1,n}} = \mu > 0, \tag{46}$$

there is a real number k such that for any real values of elements of matrix A, $\hat{A}$ (34) and $v > 0$, the system (45) will be super-stable with an super-stability margin $v > 0$.

Proof 3. In each i-th matrix row of system (45), we substitute $k = k_i, i = \overline{1,n}$. The resulting matrix will be super-stable with a margin of super-stability $v > 0$, if

$$a_{ii} + \widehat{a}_{ii} + k_i|1 + l_{ii}| \leq -(v + \sum_{j=1, j \neq i}^{n} (|a_{ij}| + \widehat{a}_{ij}) + k_i \text{sign}(k_i) \sum_{j=1, j \neq i}^{n} |l_{ij}|), \ i = \overline{1, n}.$$

Due to (46), $|1 + l_{ii}| + \text{sign}(k_i) \sum_{j=1, j \neq i}^{n} |l_{ij}| > 0$ at any sign of k_i. Taking the "worst" case into account, we obtain autonomous upper estimates for the selection of k_i:

$$k_i \leq \overline{k}_i = -\frac{v + a_{ii} + \widehat{a}_{ii} + \sum_{j=1, j \neq i}^{n} (|a_{ij}| + \widehat{a}_{ij})}{|1 + l_{ii}| - \sum_{j=1, j \neq i}^{n} |l_{ij}|}, \ i = \overline{1, n}. \tag{47}$$

Obviously, the number we are looking for is $k \leq \min\left\{\overline{k}_i\right\}_{i=\overline{1,n}}$, at which all inequalities (47) are fulfilled simultaneously, which ensures that the system (45) is super-stable with any super-stability margin $v > 0$. Lemma 3 is proved. $\square$

Using (46), we simplify the final inequality, obtaining a slightly higher estimate module for the choice of the parameter k:

$$k \leq \min_{i=\overline{1,n}}\{-(v + a_{ii} + \widehat{a}_{ii} + \sum_{j=1, j \neq i}^{n} (|a_{ij}| + \widehat{a}_{ij}))\}/\mu. \tag{48}$$

From the set of elementary parametrically indeterminate systems (40), (34), a class of systems with additional requirements (43), (46), for which there is a robust control law (44), (48), provides a solution to the problem (35) if $v = \eta_\text{d}$. Notice that condition (41) is a special case of (46).

In the next subsection, a class of systems is extracted from the set of parametrically uncertain non-elementary systems whose nominal model satisfies conditions (28), for which a guaranteed stability margin can be provided by the proposed feedback approach.

3.2. Formalisation of a Class of Acceptable Non-Elementary Systems

Let us consider the question of possibility in the combination of concepts of super-stability and RF in robust synthesis of parametrically uncertain non-elementary system (33), (34), under the assumption that in its nominal model (1), a pair (A, B) is controllable and has a controllability indicator equal to two (26). As is proved in Lemma 2, in this case, the RF of the nominal system consists of two elementary subsystems, which allows one to synthesize a super-stable closed-loop system in terms of discrepancies and, as a consequence, to provide a guaranteed stability margin in the original closed-loop system.

In order to obtain the RF structure for system (33), it is necessary to impose additional constraints on the undefined matrices $\hat{A}$ and $\hat{B}$. When fulfilled, the system (33) will not only be controllable, but it will also retain the structural properties of the nominal system (26); more specifically, it will have the same dislocation of the basis columns of the controllability matrix and, hence, the structural zeros in the RF. Thus, it is necessary to formalize the conditions under which, as a result of a non-singular linear transformation $Tx = \bar{x}$ (12), which is determined by the matrices of the nominal system (1), the indeterminate system (33) will be represented in a form similar to RF (6), (26), that is:

$$\begin{aligned}
\dot{x}_1 &= (A_{11} + \hat{A}_{11})x_1 + (A_{12} + \hat{A}_{12})x_2, \\
\dot{x}_2 &= (A_{21} + \hat{A}_{21})x_1 + (A_{22} + \hat{A}_{22})x_2 + (B_2 + \hat{B}_2)u,
\end{aligned} \tag{49}$$

where

$$\begin{aligned}
\mathrm{rank}(B_2 + \hat{B}_2) &= \mathrm{rank}B_2 = \mathrm{rank}B = \dim x_2 = m_0; \\
\mathrm{rank}(A_{12} + \hat{A}_{12}) &= \mathrm{rank}A_{12} = \dim x_1 = n - m_0,
\end{aligned} \tag{50}$$

matrices A_{ij}, B_2 are known and match the corresponding RF matrices (6) of the nominal system (1), (26), the elements of the matrices $\hat{A}_{ij}$, $\hat{B}_2$ are constant and unknown, and the limits of the intervals to which their values belong are recalculated with regard to (34) by the formulas

$$T(A + \hat{A})T^{-1} = \hat{\bar{A}}, \quad T(B + \hat{B}) = \hat{\bar{B}}. \tag{51}$$

Lemma 4. *Let the pair$(A, \ B)$ in the nominal system (1) be controllable and characterized by the controllability indices (26). If, in system (33), all uncertainty intervals (34) for pair $((A + \hat{A}), \ (B + \hat{B}))$ rank conditions are met, including*

$$\begin{aligned}
\mathrm{rank}B &= \mathrm{rank}(B + \hat{B}) = \mathrm{rank}(B \ (B + \hat{B})) = m_0, \\
(\mathrm{rank}(B \ AB) &= \mathrm{rank}((B + \hat{B}) \ (A + \hat{A})(B + \hat{B})) \\
&= \mathrm{rank}(B \ AB \ (B + \hat{B}) \ (A + \hat{A})(B + \hat{B}) \,) = m_0 + m_1 = n) \\
&\Leftrightarrow (\mathrm{rank}(B \ AB) = \mathrm{rank}(B \ AB \ (A + \hat{A})(B + \hat{B})) = m_0 + m_1 = n),
\end{aligned} \tag{52}$$

then by means of a non-singular change of the variables $Tx = \bar{x}$ (12) and transformations (51), where T depends only on the matrices of the nominal system A, B, system (33) will be represented in the form of RF (49), where conditions (50) are met.

Proof 4. First condition (52) $\mathrm{rank}B = \mathrm{rank}(B \ (B + \hat{B}))$ means that the columns of the matrix $B + \hat{B}$ are linear combinations of the columns of the matrix B; hence, the indeterminate matrix can be represented as

$$B_{n \times m} + \hat{B}_{n \times m} = B\Lambda_{0(m \times m)}, \tag{53}$$

where Λ_0 is indeterminate matrix, $m_0 \leq \mathrm{rank}\Lambda_0 \leq m$. The second condition (50), rewritten with (53) as

$$\mathrm{rank}(B \ AB) = \mathrm{rank}(B\Lambda_0 \ (A + \hat{A})B\Lambda_0) = \mathrm{rank}(B \ AB \ (A + \hat{A})B\Lambda_0) = m_0 + m_1,$$

means that the columns of the matrix $(A + \hat{A})B\Lambda_0$ are linear combinations of the columns of the matrix $(B \ AB)$ and are represented in the form of

$$(A + \hat{A})B\Lambda_0 = (B \ AB)\Lambda_1 = B\Lambda_{10} + AB\Lambda_{11}, \ \Lambda_1 = \begin{pmatrix} \Lambda_{10(m \times m)} \\ \Lambda_{11(m \times m)} \end{pmatrix}, \ \mathrm{rank}\Lambda_{11} \geq n - m_0.$$

The columns of the matrices $B\Lambda_{10}$ are linear combinations of the columns of the matrix $B\Lambda_0 = B_{n \times m} + \hat{B}_{n \times m}$ and can be represented as $B\Lambda_{10} = B\Lambda_0\Lambda_{00}$. Consequently, $(B\Lambda_0 \ AB\Lambda_{11}) \sim (B\Lambda_0 \ AB\Lambda_{11} \ B\Lambda_0\Lambda_{00})$, and then $\mathrm{rank}(B\Lambda_0 \ AB\Lambda_{11}) = m_0 + m_1 = n$.

Thus, the controllability matrix of the pair $((A + \hat{A}), (B + \hat{B}))$ when conditions (50) are fulfilled has a full rank and can be represented in the form

$$((B + \hat{B}) \ (A + \hat{A})(B + \hat{B})) = (B\Lambda_0 \ B\Lambda_0\Lambda_{00} + AB\Lambda_{11}),$$

where the matrix elements $\Lambda_0, \Lambda_{00}, \Lambda_{11}$ are unknown. Let us denote $AB = P$, swap the control matrix blocks $\hat{W} = (B\Lambda_0\Lambda_{00} + P\Lambda_{11} \ B\Lambda_0)$, and multiply this matrix on the left by the transition to RF matrix (12), which depends only on the matrix elements of the nominal system:

$$T\hat{W} = T_a T_p (B\Lambda_0\Lambda_{00} + P\Lambda_{11} \ B\Lambda_0) = T_a\left(\left(\begin{array}{c} \tilde{B}_1 \\ B_2 \end{array}\right)\Lambda_0\Lambda_{00} + \left(\begin{array}{c} \tilde{P}_1 \\ \tilde{P}_2 \end{array}\right)\Lambda_{11} \ \left(\begin{array}{c} \tilde{B}_1 \\ B_2 \end{array}\right)\Lambda_0\right)$$

$$= \left(\left(\begin{array}{c} O \\ B_2 \end{array}\right)\Lambda_0\Lambda_{00} + \left(\begin{array}{c} P_1 \\ P_2 \end{array}\right)\Lambda_{11} \ \left(\begin{array}{c} O \\ B_2 \end{array}\right)\Lambda_0\right) = \hat{\bar{W}}.$$

In the obtained matrix, the right-hand block corresponds to the transformation of the matrix $(B + \hat{B})$. With (53), it follows that

$$T(B + \hat{B}) = \left(\begin{array}{c} O \\ B_2 \end{array}\right)\Lambda_0 = \left(\begin{array}{c} O \\ B_2\Lambda_0 \end{array}\right) = \left(\begin{array}{c} O \\ B_2 + \hat{B}_2 \end{array}\right), \ \mathrm{rank}(B_2 + \hat{B}_2) = \mathrm{rank}B_2 = m_0,$$

i.e., the first condition (52) is satisfied.

According to the scheme given in Lemma 2, let us perform a similarity transformation

$$T(A + \hat{A})T^{-1} = (T((A + \hat{A})^2(B + \hat{B}) \ (A + \hat{A})(B + \hat{B}))\hat{\bar{W}}^+ = \left(\begin{array}{cc} A_{11} + \hat{A}_{11} & A_{12} + \hat{A}_{12} \\ A_{21} + \hat{A}_{21} & A_{22} + \hat{A}_{22} \end{array}\right),$$

where $A_{12} + \hat{A}_{12} = P_1\Lambda_{11}(B_2\Lambda_0)^+ \Rightarrow \mathrm{rank}A_{12} = \mathrm{rank}(A_{12} + \hat{A}_{12}) = n - m_0$, i.e., and the second condition (50) is satisfied. Hence, system (33) is representable in the form (49), whose structure corresponds to the structure of the RF of the nominal system (1), (26). Lemma 4 is proved. $\square$

Thus, a class of systems (35), (50) is defined, which can be reduced to RF (49) consisting of two elementary blocks (50) in an invariant way to the unknown parameters (34). Let us adopt without proof the inverse statement for Lemma 4, defining a constructive way to check the rank conditions (50). In system (1), the pair (A, B) is characterized by controllability indices (26). If the change of variables (12) leads system (33) to RF (49), (50), then in all uncertainty intervals (34) the rank conditions (50) for the pair $((A + \hat{A}), (B + \hat{B}))$ is fulfilled.

However, as is shown in the previous subsection, satisfaction of conditions (50) and RF (49), (50) are necessary but, in general, not sufficient for solving the problem (35) in the framework of the technique we used.

Let us first distinguish particular cases that do not require any additional constraints from the theoretical point of view.

If in (26) $n = 2$, $m_0 = 1$, then the RF will consist of two first-order subsystems, where

$$(\mathrm{rank}\,(B_2 + \hat{B}_2) = \mathrm{rank}B_2 = 1) \Leftrightarrow (b_2 \neq 0 \text{ and } b_2 + \hat{b}_2 \neq 0);$$
$$(\mathrm{rank}\,(A_{12} + \hat{A}_{12}) = \mathrm{rank}A_{12} = 1) \Leftrightarrow (a_{12} \neq 0 \text{ and } a_{12} + \hat{a}_{12} \neq 0).$$

Then, similarly to (42), using virtual control and subsequent variable change,

$$x_2 = k_1\mathrm{sign}(a_{12} + \hat{a}_{12})x_1, \ e_2 = x_2 - k_1\mathrm{sign}(a_{12} + \hat{a}_{12})x_1 \tag{54}$$

The first subsystem of the RF is stabilized, and the second subsystem is stabilized with real control $u = k_2\mathrm{sign}(b_2 + \hat{b}_2)e_2$. In another particular case, for arbitrary $m_0 \geq n - m_0 > 1$ in system (49), $\hat{A}_{12} \equiv O$ and $\hat{B}_2 \equiv O$. Then, the virtual and real control is chosen in a form similar to (37). Furthermore, the last particular case is a combination of the first two, where $m_0 = n - 1 > 1$ and $\hat{B}_2 \equiv O$.

Only for the systems with the mentioned properties is the fulfillment of conditions (52) necessary and sufficient to ensure the super-stability of the closed-loop system, with the help of the linear static feedback in terms of the discrepancies.

For the general case of systems from the considered class, sufficient conditions similar to (46) are formulated in terms of elements of the RF matrices (49). Let us first form in the system (49) the virtual and real control analogous to (44):

$$
\begin{aligned}
&x_2 = F_1 x_1 = k_1 A_{12}^+ S_1 x_1, \ e_1 := x_1, \ e_2 = x_2 - F_1 x_1, \\
&S_1 = \mathrm{diag}\{\mathrm{sign}(1 + l_{ii}^1)\}, \ L_{1(n-m_0)\times(n-m_0)} = \hat{A}_{12} A_{12}^+ = (l_{ij}^1) \ ; \\
&u = K_2 e_2 = k_2 B_2^+ S_2 e_2, \ u = Ke, \ K = (O \quad K_2), \ k_{1,2} = \mathrm{const}, \\
&S_2 = \mathrm{diag}\{\mathrm{sign}(1 + l_{ii}^2)\}, \ L_{2(m_0\times m_0)} = \hat{B}_2 B_2^+ = (l_{ij}^2),
\end{aligned}
\tag{55}
$$

and let us change the variables (14), (15) and make a closed-loop RF of the uncertain system (49), (55) in discrepancies

$$
\begin{aligned}
\dot{e}_1 &= (A_{11} + \hat{A}_{11} + k_1(I + L_1)S_1)e_1 + (A_{12} + \hat{A}_{12})e_2, \\
\dot{e}_2 &= (C_{21} + \hat{C}_{21})e_1 + (C_{22} + \hat{C}_{22} + k_2(I + L_2)S_2)e_2,
\end{aligned}
\tag{56}
$$

where the ranges of elements of the unknown matrices are assumed to be symmetric and are calculated from (34), considering the performed transformations (12), (15), which depend only on the matrices of the nominal system (1) and the selected k_1.

From Lemma 3, it follows that by successively selecting at first the parameter $k_1 = \mathrm{const}$, and then $k_2 = \mathrm{const}$, the system (56) can be made super-stable with a given margin of super-stability $\nu \geq \eta_\mathrm{d}$, if matrices $I_{n-m_0} + L_1$, $I_{m_0} + L_2$ (55) have dominant diagonals

$$
\min\{|1 + l_{ii}^1| - \sum_{j=1, j\neq i}^{n-m_0} |l_{ij}^1|\}_{i=\overline{1, n-m_0}} = \mu_1 > 0, \ \min\{|1 + l_{ii}^2| - \sum_{j=1, j\neq i}^{m_0} |l_{ij}^2|\}_{i=\overline{1, m_0}} = \mu_2 > 0. \tag{57}
$$

Then, similarly to (47), a joint system of inequalities can be obtained, based on which the feedback parameters are successively specified in the form of (48). Taking into account the notations

$$
A_{11(n-m_0)\times(n-m_0)} = (a_{ij}^{11}), A_{12(n-m_0)\times m_0} = (a_{ij}^{12}), C_{21(m_0\times(n-m_0))} = (c_{ij}^{21}), C_{22(m_0\times m_0)} = (c_{ij}^{22}),
$$

$$
\hat{A}_{11} = (\hat{a}_{ij}^{11}), \hat{A}_{12} = (\hat{a}_{ij}^{12}), \hat{C}_{21} = (\hat{c}_{ij}^{21}), \hat{C}_{22} = (\hat{c}_{ij}^{22}),
$$

$$
\left|\hat{a}_{ij}^{11}\right| \leq \widehat{a}_{ij}^{11}, \ \left|\hat{a}_{ij}^{12}\right| \leq \widehat{a}_{ij}^{12}, \ \left|\hat{c}_{ij}^{21}\right| \leq \widehat{c}_{ij}^{21}, \ \left|\hat{c}_{ij}^{22}\right| \leq \widehat{c}_{ij}^{22}
$$

we have

$$
\begin{aligned}
k_1 &\leq \min_{i=\overline{1, n-m_0}}\{-(\nu + a_{ii}^{11} + \widehat{a}_{ii}^{11} + \sum_{j=1, j\neq i}^{n-m_0}(|a_{ij}^{11}| + \widehat{a}_{ij}^{11}) + \sum_{j=1}^{m_0}(|a_{ij}^{12}| + \widehat{a}_{ij}^{12}))\}/\mu_1, \\
k_2 &\leq \min_{i=\overline{1, m_0}}\{-(\nu + c_{ii}^{22} + \widehat{c}_{ii}^{22} + \sum_{j=1, j\neq i}^{m_0}(|c_{ij}^{22}| + \widehat{c}_{ij}^{22}) + \sum_{j=1}^{n-m_0}(|c_{ij}^{21}| + \widehat{c}_{ij}^{21}))\}/\mu_2.
\end{aligned}
\tag{58}
$$

The control law based on (55) on the variables of the initial system (19) depends only on the matrices of the nominal system and selected parameters (58) and ensures stabilization of the initial parametrically uncertain system (33) with a guaranteed stability margin (35).

The theoretical statements presented in this subsection and the decomposition synthesis procedure for systems with a controllability indicator equal to two (26) can similarly be extended to non-elementary controllable systems of the general form (24).

4. Simulations

We consider a mathematical model of the control plant of the form

$$\dot{x} = Ax + Bu,\ A = \begin{pmatrix} 1 & 1 & 0 \\ 0 & 1 & 0 \\ 1 & 0 & 1 \end{pmatrix}, B = \begin{pmatrix} 1 & 0 \\ 2 & 1 \\ 0 & 1 \end{pmatrix},\ \dim x = n = 3,\ \dim u = m = 2. \quad (59)$$

Let us investigate the rank structure of the controllability matrix of the system (59) according to scheme (24):

$$\mathrm{rank}\,B = \mathrm{rank} \begin{pmatrix} 1 & 0 \\ 2 & 1 \\ 0 & 1 \end{pmatrix} = 2 \neq 0,\ \mathrm{rank}(B\ \ AB) = \mathrm{rank} \begin{pmatrix} 1 & 0 & 3 & 1 \\ 2 & 1 & 2 & 1 \\ 0 & 1 & 1 & 1 \end{pmatrix} = 2 + 1 = 3.$$

Pair $(A,\ B)$ is controllable and has a controllability indicator equal to 2. The system (59) belongs to the valid class (26), and its RF will consist of two elementary subsystems of the first and second orders. On the example of system (59), let us demonstrate the decomposition procedures developed in Sections 2 and 3 for the synthesis of modal and robust control based on the transition to the RF.

Example 1. *For the system (59), the goal is to synthesize a linear feedback that provides a given spectrum in a closed-loop system $\sigma_{\mathrm{d}} = \{-1;\ -1 \pm 3j\}$. To solve the problem, we use the synthesis of modal control based on transition to RF (Procedure 1).*

1.a. In the matrix B, the bottom two rows are linearly independent and form a basis. It is not necessary to rearrange the rows. We assume

$$B_2 = \begin{pmatrix} 2 & 1 \\ 0 & 1 \end{pmatrix},\ T_p = I, T = T_a, x = \tilde{x}.$$

1.b. Using the second Formula (10), we find the cancellation matrix

$$B_2^* = \tilde{B}_1 B_2^{-1} = \frac{1}{2}\begin{pmatrix} 1 & 0 \end{pmatrix}\begin{pmatrix} 1 & -1 \\ 0 & 2 \end{pmatrix} = \begin{pmatrix} 0.5 & -0.5 \end{pmatrix}$$

and after performing the transformation (11) to the matrix

$$T = \begin{pmatrix} 1 & -0.5 & 0.5 \\ 0 & 1 & 0 \\ 0 & 0 & 1 \end{pmatrix},\ T^{-1} = \begin{pmatrix} 1 & 0.5 & -0.5 \\ 0 & 1 & 0 \\ 0 & 0 & 1 \end{pmatrix} \quad (60)$$

we obtain an equivalent representation of system (59) in RF (6), which has the form

$$\dot{x}_1 = 1.5x_1 + (1.25\ \ -0.25)x_2,$$
$$\dot{x}_2 = \begin{pmatrix} 0 \\ 1 \end{pmatrix}x_1 + \begin{pmatrix} 1 & 0 \\ 0.5 & 0.5 \end{pmatrix}x_2 + \begin{pmatrix} 2 & 1 \\ 0 & 1 \end{pmatrix}u. \quad (61)$$

2.a. (Procedure 2) In the first subsystem, we take a valid eigenvalue from the given spectrum (61) as the reference matrix: $A_1 = -1$. The local feedback matrix $x_2 = F_{1(2\times1)}x_1$, providing (13), has infinitely many realizations. The solution obtained is similar to the first equality (5):

$$A_{11} + A_{10}F_1 = A_1 \Rightarrow F_1 = A_{10}^+(A_1 - A_{11}) = \begin{pmatrix} f_1 \\ f_2 \end{pmatrix} = \begin{pmatrix} -25/13 \\ 5/13 \end{pmatrix},\ A_{10}^+ = \begin{pmatrix} 10/13 \\ -2/13 \end{pmatrix}$$

which is inconvenient for calculations. To determine F_1, we use a direct method:

$$A_{11} + A_{10}F_1 = A_1 \Rightarrow 1.5 + \begin{pmatrix} 1.25 & -0.25 \end{pmatrix}\begin{pmatrix} f_1 \\ f_2 \end{pmatrix} = -1 \Leftrightarrow f_2 = 10 + 5f_1.$$

Let us assume, for example $F_1 = (-1 \ \ 5)^T$. After performing the transformation (15), we obtain the RF closed by the local relation (16), in the form

$$\dot{e}_1 = -e_1 + (1.25 \quad -0.25)e_2,$$

$$\dot{e}_2 = \begin{pmatrix} -2 \\ 8 \end{pmatrix} e_1 + \begin{pmatrix} 2.25 & -0.25 \\ -5.75 & 1.75 \end{pmatrix} e_2 + \begin{pmatrix} 2 & 1 \\ 0 & 1 \end{pmatrix} u.$$

2.b. For the remaining complex-conjugate pair from a given spectrum $\lambda = -1 \pm 3j$, we make a reference matrix, e.g., in the form of a Jordanian cell $A_2 = \begin{pmatrix} -1 & 3 \\ -3 & -1 \end{pmatrix}$, and generate the feedback from the second Formula (17) in the form of

$$u = \begin{pmatrix} 0.5 & -0.5 \\ 0 & 1 \end{pmatrix} \left(\begin{pmatrix} 2 \\ -8 \end{pmatrix} e_1 + \begin{pmatrix} -2.25 & 0.25 \\ -5.75 & -1.75 \end{pmatrix} e_2 + \begin{pmatrix} -1 & 3 \\ -3 & -1 \end{pmatrix} e_2 \right),$$

$$u = Ke = \begin{pmatrix} 5 & -3 & 3 \\ -8 & 2.75 & -2.75 \end{pmatrix} e,$$

which leads to a closed system of discrepancies (18), that is,

$$\dot{e}_1 = -e_1 + (1.25 \quad -0.25)e_2, \ \dot{e}_2 = \begin{pmatrix} -1 & 3 \\ -3 & -1 \end{pmatrix} e_2.$$

2.c. Considering the transformations performed, let us find the feedback matrix and form a modal state control law for the initial system in form (19)

$$F_{2\times 3} = KT_eT = \begin{pmatrix} 5 & -3 & 3 \\ -8 & 2.75 & -2.75 \end{pmatrix} \begin{pmatrix} 1 & 0 & 0 \\ 1 & 1 & 0 \\ -5 & 0 & 1 \end{pmatrix} \begin{pmatrix} 1 & -0.5 & 0.5 \\ 0 & 1 & 0 \\ 0 & 0 & 1 \end{pmatrix},$$

$$u = Fx = \begin{pmatrix} -13 & 3.5 & -3.5 \\ 8.5 & -1.5 & 1.5 \end{pmatrix} x, \tag{62}$$

which provides a solution to the problem: $\sigma(A + BF) = \sigma_d = \{-1; \ -1 \pm 3j\}$.

Figure 1 shows the behavior of the variables $x(t) = (x_1(t), x_2(t), x_3(t))^T$ and controls $u(t) = (u_1(t), u_2(t))^T$ in closed-loop system (59), (62) with $x(0) = (0.5, 0.5, 0.5)^T$.

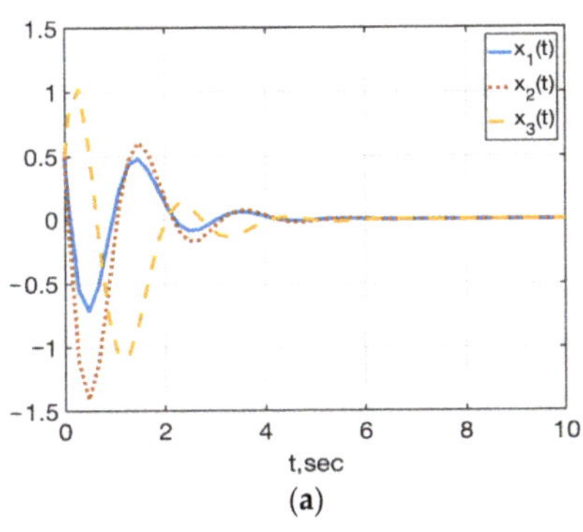

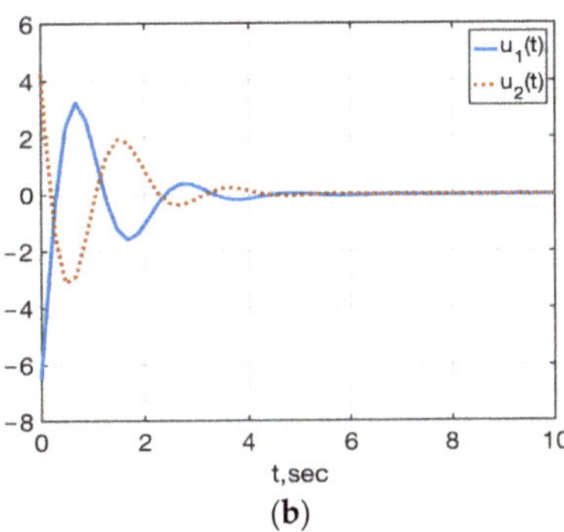

Figure 1. (**a**) Plots of $x_1(t)$, $x_2(t)$, $x_3(t)$; (**b**) Plots of $u_1(t)$, $u_2(t)$ in the closed-loop system (59), (62) with $x(0) = (0.5, 0.5, 0.5)^T$.

Example 2. *For system (59), the problem is to synthesize a linear feedback that provides a given margin of stability in the closed-loop system* $\eta \geq \eta_d = 1$. *To solve this problem, we use the procedure for synthesis of a super-stable closed-loop system (18) based on the transition to the*

RF (61). We assign the numerical values of the super-stability margin and the elements of the reference matrices of the closed-loop system (18) on the basis of equalities (32) $v = \eta_d = 1$, $A_1 = -(v + |a_{11}^{12}| + |a_{12}^{12}|) = -(1 + 1.25 + 0.25) = -2.5$; $a_1^2 = a_2^2 = -v = -1$, *which will ensure that the closed-loop system is super-stable.*

$$\dot{e}_1 = -2.5e_1 + (1.25 \ - 0.25)e_2, \ \dot{e}_2 = \begin{pmatrix} -1 & 0 \\ 0 & -1 \end{pmatrix} e_2.$$

The matrix of this system has a spectrum of $\sigma = \{-1; -1; -2, 5\}$. This spectrum, and hence a given stability margin, will be provided in the original closed-loop system (59) by the control (19). To determine the local feedback matrix F_1, we also use the direct method:

$$A_{11} + A_{10}F_1 = A_1 \Rightarrow 1.5 + 1.25f_1 - 0.25f_2 = -2.5 \Leftrightarrow f_2 = 16 + 5f_1.$$

Let us take, for example, $F_1 = (-2 \ \ 6)^T$. After performing the transformation (15), we obtain the RF of the closed-loop system (16) in the form

$$\dot{e}_1 = -2.5e_1 + (1.25 \ - 0.25)e_2,$$

$$\dot{e}_2 = \begin{pmatrix} -7 \\ 18 \end{pmatrix} e_1 + \begin{pmatrix} 3.5 & -0.5 \\ -7 & 2 \end{pmatrix} e_2 + \begin{pmatrix} 2 & 1 \\ 0 & 1 \end{pmatrix} u.$$

The second subsystem of this system gives the control laws for the transformed (17) and initial variables (19) as

$$u = \begin{pmatrix} 0.5 & -0.5 \\ 0 & 1 \end{pmatrix} \left(\begin{pmatrix} 7 \\ -18 \end{pmatrix} e_1 + \begin{pmatrix} -3.5 & 0.5 \\ 7 & -2 \end{pmatrix} e_2 + \begin{pmatrix} -1 & 0 \\ 0 & -1 \end{pmatrix} e_2 \right),$$

$$u = Ke = \begin{pmatrix} 12.5 & -5.75 & 1.75 \\ -18 & 7 & -3 \end{pmatrix} e,$$

$$F = KT_eT = \begin{pmatrix} 12.5 & -5.75 & 1.75 \\ -18 & 7 & -3 \end{pmatrix} \begin{pmatrix} 1 & 0 & 0 \\ 2 & 1 & 0 \\ -6 & 0 & 1 \end{pmatrix} \begin{pmatrix} 1 & -0.5 & 0.5 \\ 0 & 1 & 0 \\ 0 & 0 & 1 \end{pmatrix}, \tag{63}$$

$$u = Fx = \begin{pmatrix} -9.5 & -1 & -3 \\ 14 & 0 & 4 \end{pmatrix} x.$$

The matrix of a closed-loop system (59), (63), expressed as

$$A + BF = \begin{pmatrix} -8.5 & 0 & -3 \\ -5 & -1 & -2 \\ 15 & 0 & 5 \end{pmatrix}$$

is not super-stable, but the system has a given margin of stability:

$$\sigma(A + BF) = \{-1; -1; -2, 5\}, \min\{-\text{Re}\lambda_i(A + BF)\} = 1 = \eta_d.$$

Figure 2 shows the behavior of the variables $x(t) = (x_1(t), x_2(t), x_3(t))^T$ and controls $u(t) = (u_1(t), u_2(t))^T$ in a closed-loop system (59), (63) with $x(0) = (0.5, 0.5, 0.5)^T$.

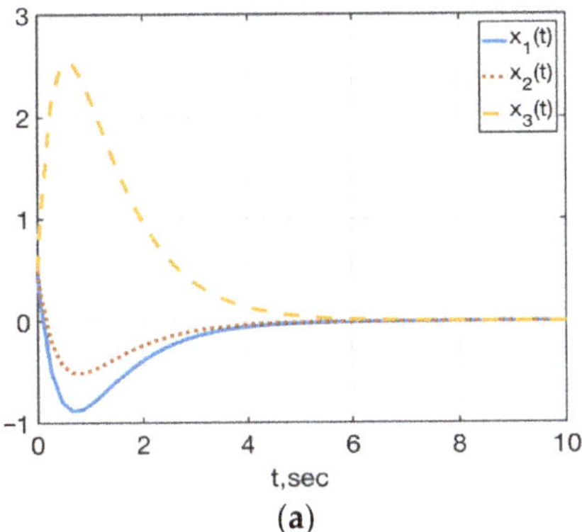

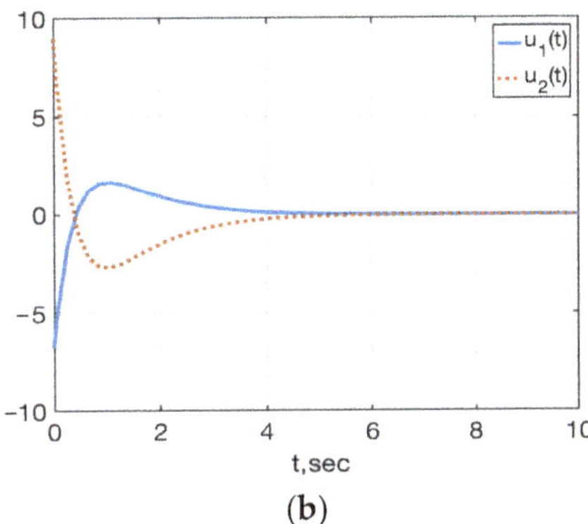

Figure 2. (**a**) Plots of $x_1(t)$, $x_2(t)$, $x_3(t)$; (**b**) Plots of $u_1(t)$, $u_2(t)$ in the closed-loop system (59), (63) with $x(0) = (0.5,\ 0.5,\ 0.5\,)^{\mathrm{T}}$.

Compared to the system (59), (62) (see Figure 1), the transients of the closed-loop system (59), (63) with real spectrum are not oscillatory but aperiodic, but the range of variation in all the variables has increased by about 2.5 times, and the time of regulation has not significantly changed.

Example 3. *With the nominal system* (59) *we will consider a parametrically indeterminate system* (33), *where* $\hat{A} = \alpha A$, $\hat{B} = \beta B$. *Parameters* α, β *are constant and unknown, their values belong to closed symmetric intervals with known boundaries:*

$$|\alpha| \le \widehat{\alpha} = 0.1,\ |\beta| \le \widehat{\beta} = 0.1. \tag{64}$$

The problem is to synthesize a linear feedback that provides a guaranteed margin of stability in a closed-loop system $\eta \ge \eta_{\mathrm{d}} = 1$ in all uncertainty intervals. In this system,

$$A + \hat{A} = A(1 + \alpha),\ B + \hat{B} = B(1 + \beta),\ \alpha \ne -1,\ \beta \ne -1, \tag{65}$$

conditions (53), (52) of Lemma 4 are met. The uncertain system is controllable in all uncertainty intervals and keeps the structural controllability properties of the nominal system (59). Hence, the uncertain system is representable in the form of RF (49)–(50) by transformation (12), (51) with matrix (60), where due to (65), $\hat{A}_{ij} = \alpha A_{ij}$, $i, j = 1, 2$, $\hat{B}_2 = \beta B_2$.

Let us check that the condition (57) is met:

$$\begin{aligned}
L_1 &= \hat{A}_{12} A_{12}^+ = \alpha(5/4\quad -1/4)\begin{pmatrix} 10/13 \\ -2/13 \end{pmatrix} = \alpha = l_{11}^1; \\
L_2 &= \hat{B}_2 B_2^{-1} = \beta\begin{pmatrix} 2 & 1 \\ 0 & 1 \end{pmatrix}\begin{pmatrix} 0.5 & -0,5 \\ 0 & 1 \end{pmatrix} = \beta I_2,\ l_{11}^2 = l_{22}^2 = \beta.
\end{aligned} \tag{66}$$

Due to (64) $1 + \alpha > 0$, $1 + \beta > 0$, the sufficient condition (57) is fulfilled, and because $\mu_1 = \mu_2 = 0.9$, in RF of an uncertain system, it is possible to provide super-stability by means of feedback (55), where

$$S_1 = \mathrm{sign}(1 + \alpha) = 1,\ S_2 = \mathrm{diag}\{\mathrm{sign}(1 + \beta)\} = I.$$

In the first subsystem of the uncertain RF $\dot{x}_1 = (6/4)(1 + \alpha)x_1 + (5/4\ -1/4)(1 + \alpha)x_2$ let us form the virtual control in the form of (55),

$$x_2 = F_1 x_1 = k_1 A_{12}^+ S_1 x_1 = k_1 \begin{pmatrix} 10/13 \\ -2/13 \end{pmatrix} x_1. \tag{67}$$

With variable changes $e_1 := x_1$, $e_2 = x_2 - F_1 x_1$ we obtain

$$\dot{e}_1 = (1+\alpha)((A_{11}+k_1)e_1 + A_{12}e_2) = (1+\alpha)((1.5+k_1)e_1 + (1.25 \quad -0.25)e_2).$$

As can be seen, in this subsystem the choice of gain k_1 does not depend on undefined parameters. Let us assume $\nu = \eta_d = 1$; then, similarly to (21), we have

$$-(1.5+k_1) - (1.25 + 0.25) \geq 1 \Rightarrow k_1 \leq -4.$$

For the convenience of the calculation (67), let us assume $k_1 = -13/2 = -6.5$, then $F_1 = (-5 \quad 1)^T$. Let us perform transformations (15) taking into account (61), (65)–(67), forming the control law in the form (55), that is,

$$u = K_2 e_2 = k_2 B_2^{-1} S_2 e_2 = k_2 \begin{pmatrix} 0.5 & -0,5 \\ 0 & 1 \end{pmatrix} e_2, \tag{68}$$

and we obtain a closed RF of the uncertain system in terms of discrepancies in the form (56), namely,

$$\dot{e}_1 = (1+\alpha)(-5e_1 + (1.25 \quad -0.25)e_2,$$
$$\dot{e}_2 = (1+\alpha)\begin{pmatrix} -30 \\ 3 \end{pmatrix} e_1 + \left((1+\alpha)\begin{pmatrix} 7.25 & -1.25 \\ -0.75 & 0.75 \end{pmatrix} + k_2(1+\beta)\begin{pmatrix} 1 & 0 \\ 0 & 1 \end{pmatrix}\right) e_2.$$

From the second inequality (58), we find the second gain

$$\bar{k}_{21} \leq -(1+(1+\widehat{\alpha})(30+7.25+1.25))/(1-\widehat{\beta}) \approx -48.2,$$
$$\bar{k}_{22} \leq -(1+(1+\widehat{\alpha})(3+0.75+0.75))/(1-\widehat{\beta}) \approx -6.62, k_2 \leq \min\{-48.2; \; -6.62\}.$$

Let us take $k_2 = -50$. Then due to (68), (19), we get

$$u = Ke, \quad K = (O \quad K_2) = \begin{pmatrix} 0 & -25 & 25 \\ 0 & 0 & -50 \end{pmatrix},$$

$$F = KT_e T = \begin{pmatrix} 0 & -25 & 25 \\ 0 & 0 & -50 \end{pmatrix}\begin{pmatrix} 1 & 0 & 0 \\ 5 & 1 & 0 \\ -1 & 0 & 1 \end{pmatrix}\begin{pmatrix} 1 & -0.5 & 0.5 \\ 0 & 1 & 0 \\ 0 & 0 & 1 \end{pmatrix}.$$

Control law

$$u = Fx = \begin{pmatrix} -150 & 50 & -50 \\ 50 & -25 & -25 \end{pmatrix} x \tag{69}$$

provides in the initial uncertain system a guaranteed margin of stability $\eta \geq \nu = \eta_d = 1$ in all uncertainty intervals, and this solves the problem. For example, in the nominal system (59) and in the uncertain system with different boundary values of parameters $\alpha = \pm 0.1$, $\beta = \pm 0,1$ we obtain

$$\sigma(A+BF) = \{-6.0531; \; -41.5559; \; -49.3910\}, \eta = 6.0531;$$
$$\sigma(1.1A+0.9BF) = \{-7.0628; \; -35.3071; \; -44.33\}, \eta = 7.0628;$$
$$\sigma(1.1A+1.1BF) = \{-6.6585; \; -45.7114; \; -54.3301\}, \eta = 6.6585;$$
$$\sigma(0.9A+1.1BF) = \{-5.2231; \; -47.625; \; -54.4519\}, \eta = 5.2231;$$
$$\sigma(0.9A+0.9BF) = \{-5.4478; \; -37.4003; \; -44.4519\}, \eta = 5.4478.$$

Figure 3 shows the behavior of the state variables $x(t) = (x_1(t), x_2(t), x_3(t))^T$ and controls $u(t) = (u_1(t), u_2(t))^T$ in the closed-loop system $\dot{x} = (1.1A+0.9BF)x$, (59), (69) with $x(0) = (0.5, 0.5, 0.5)^T$.

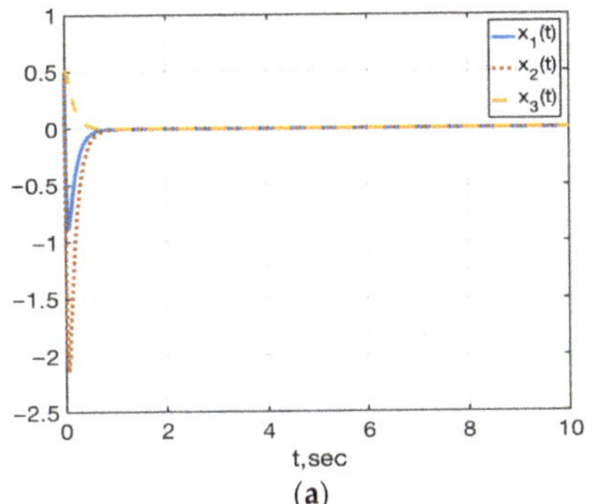 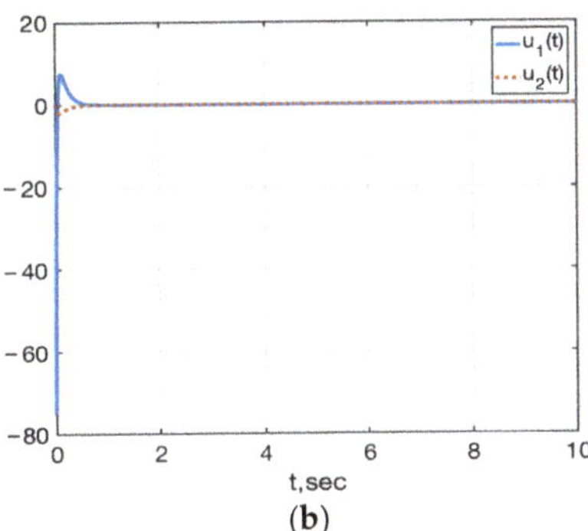

(a) (b)

Figure 3. (a) Plots of $x_1(t)$, $x_2(t)$, $x_3(t)$; (b) Plots of $u_1(t)$, $u_2(t)$ in the closed-loop system $\dot{x} = (1.1A + 0.9BF)x$, (59), (69) with $x(0) = (0.5,\ 0.5,\ 0.5\,)^{\mathrm{T}}$.

In comparison with system (59), (63) (see Figure 2), the solution norm of the closed-loop system is practically the same, but the regulation time has been reduced by about 6 times. In addition, the value of $\|u(0)\|$ has increased by about 10 times.

It should be noted that the control spikes at the beginning of the transient can be limited by piecewise linear control with saturation

$$\overline{u} = (10\mathrm{sat}(u_1),\ 10\mathrm{sat}(u_2))^{\mathrm{T}}. \tag{70}$$

Corresponding graphs for the closed-loop system $\dot{x} = (1.1A + 0.9BF)x$, (59), (69), (70) are shown in Figure 4. As can be seen from Figures 3a and 4a, the control constraint (70) had no effect on the state variable transients.

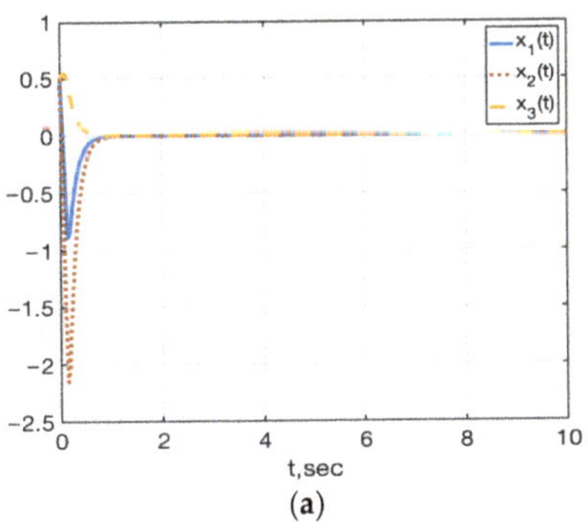 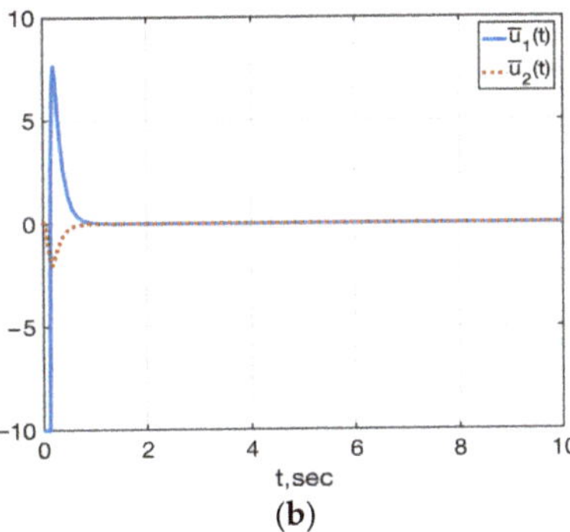

(a) (b)

Figure 4. (a) Plots of $x_1(t)$, $x_2(t)$, $x_3(t)$; (b) Plots of $\overline{u}_1(t)$, $\overline{u}_2(t)$ in the closed-loop system $\dot{x} = (1.1A + 0.9BF)x$, (59), (69), (70).

Figure 5 shows the behavior of the variables $x(t) = (x_1(t),\ x_2(t),\ x_3(t))^{\mathrm{T}}$ and control vector $u(t) = (\overline{u}_1(t),\ \overline{u}_2(t))^{\mathrm{T}}$ in a closed-loop system $\dot{x} = ((1+\alpha)A + (1+\beta)BF)x$, (59), (69), (70), $x(0) = (0.5,\ 0.5,\ 0.5\,)^{T}$, where the unknown parameters smoothly vary within the specified ranges (64): $\alpha = 0.1\sin 4t$, $\beta = 0.1\sin 2t$. As we can see, at variable parameters the nature of the transients is practically unchanged, a fact that opens perspectives for using the developed approach in relation to parametrically uncertain non-stationary control systems.

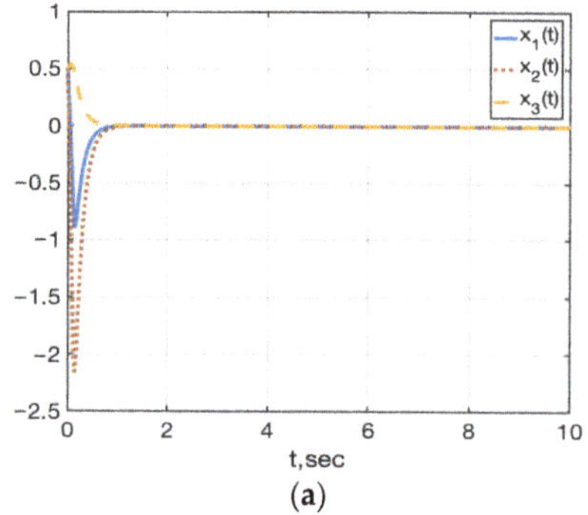
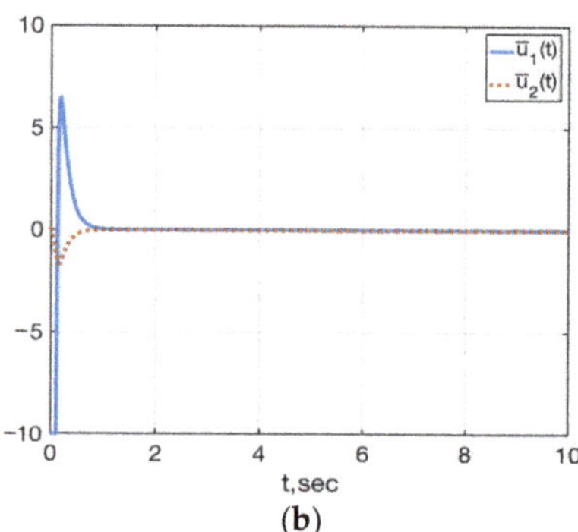

Figure 5. (**a**) Plots of $x_1(t)$, $x_2(t)$, $x_3(t)$; (**b**) Plots of $\overline{u}_1(t)$, $\overline{u}_2(t)$ in the closed-loop system $\dot{x} = ((1+\alpha)A + (1+\beta)BF)x$, (59), (69), (70), $x(0) = (0.5, 0.5, 0.5)^T$.

5. Discussion

In this paper, we propose a new approach to the synthesis of robust control for a practically significant class of linear stationary parametrically uncertain systems, in which the structural controllability properties of the nominal system do not change with parameter variation within acceptable limits. For the special case of systems with a controllability indicator equal to two, the procedures for the synthesis of a stabilizing feedback are formalized in detail, using the concepts of regular form and super-stability. The possibility of extending this approach to a general form of controllable systems is shown theoretically.

It should be noted that the tuning of the feedback coefficients, which guarantee a given margin of stability in the closed-loop system in all uncertainty intervals, is done on the basis of inequalities in terms of matrix elements rather than their eigenvalues. On the one hand, this is what allows synthesizing of a robust system. However, on the other hand, these conditions are only sufficient, and the resulting estimates are conservative. As a result, there may be spikes in the start of transients of state variables and controls that are not acceptable in practical applications.

Numerical examples show the fundamental possibility of limiting the control actions, as well as the performance of the proposed method for non-stationary systems. However, further research is needed to formalize these problems rigorously.

Author Contributions: Conceptualization, methodology, S.A.K. and V.A.U.; validation, investigation, formal analysis, Y.G.K., A.V.U., and S.A.K.; writing—original draft preparation, S.A.K. and V.A.U.; writing—review and editing, Y.G.K. and A.V.U. All authors have read and agreed to the published version of the manuscript.

Funding: This research received no external funding.

Institutional Review Board Statement: Not applicable.

Informed Consent Statement: Not applicable.

Data Availability Statement: Not applicable.

Conflicts of Interest: The authors declare no conflict of interest.

References

1. Utkin, V.A.; Utkin, A.V. Problem of Tracking in Linear Systems with Parametric Uncertainties under Unstable Zero Dynamics. *Autom. Remote Control* **2014**, *75*, 1577–1592. [CrossRef]
2. Ljung, L. Pespectives on system identification. *IFAC Annu. Rev.* **2010**, *34*, 1–12. [CrossRef]
3. Krstic, M.; Kanellakopoulos, I.; Kokotovic, P. *Nonlinear and Adaptive Control Design*; Wiley: New York, NY, USA, 1995.
4. Ackermann, J. *Robust Control: The Parameter Space Approach*; Springer: London, UK, 2002.
5. Kharitonov, V.L. Asymptotic Stability of a Family of Systems of Linear Differential Equations. *Differ. Uravn.* **1978**, *1*, 2086–2088.
6. Lao, X.X. Necessary and sufficient conditions for stability of a class of interval matrices. *Int. J. Control* **1987**, *45*, 211–214.

7. Polyak, B.T.; Tsypkin, Y.Z. Frequency Criteria of Robust Stability and Aperiodicity of Linear Systems. *Autom. Remote Control* **1990**, 9, 1192–1200.
8. Neimark, Y.I. Robust stability and *D*-partitioning. *Autom. Remote Control* **1992**, 53, 957–965.
9. Gadewadikar, J.; Lewis, F.L.; Abu-Khalaf, M. Necessary and Sufficient Conditions for H-infinity Static Output-Feedback Control. *J. Guid. Control Dyn.* **2006**, 29, 4. [CrossRef]
10. Edwards, C.; Shtessel, Y.B. Adaptive Continuous Higher Order Sliding Mode Control. *Automatica* **2016**, 65, 183–190. [CrossRef]
11. Antipov, A.S.; Krasnova, S.A.; Utkin, V.A. Methods of Ensuring Invariance with Respect to External Disturbances: Overview and New Advances. *Mathematics* **2021**, 9, 3140. [CrossRef]
12. Polyak, B.T.; Sznaider, M.; Shcherbakov, P.S.; Halpern, M. Super-stable control systems. In Proceedings of the 15th IFAC, Barcelona, Spain, 21–26 July 2002; pp. 799–805.
13. Utkin, V.I.; Yang, K.D. Methods for construction of discontinuity planes in multidimensional variable structure systems. *Autom. Remote Control* **1979**, 39, 1466–1470.
14. Drakunov, S.V.; Izosimov, D.B.; Luk'yanov, A.G.; Utkin, V.A.; Utkin, V.I. The Block Control Principle. *Autom. Remote Control* **1990**, 5, 601–608.
15. Krasnova, S.A.; Utkin, V.A.; Utkin, A.V. Block approach to analysis and design of the invariant nonlinear tracking systems. *Autom. Remote Control* **2017**, 78, 2120–2140. [CrossRef]
16. Krasnova, S.A.; Utkin, V.A.; Sirotina, T.G. A structural approach to robust control. *Autom. Remote Control* **2011**, 72, 1639–1666. [CrossRef]
17. Gantmacher, F.R. *Theory of Matrices*; Chelsea Publishing Company, Inc.: New York, NY, USA, 1959.
18. Mu, J.; Yan, X.-G.; Spurgeon, S.K.; Mao, Z. Generalized regular form based smc for nonlinear systems with application to a wmr. *IEEE Trans. Ind. Electron.* **2017**, 64, 6714–6723. [CrossRef]
19. Wonham, W.F. *Linear Multivariate Control: A Geometric Approach*; Springer: New York, NY, USA, 1985.

 *mathematics*

Article

Identification of Linear Time-Invariant Systems with Dynamic Mode Decomposition

Jan Heiland [1,†,‡] and Benjamin Unger [2,*,‡]

1 Max Planck Institute for Dynamics of Complex Technical Systems, 39106 Magdeburg, Germany; heiland@mpi-magdeburg.mpg.de
2 Stuttgart Center for Simulation Science, University of Stuttgart, 70563 Stuttgart, Germany
* Correspondence: benjamin.unger@simtech.uni-stuttgart.de
† Current address: Faculty of Mathematics, Otto von Guericke University Magdeburg, 39106 Magdeburg, Germany
‡ These authors contributed equally to this work.

Abstract: Dynamic mode decomposition (DMD) is a popular data-driven framework to extract linear dynamics from complex high-dimensional systems. In this work, we study the system identification properties of DMD. We first show that DMD is invariant under linear transformations in the image of the data matrix. If, in addition, the data are constructed from a linear time-invariant system, then we prove that DMD can recover the original dynamics under mild conditions. If the linear dynamics are discretized with the Runge–Kutta method, then we further classify the error of the DMD approximation and detail that for one-stage Runge–Kutta methods; even the continuous dynamics can be recovered with DMD. A numerical example illustrates the theoretical findings.

Keywords: dynamic mode decomposition; system identification; Runge–Kutta method

Citation: Heiland, J.; Unger, B. Identification of Linear Time-Invariant Systems with Dynamic Mode Decomposition. *Mathematics* **2022**, *10*, 418. https://doi.org/10.3390/math10030418

Academic Editor: Ioannis G. Stratis

Received: 14 September 2021
Accepted: 24 December 2021
Published: 28 January 2022

Publisher's Note: MDPI stays neutral with regard to jurisdictional claims in published maps and institutional affiliations.

1. Introduction

Dynamical systems play a fundamental role in many modern modeling approaches of physical and chemical phenomena. The need for high fidelity models often results in large-scale dynamical systems, which are computationally demanding to solve, analyze, and optimize. Thus the last three decades have seen significant efforts to replace the so-called full-order model, which is considered the *truth model*, with a computationally cheaper surrogate model. In the context of model order reduction, we refer the interested reader to the monographs [1–5]. Often, the surrogate model is constructed by projecting the dynamical system onto a low-dimensional manifold, thus requiring a state-space description of the differential equation.

If a mathematical model is not available or not suited for modification, data-driven methods, such as the *Loewner framework* [6,7], *vector fitting* [8–10], *operator inference* [11], or *dynamic mode decomposition* (DMD) [12] may be used to create a low-dimensional realization directly from the measurement or simulation data of the system. Suppose the dynamical system that creates the data is linear. In that case, the Loewner framework and vector fitting are—under some technical assumptions—able to recover the original dynamical system and hence serve as system identification tools. Despite the popularity of DMD, a similar analysis seems to be missing, and this paper aims to close this gap.

Since DMD creates a discrete, linear time-invariant dynamical system from data, we are interested in answering the following questions:

1. What is the impact of transformations of the data on the resulting DMD approximation?
2. Assume that the data used to generate the DMD approximation are obtained from a linear differential equation. Can we estimate the error between the continuous dynamics and the DMD approximation?
3. Are there situations in which we are even able to recover the original dynamical system from its DMD approximation?

It is essential to know how the data for the construction of the DMD model are generated to answer these questions. Assuming exact measurements of the solution may be valid from a theoretical perspective only. Instead, we take the view of a numerical analyst and assume that the data are obtained via time integration of the dynamics with a general *Runge–Kutta method* (RKM) with known order of convergence. We emphasize that for linear time-invariant systems, a RKM may not be the method of choice; see, for instance, [13]. Nevertheless, RKMs are a common numerical technique to solve general differential equations, which is our main reason to consider RKMs in the following.

We can summarize the questions graphically as in Figure 1. Thus, the dashed lines represent the questions that we aim to answer in this paper.

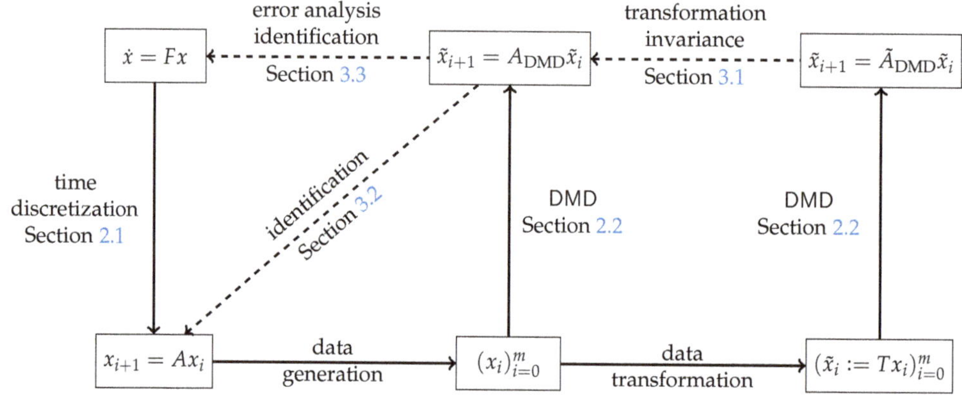

Figure 1. Problem setup.

Our main results are the following:

- We show in Theorem 1 that DMD is invariant in the image of the data under linear transformations of the data.
- Theorem 2 details that DMD is able to identify discrete-time dynamics, i.e., for every initial value in the image of the data, the DMD approximation exactly recovers the discrete-time dynamics.
- In Theorem 3, we show that if the DMD approximation is constructed from data that are obtained via a RKM, then the approximation error of DMD with respect to the ordinary differential equation is in the order of the error of the RKM. If a one-stage RKM is used and the data are sufficiently rich, then the continuous-time dynamics, i.e., the matrix F in Figure 1, can be recovered cf. Lemma 1.

To render the manuscript self-contained, we recall important definitions and results for RKM and DMD in the upcoming Sections 2.1 and 2.2, respectively, before we present our analysis in Section 3. We conclude with a numerical example to confirm the theoretical findings.

Notation

As is standard, $\mathbb{N}$, $\mathbb{R}$, and $\mathbb{R}[t]$ denote the positive integers, the real numbers, and the polynomials with real coefficients, respectively. For any $n, m \in \mathbb{N}$, we denote with $\mathbb{R}^{n \times m}$ the set of $n \times m$ matrices with real entries. The set of nonsingular matrices of size $n \times n$ is denoted with $\mathrm{GL}_n(\mathbb{R})$. Let $A = [a_{ij}] \in \mathbb{R}^{n \times m}$, $B \in \mathbb{R}^{p \times q}$, and $x_i \in \mathbb{R}^n$ ($i = 1, \ldots, k$). The transpose and the Moore–Penrose pseudoinverse of A are denoted with A^T and $A^\dagger$, respectively. The Kronecker product $\otimes$ is defined as

$$A \otimes B := \begin{bmatrix} a_{11}B & \cdots & a_{1m}B \\ \vdots & & \vdots \\ a_{n1}B & \cdots & a_{nm}B \end{bmatrix} \in \mathbb{R}^{np \times mq}.$$

We use $\mathrm{span}\{x_1,\ldots,x_k\}$ to denote the linear span of the vectors $x_1,\ldots,x_k$ and also casually write $\mathrm{span}\{X\} = \mathrm{span}\{x_1,\ldots,x_k\}$ for the column space of the matrix X with $\{x_1,\ldots,x_k\}$ as its columns. For $A \in \mathbb{R}^{n\times n}$ and a vector $x_0 \in \mathbb{R}^n$, we denote the reachable space as $\mathcal{C}(x_0, A) = \mathrm{span}\{x_0, Ax_0,\ldots,A^{n-1}x_0\}$. The Stiefel manifold of $n \times r$ dimensional matrices with real entries is denoted by

$$\mathrm{St}(n,r) := \left\{ U \in \mathbb{R}^{n\times r} \mid U^T U = I_r \right\}, \tag{1}$$

where I_r denotes the $r \times r$ identity matrix. For a continuously differentiable function $x\colon \mathbb{I} \to \mathbb{R}^n$ from the interval $\mathbb{I} \subseteq \mathbb{R}$ to the vector space $\mathbb{R}^n$, we use the notation $\dot{x} := \frac{\mathrm{d}}{\mathrm{d}t}x$ to denote the derivative with respect to the independent variable t, which we refer to as the time.

2. Preliminaries

As outlined in the introduction, DMD creates a finite-dimensional linear model to approximate the original dynamics. Thus, in view of possibly exact system identification, we need to assume that the data that are fed to the DMD algorithm are obtained from a linear ODE, which in the sequel is denoted by

$$\dot{x}(t) = Fx(t) \tag{2a}$$

with given matrix $F \in \mathbb{R}^{n\times n}$. To fix a solution of (2a), we prescribe the initial condition

$$x(0) = x_0 \in \mathbb{R}^n, \tag{2b}$$

and denote the solution of the *initial value problem* (IVP) as $x(t; x_0) := \exp(Ft)x_0$. For the analysis of DMD, we assume that the matrix F is not available. Instead, the question is to what extent DMD is able to recover the matrix F solely from measurements of the state variable x.

Remark 1. *While a DMD approximation, despite its linearity, may well reproduce trajectories of nonlinear systems (see, for example, [14]), the question of DMD being able to recover the full dynamics has to focus on linear systems. Here, the key observation is that a DMD approximation is a finite-dimensional linear map. In contrast, the encoding of nonlinear systems via a linear operator necessarily needs an infinite-dimensional mapping.*

2.1. Runge–Kutta Methods

To solve the IVP (2) numerically, we employ a RKM, which is a common one-step method to approximate ordinary and differential-algebraic equations [15,16]. More precisely, given a step size $h > 0$, the solution of the IVP (2) is approximated via the sequence $x_i \approx x(t_0 + ih)$ given by

$$x_{i+1} = x_i + h \sum_{j=1}^{s} \beta_j k_j, \tag{3a}$$

with the so-called *internal stages* $k_j \in \mathbb{R}^n$ (implicitly) defined via

$$k_j = Fx_i + h \sum_{\ell=1}^{s} \alpha_{j,\ell} Fk_\ell \qquad \text{for } j = 1,\ldots,s, \tag{3b}$$

where $s \in \mathbb{N}$ denotes the number of stages in the RKM. Using the matrix notation $\mathcal{A} = [\alpha_{j,\ell}] \in \mathbb{R}^{s\times s}$ and $\beta = [\beta_j] \in \mathbb{R}^s$, the s-stage RKM defined via (3) is conveniently summarized with the pair $(\mathcal{A}, \beta)$. Note that we restrict our presentation to linear time-invariant dynamics, and hence, do not require the full Butcher tableau.

Since the ODE (2a) is linear, we can rewrite the internal stages as

$$\begin{bmatrix} I_n - h\alpha_{1,1}F & -h\alpha_{1,2}F & \cdots & -h\alpha_{1,s}F \\ -h\alpha_{2,1}F & I_n - h\alpha_{2,2}F & \cdots & -h\alpha_{2,s}F \\ \vdots & \ddots & \ddots & \vdots \\ -h\alpha_{s,1}F & \cdots & -h\alpha_{s,s-1}F & I_n - h\alpha_{s,s}F \end{bmatrix} \begin{bmatrix} k_1 \\ k_2 \\ \vdots \\ k_s \end{bmatrix} = \begin{bmatrix} Fx_i \\ Fx_i \\ \vdots \\ Fx_i \end{bmatrix} \tag{4}$$

Setting $k := \begin{bmatrix} k_1^T & \cdots & k_s^T \end{bmatrix}^T \in \mathbb{R}^{sn}$ and $e := \begin{bmatrix} 1 & \ldots 1 \end{bmatrix}^T \in \mathbb{R}^s$, the linear system in (4) can be written as

$$(I_s \otimes I_n - h\mathcal{A} \otimes F)k = (e \otimes F)x_i, \tag{5}$$

where $\otimes$ denotes the Kronecker product. If h is small enough, the matrix $(I_s \otimes I_n - h\mathcal{A} \otimes F)$ is invertible, and thus, we obtain the discrete linear system

$$x_{i+1} = x_i + h\sum_{j=1}^{s} \beta_j k_j = x_i + h(\beta^T \otimes I_n)k$$

$$= x_i + h(\beta^T \otimes I_n)(I_s \otimes I_n - h\mathcal{A} \otimes F)^{-1}(e \otimes F)x_i = A_h x_i,$$

with (using the identity $I_s \otimes I_n = I_{sn}$)

$$A_h := I_n + h(\beta^T \otimes I_n)(I_{sn} - h\mathcal{A} \otimes F)^{-1}(e \otimes F). \tag{6}$$

Example 1. *The explicit (or forward) Euler method is given as $(\mathcal{A}, \beta) = (0, 1)$ and according to (6) we obtain the well-known formula $A_h = I_n + hF$. For the implicit (or backward) Euler method $(\mathcal{A}, \beta) = (1, 1)$ the discrete system matrix is given by*

$$A_h = I_n + h(I_n - hF)^{-1}F = (I_n - hF)^{-1}(I_n - hF + hF) = (I_n - hF)^{-1}.$$

To guarantee that the representation (6) is valid, we make the following assumption throughout the manuscript.

Assumption 1. *For any s-stage RKM $(\mathcal{A}, \beta)$ and any dynamical system matrix $F \in \mathbb{R}^{n \times n}$, we assume that the step size h is chosen such that the matrix $I_{sn} - h\mathcal{A} \otimes F$ is nonsingular.*

Remark 2. *Using Assumption 1, the matrix $I_{sn} - h\mathcal{A} \otimes F$ is nonsingular, and thus, there exists a polynomial $p = \sum_{k=0}^{sn-1} p_k t^k \in \mathbb{R}[t]$ of degree at most $sn - 1$ depending on the step size h such that*

$$(I_{sn} - h\mathcal{A} \otimes F)^{-1} = p(I_{sn} - h\mathcal{A} \otimes F) = \sum_{k=0}^{sn-1} p_k (I_{sn} - h\mathcal{A} \otimes F)^k$$

$$= \sum_{k=0}^{sn-1} p_k \sum_{\rho=0}^{k} \binom{k}{\rho}(-1)^\rho h^\rho (\mathcal{A}^\rho \otimes F^\rho),$$

where the last equality follows from the binomial theorem. Consequently, we have

$$A_h = I_n + \sum_{k=0}^{sn-1} p_k \sum_{\rho=0}^{k} \binom{k}{\rho}(-1)^\rho h^{\rho+1}\left(\beta^T \mathcal{A}^\rho e\right)F^{\rho+1}. \tag{7}$$

Rearranging the terms together with the Cayley–Hamilton theorem implies the existence of a polynomial $\tilde{p} \in \mathbb{R}[t]$ of degree at most n such that $A_h = \tilde{p}(F)$. As a direct consequence, we see that any eigenvector of F is an eigenvector of A_h and thus, A_h is diagonalizable if F is diagonalizable.

Having computed the matrix A_h, the question that remains to be answered is the quality of the approximation $\|x(ih; x_0) - x_i\|$, which yields the following well-known definition (cf. [15]).

Definition 1. *A RKM* $(\mathcal{A}, \beta)$ *has order* p *if there exists a constant* $C \geq 0$ *(independent of h) such that*

$$\|x(h; x_0) - x_1\| \leq Ch^{p+1} \tag{8}$$

holds, where $x_1 = A_h x_0$ *with* A_h *defined as in* (6).

For one-step methods, it is well known that the local errors—as estimated in (8) for the initial time step—basically sum in the global error such that the following estimate holds:

$$\|x(Nh; x_0) - x_N\| \leq Ch^p;$$

see, e.g., ([15], Thm. II.3.6).

2.2. Dynamic Mode Decomposition

For $i = 0, \ldots, m$, assume data points $x_i \in \mathbb{R}^n$ are available. If not explicitly stated, we do not make any assumption on m. The idea of DMD is to determine a linear time-invariant relation between the data, i.e., finding a matrix $A_{\mathrm{DMD}} \in \mathbb{R}^{n \times n}$ such that the data approximately satisfy

$$x_{i+1} \approx A_{\mathrm{DMD}} x_i \qquad \text{for } i = 0, 1, \ldots, m-1.$$

Following [17], we introduce

$$X := \begin{bmatrix} x_0 & \cdots & x_{m-1} \end{bmatrix} \in \mathbb{R}^{n \times m} \qquad \text{and} \qquad Z := \begin{bmatrix} x_1 & \cdots & x_m \end{bmatrix} \in \mathbb{R}^{n \times m}. \tag{9}$$

Then, the DMD approximation matrix is defined as the minimum-norm solution of

$$\min_{M \in \mathbb{R}^{n \times n}} \|Z - MX\|_F, \tag{10}$$

where $\|\cdot\|_F$ denotes the Frobenius norm. It is easy to show that the minimum-norm solution is given by $A_{\mathrm{DMD}} = ZX^\dagger$ [12], where $X^\dagger$ denotes the Moore–Penrose pseudoinverse of X. This motivates the following definition.

Definition 2. *Consider the data* $x_i \in \mathbb{R}^n$ *for* $i = 0, 1, \ldots, m$ *and associated data matrices X and Z defined in* (9). *Then the matrix* $A_{\mathrm{DMD}} := ZX^\dagger$ *is called the* DMD matrix *for* $(x_i)_{i=0}^m$. *If the eigendecomposition of* A_{DMD} *exists, then the eigenvalues and eigenvectors of* A_{DMD} *are called* DMD eigenvalues *and* DMD modes *of* $(x_i)_{i=0}^m$, *respectively.*

The Moore–Penrose pseudoinverse and, thus, also the DMD matrix can be computed via the *singular value decomposition* (SVD); see, for example, ([18], Ch. 5.5.4). Let

$$\begin{bmatrix} U & \bar{U} \end{bmatrix} \begin{bmatrix} \Sigma & 0 \\ 0 & 0 \end{bmatrix} \begin{bmatrix} V^\top \\ \bar{V}^\top \end{bmatrix} = X$$

denote the SVD of X, with $r := \mathrm{rank}(X)$, $U \in \mathrm{St}(n, r)$, $\Sigma \in \mathbb{R}^{r \times r}$ and $\mathrm{rank}(\Sigma) = r$, and $V \in \mathrm{St}(m, r)$, where we use the Stiefel manifold as defined in (1). Then

$$X^\dagger = \begin{bmatrix} V & \bar{V} \end{bmatrix} \begin{bmatrix} \Sigma^{-1} & 0 \\ 0 & 0 \end{bmatrix} \begin{bmatrix} U^\top \\ \bar{U}^\top \end{bmatrix} = V\Sigma^{-1}U^\top \tag{11}$$

and, thus,

$$A_{\mathrm{DMD}} = ZV\Sigma^{-1}U^T. \tag{12}$$

For later reference, we call $U\Sigma V^\top = X$ the *trimmed SVD* of X.

3. System Identification and Error Analysis

In this section, we present our main results. Before discussing system identification for discrete-time (cf. Section 3.2) and continuous-time (cf. Section 3.3) dynamical systems via DMD, we study the impact of transformations of the data on DMD in Section 3.1.

3.1. Data Scaling and Invariance of the DMD Approximation

Scaling and more general transformations of data are often used to improve the performance of the methods that work on the data. Since DMD is inherently related to the Moore–Penrose inverse, we first study the impact of a nonsingular matrix $T \in \mathrm{GL}_n(\mathbb{R})$ on the generalized inverse. To this purpose, consider a matrix $X \in \mathbb{R}^{n \times m}$ with $r := \mathrm{rank}(X)$. Let $X = U\Sigma V^\top$ denote the trimmed SVD of X with $U \in \mathrm{St}(n, r)$, $\Sigma \in \mathrm{GL}_r(\mathbb{R})$ and $V \in \mathrm{St}(m, r)$. Let $TU = QR$ denote the QR-decomposition of TU with $Q \in \mathbb{R}^{n \times n}$ and $R \in \mathbb{R}^{n \times r}$. We immediately obtain $\mathrm{rank}(RS) = r$. Let $R\Sigma = \widehat{U}\widehat{\Sigma}\widehat{V}^\top$ denote the trimmed SVD of $R\Sigma$ with $\widehat{U} \in \mathrm{St}(n, r)$, $\widehat{\Sigma} \in \mathrm{GL}_r(\mathbb{R})$, and $\widehat{V} \in \mathrm{St}(r, r)$. We immediately infer

$$\widehat{V}\widehat{V}^\top = I_r. \tag{13}$$

It is easy to see that the matrices $U_T := Q\widehat{U} \in \mathbb{R}^{n \times r}$, and $V_T := V\widehat{V} \in \mathbb{R}^{m \times r}$ satisfy $U_T^\top U_T = I_r = V_T^\top V_T$, i.e., $U_T \in \mathrm{St}(n, r)$ and $V_T \in \mathrm{St}(m, r)$. The trimmed SVD of TX is thus given by

$$TX = TU\Sigma V^\top = QR\Sigma V^\top = Q\widehat{U}\widehat{\Sigma}\widehat{V}^\top V^\top = U_T\widehat{\Sigma}V_T^\top.$$

We conclude

$$(TX)^\dagger TX = V_T V_T^\top = V\widehat{V}\widehat{V}^\top V^\top = VV^\top = X^\dagger X,$$

where we used the identity (13). We have thus shown the following result.

Proposition 1. *Let $X \in \mathbb{R}^{n \times m}$ and $T \in \mathrm{GL}_n(\mathbb{R})$. Then $(TX)^\dagger(TX) = X^\dagger X$.*

With these preparations, we can now show that the DMD approximation is partially invariant to general regular transformations applied to the training data. More precisely, a data transformation only affects the part of the DMD approximation that is not in the image of the data.

Theorem 1. *For given data $(x_i)_{i=0}^m$ consider the matrices X and Z as defined in (9) and the corresponding DMD matrix $A_{\mathrm{DMD}} \in \mathbb{R}^{n \times n}$. Consider $T \in \mathrm{GL}_n(\mathbb{R})$ and let*

$$\tilde{X} := TX \quad \text{and} \quad \tilde{Z} := TZ$$

be the matrices of the transformed data. Let $\tilde{A}_{\mathrm{DMD}} := \tilde{Z}\tilde{X}^\dagger$ denote the DMD matrix for the transformed data. Then the DMD matrix is invariant under the transformation in the image of X, i.e.,

$$A_{\mathrm{DMD}}X = T^{-1}\tilde{A}_{\mathrm{DMD}}TX = T^{-1}\tilde{A}_{\mathrm{DMD}}\tilde{X}.$$

Moreover, if T is unitary or $\mathrm{rank}(X) = n$, then

$$A_{\mathrm{DMD}} = T^{-1}\tilde{A}_{\mathrm{DMD}}T. \tag{14}$$

Proof. Using Proposition 1, we obtain

$$T^{-1}\tilde{A}_{\mathrm{DMD}}TX = T^{-1}TZ(TX)^\dagger TX = ZX^\dagger X = A_{\mathrm{DMD}}X.$$

If T is unitary or $\mathrm{rank}(X) = n$, then we immediately obtain $(TX)^\dagger = X^\dagger T^{-1}$, and thus

$$T^{-1}\tilde{A}_{\mathrm{DMD}}T = T^{-1}TZ(TX)^\dagger T = ZX^\dagger T^{-1}T = A_{\mathrm{DMD}},$$

which concludes the proof. $\square$

While Theorem 1 states that DMD is invariant under transformations in the image of the data matrix, the invariance in the orthogonal complement of the image of the data matrix, i.e., equality (14), is, in general, not satisfied. We illustrate this observation in the numerical simulations in Section 4 and in the following analytical example.

Example 2. *Consider the data vectors* $x_i := [i+1, 0]^\top$ *for* $i = 0, 1, 2$ *and* $T := \left[\begin{smallmatrix} 1 & 0 \\ 1 & 1 \end{smallmatrix}\right]$. *Then,*

$$X = \begin{bmatrix} 1 & 2 \\ 0 & 0 \end{bmatrix}, \quad Z = \begin{bmatrix} 2 & 3 \\ 0 & 0 \end{bmatrix}, \quad X^\dagger = \tfrac{1}{5}\begin{bmatrix} 1 & 0 \\ 2 & 0 \end{bmatrix}, \quad TX = \begin{bmatrix} 1 & 2 \\ 1 & 2 \end{bmatrix}, \quad (TX)^\dagger = \tfrac{1}{10}\begin{bmatrix} 1 & 1 \\ 2 & 2 \end{bmatrix}.$$

We thus obtain

$$A_{\mathrm{DMD}} = \tfrac{1}{5}\begin{bmatrix} 8 & 0 \\ 0 & 0 \end{bmatrix}, \quad \tilde{A}_{\mathrm{DMD}} = \tfrac{1}{5}\begin{bmatrix} 4 & 4 \\ 4 & 4 \end{bmatrix}, \quad \text{and} \quad T^{-1}\tilde{A}_{\mathrm{DMD}}T = \tfrac{1}{5}\begin{bmatrix} 8 & 4 \\ 0 & 0 \end{bmatrix},$$

confirming that DMD is invariant under transformations in the image of the data, but not in the orthogonal complement.

Remark 3. *One can show that in the setting of Theorem 1, the matrix* $\widehat{M} := TA_{\mathrm{DMD}}T^{-1}$ *is a minimizer (not necessarily the minimum-norm solution) of*

$$\min_{M \in \mathbb{R}^{n \times n}} \left\| \widehat{Z} - M\widehat{X} \right\|_{\mathrm{F}}.$$

3.2. Discrete-Time Dynamics

In this subsection, we focus on the identification of discrete-time dynamics, which are exemplified by the discrete-time system

$$x_{i+1} = Ax_i \tag{15}$$

with initial value $x_0 \in \mathbb{R}^n$ and system matrix $A \in \mathbb{R}^{n \times n}$. The question that we want to answer is to what extent DMD is able to recover the matrix A solely from data.

Proposition 2. *Consider data* $(x_i)_{i=0}^m$ *generated by (15), associated data matrices* X, Z *as defined in (9), and the corresponding DMD matrix* A_{DMD}. *Moreover let* $U\Sigma V^\top = X$ *with* $U \in \mathrm{St}(n,r)$, $\Sigma \in \mathrm{GL}_r(\mathbb{R})$, $V \in \mathrm{St}(m,r)$, *and* $r := \mathrm{rank}(X)$ *denote the trimmed SVD of* X. *Then*

$$A_{\mathrm{DMD}} = AUU^\top. \tag{16}$$

Proof. By assumption, we have $X = \begin{bmatrix} x_0 & Ax_0 & \cdots & A^{m-1}x_0 \end{bmatrix}$ and $Z = AX = AU\Sigma V^\top$. We conclude

$$A_{\mathrm{DMD}} = ZX^\dagger = AU\Sigma V^\top V\Sigma^{-1}U^\top = AUU^\top. \quad \square$$

Remark 4. *We immediately conclude that DMD recovers the true dynamics, i.e.,* $A_{\mathrm{DMD}} = A$, *whenever* $\mathrm{rank}(X) = n$. *This is the case if and only if* (A, x_0) *is controllable, i.e.,* $C(A, x_0)$ *has dimension* n, *and the data set is sufficiently rich, i.e.,* $m \geq n$.

Our next theorem identifies the part of the dynamics that is exactly recovered in the case that $\mathrm{rank}(X) < n$ that occurs for (A, x_0) is not controllable or $m < n$.

Theorem 2. *Consider the setting of Proposition 2. If* $\mathrm{span}\{U\}$ *is* A_{DMD} *invariant, then the DMD approximation is exact in the image of* U, *i.e.,*

$$(A^i - A^i_{\mathrm{DMD}})x_0 = 0 \qquad \text{for all } i \geq 0 \text{ and } x_0 \in \mathrm{span}\{U\}. \tag{17}$$

If, in addition, $\ker(A) \cap \mathrm{span}\{U\}^\perp = \{0\}$, then also the converse direction holds.

Proof. Let $x_0 \in \mathrm{span}\{U\}$. Since $\mathrm{span}\{U\}$ is A_{DMD} invariant, we conclude $A^i_{\mathrm{DMD}}x_0 \in \mathrm{span}\{U\}$ for $i \geq 0$, i.e., there exists $y_i \in \mathbb{R}^r$ such that $A^i_{\mathrm{DMD}}x = Uy_i$. Using Proposition 2 we conclude

$$A^{i+1}_{\mathrm{DMD}}x_0 = A_{\mathrm{DMD}}A^i_{\mathrm{DMD}}x_0 = A_{\mathrm{DMD}}Uy_i = Ax_i = A^{i+1}x_0.$$

The proof of (17) follows via induction over i. For the converse direction, let $x = x_U + x_U^\perp$ with $x_U \in \mathrm{span}\{U\}$ and $x_U^\perp \in \mathrm{span}\{U\}^\perp$. Proposition 2 and (17) imply

$$(A - A_{\mathrm{DMD}})x = Ax_U^\perp \neq 0,$$

which completes the proof. $\square$

Remark 5. *The proof of Theorem 2 details that $\mathrm{span}\{U\}$ is A_{DMD}-invariant if and only if $\mathrm{span}\{U\}$ is A invariant. Moreover, $\mathrm{span}\{U\} = \mathrm{span}\{X\}$ implies that this condition can be checked easily during the data-generation process. If we further assume that the data are generated via (15), then this is the case whenever*

$$\mathrm{rank}\left(\begin{bmatrix} x_0 & \cdots & x_i \end{bmatrix}\right) = \mathrm{rank}\left(\begin{bmatrix} x_0 & \cdots & x_{i+1} \end{bmatrix}\right)$$

for some $i \geq 0$.

3.3. Continuous-Time Dynamics and RK Approximation

Suppose now that the data $(x_i)_{i=0}^m$ are generated by a continuous process, i.e., via the dynamical system (2). In this case, we are interested in recovering the continuous dynamics from the DMD approximation. As a consequence of Theorem 2, we immediately obtain the following results for exact sampling.

Corollary 1. *Let A_{DMD} be the DMD matrix for the sequence $x_i = \exp(iFh)x_0 \in \mathbb{R}^n$ for $i = 1, \ldots, m$ with $m \geq n$. Then*

$$x(ih; \tilde{x}_0) = A^i_{\mathrm{DMD}}\tilde{x}_0$$

if and only if $\tilde{x}_0 \in \mathrm{span}\{x_0, \ldots, x_m\}$, where $x(t; \tilde{x}_0)$ denotes the solution of the IVP (2) with initial value $\tilde{x}_0$.

Proof. The assertion follows immediately from Proposition 2 with the observation that $\exp(iFh)$ is nonsingular. $\square$

We conclude that we can recover the continuous dynamics with the matrix logarithm (see [19] for further details), whenever $\mathrm{rank}(X) = n$. In practical applications, an exact evaluation of the flow map is typically not possible. Instead, a numerical time-integration method is used to approximate the continuous dynamics.

Suppose we use a RKM with constant step size $h > 0$ to obtain a numerical approximation $(x_i)_{i=0}^m \subseteq \mathbb{R}^n$ of the IVP (2) and use these data to construct the DMD matrix $A_{\mathrm{DMD}} \in \mathbb{R}^{n \times n}$ as in Definition 2. If we now want to use the DMD matrix to obtain an approximation for a different initial condition, say $x(0) = \tilde{x}_0$, we are interested in quantifying the error

$$\|x(ih; \tilde{x}_0) - A^i_{\mathrm{DMD}}\tilde{x}_0\|.$$

Theorem 3. *Suppose that the sequence $(x_i)_{i=0}^m$, with $x_i \in \mathbb{R}^n$ for $i = 0, \ldots, m$, is generated from the linear IVP (2) via a RKM of order p and step size $h > 0$ and satisfies*

$$\mathrm{span}\{x_0,\ldots,x_{m-1}\} = \mathrm{span}\{x_0,\ldots,x_m\}.$$

Let $A_{\mathrm{DMD}} \in \mathbb{R}^{n\times n}$ denote the associated DMD matrix. Then there exists a constant $C \geq 0$ such that

$$\|x(ih;\tilde{x}_0) - A_{\mathrm{DMD}}^i \tilde{x}_0\| \leq Ch^p \tag{18}$$

holds for any $\tilde{x}_0 \in \mathrm{span}(\{x_0,\ldots,x_{m-1}\})$.

Proof. Since the data $(x_i)_{i=0}^m$ are generated from a RKM, there exists a matrix $A_h \in \mathbb{R}^{n\times n}$ such that $x_{i+1} = A_h x_i$ for $i = 0,\ldots,m-1$. Let $\tilde{x}_0 \in \mathrm{span}(\{x_0,\ldots,x_{m-1}\})$. Then, Theorem 2 implies $A_h^i \tilde{x}_0 = A_{\mathrm{DMD}}^i \tilde{x}_0$ for any $i \geq 0$. Thus, the result follows from the classical error estimates for RKM (see, for example, [15], Thm. II.3.6) and from the equality

$$\|x(ih;\tilde{x}_0) - A_{\mathrm{DMD}}^i \tilde{x}_0\| = \|x(ih;\tilde{x}_0) - A_h^i \tilde{x}_0\| \leq Ch^p$$

for some $C \geq 0$ since the RKM is of order p. $\square$

The proof details that due to Proposition 2, we are essentially able to recover the discrete dynamics A_h obtained from the RKM via DMD, provided that $\mathrm{rank}(X) = n$. As laid out in Remark 4, this condition is equivalent to (A_h, x_0) being controllable for which the controllability of (F, x_0) is a necessary condition.

The question that remains to be answered is whether it is possible to recover the continuous dynamic matrix F from the discrete dynamics A_{DMD} (respectively A_h) provided that the Runge–Kutta scheme used to discretize the continuous dynamics is known. For any 1-stage Runge–Kutta method (α, β), i.e., $s = 1$ in (3), this is indeed the case since then (6) simplifies to

$$A_h = I_n + h\beta(I_n - h\alpha F)^{-1}F,$$

which yields

$$F = -\frac{1}{h}(I_n - A_h)(\alpha A_h + (\beta - \alpha)I_n)^{-1}.$$

Combining (19) with Proposition 2 yields the following result.

Lemma 1. *Suppose that the sequence $(x_i)_{i=0}^m \subseteq \mathbb{R}^n$ is generated from the linear IVP (2) via the 1-stage Runge-Kutta method (α, β) with step size $h > 0$. Let $A_{\mathrm{DMD}} \in \mathbb{R}^{n\times n}$ denote the associated DMD matrix. If $\mathrm{rank}(\{x_0,\ldots,x_{m-1}\}) = n$, then*

$$F = -\frac{1}{h}(I_n - A_{\mathrm{DMD}})(\alpha A_{\mathrm{DMD}} + (\beta - \alpha)I_n)^{-1}, \tag{19}$$

provided that the inverse exists.

If the assumption of Lemma 1 holds, then we can recover the continuous dynamic matrix from the DMD approximation. The corresponding formula for popular 1-stage methods is presented in Table 1.

Table 1. Identification of continuous-time systems via DMD with 1-stage Runge–Kutta methods.

Method	(α, β)	Lemma 1
explicit Euler	$(0, 1)$	$F = -\frac{1}{h}(I_n - A_{\mathrm{DMD}})$
implicit Euler	$(1, 1)$	$F = \frac{1}{h}(I_n - A_{\mathrm{DMD}}^{-1})$
implicit midpoint rule	$(\frac{1}{2}, 1)$	$F = \frac{1}{2h}(A_{\mathrm{DMD}} - I_n)(A_{\mathrm{DMD}} + I_n)^{-1}$

In this scenario, let us emphasize that we can compute the discrete dynamics with the DMD approximation for any time step.

The situation is different for $s \geq 2$, as we illustrate with the following example.

Example 3. *For given $h > 0$, consider $F_1 := 0$ and $F_2 := -\frac{2}{h}$. Then, for Heun's method, i.e., $\mathcal{A} = \begin{bmatrix} 0 & 0 \\ 1 & 0 \end{bmatrix}$ and $\beta^\top = \begin{bmatrix} \frac{1}{2} & \frac{1}{2} \end{bmatrix}$, we obtain $A_h = p(F)$ with $p(x) = 1 + hx + \frac{h^2}{2}x^2$, and thus $p(F_1) = p(F_2)$. In particular, we cannot distinguish the continuous-time dynamics in this specific scenario.*

4. Numerical Examples

To illustrate our analytical findings, we constructed a dynamical system that exhibits some fast dynamics that is stable but not exponentially stable and has a nontrivial but exactly computable flow map. In this way, we can check the approximation both qualitatively and quantitatively. In addition, the system can be scaled to arbitrary state-space dimensions. Most importantly, for our purposes, the system is designed such that for any initial value, the space not reached by the system is at least as large as the reachable space. The complete code of our numerical examples can be found in the supplementary material.

With $N \in \mathbb{N}$, $\Delta := \mathrm{diag}(0, 1, \ldots, N - 1)$ we consider the continuous-time dynamics (2) with

$$F := \begin{bmatrix} 0 & 2\Delta \\ 0 & -\frac{1}{2}\Delta \end{bmatrix} \quad \text{and} \quad \exp(tF) = \begin{bmatrix} I & 4(I - \exp(-\frac{t}{2}\Delta)) \\ 0 & \exp(-\frac{t}{2}\Delta) \end{bmatrix}.$$

Starting with an initial value $x_0 \in \mathbb{R}^{2N}$ we can thus generate exact snapshots of the solution via $x(t) = \exp(tF)x_0$, as well as the controllability space

$$\mathcal{C}(F, x_0) = \mathrm{span}\left\{ x_0, \begin{bmatrix} 0 & 2\Delta \\ 0 & -\frac{1}{2}\Delta \end{bmatrix} x_0, \begin{bmatrix} 0 & 2\Delta \\ 0 & -\frac{1}{2}\Delta \end{bmatrix}^2 x_0, \ldots, \begin{bmatrix} 0 & 2\Delta \\ 0 & -\frac{1}{2}\Delta \end{bmatrix}^{2N-1} x_0 \right\}.$$

One can confirm that $\dim(\mathcal{C}(F, x_0)) \leq N$ with equality if, for example, the initial state

$$x_0 = \begin{bmatrix} x_{0,1} \\ x_{0,2} \end{bmatrix}$$

has no zero entries in its lower part $x_{0,2} \in \mathbb{R}^N$. Due to (7), we immediately infer

$$\dim(\mathcal{C}(A_h, x_0)) \leq N$$

for any A_h obtained by a Runge–Kutta method. We conclude that DMD is at most capable of reproducing solutions that evolve in $\mathcal{C}(F, x_0)$. Indeed, as outlined in Proposition 2, all components of any other initial value $\tilde{x}_0$ that are in the orthogonal complement of $\mathcal{C}(F, x_0)$ are set to zero in the first DMD iteration.

For our numerical experiments, we set $N := 5$, $x_0 := [1, 2, \ldots, 10]^\top$, and consider the time-grid $t_i := ih$ for $i = 0, 1, \ldots, 100$ with uniform step size $h = 0.1$. A SVD of exactly sampled data

$$\begin{bmatrix} U_1 & U_2 \end{bmatrix} \begin{bmatrix} \Sigma_1 & 0 \\ 0 & 0 \end{bmatrix} V^T = \begin{bmatrix} x_0 & x(h; x_0) & x(2h; x_0) & \cdots & x(10; x_0) \end{bmatrix} \tag{20}$$

of the matrix of snapshots of the solution $x(t; x_0)$ reveals that the solution space is indeed of dimension $N = 5$ and defines the bases $U_1, U_2 \in \mathrm{St}(10, 5)$ of $\mathcal{C}(F, x_0)$ and its orthogonal complement, respectively.

For our numerical experiment, whose results are depicted in Figure 2, we choose the initial values

$$\tilde{x}_0 := U_1 e \in \mathrm{span}(U_1) \quad \text{and} \quad \hat{x}_0 := U_2 e \in \mathrm{span}(U_2) = \mathrm{span}(U_1)^\perp,$$

with $e = [1, 1, 1, 1, 1]^\top$. The exact solution for both initial values is presented in Figure 2a,b, respectively. Our simulations confirm the following:

- As predicted by Theorem 2, the DMD approximation for the initial value $\tilde{x}_0$, depicted in Figure 2c, exactly recovers the exact solution, while the DMD approximation for the initial value $\hat{x}_0$ (cf. Figure 2d) is identically zero.
- If we first transform the data with the matrix

$$
T = \begin{bmatrix} 1 & 1 & & & \\ & \ddots & & \ddots & \\ & & & \ddots & 1 \\ & & & & 1 \end{bmatrix} \in \mathrm{GL}_{2N}(\mathbb{R}),
$$

then compute the DMD approximation, and then transform the results back, the DMD approximation for $\tilde{x}_0$ remains unchanged (see Figure 2e), confirming (14) from Theorem 1. In contrast, the prediction of the dynamics for $\hat{x}_0$ changes (see Figure 2f), highlighting that DMD is not invariant under state-space transformations in the orthogonal complement of the data.

The presented numerical example is chosen to illustrate the importance of the reachable space. Computing a subspace numerically is a delicate task in particular if, as in our example, the ratio of the largest and the smallest entry in the controllability matrix is of size $\frac{(1/2)^{2N-3}(N-1)^{2N}}{(1/2)^{2N-1}} = 4(N-1)^{2N}$, which leads to huge rounding errors already for moderate N. This mainly concerns the separation of the reachable and the unreachable subspace, which, however, can be monitored in a general implementation for a general setup. Since in standard SVD implementations, the dominant directions (and, thus, the Moore–Penrose inverse) are computed with high accuracy, for quantitative approximations using DMD, these numerical issues are less severe.

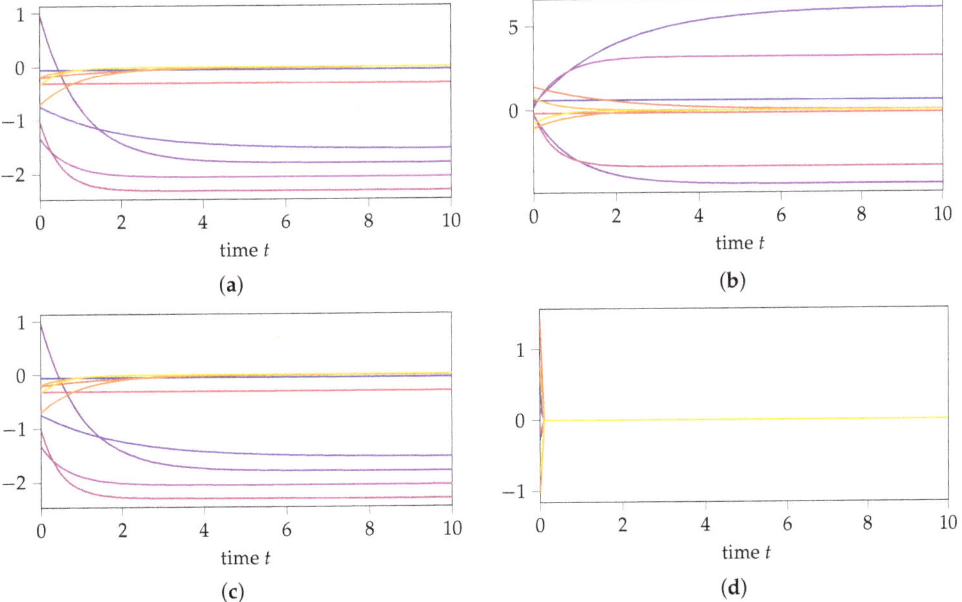

Figure 2. *Cont.*

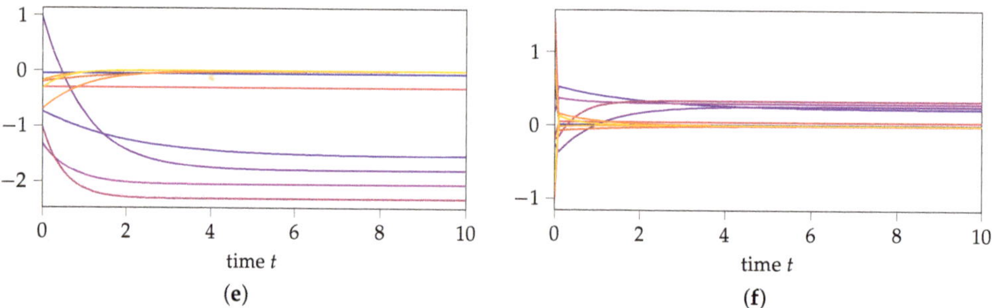

Figure 2. Comparison of the exact solution, DMD approximation, and DMD approximation based on transformed data for initial values inside the reachable subspace, i.e., $\check{x}_0 \in \mathcal{C}(F, x_0)$ and outside the reachable subspace, i.e., $\hat{x}_0 \in \mathcal{C}(F, x_0)^\perp$. (**a**) Exact solution with initial value $\check{x}_0$. (**b**) Exact solution with initial value $\hat{x}_0$. (**c**) DMD approximation with initial value $\check{x}_0$. (**d**) DMD approximation with initial value $\hat{x}_0$. (**e**) DMD with transformed data with initial value $\check{x}_0$. (**f**) DMD with transformed data with initial value $\hat{x}_0$.

5. Conclusions

This work highlighted fundamental properties of the DMD approach if applied to linear problems both in continuous and discrete times. Depending on how the initial data relate to the reachable space, the DMD can recover the exact discrete-time dynamics. If, in addition, the discrete-time data are generated from a continuous-time system via time discretization with a Runge–Kutta scheme, then the error of the DMD approximation is in the same order as the time-integration method. As a by-product of our analysis, we made a relation of the Moore–Penrose inverse and regular transformations explicit, which has not been stated so far. Although the findings mainly confirm what should be expected, the basic principles, such as controllability, will well generalize to nonlinear problems.

Supplementary Materials: The following are available at https://www.mdpi.com/article/10.3390/math10030418/s1. Python script to reproduce the numerical results.

Author Contributions: All authors have contributed equally to this work. All authors have read and agreed to the published version of the manuscript.

Funding: B. Unger acknowledges funding from the DFG under Germany's Excellence Strategy–EXC 2075–390740016 and is thankful for support by the Stuttgart Center for Simulation Science (SimTech).

Data Availability Statement: The code to produce the numerical example is attached to this manuscript as Supplementary Material.

Acknowledgments: We thank Robert Altmann for inviting us to the Sion workshop, where we started this work.

Conflicts of Interest: The authors declare no conflict of interest.

Abbreviations

The following abbreviations are used in this manuscript:

DMD	dynamic mode decomposition
IVP	initial value problem
ODE	ordinary differential equation
RKM	Runge–Kutta method
SVD	singular value decomposition

References

1. Benner, P.; Cohen, A.; Ohlberger, M.; Willcox, K. *Model Reduction and Approximation*; SIAM: Philadelphia, PA, USA, 2017. [CrossRef]
2. Quarteroni, A.; Manzoni, A.; Negri, F. *Reduced Basis Methods for Partial Differential Equations: An Introduction*; UNITEXT, Springer: Berlin, Germany, 2016. [CrossRef]
3. Antoulas, A.C. *Approximation of Large-Scale Dynamical Systems*; Advances in Design and Control; SIAM: Philadelphia, PA, USA, 2005; p. 489.
4. Hesthaven, J.S.; Rozza, G.; Stamm, B. *Certified Reduced Basis Methods for Parametrized Partial Differential Equations*; Springer: Berlin, Germany, 2016.
5. Antoulas, A.C.; Beattie, C.A.; Güğercin, S. *Interpolatory Methods for Model Reduction*; SIAM: Philadelphia, PA, USA, 2020. [CrossRef]
6. Mayo, A.J.; Antoulas, A.C. A framework for the solution of the generalized realization problem. *Linear Algebra Appl.* **2007**, *425*, 634–662. [CrossRef]
7. Beattie, C.; Gugercin, S. Realization-independent H2-approximation. In Proceedings of the 2012 IEEE 51st IEEE Conference on Decision and Control (CDC), Maui, HI, USA, 10–13 December 2012; pp. 4953–4958. [CrossRef]
8. Gustavsen, B.; Semlyen, A. Rational approximation of frequency domain responses by vector fitting. *IEEE Trans. Power Deliv.* **1999**, *14*, 1052–1061. [CrossRef]
9. Drmač, Z.; Gugercin, S.; Beattie, C. Quadrature-Based Vector Fitting for Discretized $\mathcal{H}_2$ Approximation. *SIAM J. Sci. Comput.* **2015**, *37*, A625–A652. [CrossRef]
10. Drmač, Z.; Gugercin, S.; Beattie, C. Vector Fitting for Matrix-valued Rational Approximation. *SIAM J. Sci. Comput.* **2015**, *37*, A2345–A2379. [CrossRef]
11. Peherstorfer, B.; Willcox, K. Data-driven operator inference for nonintrusive projection-based model reduction. *Comput. Methods Appl. Mech. Engrg.* **2016**, *306*, 196–215. [CrossRef]
12. Kutz, J.; Brunton, S.; Brunton, B.; Proctor, J. *Dynamic Mode Decomposition*; SIAM: Philadelphia, PA, USA, 2016.
13. Moler, C.; Van Loan, C. Nineteen Dubious Ways to Compute the Exponential of a Matrix, Twenty-Five Years Later. *SIAM Rev.* **2003**, *45*, 3–49. [CrossRef]
14. Mezić, I. Spectral Properties of Dynamical Systems, Model Reduction and Decompositions. *Nonlinear Dyn.* **2005**, *41*, 309–325. [CrossRef]
15. Hairer, E.; Nørsett, S.; Wanner, G. *Solving Ordinary Differential Equations I: Nonstiff Problems*; Springer Series in Computational Mathematics; Springer: Berlin, Germany, 2008.
16. Kunkel, P.; Mehrmann, V. *Differential-Algebraic Equations. Analysis and Numerical Solution*; European Mathematical Society: Zürich, Switzerland, 2006.
17. Tu, J.H.; Rowley, C.W.; Luchtenburg, D.M.; Brunton, S.L.; Kutz, J.N. On dynamic mode decomposition: Theory and applications. *J. Comput. Dyn.* **2014**, *1*, 391–421. [CrossRef]
18. Golub, G.H.; Van Loan, C.F. *Matrix Computations*, 3rd ed.; Johns Hopkins University Press: Baltimore, MD, USA, 1996.
19. Higham, N. *Functions of Matrices: Theory and Computation*; Other Titles in Applied Mathematics; SIAM: Philadelphia, PA, USA, 2008.

Article

Differential Neural Network-Based Nonparametric Identification of Eye Response to Enforced Head Motion

Isaac Chairez [1,2], Arthur Mukhamedov [3], Vladislav Prud [3], Olga Andrianova [4,*] and Viktor Chertopolokhov [5]

[1] Bioprocesses Department, UPIBI, Instituto Politecnico Nacional, Ciudad de Mexico 07340, Mexico; jchairezo@ipn.mx

[2] School of Engineering, Tecnologico de Monterrey, Campus Guadalajara, Monterrey 64849, Mexico

[3] Center "Supersonic", Lomonosov Moscow State University, 119991 Moscow, Russia; a.mukhamedov@vrmsu.ru (A.M.); info@vrmsu.ru (V.P.)

[4] V.A. Trapeznikov Institute of Control Sciences of RAS, 117997 Moscow, Russia

[5] Center "Supersonic", Interdisciplinary Scientific and Educational School "Mathematical Methods of Large-Scale Systems Analysis", Lomonosov Moscow State University, 119991 Moscow, Russia; psvr@vrmsu.ru

* Correspondence: andrianovaog@gmail.com; Tel.: +7-926-888-0832

Abstract: Dynamic motion simulators cannot provide the same stimulation of sensory systems as real motion. Hence, only a subset of human senses should be targeted. For simulators providing vestibular stimulus, an automatic bodily function of vestibular–ocular reflex (VOR) can objectively measure how accurate motion simulation is. This requires a model of ocular response to enforced accelerations, an attempt to create which is shown in this paper. The proposed model corresponds to a single-layer spiking differential neural network with its activation functions are based on the dynamic Izhikevich model of neuron dynamics. An experiment is proposed to collect training data corresponding to controlled accelerated motions that produce VOR, measured using an eye-tracking system. The effectiveness of the proposed identification is demonstrated by comparing its performance with a traditional sigmoidal identifier. The proposed model based on dynamic representations of activation functions produces a more accurate approximation of foveal motion as the estimation of mean square error confirms.

Keywords: nonparametric model; artificial neural network; Izhikevich artificial neuron; vestibular–ocular reflex; control Lyapunov function

MSC: 93B30; 93-10; 93D30; 93C10; 94C30

Citation: Chairez, I.; Mukhamedov, A.; Prud, V.; Andrianova, O.; Chertopolokhov, V. Differential Neural Network-Based Nonparametric Identification of Eye Response to Enforced Head Motion. *Mathematics* **2022**, *10*, 855. https://doi.org/10.3390/math10060855

Academic Editors: Natalia Bakhtadze, Igor Yadykin, Andrei Torgashov and Nikolay Korgin

Received: 10 February 2022
Accepted: 2 March 2022
Published: 8 March 2022

Publisher's Note: MDPI stays neutral with regard to jurisdictional claims in published maps and institutional affiliations.

1. Introduction

Currently, a significant multidiscipline effort deals with developing technologies that can be applied for training in simulated environments. Such training can be used in different scenarios, from studying drivers' behavior to improving road safety and pilot training, the latter of which has been one of the leading forces for the development of these systems since the early years. These technologies require understanding human sensory systems and their influence to be studied effectively with the proposer instrumentation and modeling tools.

During simulator training, body movements cannot precisely match what is being shown on screen, causing a mismatch in sensory information and leading to simulator sickness as described in [1,2]. This discrepancy is caused by several factors like delays due to tracking and rendering of the output image and physical limitations of the movement range of training systems. Consequently, attempts to overcome this problem covers several different research directions, including but not limited to dynamic motion systems, forecasting movement, and galvanic vestibular stimulation [3]. However, the problem can also be reversed, so that body reaction is used to estimate the accuracy of simulated motion.

One of such indicators is an ocular response to enforced accelerations by an external system or device, just like a flight simulator.

Due to the size and position of the fovea, which is the part of a human eye retina with a high density of light-sensitive photoreceptors, clear vision is achieved when the object of interest is moving slower than $4°/s$. A unique mechanism exists so that the region of interest on the acquired image stays on the retina as the body moves. It is called the vestibular–ocular reflex (VOR), and it is one of the interaction processes between a human body and the surrounding environment. It operates via a neural path between the vestibular and oculomotor systems: eyes compensate head rotations by rotating in the opposite direction [4].

Incorrect functioning of VOR leads to disruptions of clear vision such as the inability to compensate micromovements of the head. However, as an existing connection between external accelerations and angular velocities with the vestibular response is not entirely understood, VOR cannot be estimated directly. A natural way to study VOR is to observe it using immersive technologies (such as virtual or mixed reality) and produce reliable and accurate mathematical models of VOR with human motion as input and electrophysiological response as output. This response could be electroencephalographic signals, oculographic information, or eye motion data, among others. Despite the importance of such mathematical model design, the number and complexity of physiological aspects increase the difficulty of generating specific models for given motion cues that use a reasonably small number of parameters [5].

An alternative way to represent VOR dynamics is to use nonparametric models to reproduce the aforementioned input–output relationship while maintaining a tractable numerical complexity. Several methodologies propose nonparametric models, including adaptive autoregressive systems, polynomial approximations, swarm optimization techniques, and artificial neural networks. Nevertheless, the dynamic nature of VOR limits the applicability of the models under a wide variety of working scenarios. Dynamic approximate models can also be considered as modeling options for systems describing VOR dynamics. In particular, differential neural networks (DNNs) have been used for a long time as efficient modeling strategies of dynamic systems with uncertain mathematical models that are affected by perturbations and modeling inaccuracies. Notice that DNN based models could be well fitted to represent the VOR dynamics [6,7]. Still, the selection of activation functions could be a matter of discussion, considering that sigmoidal or other monotonical functions may not capture the complex electrophysiological VOR response.

Izhikevich model of neuron activity [8] is a bioinspired characterization of electrophysiology-based approximate mathematical models. Izhikevich artificial mathematical models have been proven to be an efficient model of diverse neuron responses [9]. Therefore, an aggregation of several Izhikevich artificial neurons is named electrophysiology-inspired approximated DNN or spiking DNNs [10,11].

Because of the modeling abilities of DNN using Izhikevich neuron dynamics, this paper proposes a method to approximate oculomotor response using the described spiking DNN model. The main contributions of this study can be summarized as follows:

- a novel modeling strategy is proposed for the ocular response on head movements based on a spiking DNN with no parameters;
- a new aggregated system is used to confirm the validity of the proposed model. It consists of an experimental system with a motion platform, inertial sensors, an eye-tracking device for acquiring data, and a neural network for processing it.

This manuscript is organized as follows. In Section 2, we provide a general description of the vestibular–ocular response. In Section 3, we introduce the uncertain model of ocular response, which is then formulated as a spiking-differential-neural-network-based nonparametric identifier in Section 4. In Section 5, we describe general modeling strategy as the process of collecting experimental data. In Section 6, we cover processing of the obtained data and assessing performance of the proposed model. Conclusions and final remarks of Section 7 close the study.

2. Description of Vestibular–Ocular Connection

As jet aviation and then crewed spaceflight progressed, they brought attention to several physiological phenomena: a vestibular–ocular reflex. Its disruption was stated to lead to deterioration of a human being in the pioneering work by A.L. Yarbus [12]. Possible causes of disorder include biological prerequisites like vestibular neuronitis [13] or congenital predisposition [14] as well as environmental change. Crewed spaceflight provided an essential context for studying the activity of the vestibular system and its connection to the rest of the body. The papers by I. Kozlovskaya and L. Kornilova (Institute of Biomedical Problems, Moscow, Russia) [15,16] examine vestibular–sensory disorders in a weightless environment and methodology for diagnosing the VOR functioning.

A general approach for detecting dysfunctions is to compare actual data with the reference. For vestibular–sensory disorders, the latter takes the form of a VOR model. The most common method of creating such models is to describe the system as a dynamic one formed by differential and difference equations. One such example is [17] that uses a bilateral model of an eye. It describes ocular dynamics based on the activity of extraocular muscles connected to the right and left sides of an eye. These muscles are more sensitive to positive difference, so they are more active when the difference is negative [18]. The downside of this model is that muscle behavior is described using a large number of parameters that require the application of genetic algorithms to improve the model accuracy [19].

An alternative method was proposed in [20]. It uses statistical methods to approximate the actual dynamics of optokinetic–vestibule–cervical and vestibular nystagmus. Typical dynamics of nystagmus' slow phase drive the values of the five parameters of the model. With known dynamics of head rotations and depending on supporting visual information, this model generates both phases of nystagmus. However, such modeling approaches do not provide enough flexibility and require vast processing power to solve the underlying optimization problem.

3. Modeling Ocular Response to Enforced Acceleration

This study is focused on developing a nonparametric model based on a single-layer DNN able to characterize ocular response. The network uses artificial neurons implemented as Izhikevich models, so it operates as a Spiking DNN or SDNN for short. The proposed model produces a vector of two angular coordinates of ocular rotation based on linear acceleration and angular velocities from a vestibular system which serves as an input. Training input data come from a tracking system and ground truth output from a bidimensional eye tracker. The two signals were resampled to have equally acquired information.

Let $\zeta = [x_{eye}, y_{eye}]^\top$ be the coordinates vector of the eye movement. Its evolution over time is forced by information from the vestibular system—linear acceleration $a = [a_x; a_y; a_z]$ and angular velocity $\omega = [\omega_x; \omega_y; \omega_z]^\top$. These values are obtained with respect the body motion.

The electrophysiological system relating inertial information with ocular movement operates using the physiological process of VOR. The continuous dynamics of ζ as the system state vector, coupled with input vector $u = [a^\top; \omega^\top]^\top$ justifies that a model of this relation has uncertain dynamics defined by the following differential equation:

$$\frac{d}{dt}\zeta(t) = f(\zeta(t), u(t)) + \eta(t). \tag{1}$$

Here $\zeta = \zeta(t)$ is the state vector, $u \in \mathbb{R}^6$ is the input vector that drives uncertain dynamics described by the proposed vector function $f : \mathbb{R}^2 \times \mathbb{R}^6 \to \mathbb{R}^2$. f is Lipschitz with respect to its first argument with a positive constant $L_f > 0$. $\eta \in \mathbb{R}^2$ is the vector of external perturbations to the system not involved in the modeling process. These perturbations belong to a subset of $\Sigma = \{\eta \mid \|\eta\|^2 \leq \eta_0, \eta_0 > 0\}$. Such class is admissible considering the nature of inputs and signals that affect the VOR dynamics.

4. Formulation of Spiking-Differential-Neural-Network-Based Model

For the vestibular–ocular system with an uncertain mathematical model (1), the SDNN formulation assumes the following form:

$$\frac{d}{dt}\zeta(t) = A\zeta(t) + W_1^o \phi_1(\zeta(t)) + W_2^o \phi_2(\zeta(t))u(t) + \tilde{f}_e(\zeta(t),t) + \eta(t),$$
$$\zeta(0) = \zeta_0 \in \mathbb{R}^2. \tag{2}$$

The vector $\zeta \in \mathbb{R}^2$ defines the SDNN state. The matrix $A \in \mathbb{R}^{2\times 2}$ describes the linear component of the network dynamics. This matrix is selected as a Hurwitz one to provide boundedness for the state ζ. The two following components form approximation of an uncertain system with traditional SDNN. $W_1^o \in \mathbb{R}^{2\times p_1}$ and $W_2^o \in \mathbb{R}^{2\times p_2}$ are the weights matrices and $\phi_1 : \mathbb{R}^2 \to \mathbb{R}^{p_1}$ and $\phi_2 : \mathbb{R}^2 \to \mathbb{R}^{p_2 \times 6}$ are the vector and matrix of activation functions respectively. Choice of the exact values of p_1 and p_2 is left to the SDNN designer, depending on the value of expected approximation error and methodologies of selecting the size of each layer of general artificial neural networks.

Dynamic nature of the real biological neural networks bioinspired the proposal in this study to use activation functions based on neuron evolution. Thus, each component of ϕ_1 and ϕ_2 is described as the output of the Izhikevich model of neuron [8]:

$$\frac{d}{dt}\varrho_i(t) = f_0(\varrho_i(t),\zeta(t)),$$

$$f_0(\varrho_i,\zeta) = \begin{bmatrix} 0.04v_i^2 + 5v_i - u_i + 140 + Z_i^{\mathrm{T}}\zeta \\ a_i(b_i v_i - u_i) \end{bmatrix}, \varrho_i = \begin{bmatrix} v_i \\ u_i \end{bmatrix}, \tag{3}$$

$$\text{if } v_i \geq 30\,\text{mV, then } \begin{cases} v_i := c_i \\ u_i := u_i + d_i. \end{cases} \tag{4}$$

Here a_i, b_i and c_i are the scalar parameters of the Izhikevich model. $\phi_{ji} = [1,0]\varrho_i$ characterizes the artificial neuron response and is used as the model output in (2). $Z_i \in \mathbb{R}^2$ is a vector of input weights.

Function $\tilde{f}_e(\zeta(t)) : \mathbb{R}^2 \times \mathbb{R} \to \mathbb{R}^2$ in (2) represents approximation error due to selection of a finite number of Izhikevich neurons in the proposed SDNN design. Based on SDNN modeling characteristics this error belongs to the following set: $\Omega = \{\tilde{f}_e \mid \|\tilde{f}_e\|^2 \leq \tilde{f}_0, \tilde{f}_0 > 0\}$. This result is a consequence of the dynamics of the Izhikevich artificial neuron.

The term $\eta \in \mathbb{R}^2$ in (2) characterises external perturbations, or elements affecting VOR system dynamics while being independent of the states values. This term can be said to belong to the set $\Sigma = \{\eta \mid \|\eta\|^2 \leq \eta_0\}$ with η_0 being a positive scalar. Together, the two terms $\tilde{f}_e$ and η represent the degree of vagueness of the underlying electrophysiological system when describing dynamic activation functions of the SDNN representation.

Based on the described approximate dynamical model, this study considers a model for uncertain dynamics of the VOR based on the design of an adaptive SDNN. The proposed approximate adaptive model can be described as follows:

$$\frac{d}{dt}\hat{\zeta}(t) = A\hat{\zeta}(t) + W_1(t)\phi_1(\hat{\zeta}(t)) + W_2(t)\phi_2(\hat{\zeta}(t))u(t), \quad \hat{\zeta}(0) = \hat{\zeta}_0 \in \mathbb{R}^2. \tag{5}$$

Vector $\hat{\zeta}$ defines the approximated dynamics of the 2 eye coordinates. The right-hand side of the VOR dynamics consists of spiking neurons and satisfies the model structure described in (2). The parameters W_1 and W_2 in (5) must be adjusted by a set of learning laws. It is necessary to have the learning laws derived in such a way so that the proposed identifier operating under these learning laws and identical input can reproduce state trajectories of (1). The aforementioned allows issuing the following problem formulation corresponding to the modeling process based on the application of Izhikevich artificial neurons.

Problem statement for the nonparametric modeling with SDNN.

The problem considered in this study is designing the nonlinear algorithm $\Sigma(x, \hat{x}, x, u)$ adjusting the weights $W = [W_1 \; W_2]$ in a way that ensures the identification error $\Delta = \zeta - \hat{\zeta}$ has a stable equilibrium point at the origin:

$$\limsup_{T \to \infty} \left\{ \sup_{\eta \in \Sigma, \; \tilde{f}_e \in \Omega} \|\Delta(T)\|_P^2 \right\} \leq \gamma \tag{6}$$

where $\gamma > 0$ defines the quality of approximation of the proposed SDNN. $P \in \mathbb{R}^{2 \times 2}$ is a positive definite matrix that adjusts influence of different components of the modeling error vector to the overall approximation quality.

This problem can be solved using Lyapunov stability theory by deriving dynamics of W_1 and W_2 from identification error Δ. To develop the stability study, the dynamics of Δ admits the following ordinary differential equation:

$$\frac{d}{dt}\Delta(t) = A\Delta(t) + W_1^* \tilde{\phi}_1(\hat{\zeta}(t)) + W_2^* \tilde{\phi}_2(\hat{\zeta}(t))u(t) + \\ \tilde{W}_1(t)\phi_1(\hat{\zeta}(t)) + \tilde{W}_2(t)\phi_2(\hat{\zeta}(t))u(t) + \tilde{f}_e(t) + \eta(t). \tag{7}$$

The process of applying Lyapunov-based stability confirms that identification error has an upper ultimate bound [21,22]. The suggested Lyapunov function has a quadratic form that depends on identification error and SDNN weights. Dynamics of these weights must be selected in such a way to ensure identification error may have an ultimate bound. The following theorem demonstrates that such a bound exists.

Theorem 1. *If there exist positive definite matrices $\Lambda_1 > 0$ and $\Lambda_2 > 0$ and positive and bounded scalar $\alpha > 0$ such that for the matrix inequality $Ric(P, \alpha) < 0$*

$$Ric(P, \alpha) := P\left(A + \frac{\alpha}{2}I_{2 \times 2}\right) + \left(A + \frac{\alpha}{2}I_{2 \times 2}\right)^\top P + PRP + Q, \tag{8}$$

$$R := \sum_{j=1}^{2} W_j^+ \left(\Lambda_j^{-1}\right) I_{2 \times 2}, \quad Q := 2I_{2 \times 2} + \sum_{j-1}^{2} L_j \Lambda_j,$$

there exists at least one positive definite solution $P \in \mathbb{R}^{2 \times 2}$, $P = P^\top > 0$ then the learning laws described by

$$\frac{d}{dt}W_j(t) = -k_j^{-1}\Omega_j(t) + \alpha \tilde{W}_j(t), \\ \Omega_j(t) = P\Delta(t)\phi_j^\top(\hat{\zeta}(t)), \tag{9}$$

$$W_1(0) = W_{1,0}, \quad W_2(0) = W_{2,0}, j = \{1, 2\},$$

with scalars $k_1, k_2 > 0$, $\tilde{W}_j = W_j^{tr} - W_j$, with W_j^{tr} any matrix satisfying $\|W_j^{tr} - W_j^0\|_F^j \leq W_j^+$ justify the identification error Δ converging to a ball with its center at the origin and an ultimate bound given by

$$\gamma \leq \frac{\eta_0 + \tilde{f}_0}{\alpha}. \tag{10}$$

Proof of Theorem 1. Taking into consideration the dynamics of the identification error Δ presented in (7), one may propose an energetic function depending on the deviation between the state ζ and $\hat{\zeta}$ as well as the deviation between the weights estimated with the identifier and the actual values of the approximation.

For the particular case of the SDNN considered in this study, the aforementioned energetic function is given by:

$$E(\Delta, \tilde{W}_1, \tilde{W}_2) = \|\Delta\|_{2,P}^2 + k_1\|\tilde{W}_1\|_F^2 + k_2\|\tilde{W}_2\|_F^2. \tag{11}$$

Here Δ is the tracking error already, for which its dynamics has been defined in (7). The symbol $\|\cdot\|_{2,P}^2$ represents the weighted l_2 norm of finite-dimensional vectors with the positive definite and symmetric matrix $P \in \mathbb{R}^{2\times 2}$. Additionally, the terms $\|\tilde{W}_j\|_F^2, j = 1,2$ are the matrix norms of the deviation weights $\tilde{W}_j$. For this study, the trace operator is selected as the matrix norms for the weights deviations. Hence, the energetic function is

$$E(\Delta, \tilde{W}_1, \tilde{W}_2) = \Delta^\top P \Delta + k_1 tr\{\tilde{W}_1^\top \tilde{W}_1\} + k_2 tr\{\tilde{W}_2^\top \tilde{W}_2\}. \tag{12}$$

Notice that the function E operates as a Lyapunov-like class with a positive definite, null value when the three arguments vanish and are radially unbounded. Now, the full-time derivative of E corresponds to

$$\frac{d}{dt}E(t) = 2\Delta^\top(t)P\frac{d}{dt}\Delta(t) + 2k_1 tr\left\{\tilde{W}_1^\top \frac{d}{dt}W_1\right\} + 2k_2 tr\left\{\tilde{W}_2^\top \frac{d}{dt}W_2\right\} \tag{13}$$

where $E(t) := E(\Delta(t), \tilde{W}_1(t), \tilde{W}_2(t))$. The term $2\Delta^\top(t)P\frac{d}{dt}\Delta(t)$ admits the following upper bound

$$2\Delta^\top(t)P\frac{d}{dt}\Delta(t) \leq \|\Delta(t)\|_{2,LM(P)}^2 + \gamma + 2k_1 tr\{\tilde{W}_1^\top \Omega_{W,1}(t)\} + 2k_2 tr\{\tilde{W}_2^\top \Omega_{W,2}(t)\} \tag{14}$$

where $LM(P) = PA + A^\top P + PRP + Q$, while the value of $\Omega_{W,1}(t)$ and $\Omega_{W,2}(t)$ have been presented in the learning laws for the proposed identifier.

Transition in (14) was obtained by applying the Young's inequality [21] $YZ^\top + ZY^\top \leq Y\Lambda Y^\top + Z\Lambda^{-1}Z^\top$, which is valid for any $Y \in \mathbb{R}^{r\times s}, Z \in \mathbb{R}^{r\times s}$ and any positive definite and symmetric matrix $\Lambda \in \mathbb{R}^{s\times s}$ a number of times. Taking the result in (14) into the right-hand side of the time derivative of $\frac{d}{dt}E(t)$, leads to

$$\frac{d}{dt}E(t) \leq \|\Delta(t)\|_{LM(P)}^2 + \gamma + 2k_1 tr\{\tilde{W}_1^\top \Omega_{W,1}(t)\} + 2k_2 tr\{\tilde{W}_2^\top \Omega_{W,2}(t)\} +$$
$$2k_1 tr\left\{\tilde{W}_1^\top \frac{d}{dt}W_1\right\} + 2k_2 tr\left\{\tilde{W}_2^\top \frac{d}{dt}W_2\right\}. \tag{15}$$

With the addition and subtraction of the following terms $\alpha\|\Delta(t)\|_P^2$, $\alpha tr\{\tilde{W}_1^\top \tilde{W}_1\}$ and $\alpha tr\{\tilde{W}_2^\top \tilde{W}_2\}$, the next right hand side holds for the time derivative of $E(t)$

$$\frac{d}{dt}E(t) \leq \|\Delta(t)\|_{Ric(P,\alpha)}^2 + \gamma - \alpha\|\Delta(t)\|_P^2 +$$
$$2k_1 tr\{\tilde{W}_1^\top \Omega_{W,1}(t)\} + 2k_2 tr\{\tilde{W}_2^\top \Omega_{W,2}(t)\} +$$
$$tr\left\{\tilde{W}_1^\top\left(2k_1\frac{d}{dt}W_1 + \alpha k_1 \tilde{W}_1\right)\right\} + tr\left\{\tilde{W}_2^\top\left(2k_2\frac{d}{dt}W_2 + \alpha k_2 \tilde{W}_2\right)\right\} -$$
$$\alpha k_1 tr\{\tilde{W}_1^\top \tilde{W}_1\} - \alpha k_2 tr\{\tilde{W}_2^\top \tilde{W}_2\}. \tag{16}$$

Using the learning laws (9) and the matrix inequality (8) presented in the theorem statement, transforms the right-hand side of the derivative of E into

$$\frac{d}{dt}E(t) \leq \gamma - \alpha\|\Delta(t)\|_P^2 - \alpha tr\{k_1 \tilde{W}_1^\top \tilde{W}_1\} - \alpha tr\{k_2 \tilde{W}_2^\top \tilde{W}_2\}. \tag{17}$$

Using the definition of the Lyapunov yields the following outcome:

$$\frac{d}{dt}E(t) \leq \gamma - \alpha E(t). \tag{18}$$

The integration of these last differential inclusions and following the convergence to an invariant set scheme presented in [21], yields to prove the ultimate boundedness of the identification error as well as the weights. $\square$

The obtained values of W_1 and W_2 that minimize the expression (6) may be fixed and used further for solving the prediction problem. The scheme of the whole process (identification and prediction) is shown in Figure 1.

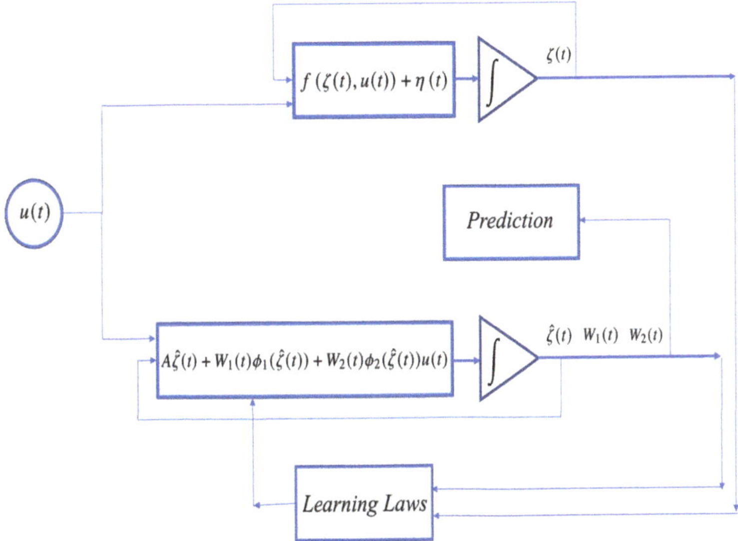

Figure 1. Identification and prediction workflow.

5. Modeling Process and Experimental Validation

The proposed approximate model was tested in an experiment that collects the data from a volunteer using an instrumented controlled acceleration motion device. The data were recorded at a predefined frequency and then injected (offline) to the proposed SDNN-based identifier. This section details all the aspects of the experiment.

A rotating dynamic platform was used to enforce controlled rotational movements on a test subject. This experiment used an XD-motion platform with 4 degrees of freedom produced by Vympel corporation. The data collecting system is based on a virtual reality headset HTC Vive Pro Eye. The headset's position and orientation quaternion in a fixed coordinate system were obtained from the SteamVR tracking system. SRanipal software gathered data provided by a built-in eye-tracking system and produced view origin and direction vectors for each eye as the output at a maximum frequency of 120 Hz. The whole experimental setup is shown in Figure 2. The resulting ocular movements and head dynamics were recorded and later processed to be modeled by the proposed SDNN.

The experimental process is as follows. First, a test subject puts on and adjusts the belts of the headset for it to stay firmly fixed on the head throughout the whole experiment. Then, the eye tracker is calibrated according to SRanipal documentation and guidelines. After finishing the calibration procedure, any adjustment of the headset by the test subject leads to resetting the experiment, according to SRanipal guidelines. The test subject is then sat on the dynamic platform straight. The platform performs rotational movements around the vertical axis, alternating clockwise and counterclockwise. Movement frequency and amplitude remain constant for 30 s, after which a 20-s break takes place, and new movement parameters are loaded. The order of these parameter sets is randomized. The test subject isn't provided any indication of these parameters. Visual and audio cues of motion are further reduced with the headset screen showing solid black and headphones playing static during the experiment.

The choice of movement pattern is based on several factors. First, horizontal semi-circular channels are stimulated more than the other two for this kind of movement, so ocular response is also primarily horizontal, allowing to focus on a single axis. Second, the platform has the most reach on this rotational axis, which allows for more diverse movement patterns. Additionally, pitch and roll rotations on this platform are performed by adjusting the length of the legs. However, this adjustment happens even in an idle state when no rotation is being performed, leading to additional platform vibrations introducing parasitic ocular response.

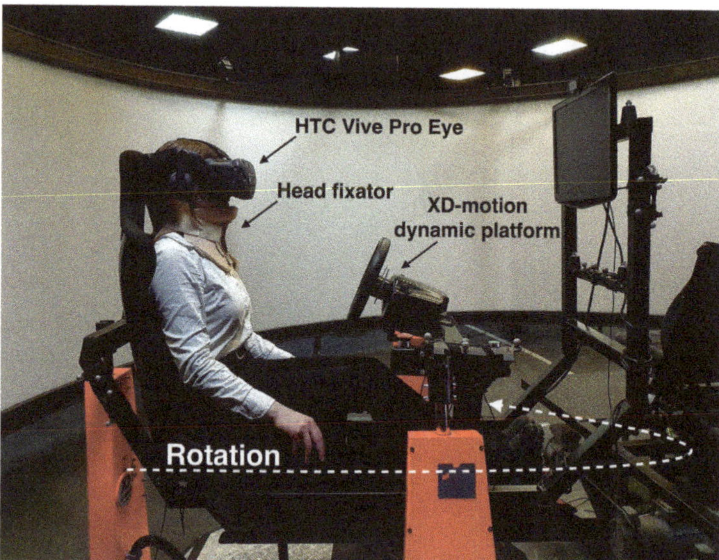

Figure 2. Experimental setup for collecting the ocular response to the controlled accelerated movements.

During the processing phase, each movement pattern is handled individually. The leading and trailing 3 s of each recording are trimmed. The view direction vector is converted from a headset coordinate system into angles of eye rotation in horizontal and vertical planes. The head coordinates data were sampled at a lower frequency than eye-tracking data, so the former were smoothed using a Gaussian filter. Head orientation quaternion was converted into Euler angles. After leaving only data corresponding to horizontal angles, angular velocity and linear acceleration were calculated.

6. Numerical Simulation

The collected data from the two motion patterns were used to test the proposed SDNN model. These two patterns are 18 25-degree rotation cycles per minute and 50-degree rotations at a rate of 4.8 cycles per minute. They are later referred to as high- and low-frequency movements. As described earlier, linear accelerations and angular velocities formed the system input u while eye rotation angles were used as a reference state ζ. Figures 3–6 compare dynamics of the proposed SDNN identifier with Izhikevich and sigmoidal activation functions on the obtained data. Figures 3a and 5a demonstrate recorded head rotation profile. Figures 3b and 5b show evolution of identification error (shown as mean square error) of the proposed identifier. In both cases, the origin is shown to be a practical stable equilibrium point for the analyzed modeling error. Direct comparison between recorded and modeled data is shown in Figures 3c and 5c. Finally, Figures 3d and 5d show evolution of the weights from initial conditions. The highlighted dashed line on both figures illustrates the work of VOR. The correspondence between ground truth eye-tracking data and identifier state shows the validity of the proposed identifier.

The identification performance of the proposed spiking identifier was compared against the traditional sigmoidal DNN-based identifier, shown in Figures 4 and 6. These figures are structured identically to Figures 3 and 5. Note the different y-axis scales between all figures on the weights dynamics plot. Parameter values for both identifiers are presented in Table 1. Numerical values are compared in Table 2 as the performance of the two approaches using mean square error (MSE), mean absolute error (MAE), and standardized mean absolute error (sMAE).

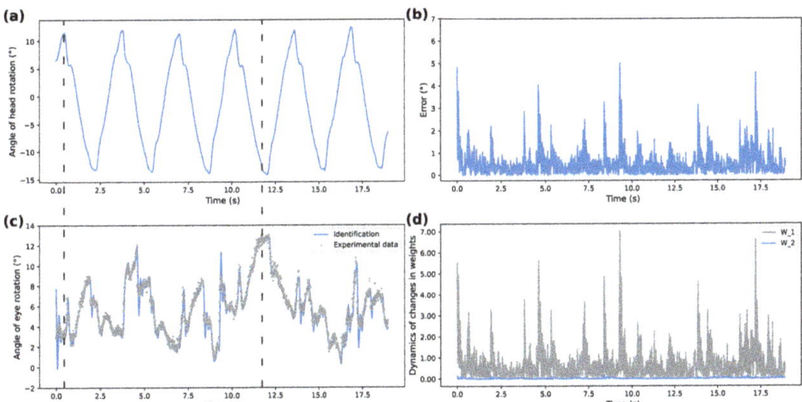

Figure 3. Identification with Izhikevich activation function for high-frequency rotations: (**a**)—recorded head rotation; (**b**)—identification error; (**c**)—recorded data and identification results comparison; (**d**)—evolution of weights.

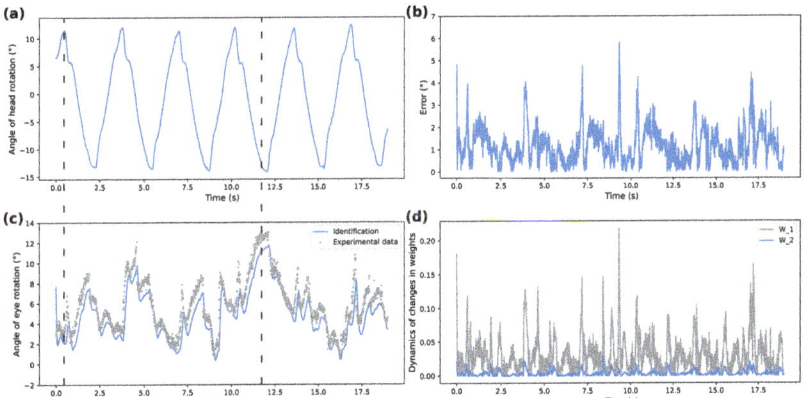

Figure 4. Identification with sigmoidal activation function for high-frequency rotations: (**a**)—recorded head rotation; (**b**)—identification error; (**c**)—recorded data and identification results comparison; (**d**)—evolution of weights.

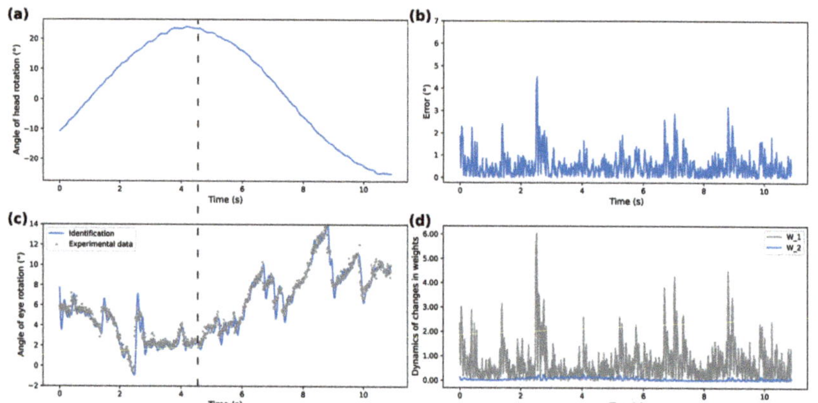

Figure 5. Identification with Izhikevich activation function for low-frequency rotations: (**a**)—recorded head rotation; (**b**)—identification error; (**c**)—recorded data and identification results comparison; (**d**)—evolution of weights.

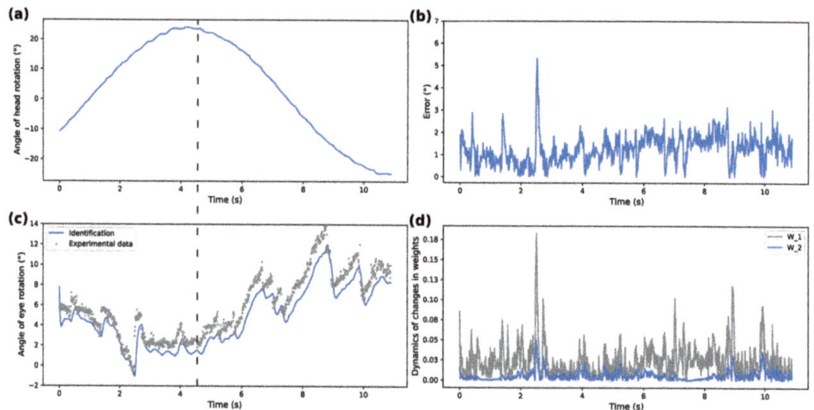

Figure 6. Identification with sigmoidal activation function for low-frequency rotations: (**a**)—recorded head rotation; (**b**)—identification error; (**c**)—recorded data and identification results comparison; (**d**)—evolution of weights.

Table 1. Parameters of the compared identifiers.

Parameter	Izhikevich	Sigmoidal
Matrix A	$20 \times diag(-1, -2)$	$20 \times diag(-2, -2)$
Matrix P	$1575.9 \times diag(60, 40)$	$1575.9 \times diag(60, 40)$
Matrix K_1	$0.15 \times diag(10, 1)$	$0.0001 \times diag(20, 10)$
Matrix K_2	$0.15 \times diag(1, 1)$	$0.0001 \times diag(20, 10)$
Matrix $W_1(0)$	$20 \times \begin{bmatrix} 1 & 1 \\ 1 & 1 \end{bmatrix}$	$0.1 \times \begin{bmatrix} 1 & 1 \\ 1 & 1 \end{bmatrix}$
Matrix $W_2(0)$	$20 \times \begin{bmatrix} 1 & 1 \\ 1 & 1 \end{bmatrix}$	$20 \times \begin{bmatrix} 1 & 1 \\ 1 & 1 \end{bmatrix}$

Table 2. Comparison of identification performance.

Identifier Type	High-Frequency Data			Low-Frequency Data		
	MSE	MAE	sMAE	MSE	MAE	sMAE
Izhikevich	0.000186	0.008948	0.119975	0.000187	0.009647	0.140333
Sigmoidal	0.000710	0.021099	0.282897	0.000588	0.021496	0.312143

Overall, correspondence between modeled behavior and ground truth data shows the applicability of the proposed system under different patterns of rotational movements. Additionally, Izhikevich activation functions for both patterns demonstrate over 50% better performance for modeling ocular response than the DNN implementing sigmoidal activation functions. This shows that SDNN can be used as a generalized approximation class for ocular response dynamics.

7. Conclusions

This study examines modeling physiological VOR systems using SDNN. The proposed nonparametric model implements an arrangement of the artificial neurons described by Izhikevich dynamics with fixed parameters to follow eye movements caused by known head accelerations. Learning laws have been derived for the proposed SDNN to ensure convergence to the origin of identification error. An experimental setup is proposed and used to obtain data and confirm the validity of the proposed SDNN-based nonparametric model. Comparison of the proposed modeling strategy and a traditional identifier with sigmoidal activation functions was performed for different experimental conditions and demonstrated the efficacy of the proposed approach. One potential use of this study is estimating the accuracy of motion cues simulation. Suppose the ground truth of the ocular motion is acquired using a model of vestibular–ocular response. In that case, it can be compared with experimental data on a dynamic platform to assess how accurate the movement was in terms of vestibule system reaction. Despite the additional computational complexity produced with the application of Izhikevich models, the identification quality improves significantly compared to the traditional sigmoidal (algebraic form) forms. This fact justifies the approximated model proposed in this study and opens novel options to create representations of complex biological systems with multirate dynamics.

8. Patents

A derivative from this work is currently undergoing software registration process.

Author Contributions: Conceptualization, I.C., O.A. and V.C.; methodology, I.C. and O.A.; software, V.P. and A.M.; validation, A.M. and V.P.; formal analysis, O.A. and I.C.; investigation, I.C.; resources, V.C.; data curation, A.M.; writing—original draft preparation, A.M. and V.P.; writing—review and editing, I.C., O.A. and V.C.; visualization, V.P.; supervision, I.C.; project administration, V.C. All authors have read and agreed to the published version of the manuscript.

Funding: This research was funded by Ministry of Science and Higher Education of the Russian Federation grant number 075-15-2020-923 "Supersonic".

Institutional Review Board Statement: Ethical review and approval were waived for this study, due to the study only considered to evaluation of motion cues with volunteers in their normal conditions.

Informed Consent Statement: Informed consent was obtained from all subjects involved in the study.

Data Availability Statement: Publicly available datasets were analyzed in this study. This data can be found here: https://github.com/cut4cut/spikennet/tree/main/data accessed on 1 February 2022.

Acknowledgments: The authors thank Alexander Poznyak and Vladimir Alexandrov for fruitful discussions and helpful suggestions and Ernest Sleptsov for valuable advices concerning literature review.

Conflicts of Interest: The authors declare no conflict of interest. The funders had no role in the design of the study; in the collection, analyses, or interpretation of data; in the writing of the manuscript, or in the decision to publish the results.

Abbreviations

The following abbreviations are used in this manuscript:

VOR	Vestibular–Ocular Reflex
DNN	Differential Neural Network
SDNN	Spiking Differential Neural Network
MSE	Mean Square Error
MAE	Mean Absolute Error
sMAE	Standardized Mean Absolute Error

References

1. Stoffreges, T.; Hettinger, L.; Haas, M.; Roe, M.; Smart, J. Postural instability and motion sickness in a fixed-base flight simulator. *Hum. Factors* **2000**, *42*, 458–469. [CrossRef] [PubMed]
2. Johnson, D.M. *Introduction to and Review of Simulator Sickness Research*; U.S. Army Research Institute for the Behavioral and Social Sciences: Fort Belvoir, VA, USA, 2005; Volume 1832.
3. Sadovnichii, V.A.; Aleksandrov, V.V.; Aleksandrova, O.V.; Vega, R.; Konovalenko, I.S.; Soto, E.; Tikhonova, K.V.; Gordillo Domingez, J.L.; Gonzalez Petlacalco, O. Galvanic Correction of Pilot's Vestibular Activity during Visual Flight Control. *Mosc. Univ. Mech. Bull.* **2019**, *74*, 1–8. [CrossRef]
4. Goldberg, J.M.; Cullen, K.E. Vestibular control of the head: Possible functions of the vestibulocollic reflex. *Exp. Brain Res.* **2011**, *210*, 331–345. [CrossRef] [PubMed]
5. Nagayama, M.; Aritake, T.; Hino, H.; Kanda, T.; Miyazaki, T.; Yanagisawa, M.; Akaho, S.; Murata, N. Detecting cell assemblies by NMF-based clustering from calcium imaging data. *Neural Netw.* **2022**, *149*, 29–39. [CrossRef] [PubMed]
6. Kumar, A.; Das, S.; Yadav, V.K. Global exponential synchronization of complex-valued recurrent neural networks in presence of uncertainty along with time-varying bounded and unbounded delay terms. *Int. J. Dyn. Control* **2021**. [CrossRef]
7. Kahloul, A.A.; Sakly, A. Constrained parameterized optimal control of switched systems based on continuous Hopfield neural networks. *Int. J. Dyn. Control* **2018**, *6*, 262–269. [CrossRef]
8. Izhikevich, E.M. Simple model of spiking neurons. *IEEE Trans. Neural Netw.* **2003**, *14*, 1569–1572. [CrossRef] [PubMed]
9. Liu, C.; Shen, W.; Zhang, L.; Du, Y.; Yuan, Z. Spike Neural Network Learning Algorithm Based on an Evolutionary Membrane Algorithm. *IEEE Access* **2021**, *9*, 17071–17082. [CrossRef]
10. Dar, M.R.; Kant, N.A.; Khanday, F.A. Dynamics and implementation techniques of fractional-order neuron models: A survey. In *Fractional Order Systems*; Elsevier: Amsterdam, The Netherlands, 2022; pp. 483–511.
11. Schumm, S.N.; Gabrieli, D.; Meaney, D.F. Plasticity impairment exposes CA3 vulnerability in a hippocampal network model of mild traumatic brain injury. *Hippocampus* **2022**, *32*, 231–250. [CrossRef] [PubMed]
12. Yarbus, A.L. *Eye Movements and Vision*; Plenum Press: New York, NY, USA, 1967.
13. Pal'chun, V.; Guseva, A.; Baybakova, E.; Makoeva, A. Recovery of vestibulo-ocular reflex in vestibular neuronitis depending on severity of vestibulo-ocular reflex damage. *Vestn. Otorinolaringol.* **2019**, *84*, 33. [CrossRef] [PubMed]
14. Gordon, C.; Spitzer, O.; Doweck, I.; Shupak, A.; Gadoth, N. The vestibulo-ocular reflex and seasickness susceptibility. *J. Vestib. Res. Equilib. Orientat.* **1996**, *6*, 229–233. [CrossRef]
15. Kornilova, L.N.; Kozlovskaya, I.B. Neurosensory Mechanisms of Space Adaptation Syndrome. *Hum. Physiol.* **2003**, *29*, 527–538. [CrossRef]
16. Naumov, I.; Kornilova, L.; Glukhikh, D.; Pavlova, A.; Khabarova, E.; Ekimovsky, G.; Vasin, A. Vestibular Function after Repeated Space Flights. *Hum. Physiol.* **2015**, *49*, 33–40. [CrossRef]
17. Broomhead, D.; Akman, O.; Abadi, R. Eye movement instabilities and nystagmus can be predicted by a nonlinear dynamics model of the saccadic system. *J. Math. Biol.* **2005**, *51*, 661–694.
18. van Opstal, A.; van Gisbergen, J. Scatter in the metrics of saccades and properties of the collicular motor map. *Vis. Res.* **1989**, *29*, 1183–1196. [CrossRef]
19. Akman, O.E.; Avramidis, E. Optimisation of an exemplar oculomotor model using multi-objective genetic algorithms executed on a GPU-CPU combination. *BMC Syst. Biol.* **2017**, *11*, 40.
20. Bokov, T.Y.; Suchalkina, A.; Yakusheva, E.; Yakushev, A. Mathematical modelling of vestibular nystagmus. Part I. The statistical model. *Russ. J. Biomech.* **2014**, *18*, 40–57.
21. Poznyak, A.; Sanchez, E.; Yu, W. *Differential Neural Networks for Robust Nonlinear Control (Identification, State Estimation an Trajectory Tracking)*; World Scientific: Singapore, 2001.
22. Fuentes-Aguilar, R.Q.; Chairez, I. Adaptive Tracking Control of State Constraint Systems Based on Differential Neural Networks: A Barrier Lyapunov Function Approach. *IEEE Trans. Neural Netw. Learn. Syst.* **2020**, *31*, 5390–5401. [CrossRef] [PubMed]

 *mathematics*

Article

Bayes Synthesis of Linear Nonstationary Stochastic Systems by Wavelet Canonical Expansions

Igor Sinitsyn [1,2], Vladimir Sinitsyn [1,2], Eduard Korepanov [1] and Tatyana Konashenkova [1,*]

[1] Federal Research Center "Computer Science and Control", Russian Academy of Sciences (FRC CSC RAS), 119333 Moscow, Russia; sinitsin@dol.ru (I.S.); vsinitsin@ipiran.ru (V.S.); ekorepanov@ipiran.ru (E.K.)
[2] Moscow Aviation Institute, National Research University, 125993 Moscow, Russia
* Correspondence: tkonashenkova64@mail.ru

Abstract: This article is devoted to analysis and optimization problems of stochastic systems based on wavelet canonical expansions. Basic new results: (i) for general Bayes criteria, a method of synthesized methodological support and a software tool for nonstationary normal (Gaussian) linear observable stochastic systems by Haar wavelet canonical expansions are presented; (ii) a method of synthesis of a linear optimal observable system for criterion of the maximal probability that a signal will not exceed a particular value in absolute magnitude is given. Applications: wavelet model building of essentially nonstationary stochastic processes and parameters calibration.

Keywords: Bayes criterion; Haar wavelets; loss function; mean risk; observable stochastic systems (OStS); stochastic process (StP); wavelet canonical expansion (WLCE)

MSC: 62C10; 65T60

Citation: Sinitsyn, I.; Sinitsyn, V.; Korepanov, E.; Konashenkova, T. Bayes Synthesis of Linear Nonstationary Stochastic Systems by Wavelet Canonical Expansions. *Mathematics* **2022**, *10*, 1517. https://doi.org/10.3390/math10091517

Academic Editors: Natalia Bakhtadze, Igor Yadykin, Andrei Torgashov and Nikolay Korgin

Received: 25 March 2022
Accepted: 27 April 2022
Published: 2 May 2022

Publisher's Note: MDPI stays neutral with regard to jurisdictional claims in published maps and institutional affiliations.

1. Introduction

Nowadays, for stochastic systems research, e.g., functioning at essentially nonstationary disturbances of complex structures, we need analytical modeling technologies for accurate analysis and synthesis. Methods of analysis and synthesis based on canonical expansions are very suitable for quick analytical modeling realizations using the first two probabilistic moments. Wavelet canonical expansions essentially increase the flexibility and accuracy of corresponding technologies.

It is known [1–3] that canonical expansion (CE) of stochastic processes (StP) is widely used to solve problems of analysis, modeling and synthesis of linear nonstationary stochastic systems (StS). For StS with high availability, corresponding software tools based on CE were worked out in [4–8]. In [4], we gave a brief review of the known algorithmic and software tools. In [5,6], the issues of instrumental software for analytical modeling of nonstationary scalar and vector random functions by means of wavelet CE (WLCE) are considered. The parameters of WLCE are expressed in terms of the coefficients of the expansion of the covariance matrix of random function over two-dimensional Dobshy wavelets. Article [7] continues the thematic cycle dedicated to analytical modeling of linear nonstationary StS based on wavelet and wavelet canonical expansions. The article describes wavelet algorithms for analytical modeling of mathematical expectation, a covariance matrix and a matrix of covariance functions, as well as wavelet algorithms for spectral and correlation-analytical express modeling.

The article [8] continues the thematic cycle devoted to software tools for analytical modeling of linear with parametric interference (Gaussian and non-Gaussian) StS based on nonlinear correlation theory (the method of normal approximation and the method of canonical expansions). Analytical methods are based on orthogonal decomposition of covariance matrix elements using a two–dimensional Dobshy wavelet with a compact carrier and Galerkin–Petrov wavelet methods.

In [5], for an essentially nonstationary StP wavelet, CE (WLCE) was proposed. Nowadays, deterministic wavelet methods are intensively applied to the problems of numerical analysis and modeling. A broad class of numerical methods based on Haar wavelets achieved great success [9]. These methods are simple in the sense of versatility and flexibility and possess less computational cost for accuracy analysis problems. The theory and practice of wavelets has attained its modern growth due to mathematical analysis of the wavelet in [10–12]. The concept of multiresolution analysis was given in [13]. In [14,15] method to construct wavelets with compact support and scaling function was developed Among the wavelet families, which are described by an analytical expression, the Haar wavelets deserve special attention. Haar wavelets, in combination with the Galerkin method, are very effective and popular for solving different classes of deterministic equations [16–25]. The application of a wavelet for CE of StP and stochastic differential and integrodifferential equations was given in [7,8,26].

In [27,28], design problems for linear mean square (MS) optimal filters are considered on the basis of WLCE. Explicit formulae for calculating the MS optimal estimate of the signal and the MS optimal estimate of the quality of the constructed linear MS optimal operator are derived. Articles [29,30] are devoted to the synthesis of wavelets in accordance with complex statistical criteria (CsC). The basic definitions of CsC and approaches are given. Methodological support is based on Haar wavelets. The main wavelet equations, algorithms, software tools and examples are given. Some particular aspects of the StS wavelet synthesis under nonstationary (for example, shock) perturbations are presented in [31].

The developed wavelet algorithms have a fairly high degree of versatility and can be used in various applied fields of science. Such complex StS describes organizations–technical–economical systems functioning in the presence of internal and external noises and stochastic factors. The developed wavelet algorithms are used for data analysis and information processing in high-availability stochastic systems, in complex data storage systems, model building and calibration.

Let us state the general problem of the Bayes synthesis of linear nonstationary normal observable StS (OStS) by WLCE means. Special attention will be paid to the synthesis of linear optimal system for criterion of the maximum probability that the signal will not exceed a particular value in absolute magnitude. For example, the results of computer experiments are presented and discussed.

2. Bayes Criteria

In practice [1,2], the choice of criterion for comparing alternative systems for the same purpose, like any question regarding the choice of criteria, is largely a matter of common sense, which can often be approached from consideration of operating conditions and purpose of any particular system.

The criterion of the maximum probability that the signal will not exceed a particular value in absolute magnitude can be represented as

$$E[l(W, W^*)] = \min. \tag{1}$$

If we take the function l as the characteristic function of the corresponding set of values of the error, the following formula is valid:

$$l(W, W^*) = \begin{cases} 1 \text{ at } |W^* - W| > W, \\ 0 \text{ at } |W^* - W| \le W. \end{cases} \tag{2}$$

In applications connected with damage accumulation (1) needs to be employed with function l in the form:

$$l(W, W^*) = 1 - e^{-k^2(W^* - W)^2}. \tag{3}$$

Thus, we get the following general principle for estimating the quality of a system and selecting the criterion of optimality. The quality of the solution of the problem in each actual case is estimated by a function $l(W, W^*)$, the value of which is determined by the actual realizations of the signal W and its estimator W^*. It is expedient to call this the loss function. The quality of the solution of the problem on average for a given realization of the signal W with all possible realizations of the estimator W^* corresponding to particular realization of the signal W is estimated by the conditional mathematical expectation of the loss function for the given realization of the signal:

$$\rho(A|W) = E[l(W, W^*|W)]. \tag{4}$$

This quantity is called conditional risk. The conditional risk depends on the operator A for the estimator W^* and on the realization of signal W. Finally, the average quality of the solution for all possible realization of W and its estimator W^* is characterized by the mathematical expectation of the conditional risk

$$R(A) = E[\rho(A|W)|W] = E[l(W, W^*)]. \tag{5}$$

This quantity is called the mean risk.

All criteria of minimum risk which correspond to the possible loss functions or functionals which may contain undetermined parameters are known as Bayes' criteria.

3. Basic formulae for Optimal Bayes Synthesis of Linear Systems

Let us consider scalar linear OStS with real StP $Z(\tau)$ ($\tau \in [t - T, t]$), which is the sum of the useful signal and the additive normal noise $X(\tau)$:

$$Z(\tau) = \sum_{r=1}^{N} U_r \xi_r(\tau) + X(\tau). \tag{6}$$

The useful signal is the linear combination of given random parameters U_r ($r = \overline{1, N}$). We need to get StP $W(t)$ in the following form:

$$W(t) = \sum_{r=1}^{N} U_r \zeta_r(t) + Y(t). \tag{7}$$

Here, $\xi_1(\tau), \ldots, \xi_N(\tau), \zeta_1(\tau), \ldots, \zeta_N(\tau)$ are known structural functions; $U_1, \ldots, U_N$ are given random variables (RV) which do not depend on noises $X(\tau)$, $Y(\tau)$ ($EX(\tau) = 0$, $EY(\tau) = 0$).

We state to construct an optimal system with operator A in cases when output StP:

$$W^*(t) = AZ \tag{8}$$

based on observation StP $Z(\tau)$ at time interval $[t - T, t]$, reproducing given output signal $W(t)$ for criteria (1) with maximal accuracy.

It is known [1–3] that the solution of this problem through CE is based on two-stage procedures based on Formulae (4) and (5).

Vector CE $\begin{bmatrix} X(\tau) & Y(\tau) \end{bmatrix}^T$ presents the linear combination of uncorrelated RV with deterministic coordinate functions:

$$X(\tau) = \sum_{v} V_v x_v(\tau), \ Y(\tau) = \sum_{v} V_v y_v(\tau) \tag{9}$$

According to [1,2] for V_v we have

$$V_v = \int_{t-T}^{t} a_v(\tau) X(\tau) d\tau + \int_{t-T}^{t} a_v(\tau) Y(\tau) d\tau \tag{10}$$

Then, coordinate functions are calculated by the following formulae:

$$x_\nu(\tau) = \frac{1}{D_\nu} \int\limits_{t-T}^{t} a_\nu(\theta) K_X(\tau,\theta) d\theta + \frac{1}{D_\nu} \int\limits_{t-T}^{t} a_\nu(\theta) K_{XY}(\tau,\theta) d\theta, \tag{11}$$

$$y_\nu(\tau) = \frac{1}{D_\nu} \int\limits_{t-T}^{t} a_\nu(\theta) K_{XY}(\theta,\tau) d\theta + \frac{1}{D_\nu} \int\limits_{t-T}^{s} a_\nu(\theta) K_Y(\tau,\theta) d\theta. \tag{12}$$

Here, $E[V_\nu] = 0$. $D_\nu = D[V_\nu]$, $K_X(\tau,\theta) = E[X(\tau) \cdot X(\theta)]$, $K_{XY}(\tau,\theta) = E[X(\tau) \cdot Y(\theta)]$, $K_Y(\tau,\theta) = E[Y(\tau) \cdot Y(\theta)]$; $a_\nu(\tau)$ is a given set of deterministic functions satisfying biorthogonality conditions:

$$\int\limits_{t-T}^{t} a_\nu(\tau) x_\mu(\tau) d\tau + \int\limits_{t-T}^{t} a_\nu(\tau) y_\mu(\tau) d\tau = \delta_{\nu\mu}. \tag{13}$$

Let us consider RV

$$Z_\nu = \int\limits_{t-T}^{t} a_\nu(\tau) Z(\tau) d\tau, \tag{14}$$

and its presentation

$$Z_\nu = \sum_{r=1}^{N} \alpha_{\nu r} U_r + V_\nu, \tag{15}$$

where

$$\alpha_{\nu r} = \int\limits_{t-T}^{t} a_\nu(\tau) \xi_r(\tau) d\tau. \tag{16}$$

The sum of RV Z_ν, multiplied by $x_\nu(\tau)$ gives the CE of StP $Z(\tau)$ ($\tau \in [t-T,t]$)

$$Z(\tau) = \sum_\nu Z_\nu x_\nu(\tau). \tag{17}$$

To find the conditional mathematical expectation of the loss function for StP $Z(\tau)$ ($\tau \in [t-T,t]$), it is necessary to find the conditional probability density of output StP relatively on input StP $Z(\tau)$. According to (4), StP $W(t)$ depends upon the given random parameters U_r ($r = \overline{1,N}$) and random noise $Y(t)$. So, we get

$$Y(t) = \sum_\nu V_\nu y_\nu(t) = \sum_\nu \left(Z_\nu - \sum_{r=1}^{N} \alpha_{\nu r} U_r \right) y_\nu(t) = \sum_\nu Z_\nu y_\nu(t) - \sum_{r=1}^{N} U_r \sum_\nu \alpha_{\nu r} y_\nu(t). \tag{18}$$

Here,

$$W(t) = \sum_{r=1}^{N} U_r \xi_r(t) + \sum_\nu Z_\nu y_\nu(t) - \sum_{r=1}^{N} U_r \sum_\nu \alpha_{\nu r} y_\nu(t). \tag{19}$$

The last formula shows that StP $W(t)$ depends upon random parameters U_r ($r = \overline{1,N}$) and the set of Z_ν.

Let us introduce the vector of RV $U = \begin{bmatrix} U_1 & U_2 & \dots & U_N \end{bmatrix}^T$. Conditional distribution of U relative StP $Z(\tau)$ coincides with the set of RV Z_ν. Conditional density $f_1(u|z_1, z_2, \dots)$ is defined by the known formula:

$$f_1(u|z_1, z_2, \dots) = \frac{f(u) f_2(z_1, z_2, \dots |u)}{\int\limits_{-\infty}^{+\infty} f(u) f_2(z_1, z_2, \dots |u) du}. \tag{20}$$

Here, $f(u)$ is a given apriority density of RV $U = \begin{bmatrix} U_1 & U_2 & \dots & U_N \end{bmatrix}^T$; $f_2(z_1, z_2, \dots | u)$ is a density of RV Z_v, relatively $U = \begin{bmatrix} U_1 & U_2 & \dots & U_N \end{bmatrix}^T$.

Taking into account that vector random noise is normal, V_v is the linear transform of vector $\begin{bmatrix} X(\tau) & Y(\tau) \end{bmatrix}^T$. We conclude that RV are not only correlated, but also independent. Joint density of V_v with zero mathematical exactions and variances D_v is expressed by formula

$$f_V(v_1, v_2, \dots) = \frac{1}{\sqrt{(2\pi)^L D_1 \cdot D_2 \cdots}} \exp\left\{ -\frac{1}{2} \sum_v \frac{v_v^2}{D_v} \right\}. \tag{21}$$

In (7), let us replace RV $U_1, \dots, U_N$ with their realizations $u_1, \dots, u_N$; then, Z_v is the linear function of RV V_v with known joint density. Expressing V_v by Z_v and using Formula (21), we get:

$$f_2(z_1, z_2, \dots | u) = \frac{1}{\sqrt{(2\pi)^L D_1 \cdot D_2 \cdots}} \exp\left\{ -\frac{1}{2} \sum_v \frac{1}{D_v} \left(z_v - \sum_{r=1}^{N} \alpha_{vr} u_r \right)^2 \right\}, \tag{22}$$

where $\alpha_v(u) = \sum_{r=1}^{N} \alpha_{vr} u_r$.

After substituting Formula (22) into (20), we get the formula for a posteriori density $f_1(u|z_1, z_2, \dots)$ of $U = \begin{bmatrix} U_1 & U_2 & \dots & U_N \end{bmatrix}^T$ for input StP $Z(\tau)$ ($\tau \in [t - T, t]$):

$$f_1(u|z_1, z_2, \dots) = \chi(z) f(u) \exp\left\{ \sum_v \frac{z_v \alpha_v(u)}{D_v} - \frac{1}{2} \sum_v \frac{\alpha_v^2(u)}{D_v} \right\}, \tag{23}$$

$$\chi(z) = \left[\int_{-\infty}^{+\infty} f(u) \exp\left\{ \sum_v \frac{z_v \alpha_v(u)}{D_v} - \frac{1}{2} \sum_v \frac{\alpha_v^2(u)}{D_v} \right\} du \right]^{-1}. \tag{24}$$

This formula may be used after observation when realization $Z(\tau)$ is available.

A posteriori mathematical expectation of loss function $l(W, W^*)$ is called conditional risk, and is denoted as $\rho(A|W)$:

$$\rho(A|W) = E[l(W, W^*)|Z] = \chi(z) \int_{-\infty}^{+\infty} l(W, W^*) f(u)$$
$$\times \exp\left\{ \sum_v \frac{z_v \alpha_v(u)}{D_v} - \frac{1}{2} \sum_v \frac{\alpha_v^2(u)}{D_v} \right\} du. \tag{25}$$

In order to solve the stated problem, it is necessary to calculate the optimal output StP $W^*(t)$ for every t from condition of minimum of integral (11).

Let us consider this integral as a function of $P^W = W^*(t)$ at fixed values of parameters

$$\eta_0 = \eta_0(z_1, z_2, \dots) = \sum_v z_v y_v(t), \quad \eta_r = \eta_r(z_1, z_2, \dots) = \sum_v \frac{\alpha_{vr} z_v}{D_v} \quad (r = \overline{1, N}) \tag{26}$$

and time t:

$$I(P^W, \eta_1, \dots, \eta_N, t) = \int_{-\infty}^{+\infty} \dots \int_{-\infty}^{+\infty} l\left(\sum_{r=1}^{N} u_r(\zeta_r(t) - b_{r0}) + \eta_0, P^W \right) f(u_1, \dots, u_N)$$
$$\times \exp\left\{ \sum_{r=1}^{N} \eta_r u_r - \frac{1}{2} \sum_{p,q=1}^{N} b_{pq} u_p u_q \right\} du_1 \dots du_N. \tag{27}$$

Here,

$$b_{p0} = \sum_v \alpha_{vp} y_v(t), \quad b_{pq} = \sum_v \frac{1}{D_v} \alpha_{vp} \alpha_{vq} \quad (q, p = \overline{1, N}). \tag{28}$$

The value of parameter $P^W = P_0^W(t, \eta_0, \eta_1, \ldots, \eta_N)$ when integral (27) reaches the minimum value defines the Bayes optimal operator for criterion (1). Changing $\eta_r, (r = \overline{0, N})$ and $P_0^W(t, \eta_0, \ldots, \eta_N)$ variables $\eta_1, \ldots, \eta_N$ and $z_1, z_2, \ldots$ with the corresponding RV $H_0, \ldots, H_N$ and $Z_1, Z_2, \ldots$, we get the required optimal operator:

$$W^*(t) = AZ = P_0^w(t, H_0, \ldots, H_N), \tag{29}$$

where

$$H_0 = \sum_v Z_v y_v(t), \ H_r = H_r(Z_1, Z_2, \ldots) = \sum_v \frac{\alpha_{vr} Z_v}{D_v} \ (r = \overline{1, N}) \tag{30}$$

The quality of the optimal operator is estimated by the mean risk [1,2]

$$
\begin{aligned}
R(A) &= E[\rho(A|W)|W] = E[l(W, W^*)] \\
&= \int\limits_{-\infty}^{+\infty} \ldots \int\limits_{-\infty}^{+\infty} l\left(\sum_{r=1}^N u_r(\zeta_r(t) - b_{r0}) + \eta_0, P_0^W \right) f_2(z_1, z_2, \ldots |u) f(u) dz_1 dz_2 \ldots du.
\end{aligned}
\tag{31}
$$

So, we get the following basic Formulae (23)–(31) necessary for wavelet canonical expansion method.

4. Wavelet Canonical Expansions Method

Let us construct an operator for an optimal linear system using the Haar wavelet CE method WLCE [5,6]:

$$\left\{ \varphi_{00}(\overline{\tau}), \ \psi_{jk}(\overline{\tau}) \right\} \tag{32}$$

where

$$\varphi_{00}(\overline{\tau}) = \varphi(\overline{\tau}) = \begin{cases} 1, \overline{\tau} \in [0, 1), \\ 0, \overline{\tau} \notin [0, 1) \end{cases} \text{ is a scaling function,} \tag{33}$$

$$\psi_{00}(\overline{\tau}) = \psi(\overline{\tau}) = \begin{cases} 1, \overline{\tau} \in \left[0, \frac{1}{2}\right), \\ -1, \overline{\tau} \in \left[\frac{1}{2}, 1\right), \\ 0, \ \tau \notin [0, 1) \end{cases} \text{ is a mother wavelet,} \tag{34}$$

$\psi_{jk}(\overline{\tau}) = \sqrt{2^j} \psi(2^j \overline{\tau} - k)$ are wavelets of level j for $j = 1, 2, \ldots, J; k = 0, 1, \ldots, 2^j - 1; J$ is maximal resolution level defined by required accuracy of approximation for any function $f(\overline{\tau}) \in L^2[0, 1]$ by finite linear combination of Haar wavelets, equal to $2^{-\frac{J}{2}}$.

Then, let us present a one-dimensional wavelet basis (32) as:

$$
\begin{aligned}
&g_1(\overline{\tau}) = \varphi_{00}(\overline{\tau}), \ g_2(\overline{\tau}) = \psi_{00}(\overline{\tau}), \ g_v(\overline{\tau}) = \psi_{jk}(\overline{\tau}), \\
&j = 1, 2, \ldots, J; \ k = 0, 1, \ldots, 2^j - 1; \ v = 2^j + k + 1; \ v = \overline{3, L}.
\end{aligned}
\tag{35}
$$

For construction of the Haar WLCE for vector $\begin{bmatrix} X(\tau) & Y(\tau) \end{bmatrix}^T$ at $\tau \in [t - T, t]$, we pass to new time variable $\overline{\tau} \in [0, 1]$, $\overline{\tau} = \frac{\tau - (t-T)}{T}$ and assume

$$
\begin{aligned}
&K_X(\tau_1, \tau_2) \in L^2([t - T, t] \times [t - T, t]), \ K_{XY}(\tau_1, \tau_2) \in L^2([t - T, t] \times [t - T, t]), \\
&K_Y(\tau_1, \tau_2) \in L^2([t - T, t] \times [t - T, t]),
\end{aligned}
\tag{36}
$$

$$
\begin{aligned}
&\overline{K}_X(\overline{\tau}_1, \overline{\tau}_2) \in L^2([0, 1] \times [0, 1]), \ \overline{K}_{XY}(\overline{\tau}_1, \overline{\tau}_2) \in L^2([0, 1] \times [0, 1]), \\
&\overline{K}_Y(\overline{\tau}_1, \overline{\tau}_2) \in L^2([0, 1] \times [0, 1]).
\end{aligned}
\tag{37}
$$

Additionally, for presentation of given covariance functions in the form of two-dimensional wavelet expansion, it is necessary to define the two-dimensional orthogonal basis through tensor composition of one-dimensional bases (32) when scaling is performed simultaneously for two variables

$$
\begin{aligned}
\Phi^A(\overline{\tau}_1,\overline{\tau}_2) &= \varphi_{00}(\overline{\tau}_1)\varphi_{00}(\overline{\tau}_2), \quad \Psi^H(\overline{\tau}_1,\overline{\tau}_2) = \varphi_{00}(\overline{\tau}_1)\psi_{00}(\overline{\tau}_2), \\
\Psi^B(\overline{\tau}_1,\overline{\tau}_2) &= \psi_{00}(\overline{\tau}_1)\varphi_{00}(\overline{\tau}_2), \quad \Psi^D_{jkn}(\overline{\tau}_1,\overline{\tau}_2) = \psi_{jk}(\overline{\tau}_1)\psi_{jn}(\overline{\tau}_2)
\end{aligned}
\tag{38}
$$

where $j = 1, 2, \ldots, J; \ k, n = 0, 1, \ldots, 2^j - 1$.

So, the two-dimensional wavelet expansion of given covariance functions takes the form

$$
\overline{K}_X(\overline{\tau}_1,\overline{\tau}_2) = a^x \Phi^A(\overline{\tau}_1,\overline{\tau}_2) + h^x \Psi^H(\overline{\tau}_1,\overline{\tau}_2) + b^x \Psi^B(\overline{\tau}_1,\overline{\tau}_2) + \sum_{j=0}^{J} \sum_{k=0}^{2^j-1} \sum_{n=0}^{2^j-1} d^x_{jkn} \Psi^D_{jkn}(\overline{\tau}_1,\overline{\tau}_2)
\tag{39}
$$

where

$$
\begin{aligned}
a^x &= \int_0^1 \int_0^1 \overline{K}_X(\overline{\tau}_1,\overline{\tau}_2)\Phi^A(\overline{\tau}_1,\overline{\tau}_2)d\overline{\tau}_1 d\overline{\tau}_2, \quad h^x = \int_0^1 \int_0^1 \overline{K}_X(\overline{\tau}_1,\overline{\tau}_2)\Psi^H(\overline{\tau}_1,\overline{\tau}_2)d\overline{\tau}_1 d\overline{\tau}_2, \\
b^x &= \int_0^1 \int_0^1 \overline{K}_X(\overline{\tau}_1,\overline{\tau}_2)\Psi^B(\overline{\tau}_1,\overline{\tau}_2)d\overline{\tau}_1 d\overline{\tau}_2, \quad d^x_{jkn} = \int_0^1 \int_0^1 \overline{K}_X(\overline{\tau}_1,\overline{\tau}_2)\Psi^D_{jkn}(\overline{\tau}_1,\overline{\tau}_2)d\overline{\tau}_1 d\overline{\tau}_2,
\end{aligned}
\tag{40}
$$

$$
\overline{K}_{XY}(\overline{\tau}_1,\overline{\tau}_2) = a^{xy} \Phi^A(\overline{\tau}_1,\overline{\tau}_2) + h^{xy} \Psi^H(\overline{\tau}_1,\overline{\tau}_2) + b^{xy} \Psi^B(\overline{\tau}_1,\overline{\tau}_2) + \sum_{j=0}^{J} \sum_{k=0}^{2^j-1} \sum_{n=0}^{2^j-1} d^{xy}_{jkn} \Psi^D_{jkn}(\overline{\tau}_1,\overline{\tau}_2)
\tag{41}
$$

where

$$
\begin{aligned}
a^{xy} &= \int_0^1 \int_0^1 \overline{K}_{XY}(\overline{\tau}_1,\overline{\tau}_2)\Phi^A(\overline{\tau}_1,\overline{\tau}_2)d\overline{\tau}_1 d\overline{\tau}_2, \quad h^{xy} = \int_0^1 \int_0^1 \overline{K}_{XY}(\overline{\tau}_1,\overline{\tau}_2)\Psi^H(\overline{\tau}_1,\overline{\tau}_2)d\overline{\tau}_1 d\overline{\tau}_2, \\
b^{xy} &= \int_0^1 \int_0^1 \overline{K}_{XY}(\overline{\tau}_1,\overline{\tau}_2)\Psi^B(\overline{\tau}_1,\overline{\tau}_2)d\overline{\tau}_1 d\overline{\tau}_2, \quad d^{xy}_{jkn} = \int_0^1 \int_0^1 \overline{K}_{XY}(\overline{\tau}_1,\overline{\tau}_2)\Psi^D_{jkn}(\overline{\tau}_1,\overline{\tau}_2)d\overline{\tau}_1 d\overline{\tau}_2,
\end{aligned}
\tag{42}
$$

$$
\overline{K}_Y(\overline{\tau}_1,\overline{\tau}_2) = a^y \Phi^A(\overline{\tau}_1,\overline{\tau}_2) + h^y \Psi^H(\overline{\tau}_1,\overline{\tau}_2) + b^y \Psi^B(\overline{\tau}_1,\overline{\tau}_2) + \sum_{j=0}^{J} \sum_{k=0}^{2^j-1} \sum_{n=0}^{2^j-1} d^y_{jkn} \Psi^D_{jkn}(\overline{\tau}_1,\overline{\tau}_2)
\tag{43}
$$

here

$$
\begin{aligned}
a^y &= \int_0^1 \int_0^1 \overline{K}_Y(\overline{\tau}_1,\overline{\tau}_2)\Phi^A(\overline{\tau}_1,\overline{\tau}_2)d\overline{\tau}_1 d\overline{\tau}_2, \quad h^y = \int_0^1 \int_0^1 \overline{K}_Y(\overline{\tau}_1,\overline{\tau}_2)\Psi^H(\overline{\tau}_1,\overline{\tau}_2)d\overline{\tau}_1 d\overline{\tau}_2, \\
b^y &= \int_0^1 \int_0^1 \overline{K}_Y(\overline{\tau}_1,\overline{\tau}_2)\Psi^B(\overline{\tau}_1,\overline{\tau}_2)d\overline{\tau}_1 d\overline{\tau}_2, \quad d^y_{jkn} = \int_0^1 \int_0^1 \overline{K}_Y(\overline{\tau}_1,\overline{\tau}_2)\Psi^D_{jkn}(\overline{\tau}_1,\overline{\tau}_2)d\overline{\tau}_1 d\overline{\tau}_2.
\end{aligned}
\tag{44}
$$

After transition to time variable $\overline{\tau} \in [0,1]$, $\overline{\tau} = \frac{\tau-(t-T)}{T}$ at $\tau = \tau(\overline{\tau}) = T\overline{\tau} + (t-T)$, expression (3) takes the form

$$
Z(\tau) = Z(\tau(\overline{\tau})) = \overline{Z}(\overline{\tau}) = \sum_{r=1}^{N} U_r \overline{\xi}_r(\overline{\tau}) + \overline{X}(\overline{\tau}).
\tag{45}
$$

Analogously, we have

$$
V_\nu = T \cdot \overline{V}_\nu; \quad \overline{V}_\nu = \int_0^1 a_\nu(\overline{\tau})\overline{X}(\overline{\tau})d\overline{\tau} + \int_0^1 a_\nu(\overline{\tau})\overline{Y}(\overline{\tau})d\overline{\tau}, \quad D_\nu = T^2 \overline{D}_\nu, \quad \overline{D}_\nu = D[\overline{V}_\nu].
\tag{46}
$$

According to [3,5], functions $a_\nu(\overline{\tau})$ may be expressed by functions:

$$
a_1(\overline{\tau}) = g_1(\overline{\tau}), \ a_\nu(\overline{\tau}) = \sum_{\lambda=1}^{\nu-1} c_{\nu\lambda} g_\lambda(\overline{\tau}) + g_\nu(\overline{\tau}) \ (\nu = \overline{2, L}).
\tag{47}
$$

Using notations:

$$\overline{x}_\nu(\overline{\tau}) = \frac{1}{\overline{D}_\nu}\int_0^1 a_\nu(\overline{\theta})\overline{K}_X(\overline{\tau},\overline{\theta})d\overline{\theta} + \frac{1}{\overline{D}_\nu}\int_0^1 a_\nu(\overline{\theta})\overline{K}_{XY}(\overline{\tau},\overline{\theta})d\overline{\theta},\tag{48}$$

$$\overline{y}_\nu(\overline{\tau}) = \frac{1}{\overline{D}_\nu}\int_0^1 a_\nu^x(\overline{\theta})\overline{K}_{XY}(\overline{\theta},\overline{\tau})d\overline{\theta} + \frac{1}{\overline{D}_\nu}\int_0^1 a_\nu^y(\overline{\theta})\overline{K}_Y(\overline{\tau},\overline{\theta})d\overline{\theta}\tag{49}$$

we get the following formulae:

$$x_\nu(\tau) = x_\nu(\tau(\overline{\tau})) = \frac{1}{T}\overline{x}_\nu(\overline{\tau}),\; y_\nu(\tau) = y_\nu(\tau(\overline{\tau})) = \frac{1}{T_y}\overline{y}_\nu(\overline{\tau}),\tag{50}$$

$$X(\tau(\overline{\tau})) = \sum_{\nu=1}^L V_\nu x_\nu(\tau(\overline{\tau})) = \sum_{\nu=1}^L T\overline{V}_\nu\frac{1}{T}\overline{x}_\nu(\overline{\tau}) = \sum_{\nu=1}^L \overline{V}_\nu\overline{x}_\nu(\overline{\tau}),\tag{51}$$

$$Y(\tau(\overline{\tau})) = \sum_{\nu=1}^L V_\nu y_\nu(\tau(\overline{\tau})) = \sum_{\nu=1}^L T\overline{V}_\nu\frac{1}{T}\overline{y}_\nu(\overline{\tau}) = \sum_{\nu=1}^L \overline{V}_\nu\overline{y}_\nu(\overline{\tau}).\tag{52}$$

Here, RV $\overline{V}_\nu$ have zero mathematical expectations, and variances coordinate functions $\overline{x}_\nu(\overline{\tau})$ and $\overline{y}_\nu(\overline{\tau})$ are successively defined by the following formulae:

$$\overline{x}_1(\overline{\tau}) = \frac{1}{\overline{D}_1}h_1^x(\overline{\tau});\;\; \overline{x}_\nu(\overline{\tau}) = \frac{1}{\overline{D}_\nu}\left(\sum_{\lambda=1}^{\nu-1}d_{\nu\lambda}h_\lambda^x(\overline{\tau}) + h_\nu^x(\overline{\tau})\right);\tag{53}$$

$$\overline{y}_1(\overline{\tau}) = \frac{1}{\overline{D}_1}h_1^y(\overline{\tau});\;\; \overline{y}_\nu(\overline{\tau}) = \frac{1}{\overline{D}_\nu}\left(\sum_{\lambda=1}^{\nu-1}d_{\nu\lambda}h_\lambda^y(\overline{\tau}) + h_\nu^y(\overline{\tau})\right);\tag{54}$$

where

$$d_{\nu\lambda} = c_{\nu\lambda} + \sum_{\mu=\lambda+1}^{\nu-1}c_{\nu\mu}d_{\mu\lambda}\;(\lambda = \overline{1,\nu-2});\; d_{\nu,\nu-1} = c_{\nu,\nu-1};\; \nu = \overline{2,L};\tag{55}$$

$$c_{\nu 1} = -\frac{k_{\nu 1}}{\overline{D}_1}\;(\nu = \overline{2,L});\; c_{\nu\mu} = -\frac{1}{\overline{D}_\mu}\left(k_{\nu\mu} - \sum_{\lambda=1}^{\mu-1}\overline{D}_\lambda c_{\mu\lambda}c_{\nu\lambda}\right)\;(\mu = \overline{2,\nu-1};\nu = \overline{3,L});$$

$$\overline{D}_1 = k_{11};\; \overline{D}_\nu = k_{\nu\nu} - \sum_{\lambda=1}^{\nu-1}\overline{D}_\lambda|c_{\nu\lambda}|^2\;(\nu = \overline{2,L}).\tag{56}$$

Parameters $k_{\nu\mu}$ are expressed by coefficients of two-dimensional wavelet expressions of covariance functions $\overline{K}_X(\overline{\tau}_1,\overline{\tau}_2)$, $\overline{K}_{XY}(\overline{\tau}_1,\overline{\tau}_2)$, and $\overline{K}_Y(\overline{\tau}_1,\overline{\tau}_2)$

$$k_{11} = a^x + 2a^{xy} + a^y,\; k_{12} = h^x + 2h^{xy} + h^y,\; k_{21} = b^x + 2b^{xy} + b^y,$$
$$k_{22} = d_{000}^x + 2d_{000}^{xy} + d_{000}^y,\; k_{\nu\mu} = d_{jkn}^x + 2d_{jkn}^{xy} + d_{jkn}^y$$
$$(\nu = 2^j + k + 1;\; \mu = 2^j + n + 1;\; j = \overline{1,J};\; k,n = 0,1,\ldots,2^j - 1).\tag{57}$$

The other $k_{\nu\mu} = 0$.

Auxiliary functions $h_\nu^x(\overline{\tau})$, $h_\nu^y(\overline{\tau})$ are expressed by basic wavelet functions (38) and coefficients of wavelet expansions of covariance functions $\overline{K}_X(\overline{\tau}_1,\overline{\tau}_2)$, $\overline{K}_{XY}(\overline{\tau}_1,\overline{\tau}_2)$, $\overline{K}_Y(\overline{\tau}_1,\overline{\tau}_2)$:

$$h_1^x(\overline{\tau}) = (a^x + a^{xy})\varphi_{00}(\overline{\tau}) + (b^x + b^{xy})\psi_{00}(\overline{\tau}),\; h_1^y(\overline{\tau}) = (a^{xy} + a^y)\varphi_{00}(\overline{\tau}) + (b^{xy} + b^y)\psi_{00}(\overline{\tau}),$$
$$h_1^x(\overline{\tau}) = (h^x + h^{xy})\varphi_{00}(\overline{\tau}) + \left(d_{000}^x + d_{000}^{xy}\right)\psi_{00}(\overline{\tau}),\; h_1^y(\overline{\tau}) = (h^{xy} + h^y)\varphi_{00}(\overline{\tau}) + \left(d_{000}^{xy} + d_{000}^y\right)\psi_{00}(\overline{\tau}),$$
$$h_\nu^x(\overline{\tau}) = \sum_{k=0}^{2^j-1}\left(d_{jkn}^x + d_{jkn}^{xy}\right)\psi_{jk}(\overline{\tau})\;(\nu = \overline{3,L};\; \nu = 2^j + n + 1;\; n = 0,1,\ldots,2^j - 1).\tag{58}$$

Considering (45), (46), we get

$$Z_\nu = T\overline{Z}_\nu, \ \overline{Z}_\nu = \sum_{r=1}^{N} \overline{\alpha}_{\nu r} U_r + \overline{V}_\nu, \tag{59}$$

$$\alpha_{\nu r} = T\overline{\alpha}_{\nu r}, \ \overline{\alpha}_{\nu r} = \int_0^1 a_\nu(\overline{\tau})\overline{\xi}_r(\overline{\tau})d\overline{\tau}. \tag{60}$$

If functions $\xi_1(\tau),\ldots,\xi_N(\tau) \in L^2[t-T,t]$, then $\overline{\xi}_1(\overline{\tau}),\ldots,\overline{\xi}_N(\overline{\tau}) \in L^2[0,1]$ and have wavelet expansions

$$\overline{\xi}_r(\overline{\tau}) = a_r^\xi \varphi_{00}(\overline{\tau}) + \sum_{j=0}^{J} \sum_{k=0}^{2^j-1} d_{rjk}^\xi \psi_{jk}(\overline{\tau}) \ (r=1,\ldots,N), \tag{61}$$

$$a_r^\xi = \int_0^1 \overline{\xi}_r(\overline{\tau})\varphi_{00}(\overline{\tau})d\overline{\tau}, \ d_{rjk}^\xi = \int_0^1 \overline{\xi}_r(\overline{\tau})\psi_{jk}(\overline{\tau})d\overline{\tau}, \tag{62}$$

Using notation (38) we get from (61), (62)

$$\overline{\xi}_r(\overline{\tau}) = c_{r1}^\xi g_1(\overline{\tau}) + \sum_{\nu=2}^{L} c_{r\nu}^\xi g_\nu(\overline{\tau}) \ (r=1,\ldots,N), \tag{63}$$

$$(\nu = 2^j + k + 1; j = \overline{0,J}; k = 0,1,\ldots,2^j-1)$$

$$c_{r1}^\xi = a_r^\xi, \ c_{r\nu}^\xi = d_{rjk}^\xi. \tag{64}$$

From (60), (62), (64), we have

$$\overline{\alpha}_{1r} = c_{r1}^\xi; \ \overline{\alpha}_{\nu r} = \sum_{\lambda=1}^{\nu-1} c_{\nu\lambda} c_{r\lambda}^\xi + c_{r\nu}^\xi \ (\nu = \overline{2,L}). \tag{65}$$

Finally, using formulae

$$\sum_{\nu=1}^{L} Z_\nu x_\nu(\tau) = \sum_{\nu=1}^{L} (T\overline{Z}_\nu)\left(\frac{1}{T}\overline{x}_\nu(\overline{\tau})\right) = \sum_{\nu=1}^{L} \overline{Z}_\nu \overline{x}_\nu(\overline{\tau}) \tag{66}$$

we get the required WLCE for StP $Z(\tau)$ $(\tau \in [t-T,t])$:

$$Z(\tau) = Z(\tau(\overline{\tau})) = \overline{Z}(\overline{\tau}) = \sum_{\nu=1}^{L} \overline{Z}_\nu \overline{x}_\nu(\overline{\tau}). \tag{67}$$

In basic Formulae (23)–(31), the parameters are expressed as follows:

$$\eta_0 = \sum_{\nu=1}^{L} z_\nu y_\nu(\tau) = \sum_{\nu=1}^{L} (T\overline{z}_\nu)\left(\frac{1}{T}\overline{y}_\nu(\overline{\tau})\right) = \sum_{\nu=1}^{L} \overline{z}_\nu \overline{y}_\nu(\overline{\tau}), \tag{68}$$

$$\eta_r = \sum_{\nu=1}^{L} \frac{\alpha_{\nu r} z_\nu}{D_\nu} = \sum_{\nu=1}^{L} \frac{(T\overline{\alpha}_{\nu r})(T\overline{z}_\nu)}{T^2 \overline{D}_\nu} = \sum_{\nu=1}^{L} \frac{\overline{\alpha}_{\nu r}\overline{z}_\nu}{\overline{D}_\nu} \ (r = \overline{1,N}), \tag{69}$$

$$b_{p0} = \sum_{\nu=1}^{L} \alpha_{\nu p} y_\nu(\tau) = \sum_{\nu=1}^{L} (T\overline{\alpha}_{\nu p})\left(\frac{1}{T}\overline{y}_\nu(\overline{\tau})\right) = \sum_{\nu=1}^{L} \overline{\alpha}_{\nu p}\overline{y}_\nu(\overline{\tau}), \tag{70}$$

$$b_{pq} = \sum_{\nu=1}^{L} \frac{1}{D_\nu}\alpha_{\nu p}\alpha_{\nu q} = \sum_{\nu=1}^{L} \frac{1}{T^2 \overline{D}_\nu}(T\overline{\alpha}_{\nu p})(T\overline{\alpha}_{\nu q}) = \sum_{\nu=1}^{L} \frac{1}{\overline{D}_\nu}\overline{\alpha}_{\nu p}\overline{\alpha}_{\nu q}. \tag{71}$$

Note that expression $P_0^W(t,\eta_0,\ldots,\eta_N)$ depends on fixed values $\overline{z}_1,\ldots,\overline{z}_L$ of $\overline{Z}_1,\overline{Z}_2,\ldots,\overline{Z}_L$.

So, the WLCE method is defined by Formulae (67)–(71) at conditions (61)–(65).

5. Synthesis of a Linear Optimal System for Criterion of the Maximum Probability That Signal Will Not Exceed a Particular Value in Absolute Magnitude

Conditional risk $\rho(A|W)$ in case (2) is equal from interval to probability of error exit

$$\rho(A|W) = E[l(W, W^*)|W] = P(|W^* - W| \geq w(t)) = 1 - P(|W^* - W| < w(t)). \quad (72)$$

A priori density $f(u) = f(u_1, \ldots, u_N)$ of RV $U = [U_1\, U_2\, \ldots\, U_N]^T$ is defined by formula

$$f(u_1, \ldots, u_N) = \left[(2\pi)^N |K|\right]^{-\frac{1}{2}} \exp\left\{-\frac{1}{2} \sum_{p,q=1}^{N} c_{pq} u_p u_q\right\} \quad (73)$$

where K is the covariance matrix of U, c_{pq} $(p, q = \overline{1, N})$ is K^{-1} elements.

Let us find minimum of the integral

$$I(P^W, \eta_0, \ldots, \eta_N, t) = \left[(2\pi)^N |K|\right]^{-\frac{1}{2}}$$
$$\times \iint\limits_{|\sum\limits_{r=1}^{N} u_r(\zeta_r(t)-b_{r0})+\eta_0-P^W|\geq w(t)} \exp\left\{\sum_{r=1}^{N} \eta_r u_r - \frac{1}{2} \sum_{p,q=1}^{N} (c_{pq} + b_{pq}) u_p u_q\right\} du_1 \ldots du_N. \quad (74)$$

Integral (74) is propositional to the probability of the normal point $(U_1, U_2, \ldots, U_N)$, and does not get into the subspace defined by inequality $|\sum\limits_{r=1}^{N} u_r(\zeta_r(t) - b_{r0}) + \eta_0 - P^W| < w(t)$. This probability has a minimum, if its mathematical expectation lies on line $\sum\limits_{r=1}^{N} u_r(\zeta_r(t) - b_{r0}) + \eta_0 - P^W = 0$. Normal density has maximum mathematical expectation. So, for definition of mathematical expectation, it is enough to equate partial derivatives in (74) to zero for $u_1, u_2, \ldots, u_N$. The (74) minimization value $P_0(t, \eta_0, \ldots, \eta_N)$ is equal to:

$$P_0^W = \sum_{r=1}^{N} \lambda_r(t)(\zeta_r(t) - b_{r0}) + \eta_0. \quad (75)$$

For solution of functions $\lambda_1(t), \lambda_2(t), \ldots, \lambda_N(t)$ it is necessary to solve the system of linear algebraic equations:

$$\sum_{p=1}^{N} \lambda_p(t)(c_{pq} + b_{pq}) = \eta_q(t) \, (q = \overline{1, N}). \quad (76)$$

In matrix form, Equation (76) is as follows:

$$C_1 \cdot \Lambda = A_1^T \cdot Z_1 \quad (77)$$

where

$$C_1 = (c_{ij} + b_{ij})_{i,j=1}^{N}, \; A_1 = \left(\frac{\overline{\alpha}_{ij}}{\overline{D}_i}\right)_{i,j=1}^{L,N}, \; Z_1 = [\overline{z}_1, \overline{z}_2, \ldots, \overline{z}_L]^T, \; \Lambda = [\lambda_1(t), \ldots, \lambda_N(t)]^T. \quad (78)$$

Hence,

$$\Lambda = C_1^{-1} \cdot A_1^T \cdot Z_1. \quad (79)$$

Using notations

$$B_1 = \begin{pmatrix} \zeta_1(t) - b_{10} \\ \dots \\ \zeta_N(t) - b_{N0} \end{pmatrix}, \ Y_1 = \begin{pmatrix} \overline{y}_1(t) \\ \dots \\ \overline{y}_N(t) \end{pmatrix} \tag{80}$$

we get the Bayes optimal operator in matrix form:

$$A = B_1^T \cdot C_1^{-1} \cdot A_1^T + Y_1^T. \tag{81}$$

The Bayes optimal estimate of output StP is defined by

$$W^*(t) = A \cdot Z_1. \tag{82}$$

The mean risk is at

$$R(A) = \left[(2\pi)^{N+L} \cdot D_1 \cdot \dots \cdot D_L \cdot |K| \right]^{-\frac{1}{2}} \iint\limits_{|\sum\limits_{r=1}^{N} u_r(\zeta_r(t)-b_{r0})+\eta_0-P_0^W| \geq w(t)} \exp\{-\tfrac{1}{2}\sum\limits_{v=1}^{L} \tfrac{z_v^2}{D_v} -$$

$$- \sum\limits_{v=1}^{L}\sum\limits_{r=1}^{N} \tfrac{\alpha_{vr}}{D_v} z_v u_r - \tfrac{1}{2} \sum\limits_{p,q=1}^{N} \left(c_{pq} + b_{pq} \right) u_p u_q \} du_1 \dots du_N dz_1 \dots dz_L =$$

$$= 1 - \left[(2\pi)^{N+L} \cdot D_1 \cdot \dots \cdot D_L \cdot |K| \right]^{-\frac{1}{2}} \iint\limits_{|\sum\limits_{r=1}^{N} u_r(\zeta_r(t)-b_{r0})+\eta_0-P_0^W| < w(t)} \exp\{-\tfrac{1}{2}\sum\limits_{v=1}^{L} \tfrac{z_v^2}{D_v} -$$

$$- \sum\limits_{v=1}^{L}\sum\limits_{r=1}^{N} \tfrac{\alpha_{vr}}{D_v} z_v u_r - \tfrac{1}{2} \sum\limits_{p,q=1}^{N} \left(c_{pq} + b_{pq} \right) u_p u_q \} du_1 \dots du_N dz_1 \dots dz_L. \tag{83}$$

Equations (75)–(83) define the method of synthesis of a linear system for criterion of maximum probability that the signal will not exceed a particular value in absolute magnitude.

New results generalize the following particular results [27–31] for different Bayes criteria in OStS:

- Mean square error;
- Complex statistical criteria;
- Criterion of maximum probability that the signal not exceed particular value in absolute magnitude.

6. Example

The designed software tools based on results of Section 5 provide the possibility to compare mathematical models of different classes of linear OStS, its optimal instrumental potential accuracy in case of stochastic factors and noises.

Let us consider the extrapolator for a radar-location device described by the following equations:

$$Z(\tau) = U_1 + U_2\tau + X(\tau), \ W(t) = U_1 + U_2(t + \triangle), \ \tau \in [t - T, t] \tag{84}$$

Here, U_1 and U_2 are random calibration parameters for the calibration device, and X is the colored noise. For the criterion of the maximum probability that the signal will not exceed a particular value a in absolute magnitude, we use algorithm (82).

Suppose that:

- The noise $X(t)$ is normal $EX(t) = 0$, $K_X(\tau_1, \tau_2) = D \exp\{-\alpha|\tau_2 - \tau_1|\}$;
- Random parameters U_1, U_2 are normal with joint density:

$$f(u_1, u_2) = \frac{\sqrt{c_{11}c_{22} - c_{12}^2}}{2\pi} \exp\left\{ -\frac{1}{2} \sum\limits_{p,q=1}^{2} c_{pq} u_p u_q \right\} \tag{85}$$

(c_{pq} are elements of the inverse covariance matrix K^{-1});

- Input data:

$t \in [9; 18], \quad T = 8, \quad \triangle = 1,$

$D = 1, \quad \alpha = 1, K = \begin{bmatrix} 1 & 0 \\ 0 & 1 \end{bmatrix},$

$\xi_1(\tau) = 1, \xi_2(\tau) = \tau; \xi_1(t) = 1, \xi_2(t) = t + \triangle,$

$J = 2, L = 8.$

A typical realization method demonstrates high accuracy in Figure 1. As practice for quick calibration of typical devices we use, algorithms more simple than (82) were developed, computed and compared. This information is necessary for passport documentation.

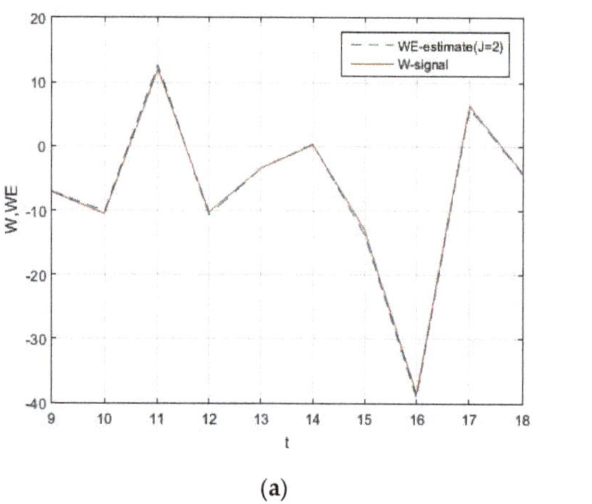

(a)

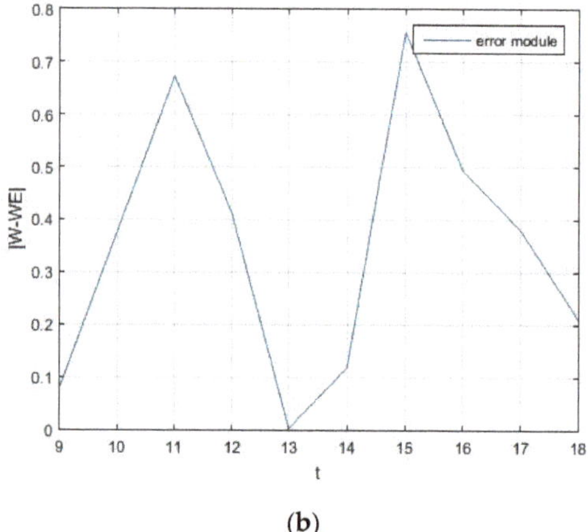

(b)

Figure 1. Graphs of: (**a**) signal extrapolation W and estimate extrapolation W^*; (**b**) module $|W^* - W|$.

The extrapolator takes values from -38.6099 to 11.9854. At the same time, the extrapolator error modulus does not exceed 0.7568 (Figure 1).

7. Conclusions

This article is devoted to problems with optimizing observable stochastic systems based on wavelet canonical expansions. Section 2 is devoted to different Bayes criteria in terms of risk theory. Following [1,2], in Section 3, basic formulae for optimal Bayes synthesis based on canonical expansions are given. Section 4 is dedicated to the solution of a general optimization problem using wavelet canonical expansions in case of complex nonstationary linear systems. In Section 5, a basic algorithm is given for the criterion of maximal probability that the signal will not exceed a particular value in absolute magnitude. An example of a radar-location extrapolator device is discussed.

The developed optimization methodology "quick probabilistic analytical numerical optimization" does not use statistical Monte Carlo methods.

Directions of future generalizations and implementations:

- New models of scalar and vector OStS (nonlinear, with parametric noises, etc.):
- New classes of the Bayes criteria.

The research was carried out using the infrastructure of the Shared Research Facilities "High Performance Computing and Big Data" (CKP "Informatics") of FRC CSC RAS (Moscow).

Author Contributions: Conceptualization, I.S.; methodology, I.S., V.S., T.K.; software, E.K., T.K. All authors have read and agreed to the published version of the manuscript.

Funding: The research received no external funding.

Institutional Review Board Statement: Not applicable.

Informed Consent Statement: Not applicable.

Data Availability Statement: Not applicable.

Conflicts of Interest: The authors declare no conflict of interest.

Abbreviations

$X(t)$	random function, noise
$Y(t)$	random function, noise
$EX(t)$	mathematical expectation of random function $X(t)$
$Z(t)$	input stochastic process
$W(t)$	output stochastic process
$W^*(t)$	estimator $W(t)$
$l(W, W^*)$	loss function
A	system operator
$\rho(A|W)$	conditional risk
$R(A)$	mean risk
U_r	random parameter
$\xi_r(\tau), \zeta_r(\tau)$	structural functions
V_ν	random variable of canonical expansion of random vector $\begin{bmatrix} X(t) & Y(t) \end{bmatrix}^T$
$x_\nu(t)$	coordinate function of canonical expansion of random function $X(t)$
$y_\nu(t)$	coordinate function of canonical expansion of random function $Y(t)$
D_ν	variance of random variable V_ν
$K_X(t_1, t_2)$	covariance function of random function $X(t)$
Z_ν	random variable of canonical expansion of StP $Z(t)$
$f(u)$	probability density of random vector $U = \begin{bmatrix} U_1 & U_2 & \dots & U_N \end{bmatrix}^T$
$f_1(u|z_1, z_2, \dots)$	conditional probability density of random vector $U = \begin{bmatrix} U_1 & U_2 & \dots & U_N \end{bmatrix}^T$ relative to random variables Z_ν
$f_V(v_1, v_2, \dots)$	joint probability density of random variables V_ν
$f_2(z_1, z_2, \dots |u)$	conditional probability density of random variables Z_ν relative to random vector $U = \begin{bmatrix} U_1 & U_2 & \dots & U_N \end{bmatrix}^T$
$\varphi_{00}(t)$	Haar scaling function
$\psi_{00}(\overline{\tau})$	Haar mother wavelet
CE	Canonical Expansion
CsC	complex statistical criteria
OStS	observable Stochastic System
RV	random variables
StP	Stochastic Process
StS	Stochastic System
WLCE	Wavelet Canonical Expansion

References

1. Pugachev, V.S. *Theory of Random Functions and Its Applications to Control Problems*; Pergamon Press: Oxford, UK, 1965; 833p.
2. Pugachev, V.S.; Sinitsyn, I.N. *Stochastic Systems Theory and Applications*; World Scientific: Singapore, 2001.
3. Sinitsyn, I. *Canonical Expansion of Random Functions and Its Application to Scientific Computer-Aided Support*; Torus Press: Moscow, Russia, 2009. (In Russian)
4. Sinitsyn, I.N.; Sinitsyn, V.I.; Korepanov, E.R.; Belousov, V.V.; Sergeev, I.V. Development of Algorithmic Support for the Analysis of Stochastic Systems Based on Canonical Expansions of Random Functions. *Autom. Remote Control* **2011**, *72*, 405–415. [CrossRef]
5. Sinitsyn, I.N.; Sinitsyn, V.I.; Korepanov, E.R.; Konashenkova, T.D. Software Tools for Analysis and Synthesis of Stochastic Systems with High Availability (IV). *Highly Available Syst.* **2017**, *13*, 55–69. (In Russian)
6. Sinitsyn, I.N.; Sinitsyn, V.I.; Korepanov, E.R.; Konashenkova, T.D. Software Tools for Analysis and Synthesis of Stochastic Systems with High Availability (V). *Highly Available Syst.* **2018**, *14*, 59–70. (In Russian)
7. Sinitsyn, I.N.; Sinitsyn, V.I.; Korepanov, E.R.; Konashenkova, T.D. Software Tools for Analysis and Synthesis of Stochastic Systems with High Availability (VI). *Highly Available Syst.* **2018**, *14*, 40–56. (In Russian)
8. Sinitsyn, I.N.; Sinitsyn, V.I.; Korepanov, E.R.; Konashenkova, T.D. Software Tools for Analysis and Synthesis of Stochastic Systems with High Availability (VII). *Highly Available Syst.* **2019**, *15*, 47–61. (In Russian)

9. Arora, S.; Singh Brar, Y.; Kumar, S. Haar Wavelet Matrices for the Numerical Solutions of Differential Equations. *Int. J. Comput. Appl.* **2014**, *97*, 33–36. [CrossRef]
10. Stromberg, J.O. A modified Franklin system and higher-order spline systems on Rn as unconditional bases for Hardy spaces. In Proceedings of the Conference on Harmonic Analysis in Honor of Antoni Zygmund, Chicago, IL, USA, 23–28 March 1981; pp. 475–494.
11. Grossmann, A.; Morlet, J. Decomposition of Hardy Functions into Square Integrable Wavelets of Constant Shape. *SIAM J. Math. Anal.* **1984**, *15*, 723–736. [CrossRef]
12. Meyer, Y. *Analysis at Urbana 1: Analysis in Function Spaces*; Cambridge University Press: Cambridge, UK, 1989.
13. Mallat, S.G. Multiresolution approximations and wavelet orthonormal bases of L^2 (R). *Trans. Am. Math. Soc.* **1989**, *315*, 69–87.
14. Daubechies, I. Orthonormal bases of compactly supported wavelets. *Commun. Pure Appl. Math.* **1988**, *41*, 909–996. [CrossRef]
15. Strang, G. Wavelets and dilation equations: A brief introduction. *SIAM Rev.* **1989**, *31*, 614–627. [CrossRef]
16. Hsiao, C.H. Haar wavelet approach to linear stiff systems. *Math. Comput. Simul.* **2004**, *64*, 561–567. [CrossRef]
17. Daubechies, I. *Ten Lectures on Wavelets*; SIAM: Philadelphia, PA, USA, 1992.
18. Chui, C.K. *An Introduction to Wavelets*; Academic Press: Boston, MA, USA, 1992.
19. Lepik, U. Numerical solution of differential equations using Haar wavelets. *Math. Comput. Simul.* **2005**, *68*, 127–143. [CrossRef]
20. Lepik, U. Numerical Solution of Evolution Equations by the Haar Wavelet Method. *Appl. Math. Comput.* **2007**, *185*, 695–704. [CrossRef]
21. Chen, C.F.; Hsiao, C.H. Haar Wavelet Method for Solving Lumped and Distributed Parameter Systems. *IEE Proc. Control Theory Appl.* **1987**, *144*, 87–94. [CrossRef]
22. Hsiao, C.H. State Analysis of Linear Time Delayed Systems via Haar Wavelets. *Math. Comput. Simul.* **1997**, *44*, 457–470. [CrossRef]
23. Cattani, C. Haar Wavelets Based Technique in Evolution Problems. *Proc.-Est. Acad. Sci. Phys. Math.* **2004**, *1*, 45–63. [CrossRef]
24. Hariharan, G. An Overview of Haar Wavelet Method for Solving Differential and Integral Equations. *World Appl. Sci. J.* **2013**, *23*, 1–14.
25. Hsiao, C.H.; Wu, S.P. Numerical Solution of Time-Varying Functional Differential Equations via Haar Wavelets. *Appl. Math. Comput.* **2007**, *188*, 1049–1058. [CrossRef]
26. Sinitsyn, I.; Sinitsyn, V.; Korepanov, E.; Konashenkova, T. Wavelet Modeling of Control Stochastic Systems at Complex Shock Disturbances. *Mathematics* **2021**, *9*, 2544. [CrossRef]
27. Sinitsyn, I.; Sinitsyn, V.; Korepanov, E.; Konashenkova, T. Optimization of Linear Stochastic Systems Based on Canonical Wavelet Expansions. *Autom. Remote Control* **2020**, *81*, 2046–2061. [CrossRef]
28. Sinitsyn, I.N.; Sinitsyn, V.I.; Korepanov, E.R.; Konashenkova, T.D. Software Tools for Analysis and Synthesis of Stochastic Systems with High Availability (XII). *Highly Available Syst.* **2021**, *17*, 26–44. (In Russian)
29. Sinitsyn, I.N.; Sinitsyn, V.I.; Korepanov, E.R.; Konashenkova, T.D. Software Tools for Analysis and Synthesis of Stochastic Systems with High Availability (XI). *Highly Available Syst.* **2021**, *17*, 25–40. (In Russian) [CrossRef]
30. Sinitsyn, I.N.; Sinitsyn, V.I.; Korepanov, E.R.; Konashenkova, T.D. Software Tools for Analysis and Synthesis of Stochastic Systems with High Availability (XIII). *Highly Available Syst.* **2021**, *17*, 16–35. (In Russian) [CrossRef]
31. Sinitsyn, I.N.; Sinitsyn, V.I.; Korepanov, E.R.; Konashenkova, T.D. Software Tools for Analysis and Synthesis of Stochastic Systems with High Availability (XV). *Highly Available Syst.* **2022**, *18*, 47–61. (In Russian) [CrossRef]

 *mathematics*

Article

Identification of Quadratic Volterra Polynomials in the "Input–Output" Models of Nonlinear Systems

Yury Voscoboynikov [1,2], Svetlana Solodusha [3,*], Evgeniia Markova [3], Ekaterina Antipina [3,4] and Vasilisa Boeva [1]

[1] Department of Applied Mathematics, Novosibirsk State University of Architecture and Civil Engineering, 630008 Novosibirsk, Russia; voscob@mail.ru (Y.V.); v.boyeva@sibstrin.ru (V.B.)
[2] Department of Automation, Novosibirsk State Technical University, 630087 Novosibirsk, Russia
[3] Department of Applied Mathematics, Melentiev Energy Systems Institute, Siberian Branch of Russian Academy of Sciences, 664033 Irkutsk, Russia; markova@isem.irk.ru (E.M.); kate19961231@gmail.com (E.A.)
[4] Department of Mathematical Analysis and Differential Equations, Irkutsk State University, 664003 Irkutsk, Russia
* Correspondence: solodusha@isem.irk.ru

Abstract: In this paper, we propose a new algorithm for constructing an integral model of a nonlinear dynamic system of the "input–output" type in the form of a quadratic segment of the Volterra integro-power series (polynomial). We consider nonparametric identification of models using physically realizable piecewise linear test signals in the time domain. The advantage of the presented approach is to obtain explicit formulas for calculating the transient responses (Volterra kernels), which determine the unique solution of the Volterra integral equations of the first kind with two variable integration limits. The numerical method proposed in the paper for solving the corresponding equations includes the use of smoothing splines. An important result is that the constructed identification algorithm has a low methodological error.

Keywords: nonparametric identification; dynamic system; integral model; Volterra equations; smoothing cubic splines; selection of the smoothing option

MSC: 45D05

Citation: Voscoboynikov, Y.; Solodusha, S.; Markova, E.; Antipina, E.; Boeva, V. Identification of Quadratic Volterra Polynomials in the "Input–Output" Models of Nonlinear Systems. *Mathematics* 2022, 10, 1836. https://doi.org/10.3390/math10111836

Academic Editors: Natalia Bakhtadze, Igor Yadykin, Andrei Torgashov and Nikolay Korgin

Received: 12 April 2022
Accepted: 24 May 2022
Published: 26 May 2022

Publisher's Note: MDPI stays neutral with regard to jurisdictional claims in published maps and institutional affiliations.

1. Introduction

The development of the theory of dynamical systems, taking into account the specifics of applied problems, aims to create new mathematical methods. This paper is devoted to the develop mathematical tools for studying inverse problems in the theory of dynamical systems. The work aims to develop a methodology and algorithms for identifying Volterra polynomials (finite segments of Volterra series) [1].

$$y(t) = \sum_{n=1}^{N} \int_0^t \ldots \int_0^t K_n(t, s_1, \ldots, s_n) \prod_k^n x(s_k) ds_k, \, t \in [0, T]. \tag{1}$$

The Volterra integro-power series is well known in the theory of mathematical modeling of nonlinear dynamic systems of the "input–output" type. However, modern and classical studies in this area do not provide a universal mathematical apparatus for studying problems with restrictions on the dynamic characteristics of systems.

Reference [2] contains an extensive list of references on methods for identifying nonlinear objects using Volterra integral equations. References [3–7] are devoted to methods for constructing dynamic models using Volterra polynomials. Models based on the Volterra theory are used to describe stochastic systems [8], as well as for the structural identification of nonlinear dynamic systems [9]. A systematic approach to modeling nonlinear dynamic systems by formalizing the relationship between input $x(t)$ and output $y(t)$ was first implemented by Norbert Wiener [10]. He applied the Volterra series in the analysis of nonlinear electronic circuits. He developed efficient identification algorithms for the case of an input signal in the form of Gaussian white noise. Wiener's research was continued in the works of Marmarelis, Schetzen, Rugh, and other researchers (see, for example, the reviews in [11,12]). The system responses to test signals in the form of ideal white noise are used to identify the Wiener kernels. In practice, the implementation of such input actions is carried out with inevitable errors, which are compensated by choosing the optimal range in test disturbances [13]. When solving inverse quantum mechanical problems, researchers use wave functions [14] to construct Volterra integral models. The identification of Volterra kernels is based on minimizing the root-mean-square error from the response of the dynamic system tested. This approach is associated with the extreme complexity of practical implementation [15].

In this regard, they strive to achieve a simplification of the methods (see, for example, [16–19]). In particular, the authors of [18] implemented the case where Volterra kernels are assumed to be separable,

$$K_i(s_1,\ldots,s_i) = \prod_{n=1}^{i} g(s_n), i = \overline{1,3}, \tag{2}$$

as well as the satisfiability of a priori conditions,

$$K_n(s_1,\ldots,s_n) = 0, n > 3. \tag{3}$$

Reference [16] considered a modified discrete analog of the cubic Volterra polynomial.

$$\begin{aligned}
y(t_i) = & \sum_{m_1=0}^{N_1-1} K_1(t_{m_1})x(t_{i-m_1}) + \sum_{m_1=0}^{N_2-1}\sum_{m_2=m_1}^{N_2-1} K_2(t_{m_1},t_{m_2})x(t_{i-m_1})x(t_{i-m_2}) + \\
& + \sum_{m_1=0}^{N_3-1}\sum_{m_2=m_1}^{N_3-1}\sum_{m_3=m_2}^{N_3-1} K_3(t_{m_1},t_{m_2},t_{m_3})x(t_{i-m_1})x(t_{i-m_2})x(t_{i-m_3}),
\end{aligned} \tag{4}$$

where the symmetric kernels K_2 and K_3 are defined only on one of the subdomains $0 \leq m_1 \leq m_2 \leq N_2 - 1$ and $0 \leq m_1 \leq m_2 \leq m_3 \leq N_3 - 1$, respectively. To reduce computational costs, the authors of [16] proposed a transition from (4) to relations

$$y(t_i) = \sum_{m_1=0}^{N_1-1} K_1(t_{m_1})x(t_{i-m_1}) + \sum_{m_1=0}^{N_2-1}\sum_{m_2=m_1}^{N_2-1} K_2(t_{m_1},t_{m_2})x(t_{i-m_1})x(t_{i-m_2}) + \sum_{m=0}^{N_3-1} \widetilde{K}_3(t_m)x^3(t_{i-m}) \tag{5}$$

or

$$y(t_i) = \sum_{m_1=0}^{N_1-1} K_1(t_{m_1})x(t_{i-m_1}) + \sum_{m=0}^{N_2-1} \widetilde{K}_2(t_m)x^2(t_{i-m}) + \sum_{m=0}^{N_3-1} \widetilde{K}_3(t_m)x^3(t_{i-m}). \tag{6}$$

It depends on the statistical properties of the input signals. In this case, they solve the problem of restoring the functions $\widetilde{K}_n$ of one variable instead of the problem of determining in (4) the functions K_n, $n = 2,3$, of many variables in (5) and (6). Moreover, instead of searching for $K_n(t,s_1,\ldots,s_n)$ on the entire domain of definition $0 \leq s_1,\ldots,s_n \leq t \leq T$, researchers confine themselves to the values of the function at fixed values $s_1 = s_2 = \ldots = s_n = t$, $t \in [0, T]$. In particular, this approach was applied in [20] (p. 1387) and [21] (p. 1078). The critical review of [22] (pp. 178–179) explained the difference between these problems in detail using the approaches described in [23,24] as an example.

As noted in [25], "for the presentation of information in the time domain, the expediency of using pulsed and stepped test signals is obvious". A method based on the

δ-functions use was proposed in [26] and developed later in [27]. It suggests using the $(n-1)$-parametric family,

$$x_{\omega_1,\ldots,\omega_{n-1}}(t) = \sum_{j=0}^{n-1} \delta(t - \omega_j), \omega_0 = 0, \omega_j \geq 0, \sum_{j=0}^{n-1} \omega_j \leq t \leq T, \tag{7}$$

where $\delta(s)$ is the Dirac δ-function,

$$\delta(s) = \begin{cases} 0, s \neq 0, \\ \infty, s = 0, \end{cases}$$

as test actions for identifying the $K_n(s_1, \ldots, s_n)$.

A discrete analog of this approach is the numerical algorithm proposed in [28]. Note that the technique based on (6) has a limited scope. An explanation for this can be found in [29] (p. 142): "... this simple idea is impulse-response analysis. Its basic weakness is that many physical processes do not allow pulse inputs ... Moreover, such input could make the system exhibit nonlinear effect that would disturb the linearized behavior we have set out to model". Readers can find a detailed review of identification methods based on impulse disturbances [27,30].

Let us now turn to methods based on the application of Heaviside functions $e(t)$. Reference [31] considered an approach related to approximating on $[0, T]$ a periodic test signal by discretely given stepwise one with a constant quantization step. It is assumed the initial continuous input signal has a constant period T. This technique was further developed in [32,33], in which

$$x_{\omega_1,\ldots,\omega_{n-1}}(t) = \sum_{j=1}^{n} C_{\omega_j} \alpha e(t - \omega_j), \omega_j \geq 0, \sum_{j=1}^{n} \omega_j \leq t \leq T,$$

was used as the test signal for identifying $K_n, n \geq 2$, where α is the signal amplitude (height), and C_{ω_j} is a logical variable equal to zero if

$$\omega_j = 0.$$

In [34], a modification was made for a dynamical system with two inputs. Here, the identification process included a heuristic algorithm for dividing the system response $y(t)$ into components due to the influence of a separate integral term of the quadratic Volterra model.

In this paper, we consider dynamic systems, the transient characteristics of which are presented in the time domain. The possibility of scaling in time makes it possible to study fast processes that are typical for many technical (energy) systems. The method of finding the transient characteristics of the system is deterministic. Fewer data are required to formalize the mathematical model in comparison with the probabilistic method. The collection of initial data occurs during the execution of an active experiment, which implies the possibility of influencing the system with test input signals. In comparison with a passive experiment (observation), this method allows one to reduce the time for collecting initial data and specify the type of test signal.

Reference [3] presented a method for identifying Volterra kernels using a combination of Heaviside functions with a deviating argument as test signals. Its advantage lies in the transition from the original problem to the solution of such special multidimensional Volterra equations of the first kind with variable upper and lower integration limits, which have explicit inversion formulas. The scope of this technique for modeling the dynamics of real-life technical objects is limited by the complexity of the formation of piecewise constant test signals. Reference [35] considered the possibility of using test signals of a piecewise linear form,

$$x(t) \equiv x_v(t) = \begin{cases} 0, & t \le 0, \\ \frac{t}{v}, & 0 < t \le v, \\ 1, & t > v, \end{cases} \tag{8}$$

in the problem of identifying a two-dimensional continuum of unknowns from a linear Volterra equation of the first kind with a nonstationary kernel. Figure 1 shows the form of the input signal (8).

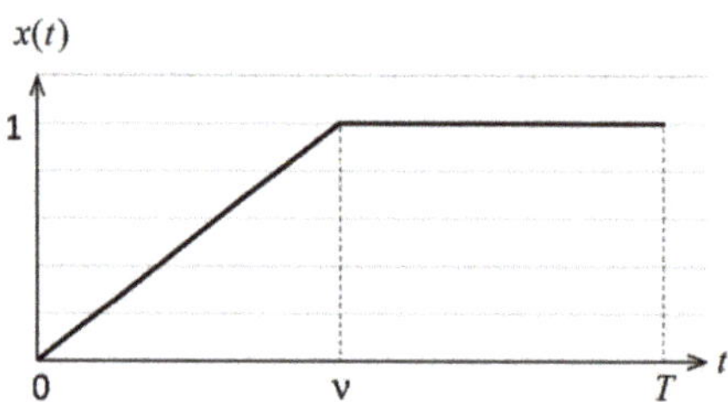

Figure 1. The form of the input signal (8).

The chosen modification of the input signals simplifies their formation in practice, and the distinguished Volterra integral equations of the first kind, as before, have a unique solution in the class of continuous functions.

The identification method was developed to further apply it for numerical modeling the process of automatic simulation of the nonlinear dynamics of heat and electric power industry objects based on Volterra polynomials with a vector input.

The purpose of this work is, firstly, to use the reserve for increasing the accuracy of constructing an integral model, presented as a modified quadratic Volterra polynomial, through the use of piecewise linear signals close to real-life dynamic systems, and secondly, to develop measurement noise-resistant algorithms for identifying functions two variables.

The paper is organized as follows: Section 2 describes the technique for building an integral model using piecewise linear test signals. It also presents an example illustrating the effect of increasing the accuracy of modeling the linear term by applying piecewise linear signals. Section 3 contains a numerical algorithm for identifying the quadratic term of the Volterra series based on smoothing cubic splines. Section 4 considers the implementation of the numerical solution algorithm using the quadrature method. Section 5 suggests directions for future work. Section 6 contains the main results.

2. Method for Constructing a Quadratic Volterra Polynomial

Let us consider a quadratic model containing a linear nonstationary component,

$$y(t) = \int_0^t K_1(t,s)x(s)ds + \int_0^t \int_0^t K_2(s_1,s_2)x(t-s_1)x(t-s_2)ds_1 ds_2, t \in [0,T]. \tag{9}$$

To identify the Volterra kernels $K_1(t,s), 0 \le s \le t \le T, K_2(s_1,s_2), 0 \le s_1,s_2 \le t \le T,$ the authors of [36] used test signals

$$x(t) \equiv x_v^{\alpha_{1,2}}(t) = \alpha_{1,2}(e(t) - e(t-v)), 0 \le v \le t \le T, \tag{10}$$

where $\alpha_1 \ne \alpha_2$. Figure 2 shows the form of the input signal (10) when the signal amplitude is equal to 1.

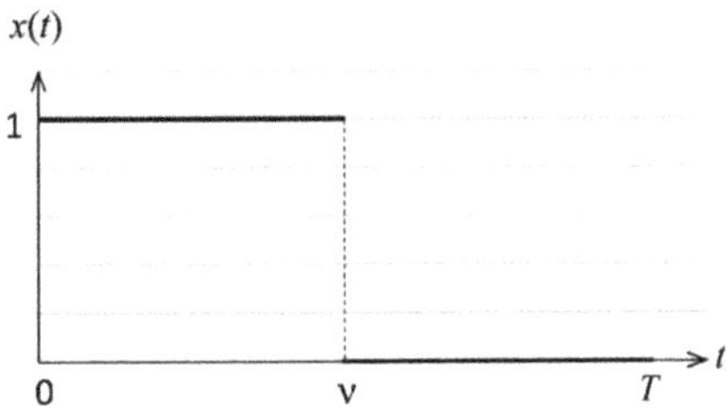

Figure 2. The form of the input signal (10).

Substituting (10) in (9) leads to the following system:

$$\alpha_1 \int_0^v K_1(t,s)ds + \alpha_1^2 \int_{t-v}^t \int_{t-v}^t K_2(s_1,s_2)ds_1ds_2 = y^{\alpha_1}(t,v),$$
$$\alpha_2 \int_0^v K_1(t,s)ds + \alpha_2^2 \int_{t-v}^t \int_{t-v}^t K_2(s_1,s_2)ds_1ds_2 = y^{\alpha_2}(t,v),$$
(11)

where $\alpha_1 \neq \alpha_2, 0 \leq v \leq t \leq T$, which implies that

$$K_1(t,v) = f'_{1v}(t,v),$$
(12)

$$K_2(t,t-v) = \frac{1}{2}\left(f''_{2tv}(t,v) + f''_{2v^2}(t,v)\right),$$
(13)

where

$$f_1(t,v) = \frac{\alpha_2^2 y^{\alpha_1}(t,v) - \alpha_1^2 y^{\alpha_2}(t,v)}{\alpha_1\alpha_2(\alpha_2 - \alpha_1)},$$
(14)

$$f_2(t,v) = \frac{\alpha_1 y^{\alpha_2}(t,v) - \alpha_2 y^{\alpha_1}(t,v)}{\alpha_1\alpha_2(\alpha_2 - \alpha_1)}.$$
(15)

Let us carry out the procedure for identifying the Volterra kernel $K_2(s_1,s_2)$ symmetric in variables s_1, s_2, using Equations (13) and (15). Then the problem of identifying $K_1(t,s)$ from (9) reduces to solving

$$\int_0^t K_1(t,s)x(s)ds = q(t),$$
$$q(t) = y(t) - \int_0^t \int_0^t K_2(s_1,s_2)x(t-s_1)x(t-s_2)ds_1ds_2,$$
(16)

where $K_2(s_1,s_2)$ is known. Applying test signals (8) in addition to (10), we obtain Equation (16), where

$$q(t) \equiv q_v(t) = \begin{cases} 0, & t = 0, v = 0, \\ g(t,v), & 0 < v \leq t, \end{cases}$$

which can be represented in the form

$$\int_0^v K_1(t,s)\frac{s}{v}ds + \int_v^t K_1(t,s)ds = q(t,v),$$
(17)

$$q(t,v) = g(t,v) - \int_{t-v}^t \int_{t-v}^t K_2(s_1,s_2)\frac{t-s_1}{v}\frac{t-s_2}{v}ds_1ds_2 -$$
$$-2\int_{t-v}^t ds_1 \int_0^{t-v} K_2(s_1,s_2)\frac{t-s_2}{v}ds_2 - \int_0^{t-v}\int_0^{t-v} K_2(s_1,s_2)ds_1ds_2.$$

Here, $g(t, v)$ is the response of a dynamic object to a signal (8) at $0 \leq v \leq t \leq T$. Following [35,37], the inversion Formula (17) has the form

$$K_1(t, v) = -\left(2g'_v(t, v) + vg''_{v^2}(t, v)\right). \tag{18}$$

Let us compare the effect of using test signals (8) and (10) when building an integral model (9).

The below example demonstrates the effect of increasing the simulation accuracy when using test signals of the form (8). Let the "reference" dynamical system be represented by a cubic Volterra polynomial with kernels $K_1 = 1$, $K_2 = \frac{1}{2}$, $K_3 = \frac{1}{3!}$, so that

$$y_{et}(t) = \int_0^t x(s)ds + \frac{1}{2}\left(\int_0^t x(s)ds\right)^2 + \frac{1}{3!}\left(\int_0^t x(s)ds\right)^3. \tag{19}$$

The technique for constructing quadratic and cubic Volterra polynomials, based on the use of piecewise constant test signals of type (10), has been successfully tested on dynamic systems of various physical nature, including a mathematical model of type (19), as well as in modeling the dynamics of a heat exchanger element and wind power plant [38]. Note that (19) is a partial sum of the series for the function

$$e^{\int_0^t x(s)ds} - 1.$$

This function has proven itself well in the study of the areas of applicability of identification algorithms for quadratic and cubic Volterra polynomials [38,39]. We apply the procedure for identifying kernels by using test signals (10) with amplitudes $\alpha_1 = -\alpha_2 = \alpha > 0$ and, instead of (9), obtain

$$y_1(t) = \int_0^t \left(1 + \frac{\alpha^2}{2}s^2\right)x(s)ds + \frac{1}{2}\left(\int_0^t x(t-s)ds\right)^2, \tag{20}$$

where the Volterra kernels were restored using Equations (12) and (13), respectively.

The combined model (9) with the addition to (10) test signals (8) with amplitude α for identification $K_1(t, s)$ has the form

$$y_2(t) = \int_0^t \left(1 + \alpha^2\left(\frac{1}{4}s^2 - \frac{3}{4}ts + \frac{1}{2}t^2\right)\right)x(s)ds + \frac{1}{2}\left(\int_0^t x(t-s)ds\right)^2, \tag{21}$$

where the kernel identification was performed using Equations (18) and (13), respectively. On signals $x^\beta(t) = \frac{t}{\beta}$, $\beta = k \cdot \alpha \cdot 0.01$, $k = \overline{1, B}$, model (20) gives residual

$$n_1(t) = y_{et}^\beta(t) - y_1^\beta(t) = \frac{t^6}{48\beta^3} - \frac{\alpha^2 t^4}{8\beta},$$

and model (21) gives residual

$$n_2(t) = y_{et}^\beta(t) - y_2^\beta(t) = \frac{t^6}{48\beta^3} - \frac{\alpha^2 t^4}{16\beta},$$

where y_{et}^β is the response (19) to signal $x^\beta(t)$.

Let us present an algorithm for constructing the polynomial (9) for modeling the response of the dynamic system represented in the form (19).

Step 1. Calculation of the values of $y_{et}^{\alpha}(t,v)$ and $y_{et}^{-\alpha}(t,v)$ using substitution (10) with amplitude $\alpha_1 = -\alpha_2 = \alpha > 0$ into the right-hand side of (19).

Step 2. Calculation by (15) of the values of the right-hand side of the integral equation,

$$\int\limits_{t-v}^{t}\int\limits_{t-v}^{t} K_2(s_1,s_2)ds_1ds_2 = f_2(t,v)\,, 0 \leq v \leq t \leq T.$$

Step 3. Application of Equation (13) for identifying $K_2(s_1,s_2), 0 \leq s_1, s_2 \leq T$.

Step 4. Calculation of values $y_{et}^{\alpha}(t,v)$ using substitution (8) with an amplitude α into the right-hand side of (19).

Step 5. Calculation of the right-hand side of (17) $q(t,v)$, where $K_2(s_1,s_2)$ and $q(t,v) \equiv y_{et}^{\alpha}(t,v)$ are obtained in the previous steps 3 and 4, respectively.

Step 6. Application of Equation (18) for identifying $K_1(t,v), 0 \leq v \leq t \leq T$.

Step 7. Substitution of kernels $K_2(s_1,s_2)$ and $K_1(t,v)$ obtained in steps 3 and 6, respectively, into the right-hand side of (9). This leads to (21).

Modeling accuracy $y_1(t)$ was compared with response $y_2(t)$. The value of the "mean absolute error" coefficient was chosen as a criterion for modeling accuracy.

$$MAE_r(t) = \frac{1}{B}\sum_{\beta=1}^{B}|n_r(t)|,\ r = 1, 2,\ t \in [0, 15].$$

In Figure 3, black color shows the areas of fulfillment of the inequality $MAE_2(t) < MAE_1(t)$ for $B = 10, 25, 40$ with an accuracy of $\delta = 10^{-2}$.

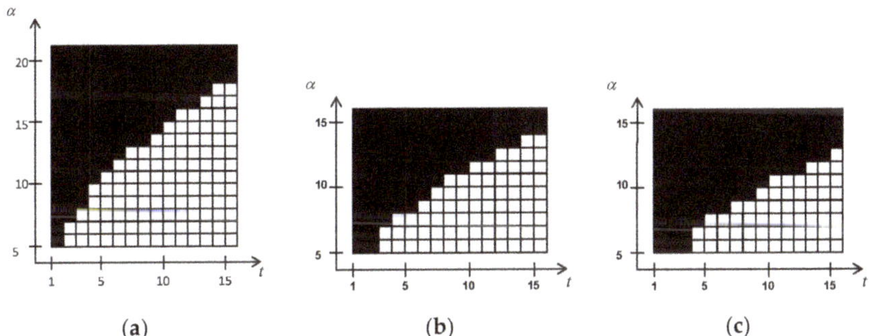

Figure 3. Areas of fulfillment of the inequality $MAE_2(t) < MAE_1(t)$ for **(a)** $B = 10$, **(b)** $B = 25$, and **(c)** $B = 40$.

The computational experiment showed that the areas of efficiency of the integral models (20) and (21) depend on the length of the segment T, the amplitude of the test signals α used to identify the Volterra kernels, and the accuracy of the calculations δ.

Note that we assumed the quadratic term, the two-dimensional kernel $K_2(t,v)$, in Equation (18) to be known. Therefore, in the next section, we consider an algorithm for identifying this term using Equation (13).

3. Identification Algorithm for Quadratic Term

Unfortunately, the implementation of the obtained inversion Equation (13) in practice faces a fundamental difficulty: the differentiation operation is an ill-posed one [40]. One of the manifestations of ill-posedness is large errors in calculating the derivative, even for very small errors in specifying a differentiable function. Note that the operation of subtraction in (15) of the registration errors of two functions leads to an increase in the variance of the total error in setting the function $f_2(t,v)$. Thus, stable differentiation of noisy data becomes an urgent problem for the implementation of formula (13) in practice.

Reference [41] constructed a stable identification algorithm on the basis of Equation (12) (a stable identification algorithm is an algorithm in which the relative identification error is comparable to the relative error of the initial data). There, a smoothing cubic spline (SCS) of a defect unit was used for a stable calculation of the first derivative. The smoothing parameter was chosen from the condition of the minimum root-mean-square smoothing error. The use of smoothing splines becomes much more complicated in the case of identifying the quadratic kernel $K_2(\tau, s)$. First, to calculate the second-order mixed derivative $f''_{2tv}(t, v)$, we need to build a smoothing bicubic spline (SBS), which is a function of two variables t, v. Secondly, the boundary conditions are now given not at two extreme points of the SCS construction interval, but on four straight lines, which are the boundaries of the rectangular area of the SCS construction. Thirdly, due to the different "smoothness" of the function $f_2(t, v)$ in different variables, we now have to choose two smoothing parameters from the condition for the minimum smoothing error. These difficulties caused the main problems that were not solved in the corresponding scientific publications and which are addressed in this section.

Suppose that the values of the function $f_2(t, v)$ are determined at the nodes of a rectangular grid. To take into account possible errors (noise) of measurements, the following representation of noisy measurements $\widetilde{f}_2(t_i, v_j)$ is taken:

$$\widetilde{f}_2(t_i, v_j) = f_2(t_i, v_j) + \eta_{i,j}, \; i = 1, \ldots, N_t, j = 1, \ldots, N_v,$$

where $\eta_{i,j}$ is random measurement noise with zero mean value and variance σ_η^2 (equally accurate measurements). Note that nodes t_i and v_j may not have the same or equal steps. It is required to calculate the values of derivatives $f''_{2tv}(t, v)$, $f''_{2v^2}(t, v)$ at the given nodes from the initial data $\left\{ \widetilde{f}_2(t_i, v_j) \right\}$.

For a stable calculation of these derivatives, we turn to SCS [42] widely used in the processing of experimental data [43,44]. Suppose we have N_v nodes $V_1 = v_1 < v_2 < \ldots < v_{N_v} = V_2$ at some interval $[V_1, V_2]$. In these nodes, the values of the function (signal) $f(v)$ are measured as follows:

$$\widetilde{f}_j = f(v_j) + \eta_j, j = 1 \ldots N_v, \tag{22}$$

where η_j is the random measurement noise with zero mean and variance σ_η^2 (equally accurate measurements). The smoothing cubic spline $S_{N_v,\alpha}(v)$ of a defect unit on each segment $[v_j, v_{j+1})$ can be represented by a cubic polynomial of the following form [42]:

$$S_{N_v,\alpha}(v) = a_j + b_j \cdot (v - v_j) + c_j \cdot (v - v_j)^2 + d_j \cdot (v - v_j)^3. \tag{23}$$

Moreover, the function $S_{N_v,\alpha}(v)$ must be twice continuously differentiable on the entire interval $[V_1, V_2]$ of its definition. Note that, in contrast to the interpolation spline (passing through the points $\left(v_j, \widetilde{f}_j\right)$), the smoothing cubic spline $S_{N_v,\alpha}(v)$ generally does not pass through these points, but passes more "smoothly" in some neighborhoods of these points (depending on the smoothing parameter α), thereby providing smoothing (filtering) of measurement noise.

To uniquely calculate the spline coefficients a_j, b_j, c_j, d_j, boundary conditions are set at the nodes v_1, v_{N_v}. The following conditions are most often used [42,44]:

- conditions on zero second derivatives of the spline (natural boundary conditions),

$$S''_{N_v,\alpha}(v_1) = 0; \; S''_{N_v,\alpha}(v_{N_v}) = 0, \tag{24}$$

- conditions on the first derivatives of the spline,

$$S'_{N_v,\alpha}(v_1) = s'_1; \; S'_{N_v,\alpha}(v_{N_v}) = s'_{N_v}, \tag{25}$$

as well as a combination of these conditions (for example, condition (25) is on the left, condition (24) is on the right). It was shown [42] the SCS constructed under these conditions provides a minimum to the functional

$$F_\alpha(S) = \alpha \cdot \int_{v_1}^{v_{N_v}} |S''(v)|^2 dv + \sum_{j=1}^{N_v} p_j^{-1} \cdot (\tilde{f}_j - S(v_j))^2, \tag{26}$$

where p_j denotes the weight factors reflecting the accuracy of the j-th measurement $\tilde{f}_j$ (they are given the same in the case of equally accurate measurements).

To calculate the spline coefficients (for a given smoothing parameter), it is necessary to compose a system of linear algebraic equations with a five-diagonal matrix concerning some vector (as a rule, these are the values of the second derivative of the spline at the nodes $\{v_j\}$), through which all the spline coefficients are then found (for details, see [42,44]).

The smoothing parameter α "controls" the smoothness of the spline, and the smoothing error (as well as the differentiation error) depends significantly on the value of this parameter [44,45]. There is a parameter value (let us call it optimal) for which the smoothing error (in the accepted norm) is minimal [45]. Let us temporarily assume that we have found an acceptable (in terms of the minimum smoothing error) value of the smoothing parameter (the choice of the parameter is discussed in the next section).

Remark 1. *It follows from the form of the integrals (11) that the function $f_2(t,v)$ takes nonzero values for the arguments satisfying the condition $v \le t$. For other values of v, t, the function is equal to zero due to the condition of the technical feasibility of the system with negative values of the arguments, i.e., $k_2(t,v) \equiv 0$, if $v < 0$, $t < 0$.*

To eliminate the discontinuity of the first kind at $v = t$ values when constructing a smoothing spline, we propose to supplement the values of the function $f_2(t,v)$ for $v > t$ according to the following rule:

$$f_2(t, t + \Delta v) = \begin{cases} 2f_2(t,t) - f_2(t, t - \Delta v), & 0\Delta v \le t; \\ 2f_2(t,t), & t\Delta v \le T - t. \end{cases}$$

We denote the function supplemented in this way as $f_2^*(t,v)$.

Initially, we focus on the algorithm for calculating the values of the derivative $f''_{2v^2}(t,v)$. It can be represented by the following steps:

Step 1. We set the boundary conditions, the combination of which at the extreme points v_1, v_{N_v} of the construction interval is determined on the basis of available a priori information about the function $f_2^*(t,v)$. If such reliable information is not available, then one should turn to the natural boundary conditions (24).

Step 2. For each $i = 1, \ldots, N_t$, we form a dataset

$$\left\{ v_j, \tilde{f1}_j^{(i)} = \tilde{f}_2^*(t_i, v_j), j = 1, \ldots, N_v \right\},$$

select the smoothing parameter $\alpha1^{(i)}$, and build the SCS $S1_{N_v, \alpha1^{(i)}}^{(i)}(v)$, from which we then calculate the first derivative $\hat{f}'_{2v}(t_i, v_j) = \frac{d}{dv} S1_{N_v, \alpha1^{(i)}}^{(i)}(v)|_{v=v_j} = b1_j^{(i)}$ (an estimate of the derivative $f'_{2v}(t_i, v_j)$), where $b1_j^{(i)}$ is the coefficient of spline $S1_{N_v, \alpha1^{(i)}}^{(i)}(v)$ in representation (23).

Step 3. For each Y, we again form the dataset

$$\left\{ v_j, \tilde{f2}_j^{(i)} = \hat{f}'_{2v}(t_i, v_j), j = 1, \ldots, N_v \right\},$$

select the smoothing parameter $\alpha2^{(i)}$, and build the SCS $S2^{(i)}_{N_v,\alpha2^{(i)}}(v)$, the first derivative of which is the estimate $\hat{f}''_{2v^2}(t_i,v_j) = \frac{d}{dv}S2^{(i)}_{N_v,\alpha2^{(i)}}(v)|_{v=v_j} = b2^{(i)}_j$ for the second derivative $f''_{2v^2}(t_i,v_j)$, where $b2^{(i)}_j$ is the coefficient of spline $S2^{(i)}_{N_v,\alpha2^{(i)}}(v)$ in representation (23).

Thus, we calculate estimates of the second derivative $f''_{2v^2}(t_i,v_j)$ for t_i, $i = 1,\ldots,N_t$.

Let us proceed to the construction (following the technique of [46]) of a bicubic smoothing spline for calculating the mixed derivative $f''_{2tv}(t_i,v_j)$. We use the following algorithm:

Step 1. For each $j = 1,\ldots,N_v$, we again form a dataset (fix the value of v_j)

$$\left\{t_i, \tilde{f3}^{(j)}_i = \tilde{f}^*_2(t_i,v_j), i = 1,\ldots,N_t\right\},$$

select the smoothing parameter $\alpha3^{(j)}$, build the SCS $S3^{(j)}_{N_t,\alpha3^{(j)}}(t)$, from which we then calculate the first derivative $\hat{f}'_{2t}(t_i,v_j) = \frac{d}{dt}S3^{(j)}_{N_t,\alpha3^{(j)}}(t)|_{t=t_i} = b3^{(j)}_i$ (estimation of the derivative $f'_{2t}(t_i,v_j)$), where $b3^{(j)}_i$ is the coefficient of spline $S3^{(j)}_{N_t,\alpha3^{(j)}}(t)$ in representation (23).

Step 2. For each Y, we form a dataset

$$\left\{v_j, \tilde{f4}^{(i)}_j = \hat{f}'_{2t}(t_i,v_j), j = 1,\ldots,N_v\right\},$$

select a smoothing parameter $\alpha4^{(i)}$, build an SCS $S4^{(i)}_{N_v,\alpha4^{(i)}}(v)$, the first derivative of which is an estimate $\hat{f}''_{2tv}(t_i,v_j) = \frac{d}{dv}S4^{(i)}_{N_v,\alpha4^{(i)}}(v)|_{v=v_j} = b4^{(i)}_j$ for the mixed derivative $f''_{2tv}(t_i,v_j)$, where $b4^{(i)}_j$ is the coefficient of spline $S4^{(i)}_{N_v,\alpha4^{(i)}}(v)$ in representation (23).

Thus, we repeat step 1 for $v_j, j = 1,\ldots,N_v$, and step 2 for $t_i, i = 1,\ldots,N_t$. After calculating the estimates $\hat{f}''_{2v^2}(t_i,v_j)$, $\hat{f}''_{2tv}(t_i,v_j)$ using Equation (13), we find the estimate $\hat{k}_2(t_i - v_j, t_i)$ for the values $v_j \leq t_i$.

Remark 2. *The inversion Equation (13) determines the value of the quadratic kernel $K_2(t,v)$ for the arguments $0 \leq v \leq t \leq T$, i.e., for the values of the argument $v \leq t$. The line $v = t$ is the axis of symmetry of the kernel $K_2(t,v)$ (follows from the one-dimensionality of the input signal); therefore, to determine the values of the kernel for $v = t + \Delta v > t$, where $\Delta v > 0$, we propose a symmetrical supplement of the kernel values according to the formula $K_2(t,t + \Delta v) = K_2(t + \Delta v, t)$.*

Remark 3. *Since the construction of the SCS by the variable v requires approximately $C_{oper} \cdot N_v$ arithmetic operations, where $C_{oper} \approx 30$ [42], the proposed algorithm for calculating derivatives requires approximately $C^4_{oper} \cdot N^3_v \cdot N_t$ operations. Therefore, the proposed algorithms for calculating derivatives have a high computational efficiency even with a large dimension of the grid (t_i,v_j).*

Previously, the values of the smoothing parameters $\alpha1^{(i)}$, $\alpha2^{(i)}$, $\alpha3^{(j)}$, $\alpha4^{(i)}$ selected were assumed (i.e., determined). Therefore, the question of how to choose these parameters arises, which will significantly affect the error of smoothing and differentiation. If the variance σ^2_η of the measurement noise (see (22)) were reliably known (at least with an accuracy of 5–8%), then the selection algorithm constructed on the basis of checking the optimality criterion of the linear filtering algorithm would allow, with acceptable accuracy (5–8%), to estimate the values of the optimal smoothing parameter that minimizes the value of the root-mean-square smoothing error (see [44] (pp. 60–67), [45]). It is obvious that the situation with unknown noise dispersion is most characteristic in solving practical identification problems. Therefore, to choose a parameter in this case, we turn to the L-curve method used to choose the regularization parameter in algorithms for solving linear ill-posed problems (for example, [47,48]). In [49], a modification of the L-curve method was proposed for choosing the smoothing parameter.

Let us talk briefly about the essence of this selection algorithm. Let us introduce the following functionals (see [49]):

$$\rho(\alpha) = \sum_{j=1}^{N_v} p_i^{-1} \cdot (\widetilde{f}_j - S_{n,\alpha}(v_j))^2, \quad \gamma(\alpha) = \int_{v_1}^{v_{N_v}} \left| S_{N_v,\alpha}''(v) \right|^2 dv.$$

Then, an L-curve (whose shape resembles the outline of the Latin letter L) is a parametric curve with coordinates $(\rho(\alpha), \gamma(\alpha))$. It can be shown that the curvature of an L-curve is given by the following formula:

$$k_L(\alpha) = 2 \cdot \frac{\hat{\rho}'(\alpha) \cdot \hat{\gamma}''(\alpha) - \hat{\rho}''(\alpha) \cdot \hat{\gamma}'(\alpha)}{\left[(\hat{\rho}'(\alpha))^2 + (\hat{\gamma}'(\alpha))^2 \right]^{\frac{3}{2}}}, \tag{27}$$

where $\hat{\rho}(\alpha) = \ln \rho(\alpha)$, $\hat{\gamma}(\alpha) = \ln \gamma(\alpha)$. The smoothing parameter is the value α_L for which the curvature $k_L(\alpha)$ takes on the maximum value. To effectively calculate the value of the functional $\gamma(\alpha)$, the following formula is proposed:

$$\gamma(\alpha) = \sum_{i=1}^{n-1} \left(4c_i^2 \cdot h_i + 12c_i \cdot d_i \cdot h_i^2 + 12d_i^2 \cdot h_i^3 \right),$$

where $h_i = t_{i+1} - t_i, i = 1, \ldots, n-1$, c_i, d_i are the SCS coefficients in representation (23), calculated for a given parameter α. To calculate the curvature value using Equation (27), an approach is proposed that uses cubic interpolation splines to approximate the dependences $\hat{\rho}(\alpha)$, $\hat{\gamma}(\alpha)$ (for details, see [49]). An extensive computational experiment was also carried out there to answer the following question: Is the loss due to smoothing error large when α_L is used instead of the optimal α_{opt} (which can only be determined in a computational experiment)? The experiment was carried out with functions that are "typical" output signals of a dynamic system when step signals are applied to the input. The analysis of the results of the experiment showed that the algorithm for selecting the smoothing parameter on the basis of the L-curve method makes it possible to estimate the optimal value of the smoothing parameter quite well. The increase in the smoothing error when using the parameter α_L does not exceed 5–15% on average compared to α_{opt}, the calculation of which is impossible in practice. Therefore, to calculate the smoothing parameters $\alpha 1^{(i)}$, $\alpha 2^{(i)}$, $\alpha 3^{(j)}$, and $\alpha 4^{(i)}$, it is proposed to use the described algorithm for choosing the smoothing parameter on the basis of the L-curve method.

To test the proposed algorithm of identifying quadratic kernel, a numerical experiment was carried out, some of the results of which we present in this paper. The test quadratic kernel $K_2(\tau, s)$ is a function used to describe the dynamics of some type of heat exchangers [50]. Figure 4a shows the surface of this function, and Figure 4b shows isolines. The time interval boundary was $T = 1$, while the number of nodes was $N_t = 80$, $N_v = 80$.

First, we define the methodological error of the identification algorithm. To do this, we calculated the values of the function (15) at the nodes $t_i, i = 1, \ldots, N_t, v_j, j = 1, \ldots, N_v$, which were interpreted as the exact values of the function $f_2(t_i, v_j)$. These data, presented as a matrix F with dimensions 80×80 with elements $F_{i,j} = f_2(t_i, v_j)$, were the initial data for the proposed identification algorithm. Since these initial data were taken as exact, instead of SCS, we built interpolating cubic splines (including the bicubic spline) with boundary conditions (24). We calculated estimates for the derivatives $\hat{f}_{2v^2}''(t_i, v_j)$ and $\hat{f}_{2tv}''(t_i, v_j)$ on the basis of these splines and then constructed an estimate for the quadratic kernel using Equation (9) (see Remark 2). Figure 5 shows the isolines of this estimate, having a relative identification error $\delta_K = \frac{\|K_2 - \hat{K}_2\|}{\|K_2\|} = 0.011$, where K_2, $\hat{K}_2$ are matrices composed of the values of the exact kernel $K_2(t_i, v_j)$ and its estimates $\hat{K}_2(t_i, v_j)$, respectively, and $\|\cdot\|$ is the Euclidean norm of the matrix. Approximately the same error was observed for other grid sizes in t, v. Therefore, we can conclude the proposed identification algorithm has a low methodological error.

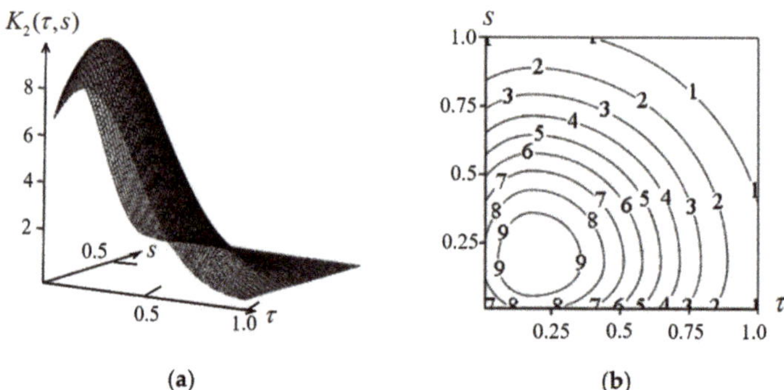

Figure 4. Test quadratic kernel: (**a**) the surface of $K_2(\tau, s)$; (**b**) isolines.

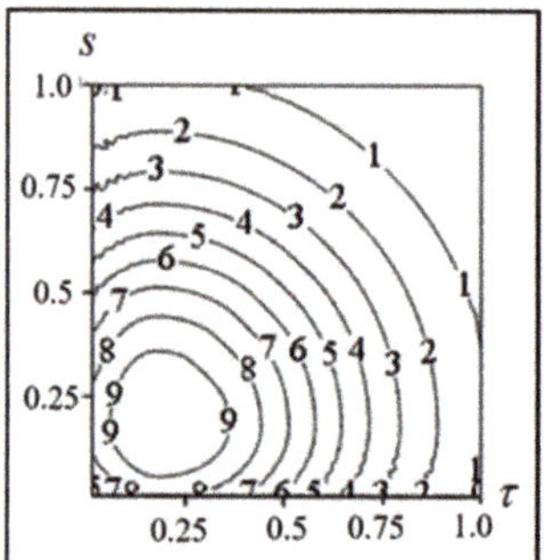

Figure 5. Estimation of the kernel $\hat{K}_2(\tau, s)$, built on exact data.

Let us consider the influence of the measurement noise of the function $f_2(t, v)$ on the accuracy of identification. To do this, we distorted all elements of the "exact" matrix F with normally distributed noise with a relative level $\delta_F = \dfrac{\|F - \tilde{F}\|}{\|F\|}$, where $\tilde{F}$ is a matrix with "noisy" elements. The matrix $\tilde{F}$ thus formed was used as initial data for the previously described identification algorithm. We chose the smoothing parameter at all steps of calculating derivatives using the L-curve method described above. Figure 6 shows the isolines of the estimate $\hat{K}_2(t_i, v_j)$, built at a noise level of 0.02. The relative identification error was $\delta_K = 0.044$, which indicates the acceptable accuracy of quadratic term identification by the proposed algorithm.

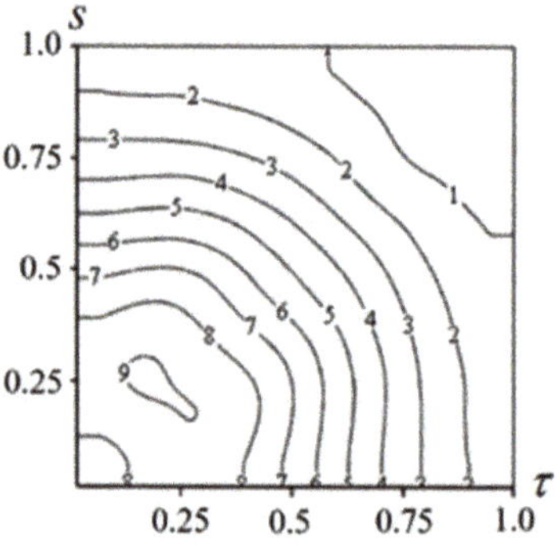

Figure 6. Estimation of the kernel $\hat{K}_2(\tau, s)$, built on noisy data.

4. Difference Scheme for Finding a Linear Nonstationary Kernel Using the Quadrature Method

It often happens in practice that the responses of the system (the right-hand side of equations) are given not analytically, but in the form of a series of numbers. In this case, we have to turn to the numerical solution. The procedure for the numerical identification of the Volterra polynomial (9) using piecewise constant test signals (10) was considered in detail earlier in [36]. This approach to constructing a quadratic polynomial was tested in applications for thermal power objects [51]. As shown in the previous section, using signals of a new type with a rising edge of the form (8) makes it possible to improve the accuracy of modeling, even if they are used to identify only one of the polynomial kernels (9). Therefore, in this section, we restrict ourselves to the procedure for numerical identification of a nonstationary linear term from (9) based on test signals of the form (8).

As shown in Section 2, if we assume that identifying the kernel $K_2(s_1, s_2)$ in the quadratic term of the polynomial (9) has already been achieved in one way or another, then the substitution of (8) into (16) leads to (17). We present a difference scheme for finding a linear nonstationary kernel from (17) with a known right-hand side. To do this, we introduce on the interval $[0, T]$ a uniform grid $t_i = ih$, $i = \overline{0, N}$ and a subgrid $t_{i-1/2} = (i - 1/2)h$, $i = \overline{1, N}$, while we denote by $K_{i,j}^h$ the grid approximation of the kernel $K_1(t_i, t_j)$. To approximate the integrals in (17), we use the middle rectangle rule, taking into account $v \leq t$,

$$h \sum_{k=1}^{j} K_{i,\, k-1/2}^h \frac{t_{k-1/2}}{t_j} + h \sum_{k=j+1}^{i} K_{i,\, k-1/2}^h = q(t_i, t_j), i = \overline{1, N}, j = \overline{1, i}. \tag{28}$$

At each step $i = \overline{1, N}$, one has to solve a system of linear algebraic equations of dimension $(i \times i)$ with respect to $K_{i,\, k-1/2}^h, k = \overline{1, i}$.

Consider the application of the difference scheme (28) with help of a test example. Let the right side of (17) have the form

$$q(t, v) = t - \frac{v}{2} + \frac{5t^3}{24} - \frac{v^3}{48} + \frac{tv^2}{8} - \frac{t^2 v}{4}. \tag{29}$$

This right side will correspond to the kernel $K_1(t, v)$ from example (21). Table 1 shows the results of numerical calculations obtained using the difference scheme (28). Here,

$$\varepsilon = \max_{1 \leq j \leq i \leq N} \left| K_1\left(t_i, t_{j-1/2}\right) - K_{i,\, j-1/2}^h \right|$$

denotes the errors of the numerical solution. The last column of the table shows the number of nodes in which the maximum error is achieved. The table shows that the proposed algorithm has a linear order of convergence.

Table 1. The error of the numerical solution to (17) with the right side (29).

h	ε	Node Number, (i, j)
1/8	0.00553385	$(8, 2)$
1/16	0.00268555	$(16, 4)$
1/32	0.00132243	$(32, 8)$
1/64	0.00065613	$(64, 6)$

Thus, the numerical construction of the quadratic Volterra polynomial using the quadrature of the middle rectangles can be implemented by the formula

$$h \sum_{j=1}^{i} K_1^h\left(t_i, t_{j-1/2}\right) x(t_j) + h^2 \sum_{k=1}^{i} \sum_{l=1}^{i} K_2^h(t_{k-1/2}, t_{l-1/2}) x(t_i - t_{k-1/2}) x(t_i - t_{l-1/2}) = g(t_i), i = \overline{1, N},$$

where the kernels $K_1^h\left(t_i, t_{j-1/2}\right)$ are obtained using the difference Equation (28).

5. Future Research

This section is devoted to interpreting the identification method for nonsymmetric kernel $K_1(t,s)$ presented in Section 2 for solving the reconstruction problem for symmetric function $K_2(s_1,s_2)$. For this, we introduce the system of integral Equation (9), where the functions $x(t)$ and $y(t)$ have the form

$$
x(t) \equiv x_v^{\alpha_{1,2}}(t) = \begin{cases} 0, & t \le 0, \\ \alpha_{1,2}\frac{t}{v}, & 0 < t \le v, \\ \alpha_{1,2}, & t > v, \end{cases}
\tag{30}
$$

$$
y(t) \equiv y_v^{\alpha_{1,2}}(t) = \begin{cases} 0, & t = 0, v = 0, \\ g^{\alpha_{1,2}}(t,v), & 0 < v \le t, \end{cases}
\tag{31}
$$

where $\alpha_1 \ne \alpha_2$, and $g_v^{\alpha_{1,2}}(t)$ is a sufficiently smooth function. Assuming that in (9) the kernel $K_2(s_1,s_2) = \varphi(s_1)\varphi(s_2)$ is a separable function, such that $\varphi(s) \in C_\Omega$, C_Ω is the space of continuous functions symmetric on the square $\Omega = \{s_1, s_2 : 0 \le s_1, s_2 \le T\}$; then, system (9) can be transformed to the form

$$
\int_0^t K_1(t,s)x(s)ds + \left(\int_0^t \varphi(s)x(t-s)ds\right)^2 = y(t),
$$

or, taking into account (30) and (31), into the system

$$
\alpha_{1,2}\left(\int_0^v K_1(t,s)\frac{s}{v}ds + \int_v^t K_1(t,s)ds\right) + \alpha_{1,2}^2\left(\int_0^v \varphi(t-s)\frac{s}{v}ds + \int_v^t \varphi(t-s)ds\right)^2 = g^{\alpha_{1,2}}(t,v).
\tag{32}
$$

We introduce the following functions $f_1(t,v)$, $f_2(t,v)$:

$$
f_1(t,v) = \int_0^v K_1(t,s)\frac{s}{v}ds + \int_v^t K_1(t,s)ds,
\tag{33}
$$

$$
f_2(t,v) = \int_0^v \varphi(t-s)\frac{s}{v}ds + \int_v^t \varphi(t-s)ds.
\tag{34}
$$

The system of linear functional equations of the form (32), presented with the designations (33) and (34),

$$
\begin{cases} \alpha_1 f_1(t,v) + \alpha_1^2 f_2^2(t,v) = g^{\alpha_1}(t,v), \\ \alpha_2 f_1(t,v) + \alpha_2^2 f_2^2(t,v) = g^{\alpha_2}(t,v), \end{cases}
$$

where $\alpha_1 \ne \alpha_2$, has a unique solution

$$
f_1(t,v) = \frac{\alpha_2^2 g^{\alpha_1}(t,v) - \alpha_1^2 g^{\alpha_2}(t,v)}{\alpha_1 \alpha_2^2 - \alpha_1^2 \alpha_2},
\tag{35}
$$

$$
f_2^2(t,v) = \frac{\alpha_1 g^{\alpha_2}(t,v) - \alpha_2 g^{\alpha_1}(t,v)}{\alpha_1 \alpha_2^2 - \alpha_1^2 \alpha_2}.
\tag{36}
$$

According to [35], the inversion formula for (33) has the form

$$
K_1(t,v) = -2\frac{\partial f_1(t,v)}{\partial v} - v\frac{\partial^2 f_1(t,v)}{\partial^2 v},
$$

or, introducing the differentiation operator $D_2 = 2\frac{\partial}{\partial v} + v\frac{\partial^2}{\partial^2 v}1$,

$$K_1(t,v) = -D_2(f_1(t,v)).$$

Similarly, for (34) we have

$$\varphi(t-v) = -D_2(f_2(t,v)).$$

Here, the functions $f_1(t,v)$ and $f_2(t,v)$ are determined by (35) and (36), respectively.

6. Conclusions

This paper generalized the experience of using piecewise-specified test signals to identify nonlinear dynamic systems of the input–output type, represented as quadratic Volterra polynomials, taking into account the nonstationary properties of the object. The development of this direction is associated with the introduction of test signals with a rising edge, which are characteristic of input actions that occur in practice. The type of test signals introduced in this paper can be used to identify the Volterra kernels included in the quadratic Volterra polynomial.

The new approach to constructing a quadratic Volterra polynomial in the time domain is based on the use of physically realizable test signals, which is very promising for applications. Volterra integral equations of the first kind, to which the problem of identifying Volterra kernels is reduced, have explicit inversion formulas, which ensures the construction of high-speed computational procedures. These formulas include mixed partial derivatives. A new method is proposed for choosing the smoothing parameter of a cubic spline for a stable numerical calculation of the derivatives included in the constructed inversion formula. This choice of parameter provides effective filtering of measurement noise. The results of the computational experiment showed that the relative identification error is comparable to the relative error of the initial data error; at a noise level of the initial data of 2%, the methodological error in the identification of the Volterra kernel was 4.4%.

Author Contributions: Conceptualization, Y.V. and S.S.; methodology, Y.V. and S.S.; software, E.M., E.A. and V.B.; validation, Y.V., S.S., E.M., E.A. and V.B.; formal analysis, Y.V., S.S., E.M., E.A. and V.B.; investigation, Y.V. and S.S.; resources, Y.V., S.S., E.M., E.A. and V.B.; data curation, E.M. and V.B.; writing—original draft preparation, Y.V., S.S., E.M., E.A. and V.B.; writing—review and editing, Y.V., S.S., E.M., E.A. and V.B.; visualization, Y.V., S.S., E.M., E.A. and V.B.; supervision, Y.V., S.S., E.M., E.A. and V.B.; project administration, Y.V. and S.S.; funding acquisition, Y.V. and S.S. All authors have read and agreed to the published version of the manuscript.

Funding: This research was funded by Russian Science Foundation, grant number 22-21-00409.

Institutional Review Board Statement: Not applicable.

Informed Consent Statement: Not applicable.

Data Availability Statement: Not applicable.

Conflicts of Interest: The authors declare no conflict of interest.

References

1. Volterra, V. *A Theory of Functionals and of Integral and Integro-Differential Equations*; Dover Publications: New York, NY, USA, 1959; ISBN 0486442845.
2. Brunner, H. *Volterra Integral Equations: An Introduction to Theory and Applications*; Cambridge University Press: New York, NY, USA, 2017.
3. Apartsyn, A.S. *Nonclassical Linear Volterra Equations of the First Kind*; De Gruyter Publisher: Utrecht, The Netherlands; Boston, MA, USA, 2003. [CrossRef]
4. Boikov, I.V.; Krivulin, N.P. *Analytical and Numerical Methods for Identification of Dynamical Systems*; Penza State University: Penza, Russia, 2016.
5. Doyle, F., III; Pearson, R.; Ogunnaike, B. *Identification and Control Using Volterra Models*; Springer: Berlin, Germany, 2002.
6. Ogunfunmi, T. *Adaptive Nonlinear System Identification: The Volterra and Wiener Model Approaches*; Springer: Berlin, Germany, 2007.

7. Rugh, W.J. *Nonlinear System Theory: The Volterra/Weiner Approach*; John Hopkins Press: Baltimore, MD, USA, 1981.
8. Elloum, M.; Gassara, H.; Naifar, O. An Overview on Modelling of Complex Interconnected Nonlinear Systems. *Math. Probl. Eng.* **2022**, *2022*, 4789405. [CrossRef]
9. Szlobodnyik, G.; Szederkényi, G. Structural identifiability analysis of nonlinear time delayed systems with generalized frequency response functions. *Kybernetika* **2021**, *57*, 939–957. [CrossRef]
10. Wiener, N. *Nonlinear Problems in Random Theory*; The Technology Press of M.I.T.: New York, NY, USA; John Wiley & Sons, Inc.: Hoboken, NJ, USA, 1958.
11. Borys, A. On Modelling of Nonlinear Systems and Phenomena with the Use of Volterra and Wiener Series. *TransNav Int. J. Mar. Navig. Saf. Sea Transp.* **2015**, *9*, 91–98. [CrossRef]
12. Skyvulstad, H.; Petersen, Ø.W.; Argentini, T.; Zasso, A.; Øiseth, O. The use of a Laguerrian expansion basis as Volterra kernels for the efficient modeling of nonlinear self-excited forces on bridge decks. *J. Wind Eng. Ind. Aerodyn.* **2021**, *219*, 104805. [CrossRef]
13. Orcioni, S. Improving the approximation ability of Volterra series identified with a cross-correlation method. *Nonlinear Dyn.* **2014**, *78*, 2861–2869. [CrossRef]
14. Balassa, G. Estimating Scattering Potentials in Inverse Problems with a Non-Causal Volterra Model. *Mathematics* **2022**, *10*, 1257. [CrossRef]
15. Tsibizova, T.Y. Identification of nonlinear automatic control systems via Volterra filters. *Basic Res.* **2015**, *2*, 3070–3074.
16. Menshikov, B.N.; Priorov, A.L. Nonlinear echo-elimination on the basis of adaptive polynomial Volterra filter with a dynamically readjusted structure. *Digital Signal Processing* **2006**, *3*, 20–25.
17. Tsibizova, T.Y. Adaptive algorithm for identification of nonlinear systems by Volterra series. *Basic Res.* **2016**, *10*, 102–106.
18. Marmarelis, V.Z. Identification of nonlinear systems by use of nonstationary white-noise inputs. *Appl. Math. Model.* **1980**, *4*, 117–124. [CrossRef]
19. Mirri, D.; Iuculano, G.; Traverso, P.A.; Pasini, G.; Filicori, F. Non-linear dynamic system modelling based on modified Volterra series approaches. *Measurement* **2003**, *33*, 9–21. [CrossRef]
20. Liu, Q.; Xie, M.; Lim, M.-K. Volterra Series Models for Nonlinear System Control. In Proceedings of the 32nd ISR (International Symposium on Robotics), Seoul, Korea, 19–21 April 2001; pp. 1386–1391.
21. Medvedew, A.; Fomin, O.; Pavlenko, V.; Speranskyy, V. Diagnostic features space construction using Volterra kernels wavelet transforms. In Proceedings of the 2017 9th IEEE International Conference on Intelligent Data Acquisition and Advanced Computing Systems: Technology and Applications (IDAACS), Bucharest, Romania, 21–23 September 2017; pp. 1077–1081. [CrossRef]
22. Apartsyn, A.S. Nonclassical Volterra Equations of the First Kind in Integral Models of Dynamical Systems: Theory, Numerical Methods, Applications. Ph.D. Thesis, Irkutsk State University, Irkutsk, Russia, 2000.
23. Venikov, V.A.; Sukhanov, O.A.; Guseynov, A.F. Functional representation of subsystems in cybernetic modeling. In *Cybernetics of Electric Power Systems*; USSR Academy of Sciences: Bryansk, Russia, 1974; pp. 39–46.
24. Galin, N.M.; Zyabirov, F.I. Method for solving nonlinear problems of heat transfer using the Volterra functional series. In *Hydrodynamics and Heat Transfer in Single-Phase and Two-Phase Flows*; Moscow Energy Institute: Moscow, Russia, 1987; pp. 34–48.
25. Eykhoff, P. *System Identification: Parameter and State Estimation*; Wiley: Chichester, UK, 1974; p. 555.
26. Schetzen, M. Measurement of the Kernels of a Nonlinear System of Finite Order. *Int. J. Control* **1965**, *1*, 251–263. [CrossRef]
27. Danilov, L.V.; Matkhanov, P.N.; Filippov, E.S. *Theory of Nonlinear Electrical Circuits*; Energoatomizdat: Leningrad, Russia, 1990.
28. Venikov, V.A.; Sukhanov, O.A. *Cybernetic Models of Power Systems*; Energoizdat: Moscow, Russia, 1982.
29. Ljung, L. *System Identification: Theory for the User*; Prentice Hall, Inc.: Upper Sadle River, NJ, USA, 1987.
30. Pavlenko, S.V. Methods and Tools for Identifying Nonlinear Dynamic Systems Based on Volterra Models. Ph.D. Thesis, Odessa National Polytechnic University, Odessa, Ukraine, 2017.
31. Fujii, K.; Nakao, K. Identification of nonlinear dynamic systems without self–regulation using Volterra functional series. *Trans. Soc. Instrum. Control Eng.* **1971**, *7*, 129–136. [CrossRef]
32. Masri, M.M. Methods and Tools for Constructing Information Models of Nonlinear Dynamic Objects for Diagnostic Purposes. Ph.D. Thesis, Odessa National Polytechnic University, Odessa, Ukraine, 2015.
33. Pavlenko, V.D. Compensation method for identification of nonlinear dynamical systems in the form of Volterra kernels. *Proc. Odessa Polytech. Univ.* **2009**, *2*, 121–129.
34. Fedorova, A.N.; Fomin, A.A.; Pavlenko, V.D. The method of constructing multidimensional Volterra model of the oculo-motor apparatus. *Electr. Comput. Syst.* **2015**, *19*, 296–301. [CrossRef]
35. Solodusha, S.V. New Classes of Volterra Integral Equations of the First Kind Related to the Modeling of the Wind Turbine Dynamics. In Proceedings of the 2020 15th International Conference on Stability and Oscillations of Nonlinear Control Systems (Pyatnitskiy's Conference) (STAB), Moscow, Russia, 3–5 June 2020. [CrossRef]
36. Apartsyn, A.S. On increasing the accuracy of modeling the nonlinear dynamic systems with Volterra polynomials. *Electron. Modeling* **2001**, *23*, 3–12.
37. Voskoboynikov, Y.E.; Solodusha, S.V. Problem and algorithm for nonparametric identification of the combined quadratic Volterra polynomial using cubic splines. *Numer. Anal. Appl.* **2022**, *in press*.

38. Solodusha, S.V.; Orlova, I.V. Integral models of non-linear non-stationary systems and their applications. In Proceedings of the 2017 International Conference on Industrial Engineering, Applications and Manufacturing, ICIEAM 2017, Chelyabinsk, Russia, 16–19 May 2017; p. 8076419. [CrossRef]
39. Solodusha, S.V. Quadratic and cubic Volterra polynomials: Identification and application. *Vestn. St. Petersburg Univ. Appl. Math. Comput. Sci. Control. Processes* **2018**, *14*, 131–144. [CrossRef]
40. Tikhonov, A.N.; Arsenin, V.Y. *Solutions of Ill-Posed Problems*; Winston and Sons: Washington, DC, USA, 1977.
41. Voskoboynikov, Y.E.; Boeva, V.A. Non-parametric identification algorithms for complex engineering systems. *Sci. Bull. Novosib. State Tech. Univ.* **2020**, *4*, 47–64. [CrossRef]
42. Zavyalov, Y.S.; Kvasov, B.I.; Miroshnichenko, V.L. *Methods of Spline Functions*; Nauka: Moscow, Russia, 1980; p. 345.
43. Wang, Y. *Smoothing Splines Methods and Applications*; Ser. Monographs on Statistics and Applied Probability; CRC Press: Boca Raton, FL, USA, 2011; Volume 121, p. 347.
44. Voskoboynikov, Y.E.; Preobrazhensky, N.G.; Sedelnikov, A.I. *Mathematical Processing of Experiment in Molecular Gas Dynamics*; Nauka: Novosibirsk, Russia, 1984; p. 238.
45. Voskoboynikov, Y.E.; Boeva, V.A. Synthesis of smoothing cubic spline in non-parametric identification technical systems' algorithm. In Proceedings of the IOP Conference Series: Materials Science and Engineering. XIII International Scientific Conference Architecture and Construction, Novosibirsk, Russia, 22–24 September 2020; Institute of Physics Publishing: Bristol, UK, 2020; p. 012035. [CrossRef]
46. Voskoboynikov, Y.E.; Boeva, V.A. Stable algorithm for computing mixed derivatives in problems of nonparametric identification of nonlinear systems. *Mod. High Technol.* **2021**, *4*, 25–29. [CrossRef]
47. Rezghi, M.; Hosseini, S.M. A new variant of L-curve for Tikhonov regularization. *J. Comput. Appl. Math.* **2012**, *231*, 914–924. [CrossRef]
48. Cultrera, A.; Callegaro, L. A simple algorithm to find the L-curve corner in the regularization of ill-posed inverse problems. *IOP SciNotes* **2020**, *1*, 32–39. [CrossRef]
49. Voskoboynikov, Y.E.; Boeva, V.A. L-curve method for evaluating the optimal parameter of a smoothing cubic spline. *Int. Res. J.* **2021**, *11*, 6–13. [CrossRef]
50. Solodusha, S.V. Modeling heat exchangers by quadratic Volterra polynomials. *Autom. Remote Control* **2014**, *75*, 87–94. [CrossRef]
51. Apartsyn, A.S.; Solodusha, S.V.; Spiryaev, V.A. Modeling of Nonlinear Dynamic Systems with Volterra Polynomials: Elements of Theory and Applications. *Int. J. Energy Optim. Eng.* **2013**, *2*, 16–43. [CrossRef]

 *mathematics*

Article

Choice of Regularization Methods in Experiment Processing: Solving Inverse Problems of Thermal Conductivity

Alexander Sokolov [1,*] **and Irina Nikulina** [2]

[1] Institute for Information Transmission Problem (Kharkevitch Insitute) RAS, Bolshoy Karetny per. 19, Build.1, Moscow 127051, Russia
[2] V. A. Trapeznikov Institute of Control Sciences of RAS, 65 Profsoyuznaya Street, Moscow 117997, Russia
* Correspondence: abc@iitp.ru

Abstract: This work is aimed at numerical studies of inverse problems of experiment processing (identification of unknown parameters of mathematical models from experimental data) based on the balanced identification technology. Such problems are inverse in their nature and often turn out to be ill-posed. To solve them, various regularization methods are used, which differ in regularizing additions and methods for choosing the values of the regularization parameters. Balanced identification technology uses the cross-validation root-mean-square error to select the values of the regularization parameters. Its minimization leads to an optimally balanced solution, and the obtained value is used as a quantitative criterion for the correspondence of the model and the regularization method to the data. The approach is illustrated by the problem of identifying the heat-conduction coefficient on temperature. A mixed one-dimensional nonlinear heat conduction problem was chosen as a model. The one-dimensional problem was chosen based on the convenience of the graphical presentation of the results. The experimental data are synthetic data obtained on the basis of a known exact solution with added random errors. In total, nine problems (some original) were considered, differing in data sets and criteria for choosing solutions. This is the first time such a comprehensive study with error analysis has been carried out. Various estimates of the modeling errors are given and show a good agreement with the characteristics of the synthetic data errors. The effectiveness of the technology is confirmed by comparing numerical solutions with exact ones.

Keywords: modeling; regularization; inverse problems; balanced identification; error analysis; one-dimensional heat equation

MSC: 93B30

Citation: Sokolov, A.; Nikulina, I. Choice of Regularization Methods in Experiment Processing: Solving Inverse Problems of Thermal Conductivity. *Mathematics* **2022**, *10*, 4221. https://doi.org/10.3390/math10224221

Academic Editor: Dimplekumar N. Chalishajar

Received: 15 September 2022
Accepted: 8 November 2022
Published: 11 November 2022

Publisher's Note: MDPI stays neutral with regard to jurisdictional claims in published maps and institutional affiliations.

1. Introduction

The experiment preparation and processing of the results involve an extensive use of mathematical models of the objects under study. To save costs, they must be carefully planned: one should determine what, when, where and with what accuracy is to be measured to estimate the sought parameters with the given accuracy. These questions can be answered by "rehearsing" the experiment and its processing on a mathematical model simulating the behavior of the object.

Usually, the purpose of an experiment is to evaluate some of the object's parameters. In the case of an indirect experiment, some parameters are measured, while others are to be evaluated. The relationship between the parameters can be described by complex mathematical models. The formalization of this approach leads to identification problems that are by their nature inverse. Those problems often turn out to be ill-posed, and specific approaches using regularization methods are required for the solution [1]. One of the problems with regularization methods is the choice of regularization weights (penalties): weights that are too large lead to unreasonable simplification (and distortion) of the model, and those that are too small lead to overtraining, an excessive fitting of the model's trajectory to experimental data. In the balanced identification method [2], the choice of regularization weights is carried out by minimizing the cross-validation error. This makes it possible to find a balanced solution that implements the optimal (in the sense of minimizing the cross-validation error) compromise between the proximity of the model to the data and the simplicity of the model [3], formalized in a regularizing additive.

Usually, for each specific identification problem (see examples of modeling pollutants moving in the river corridor [4], parameter identification in nonlinear mechanical systems [5], identification of conductivity coefficient in heat equation [6–8]), a separate special study is carried out, including goal setting, mathematical formalization of the problem, its study, creating a numerical model, preparing a computer program, solving a numerical problem and studying the results, including error estimation, etc.

However, such problems have much in common: the mathematical model description, assignment of operators linking measurements with model variables, formalization of the solution selection criterion, program preparation, error estimation, etc. Additionally, the abundance of similar tasks invariably necessitates a technology that summarizes the accumulated experience.

Balanced Identification Technology or SvF (Simplicity versus Fitting) technology is a step in this direction.

Here is the general "human–computer" scheme of the SvF technology, which implements the balanced identification method (a more detailed description of the technical issues of the technology implementation and the corresponding flowchart can be found in [2]). At the user level, an expert (with knowledge about the object under study) prepares data files and a task file. The data files contain tables with experimental data (as plain text or in MS Excel or MS Access formats). The task file usually contains the data file names, a mathematical description of the object (formalization of the model in a notation close to mathematical, see Appendix A), including a list of unknown parameters, as well as specifications of the cross-validation procedure (CV). These files are transferred to the client program, which replaces the variational problems with discrete ones, creates various sets (training and testing) for the CV procedure, formulates a number of NLP (nonlinear mathematical programming) problems and writes (formalizes) them in the Pyomo package language [9]. The constructed data structures are transferred to a two-level optimization routine that implements an iterative numerical search for unknown model parameters and regularization coefficients to minimize the error of cross-validation. This subroutine can use the parallel solution of mathematical programming problems in a distributed environment of Everest optimization services [10], namely SSOP applications [11]. The Pyomo package converts the NLP description into so-called NL files, which are processed at the server level by special Ipopt solvers [12]. The solutions are then collected and sent back to the client level and subsequently analyzed (for example, complete iterative process conditions are checked). If the iterative process is completed, the program prepares the results (calculates errors, creates solution files, draws graphs of the functions found) and presents them to the researcher (who may not know about the long chain of the tasks preceding the result).

The experts then utilize the results (especially the values of modeling errors–root-mean-square errors of cross validation) for choosing a new (or modified) model or deciding to cease calculations.

The software package together with examples (including some examples of this article) is freely available online (file SvF-2021-11.zip in the Git repository https://github.com/distcomp/SvF, accessed on 1 September 2022).

SvF technology has been successfully applied in various scientific fields (mechanics, plasma physics, biology, plant physiology, epidemiology, meteorology, atmospheric pollution transfer, etc., and a more detailed enumeration can be found in [2]) as an inverse problem solving method. In these studies, the main attention was paid to the construction of object models using specific regularization methods. This article, in contrast, focuses on the study of the regularization methods themselves, and the problem of heat conduction is chosen as a convenient example.

The problem of thermal conductivity is chosen to illustrate the technology. This is a classic problem in mathematical physics. It is well studied, and the one-dimensionality allows you to present the results in the form of graphs. Literature reviews can be found in [7,8]. The main task is to find the dependence of the thermal conductivity coefficient on temperature based on an array of experimental data. In total, nine problems were considered, differing in data sets and criteria for choosing solutions. Some of them are original. This is the first time such a comprehensive study with error analysis has been carried out. Various estimates of the modeling errors are given and turn out to be in good agreement with the characteristics of the synthetic data errors.

2. Mixed One-Dimensional Thermal Conductivity Problem

Let us denote $M = 0$ a set of mathematical statements defining the investigated model of thermal conductivity:

$$M = 0 : \begin{cases} x \in [0,2], \ t \in [0,5] \\ \frac{\partial T}{\partial t} = \frac{\partial}{\partial x}\left(K(T)\frac{\partial T}{\partial x}\right) \\ T(x,0) = \varphi(x) \\ T(0,t) = l(t) \\ T(2,t) = r(t) \end{cases} \tag{1}$$

where x and t are the spatial and temporal coordinates, $T(x,t)$ is the temperature, $K(T)$ is the (temperature-dependent) thermal conductivity coefficient, $\varphi(t)$ is the initial condition, $l(t)$ and $r(t)$ are the left and right boundary conditions.

In what follows, all functions in various (non-difference) statements are considered twice continuously differentiable.

Remark. The formulas in (1) actually coincide with the records (descriptions of the model) in the text of the task file (a set of instructions for obtaining a numerical solution) given in Appendix A.

When conducting numerical experiments, the exact solution of the mathematical model (1)

$$\begin{aligned} Ts(x,t) &= \frac{200(t+1)}{(x+1)^2 + (t+1)^2} \\ Ks(T) &= \frac{100}{T} \\ \varphi s(x) &= \frac{200}{(x+1)^2 + 1} \\ ls(t) &= \frac{200(t+1)}{1 + (t+1)^2} \\ rs(t) &= \frac{200(t+1)}{9 + (t+1)^2} \end{aligned} \tag{2}$$

is used for the generation of pseudo-experimental data sets (observations) and for comparison with the numerical solution (calculation of errors).

In the notation of the functions of the exact solution, $'s'$ is used (short for solution). The functions of the exact solution are shown in Figure 1.

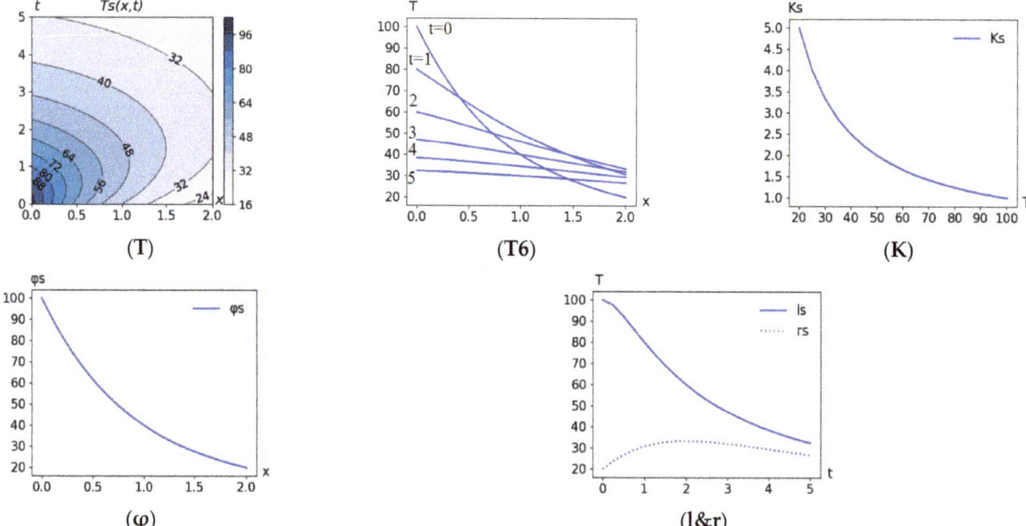

Figure 1. Functions of the exact solution: (**T**) contour lines of $Ts(x,t)$; (**T6**) 6 time slices of $Ts(x,t)$: $Ts(x,0), Ts(x,1), \dots , Ts(x,5)$; (**K**) thermal conductivity $K(T)$; (φ) initial condition $\varphi s(t)$; (**l&r**) left $ls(x)$ and right $rs(x)$ boundary conditions.

3. Data Sets

Formalizing the concept of a data set (observations or measurements set):

$$D: \quad \{x_i, t_i, T_i,\}, \ i \in I, \ I = 0..i_{max},$$

where T_i is the temperature measurement at point x_i at time t_i.

For vectors of dimension $|D|$, introduce the notation

$$\|a_i\|_D = \|a\|_D = \sqrt{\frac{1}{|D|} \sum_{i \in I} a_i^2}$$

Below, for numerical experiments, pseudo-experimental data are used, prepared on the basis of the exact solution (2) using pseudo-random number generators. The prepared 4 data sets were chosen as the most illustrative.

A basic data set was generated on a regular 11×11 grid (11 points in space 0, 0.2, 0.4 $\dots$, 2 and 11 points in time 0, 0.5, 1, $\dots$ 5)

$$D\_reg11x11: \quad \{x_i = n * 0.2, \ t_i = j * 0.5, \ T_i = Ts(x_i, t_i) + \varepsilon_i\},$$

$$i = 11 * j + n, \ n = 0..10, \ j = 0..10,$$

where $Ts(x_i,t_i)$ are the values of the exact solution, ε_i is the random error with variance

$$\sigma_d = \|\varepsilon\|_D.$$

To generate ε_i, a normal distribution random number generator (gauss (0.2)) with zero mean and variance equal to 2 (degrees) was used. As a result, the distribution ε_i was obtained with average $m_d = -0.10$ (degrees) and variance $\sigma_d = 2.06$ (degrees). These characteristics of errors are not used in calculations but are taken into account when considering the results.

By analogy, we introduce a data set of exact measurements:

$$D\_reg11x11(\varepsilon = 0)$$

with zero errors $\varepsilon_i = 0$.

Let us define a data set containing 121 points randomly distributed on the x,t plane:

$$D\_rnd121: \quad \{x_i = uniform(0, 2), t_i = uniform(0, 5), T_i = Ts(x_i, t_i) + \varepsilon_i\}, \ j = 0..121.$$

To do this, use *uniform*(*a*, *b*)—a generator of random numbers uniformly distributed over the interval (*a*,*b*). The obtained characteristics of the normal distribution of temperature measurements are: $m_d = -0.19$ (degrees) and $\sigma_d = 2.14$ (degrees).

Finally, let us define a data set containing 1000 points, distributed in a random way:

$$D\_rnd1000: \quad \{x_i = uniform(0, 2), t_i = uniform(0, 5), T_i = Ts(x_i, t_i) + \varepsilon_i\}, \ j = 0..1000,$$

with the characteristics of the normal distribution of temperature measurements: $m_d = -0.02$ (degrees) and $\sigma_d = 2.01$ (degrees).

The location of the measurement points of the $D\_reg11x11$, D_rnd121 and $D\_rnd1000$ sets on the x, t plane can be seen in Figure 2.

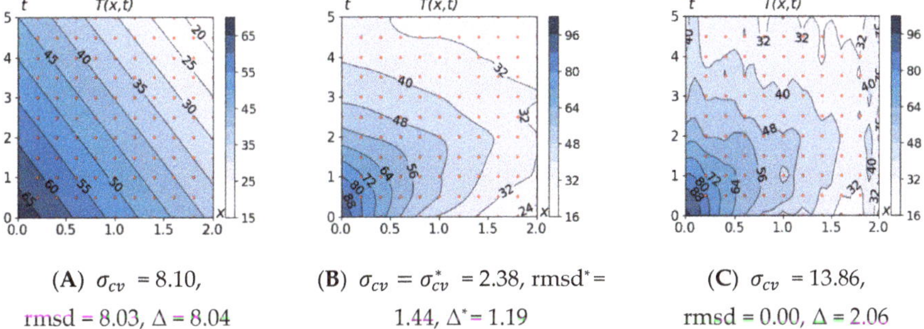

(**A**) $\sigma_{cv} = 8.10$, rmsd = 8.03, $\Delta = 8.04$

(**B**) $\sigma_{cv} = \sigma_{cv}^{*} = 2.38$, rmsd* = 1.44, $\Delta^{*} = 1.19$

(**C**) $\sigma_{cv} = 13.86$, rmsd = 0.00, $\Delta = 2.06$

Figure 2. Solutions with different weights of regularization (penalties): (**A**) too big a penalty (undertrained solution); (**B**) optimally balanced SvF solution; (**C**) too small a penalty (overtrained solution).

The data set files can be found in file SvF-2021-11.zip in the Git repository https://github.com/distcomp/SvF (accessed on 1 September 2022).

4. Method of Balanced Identification

The general problem is finding a function $T(x,t)$ (and other functions of model (1)) that approximates the data set D and, possibly, satisfies additional conditions (for example, the heat equation). To formalize it, we define an objective function (or selection criterion), which is a weighted sum of two terms: one formalizing the concept of the proximity of the model trajectory to the corresponding observations, the other formalizing the concept of the complexity of the model, expressed in this case through the measure of curvature included in the statement of functions.

Let us introduce a measure of the proximity of the trajectory of the model to measurements (data set D) or the approximation error:

$$MSD(D, T) = \frac{1}{|D|} \sum_{i \in I} (T_i - T(x_i, t_i))^2 = \|T_i - T(x_i, t_i)\|_{D}^2,$$

where $|D|$ is the number of elements of the set D,

and a measure of curvature (complexity) of functions of one variable

$$Curv(f(x), \alpha) = \alpha \int_a^b \left(f''(x)\right)^2 dx \, ,$$

where $[a, b]$ is the domain of the function $f(x)$, and two variables

$$Curv(f(x,y), \alpha_x, \alpha_y) = \int\limits_{x_{min}}^{x_{max}} \int\limits_{y_{min}}^{y_{max}} \left(\alpha_x^2 \left(f''_{xx}\right)^2 + 2\alpha_x \alpha_y \left(f''_{xy}\right)^2 + \alpha_y^2 \left(f''_{yy}\right)^2\right) dx dy.$$

The objective function is a combination of the measures introduced above. Let us give, as an example, the objective function

$$Obj(T, D, \alpha_x, \alpha_t) = MSD(D, T) + Curv(T(x,y), \alpha_x, \alpha_t).$$

The second term is the regularizing addition that makes the problem (of the search for a continuous function) correct. The choice of its value determines the quality of the solution. Figure 2 shows two unsuccessful options (A—weights that are too large, C—too small) and one successful (B—optimal weights chosen to minimize the cross-validation error).

Hereinafter, the following designations are used:

$rmsd = \| T_i - T(x_i, t_i) \|_D$ – the standard deviation of the solution from the measurements;

$rmsd^*$ – standard deviation of the balanced solution from measurements;

$Err(x,t) = T(x,t) - Ts(x,t)$ – deviation of the solution from the exact solution;

$\Delta = \| Err(x_i, t_i) \|_D$ – the standard deviation of the SvF solution from the exact solution;

Δ^* – estimation of Δ;

$\sigma_{cv} = \| T_i - T_\alpha^i(x_i, t_i) \|_D$ – error (mean square error) of cross-validation,

where $T_\alpha^i(x_i, t_i)$ is the solution obtained by minimizing the objective functional for given α on the set D without point (x_i, t_i). A more detailed (and more general) description of the cross-validation procedure can be found in [2].

An optimally balanced SvF solution is obtained by minimizing the cross-validation error by regularization coefficients (α):

$$\sigma_{cv}^* = \min_\alpha \| T_i - T_\alpha^i(x_i, t_i) \|_D$$

As a justification for using the minimization of σ_{cv} to choose a model (regularization weights), we present the following reasoning (here $(\cdot_i)$ stands for (x_i, t_i)):

$$\sigma_{cv}^2 = \frac{1}{|D|} \sum_{i \in I} \left(T_i - T_\alpha^i(\cdot_i)\right)^2 = \frac{1}{|D|} \sum_{i \in I} \left(T_i - Ts(\cdot_i) - \left(T_\alpha^i(\cdot_i) - Ts(\cdot_i)\right)\right)^2$$

$$\sigma_{cv}^2 = \frac{1}{|D|} \sum_{i \in I} (\varepsilon_i)^2 - \frac{2}{|D|} \sum_{i \in I} \varepsilon_i \cdot \left(T_\alpha^i(\cdot_i) - Ts(\cdot_i)\right) + \frac{1}{|D|} \sum_{i \in I} \left(T_\alpha^i(\cdot_i) - Ts(\cdot_i)\right)^2$$

The second term represents the sum of the products of random variables ε_i by an expression in parentheses, with the value of ε_i excluded from the calculation (point i was removed from the data set). It is expected to tend to zero with an increase of the observations' number. Similarly, with an increase of the observations' number (everywhere dense in space (x,t)), the third term tends to Δ^2, since $T_\alpha^i(\cdot_i) \to T(\cdot_i)$. As a result, we obtain the estimate

$$\sigma_{cv}^2 \approx \sigma_D^2 + \Delta^2.$$

Thus, cross-validation error minimizing leads (if a number of observations go to infinity) to minimizing the deviation of the solution found from the (unknown) exact solution. To assess such a deviation, introduce the designation:

$$\Delta^* = \sqrt{\sigma_{cv}^{*2} - \sigma_D^2}. \tag{3}$$

Remark. The payment for the problem regularization, as a rule, is the distortion of the solution. Moreover, the greater the weight of the regularization, the greater the distortion. In the case under consideration, the distortion consists in "straightening" the solution. The extreme case of "straightening" is shown in Figure 2A.

5. Various Identification Problems and Their Numerical Solution

Nine different identification tasks are discussed below. They differ in choices of data sets, minimization criteria (various regularizing additives) and additional conditions. For example, in Problem 5.1 *MSD(D_reg11x11) + Curv(T):M = 0*, the minimization criterion is used:

$$(T, K, \varphi, l, r) = \underset{T,K,\varphi,l,r}{Argmin} \{MSD(Dreg11x6, T) + Curv(T, \alpha_x, \alpha_t) : M = 0\},$$

which means for the given regularization weights α_x, α_t and a given data set *D_reg11x11*, find a set of functions (T, K, φ, l, r) that minimizes the functional *MSD(D_reg11x11,T) + Curv(T,α_x,α_t)*, and the sought functions must satisfy the equations of the model *M = 0*. This criterion is used to minimize the error of cross-validation, which makes it possible to find the regularization weights and the corresponding balanced SvF solution (T, K, φ, l, r).

To reduce the size of the formulas, a more compact notation for the selection criterion is used:

$$MSD(D\_reg11x11,T) + Curv(T,\alpha_x,\alpha_y) \rightarrow min:(M = 0).$$

The same notation will be used for the other problems.

The mathematical study of the variational problems is not the subject of the article. Note that even the original inverse problems of this type can have a non-unique solution, in particular, there are different heat conductivity coefficients leading to the same solution $T(x,t)$ [7,8]. Only Problem 5.0 (a spline approximation problem) is known to have a unique solution under rather simple conditions [13].

To find approximate solutions, we will use numerical models, which are obtained from analytical ones by replacing arbitrary mathematical functions with functions specified on the grid or polynomials (only for $K(T)$), derivatives with their difference analogs, integrals with the sums. Note that the grid used for the numerical model (41 points in x with a step equal to 0.05 and 21 points in t with a step equal to 0.25) is not tied to the measurement points in any way. For simplicity (and stability of calculations), an implicit four-point scheme was chosen [14]. The choice of scheme requires a separate study and is not carried out here. However, apparently, the optimization algorithm used for solving the problem as a whole (residual minimization) makes it possible to avoid a number of problems associated with the stability of calculations.

For the graphs of the exact solution, blue lines will be used, and for the SvF solution, red.

5.0. Problem MSD(D_reg11x11) + Curv(T)

Generally speaking, this simplest problem has nothing to do with the heat equation (therefore, its number is 0). It consists of finding a compromise between the proximity of the surface $T(x,t)$ to observations and its complexity (expressed in terms of the curvature $T(x,t)$) based on the minimization functional:

$$MSD(D\_reg11x11,T) + Curv(T,\alpha_x,\alpha_y) \rightarrow min \tag{4}$$

The results of the numerical solution of the identification problem are shown in Figure 3. The estimates obtained (resulting errors)

$$\sigma_{cv}^* \ 2.38, \ \text{rmsd} * = 1.44, \ \Delta^* = 1.19$$

are benchmarks for assessing the errors of further problems.

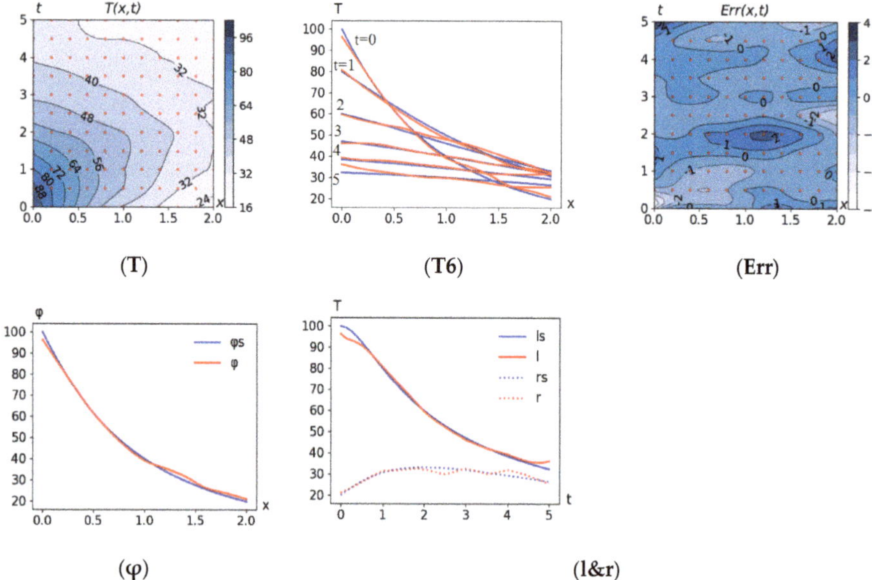

Figure 3. SvF solution of Problem 5.0: (**T**) contour lines of $T(x,t)$; (**T6**) 6 slices of $T(x,t)$; (**Err**) $Err(x,t) = T(x,t) - Ts(x,t)$ – deviation of the SvF solution from the exact solution; (**φ**) is the initial condition; (**l&r**) left and right boundary conditions.

5.1. Problem MSD(D_reg11x11) + Curv(T): M = 0

Now, the identification problem is related to the heat conduction equation. It consists of minimizing the cross-validation error, provided that the solution sought satisfies the thermal conductivity equation ($M = 0$), based on the criterion:

$$MSD(D\_reg11x11,T) + Curv(T,\alpha_x,\alpha_y) \rightarrow min:(M = 0)$$

The results are shown in Figure 4.

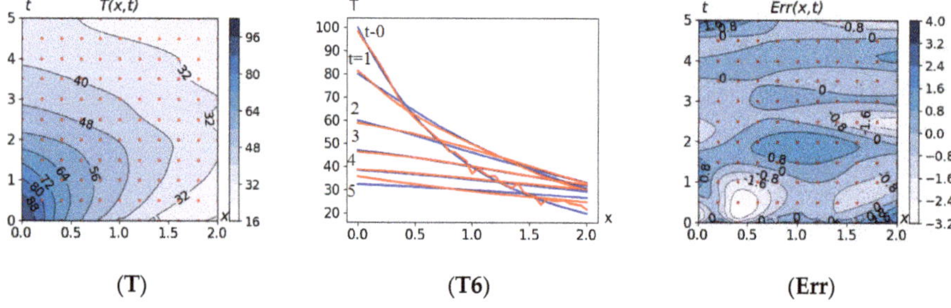

Figure 4. *Cont.*

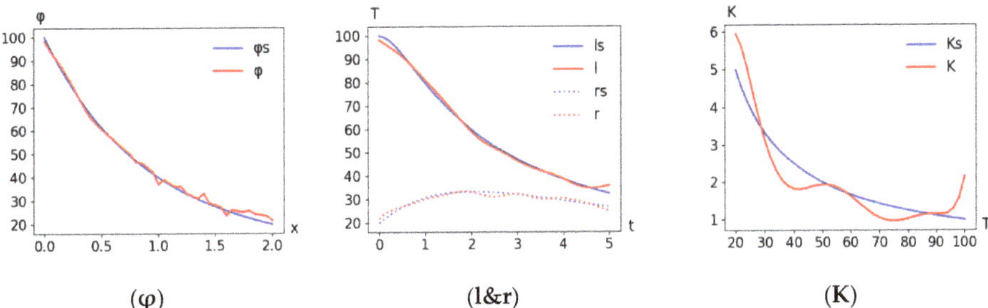

Figure 4. SvF solution of Problem 5.1: (**T**) contour lines of *T(x,t)*; (**T6**) 6 slices of *T(x,t)*; (**Err**) *Err(x,t) = T(x,t)-Ts(x,t)*; (**φ**) the initial condition; (**l&r**) boundary conditions; (**K**) the thermal conductivity coefficient *K(t)*.

Errors: $\sigma_{cv}^* = 2.24$, *rmsd** = 1.58, Δ* = 0.86.

5.2. Problem MSD(D_reg11x11) + Curv(T): M = 0, l = ls, r = rs

Two additional conditions *l = ls, r = rs* mean that the SvF solution must coincide with the exact one on the boundaries:

$$MSD(D\_reg11x11,T) + Curv(T,\alpha_x,\alpha_y) \rightarrow min:(M = 0, l = ls, r = rs)$$

Here and below, the figures show not the entire set of functions, but only the essential ones (the rest do not change much). The results are shown in Figure 5.

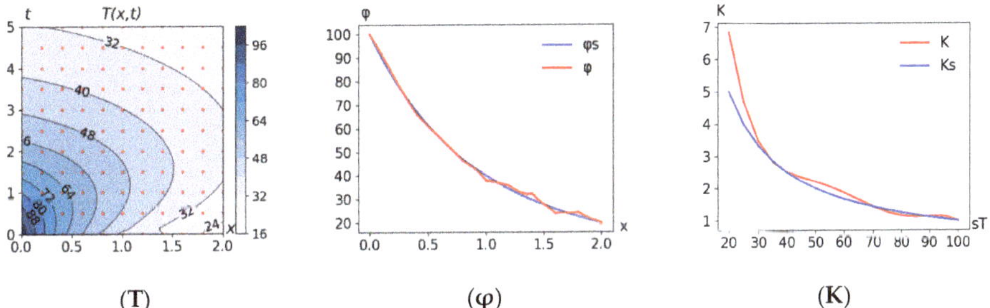

Figure 5. SvF solution of Problem 5.2: (**T**) contour lines of *T(x,t)*; (**φ**) the initial condition; (**K**) the thermal conductivity coefficient *K(t)*.

Errors: $\sigma_{cv}^* = 2.15$, *rmsd** = 1.86, Δ* = 0.61.

5.3. Problem MSD(D_reg11x11) + Curv(T): M = 0, l = ls, r = rs, φ = φs

Suppose that the initial condition is also known:

$$MSD(D\_reg11x11,T) + Curv(T,\alpha_x,\alpha_y) \rightarrow min:(M = 0, l = ls, r = rs, \varphi = \varphi s)$$

Some results are shown in Figure 6.

Errors: $\sigma_{cv}^* = 2.06$, *rmsd** = 2.01, Δ* = 0.49.

5.4. Problem MSD(D_reg11x11) + Curv(φ) + Curv(l) + Curv(r) + Curv(K):M = 0

The problem differs from Problem 5.1 by the penalties of four functions *φ, l, r* and *K*, that determine the solution, replacing the penalty for the curvature of the solution *T(x,t)*:

$$MSD(D\_reg11x11,T) + Curv(\varphi,\alpha_1) + Curv(l,\alpha_2) + Curv(r,\alpha_3) + Curv(K,\alpha_4) \rightarrow min:(M = 0).$$

The formulation seems to be more consistent with the physics of the phenomenon—regularization occurs at the level of functions that determine the solution, and not at the solution itself.

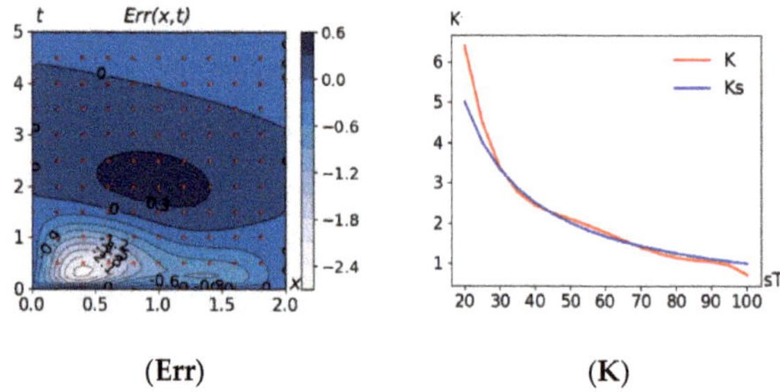

(Err)   (K)

Figure 6. SvF solution of Problem 5.3: (**Err**) *Err(x,t) = T(x,t)-Ts(x,t)*; (**K**) the thermal conductivity coefficient *K(t)*.

Errors: $\sigma_{cv}^* = 2.22$, *rmsd** = 1.82, $\Delta^* = 0.83$.

Attention should be paid to the incorrect behavior of the thermal conductivity coefficient near the right border of the graph in Figure 7K.

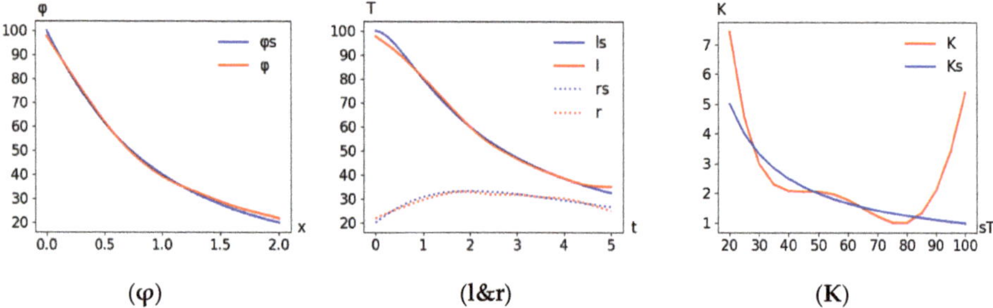

(φ)   (l&r)   (K)

Figure 7. SvF solution of Problem 5.4: (**φ**) the initial condition; (**l&r**) boundary conditions; (**K**) the thermal conductivity coefficient.

5.5. Problem MSD(D_reg11x11) + Curv(φ) +Curv(l) + Curv(r) + Curv(K): M = 0, dK/dT <= 0

Let it be additionally known that the thermal conductivity does not increase with increasing temperature *dK/dT <= 0*:

$$MSD(D\_reg11x11,T) + Curv(\varphi,\alpha_1) + Curv(l,\alpha_2) + Curv(r,\alpha_3) + Curv(K,\alpha_4) \rightarrow min:(M = 0, dK/dT <= 0)$$

This is an attempt to correct the solution by adding to the formulation of the minimization problem an additional condition formalizing a priori knowledge of the behavior of the coefficient *K(T)* (see Figures 7K and 8K).

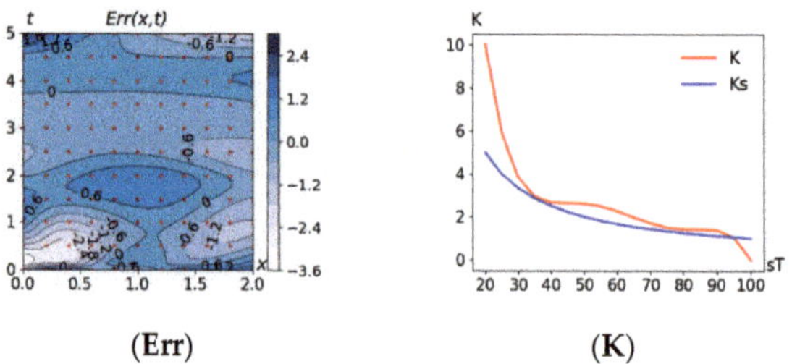

(Err)   (K)

Figure 8. SvF solution of Problem 5.5: (**Err**) *Err(x,t) = T(x,t)-Ts(x,t)*; (**K**) the thermal conductivity coefficient.

Errors: $\sigma_{cv}^* = 2.23$, *rmsd** = 1.80, $\Delta^* = 0.85$.

5.6. Problem MSD(D_rnd121) + Curv(T): M = 0, l = ls, r = rs, φ = φs

The problem is similar to Problem 5.3, except the data set consists of 121 points on an irregular grid:

$$MSD(D\_rnd121,T) + Curv(T,\alpha_x,\alpha_y) \rightarrow min{:}(M = 0, l = ls, r = rs, \varphi = \varphi s)$$

Some results are shown in Figure 9.

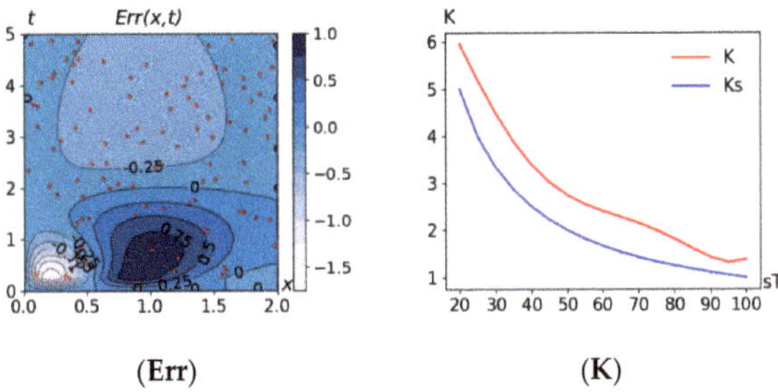

(Err)   (K)

Figure 9. SvF solution of Problem 5.6: (**Err**) $Err(x,t) = T(x,t){-}Ts(x,t)$; (**K**) the thermal conductivity coefficient.

Errors: $\sigma^*_{cv} = 2.13$, $rmsd^* = 2.05$, $\Delta^* = 0.39$.

5.7. Problem MSD(D_rnd1000) + Curv(T): M = 0, l = ls, r = rs , $\varphi = \varphi s$

The problem is similar to problem 5.6, except the data set consists of 1000 points:

$$MSD(D\_rnd1000,T) + Curv(T,\alpha_x,\alpha_y) \rightarrow min{:}(M = 0, l = ls, r = rs, \varphi = \varphi s)$$

The results are shown in Figure 10.

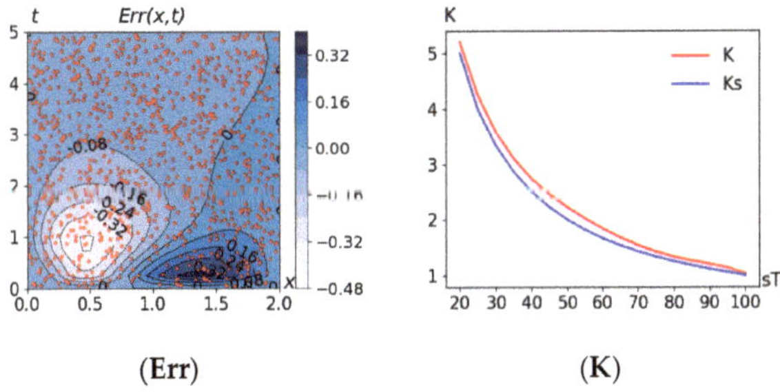

(Err)   (K)

Figure 10. SvF solution of Problem 5.7: (**Err**) $Err(x,t) = T(x,t){-}Ts(x,t)$; (**K**) the thermal conductivity coefficient.

Errors: $\sigma^*_{cv} = 2.02$, $rmsd^* = 2.01$, $\Delta^* = 0.15$.

5.8. Problem MSD(D_reg11x11($\varepsilon = 0$)) + Curv(φ) + Curv(l) + Curv(r) + Curv(K):M = 0

The problem is similar to Problem 5.4, but with a set of exact measurements ($\varepsilon_i = 0$):

$$MSD(D\_reg11x11(\varepsilon = 0)),T) + Curv(\varphi,\alpha_1) + Curv(l,\alpha_2) + Curv(r,\alpha_3) + Curv(K,\alpha_4) \rightarrow min{:}(M = 0).$$

Some results are shown in Figure 11.

Errors: $\sigma^*_{cv} = 0.06$, $rmsd^* = 0.004$, $\Delta^* = 0$.

The graphs of the boundary and initial conditions are not shown, since the SvF solutions actually coincide with the exact one.

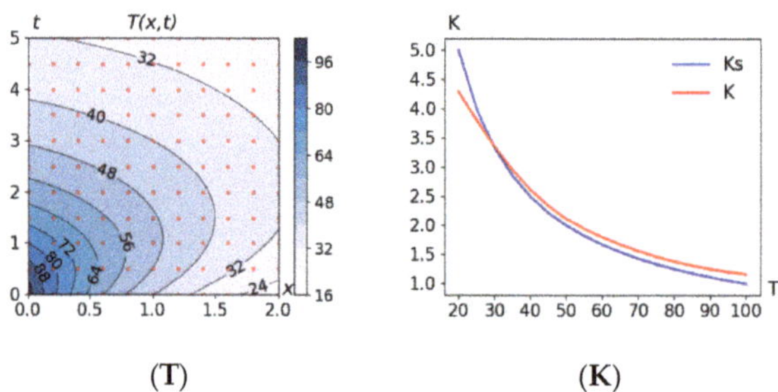

(**T**)   (**K**)

Figure 11. SvF solution of Problem 5.8: (**T**) contour lines of *T(x,t)*; (**K**) the thermal conductivity coefficient.

6. Discussion

The errors obtained during problem solving are summarized in Table 1. Analyzing the table allowed us to identify some of the patterns that appeared during problem modification.

Table 1. Errors: σ_{cv}^* –error of cross-validation, the main indicator of the "quality" of the constructed model; $rmsd^*$ is the standard deviation of the SvF solution from observations, σ_d is the data error, Δ is the standard deviation of the SvF solution from the exact solution, Δ^* is the estimate of Δ determined by Formula (3).

#	Problem	σ_{cv}^*	$rmsd^*$	σ_d	Δ	Δ^*
0	*MSD(D_reg11x11) + Curv(T)*	2.38	1.44	2.06	1.08	1.19
1	*MSD(D_reg11x11) + Curv(T): M = 0*	2.24	1.58	2.06	1.06	0.89
2	*MSD(D_reg11x11) + Curv(T): M = 0, l = ls, r = rs*	2.15	1.86	2.06	0.61	0.61
3	*MSD(D_reg11x11) + Curv(T): M = 0, l = ls, r = rs, φ = φs*	2.06	2.01	2.06	0.42	0
4	*MSD(D_reg11x11) + Curv(φ) + Curv(l) + Curv(r) + Curv(K): M = 0*	2.22	1.82	2.06	0.83	0.83
5	*MSD(D_reg11x11) + Curv(φ) + Curv(l) + Curv(r) + Curv(K): M = 0, K/dT<=0*	2.23	1.80	2.06	0.83	0.85
6	*MSD(D_rnd121) + Curv(T): M = 0, l = ls, r = rs , φ = φs*	2.13	2.05	2.08	0.24	0.39
7	*MSD(D_rnd1000) + Curv(T): M = 0, l = ls, r = rs , φ = φs*	2.02	2.01	2.01	0.13	0.15
8	*MSD(D_reg11x11(ε = 0)) + Curv(φ) + Curv(l) + Curv(r) + Curv(K): M = 0*	0.06	0.004	0	0.06	0

Lines 0–3. Lines 0–3 of Table 1 show some patterns of successive model modifications. As expected, adding the "correct" additional conditions leads to a more accurate (see column Δ) modification of the model. These conditions reduce the set of feasible solutions of the optimization problem, while adding "correct" conditions cuts off unnecessary (non-essential) parts from it. In the technology used, this leads to a decrease in the σ_{cv}^* cross-validation error.

The growth of the $rmsd^*$ error seems paradoxical: the more accurate the model, the greater its root mean square deviation from observations. However, it is easy to explain. First of all, $rmsd^*$ is within the error limits of the initial data σ_d. Second, the better the model, the closer it is to the exact solution, and for the exact solution $rmsd = \sigma_d$. Of course, if regularization penalties that are too large are chosen, the solution will be distorted so that $rmsd$ will be greater than σ_d. This situation is shown in Figure 2A.

During modification, every subsequent model (from 0 to 3) is a follow up of the previous one. Previously found solutions are used as initial approximations, which allows us to find solutions faster as well as avoid poorly interpreted solutions.

Lines 4–5. The problems considered differ from Problem 5.1 by the selection criterion: instead of the solution *T*, the functions *φ, l, r,* and *K* (defining the solution) are used for regularization. This formulation seems to be more consistent with the physics of the phenomenon—a penalty imposed on the original functions determining the dynamics of the process, and not on their consequence (solution). The estimates of the cross-validation error (σ_{cv}) obtained are similar to Problem 5.1 but with smaller deviation from the exact solution Δ. The decrease in deviation may be associated with a special case of generated errors. The issue requires further research.

In Problem 5.4, the obtained solution of the thermal conductivity coefficient $K\,(T)$ (see Figure 7K) rises sharply to the right border. Suppose it is known in advance that the coefficient is not to increase. This knowledge can be easily added to the model as an additional condition ($dK/dT <= 0$). As a result (Problem 5.5), $K(T)$ changed (see Figure 8K). At the same time, the accuracy indicators (line 5) practically stayed unchanged, which indicates that such an additional condition does not contradict the model and observations.

Line 6. Problem similar to Problem 5.3 but with a data set with a random arrangement of observations in space and time. The same number of observations leads to the same error estimates but the deviation from the exact solution is noticeably smaller. The use of such data sets should be carefully considered.

Line 7. Increasing the number of observations to 1000 significantly improves the accuracy of the solution.

Line 8. Using a data set with precise measurements allows us to get a close-to-exact solution.

General notes. The Δ^{*} estimate generally describes Δ (the standard deviation of the SvF solution from the exact one) well enough. Note, that the data error σ_d (usually unknown) is used for the calculations.

Figures 4Err, 6Err, 8Err, 9T and 10Err show how the regularization distorts the solution. As expected, distortions are mainly observed in regions with high curvature (large values of the squares of the second derivatives).

It is easy to see that almost for all problems (except problem 5.8), the following inequalities hold:

$$\sigma_{cv}^{*} \geq \sigma_{d} \geq \text{rmsd}^{*}.$$

It appears to be true when the model used, the regularization method, and the chosen cross-validation procedure are consistent with the data used and the physics of the phenomenon. At least, if the wrong model is chosen for describing the data (an incorrect mathematical description or too severe a regularization penalty), then the right-hand side of the inequality does not hold. If the errors in setting the data are not random (for example, space position related) or the cross-validation procedure is chosen incorrectly, the left side of the inequality will be violated. Thus, the violation of the inequality above is a sign of something going wrong.

7. Conclusions

The problems (and their solution) considered in the article illustrate the effectiveness of the application of regularization methods and, in particular, the use of balanced identification technology.

The results above confirm the thesis: the more data, the higher the accuracy, and the more knowledge about the object, the more complex and accurate models can be constructed. The technology used allows us to organize the evolutionary process of building models, from simple to complex. In this case, the indicator determining "the winner in the competitive struggle of models" is the error of cross-validation—reducing the error is a big argument in favor of this model.

In addition, this gradual (evolutionary) modification is highly desirable as the formulations under consideration are complex two-level (possibly multi-extreme) optimization problems and their solution requires significant resources. Thus, finding a solution without a "plausible" initial approximation would require computational resources that are too large and, in addition, one cannot be sure that the solution found (one of the local minima of the optimization problem) will have a subject interpretation that satisfies the researcher.

This step-by-step complication of the problem, together with specific techniques such as doubling the number of grid nodes, can significantly save computational resources. All of this work's results were obtained on a modern laptop (CORE i5 processor) within a reasonable time (up to 1 h). The two-level optimization problem, which in this case allows parallelization, consumes the majority of the resources. Tools for the solution of more complex resource-intensive tasks exist for high-performance multiprocessor complexes [10,11].

As for computing resources, SvF technology is resource intensive. This is justified as it is aimed at saving the researcher's time.

Appendix A contains a listing of the task file. The notation used is close to the mathematical one—a formal description of the model for calculations practically coincides with the formulas of the model (1). This allows for an easy model modification (no "manual" program code rewriting). For example, to take into account the heat flux at the border, a corresponding condition defining the derivative at the border has to be added to the task file.

Let us take a look at unsolved problems and possible solutions.

One problem is possible local minima. However, there are special solvers designed to search for global extrema, for example, SCIP [15] (source codes are available) which implements the branch-and-bound algorithm, including global optimization problems with continuous variables. Perhaps, if a previously found solution is used as an initial approximation, a confirmation that the found minimum is global might be obtained in a reasonable time.

Finally, the paper considers various errors' estimates of solution T(x,t) only and not the other functions' identification accuracy. The evaluation of the accuracy of determining the thermal conductivity coefficient is particularly interesting. Another problem is the formalization of errors that arise when replacing a real physical object with a mathematical model and real observations with a measurement error model. In the future, these issues should be researched.

Author Contributions: Conceptualization, A.S.; methodology, A.S.; software, A.S. and I.N.; validation, A.S. and I.N.; formal analysis, A.S. and I.N.; investigation, A.S. and I.N.; resources, A.S. and I.N.; data curation, A.S. and I.N.; writing—original draft preparation, A.S. and I.N.; writing—review and editing, A.S.; visualization, A.S. and I.N.; supervision, A.S. and I.N.; project administration, A.S. and I.N.; funding acquisition, A.S. All authors have read and agreed to the published version of the manuscript.

Funding: This work was supported by the Russian Science Foundation under grant no. 22-11-00317, https://rscf.ru/project/22-11-00317/, accessed on 1 November 2022. This work has been carried out using computing resources of the federal collective usage center Complex for Simulation and Data Processing for Megascience Facilities at NRC "Kurchatov Institute".

Institutional Review Board Statement: Not applicable.

Informed Consent Statement: Not applicable.

Data Availability Statement: The software package together with a task file (MSD(D_reg11x11) + Curv(T):M = 0.odt) is freely available online in the Git repository https://github.com/distcomp/SvF, accessed on 1 November 2022 (file SvF-2021-11.zip).

Conflicts of Interest: The authors declare no conflict of interest. The funders had no role in the design of the study; in the collection, analyses, or interpretation of data; in the writing of the manuscript; or in the decision to publish the results.

Appendix A. Task File Sample

The software package together with the considered task file (MSD(D_reg11x11) + Curv(T):M = 0.odt) is freely available online in the Git repository https://github.com/distcomp/SvF, accessed on 1 November 2022 (file SvF-2021-11.zip) (accessed on 1 September 2022).

Format: .odt-Open/Libre Office.

The file contains a complete formal description of Problem 5.1 (identification of unknown functions of the mathematical model *MSD(D_reg11x11) + Curv(T):M = 0* and a number of service instructions required for a numerical solution based on the balanced identification technology.

The first line (see Figure A1) specifies the maximum number of iterations, the second specifies the difference scheme, the third specifies the data source (data set), and the fourth specifies the cross-validation procedure parameters. The following describes the mathematical model: *Set:* defines the sets, *Var:* defines unknown variables—functions to be identified, *EQ:* equations of the mathematical model, *Obj:* objective function (selection criterion). Note that the first equation was made in the formula editor (Tex notation). A different, less visual encoding of formulas (commented out line, marked with a # symbol) can be used instead.

```
BoF-SvF
CVNumOfIter = 100
SchemeD1    = 'Backward'  #'Forward'  # Central
Data = Select x, t, Terr as T, ROWNUM as npp from ../Exp3.dat
SvF_MakeSets_byParam ( Data.npp, 8, 0 )

Set:   x  ∈ [0, 2, -40]|
       t  ∈ [0, 5, -40]
       sT ∈ [20, 100, 5]

Var:   T(x,t)  >=0
       φ(x)    >=0
       l(t)    >=0
       r(t)    >=0
       K(sT)   >=0; <= 10; PolyPow = 7
```

$$\text{EQ:} \quad \frac{\partial}{\partial t}(T) = K(T) \cdot \frac{\partial^2}{\partial x^2}(T) + \frac{\partial}{\partial T}(K(T)) \cdot (\frac{\partial}{\partial x}(T)) * *2$$

```
       T(0,t) = l(t)
       T(2,t) = r(t)
       T(x,0) = φ(x)
#EQ:   d/dt(T(x,t)) = K(T)*d2/dx2(T(x,t)) + d/dT(K(T))*(d/dx(T(x,t)))**2

Obj:   T.ComplSig2( Penal[0],Penal[1] ) + T.MSD()

Draw
EOF       #-------------------------------------------------------
```

Figure A1. Listing of the example task file.

References

1. Tikhonov, A.N.; Goncharsky, A.V.; Stepanov, V.V.; Yagola, A.G. *Numerical Methods for the Solution of Ill-Posed Problems*; Springer: Berlin/Heidelberg, Germany, 1995; 262p.
2. Sokolov, A.V.; Voloshinov, V.V. Model Selection by Balanced Identification: The Interplay of Optimization and Distributed Computing. *Open Comput. Sci.* **2020**, *10*, 283–295. [CrossRef]
3. Tikhonov, A.N. On mathematical methods for automating the processing of observations. In *Computational Mathematics Problems*; Moscow State University Publishing House: Moscow, Russia, 1980; pp. 3–17.
4. Zhang, Y.; Zhou, D.; Wei, W.; Frame, J.M.; Sun, H.; Sun, A.Y.; Chen, X. Hierarchical Fractional Advection-Dispersion Equation (FADE) to Quantify Anomalous Transport in River Corridor over a Broad Spectrum of Scales. *Mathematics* **2021**, *9*, 790. [CrossRef]
5. Manikantan, R.; Chakraborty, S.; Uchida, T.K.; Vyasarayani, C.P. Parameter Identification in Nonlinear Mechanical Systems with Noisy Partial State Measurement Using PID-Controller Penalty Functions. *Mathematics* **2020**, *8*, 1084. [CrossRef]
6. Kolesnik, S.A.; Stifeev, E.M. Inverse retrospective problem for nonlinear heat conduction equations. In Proceedings of the XXII International Conference on Computational Mechanics and Modern Applied Software Systems, Alushta, Russia, 4–13 September 2021; Moscow Aviation University Publishing House: Moscow, Russia, 2021; pp. 43–45.
7. Albu, A.F.; Zubov, V.I. Identification of Thermal Conductivity Coefficient Using a Given Temperature Field. *Comput. Math. Math. Phys.* **2018**, *58*, 1585–1599. [CrossRef]
8. Albu, A.F.; Zubov, V.I. Identification of the Thermal Conductivity Coefficient in the Three-Dimensional Case by Solving a Corresponding Optimization Problem. *Comput. Math. Math. Phys.* **2021**, *61*, 1416–1431. [CrossRef]
9. Python Optimization Modeling Objects. Available online: http://www.pyomo.org (accessed on 1 September 2022).
10. Sukhoroslov, O.; Volkov, S.; Afanasiev, A. A Web-Based Platform for Publication and Distributed Execution of Computing Applications. In Proceedings of the Parallel and Distributed Computing, 14th International Symposium on IEEE, Limassol, Cyprus, 29 June–2 July 2015; pp. 175–184.
11. SSOP (Solve Set of Optimization Problems). Available online: https://optmod.distcomp.org/apps/vladimirv/SSOP (accessed on 1 September 2022).

12. Ipopt (Coin-OR Interior Point Optimizer, NLP). Available online: https://github.com/coin-or/Ipopt (accessed on 1 September 2022).
13. Rozhenko, A.I. *Theory and Algorithms of Variational Spline-Approximation*; ICM&MG SB RAS Publishing: Novosibirsk, Russia, 2005; 244p.
14. Samarskii, A.A. *The Theory of Difference Schemes*; Marcel Dekker, Inc.: New York, NY, USA, 2001; 762p.
15. SCIP. Available online: https://www.scipopt.org/ (accessed on 1 September 2022).

250

MDPI
St. Alban-Anlage 66
4052 Basel
Switzerland
Tel. +41 61 683 77 34
Fax +41 61 302 89 18
www.mdpi.com

Mathematics Editorial Office
E-mail: mathematics@mdpi.com
www.mdpi.com/journal/mathematics